Pain Management Psychotherapy

A Practical Guide

Bruce N. Eimer, Ph.D., ABPP
Arthur Freeman, Ed.D., ABPP

John Wiley & Sons, Inc.

New York • Chichester • Weinheim • Brisbane • Singapore • Toronto

Library of Congress Cataloging in Publication Data:
Eimer, Bruce N., 1953–
    Pain management psychotherapy : a practical guide / Bruce N.
Eimer, Arthur Freeman.
      p.   cm.
    Includes bibliographical references and index.
    ISBN 0-471-15708-2 (cloth : alk. paper)
    1. Pain—Treatment.   2. Cognitive therapy.   3. Hypnotism—
Therapeutic use. I. Freeman, Arthur M. II. Title.
RB127.E36   1998
616′.0472—dc21   97-15702

Printed in the United States of America

10 9 8 7 6 5 4 3 2 1

I DEDICATE this book in loving memory of my father, Joe Eimer (May 10, 1913–September 1, 1996). Born in Poland and raised in Vienna, he was a survivor of the Holocaust who still cherished solid values of the Old World. My father loved life and knew how to enjoy it. An active and energetic man, he built a new life and family in America after the war, while remaining connected to what was left of his family of origin, which had been decimated by the Nazis. Despite the traumas of his youth, my father was a warm, loving, sacrificing, and ambitious man who knew how to turn adversity to advantage.

My father died ravaged by a painful form of prostate cancer. He lived the last year of his life with the same courage and strength of spirit that had enabled him to survive the Holocaust. When he finally admitted defeat, he surrendered gracefully. He spent his last three weeks under palliative care, in an angelic place called Hospice By the Sea, in Boca Raton, Florida. I also dedicate this book to Hospice By the Sea, an organization that exemplifies loving compassion and professional pain control. Their well-trained and compassionate staff helped make our pain a bit more bearable and served as a powerful reminder that pain management is a noble profession.

B. N. E.

Preface

There are some remedies worse than the disease.

—Publilius Šyrus

THE TERM *to soothe* means "to reduce the force or intensity of pain," "to soften or mitigate an unpleasant experience," "to render an experience less objectionable or offensive," and "to restore to a tranquil condition" (*Oxford English Dictionary*, 1971); in other words, to alter the perception of pain. This book is about the psychological treatment of people with persistent physical pain. The prevalent problem of pain is frequently undertreated behaviorally and psychologically. This may be because of inadequate available resources or knowledge about how to treat chronic pain; however, it can also be due to a disbelief in the potential of psychological methods to reduce pain. This disbelief can stem from the conviction that altering the perception of pain is somehow less valid or objective than physically correcting or removing its noxious source. Yet, it is not always possible even to identify such a noxious source, much less to correct or remove it. Many chronic pain states are markedly disproportionate to any identifiable tissue injury.

Some medicinal and medical-surgical treatments can produce their intended results despite unfavorable psychological conditions. The patient's psychological condition, however, is still of central importance, because it can affect whether the patient will benefit from the treatment and how well the patient will deal with potential side effects. Many medicinal and medical-surgical treatments produce favorable treatment outcomes, but only up to a point. After reaching that stage in recuperation, patients may have to manage on their own. Therefore, patients' expectations and beliefs play an important role in their recovery from an illness or injury. Mind and body are not separate—psychological and physical processes constantly influence each other.

Chronic pain patients have been seen as a difficult group to treat, partly because their complex problems often rule out easily applied or mechanical treatment techniques following the traditional medical illness model. However, chronic and persistent pain syndromes are more than just physical or medical problems. They are also behavioral and psychological problems. In this book we offer a partial remedy by providing accessible technical knowledge that will allow practitioners to alleviate unnecessary pain and suffering.

Our primary audience is behavioral and mental health professionals who work with acute, subacute, or chronic pain patients in medical, psychiatric, or physical rehabilitation settings. Much of the information will also be useful to physicians and physical rehabilitation specialists and to insurance claims adjusters, disability and case managers, and utilization reviewers who want a better understanding of the psychological aspects of persistent pain and the important role of psychological treatments.

We define Pain Management Psychotherapy (PMP), as the clinical application of behavioral and psychological methods, in a professional context, for alleviating emotional suffering, improving pain relief, and promoting pain management. In keeping with prevailing practice, our orientation is both cognitive-behavioral and hypnotherapeutic, or hypno-behavioral, as it is sometimes called (Barber, 1996; Gatchel & Turk, 1996; Philips & Rachman, 1996; Roth-Roemer, Abrams, & Syrjala, 1996; Schafer, 1996; Tunks & Merskey, 1990; Turk, Meichenbaum, & Genest, 1983; Turner & Romano, 1990).

Cognitive-behavior therapy and hypnotherapy can provide a framework and techniques for helping pain patients, but it is the psychotherapist's job to select the best methods and strategies for helping pain patients cope with their pain. PMP is not a substitute for adequate medical evaluation, treatment, and follow-up care. It should serve as an adjunct to good medical care. It addresses the behavioral, emotional, cognitive, and interpersonal aspects of pain problems with the goal of reducing emotional distress and suffering associated with pain.

Readers who are not formally trained in cognitive-behavior therapy or clinical hypnosis should not view this book as a substitute for formal training and supervision. Clinical skills and experience cannot be obtained solely from reading a book.

ORGANIZATION OF THIS BOOK

This book is organized into 11 chapters. Chapter 1 is an introduction to pain problems; it discusses the medical necessity of psychological intervention, defines basic terms, and sets the book's focus. Part One of the book comprises Chapters 2 through 4 and deals with assessment and treatment planning. Chapter 2 covers the use of structured clinical interviews, mental status examination, pain assessment checklists, and pain intensity rating scales. Chapter 3 deals with the assessment of pain-related disability, pain beliefs, coping strategies, personality, adjustment/maladjustment, and psychopathology. Chapter 4 explains how to integrate assessment findings, case conceptualization, and treatment planning. Many of the clinical instruments and forms discussed in these chapters are included in the Appendixes.

Part Two, "Cognitive-Behavioral Pain Management," includes Chapters 5 through 8. Chapter 5 presents a cognitive-behavioral model of pain and suffering, and introduces the applications of cognitive therapy for pain management. Chapter 6, which focuses on implementation, introduces an array of cognitive intervention techniques for assessing and modifying maladaptive attitudes and negative beliefs related to pain, and for alleviating the attendant emotional suffering. This chapter also describes techniques for training pain patients to use cognitive coping strategies and self-management skills such as self-monitoring, cognitive disputation and cognitive restructuring, and self-instructional and stress inoculation training. Chapter 7 covers assessment and intervention on the level of patient beliefs about pain. It also describes the applications of the new technique Eye Movement Desensitization and Reprocessing (EMDR) to PMP. It shows how EMDR can be used to help pain patients process the negative emotional states and negative cognitions associated with their pain.

Chapter 8 covers the assessment and reduction of pain behaviors, and the assessment and treatment of common behavioral problems (e.g., noncompliance, overreliance on pain medications, sleep problems, anger, deconditioning, avoidance, and assertiveness deficits). Various operant and respondent behavioral coaching principles for effective PMP are also described and illustrated.

Part Three, "Hypno-Behavioral Pain Management," is devoted to hypnotherapeutic techniques and strategies. In Chapter 9, basic hypnotherapy terms are defined, and the applicability of hypnotherapy for pain management is discussed. Then, hypnotic and imagery strategies for managing pain symptoms and uncovering emotional factors associated with persistent pain states are described. Chapters 10 and 11 cover the formal assessment of hypnotic ability and responsiveness, hypnosis induction strategies, the nuts and bolts of strategically using hypnosis for pain control, and the use of biofeedback instruments in PMP.

The Epilogue pulls together the key issues in Pain Management Psychotherapy.

ACKNOWLEDGMENTS

Bringing a book like this to fruition demands the help of many people. First, we gratefully acknowledge the expert help, patient assistance, and continual support of our editors at John Wiley & Sons, Jo Ann Miller, Tracey Thornblade, Linda Indig, and Dorothy Lin, who made this project possible. Special thanks are due Nancy M. Land, Pamela Blackmon, and Charlotte Saikia whose wise copy-editing helped ease our book into its final form. We thank HarperCollins/Basic Books for their permission to reprint and adapt excerpts from the Spiegel Hypnotic Induction Profile for inclusion in the Hypnotic Ability and Response Profile, and reprint the Spiegel AOD Personality Inventory. We thank Ronald Melzack, Ph.D., for his permission to reprint the McGill Pain Questionnaire and the Short Form-McGill Pain Questionnaire. We also thank Dr. Melzack for his permission to adapt some of the original MPQ verbal descriptors for inclusion in the Philadelphia Pain Questionnaire. We thank Dennis Turk, Ph.D., for his permission to reprint the Pain Experience Scale. We thank David Williams, Ph.D., for his permission to reprint the Pain Beliefs and Perceptions Inventory. We thank Beverly Thorn, Ph.D., for her permission to adapt her Pain Diary. We thank Robert F. Heller, Ed.D., for permission to adapt items from the Hypnosis Belief Survey.

We gratefully acknowledge Marc Oster, Psy.D., ABPH, for helping us edit the clinical hypnosis chapters in Part Three. Dr. Oster's incisive editorial assistance and academic/clinical feedback helped make those chapters more readable. Dr. Oster also coauthored the Hypnotic Ability and Response Profile (HARP) (Eimer & Oster, 1996) and provided the preliminary data reported in Chapter 10.

We thank Herbert Spiegel, M.D., for reading and commenting on portions of the manuscript, and for providing B.N.E. with personal training in administering and using the Spiegel Hypnotic Induction Profile. We thank Dabney Ewin, M.D., for commenting on portions of the manuscript. We also thank Philip Friedman, Ph.D., the author of GB-STAT, for assisting in some of the data analyses.

B.N.E. thanks his wife, Andrea, and daughters, Marisa and Allison, for loving and standing by him over the past two years during this book's preparation which took away precious time from them. B.N.E. thanks his friend, Lyle A. Allen III, M.A., president of CogniSyst, Inc., for his unwavering friendship and collaboration. B.N.E. also thanks his mother, Cecile Eimer, for never losing faith in him, and for providing a quiet hideaway for writing in beautiful Delray Beach, Florida. B.N.E. gratefully acknowledges his co-author, Arthur Freeman, who as his clinical supervisor and mentor years ago, helped open the door to the art and science of cognitive therapy. This book, in part, owes its existence to Dr. Freeman, who early on, saw the promise of this work and wanted to be a part of its conception, development, and birth. B.N.E. gratefully acknowledges a personal and intellectual debt to Arnold Lazarus, Ph.D., who taught him the real meaning of the term "eclectic" and helped him become a multimodal psychotherapist. B.N.E. also gratefully acknowledges a personal debt to the late David Cheek, M.D., a gently, courageous, pioneering giant of hypnosis, for his kind and generous mentoring.

The publication of this volume marks the beginning of a new life experience for A.F. who acknowledges his wife, Sharon, and daughters, Heather, April, and Laura, who became part of his family along with Andrew, Russell, Aaron, and Rebecca.

We also gratefully acknowledge our patients who have entrusted us with their secrets in the hope that we might help them obtain relief from their persistent pain.

Contents

CHAPTER 1

Introduction: The Medical Necessity of Psychotherapy for Pain Management

But that I can save him from days of torture, that is what I feel is my great and ever new privilege. Pain is a more terrible lord of mankind than even death itself.

—Dr. Albert Schweitzer

PAIN IS a fact of life. Yet despite the enormous advances in our understanding over the past two decades, knowledge about its complex mechanisms and multiple determinants is still rudimentary (AMA, 1995; Wall, 1994). As stated in the chapter "Pain" in the American Medical Association's (1995) *Guides to the Evaluation of Permanent Impairment*, "Pain is endemic in the United States population," and "the medical, social, and economic consequences of pain are enormous" (p. 303). Bonica (1987), a pioneer in the field of modern pain management, estimated that approximately 30% of the population in economically developed countries suffer from chronic pain (Fordyce, 1995). A report published by the International Association for the Study of Pain stated, "Seventy million Americans report chronic pain, of whom more than fifty million are partially or totally disabled for periods ranging from a few days to weeks or months. Some are permanently disabled" (Fordyce, 1995, p. 5).

Estimates vary concerning the number of patients making new and follow-up office visits to physicians each year for treatment of acute and chronic pain (AMA, 1995; Social Security Administration, 1987; Turk & Melzack, 1992), but they probably exceed 100 million. The economic repercussions of chronic pain—lost workdays, disability, compensation,

1

and medical and surgical treatments—are staggering (AMA, 1995; Fordyce, 1995; Osterweis, Kleinman, & Mechanic, 1987). Yet, chronic pain's greatest cost must be measured in the untold human suffering that it causes. In Wall's introduction to the third edition of Wall and Melzack's (1994) classic *Textbook of Pain*, he highlights the intractable pain problems of patients who suffer from peripheral and central nerve damage (e.g., amputees, nerve injury cases, and people with various neuropathies, meaning pathological nerve changes and damage). He presents a vivid metaphor characterizing how these pain patients

> . . . move on like draught horses, uncomplaining, heads down in continuous driving snow. Not only have their multiple treatments failed but they have suffered the indignity of being told that their pain will go away and/or that it is all in their head. They have learnt that to continue to complain is to alienate and isolate. These stoical characters plod on, often counted as cured because they no longer go to the doctors or take their ineffective medicine. (Wall & Melzack, 1994, p. 1)

Another major aspect of the problem of chronic pain is that many chronic pain conditions such as arthritis are only medically treatable up to a point. Referring to the pain of arthritis, Wall (Wall & Melzack, 1994, p. 2) asserts, "Medicinal treatments ameliorate the pain in most patients but there are few who can tolerate the long-term side-effects of the full doses which completely relieve the minority."

Chronic pain is an enormous problem for which there are inadequate effective treatments. The U.S. Department of Health and Human Services formally recognized the impact of the problem by setting up in 1985, a formal Commission on the Evaluation of Pain (AMA, 1995; Osterweis et al., 1987; Social Security Administration, 1987). This commission "concluded that chronic pain is not a psychiatric disorder" (AMA, 1995, p. 303). However, the commission also acknowledged the central role of psychological and psychosocial factors.

The AMA's (1995) stated basic assumptions about pain evaluation emphasize that (a) pain evaluation does not lend itself to strict, nonsubjective, physical laboratory standards, (b) chronic pain is not detectable or measurable on the basis of the traditional, physical, tissue-oriented, medical disease model, and (c) "pain evaluation requires acknowledging and understanding a multifaceted, biopsychosocial model that transcends the usual, more limited disease model" (p. 304). The U.S. Department of Health and Human Services' 1985 Commission on the Evaluation of Pain (Osterweis et al., 1987; Social Security Administration, 1987) defined pain as a "complex experience, embracing physical, mental, social, and behavioral processes, which compromises the quality of life of many individuals" (AMA, 1995, p. 304).

Given the pressing need for effective pain management services and the tremendous costs of ignoring the problem, affording pain patients access to practical, efficient and cost-effective short-term interventions for pain management should be a top priority. Over the past two decades, newly developed behavioral and psychological interventions have reflected the growing recognition that many pain problems are partially maintained or exacerbated by psychological, psychosocial, and behavioral factors (Barber, 1996; Catalano & Hardin, 1996; Caudill, 1995; Eimer, 1988, 1989; Fordyce, 1976; Gatchel & Turk, 1996; Hanson & Gerber, 1990; Melzack & Wall, 1982; Turk et al., 1983). Yet, despite their availability, psychological interventions have been underemployed. Only a small percentage of pain sufferers seek out or are offered psychological therapy as a routine component of their care, with the result that many people whose pain is intractable, medically untreatable, or only partially treatable are denied the psychological health care that could afford them significant relief.

This situation is due in part to several widespread misconceptions such as that pain is solely a physical problem or, conversely that it is caused by an underlying psychiatric disorder. Others mistakenly believe it is maintained by secondary gains, such as financial compensation, disability payments or time out of work. Another belief, which if erroneous, is certainly grossly exaggerated, is that a societal stigma is associated with receiving any kind of psychological, psychiatric, or mental health care.

Each of these beliefs fosters the myth that the mind and the body are separate entities, and that physical-medical care for physically manifested problems is legitimate and psychological care is not. Where pain is concerned, health care should seldom involve an either/or proposition of providing physical care versus mental care.

This book has been designed to provide a practical guide for implementing psychological and behavioral interventions with pain patients that can enhance pain management. Throughout this book, we refer to Pain Management Psychotherapy as PMP, and we identify the clinician who implements psychological and behavioral pain management interventions with pain patients as a Pain Management Psychotherapist, PMP therapist, or PMP clinician.

This book is technique oriented and primarily directed to the needs of the psychotherapist who wants to conduct Pain Management Psychotherapy. Psychological assessment and intervention procedures for pain management are presented with case examples and in sufficient detail to allow trouble-free implementation by an experienced psychotherapist. We have developed, refined, or modified many of these techniques in our clinical practice; our pain patients have found them to be useful and effective.

The segments of the pain patient population that Wall (1994) has termed "medically treatable up to a point," and the segments that have been termed "intractable," or "medically untreatable," represent the majority of pain sufferers, and many of these patients can benefit from Pain Management Psychotherapy. Our definitions of pain also underscore that duration of persistent pain is not the only, or best, criterion for deciding whether or when to intervene psychologically and behaviorally.

PATIENT ASSESSMENT

Initially, we direct considerable attention to assessing psychological adjustment, maladjustment, psychopathology, and symptom magnification, as they relate to the primary complaint of pain. This is because attempts to distinguish between psychogenic and objective pain complaints have created much confusion in the pain management field (Gatchel, 1996; Hendler, 1981; Turk, 1996; Turk & Melzack, 1992). Also, alienation, resentment, anger, and maladjustment are frequent iatrogenic outcomes in patients who repeatedly fail to obtain pain relief despite numerous medical treatments (Eimer, 1988, 1989; Eimer & Allen, 1995).

THE PROBLEM OF DUAL DIAGNOSES

It is a misleading oversimplification to label pain as psychogenic or objective, one or the other. A more precise and useful conceptualization is the idea of "dual diagnoses," as employed in the contexts of substance abuse and mental health treatment. Thus, patients whose primary, initial, presenting complaint is pain may also have underlying, comorbid, character pathology or substance abuse disorders that predate their pain problems. Patients with dual diagnoses are usually harder to treat effectively for their pain problems than are pain patients who do not have preexistent psychiatric pathology. Often, the underlying behavioral health problems sabotage all efforts at pain management; the psychopathology and addictive disorders must be treated before attempting pain management. True psychopathology and characterologic pathology ought not to be confused with chronic pain syndromes, although they often exist side by side. Where the chronic pain syndrome is the secondary diagnosis, the primary diagnosis usually needs to be addressed first.

THE PROBLEM OF ALIENATION

Chronic pain patients' levels of alienation, resentment, depression, anger, and hostility need accurate assessment because their presence can provide a breeding ground for treatment noncompliance and resistance. High levels of these factors can be a harbinger of negative pain treatment outcomes. Foreknowledge may allow the therapist to address these potential treatment-sabotaging factors and avoid wasting resources by applying expensive treatments that have little chance of success.

TREATMENT PLANNING

A Primary Diagnosis of Chronic Pain Syndrome

If a patient's primary diagnosis is a chronic pain syndrome, the way is usually clear to proceed with an individually paced, short-term program of Pain Management Psychotherapy (PMP) and coping skills training. The PMP Treatment Plan is formulated to target the psychological, psychosocial, cognitive, behavioral, emotional, and physical factors that can block effective pain relief and impede highest possible levels of coping, functionality, and quality of life. Treatment planning is the subject of Chapter 4. Following the chapters on assessment and treatment planning, the rest of this book covers cognitive, behavioral, emotive, psychophysiological, and hypnotherapeutic, or hypno-behavioral, interventions for pain management.

The Medical Necessity of Pain Management Psychotherapy

Effective pain management requires considering the psychological factors involved because pain does not exist in a physiological vacuum. The psychological and behavioral factors that affect pain's presentation, severity, and course require intervention; evaluation and psychotherapy are medically necessary components of the effective management of many pain problems. This specialty component of medical pain management, which we term Pain Management Psychotherapy (PMP), is focused, structured, and usually short-term.

Indications for Psychological Evaluation

A psychological evaluation for PMP is indicated (a) whenever a patient with acute or subacute pain presents with a negative, exaggerated, emotional, or behavioral reaction to the pain; (b) whenever a pain patient does not seem to be progressing with medical or medicinal treatment, and (c) whenever medical or medicinal treatments are only partially effective leaving the patient with the need to manage substantial pain.

To select appropriate psychological interventions, an initial evaluation should assess several patient variables: (a) severity of distress, (b) level of suffering, (c) pain interference, (d) depression, (e) alienation and maladjustment, (f) psychological motivation for treatment, (g) general psychological adjustment, (h) self-efficacy, and (i) psychological and behavioral coping strategies. Cognitive, behavioral, emotive, psychophysiological, and hypnotherapeutic methods can relieve much suffering by addressing and processing attendant emotional factors, identifying and modifying cognitive distortions and maladaptive behaviors, and helping the patient develop a repertoire of pain coping skills.

Caution: PMP Is an Adjuvant Therapy

Pain Management Psychotherapy is an adjuvant to the comprehensive medical management of pain problems. Nonphysician clinicians and psychotherapists must refrain from treating pain problems that have not been adequately worked up and assessed medically. It is essential to review patients' prior medical records. Failure to obtain background medical information constitutes negligence. If a person seeking treatment for pain does not provide medical records of prior evaluations and treatment, the nonphysician therapist should request permission to obtain them.

Before treating any pain problems, it is judicious to obtain a patient's permission to confer with his or her currently treating physician or physicians. If a patient does not have an up-to-date medical history, prudence demands that the clinician advise the patient to obtain medical consultation before proceeding with psychological interventions. It is irresponsible to attempt to alleviate pain symptoms employing solely psychological methods when those symptoms may represent an underlying, medically treatable, physical problem. A medical workup is a prerequisite for implementing psychological interventions. Physicians serving as pain clinicians should take the same precautions: Obtain a thorough medical history before proceeding with any new pain treatments.

Attempting to help a patient manage pain that is a physical symptom of a treatable, underlying, but as yet undiagnosed, physical condition may constitute malpractice if the clinician fails to take at least one of the following courses of action: (a) obtaining and reviewing prior medical records, (b) if there are no prior medical records, recommending that the patient obtain medical consultation before beginning pain treatment, or (c) if the patient has been receiving medical treatment or has been referred by a physician, conferring with the patient's treating physician or physicians. If a new patient does not have a physician, the clinician should provide the patient with medical referral options and should NOT begin any psychological pain treatment until the patient obtains a medical evaluation, the results of which can be reviewed.

BASIC DEFINITIONS

PAIN'S SIGNALING FUNCTION

Adaptive pain performs a basic biological and psychological signaling function by providing the organism with biologically and psychologically informative feedback (Portenoy & Kanner, 1996a). *Acute* (recent onset) pain serves to notify a person of present or potential physical harm (e.g., a fractured ankle, a burned finger, physical exhaustion from overactivity). Because acute pain offers a biologically protective opportunity to remove oneself from harm's way and to relieve the cause of the discomfort, it is a primary symptom that motivates people to seek medical treatment (Turk & Melzack, 1992). However, when pain persists long after it has served its primary signaling function, it can be maladaptive and impair the quality of life. After appropriate medical care has been rendered, pain that does not remit must be managed.

DEFINING PAIN

The formal definition of pain developed by the International Association for the Study of Pain (IASP) states, "Pain is an unpleasant sensory and emotional experience associated with actual or potential tissue damage or described in terms of such damage" (Merskey & Bogduk, 1994, p. 210). This definition highlights that pain is an "unpleasant experience" with both "sensory" and "emotional" aspects. The sensory aspect of pain refers to the stimulation and activation of specialized sensory receptors in the nervous system by noxious stimuli (Melzack & Wall, 1965, 1982; Portenoy & Kanner, 1996a). The activation of these receptors creates what is termed *nociceptive sensory input,* and this in turn, is transformed neurochemically into nerve signals. Specific neural pathways in the spinal cord transmit these signals to the brain, where they are interpreted (Bromm & Desmedt, 1995; Melzack & Wall, 1965, 1982; Portenoy, 1996a).

Emotional and psychological factors affect the way a person interprets or perceives these neurochemically transmitted signals of noxious stimulation, and conversely, perceptions of the noxious stimuli determine that person's emotional and psychological reactions to the physical sensations. This interactive complex is one way of schematizing the experience of pain.

This conceptualization views pain as much more than an unpleasant sensation experienced solely in the present tense. It implies that a person's present experience is likely to be influenced by her memories of the past and expectations for future, or potential, bodily injury or tissue damage. It emphasizes that pain is more a perception than a sensation and is mediated by sensory, physiological, cognitive, emotional, behavioral, interpersonal, and environmental-situational factors.

THE SUBJECTIVITY OF PAIN

Because the perception of pain is a personal and individual experience, no two people can or will feel pain in exactly the same way. Similarly, a person's perceptions of pain at different points in time are likely to vary as a function of psychological and situational circumstances. Thus, it is a truism that no person, no matter how empathic, can ever truly experience another person's pain.

ACUTE PAIN

Acute pain may be defined as "pain of recent onset and probable limited duration" (Portenoy & Kanner, 1996a; Portenoy & Payne, 1992; Turk & Melzack, 1992). Typically, it has an identifiable temporal and causal relationship to a physical injury or disease process (e.g., pain associated with a broken arm, postsurgical pain). Thus, acute pain begins with a physical insult to some structures or tissues of the body and is time limited to hours, days, or weeks. Its intensity is usually greatest at the time of onset. As healing or tissue repair takes place, there usually is a corresponding gradual reduction in nociception and acute pain sensation. By definition, acute pain eventually remits, either spontaneously, or with some form of treatment that addresses the associated injury or disease.

INDIVIDUAL PSYCHOLOGICAL RESPONSES TO PAIN

The psychological and situational context mediate a person's response to acute pain, as well as the pain's course and duration. Myriad factors affect people's psychological responses including the understood cause of the pain, the circumstances of onset, and its understood medical prognosis (Toomey, Seville, Abashian, Finkel, & Mann, 1994). Acute (recent onset) and subacute (relatively recent onset) pain associated with strong negative emotions such as fear, grief, or anger can persist long after a precipitating physical injury has been treated (Geisser, Robinson, Keefe, & Weiner, 1994; Schreiber & Galai-Gat, 1993). Furthermore, situations that trigger strong negative emotions, feelings of lack of control, or conflictual feelings (e.g., guilt, anger, secondary gains) can impair a person's recovery from pain (Fernandez & Turk, 1995; Geisser, Roth, Bachman, & Eckert, 1996; Kerns & Haythornthwaite, 1988; Turk, Okifuji, & Scharff, 1995).

The pain of relatively minor physical injuries sustained in a psychologically traumatic event (e.g., a motor vehicle accident or a physical assault) may have a prolonged course (Geisser et al., 1996; Harness & Donlon, 1988; Hickling, Blauchard, Silverman, & Schwartz, 1992; Muse, 1986; Pilowsky, 1985) compared with the pain of comparably greater physical injuries from a less traumatic incident (e.g., fracturing an arm in an athletic event). In the former instance, the painful injuries are associated with psychological distress. In the latter example, the painful injury is not associated with significant psychological disruption.

CHRONIC PAIN

In contrast to acute pain, *chronic pain* is defined as "pain lasting for long periods of time." As discussed by Portenoy and Kanner (1996a), early definitions represented chronic pain as pain persisting for greater than 3 to 6 months. However, Bonica's (1990) improved definition states, "Pain is chronic if it persists for a month beyond the usual course of an acute illness or a reasonable duration for an injury to heal, if it is associated with a chronic pathologic process, or if it recurs at intervals for months and years." Thus, chronic pain is persistent pain that is insufficiently responsive to medical treatment (Portenoy & Kanner, 1996a; Turk & Melzack, 1992). It persists for extended periods (months or years) despite all efforts to treat the underlying physical pathology as it is understood.

This definition provides a more functional and realistic treatment of time or duration since pain's onset. To set 3 or 6 months since pain onset as a criterion for calling a pain complaint chronic, is essentially arbitrary. On the other hand, clinicians can obtain medically valuable information relevant to treatment by evaluating (a) whether a pain complaint is reasonable based on the usual or customary time course of an illness or an injury's healing, (b) whether the pain complaint is associated with a chronic, pathological process, or (c) whether the pain tends to recur over an extended period. Once again, the evaluation of these criteria requires medical input.

Classifying Chronic Pain

Chronic pain may further be classified:

- The term *objective* may be used to describe chronic pain associated with a medically verifiable disease process or physical injury, if the pain's severity is considered to be relatively proportionate to objective measures of the severity of the underlying disease or injury.
- In contrast, the term *psychogenic* typically characterizes chronic pain that is considered disproportionate to objective measures of the severity of the underlying disease or injury, or when no underlying disease or injury can be verified medically to account for the pain.

- The term *chronic, benign pain* typically refers to chronic pain that is secondary to benign (non-cancer-related) diseases or physical conditions (e.g., physical or emotional trauma, mechanical degeneration, inflammation, psychophysiological factors). Nonmalignant, chronic pain is not always psychologically benign. It often presents with a level of physical severity disproportionately in excess of the objective physical findings indicative of ongoing nociceptive input and frequently is associated with significant emotional distress. Thus, it creates a quandary for many treating physicians who are trained to focus on acute physical pathology and cure disease.

- *Chronic, malignant pain* refers to chronic pain that is secondary to a malignant, progressive process (e.g., metastatic cancer, tumor growth).

- *Progressive* refers to chronic pain associated with an underlying disease process that is gradually worsening (i.e., progressing). The underlying, worsening disease may be cancer (e.g., metastatic disease), but it also may be another nononcologic, progressive disease such as chronic obstructive pulmonary disease or multiple sclerosis.

- *Recurrent chronic pain* refers to pain that recurs episodically (e.g., chronic migraine or tension headaches) and is resistant to treatment efforts. The term *intermittent* also might characterize pain that comes and goes (i.e., recurs) in relatively discrete episodes.

- In contrast, *continuous* refers to pain that is always there, although its severity or magnitude may vary (e.g., mechanical, low back pain).

Chronic Pain and Symptoms of Posttraumatic Stress

Investigators have reported a marked prevalence of symptoms of posttraumatic stress disorder in people with chronic pain (Benedikt & Kolb, 1986; Blanchard & Hickling, 1997; Geisser et al., 1996; Lebovits, Yarmush, & Lefkowitz, 1990; Muse, 1986; Pilowsky, 1985; Schreiber & Galai-Gat, 1993). Research by Blanchard and Hickling (1997) and Geisser et al. (1996) with motor vehicle and other accident victims revealed that PTSD symptoms are associated with increased self-reports of chronic pain, affective distress, and functional disability. Hickling et al. (1992) have reported PTSD prevalence rates as high as 75% for consecutive patients referred for psychological evaluation and treatment of motor vehicle accident related pain. These studies suggest that injured persons who initially register high levels of serious emotional distress show a slower recovery from their physical injuries than those who have less initial distress. In Blanchard and Hickling's (1997) study of motor vehicle accident survivors, "the subgroup of individuals who continued to meet the criteria for full PTSD at 12 months plateaued with regard to remission of injuries" (p. 166). As stated by Blanchard and Hickling (1997), "It is as if the physical injuries in those who continued to be symptomatic enough to qualify as full PTSD have ceased to improve" (p. 167). Physically injured individuals who are significantly emotionally distressed likely are vulnerable to additional stressors and thus require more psychologically oriented treatment.

Patients' Appraisals of Their Pain

In a much cited study, Beecher (1946) compared the reactions of World War II soldiers whose painful wounds occasioned their leaving the battle zone, with the reactions to pain of civilians awaiting surgery. The soldiers reported less pain and fewer requested narcotics than did the civilians. Beecher's interpretation of these findings was that the soldiers viewed their painful wounds as a ticket out of the line of fire. Thus, their pain was associated with positive expectations and emotions such as happiness, hope, and relief. On the other hand, negative expectations and emotions such as worry, anxiety, and fear affected the civilians' more negative reactions to their pain.

Research by Turk and his colleagues (Fernandez & Turk, 1995; Rudy, Kerns, & Turk, 1988; Turk et al., 1995) suggests that patients' appraisals of the impact of pain on their lives and their ability to control the pain affect whether or not patients become depressed. The connection between depression and the exacerbation of pain requires further exploration, but our clinical experience has been that depression, anxiety, anger, and hostility complicate and often impede pain rehabilitation and recovery (Ahles, Yunus, & Masi, 1987; Beutler, Engle, Oro-Beutler, Daldrup, & Meredith, 1986; Blumer & Heilbronn, 1989; Brown, 1990; Burns, Johnson, Mahoney, Devine, & Pawl, 1996). In a related line of research, anger and hostility have been widely observed in persons with chronic pain, and these reactions have been found to account for significant variance in measures of pain severity, pain interference, and frequency of pain behaviors (Burns et al., 1996; Eimer & Allen, 1995; Fernandez & Turk, 1995; Kerns, Rosenberg, & Jacob, 1994).

CANCER PAIN

Malignant chronic pain, secondary to the progression of cancer (tumor growth and metastasis), presents a unique constellation of challenging psychological problems related to the fear of bodily decline and death. Nevertheless, the majority of psychological pain management techniques in this book, if applied in an appropriate treatment context, are relevant to the management of both cancer and noncancer pain. Evidence is growing that nonpharmacological behavioral and psychological methods have an important adjuvant role in the management of cancer pain (Roth-Roemer, Abrams, & Syrjala, 1996). In particular, hypnosis and imagery, in conjunction with cognitive-behavioral methods, have emerged as effective therapeutic tools (Fawzy, Fawzy, Arndt, & Pasnau, 1995; Syrjala & Abrams, 1996; Turk et al., 1983).

THE CHRONIC PAIN SYNDROME

Chronic pain syndrome refers to a condition characterized by non-cancer-related, enduring pain associated with significant suffering, emotional distress, behavioral dysfunction, physical deconditioning, and disability. It is persistent and unremitting despite extensive medical care and treatment, and its severity and degree of behavioral disruption are often markedly in excess of any objective medical findings of tissue pathology.

THE EVOLUTION OF A CHRONIC PAIN SYNDROME

When a treating physician's efforts fail to help a patient obtain adequate, enduring pain relief, both patient and physician face a dilemma: The physician must decide whether to refer the patient to another health care professional; the patient wonders whether to continue treating with the physician, seek help from someone else, or just cease seeking help and suffer. Most patients in this situation opt to seek help elsewhere hoping to find out how to obtain adequate, enduring pain relief. Frequently, they consult numerous doctors, and frustration mounts when satisfactory answers are not forthcoming.

THE "SIX DYSFUNCTIONAL DS" OF CHRONIC PAIN SYNDROMES

Going from doctor to doctor takes its toll on a person. First, medical visits take up time and cost money. Second, compliance with medical treatment regimens uses up energy—something that people with persistent pain typically do not have in abundance. Third, each time answers are inadequate and treatment fails, patients become less hopeful. In time, after a fruitless search for answers and numerous treatment failures, many people with chronic, persistent pain come to expect little from health care professionals. A state of learned helplessness (Seligman, 1975) may develop that can significantly alter a person's lifestyle. For many people with chronic pain syndromes, this state frequently is marked by dysfunction in the form of (a) emotional *d*istress (e.g., anxiety, conflict, anger, hostility, resentment, alienation), (b) behavioral and cognitive *d*eficits (e.g., deficits in impulse control, assertiveness, attention, concentration, memory, and judgment), (c) varying degrees of *d*isability related to work, (d) *d*epression, (e) physical *d*econditioning, and (f) *d*isturbed sleep patterns (Gatchel, 1996).

The Six Dysfunctional Ds are present in many chronic persistent pain syndromes. Effective medical treatment of a patient's pain problem requires assessing and addressing them. These psychological and behavioral issues can then be confronted and remediated most successfully in a psychotherapy context.

Often, a person with acute or subacute pain enters a state of learned helplessness and becomes a chronic pain patient in an insidious process involving multiple, interacting factors (Gatchel, 1996; Hendler, 1981; Skevington, 1996; Turk, 1996). Initially, pain as a signal of potential harm produces a psychological distress reaction. The distress does not get resolved but, instead, rises as the pain does not remit. Initial concern, preoccupation with symptoms, and anxiety may evolve into greater anxiety, fear, and frustration. Depending on the situational context, frustration may turn into anger and resentment. Over time, as pain-related problems mount, depression may set in. The particular psychological disorder that emerges depends on a person's premorbid personality traits, psychological characteristics, medical condition, and situational-contextual factors such as psychosocial and socioeconomic conditions (Gatchel, 1996; Linton & Bradley, 1996; Turk, 1996).

RISK FACTORS FOR CHRONIC PAIN SYNDROME

In the past decade, investigators have learned much about psychosocial and psychological risk factors that can create barriers to recovery from acute pain and predispose a person to develop a chronic pain syndrome (Dworkin, 1991; Elliot, 1996; Gatchel, 1996; Linton & Bradley, 1996; Sanders, 1995b; Skevington, 1996). These include (a) pain duration greater than 2 years, and multiple invasive treatments (Linton & Bradley, 1996), (b) a history of prolonged recovery from similar or other types of pain (Grzesiak, Ury, & Dworkin, 1996), (c) job dissatisfaction (Feuerstein & Zastowny, 1996; Linton & Bradley, 1996; Sanders, 1995b), (d) a history of emotional or physical trauma (Geisser et al., 1996; Grzesiak et al., 1996; Harness & Donlon, 1988; Muse, 1986), (e) a history of physical, emotional, or sexual abuse (Scarinci, Haile, Bradley, & Richter, 1994; Walker et al., 1988), (f) low levels of activity, excessive pain behaviors, and solicitous or exceptionally punitive family members' responses to such behaviors (Fordyce, 1976; Sanders, 1996), (g) negative, fear-based beliefs about pain and activity (Waddell, Newton, Henderson, Somerville, & Main, 1993; Waddell & Turk, 1992), and (h) premorbid affective, anxiety, substance abuse, or personality disorders (Blumer & Heilbronn, 1989; Ciccone & Lenzi, 1994; Dworkin, 1991; Engel, 1959; Grzesiak et al., 1996; Hendler, 1981).

When any of the preceding risk factors are present, a psychological evaluation is indicated to identify potential barriers to recovery and ways to surmount them. Some of the factors are modifiable; others are not. Although it is impossible to modify a person's history, the therapist may be able to modify a person's behavior and reactions to that history. Timely behavioral and psychological intervention to address the behavior and reactions associated with pain-related disability may help prevent acute pain from evolving into a chronic pain syndrome (Feuerstein & Zastowny, 1996; Gatchel, 1996; Linton & Bradley, 1996; Sanders, 1995b). Evidence has mounted that focused psychological intervention can improve pain management outcomes by helping pain patients learn self-management techniques and build coping skills (Caudill, 1995; Hanson & Gerber, 1990; Linton & Bradley, 1996; Philips & Rachman, 1996; Turk, 1996; Turk et al., 1983).

THE NEED FOR PAIN MANAGEMENT PSYCHOTHERAPY TO BE CONTEXTUALLY RELEVANT

In the current climate of health care, psychotherapists and other health care practitioners are under increasing pressure to document and justify their interventions. This calls for a conceptually guided, *contextually relevant* approach to PMP that incorporates what A. Lazarus (1989), the author of multimodal therapy, has termed *technical eclecticism.* Embracing technical eclecticism means being willing to select from and use a wide range of psychological techniques, based on their potential to produce positive therapeutic outcomes, regardless of any technique's theoretical origins. Therapeutic interventions are based on the clinician's conceptualization of a patient's presenting problems and goals for treatment. We define contextually relevant psychotherapy as psychological treatment that is (a) consistent with a patient's relevant beliefs and treatment expectations, (b) appropriate to the context and circumstances of a patient's problems, and (c) reasonable from the standpoint of available resources, operating influences, and what is likely to be achieved. Psychological and behavioral interventions need to be planned and implemented based on these contextual factors.

Contextually relevant PMP begins with a focused psychological assessment of the patient. The data from the initial assessment guide the clinician in formulating a treatment plan that translates the patient's presenting complaints into specific pain treatment goals and objectives. Then, based on the therapeutic context, the therapist negotiates with the patient which treatment objectives to target, in what order, employing which interventions.

When time, office space, and insurance resources are limited, as they often are in a busy medical setting, psychological interventions need to be brief and focused. To be effective, psychotherapists in medical settings must "think on their feet," as do their physician colleagues and quickly select interventions from a readily accessible clinical tool box of interventional modalities and strategies. Even when a clinician has the luxury of a full 50-minute hour (or even a 90-minute session), limitations on session numbers and third-party demands for accountability necessitate short-term, solution-focused treatment.

Definition of Pain Patient

A *pain patient* is one whose primary presenting complaint is persistent pain and whose primary reason for seeking treatment is to ameliorate this persistent pain and other associated symptoms. Pain patients often complain that health care professionals do not adequately explain the causes of their pain, or rationales for its management (DeGood, 1983; DeGood & Shutty, 1992). This frequently leads to dissatisfaction with pain treatment. Effective psychotherapy for pain patients (i.e., PMP) should address the patient's need for answers. It should examine the interrelationship between a patient's beliefs about pain and suffering, beliefs about himself or herself, idiosyncratic understanding of the causes and meaning of the pain, attitudes about treatment, and expectations for the future.

Effective Pain Management Psychotherapy

Effective psychotherapy in general and PMP in particular are contextually relevant by providing patients with understandable and acceptable rationales for assessment procedures and therapeutic interventions (Turk et al., 1983). The technical components of PMP include:

1. Adequate initial and ongoing assessments of baseline status and therapy progress.
2. Structured, psychoeducational teaching to provide the patient with an understandable rationale for the therapy, an understandable model of pain mechanisms, and an acceptable rationale for making recommended lifestyle changes.
3. Cognitive therapy (J. Beck, 1995; Beck, Rush, Shaw, & Emery, 1979; Eimer, 1989, 1992; Freeman, Pretzer, Fleming, & Simon, 1990; Turk et al., 1983) to help the patient identify and modify depressogenic and distress-producing negative thinking patterns.

4. Behavioral reactivation therapy for restoring physical conditioning and increasing levels of positively reinforcing activities.

5. Coping skills therapy (or training) to help the patient develop coping strategies and pain management skills.

6. Psychophysiological self-regulation therapy to teach relaxation skills.

7. Hypnotherapy, or imagery work, for modifying thoughts and images associated with pain and suffering and building an adaptive repertoire of thoughts and images associated with pain relief (Barber, 1996; Schafer, 1996).

8. Cognitive-emotive reprocessing of upsetting or traumatic memories associated with pain and pain treatment (Cheek, 1994; Eimer, 1993a, 1993b; Shapiro, 1995).

PMP does not always include all eight components. Many patients receive Components 1 through 7. Component 8 is included and integrated into the treatment plan when appropriate. Some patients, who are referred for an evaluation only, just receive the first two components. Many patients who are referred for biofeedback or relaxation therapy, receive Components 3 (cognitive therapy), 5 (coping skills therapy), 6 (psychophysiological), and 7 (imagery work). The important point is that patients receive those components for which they are referred.

THE IATROGENIC EFFECTS OF CERTAIN TRAIT-BASED SUMMARY LABELS

Pain patients often have seen numerous health care practitioners before their first evaluation by a psychotherapist and may already have been labeled as treatment failures. Some patients' presenting behaviors and past histories may suggest that they sabotaged previous treatment efforts, which can lead a clinician into thinking in terms of negative, personality or trait-based labels such as "pain-prone," "addictive," "manipulative," or "borderline." Such trait-based labeling seldom contributes anything worthwhile to the formulation of an implementable treatment plan. Conceptualizing a patient as a pain treatment failure because of a characterologic disorder stands in sharp contrast to formulating a patient's condition as an evolved combination of unfortunate medical, socioeconomic, and psychological circumstances. Because negative trait terms imply permanent dysfunction, they leave little room for modifiability or improvement.

Conceptualizing a patient as having a "pain-prone personality," or as being a "low-back loser" (Engel, 1959; Sternbach, 1974) implies that the patient's current suffering (learned helplessness) represents an unmodifiable trait as opposed to a potentially modifiable state. This attributional process can lead to a treatment stalemate and unfavorable outcome. A clinician who views a patient this way may subsequently operate from a negative expectancy about the patient's potential to learn how to manage pain more effectively.

In addition to personality variables, other factors influence the development of a chronic pain syndrome and some of these are more readily modified, such as behavioral and psychological variables and management of the patient's medical condition. To date, there is no compelling evidence for the existence of a unitary entity that could be called a pain-prone personality (Gatchel, 1996; Grzesiak et al., 1996; Turk, 1996). Evidence is emerging, however, for constellations of risk factors that can make a person vulnerable to developing a chronic pain syndrome. Additionally, certain personality traits appear to make a person more vulnerable to pain and suffering including hysteria, hypochondriasis, long-standing depression, anger, resentment, hostility, and social anxiety (Blumer & Heilbronn, 1989; Grzesiak et al., 1996; Sanders, 1995b). Our basic premise, however, is that currently modifiable, behavioral and psychological factors should be the main targets of intervention.

THE WEAR, TEAR, AND FEAR OF PAIN

The fear of pain is a universal phenomenon because pain is an unpleasant experience associated with physical injury. In fact, severe, unremitting, or worsening pain frequently is related to physical decline, and sometimes with dying or death. In advanced cases of cancer-related pain, increasing pain severity often signals progression of disease and tumor growth. People who are terminally ill sometimes perceive constant, physical pain to be a greater adversity than imminent or eventual death. On the other hand, increases in the intensity of chronic, benign (non-cancer-related) pain do not typically correlate with disease progression, although persistent pain typically is associated with physical decline, physical impairment, disability, and emotional distress. Yet, there is no simple and direct relationship between the severity of chronic, benign pain and the magnitude of a person's underlying physical problems. Variations in pain intensity are usually a fact of life with chronic, benign pain.

Living in a persistent pain state exacts a huge toll; people with chronic pain commonly live in a state of tension and anxiety. Constant pain consumes energy and demands attention draining a person's physical, emotional, and cognitive resources. It can disrupt sleep, appetite, and other basic biological functions. People who live in pain typically fear it will get worse. The medical consequences of such distress often include significant wear and tear on the body. When pain is episodic or intermittent (e.g., migraine headaches, crises of sickle cell anemia), people often live in fear that the next recurrence may be more severe and disabling than the last. It is not uncommon for people to blame themselves, to some degree, for flare-ups.

EMOTIONAL FACTORS, PERSISTENT PAIN, AND SUFFERING

Emotional, psychological, and behavioral factors play a major role in the maintenance and perpetuation of suffering related to persistent pain. With lives that are disrupted severely by their painful conditions, and no relief on the horizon, many people understandably become anxious, angry, and depressed. However, the onset and perpetuation of significant emotional disturbance makes it less likely that a pain-sufferer will be able to escape from a "prison of pain." The following prototypical case summaries introduce three typical pain scenarios: (a) a continual, mechanical low back pain condition associated with a work-related injury; (b) advanced cancer pain, and (c) recurrent, mixed headache pain. Each case summary provides a list of the key issues that the psychotherapist needs to address.

Case 1. Living with Constant, Low Back and Leg Pain

Jim was a 36-year-old married, former maintenance mechanic who had injured his back in a work-related, lifting accident three years previously. He had sustained a lumbosacral strain injury, as well as several lumbar disc herniations, which left him in a persistent state of low back and leg pain. Initial, conservative care had not remitted his severe pain, and eventually, he went on to have several back operations that failed to relieve his low back and leg pain syndrome. His underlying lumbar pathology and failed back surgeries resulted in a chronic, intractable state of nerve root damage and arachnoiditis, with muscle weakness, sensory loss, and a gait disorder. He had seen numerous orthopedic and neurosurgical specialists, but had not benefited from any enduring solution to his intractable pain problem. Currently, he was being evaluated for implantation of a dorsal column, spinal cord stimulator and had been referred for a psychological evaluation to assist the anesthesiologist in determining Jim's psychological suitability for such a procedure.

Jim described his pain as "constant, throbbing, shooting, stabbing, sharp, nagging, intense, cramping, and agonizing." He experienced it as radiating from his low back down the back of both legs. Jim had been out of work since the accident. He stated that he could no longer work, as a result of his pain, stiffness, weakness, and associated symptoms. Jim told the psychologist that he awoke every day with severe back, leg, and neck pain; he looked forward to sleep as his only respite from pain. Because of severe pain, he had to lie down and rest on numerous occasions throughout the day and took excessive amounts of pain medication. The pain medication made him tired, but nevertheless, he was unable to obtain restful or restorative sleep because of the constant pain.

At the time of his psychological pain evaluation, Jim stated that he could not sit for more than a few minutes at a time because sitting intensified his back and leg pain. He also complained of feeling "stiff and cramped up" all the time. Bending was difficult, as was lifting anything weighing more than 15 pounds, because of the stress and strain these activities placed on his back, hips, and legs. Jim tried to walk as much as he could on a daily basis but could not walk for more than a few minutes without experiencing worsening pain. He walked with a cane, which he said was necessary to compensate for the weakness and sensory loss in his left leg. The pain had forced him to give up several leisure activities he used to enjoy, such as hunting, fishing, and coaching his son's Little League and soccer teams.

Despite his suffering, Jim believed that others doubted the validity of his pain complaints and thought he was a malingerer. He described his wife as punitive and resentful at times. In addition, his 9-year-old daughter and 13-year-old son had become spiteful and seemed increasingly to avoid him. The insurance company responsible for paying workers' compensation benefits had tried to cut off his benefits several times, which motivated Jim to hire an attorney.

Jim felt resigned to living the rest of his life in a state of continual pain, but he feared his condition would gradually worsen, and this frightened him. He also feared that his workers' compensation subsidy and medical benefits would end, and that he and his family would be destitute. Jim admitted to suppressing a good deal of anger about not getting better, his history of failed treatments, the insurance company's actions, and some of his family's responses to his condition.

Conferral with Jim's treating physicians revealed that Jim had been a compliant patient who had followed through with his doctors' prescriptive treatments. Most of his doctors, however, expressed the view that there was little more that they could do for him medically. The surgical implantation of a dorsal spinal column stimulator was a final treatment possibility for pain relief—a "court of last resort."

On psychological evaluation, Jim admitted to feeling demoralized and moderately depressed. His score of 14 on the Beck Depression Inventory (BDI; A. Beck, 1987/1993; Beck, Ward, Mendelson, Mock, & Erlbaugh, 1961), is considered to fall in the "mild" range of depressive symptomology. Nevertheless, he indicated that pain interfered markedly with his activities of daily living. Further psychodiagnostic evaluation and psychological testing with the Pain Patient Profile (P-3) (Tollison & Langley, 1995) revealed a high level of somatic preoccupation and distress (termed "somatization"), a mild-to-moderate level of depression, but a normative level of anxiety, when compared with a chronic pain reference group. No other marked signs of psychopathology were evident.

Summary. Jim presented as mildly to moderately disabled physically, mildly to moderately depressed, very somatically preoccupied, and no more anxious than the typical low back pain patient. He admitted that he feared that spinal cord stimulation might turn out to be another treatment failure. The key issues for psychotherapeutic consideration were:

- The experience of being in constant pain over which Jim felt he had little control.
- Disrupted, nonrestorative sleep and constant fatigue.
- Too much "downtime" (e.g., frequent lying down to escape from pain).
- Markedly limited physical endurance and marked deconditioning.
- Excessive levels of disability relative to work and activities of daily living.
- Maladaptive control of his activity levels by pain and fear of more pain.
- Jim's internalized and unexpressed anger.
- A dearth of rewarding leisure activities, and a marked loss of pleasure.
- A strained marital relationship, and an increasingly alienated relationship with his daughter and son.
- An adversarial, stressful relationship with his insurance company.
- Mild-to-moderate symptoms of depression (e.g., concentration difficulties, loss of interest, hopelessness, feelings of guilt, decreased self-esteem, feelings of having failed, social withdrawal, inertia).
- High levels of somatization.

Case 2. Living with Progressive Cancer Pain

Tom, an 81-year-old married, retired man, was suffering from metastatic prostate cancer. He had been initially diagnosed with prostate cancer approximately 5 years previously but, at that time, was minimally symptomatic. Following an observational period of no treatment (about 2 years), Tom was treated with hormonal suppression therapy after he began to develop urinary and bladder symptoms, and after his prostate specific antigen (PSA) level began to rise. He subsequently was advised to undergo a course of pelvic radiation therapy of the prostate tumor, which he did.

Following irradiation of his tumor, Tom's PSA level went down, and for about 2 years, he remained minimally symptomatic. He continued to receive hormonal suppression therapy in the form of monthly injections of the drug, Lupron, at his urologist's office. Approximately 1 year previous to his current problems, he developed hematuria (bloody urine), progressive urinary problems (trouble voiding), and worsening anal and perineal spasms. Tom next had several surgeries performed [transurethral resections of the prostate (TURPs)] in which his doctors attempted to resect his massive, growing tumor. Nevertheless, his condition continued to worsen.

There was no previous history of depression, nor of any other psychiatric or psychological adjustment problems. However, Tom's doctors had recently told him that his cancer had become aggressive and was progressing quickly now, despite treatment. Tom's physical condition had worsened, along with his spirits. When referred for psychological consultation, Tom was experiencing a severe postradiation pain syndrome marked by hematuria, progressively worsening perineal and rectal pain, burning pain in his scrotum and penis, and proctitis (rectal inflammation, irritation, and pain). The constant, sharp, burning, and pressing pain made it extremely difficult for him to sit. The pain was rated as severe to excruciating.

Tom's pain was only partially controlled pharmaceutically with regularly scheduled and "as-needed" oral dosing of opioid pain medication, and epidural dosing with a sustained-release opioid (Fentanyl) skin patch. At times, Tom described the intensity of his breakthrough pain as agonizing, and he would tell his wife that he wanted to die. Tom had also become incontinent of urine; he had to self-catheterize and was unable to move his bowels without taking enemas and laxatives. The demands of his daily self-care were exhausting to both Tom and his wife, Sally. He was sleeping through much of the day, while Sally, although exhausted, could not sleep well. Tom had also lost most of his formerly excellent appetite and was losing weight steadily.

Despite all his medical problems, Tom continued to live at home with his dedicated wife of 50 years, who was feeling increasingly helpless in the face of their mutual ordeal. The couple also had two grown, married children. Their daughter, who lived in town, provided some emotional support. She spoke with her parents on the telephone on a daily basis, and visited several times per week. Their son lived out of town.

Two of Tom's doctors eventually suggested that hospice care might be the best option, but neither Tom nor Sally was ready to consider this option. By now, both Tom and Sally were feeling increasingly abandoned by their health care providers, who had failed to arrest the cancer's progression. They were also angry at the health care providers whom they perceived to be uncaring, insensitive, and "just in it for the Medicare money." Tom was referred for psychological consultation by his oncologist who hoped that some psychological techniques could help Tom manage his depression, as well as his pain. The oncologist also thought that the couple needed supportive counseling.

On their first visit, Tom told the psychologist he could accept that he probably had a limited time left to live, given the progression of his prostate cancer. He stated that although he could tolerate pain, his greatest fear was of suffering from agonizing, uncontrolled pain, and his pain was getting worse. Tom could no longer find a place for himself to get comfortable. He could not sit still, or in one position, for more than a few minutes, and felt agitated most of the time. Tom told the psychologist that his first wish was for freedom from pain and that this wish came before his wish for life extension. He dreaded the recurrences of sharp, agonizing pain that broke through numerous times each day, despite his pharmaceutical pain control regimen. The level of his pain was judged to be intolerable. Tom stated that, if the situation worsened, he would be willing to go into a hospice. He also complained about doctors and other health care providers being insensitive and admitted to harboring considerable anger about this.

Summary. Tom presented as very medically ill, with a secondary depressive and anxiety reaction to his physically debilitated condition. He was in constant physical pain, and the pain was getting worse. Both Tom and his wife were physically exhausted and scared. They felt let down and abandoned by Tom's doctors, and they were angry. To both Tom and his wife, the worsening pain signified the progression of his disease and the approach of death, as well as the continuation of a life filled with increasing pain and exhausting daily self-care ordeals.

Minimal psychological testing was performed because of this patient's limited physical and mental endurance and concentration. There was minimal evidence of cognitive dementia based on administration of the Mini-Mental State Examination (Folstein, Folstein, & McHugh, 1975) on which he earned a score of 26 out of a maximum possible total of 30. On the Beck Depression Inventory (BDI), Tom's total BDI score came to 42 out of a maximum possible total of 63, placing him in the severe range of depression. Tom's key depressive symptoms included sadness, hopelessness, anhedonia, feelings of being punished, anger, serious thoughts of ending his life, crying spells, irritability, loss of social interest, concentration problems, inertia, anorexia, crushing fatigue, and preoccupation with pain and the disease. Some of the depressive symptoms were due to physical factors associated with Tom's medical status (e.g., inertia, anorexia, crushing fatigue).

The key issues for psychotherapeutic consideration were:

- Tom's fear of dying and death.
- Sally's fear of witnessing Tom's death; Also, her feelings of guilt secondary to the thought that she was not doing enough for Tom.
- Tom and Sally's feelings of abandonment by their doctors, and their resultant anger.
- Tom and Sally's anger at the illness.
- Tom's preparations for dying, and his grieving over the imminent prospect of leaving his loved ones.
- Tom's experience of being in constant pain over which he felt he had little control and his constant association of the pain with being victimized, and with dying.
- Tom's heightened psychophysiological level of anxiety, manifested in his hyperventilation, irritability, episodes of mild agitation, and inability to relax, sit still, or "find a place for himself."
- Tom's depressive symptoms (e.g., his feelings of helplessness and hopelessness, and of being punished; his anger, his inertia, and preoccupation with the pain).

Case 3. Living with Chronic, Recurrent Headaches

Sara was a 42-year-old married secretary who suffered from chronic headaches. Her family physician and her neurologist referred her for biofeedback and stress reduction therapy. On her initial visit, Sara told the psychologist that she had one to two "sick headache" episodes per week, but that she had headaches, pain, and tension every day. She stated that she woke up every day with a headache and that if she did not have a headache on awakening in the morning, she would have a tension headache on arriving at work. Her sick headaches appeared to be triggered by, among other things, interpersonal and work stress, certain foods, changes in her sleep patterns (i.e., too little or too much sleep), weekends and holidays, trips, visual strain (as from reading too much), and even the occurrence of something unexpectedly pleasant.

Sara had seen numerous physicians, neurologists, and pain specialists, none of whom had been able to help her control her headaches. Her medical records revealed the following diagnoses: common migraine headaches, muscle contraction/tension headaches, mixed headache syndrome, sinus headaches (she had corrective surgery for a deviated septum), allergic headaches, cervical cephalgia, and postconcussive headaches (she had been in a motor vehicle accident approximately 3 years previously). Sara had been tried on numerous pharmacological preparations that had either not worked or gave rise to undesirable side effects. Sara also had been told by one of her doctors that she probably was suffering from analgesic rebound headaches, which perpetuated her headache problem, and made her refractory to treatment.

Sara admitted that she felt hopelessly addicted to her daily medicine cabinet combination of nonsteroidal anti-inflammatory drugs (NSAIDs; e.g., Motrin), narcotic and nonnarcotic pain relievers (e.g., Tylenol with codeine, Percocet, Extra-Strength Tylenol), anxiolytic tranquilizers (e.g., Xanax), ergotamine-caffeine compounds (e.g., Cafergot), and analgesic-barbiturate-caffeine compounds (e.g., Fiorinal). She also admitted to making frequent (sometimes weekly) trips to the local hospital's emergency room, for intramuscular, (IM) injections of a serotonin-agonist drug such as Imitrex (sumatriptan). She believed that these medicines were the only treatments on which she could rely to lessen her headaches' impact and help her get to sleep. After an injection, she would go home and "sleep it off." Then, she would awaken, soon have another headache, and the cycle would be repeated.

Some of Sara's doctors were now suggesting that psychological factors were probably responsible for her poor response to medical treatment. She interpreted this to mean that they thought that her headaches were "all in her head" (i.e., psychologically based). This implication made her feel at various times, annoyed, angry, guilty, depressed, and more distressed.

Sara had been hospitalized several times on a dedicated headache pain treatment unit for medicine detoxification, but within months after each discharge, the cycle began again. She lived in constant fear of having her next debilitating headache episode. When she had such an episode, she usually was disabled for up to 12 hours and had to lie down in a dark, quiet room in the hope that she could "get to sleep and sleep it off." When her sick headache pain started, it was so severe that she wished that she was unconscious. Thus, she was always vigilant for signs of an impending episode. This affected her motivation and initiative, impaired her quality of life, and markedly constricted her activities. She often thought to herself, "Why bother doing anything?" as she expected an incapacitating headache to disrupt whatever enjoyment or satisfaction she obtained from an activity.

Sara described the main symptoms of her sick headaches (migraines) as nausea, vertigo, blurred vision, inability to sit up, cold and clammy hands and feet, photosensitivity and audiosensitivity ("photophobia" and "phono-phobia"), and an intense throbbing, pounding, pulsating, and aching pain spreading from around one of her eyes (worse around the left eye), up into her forehead, into the back of her head, and down into her neck and shoulders. The main symptoms of her daily tension headaches included tightness in her scalp; severe pain and stiffness in her neck and shoulders; extreme tenderness, pulsing, and sensitivity in her temples and in the back of her head; and some dizziness or light-headedness. As a result of her headache problem, Sara had missed many workdays, and her supervisor had threatened to have her fired several times. Lately, the headaches had increased in frequency and severity.

Sara was married, but had no children. She stated that although her husband usually did her chores around the house and catered to her when she had a bad headache, she was afraid he was losing patience. She felt that their marriage had been on shaky ground for some time because she was "always sick with a headache."

Summary. Sara felt little hope about the prospects of a cure for her headaches. She felt sick and in pain much of the time. She was consuming a large amount of pain medication on a daily basis. She was angry at doctors for being peremptory, but nevertheless failing to help her, and also in her opinion, for negatively labeling her. She did not expect much from psychological counseling or biofeedback. Nevertheless, she agreed to give it a chance (two to three sessions to "see if the psychologist made any sense"). She hated her job and found work stressful. Her quality of life was rated as poor. She was afraid her husband might "get fed up and leave." She also stated that she did not sleep well, and that she felt tired and depressed much of the time.

On the Beck Depression Inventory, she scored in the low-grade range of depression (BDI = 15 out of 63). She admitted to feelings of discouragement, failure, and self-disappointment. She did not obtain pleasure from things anymore, was irritable, unmotivated to do things, tired most of the time, and often felt helpless and hopeless. She blamed most of her problems on her headaches. Her expressed level of psychological insight was low. She believed the cause of her headaches was largely some undiagnosed "biochemical imbalance" that needed to be treated. On the Pain Beliefs and Perceptions Inventory (Williams & Keefe, 1991), she revealed that she viewed her headache pain as mysterious, continuous, and permanent. On the McGill Pain Questionnaire (Melzack & Katz, 1992), she scored as high on the evaluative and affective descriptive dimensions of her pain as she did on the sensory descriptive dimension.

The key issues for psychotherapeutic consideration were:

- Sara's extreme difficulty relaxing.
- Sara's extreme overuse of medications, especially pain medications.
- Sara's anger and hostility.
- Sara's negative thinking patterns, which were associated with her depression, hostility, and continued headaches.
- Sara's expectation and fear of having one sick headache after another.

- Sara's feeling and perception of having little control over her headaches. Indeed, she had one continuous headache marked by intermittent sick headache episodes.
- The frequency and extended duration of her sick headaches, and the extent of her resultant disablement.
- Sara's elevated psychophysiological level of anxiety, manifested by an inability to relax, hypervigilance, heightened arousal, hyperventilation, muscle tension, and irritability.
- Depressive symptoms (e.g., feelings of discouragement, failure, and self-disappointment; lack of a sense of pleasure or mastery from things and few rewarding activities; irritability, lack of motivation, and fatigue; feelings of helplessness and hopelessness; preoccupation with pain).
- Sara's job dissatisfaction and conflicts at work.
- The dynamics of Sara's relationship with her husband, especially his tendency to take over for her whenever she was sick.

THE COMPLEXITY OF CHRONIC PAIN

Each of these studies illustrates the psychological ramifications of chronic pain. Cases 1 and 3 illustrate "chronic, benign pain," whereas Case 2 illustrates chronic, progressive, malignant pain. However, the psychological ramifications in Cases 1 and 3 are not benign! The past two decades have yielded marked technological advances in the medical, pharmacological, and surgical treatment of acute disease, and in the medical management of many chronic conditions. Remarkable progress has also been made in the medical and medicinal management of acute pain (American Pain Society, 1992; Ready & Edwards, 1992; Williams, 1996). Treatment of chronic pain has been less progressive. Medical, pharmacological, and surgical interventions used effectively for acute conditions often fail to provide patients with long-lasting relief from chronic, persistent pain, and associated emotional suffering.

Chronic pain is complex and multidimensional. Behavioral and psychological interventions address its psychological and psychosocial toll, but medical patients frequently interpret a referral for psychological consultation to imply that their pain is in some sense not valid or real. They then feel angry and resentful toward health care providers, who may no longer seem to be collaborators.

Chronic pain tends to generalize across a pain sufferer's life (Bellissimo & Tunks, 1984; Eimer & Allen, 1995). One low back pain patient stated, three months after her injury, "This whole situation has affected my whole life. I had to drop out of school. I can't sleep. I can hardly work. I feel I've been beaten down so much!" Although psychological factors always affect the perception of pain, the psychological ramifications can become complex when acute pain proves to be unremitting and treatment-resistant (chronic), as with this patient. Psychological and physical factors can become closely entwined and difficult to disentangle. Interactions with premorbid psychosocial stressors such as dysfunctional personality traits, maladaptive coping behaviors, and negative experiences can magnify suffering (Gatchel, 1996; Hendler, 1981; Maruta, Swanson, & Swenson, 1979; Sternbach, 1974; Turk, 1996). Additionally, when physical or psychological disability results from or causes chronic pain, this primary problem can interact with factors having the potential to produce secondary gains. These factors include litigation, disability payments, the contingent attention provided in response to "pain behaviors," and adversarial relationships with health care providers and third parties (DeGood & Dane, 1996; Feuerstein & Zastowny, 1996; Linton & Bradley, 1996; Pilowsky, 1995).

BELIEFS, COPING STRATEGIES, AND ADJUSTMENT

Investigators have demonstrated a close association between pain-related beliefs, pain coping strategies, and emotional adjustment in persons suffering from chronic pain (DeGood & Shutty, 1992; Eimer, 1989; Eimer & Allen, 1995; Hill, Niven, & Knussen, 1995; Jensen & Karoly, 1991; Jensen, Turner, Romano, & Lawler, 1994; Keefe, Dunsmore, & Burnett, 1992; Turk, 1996; Williams & Keefe, 1991). This line of research has identified catastrophizing as one of the most significant predictors of poor coping and adjustment to living with pain (Rosenstiel & Keefe, 1983; Sullivan & D'Eon, 1990). The term *catastrophizing* means "dwelling on and magnifying the negative aspects of a situation." Simply put, patients who expect the worst, cope poorly and fare poorly. This tends to reduce their ability to obtain pain relief, and decrease their sense of self-efficacy (Schiafino, Revenson, & Gibofsky, 1991). Negative beliefs lead to negative (i.e., maladaptive) coping strategies, which in turn foster maladjustment and eventually alienation:

Case Example

A 38-year-old divorced woman who had sustained neck and back injuries in a motor vehicle accident 4½ months earlier was referred for psychological consultation based on her extremely negative and hostile attitude, and hypersensitivity to being touched (hyperesthesia) due to allodynia (low pain threshold for normally, nonpainful tactile stimuli). After 4 months of physical and occupational therapy, she appeared to be getting worse rather than better and was ingesting excessive quantities of pain medication. When first seen by the psychologist, this patient expressed the belief that she was "under a bad star" because an unfortunate series of events had preceded her car accident.

She also believed that she had been exploited and transferred this belief into the present treatment context. As a result, she expressed much resentment and tended to be snappy, negative, and irritable during physical and occupational therapy, where she maintained a tense and defensive posture. She also was inconsistent in keeping her appointments, and noncompliant in following her therapists' prescriptions. She would state that she was "too stressed out to be a nice, little, compliant patient."

When she left after her first evaluation session, she was noncommittal about coming back, but she called the psychologist for a second appointment a week later, stating that she needed help because she felt "so miserable." She was subsequently seen for a total of 10 PMP sessions. A good part of her PMP involved examining her beliefs and her coping strategies. She was helped to realize that some of her beliefs led her to use harmful coping strategies; for example, the belief that she was being exploited led her to overinterpret events as indicative of exploitation, creating a self-fulfilling prophecy. By the end of 10 PMP sessions, this patient reported, her self-monitoring records showed, and her physical and occupational therapists' notes documented a marked reduction in catastrophizing, activity avoidance, ingestion of pain medication, complaining, manifest hostility, muscle bracing, allodynia, and hyperesthesia. There was a correspondent improvement in her compliance, and a notable increase in her use of coping self-statements and activity pacing. Her depression was also much less severe.

This case exemplifies the relationships among pain beliefs, coping, and adjustment repeatedly reported in the research literature cited previously and in the following chapters. These findings highlight the importance of helping patients examine their pain-related beliefs and coping strategies empirically. However, the process of doing so is often nonlinear because negatively motivated pain patients may resist a straightforward approach. In fact, because many pain patients do not follow through with formal PMP, positive treatment outcomes often may not be attributed to the PMP therapist who initiated them. Many hostile and angry pain patients obtain therapeutically helpful information from a one-time consultation and evaluation. They may not intend to obtain PMP. They may not even acknowledge the evaluation as helpful and may leave feeling resentful. However, follow-up with the referral source 2 weeks to 1 month later may reveal positive changes that can be attributed to the psychological consultation.

Case Example

A low back pain patient initially asked the question, "Am I holding myself back?" but she was unwilling to begin a program of PMP. The psychologist evaluating her discovered that her main pain-related beliefs were (a) that her pain was continuous, (b) that her pain was going to be permanent, and (c) that no medical, physical, or psychological therapies could help her. Correspondingly, her main coping strategies were catastrophizing, activity avoidance, frequent downtime, and as-needed ingestion of analgesic medications based on pain. Her level of adjustment was very poor. She was severely depressed and contemplated suicide. Her constellation of beliefs and coping strategies was preventing her from improving her level of functionality.

Initial intervention was directed at helping her reach her own conclusion that she was in fact holding herself back. The evaluation revealed a number of significant risk factors for the development of a chronic pain syndrome and continued disability that were reviewed with the patient. Nevertheless, she did not elect to come back for a course of PMP. However, follow-up 1 month later with the referral source revealed a notable improvement in the patient's status that the patient did not specifically attribute to the psychological consultation. The patient was reported to have requested a change in the focus of her physical therapy which led to a modification in her corrective exercise program, and in the physical therapy modalities employed. This patient actually began to take more responsibility for her role in her treatment. She also started to manifest a slightly more favorable attitude, which was also reflected in reports of decreased pain, and in an increase in the number of hours she worked per week.

PMP therapists need to employ a range of modalities and strategies to positively motivate alienated and depressed patients. PMP therapists also need to adjust their expectations about treatment modalities and appropriate outcome measures to the patient. Just as on a macrolevel, pain clinics offering integrated, multidisciplinary programs often document positive rehabilitation outcomes (DeGood & Dane, 1996; Feuerstein & Zastowny, 1996; Flor, Fydrich, & Turk, 1992), on a microlevel, individual pain practitioners who use a multimodal and flexible approach have the best chances of success with individual pain patients. This book's primary purpose is to offer multimodal methods and strategies for the Pain Management Psychotherapist.

PART ONE

PAIN ASSESSMENT AND TREATMENT PLANNING

CHAPTER 2

Assessment through Structured Interviews, Checklists, and Pain Rating Scales

Symptoms, then, are in reality nothing but the cry from suffering organs.

—Jean-Martin Charcot

THE INITIAL PSYCHOLOGICAL WORKUP

The initial psychological workup of a pain patient entails obtaining an informative pain history and assessing the person's current mental status and pain condition. This information is usually assembled from several data sources including (a) patient interview; (b) interview of significant others, when relevant; (c) review of relevant medical records (e.g., previous medical evaluation reports, past and ongoing medical treatment notes, medical discharge summaries, and medicolegal documents); (d) review of records of any past psychological or psychiatric evaluations and treatment; and (e) administration of a relevant battery of psychological and pain assessment tests. We ask new patients either to bring their medical records to the initial appointment or have them sent to our office so we can examine them before seeing the patient.

CLINICAL INTAKE FORMS

New patients at our office fill out two administrative forms and several pages of clinical intake forms before their initial interview. The first administrative form, "New Patient Information," is displayed in

Appendix A. This standard one-page form gathers essential identifying, demographic, and insurance information. The second one-page administrative form, "Signed Authorizations and Informed Consents," is displayed in Appendix B. This form serves to record the patient's written consent and authorization (a) to release information regarding the results of his or her evaluation and treatment to appropriate parties (e.g., referring or treating physicians, the patient's attorney); (b) to receive relevant medical records; and (c) to bill relevant third-party payors for services rendered. The form also includes the patient's informed consent to psychological evaluation and treatment.

Next, the patient fills out a seven-page pain assessment intake form entitled the Philadelphia Pain Questionnaire (PPQ) and the two-page Beck Depression Inventory (BDI). The PPQ is displayed in its entirety in Appendix C. Its development, content, scoring, and interpretation are discussed in detail in this chapter. The BDI is published by the Psychological Corporation and can be obtained from the publisher (Beck, 1987/1993; Beck et al., 1961). It is discussed briefly.

The first section of the PPQ is a 4-page pain history and status questionnaire. This questionnaire gathers important demographic and clinical data by asking the patient to respond to these 65 items: basic identifying information and demographics (1–5, 14–16); referral source, reason for referral, and purpose of the visit (6–10); pain description and locations (11, 12); the assumed or inferred cause(s) of pain condition and medical diagnoses (17–19, 21); how long the pain has persisted (22, 23); percentage of time in pain (20); current work status and disability ratings (24–29, 38, 39, 55–61); litigation status (30); current medications (31); medical and surgical treatment history (33, 34); medical history and symptom checklist (62); presence of a concussive episode or head injury (32); experienced cognitive problems and possible symptoms of postconcussive syndrome (44–54); psychological/psychiatric treatment history (43); pain intensity and severity (13, 35); factors that relieve and worsen pain (36, 37, 40); estimated percentage relief obtained from pain medications and current treatments (41, 42); and ability to use relaxation methods when tense (63–65).

The Brief Pain Status Questionnaire

To aid in tracking treatment progress and outcomes, a 2-page version of the pain history and status portion of the PPQ was also constructed. This questionnaire, called the Brief Pain Status Questionnaire (BPSQ), is displayed in Appendix D.

The 25 items on the BPSQ track a patient's qualitative description of the pain (1), percentage of time in pain (2), pain locations (3), severity of pain in each noted location (4), medications used, dosages, and frequencies of use (5), work status (6, 7, 15, 16), pain intensity ratings at different times of day (8, 17), pain's temporal pattern (21), present pain intensity (4, 8a, 22), pain relievers (9), pain triggers (10), pain interference and pain impairment ratings (11–14, 16), percentage relief obtained from current medications (18), percentage relief obtained from current pain treatments (20), and use of relaxation methods (23–25).

THE CLINICAL INTERVIEW

The 4-page pain history and status section of the Philadelphia Pain Questionnaire (PPQ) can also be administered as a structured interview with patients who cannot fill out the form on their own. However, most patients first fill the form out, and then complete the remainder of the Philadelphia Pain Questionnaire (containing a pain adjective checklist, several pain intensity rating scales, and instructions for making a pain drawing—to be discussed), as well as the Beck Depression Inventory (BDI). We go over these forms with the patient during the clinical interview, to clarify the patient's responses and obtain more detailed or specific information.

At the clinical interview, the therapist seeks to determine firsthand the patient's understanding of the purpose of the visit, identify and conceptually formulate the presenting problems and goals, obtain a detailed description of the pain experience, obtain a pain history, and evaluate the patient's mental status. Table 2.1 summarizes the major areas to be covered.

The Pain Imagery Interview (PII) displayed in Appendix E is a useful guide and checklist for conducting an initial structured or semistructured, clinical pain interview. The interview addresses the patient's pain condition and how it has affected the person; it is not quantitatively scored. The clinical information obtained is used to formulate a case conceptualization and PMP treatment plan (see Chapter 4).

The PII was constructed to elicit personal historical information (a pain history), as well as the patient's personal constructs related to the pain symptoms and condition. The therapist needs to ask open-ended, projective questions aimed at eliciting affect-laden material, such as the patient's implicit pain imagery and personal associations about the pain's effects on the patient's past, present, and future. The PII covers the presenting complaint, the patient's pain experience, pain onset, pain imagery and pain relief imagery, pain triggers and relievers, pain severity and interference, negative and positive cognitions, primary losses, secondary gains, work and disability issues, social supports, associated fears, associated symptoms, past vulnerability factors, coping issues, and motivation (see Appendix E).

Table 2.1
Concise Initial Interview Guide

I. Presenting Problem. Nature of problem(s), precipitants, course, patient's understanding of problem(s), previous attempts at dealing with problem(s).

   1. What is the problem? How can I be of help? Why are you seeking help now?

   2. When did you have pain for the first time?

   3. How often do you have pain? How long does it last?

   4. Describe the pain. Where does it start and where does it travel?

   5. What brings the pain on? Does anything aggravate it, increase it, or make it worse?

   6. What lessens it?

   7. What have you done to lessen it?

   8. What previous treatment have you had for the pain?

   9. What do you think caused the pain originally? What is causing the pain now?

  10. What do you think the future holds for you?

  11. How bad is the pain?

  12. What could you do if you did not have this problem?

  13. Inquire about happiest, most anxious, saddest, angriest, most shameful experiences.

II. Current Life Situation. Living situation, work, interests, leisure time, relationships, life satisfaction.

III. Developmental History. Relationship with parents, sibling relationships, major childhood events.

IV. School/Occupational History. Achievement, satisfaction, career choices, problems.

V. Social History. Peer relationships during development and currently; sexual relationships.

VI. Traumatic Experiences. Family disruptions; medical, psychological, substance abuse problems within the family; physical or sexual abuse; instances of physical or emotional trauma.

VII. Medical History. Pain treatment history; current medications; current and previous medical problems; substance abuse; family medical history, psychological problems, and/or substance abuse in the family.

VIII. Psychiatric History. Previous therapy (when? where? with whom? why? helpful or not helpful? any problems with the therapy?); previous occurrence of current problems; their course and outcome.

IX. Mental Status. Appearance, attitude, behavior, mood, affect, speech, thought, perception, cognitive functioning.

X. Patients' Goals for Therapy and Concerns. Prioritize; (ask, "anything else I should know?")

ASSESSING VULNERABILITY TO PAIN TRIGGERS

To create a clinical tool for collecting information about a patient's perceptions of vulnerability to pain triggers and precipitants, we developed an instrument called the Pain Vulnerability Checklist (PVCL; see Appendix F). The PVCL is given to patients who are intrinsically self-motivated to learn how their cognitions and behaviors are related to their pain levels. They are asked to fill it out between their initial and second visits.

The PVCL contains 85 items representing behaviors, behavioral deficits, behavioral excesses, feelings, affective reactions, cognitive evaluations, thinking patterns, interpersonal reactions, motivational tendencies, and health-related behaviors (e.g., eating behaviors, physical exercise, medication use, drug and alcohol use) that we have found to be associated with vulnerability to pain flare-ups. Patients are asked to estimate how many days they have felt or done the listed items, over the past 7 days. They are also requested to record their perceptions on a "0 to 3" scale of how vulnerable each item might have made them to having a pain flare-up. The checklist is not quantitatively scored. It is a tool for talking with patients about these vulnerability factors.

ASSESSING TRAUMA HISTORY

An additional area that should be screened in an initial clinical interview is the possible connection of a patient's persistent pain syndrome to a past history of emotional, physical, or sexual trauma. Many studies suggest a high prevalence of symptoms of posttraumatic stress disorder (PTSD) among individuals with chronic pain (Benedikt & Kolb, 1986; Blanchard & Hickling, 1997; Chibnall & Duckro, 1994; Geisser et al., 1996; Grzesiak et al., 1996; Haber & Roos, 1985; Harness & Donlon, 1988; Hickling et al., 1992; Lebovits et al., 1990; Muse, 1986; Pilowsky, 1985; Schreiber & Galai-Gat, 1993; Walker et al., 1988). Therefore, the initial workup of a chronic pain patient should include an assessment for the possible presence of a manifest or hidden posttraumatic stress disorder, also termed *"cryptotrauma"* (Harness & Donlon, 1988; Pilowsky, 1985).

The clinician should assess the patient for the presence of PTSD symptoms as well as for any past history of trauma. These kinds of questions are best asked after establishing rapport in a clinical interview (as opposed to being asked on a paper-and-pencil questionnaire). Because patients with old histories of untreated or unhealed trauma may have strong emotional reactions or abreactions based on associations and memories that are brought up by this line of questioning, the clinician should be prepared to deal with such reactions. In Chapters 7 and 9, we cover procedures and strategies for assessing and reprocessing cryptotrauma associated with persistent pain (Harness & Donlon, 1988; Pilowsky, 1985). In Chapter 3, we cover a number of psychometric instruments for assessing symptoms of PTSD. During an initial clinical interview and workup, the clinician needs to project understanding, empathy, and reassurance, while working to limit the extent to which a patient goes back into the old state-dependent material. The clinician needs to be prepared to redirect the patient back to the present context.

The PII (see Appendix E) contains many questions designed to screen for this type of material (6–9, 14, 20, 24, 25, 30, 32, 33, 36, 38, 39, 46–48, 51, 52–57, 63). In addition, the pain history and status section of the Philadelphia Pain Questionnaire (PPQ) (see Appendix C) contains several questions that address the issues of pain causality (questions 17–19, 21, 30, 32, 34, 43), and possible PTSD symptoms and outcomes (44–57, 60, 62).

THE CLINICAL MENTAL STATUS EXAMINATION

Formal mental status testing should be distinguished from the assessment of mental status during pain history taking. A formal mental status interview examination to evaluate a patient's cognitive and/or psychiatric status is often necessary when assessing infirmed elderly pain patients and substance abusers or when a severe psychiatric disturbance is suspected (e.g., major depressive disorder, a psychosis). Several available sources provide excellent guidelines for formal mental status testing (Maxmen & Ward, 1995; Schinka, 1986; Strub & Black, 1985/1993; Zimmerman, 1994). Typically, we assess a patient's mental status during our history taking and document our findings. The following list describes the major areas in a comprehensive assessment of mental status. It is rarely necessary to cover all the areas listed. The clinician can note the important aspects of the patient's presentation and behavior and assess whatever is relevant.

The major areas of mental status assessment include:

- *The Patient's Appearance.* Level of nourishment, weight, personal grooming, attire, hygiene.
- *Level of Orientation in the Three Cognitive Spheres (person, place, time).* The patient's knowledge and awareness of his or her personal identity, age, birthdate, current location and place, and time of day, day of the week, month, and year.
- *Level of Responsiveness.* Alert, hypervigilant, drowsy, lethargic, obtunded, confused, stuporous.
- *Manner of Presentation and Interaction, Attitude, and Facial Expressions.* Friendly, pleasant, cooperative, personable, willing to interact, active versus passive, hostile, guarded, suspicious, paranoid, annoyed,

irritable, withdrawn, resentful, angry, uncooperative, sarcastic, unmotivated, displaying any bizarre or unusual aspects.

- *Affect and Mood.* Labile, constricted, appropriate, depressed, scared, anxious, hostile, angry.
- *Motor Behavior and Motor Coordination.* Calm, agitated, restless, jumpy, slowed, fidgety, gait, manner of ambulation with or without an assistive device.
- *Presenting Complaints.* Panic attacks, sleep problems, pain, depression, loss of libido, anergia, appetite changes, inertia, anhedonia, loss of drive, anger, resentment, blaming others, self-blame, worries, anxieties; symptoms of posttraumatic stress: flashbacks, severe anxiety, nightmares, withdrawal, dissociation and numbing, hypervigilance, shame, phobic and avoidance reactions, somatic or pain preoccupations, fatigue; cognitive problems: memory, concentration, loss of efficiency, word-finding difficulties, speech problems; neurological problems: dizziness, lightheadedness, numbness, paresthesias, loss of sensations, tinnitus, clumsiness, tremors.
- *Pain Behaviors.* Muscle guarding and bracing, groaning, rubbing body parts, posture: tense; rigid; slouched; bent; sitting and standing tolerance.
- *Speech and Conversation.* Normal speech, pressured, effort, quantity, organization, purposiveness and goal-directedness, articulation; conversation limited, self-initiating, difficult to establish or maintain.
- *Other Cognitive Performance Variables:*
  1. Fund of information (e.g., ask for names of the last five Presidents, U.S. Presidents during the Civil War and World War II, and who Albert Einstein was).
  2. Abstraction ability (e.g., "How are a car and a bicycle similar?" Ask the patient to interpret various proverbs).
  3. Judgment (e.g., "What should you do if you are in a mall and you see a small child crying and wandering by herself?"; "What should you do if you are running late for an appointment?").
  4. Psychological insight (inquire about the patient's understanding of the reasons for his or her psychological and mood states).
  5. Mental computational skills (e.g., counting to 200 by thirteens, counting backward from 100 by sevens, or from 20 by threes, counting out loud by threes, reciting the alphabet, or alternating in reciting the alphabet and counting by threes out loud).
  6. Memory and concentration (e.g., immediate and delayed retention for five words after 5-minute, 10-minute, and 30-minute intervals; immediate sequential recall for digits in forward and reverse order).

7. Immediate, short-term and remote recall for personal and non-personal information.
8. Task focus (e.g., observed attention and concentration, task persistence, task frustration tolerance, ability to delay gratification, interest in feedback, reactions to feedback, praise, and reinforcement).

- *Evaluating for Chemical Addictions and Medicine Abuse.* Opioid addiction, alcohol abuse, abuse of street drugs, abuse of over-the-counter or prescription medications.
- *Present Effects.* Effects of any chemicals, substances, or medications the patient may have taken before the interview.
- *Signs of Emotional Distress.* Weeping, pacing, shaking, crying uncontrollably, abreactions.
- *Suicide Risk* (see Beck, Kovacs, & Weissman, 1979; Freeman & Reinecke, 1993).
- *Thought Content.* Delusions, homicidal ideation, suicidal ideation and degree of intent, preoccupations, obsessions, compulsions.
- *Validity of the Patient's Pain Complaints and Task Performance.* Probability of malingering, secondary gains, symptom exaggeration, response bias, consistency of patient's responses on tasks and to interview questions.
- *Legal and Medicolegal Problems.* History of violence or aggression, past or present criminal activity, marital status, including divorce or custody proceedings, current living situation, civil litigation, workers' compensation issues, motor vehicle accident liability and litigation issues.
- *Quality of Life.* Current living situation, hobbies, and leisure activities.
- *Vocational and Financial Issues.*
- *Employment and Education History.*
- *Past Medical and Psychiatric Treatment History.*

The preceding list can function as a checklist for patient interviews. When problems are suspected or observed in certain areas, they can be noted and documented. If they are relevant to the reason for referral these problems should be included in the Report of Evaluation.

COGNITIVE AND NEUROPSYCHOLOGICAL TESTING

When the therapist suspects that cognitive problems need to be addressed as part of a patient's treatment, it is appropriate to supplement the clinical interview and informal mental status examination with formal mental status testing or neuropsychological testing. Completing Strub and

Black's (1985/1993) very thorough formal mental status examination usually takes anywhere from 30 to 45 minutes. For a severely disturbed or an elderly patient, the clinician can administer Folstein et al.'s (1975) brief Mini-Mental State Examination. Mattis's (1976, 1988) Dementia Rating Scale, or Kiernan, Mueller, Langston, and VanDyke's (1987) Neurobehavioral Cognitive Status Examination are useful for a more comprehensive neuropsychological screening of an elderly pain patient's cognitive status. More extensive cognitive assessment may require formal neuropsychological testing. Several excellent general sourcebooks provide detailed treatment of this vast specialty area (Adams, Parsons, Culbertson, & Nixon, 1996; R. Anderson, 1994; Grant & Adams, 1996; Lezak, 1995; Spreen & Strauss, 1991).

In addition to the clinical interview and observation, evaluation of the patient should include the administration of relevant psychological assessment instruments. Confidence in clinical assessment findings is strengthened when they are corroborated by several measures.

ASSESSING COGNITIVELY IMPAIRED PATIENTS' PAIN

Despite reports of greater health care utilization by the elderly compared with that of younger populations, persistent pain problems may be underreported and undertreated in some elderly populations (Harkins & Price, 1992; Kee, Middaugh, & Pawlick, 1996). Although research suggests that the prevalence of chronic pain increases in old age (Harkins & Price, 1992; Kee et al., 1996; Melding, 1991; Williamson & Schultz, 1992), the cognitively impaired elderly have serious problems communicating their pain experience to caregivers and health care professionals (Bruce et al., 1992).

In certain health care settings, clinicians often encounter patients in severe pain who are too cognitively impaired to describe their pain articulately or even understandably (Bruce et al., 1992; Harkins & Price, 1992). Many of these patients are unable to fill out a questionnaire, checklist, or rating scale. Formal mental status testing with any of the cognitive screening instruments mentioned earlier typically documents marked cognitive impairment and associated cognitive performance limitations. This clinical situation frequently confronts clinicians who evaluate hospitalized patients at bedside, or elderly patients in pain who reside in skilled nursing facilities and nursing homes.

One way of beginning to solve this problem is to develop methods for identifying and assessing pain in geriatric and other cognitively impaired patient populations. The clinician's challenge is to enable the cognitively impaired patient to communicate his or her pain complaints and experience. Adequate rapport must quickly be established to prevent the patient from becoming agitated or more confused. The clinician must ask the patient nonthreatening questions with good face validity, and must phrase them in a simple, unambiguous, and easy-to-answer format. Open-ended questions seeking elaborated responses are usually contraindicated with this population because they tend to exceed and overwhelm such a patient's cognitive capacities, and lead to more confusion. More success is likely with simply worded, yes/no questions. To this end, we have developed a structured interview called the Geriatric Pain Assessment Interview (GPAI), displayed in Appendix G.

The Geriatric Pain Assessment Interview

The GPAI contains 50 yes/no questions about pain (and 12 questions requiring other answers) arranged in seven sections or categories that assess the pain's temporal pattern, severity, spatial pattern and distribution, descriptive characteristics, triggers, relievers, and emotional consequents. This instrument was constructed based on hundreds of interviews we have conducted with geriatric pain patients in skilled nursing and hospital settings. A much larger initial item pool was developed to assess what we considered to be important issues relative to pain experienced by elderly persons in acute inpatient and skilled nursing facility settings. This pool was eventually honed down to the current 62 questions based on feedback from patients, facility nursing and medical staff, and psychologists who administered earlier versions of the interview.

Scoring and Interpretation

A preliminary quantitative scoring system has been developed for the GPAI. Patients' responses to the GPAI questions are scored "0" or "1" based on their yes/no responses to each question. Numerical scores of 1 are assigned to yes/no responses in the direction of more pain, suffering, or emotional disturbance as opposed to less pain, suffering, or emotional disturbance (which receive numerical scores of 0). A GPAI Total Pain Severity Score and seven category scores may then be calculated by summing the numerical scores for all the items within each category. These sums can be recorded on a scoring profile form that constitutes the third page of the GPAI. Percentages for each category can be computed and plotted on a simple Graphic Profile on the scoring page (see Appendix G). Higher scores (percentages) are associated with greater pain problems.

This quantitative scoring system is preliminary. Total pain severity and category scores should be used to generate clinical hypotheses because the GPAI is not primarily intended to be a quantitatively scored instrument. Its administration primarily is meant to elicit qualitative clinical information from the patient about his or her pain experience. Although the questions are intentionally closed-ended (yes/no) for this population, the clinician should add open-ended questions if he or she judges that answers will be clinically informative and useful.

A consultation form for recording a Report of Psychological Evaluation conducted in a hospital or residential care setting is also provided in Appendix G.

PAIN DIARIES, PAIN ADJECTIVE CHECKLISTS, AND PAIN RATING SCALES

PAIN DIARIES

Pain diaries enable a clinician to gather data about a patient's pain levels and other variables of clinical interest that occur between sessions (e.g., medication use, coping methods, negative thinking, downtime). As such, they play an important role in a patient's initial workup. Because pain diaries can help patients become better observers of their own experience, diary self-monitoring often is an important component of cognitive and behavioral self-control training. This topic is covered more fully in Chapters 6 and 8.

We generally give our patients a pain diary to take home with them after the first visit. After instructing them on its use, we ask that they record the requested data between their first and second sessions. They bring their filled-in diary sheets with them to their second visit. The Pain Tracking Diary (PTD) that we give patients after the initial interview is displayed in Appendix R-2. It is an adaptation and variation of a format described by Thorn and Williams (1993). A 10-point verbally anchored, numerical rating scale helps patients make their pain intensity ratings on the diary form. Patients rate their pain levels at four fixed times each day, record their daily pain medication use, the coping methods they used, and the amount of downtime. Each diary sheet allows a patient to record data for 4 days. We generally give patients two to four diary sheets to take home. An alternative "Daily Pain Diary" form employing Melzack's (1975) 6-point Present Pain Index is displayed in Appendix H. It allows patients to make separate ratings of their pain's intensity and their emotional distress every two hours, and to record other variables of interest.

Following Thorn and Williams (1993), we have found that patients are most likely to be compliant with diary self-monitoring if they are asked to record their pain levels at routine times each day, generally mealtimes and bedtime. Patients who have irregular daily routines and missed mealtimes make their diary recodings within an hour of awakening in the morning, at around noon, at around 5:00 P.M. to 6:00 P.M., and at around 10:00 P.M. to 11:00 P.M. or at bed-time. As discussed in Chapter 8, patients learn that it is important to make their daily routines more regular and disciplined in the service of pain management. Patients' compliance or lack of compliance with diary self-monitoring provides important information relevant to case formulation and treatment planning. Other pain diary forms that can be used in treatment are discussed in Chapters 4, 6, and 8.

PAIN ADJECTIVE CHECKLISTS AND RATING INSTRUMENTS

Pain adjective checklists and rating instruments enable a clinician to obtain patients' descriptions of the quality and intensity of their pain experience. They can provide data that complement a good clinical interview, mental status examination, and history and thus should be a part of most pain evaluations. The best known pain evaluation questionnaire is the McGill Pain Questionnaire (MPQ), a pain adjective checklist developed by Ronald Melzack (Melzack, 1975; Melzack & Katz, 1992; Melzack & Torgerson, 1971).

The McGill Pain Questionnaire

This brief adjective checklist has been widely used and translated into several languages (Melzack & Katz, 1992). The MPQ is clinically useful because it is brief and enables a clinician to help a patient describe his or her pain experience using a range of verbal descriptors and adjectives. The MPQ categorizes pain adjectives into four major groups: *sensory-discriminative* (e.g., "throbbing, stabbing"), *affective-motivational* (e.g., "exhausting, fearful"), *cognitive-evaluative* (e.g., "miserable, intense, unbearable,"), and *miscellaneous* (e.g., "spreading, nagging"). The patient selects descriptors supplied on a picklist or checklist. The MPQ can be self-administered in 5 to 10 minutes and is easily scored. Alternatively, the verbal descriptors on the MPQ can be read aloud to the patient who is asked to choose only those words describing his or her feelings and pain sensations at the present moment.

   The Original MPQ: The original MPQ contains 20 sets of verbal pain descriptors containing a total of 78 adjectives (see Table 2.2). In addition, Row 21 provides pain intensity descriptors and Row 22 refers to temporal qualities of the pain. The order of the pain adjectives in each row is based on their ranked intensity, which was determined in studies conducted by Melzack and his associates (Melzack, 1975; Melzack & Katz, 1992; Melzack & Torgerson, 1971). The first word in a row corresponds to the lowest intensity ranking or rating for that row, and it is assigned a numerical value of 1. The last word in a row corresponds to the highest intensity rating for that row, and it is assigned the highest numerical value. For example, Item 6 contains the words *tugging, pulling,* and *wrenching.*

Table 2.2

McGill Pain Questionnaire Pain Adjective Checklist

Instructions: For each row of words, place an "X" next to the one word that best describes your present pain. Choose no more than *one* word in each row. If no words in a row describe your pain, then do not choose any words in that row.

NAME: _____ DATE: _____ MEDICAL DIAGNOSIS: _____

1. flickering	quivering	pulsing	throbbing	beating	pounding
2. jumping	flashing	shooting			
3. pricking	boring	drilling	stabbing	lancinating	
4. sharp	cutting	lacerating			
5. pinching	pressing	gnawing	cramping	crushing	
6. tugging	pulling	wrenching			
7. hot	burning	scalding	searing		
8. tingling	itchy	smarting	stinging		
9. dull	sore	hurting	aching	heavy	
10. tender	taut	rasping	splitting		
11. tiring	exhausting				
12. sickening	suffocating				
13. fearful	frightful	terrifying			
14. punishing	grueling	cruel	vicious	killing	
15. wretched	blinding				
16. annoying	troublesome	miserable	intense	unbearable	
17. spreading	radiating	penetrating	piercing		
18. tight	numb	drawing	squeezing	tearing	
19. cool	cold	freezing			
20. nagging	nauseating	agonizing	dreadful	torturing	
21. no pain	mild	discomforting	distressing	horrible	excruciating
22. brief	intermittent	constant	*****PLEASE STOP HERE*****		

PRI: S (1–10) _____ A (11–15) _____ E (16) _____ M (17–20) _____

PRI-TOTAL (1–20) _____ PPI _____

Note. Adapted with permission from the McGill Pain Questionnaire. Copyright © 1975 by Ronald Melzack.

Tugging is assigned a value of 1, pulling is assigned a value of 2, and wrenching is assigned a value of 3.

The patient selects only those words on the checklist that apply, but selects no more than one word from each row. A summative Pain Rating Index (PRI) is computed by adding the ranked numerical values of all selected descriptive words. Separate PRIs are also obtained for the 10 sets of sensory words (Rows 1–10), the 5 sets of affective words (Rows 11–15), the evaluative set (Row 16), and the 4 miscellaneous sets (Rows 17–20). Each of these category-specific PRIs is calculated by adding the ranked numerical values of all the selected adjectives in each category.

In addition to the PRIs, other indices are obtained including the total Number of Words Chosen (NWC), and the Present Pain Index (PPI), which is the pain intensity descriptor checked in Row 21. The PPI is coded with the numerical value associated with the word selected. The numerical value and intensity word combinations are: 0 ("no pain"), 1 ("mild"), 2 ("discomforting"), 3 ("distressing"), 4 ("horrible"), and 5 ("excruciating"). The patient also chooses one word in Row 22 to indicate whether the pain is brief, intermittent, or constant.

Limitations of the Original MPQ: Although the MPQ is a clinically useful and easy-to-administer test, the reading-vocabulary level is too advanced for some patients. Also, many patients have difficulty associating descriptive words on the test with their own subjective experience, the McGill's standardized list of descriptive terms may not be relevant to the way an individual patient characterizes pain. To address these concerns, the test should be supplemented with a good clinical pain interview as well as with other relevant tests.

Another problem with the original form of the MPQ has to do with the interpretation of the total Pain Rating Index (PRI-Total) and the summative indices for each category (e.g., PRI-Sensory, PRI-Affective). Many patients do not agree with the intensity rankings of the descriptive words within each set or row. Because the severity/intensity ranking of each descriptor is equal to its order in its set or row, the first word in a set is ranked 1, the second word is ranked 2, and so on. Thus, in the sensory set containing the ordered words, *pricking, boring, drilling, stabbing,* and *lancinating,* the final word, lancinating (ranked 5), is ranked higher (as more intense) than is stabbing (ranked 4) or drilling (ranked 3). However, a patient who selects drilling from this set as most descriptive of his or her present pain may nevertheless, subjectively view that word to be a more intense or severe characterization of pain than stabbing or lancinating, both of which are ranked higher. In fact, the patient may not even understand the meaning (or appreciate the connotation) of the word lancinating, which has the highest ranking in the set.

The preceding problem raises this question: Given that the descriptors are numerically ranked in this questionnaire, are some aspects of the pain of a patient who chooses words such as drilling and burning less intense than the same aspects of the pain of another patient who for the same sets, chooses words such as lancinating and searing? The words lancinating and searing are ranked numerically higher in intensity/severity within their respective sets than are the words drilling and burning. In our clinical experience with the original MPQ, some patients who choose less intensely ranked sensory descriptors nevertheless report overall perceptions of more severe pain than other patients who select more intensely ranked sensory descriptors. Thus, higher pain rating indices may not always be associated with patients' perceptions of greater pain severity or intensity.

The Short Form McGill Pain Questionnaire: Based on these concerns as well as the desire to create a shorter measure that would be easy to use and interpret, Melzack (1987) developed the short form McGill Pain Questionnaire (SF-MPQ). It uses fewer pain descriptors (15 items) than the original instrument (78 items), and it presents the items in the form of simple rating scales. The SF-MPQ is displayed in Table 2.3.

On the SF-MPQ, Items 1 through 11 represent the sensory dimension, and Items 12 through 15 represent the affective and evaluative dimensions of pain. The SF-MPQ can be self-administered as a paper-and-pencil instrument, or alternatively, verbally administered by the clinician. The patient rates or ranks each item (descriptive quality) on a 0 to 3 intensity scale, with 0 representing "none" of that descriptive quality, 1 representing a "mild" perceived level of intensity, 2 representing a "moderate" intensity, and 3 representing a "severe" intensity.

The patient's responses on the SF-MPQ can be summarized and analyzed five ways:

1. The number of ratings per category (NRPC) of pain intensity (none, mild, moderate, severe) can be compared.
2. A total summed score, or Pain Rating Index (PRI), can be computed by adding all the ratings. This can be converted to a percentage by dividing the sum of all the ratings by the maximum possible score (i.e., 15 items $\times$ 3 = 45) and multiplying the quotient by 100. An average rating can also be calculated (i.e., sum of all the ratings divided by 15).
3. A total summed score, or PRI, can be computed for the 11 sensory descriptors and can also be converted to a percentage and an average rating.
4. A total summed score, or PRI, can be computed for the four affective-evaluative descriptors and again can be converted to a percentage and an average rating.
5. The rating trend for the sensory items can be compared with the rating trend for the affective-evaluative items. However, because there are so few total items (15), and such an uneven number of sensory items (11) compared with affective-evaluative items (4), this comparison has its limitations.

The SF-MPQ is a clinically useful instrument that is brief, easy to administer and interpret, and yields intensity ratings for each of the pain descriptors on the checklist based on a uniform pain intensity scale. Melzack and Katz (1992) report that the SF-MPQ correlates highly with

Table 2.3
Short-Form McGill Pain Questionnaire

Patient's Name _____ Date _____

Instructions: Each of the words in the left column describes a *quality* that pain can have. For *each* pain quality, check *the number* in that row that tells how much of that specific *quality* your pain has. Rate *every* pain quality.

Pain Quality	None	Mild	Moderate	Severe
1. Throbbing	(0)_____	(1)_____	(2)_____	(3)_____
2. Shooting	(0)_____	(1)_____	(2)_____	(3)_____
3. Stabbing	(0)_____	(1)_____	(2)_____	(3)_____
4. Sharp	(0)_____	(1)_____	(2)_____	(3)_____
5. Cramping	(0)_____	(1)_____	(2)_____	(3)_____
6. Gnawing	(0)_____	(1)_____	(2)_____	(3)_____
7. Hot-burning	(0)_____	(1)_____	(2)_____	(3)_____
8. Aching	(0)_____	(1)_____	(2)_____	(3)_____
9. Heavy	(0)_____	(1)_____	(2)_____	(3)_____
10. Tender	(0)_____	(1)_____	(2)_____	(3)_____
11. Splitting	(0)_____	(1)_____	(2)_____	(3)_____
12. Tiring-exhausting	(0)_____	(1)_____	(2)_____	(3)_____
13. Sickening	(0)_____	(1)_____	(2)_____	(3)_____
14. Fearful	(0)_____	(1)_____	(2)_____	(3)_____
15. Punishing-cruel	(0)_____	(1)_____	(2)_____	(3)_____

A. Please make an "x" on the line below to show how bad your pain is right now.

NO PAIN   WORST POSSIBLE PAIN

B. For each column below, please check the *one* descriptor below that best describes your present pain.

Mark Your Present Pain Intensity: My Pain Is Usually Present:

0	No pain	_____
1	Mild	_____
2	Discomforting	_____
3	Distressing	_____
4	Horrible	_____
5	Excruciating	_____

_____ 1 Briefly
_____ 2 It comes and goes
_____ 3 Its constant

Note. Adapted with permission from the "short-form McGill Pain Questionnaire." Copyright © 1987 by Ronald Melzack.

the major pain rating indices of the original MPQ, and is sensitive in measuring pain treatment changes and outcomes. We have found the short form to be easier and more straightforward than the original form to use and interpret with pain populations. It is, however, more therapeutically useful in a qualitative way than in a diagnostic, or statistically quantitative way. Its main clinical limitation has been the limited sampling of pain descriptors, especially within the affective and evaluative domains.

The Philadelphia Pain Questionnaire-Pain Adjective Checklist (PPQ-PAC)

Taking into account the strengths and limitations of the original and short forms of the MPQ, Eimer and Allen (1996) adapted 49 of the 78 pain descriptors from the MPQ to develop the Philadelphia Pain Questionnaire-Pain Adjective Checklist (PPQ-PAC). This self-report, paper-and-pencil form is a new measure in development, and an evolutionary extension of the pain adjective checklists and rating scales developed by Melzack and his associates (Melzack, 1975, 1987; Melzack & Katz, 1992). The PPQ-PAC includes a relatively balanced sampling of pain descriptors from within the sensory-descriptive and affective-evaluative domains. The PPQ-PAC follows the PPQ Pain History and Status Questionnaire (see pp. 5–6 of the PPQ in Appendix C).

Following Melzack and Katz's (1992) call for "further development and refinement of pain measurement techniques [in order to construct] increasingly accurate tools with greater predictive powers" (p. 164), the PPQ-PAC addresses eight issues relevant to assessing and describing patients' pain experience:

1. Creating a pain assessment test that is clinically applicable and relevant to the widest possible range of pain patients.
2. Making the test brief and easy to administer, score, and interpret.
3. Developing a uniform rating scale for quantifying pain intensity on relevant pain dimensions.
4. Writing the test so that it can be administered by a clinician orally, or self-administered by a patient in written form.
5. Retaining the same simple scoring system for both oral and written versions of the test.
6. Making it possible for both versions of the test to elicit both qualitative and quantitative information about a patient's pain.
7. Allowing quantitative comparisons to be made between affective, evaluative, and sensory aspects of a patient's pain experience.
8. Enabling the test to yield information about possible response bias and potential symptom magnification.

Overview of the PPQ-PAC: The seven-page Philadelphia Pain Questionnaire (PPQ) is provided in its entirety in Appendix C for the reader's clinical use. The first section of the PPQ, the *Pain History and Status Questionnaire* (pp. 1–4 of the form) was reviewed earlier. The PPQ-PAC, which appears on pages 5 and 6 of the form, contains 52 pain descriptors. Half of these (Section I of the PPQ-PAC) are considered affective and evaluative words; the remaining 26 descriptors (Section II of the PPQ-PAC) are considered sensory words. The patient is instructed to respond to the words in two stages. First, the patient is asked to "mark an X next to the qualities that your pain has." After selecting those words that are relevant to his or her condition, the patient is then asked to rate each selected word on a 4-point scale to depict *"how much* of that quality your pain has, *how bad* that quality is, or *how well* that quality describes your pain." For each pain descriptor marked as relevant, the patient selects a number/word combination representing a particular degree of intensity or descriptiveness. The numerical value and word combinations are: 1 ("a little bit"), 2 ("somewhat"), 3 ("quite a bit"), and 4 ("very much/a lot").

Applicability of the PPQ-PAC to a Wide Range of Patients: The preceding instructions and format promote the instrument's applicability to a wide range of pain patients because they do not need to rate every item individually. This also can reduce the instrument's administration time. These instructions usually make it possible to obtain clinically valuable information even when a patient is too cognitively compromised, emotionally distressed, or distracted by pain to rate the items. Most patients can indicate which of the listed qualities their pain has (whether verbally through oral administration of the test, or in written form, through self-administration). Furthermore, asking patients to rate the intensity, degree of badness, or descriptiveness of only the items that they have marked makes the task and the resulting data more meaningful. This format seems to optimize the test's face validity, which can improve rapport with angry, resistant, or cognitively compromised pain patients.

Oral Administration of the PPQ-PAC: The PPQ-PAC can easily be administered orally to patients who for some reason are unable to self-administer the test in written form. The oral version lends itself to being given at bedside in a hospital or nursing facility and also may be the best choice in outpatient settings, when time is limited, or when asking a patient to self-administer written forms would sacrifice rapport. Appendix I provides verbatim instructions for oral administration of the PPQ-PAC. Essentially, the clinician goes down the entire list of pain adjectives, inserting each adjective in one or both of the following questions: "Is your pain [insert the word]?" Or, "Would you use the word [insert the word] to describe your pain?" Then, for each word that the patient indicates is a relevant descriptive pain quality, the clinician asks: "How [insert the relevant word] is your pain? Is it 'a little bit' [insert word]? Is it 'somewhat' [insert word]? Is it 'quite a bit' [insert word]? Or, is it 'very much/a lot' [insert word]?"

Ease of Scoring and Interpretation: The PPQ-PAC format makes it easy to score and interpret. The relatively balanced sampling of items between affective-evaluative and sensory categories and the uniformity of the scale for making intensity ratings allow the raw data to provide a graphic picture of the quality and intensity of a patient's pain experience. Scoring and interpretation are discussed in detail later in the chapter.

PAIN INTENSITY RATINGS AND PAIN DRAWINGS

Pain Rating Scales

The most common method for obtaining direct information from patients about the intensity or severity of their pain has been to use either *visual analogue scales* (VASs) for showing pain intensity, or *numerical rating scales* (NRSs) for rating pain intensity (Jensen & Karoly, 1992; Karoly & Jensen, 1987; Sriwatanakul et al., 1983). The most common VAS asks that a patient make a mark somewhere along a 100 mm line to indicate the amount of pain that he or she is experiencing. Other types of VASs include "pain thermometers" (with the bulb at the bottom representing "no pain," and the top of the thermometer signifying "pain as bad as it can be," or "worst imaginable pain"), and lines segmented at equal intervals with numbers or intensity-denoting adjectives. Figure 2.1 displays some typical, VAS formats.

The numerical rating scale format also permits a patient to record pain intensity. In contrast to a visual analogue scale, it uses numbers such as 0 to 10. The numbers 0 or 1 typically represent "no pain" or "least pain," and the number 10 typically represents "worst or most pain imaginable." Often, numerical and visual analogue scales are combined when patients are asked to rate the intensity of their pain.

These approaches to measuring pain severity, intensity, or strength also allow comparisons of perceived pain intensity at different points in time. Thus, a patient can be asked to represent the typical or average level of pain experienced, as well as pain at its worst, and at its least. Such ratings can be made before and after treatment to measure treatment effects.

A. PURE VAS (100 mm line)

Please make an "X" on the line below to show how bad your pain is right now.

NO PAIN |————————————————————————| WORST POSSIBLE PAIN

B. VERBAL RATING VAS

Please make an "X" on the line below to show how bad your pain is right now.

|————————————|————————————|————————————|————————————|

No pain   Mild   Moderate   Severe   Worst pain imaginable

C. NUMERICAL RATING VAS

Please make an "X" on the line below to show how bad your pain is right now.

No Pain 0——1——2——3——4——5——6——7——8——9——10 WORST POSSIBLE

Figure 2.1 Some Visual Analogue Scales (VASs) for Measuring Pain Intensity.

Additionally, numerical or visual analogue scales can enable a patient to answer questions about the pain's continuity and duration. A patient can rate or depict the percentage of time the pain is present, or how frequently the pain gets worse. Another use of a percentage VAS is to ask a patient to rate the percentage relief obtained from pain medication, or from other pain treatments. These types of rating scales are included in the pain history and status section of the PPQ (see pp. 1–4 of the form, Appendix C), and on the last page of the PPQ-PAC (p. 7 of the form, Appendix C).

Reliability and Validity of VASs and NRSs

There is much evidence supporting the clinical utility and validity of VASs for registering pain intensity (Jensen & Karoly, 1992; Karoly & Jensen, 1987; Sriwatanakul et al., 1983). They are intuitively simple to use, easy for most patients to comprehend, and easy to score. Despite the widespread use of these scales, however, their reliability can vary and, under some circumstances, may be questionable. There simply is no way to assess the veracity of a patient's ratings—all pain is subjective. Also, many factors affect patients' ratings: personality style, the demand characteristics of the situation, a patient's current mood state, and whether or not secondary gains are likely if the pain is reported as very bad, intense, or severe. Despite these limitations, visual analogue and numerical pain rating scales provide useful tools for assessing important dimensions of the physical and temporal aspects of experienced pain. They allow a patient to state directly, how bad the pain is.

Obtaining a Global Composite Pain Score

Visual analogue scales (VASs), numerical rating scales (NRSs), and verbal rating scales (VRSs) such as the Present Pain Index (PPI) of the McGill Pain Questionnaire can be combined to obtain a numerical composite or Global Pain Score (GPS; Poulain, Langlade, & Goldberg, 1997). Combining several simple, cognitively undemanding, specific, and quickly administered pain rating measures into one numerical composite pain rating assessment tool may increase the reliability and consistency of the clinical measurement of pain. The GPS offered by Poulain, Langlade, and Goldberg can range from a sum of 0, which indicates that there is no pain at all, to a sum of 10, which indicates maximum, increasing pain. The GPS may prove especially useful in settings where there is little time for extensive testing, but where a simple and accurate method of assessing pain is necessary (e.g., inpatient and geriatric settings, palliative care settings). Its brevity of administration and computational simplicity make the GPS useful as a quick and convenient treatment outcome measure, and as a means of summarizing PMP progress. It is computed as the arithmetic sum of the three numerically scored pain ratings in the following list:

1. *Visual Analogue Scale (VAS).* The patient's current VAS rating is compared with his or her previous one. A numerical score of "0" is assigned if the VAS has decreased, a "1" is assigned if the VAS is unchanged, and a "2" is assigned if the VAS has increased.

2. *Verbal Rating Scale (VRS).* The patient is asked to rate his or her "present pain intensity" on the following VRS: "no pain" = 0; "mild pain" = 1; "moderate pain" = 2; "severe pain" = 3; and "excruciating pain" = 4.

3. *Percentage Pain Relief.* The patient is asked how much pain relief he or she has obtained as a result of treatment. The scale is as follows: "0% to 30% relief" = 4; "30% to 49% relief" = 3; "50% to 79% relief" = 2; "80% to 99% relief" = 1; and "100% relief" = 0.

PPQ-PAC PAIN INTENSITY RATINGS AND PAIN DRAWINGS

The third and last section of the PPQ (see p. 7, Appendix C) is entitled Pain Intensity Ratings and Pain Drawings. It contains six items (A–F). Item A is a visual analogue scale (VAS) in the form of a 100 millimeter line for recording a Present Pain Index. One end of the line is labeled "no pain," and the other end is labeled "worst possible pain." The patient is instructed to "make an 'X' on the line to show how bad your pain is now." Item B is a numerical-verbal "0 to 5" rating scale for registering present pain intensity, which uses the same numerical value-intensity word combinations as appear on the original MPQ (Melzack, 1975) (also see Item 21, Table 2.2; and Item B, Table 2.3). Item C is a verbal picklist—the patient responds by circling all the words that describe the pain's temporal qualities (i.e., brief, comes and goes, continuous, constant, always there, never goes away, appears and disappears, intermittent). Item D asks the patient to circle the percentage of time he or she is in pain. This request appears earlier in the PPQ as Question 20 in the pain history and status section. The repetition is a check on the reliability of a patient's rating. Item E consists of instructions for mapping the pain on a pain drawing (both front and rear views). The patient is instructed to draw symbols on the human figure drawings to depict the locations of pain, pins and needles, and numbness. Finally, Item F requests that the patient describe the specific qualities of the pain felt in the marked bodily locations on the drawings. The form provides blank lines for recording the relevant pain descriptors. The patient is cued to begin by recording the pain qualities associated with the most painful area marked on the drawings, and to work down to the least painful area. That concludes the administration of the PPQ and the PPQ-PAC.

CLINICAL UTILITY OF PAIN DRAWINGS

Pain drawings or diagrams have a rich clinical tradition of use in the assessment of pain (Ransford, Cairns, & Mooney, 1976; Toomey, Gover, & Jones, 1983; Waddell & Turk, 1992). The procedure can be helpful for categorizing and localizing experienced pain into symptom clusters relevant to the clinical pain population being assessed (e.g., numbness, pins and needles, shooting, burning, aching, or stabbing for low back pain patients). These symptom clusters are represented on the pain drawing in locations corresponding to where they are physically felt.

Emotional factors often influence the particular way in which patients represent their pain in a drawing. Patients who fill in a pain drawing by marking widespread and nonanatomically related areas often are communicating their emotional distress as opposed to purely the physical-sensory characteristics of their pain. Ransford et al. (1976) found that patients with abnormal drawings had higher scores on the Hysteria *(Hy)* and Hypochondriasis *(Hs)* scales of the MMPI. Toomey et al. (1983) found that the number of areas marked as pain locations on a drawing was related to such clinically significant variables as the number of words chosen (NWC) on the MPQ, the total and sensory Pain Rating Indices (PRI), pain interference with activities of daily living, and medication use.

DERIVATION AND CLASSIFICATION OF PPQ-PAC PAIN DESCRIPTORS

Section I of the PPQ-PAC contains 26 affective and evaluative words, 21 of which (1–3, 5–22) were derived from the original form of the MPQ (see p. 5 of the form, Appendix C). Items 1 through 15 are categorized as affective descriptors, and Items 16 through 26 are categorized as evaluative descriptors. Items 4 and 23 through 26 were derived based on clinical considerations and interviews with pain patients.

The assignment of the words to the major categories of affective versus evaluative, and to specific affective and evaluative subcategories, was based on previous work by Melzack and his associates (Melzack, 1975; Melzack & Katz, 1992; Melzack & Torgerson, 1971), Hase (1992), Hand and Reading (1986), Fernandez and Towery (1996), and the PPQ-PAC authors' clinical judgment (Eimer & Allen, 1996). In several cases, previous researchers differed in the categories and subcategories to which certain affective-evaluative words were assigned. Such differences were resolved based on the PPQ-PAC authors' clinical judgment. The distinctions between affective and evaluative words are not always clear-cut because considerable overlap exists between the two categories: Affective words usually are strongly evaluatively loaded, and evaluative words usually are strongly affectively or emotionally loaded.

Section II of the PPQ-PAC (see p. 6 of the form, Appendix C) contains 26 sensory words or word combinations (Items 42 and 52), all of which were derived from the original MPQ (Melzack, 1975). As with the affective and evaluative words in Section I, the assignment of sensory words to specific sensory subcategories was guided by the previous work of Melzack and his associates (Melzack, 1975; Melzack & Katz, 1992; Melzack & Torgerson, 1971), other authors such as Hase (1992), Fernandez and Towery (1996), and Hand and Reading (1986), and the PPQ-PAC authors' clinical judgment. Once again, differences between studies in the subcategorization of sensory words incorporated in the PPQ-PAC were resolved based on the PPQ-PAC authors' clinical judgment.

COMPARING AFFECTIVE AND EVALUATIVE WITH SENSORY RATINGS

Eimer and Allen (1996) chose to present the affective and evaluative descriptive words before the sensory descriptive words on the PPQ-PAC for several reasons.

First, we noted that many chronic pain patients are alexithymic, meaning restricted in their ability to label and communicate their emotional and affective experience (Blumer & Heilbronn, 1989; Eimer, 1989; Engel, 1959; Grzesiak et al., 1996). We have encountered this phenomenon with a significant number of chronic pain patients, and thus consider it important to assess a range of potential emotional reactions and evaluative responses to persistent pain states. Placing the affective and evaluative items first means that patients label and quantify their emotional and affective experience of pain before establishing any rating response bias that might result from rating their sensory descriptors first.

Second, it has been our clinical experience that rapport with angry and resentful chronic pain patients is enhanced when a clinician acknowledges early in an interview the importance of the patient's perceptions of pain's effects on his or her life. This may entail exploring with the patient how the pain has affected the patient emotionally.

Third, there is a relationship between patients' affective and evaluative responses to persistent pain and their sensory perceptions of pain. In designing the PPQ-PAC, it was considered important to obtain a relatively equal sampling of affective-evaluative and sensory pain perceptions. However, some chronic pain patients show a tendency to exaggerate or magnify pain-related symptoms. When sensory words are presented first, followed by affective-evaluative words, patients may get the message that purely sensory-descriptive words are being compared with affective-evaluative words. Some patients also may get the idea that the examiner is asking them to assess their pain using both more objective, sensory criteria as well as less objective, and more subjective, evaluative criteria. Presenting affective and evaluative words first avoids alerting patients to these possibilities.

Based on the preceding considerations, it was hypothesized that some patients with a significant emotional component to their pain might be apt to register more extreme ratings on affective and evaluative dimensions when asked to consider these first than they would if asked to consider these last. It was thought that some patients might register less extreme affective-evaluative ratings if they rated the affective and evaluative aspects of their pain after its sensory aspects.

SELECTION OF THE PPQ-PAC PAIN DESCRIPTORS

The selection of the 52 pain descriptor words for inclusion in the PPQ-PAC was based on three main criteria: (a) relevance, (b) perceived intensity and frequency of association, and (c) vocabulary and reading level.

Relevance to Common Clinical Pain Syndromes

Relevance to and frequency of association with several common clinical pain syndromes was the first criterion relative to which potential sensory descriptor items were judged. This criterion was evaluated based on the authors' clinical experience, and on the findings reported by Dubuisson and Melzack (1976), which are also reviewed by Melzack and Katz (1992). These common clinical pain syndromes included menstrual pain, arthritic pain, labor pain, discogenic disease pain, dental pain, cancer pain, phantom limb pain, and postherpetic pain.

Perceived Intensity and Frequency of Association with Specific Sensory, Affective, and Evaluative Subcategories of Pain Descriptors

Perceived intensity and frequency of association with specific sensory, affective, and evaluative categories of pain descriptors was the second criterion relative to which potential items were judged. Based on findings reported in a recent study by Fernandez and Towery (1996), and in an early study by Melzack and Torgerson (1971), sensory descriptors were selected based on their rated mean intensity and relative frequency (in their study). The items showing the highest mean intensities and relative frequencies of association with each subcategory of sensory descriptors were considered for inclusion in the PPQ-PAC. Hase's (1992) findings were also taken into account in evaluating potential items according to this criterion. However, certain descriptors were selected even though they did not have the highest mean intensities or relative frequencies in the cited studies. The basis for this was the PPQ-PAC authors' judgment that these descriptors were clinically relevant and important.

PPQ-PAC Affective and Evaluative Subcategories: Drawing on studies by Dubuisson and Melzack (1976), Melzack (1987), Melzack and Katz (1992), Melzack, Terrence, Fromm, and Amsel (1986), and Melzack and Torgerson (1971), Hase's (1992) previous work, and the PPQ-PAC authors' clinical experience, affective and evaluative descriptors were chosen to sample clinically relevant affective and evaluative subcategories of pain experience. Eimer and Allen (1996) settled on a total of four affective descriptor subcategories, and three evaluative descriptor subcategories. The affective subcategories (along with their shorthand labels in parentheses) are *fatigue* (aFa), *autonomic distress* (aAu), *punitiveness* (aPu), and *fear* (aFe). The evaluative subcategories are: *misery* (eMi), *suffering* (eSu), and a *miscellaneous* (eMs) subcategory. The miscellaneous subgroup was included based on the authors' frequent clinical experience with four evaluatively loaded issues associated with chronic pain: the perceptions of pain as *mysterious, out of control, hopeless,* and *disabling.* These seven affective and evaluative subcategories cover some of the "dysfunctional Ds" of chronic pain discussed in Chapter 1.

The subcategory symbols appear in Section I of the PPQ-PAC in the final column (see p. 5 of the form, Appendix C). The subcategory symbols (e.g., aFa) appear in the same row as the last word in each subcategory.

PPQ-PAC Sensory Subcategories: Also drawing on the previously cited sources, 10 sensory descriptor subcategories were selected for inclusion on the PPQ-PAC. They represent the sensory properties that in the authors' clinical experience are most commonly encountered: *sensory-temporal* (sTe), *sensory-spatial* (sSp), *sensory-punctate pressure* (sPP), *sensory-incisive pressure* (sIP), *sensory-constrictive pressure* (sCP), *sensory-traction pressure* (sTP), *sensory-hotness* (sHo), *sensory-additive* or *cumulative pressure* (sAP), sensations of *soreness* or *dullness* (sSo), and sensations of *coldness* or *numbness* (sCo).

Vocabulary and Reading Level

Judged vocabulary and reading level constituted the third criterion for judging potential items. This criterion was established by having eight independent raters rate all of the proposed items on a 1-to-4 scale of readability or difficulty. A rating of "1" represented that the word was perceived to be "very clear, very easy to read, and very easy to understand," a rating of "2" represented "clear, easy to read, and easy to understand," a rating of "3" represented "fairly clear, fairly easy to read, and fairly easy to understand," and finally, a rating of "4" represented "not clear, and hard to read, comprehend, represent, or understand." Any items receiving a rating of 4 by three or more raters were to be discarded.

None of the items that met the first two criteria and reached this level received a rating of 4 by three or more raters, and therefore, none needed to be eliminated.

DETECTING POSSIBLE EXTREME RESPONSE BIAS

Melzack and his associates ordered and ranked the MPQ adjectives within each adjective set on the MPQ based on the words' relative scale values or mean intensity ratings, as reported in the original Melzack and Torgerson (1971) study. Other authors who have developed alternative versions of the MPQ (e.g., Hase, 1992) also arranged their items within sets or subclasses in order of the words' assumed or mean intensity ratings. Drawing on these earlier studies (Hase, 1992; Melzack, 1975; Melzack & Katz, 1992; Melzack & Torgerson, 1971), Eimer and Allen (1996) arranged their affective, evaluative, and sensory descriptors within each set or subcategory on the PPQ-PAC, in order of their intensity connotations. When there was disagreement between studies on the rankings of particular words, Eimer and Allen used their clinical judgment to determine the final order. It was hoped that ordering the words based on their assumed intensity would help in detecting possible symptom exaggeration, pain magnification, and invalid pain complaints. The rationale behind this was the hypothesis that some patients who exaggerate or magnify their pain complaints will show a tendency, trend, or bias to make more extreme ratings on more intense descriptors. The viability of this hypothesis can only be established through research with the test.

SUMMARIZING THE PPQ-PAC DATA

The sensory, affective, and evaluative descriptors that a patient selects on the PPQ-PAC can assist a clinician in evaluating how that patient qualitatively experiences his or her pain. These ratings can assist a clinician in evaluating how intensely a patient experiences the relevant qualities or properties of his or her pain.

PAIN RATING INDICES CALCULATED ON THE PPQ-PAC

Various summary indices, or Pain Rating Indices (PRIs), for each category of adjective descriptors can be computed from a patient's responses on the PPQ-PAC. Each category-specific PRI quantifies a patient's reported, subjectively experienced intensity of that category of pain experience or distress. The main categories are (a) the entire set of all 52 descriptors, (b) the 26 Affective-Evaluative descriptors, (c) the 11 Evaluative descriptors, (d) the 15 Affective descriptors, and (e) the 26 Sensory descriptors.

Appendix J displays a graphic profiling form that also contains the formulas for calculating the Pain Rating Indices (PRIs) associated with the PPQ-PAC categories. This form allows a clinician to graphically plot the following PRI percentages: Sensory, Affective, Evaluative, Affective-Evaluative, Total, PPI Percentage marked on the VAS, and the Percentage of Words Chosen.

A computer scoring program is also available that produces a three-page report containing all the major category and subcategory PRIs and a graphic profile. It can be obtained from the publisher CogniSyst, Inc., of Durham, North Carolina (Tel: 919-489-4434).

- *Sum of Ratings.* For each of the five major categories of PPQ-PAC pain descriptors, a total Sum of the Ratings is calculated for those items selected and rated in each category. The computational formula is simply to *add up* the numerical ratings of the words selected and rated. Following suggestions offered by Melzack and Katz (1992), the Summed Ratings in each category are also converted to Percent Scores and Average Ratings.
- *Percent Scores.* Compute Percent Scores for each category using the following formula: Calculate the Sum of the Ratings for the words selected in a given category, *divide that sum by* the Maximum Possible Sum of the Ratings for the words selected in that category (i.e., the number of items rated × 4), and *multiply by* 100.
- *Average Ratings.* Compute Average Ratings for each category using the following formula: Calculate the Sum of the Ratings for the words selected in a given category, and *divide that sum by* the Number of Words Rated in that category.

MISSING (NONRATED) ITEMS NOT INCLUDED IN COMPUTING INDICES

To facilitate comparability and standardization of PPQ-PAC scores, missing (i.e., nonselected and nonrated) items are not included in any calculations. All category and subcategory totals (sums), percentages, and averages are calculated based solely on the items that a patient selected and then rated (as indicated in the formulas). The specific denominators in each formula are based on the number of items selected and rated.

COMPUTATIONAL FORMULAS FOR PRIs

The following list provides the formula for each PRI, with N being equal to the number of items selected and rated in a given category (also see Appendix J):

1. Affective-Evaluative PRI Sum of Ratings = summed ratings of selected items 1–26.
2. Affective-Evaluative PRI Percent Score = (summed ratings of selected items / $N \times 4$) $\times$ 100.
3. Affective-Evaluative PRI Average = summed ratings of selected items / N.
4. Affective PRI Sum of Ratings = sum of ratings of selected items 1–15.
5. Affective PRI Percentage Score = (summed ratings of selected items / $N \times 4$) $\times$ 100.
6. Affective PRI Average = summed ratings of selected items / N.
7. Evaluative PRI Sum of Ratings = sum of ratings of selected items 16–26.
8. Evaluative PRI Percentage Score = (summed ratings of selected items / $N \times 4$) $\times$ 100.
9. Evaluative PRI Average = summed ratings of selected items / N.
10. Sensory PRI Sum of Ratings = sum of ratings of selected items 27–52.
11. Sensory PRI Percentage Score = (summed ratings of selected items / $N \times 4$) $\times$ 100.
12. Sensory PRI Average = summed ratings of selected items / N.
13. Total PRI Sum of Ratings = sum of ratings of selected items 1–52.
14. Total PRI Percentage Score = (summed ratings of selected items / $N \times 4$) $\times$ 100.
15. Total PRI Average = summed ratings of selected items / N.

PPQ-PAC Subcategory Scores

For each of the adjective subcategories within the major Sensory, Affective, and Evaluative categories on the PPQ-PAC, subcategory PRI Sums of Ratings, PRI Percentage Scores, and PRI Averages can also be calculated for the items selected and rated. Table 2.4 displays the items that compose each PPQ-PAC subcategory PRI. The computational formulas for the subcategory PRI Sums of Ratings, Percentages, and Averages are identical to those in the preceding section.

Additional PPQ-PAC Indices

Several additional PPQ-PAC indices can be calculated including (a) the Percentage of Words Chosen out of the 52 pain adjectives (PWC), (b) the Number of Body Locations marked (NBL) on the pain drawings, and (c) the Number of [unique] Words Chosen (NWC) to describe the pain in the bodily locations marked.

Table 2.4
Items Composing Each PPQ-PAC Subcategory Pain Rating Index

Category	Subcategory	Items
Affective	Fatigue (aFa)	1, 2, 3, 4
	Autonomic (aAu)	5, 6, 7
	Punishing (aPu)	8, 9, 10, 11
	Fear (aFe)	12, 13, 14, 15
Evaluative	Misery (eMi)	16, 17, 18
	Suffering (eSu)	19, 20, 21, 22
	Miscellaneous (eMs)	23, 24, 25, 26
Sensory	Temporal (sTe)	27, 28
	Spatial (sSp)	29, 30, 31
	Punctate Pressure (sPP)	32, 33
	Incisive Pressure (sIP)	34, 35
	Constrictive Pressure (sCP)	36, 37, 38, 39
	Traction Pressure (sTP)	40, 41
	Hotness (sHo)	42, 43
	Additive Pressure (sAP)	44, 45
	Soreness (sSo)	46, 47, 48, 49
	Coldness (sCo)	50, 51, 52

Note. A PRI Sum of Ratings, Percentage, and Average can be calculated for each subcategory (see text for the computational formulas). Nonselected and nonrated items are not included in the calculations of these PRIs.

Visual Analogue Scale and Numerical-Verbal PPIs

Two additional Present Pain Indices (PPIs) are also calculated. The first one is derived from a patient's Visual Analogue Scale (VAS) pain intensity marking and is computed by measuring the number of millimeters to the left of the patient's "X" on the 100 millimeter line, and then dividing this number by 100, to yield a VAS PPI Percentage. The second PPI is a numerical score, or PPI Intensity Percentage, derived from a patient's selected PPI intensity descriptor on the 6-point Numerical-Verbal Rating Scale that appears as Item B, on page 7 of the PPQ (see Appendix C). This numerical score is computed by dividing the number associated with the patient's chosen pain intensity word (range: 0 through 5) by 5, and then multiplying by 100. For example, if "discomforting," which is associated with the number 2, is selected, then 2 would be divided by 5, and then multiplied by 100, to yield a PPI Percentage of 40%.

PRELIMINARY NORMS FOR THE PPQ-PAC

Based on a mixed sample of 80 chronic pain patients, Eimer and Allen (1996) developed a preliminary normative database for the PPQ-PAC. The reference sample consisted of pain patients seen in medical office settings for pain treatment. There were 24 men and 56 women in the sample, ranging in age from 19 to 78 years (median age = 52 years). Average pain duration in months for the sample was 96 months (Range = .25 to 384 months).

Within this sample, 12 patients, or 15%, identified the primary cause of their current or acute pain as being secondary to a motor vehicle accident, and 3 patients (4%) identified the primary cause of their current pain as being secondary to a work-related injury. Twenty patients (25% of the sample) identified a rheumatic condition as being the primary cause of their chronic pain, and 17 additional patients (21%) identified their primary cause as chronic fatigue syndrome or fibromyalgia. The remaining 35% of the sample reported mixed causes which included repetitive strain injuries, peripheral neuropathy, previous surgeries, and unknown etiologies.

The primary pain diagnoses in this sample were mixed arthritis pain ($N = 24$, 30% of the sample), discogenic disease pain ($N = 17$, 21%), chronic fatigue syndrome/fibromyalgia ($N = 18$, 23%), peripheral neuropathy ($N = 8$, 10%), musculo-skeletal injuries in the hands or feet ($N = 8$, 10%), chronic headaches ($N = 3$, 4%), and *unknown* ($N = 2$, 2%). All the rheumatologic patients were actively treating with a rheumatologist who assisted in providing these data. The rheumatologic patients evidenced the most chronic duration of pain (arthritis mean duration = 145 months, range = 10 to 470; CFS/fibromyalgia mean = 142 months, range = 36 to 348). The data for the other diagnostic groups of patients were provided by several family physicians specializing in pain treatment, and a podiatrist. Seven cases in the data set were included from our practice.

Table 2.5 presents preliminary PPQ-PAC norms based on the entire mixed sample of 80 chronic pain patients. The data are presented in the form of means, standard deviations, and percentiles for Pain Rating Indices (PRIs) and Percentages of Words Chosen (PWCs), in each major PPQ-PAC category (Total, Sensory, Affective-Evaluative, Affective, and Evaluative). The PRIs are presented in the form of Summed Ratings, Average Ratings, and Percentage Scores. Table 2.5 also presents means, standard deviations, and percentiles for VAS ratings and PPIs.

Table 2.6 presents PPQ-PAC means, standard deviations, and percentiles for PRIs, PWCs, VAS ratings, and PPIs by pain type, based on the following four pain diagnostic groups: (a) mixed arthritis pain, (b) discogenic disease, (c) chronic fatigue syndrome/fibromyalgia, and (d) peripheral neuropathy.

Table 2.7 presents PRI Percentage Score means, standard deviations, and percentiles for each PPQ-PAC subcategory based on the entire mixed sample. As discussed, these subcategory PRI Percentage Scores can be computed using the same basic formula employed to compute the major

Table 2.5

PPQ-PAC Means, Standard Deviations, and Percentiles for
Pain Rating Indices, Percentages of Words Chosen, VAS Ratings,
and Present Pain Indices in a Mixed Sample of 80 Pain Patients

Index	Mean	SD	Percentiles				
			10th	25th	50th	75th	90th
VAS	40.17	28.55	0	13	35	70	80
PPI	2.01	1.18	0	1	2	3	4
Total PRI SR	41.46	32.99	6	18	31.5	58	96
Total PRI Ave	2.56	0.71	1.67	2.00	2.50	3.07	3.50
Total PRI Pct	63.89	17.66	41.67	50.00	62.50	76.67	87.50
Total PWC	30.67	24.52	5.77	13.46	23.08	36.54	73.08
Sensory PRI SR	20.78	16.90	4.00	8.00	16.00	32.00	50.00
Sensory PRI Ave	2.53	0.91	1.33	2.00	2.64	3.13	3.67
Sensory PRI Pct	63.37	22.76	33.33	50.00	65.84	78.13	91.67
Sensory PWC	30.63	25.34	7.69	11.54	23.08	38.46	73.08
Affective-Evaluative PRI SR	20.69	17.95	2.00	7.00	15.00	29.00	48.00
Affective-Evaluative PRI Ave	2.44	0.88	1.00	2.00	2.50	3.00	3.70
Affective-Evaluative PRI Pct	60.89	21.94	25.00	50.00	62.50	75.00	92.50
Affective-Evaluative PWC	30.72	25.55	3.85	15.38	23.08	38.46	76.92
Affective PRI SR	10.56	9.85	1.00	3.00	8.00	14.00	25.00
Affective PRI Ave	2.27	1.04	1.00	1.75	2.40	3.00	3.67
Affective PRI Pct	56.84	26.00	25.00	43.75	60.00	75.00	91.67
Affective PWC	28.08	25.43	6.67	13.33	23.33	33.33	80.00
Evaluative PRI SR	10.13	9.08	1.00	3.00	8.00	15.00	24.00
Evaluative PRI Ave	2.50	1.01	1.00	2.00	2.50	3.33	4.00
Evaluative PRI Pct	62.62	25.25	25.00	50.00	62.50	83.33	100.00
Evaluative PWC	34.32	28.42	9.09	9.09	27.27	45.45	81.82

Note. PRI = Pain Rating Index; PWC = Percentage of Words' Chosen; SR = Summed Ratings; VAS = Visual Analogue Scale; Ave = Average; Pct = Percent of Maximum PRI for words selected.

category PRI Percentage Scores. Each Subcategory Percentage Score calculated can be recorded on the appropriate blank line next to its symbol on the right margin of page 5 or 6 of the PPQ-PAC response form (see Appendix C).

INTERPRETATION OF THE PPQ-PAC

The original form of the MPQ has been shown to discriminate between different types of pain syndromes (Dubuisson & Melzack, 1976; Masson, Hunt, Gem, & Boulton, 1989; Melzack & Katz, 1992; Melzack et al., 1986). Each type of pain syndrome studied (e.g., phantom limb pain, degenerative disc disease) appears to have certain characteristic pain descriptors associated with it. Likewise, the original form of the MPQ has enabled some investigators (Melzack et al., 1986) to differentiate between pain

Table 2.6

PPQ-PAC Means, Standard Deviations, and Percentiles for
Pain Rating Indices, Percentages of Words Chosen, VAS Ratings,
and Present Pain Indices by Type of Pain

Index	Mean	SD	Percentiles				
			10th	25th	50th	75th	90th
Mixed arthritis (*N* = 24)							
VAS	32.16	26.06	0	5	25	50	75
PPI	1.95	1.00	1	1	2	2	3
Total PWC	23.56	21.83	5.77	11.54	18.27	25	59.62
Total PRI Pct	58.41	15.41	37.71	45.59	58.78	71.88	75.74
Sensory PRI Pct	59.66	22.61	29.17	49.04	60.42	75	90
Affective-Evaluative PRI Pct	52.28	21.08	25	37.5	53.13	70	75
Affective PRI Pct	47.86	25.42	0	28.57	50	68.75	75
Evaluative PRI Pct	54.53	23.49	25	35	57.63	75	78.13
Discogenic Disease (*N* = 17)							
VAS	54.5	21.86	30	40	52.5	75	80
PPI	2.53	1.01	2	2	2	3	4
Total PWC	39.14	32.61	9.62	15.38	25	59.62	98.08
Total PRI Pct	66.11	17.48	47.06	50.68	62.5	79.87	95.83
Sensory PRI Pct	63.66	24.16	45	50	63	82.5	95
Affective-Evaluative PRI Pct	62.30	23.64	43.27	50.63	62.5	75.45	97.73
Affective PRI Pct	56.46	26.55	0	50	58.33	75	91.67
Evaluative PRI Pct	63.91	26.78	37.5	46.59	66.67	83.93	100
CFS/Fibromyalgia (*N* = 18)							
VAS	42.47	28.42	3	10	48	72.5	80
PPI	2.17	1.20	1	2	2	2	4
Total PWC	34.19	18.93	11.54	23.08	34.62	40.38	65.38
Total PRI Pct	70.98	14.42	50	58.33	73.22	80.83	87.5
Sensory PRI Pct	73.61	12.41	55	64.29	75	81.82	90
Affective-Evaluative PRI Pct	68.65	18.07	50	56.25	71.13	82.81	92.5
Affective PRI Pct	65.25	25.25	25	50	66.03	82.14	95
Evaluative PRI Pct	70.47	21.02	50	58.33	68.75	88.89	100
Peripheral Neuropathy (*N* = 8)							
VAS	37.17	37.39	0	0	30	73	90
PPI	1.25	1.16	0	0	1.5	2	3
Total PWC	32.21	26.58	3.85	5.77	26.92	57.69	80.77
Total PRI Pct	60.81	22.30	25	43.45	57.92	82.5	93.06
Sensory PRI Pct	54.82	31.51	0	25	57.74	83.33	100
Affective-Evaluative PRI Pct	59.48	23.57	25	35.94	58.33	86.11	95.45
Affective PRI Pct	59.3	24.29	25	33.33	58.04	75	100
Evaluative PRI Pct	57.97	32.36	0	39.29	50	94.44	95

Note. PRI = Pain Rating Index; PWC = Percentage of Words Chosen; PPI = Present Pain Index; VAS = Visual Analogue Scale; Pct = Percent of Maximum PRI for adjectives selected.

Table 2.7

Means, SDs, and Percentiles for Pain Rating Index Percentage Scores
by PPQ-PAC Subcategory in a Mixed Sample of 80 Pain Patients

| Index | Mean | SD | Percentiles | | | | |
			10th	25th	50th	75th	90th
Affective Subcategories							
1. Fatigue (items 1–4)	60.68	27.55	25	50	67.71	81.25	93.75
2. Autonomic Distress (items 5–7)	11.35	23.54	0	0	0	0	50
3. Punitiveness (items 8–11)	16.90	30.20	0	0	0	25	75
4. Fear (items 12–15)	19.77	30.64	0	0	0	50	75
Evaluative Subcategories							
1. Misery (items 16–18)	63.23	30.04	25	50	75	91.67	100
2. Suffering (items 19–22)	32.08	36.42	0	0	12.5	62.5	91.67
3. Miscellaneous (items 23–26)	27.81	35.46	0	0	0	56.25	87.5
Sensory Subcategories							
1. Temporal (items 27, 28)	34.69	36.51	0	0	25	75	87.5
2. Spatial (items 29–31)	30.57	35.93	0	0	0	50	100
3. Punctate Pressure (items 32, 33)	23.59	34.04	0	0	0	50	75
4. Incisive Pressure (items 34, 35)	24.53	34.01	0	0	0	62.5	75
5. Constrictive Pressure (items 36–39)	32.84	33.36	0	0	40.63	56.25	75
6. Traction Pressure (items 40, 41)	14.06	26.64	0	0	0	25	75
7. Hotness (items 42, 43)	22.66	33.05	0	0	0	50	75
8. Additive Pressure (items 44, 45)	21.25	34.07	0	0	0	50	75
9. Soreness (items 46–49)	64.66	32.09	0	50	75	100	100
10. Coldness/Numbness (items 50–52)	31.77	35.55	0	0	25	62.5	87.5

syndromes with and without clear-cut physical causes. As more data from the PPQ-PAC become available, it should become possible to empirically derive prototypical profiles associated with different pain syndromes.

Based on the PRIs and other indices, a clinician can obtain from a patient's PPQ-PAC, quantitative data on the intensity of clinically significant dimensions of the patient's pain experience. At this juncture in this instrument's development, based on the currently available norms, the following preliminary interpretive guidelines may be followed:

1. Graphically plot a patient's PRI Percentage Scores for each of the five major PPQ-PAC categories (Total, Sensory, Affective, Evaluative, Affective-Evaluative) on the form in Appendix J. Also, plot a patient's VAS Percentage Score, PPI Percentage Score, and Overall Percentage of Words Chosen (PWC).

2. For each of the five major PPQ-PAC categories, compare the patient's PRI Percentage Scores with the mean and percentile values for the total normative sample, and the relevant pain-specific sample. For each score plotted on the graphic profile, record its nearest, normative percentile value. Total PRIs of 90% or more are suggestive of a strong psychogenic or emotional component to a patient's pain.

3. Compare the magnitude of the patient's Sensory PRI with the patient's Affective and Evaluative PRIs, taking into account the normative mean and percentile values. High Affective and Evaluative PRIs in the presence of a low Sensory PRI suggests a primary influence of emotional components underlying a patient's pain complaints. Affective and Evaluative PRIs of 90% or more strongly suggest that there are emotional components to a patient's pain.

4. Extreme Affective and Evaluative Subcategory PRIs can suggest symptom magnification or exaggeration and are associated with a substantive emotional component underlying the pain complaint. The Subcategory PRIs should be computed and recorded on the PPQ-PAC patient response form. Then, the clinician should compare the calculated Subcategory PRIs with the preliminary normative means and percentiles in Table 2.7. The table shows that for this normative sample, high endorsement of the words within certain subcategories is rare (e.g., see *autonomic distress, punitiveness, fear,* and *miscellaneous* Affective and Evaluative subcategories, and the *pressure* and *hotness* sensory subcategories). This is especially true for the four Affective-Evaluative subcategories given above. If a patient intensely endorses the words in one or more of these rarely endorsed Affective-Evaluative subcategories, this raises a red flag for a possibly exaggerated or biased pain complaint.

5. Note and compare the magnitude of the Percentages of Words Chosen (PWCs) for each of the PPQ-PAC categories. High PWCs for Affective

and Evaluative categories in the presence of low PWCs for the Sensory category also suggest a strong psychogenic or emotional component to a patient's pain.

6. Patients who have a Present Pain Intensity (PPI) Index of 4 or 5 (item B, p. 7 on the PPQ) are very likely to have a significant psychogenic component to their pain complaint.

7. Patients who have a VAS of 80 or above (item A, p. 7 on the PPQ) are also very likely to have a significant psychogenic component to their pain complaint.

8. Patients who—in response to Question 20 on the PPQ pain history and status section and to Item D under Pain Intensity Ratings and Pain Drawings—indicate that their pain is present 100% of the time, may have what has been termed a "constant pain syndrome" (Ewin, 1986, 1992). Also, look at the temporal words circled for Item C under Pain Intensity Ratings and Pain Drawings. If the words *continuous, never goes away, constant,* and *always there* are all circled, the patient is probably communicating a perception of constant pain. Pain that never goes away may suggest a psychological basis, or an invalid pain complaint (see discussions of symptom invalidity measures in Chapter 3).

CHAPTER 3

Assessing Disability, Pain Beliefs, Coping, and Maladjustment

It is much more important to know what sort of a patient has a disease than what sort of disease a patient has.

—William Osler

AFTER EVALUATING a patient's pain history and status, the clinician next must assess behavioral and psychological functioning by examining the patient's (a) *impairment* and *disablement* due to pain, (b) *pain beliefs,* (c) *coping strategies,* and (d) the presence and extent of any *psychological maladjustment* and *psychopathology.* Psychometrically sound and clinically useful instruments have been developed for evaluating each of the areas (Bradley, Haile, & Jaworski, 1992; DeGood & Shutty, 1992; Kerns & Jacob, 1992; Turk & Melzack, 1992). In this chapter, we cover the clinical assessment of these areas, and also introduce a new, comprehensive pain assessment instrument called the Pain Coping Inventory (PCI) (Eimer & Allen, 1995).

DEFINITIONS

IMPAIRMENT

The fourth edition of the American Medical Association's *Guides to the Evaluation of Permanent Impairment* (AMA, 1995) defines impairment as "the loss, loss of use, or derangement of any body part, system, or function," and as "an alteration in a person's health status that can be assessed medically and objectively through clinical and/or laboratory procedures" (p. 315). Examples of physical impairment would be decreased range of motion, strength, flexion, or extension from a lumbosacral strain or herniated lumbar disc, and decreased or altered sensation from a nerve root injury. Medical assessments are necessary for evaluating anatomical and physiological abnormalities or losses. Psychological impairments include a patient's phobias, depression, anxiety, anger, sleep disruption, or emotional distress and suffering after a traumatic event; these require psychological methods of evaluation. Likewise, a patient's cognitive deficiencies (e.g., memory loss), personality alterations, and maladaptive behavioral changes following a closed head injury or concussion would be considered *neuropsychological* impairments, calling for neuropsychological methods of evaluation (Adams et al., 1996; R. Anderson, 1994; Grant & Adams, 1996; Lezak, 1995). Typically, physical and psychological impairments manifest as functional limitations that need to be evaluated to quantify degree of impairment.

FUNCTIONAL LIMITATIONS

The term *functional limitation* is defined by Vasudevan (1992) as "a restriction or the lack of ability to perform an activity or function in the manner within the range considered normal for that person, that results from an impairment . . . Thus, functional limitations are manifestations of impairment translated in terms of function" (p. 102). In reality, however, the terms functional limitation and impairment are used interchangeably.

TWO DIMENSIONS OF VARIATION IN IMPAIRMENT

Physical, psychological, and neuropsychological impairments vary along two main dimensions: the *temporary-permanent* continuum, and the *degree of impairment* or *severity* continuum. Many impairments can be temporary, lasting during a phase of active pathology, or they may be permanent, continuing long after any active pathology has been treated and resolved (Vasudevan, 1992). The AMA (1995) defines permanent impairment as "impairment that has become static or well stabilized with or without medical treatment and is not likely to remit despite medical treatment" (p. 315). Some impairments may be relatively minor, whereas others can be severe. Both dimensions of impairment are usually closely related to the concept of pathology.

IMPAIRMENTS, FUNCTIONAL LIMITATIONS, AND PATHOLOGY

Physical pathology is defined as "altered anatomy and/or physiology that underlies and causes physical dysfunction and impairment" (Vasudevan, 1992). It can result from trauma, infection, inflammation, degeneration, a metabolic disorder, and so on. *Psychological pathology* (psychopathology), on the other hand, refers to the *"manifestations* of mental disorders . . . Psychopathology involves *impairments, deviance,* and *distress,* but not all impairments, deviance, and distress are psychopathology . . . According to DSM-IV, mental disorders must produce clinically significant *impairment* or *distress* in one's personal, social, or occupational life" (Maxmen & Ward, 1995, p. 5). Although it may or may not result from biological causes such as trauma, infection, or metabolic disorders, psychopathology can also result in or produce symptoms of physical disorder (e.g., pain, autonomic arousal).

It is typically assumed that some form of identifiable pathology underlies objective indices of impairment. For example, brain injury or brain damage (pathology) may underlie cognitive impairment and dysfunction that is organically caused. Permanent cognitive impairment may be related to permanent alterations in brain neurophysiology (e.g., the consequences of a traumatic brain injury or stroke). In contrast, temporary cognitive impairment is often relatable to acute or temporary, psychological conditions affecting mentation (e.g., a major depressive episode, or acute stress disorder). Psychological impairment can result from physical or psychological (nonorganically based) forms of pathology. Physical impairment often results from clinically significant physical pathology (e.g., a broken leg). However, this is not always the case. Often, physical impairment is evidenced to a degree that cannot be accounted for by the medically diagnosed physical pathology.

IMPAIRMENT IN EXCESS OF DOCUMENTED PATHOLOGY

In the realm of chronic pain, neither degree of impairment or pain are typically commensurate with medically documentable levels of physical pathology. Because all pain is subjective, it is not even possible to measure pain impairment in the same way that many other forms of impairment can be measured (e.g., functional capacity testing, muscle strength, blood flow, pulmonary function). Essentially, we are dependent on patient self-report and observations of patient behaviors. The relationship between persistent pain, physical pathology, and functional impairment is generally not clear-cut. This is where the evaluation of psychological factors and disability is applicable.

DISABILITY

Disability is defined as "the inability of the individual to perform his or her usual activities and to assume usual obligations" (Vasudevan, 1992,

p. 102). The AMA (1995) defines it as a "decrease in, or the loss or absence of, the capacity of an individual to meet personal, social, or occupational demands, or to meet statutory or regulatory requirements" (p. 317). Disability is usually assumed to arise out of an underlying impairment, (e.g., pain, altered physiology, psychopathology) that limits an individual's ability to perform his or her usual role and activities. However, there is no invariant, one-to-one relationship between the variables of pain, tissue pathology, functional impairment, and level of disability.

In contrast to the concept of impairment which, at least by the AMA's (1995) definition, is considered objectively determinable by medical, clinical, or laboratory measures, the concept of disability refers to a judgment that often is mired in subjectivity and potential response bias. Some patients may be biased in reporting their impairments, functional limitations, and disability for purposes of secondary gain, or for other reasons. The key to understanding a patient's impairments and disability is to develop an adequate understanding of the underlying forms of pathology (physical and psychological) that are likely to be operative. Valid determinations of disability demand that clinicians administer several procedures to obtain a multidimensional or multifactorial picture of a patient's relevant problems. Thus, within the realm of chronic pain and disability, it is often necessary to evaluate a patient's pain history, pain experience, mental status, cognitive status, pain beliefs, coping strategies, types and degrees of impairment, physical pathology, psychopathology, and disability, to understand the patient and recommend appropriate treatment.

PSYCHOMETRIC INSTRUMENTS FOR EVALUATING PAIN IMPAIRMENT AND DISABILITY

THE MULTIDIMENSIONAL PAIN INVENTORY

The Multidimensional Pain Inventory, or MPI (Kerns, Turk, & Rudy, 1985; Rudy, 1989), is a 61-item, self-report questionnaire that assesses functional pain impairment in the form of 13 dimensions operationalized as scales. Section I of the questionnaire covers pain severity, activity interference, perceived life control, affective distress, and perceived level of social support. Section II assesses perceived responses of significant others including punitive, solicitous, and distracting responses. Section III assesses frequency of engagement in various activities of daily living which covers household chores, outdoor work, activities away from home, social activities, and general activity level. Based on their pattern of responses on the test, patients are classified into one of five coping profile categories ("dysfunctional coper," "interpersonally distressed," "adaptive coper," "hybrid profile," and "anomalous") that according to the test's developers, form an empirically derived pain patient taxonomy (Turk & Rudy, 1992). The MPI is a unique and well-conceptualized instrument grounded in a cognitive-behavioral, multifactor model of pain and its effects. The information the test provides can be useful in treatment planning.

THE SICKNESS IMPACT PROFILE

The Sickness Impact Profile (SIP) is a 136-item self-report questionnaire (Bergner, Bobbitt, Carter, & Gilson, 1981) that profiles impairment and disability along 12 functional dimensions: ambulation, mobility, body care and movement, social interaction, communication, alertness, emotional behavior, sleep and rest, eating, work, home management, and recreation. These dimensions are clustered to form Physical, Psychosocial, and Total Disability scales. Studies have shown the SIP to be a sensitive measure of treatment-mediated changes in patient mobility, sociability, and global functioning, and the test has been reported to correlate well with pain patients' self-reports of pain, physical examination measures, and several other functional disability measures (Bradley et al., 1992; Deyo, 1986; Follick, Smith, & Ahern, 1985).

THE ROLAND AND MORRIS DISABILITY QUESTIONNAIRE

Another instrument developed to measure perceived degree of disability associated with chronic back pain is the Roland and Morris Disability Questionnaire (Roland & Morris, 1983). It has 24 items derived from the Sickness Impact Profile and was developed to provide a briefer, more easily interpretable instrument. In an unpublished study reported by Waddell and Turk (1992), the Roland and Morris instrument was found to have "better factor structure" and clinical utility than the Oswestry Disability Questionnaire.

THE OSWESTRY DISABILITY QUESTIONNAIRE

The Oswestry Disability Questionnaire (ODQ; Fairbank, Couper, Davies, & O'Brien, 1980) is a brief self-report instrument specifically designed to assess a back pain patient's perceived degree of disability. The patient rates his or her degree of dysfunction and limitations in 10 areas: pain intensity, personal care, lifting, walking, sitting, standing, sleeping, sexual activity, social life, and traveling. The ODQ yields a total score representing degree of dysfunction in the aforementioned activities of daily living.

It is a widely used instrument because of its clarity, brevity, and ease of administration and interpretation.

THE ILLNESS BEHAVIOR QUESTIONNAIRE

Another self-report instrument designed to assess pain-related disability and abnormal illness behavior is the Illness Behavior Questionnaire (IBQ; Pilowsky, 1995; Pilowsky, Spence, Cobb, & Katsikitis, 1984). This 62-item, true-false, self-report questionnaire assesses seven dimensions: General Hypochondriasis; Conviction of Disease; Psychological versus Somatic Focus of Disease; Affective Inhibition; Affective Disturbance; Denial of Life Problems Unrelated to Pain, and Irritability. Research has shown that the test is capable of detecting pain patients with no demonstrable organic pathology as they evidence high IBQ scores (Pilowsky, Chapman, & Bonica, 1977; Speculand, Goss, Spence, & Pilowsky, 1981). The test is particularly useful for assessing hypochondriacal tendencies.

THE PAIN INTERFERENCE AND IMPAIRMENT INDEX

We have developed the Pain Interference and Impairment Index (PIII) displayed in Appendix K to provide a straightforward, clinically useful, patient self-report measure of both the intensity and frequency of pain's interference with common activities of daily living. It was inspired by the fourth edition of the American Medical Association's *Guides to the Evaluation of Permanent Impairment* (1995), which proposes two major dimensions for evaluating *degree* of pain-related impairment: intensity or severity and frequency. On the PIII, each activity is rated on two Likert scales—a 4-point, 0-to-3 scale of pain interference intensity, and a 4-point, 0-to-3 scale of pain interference frequency. For each of the 36 items, a patient is asked to "circle the number of the response that shows *how much* [intensity] and *how often* [frequency] pain interferes with that activity." The 36 activities on the PIII sample ten major categories of activities of daily living—the AMA *Guides* suggest nine of these (AMA, 1995): personal care, communicating, movement and physical activity, sensory functions, hand use, travel, sexual functioning, sleep, and social and recreational activities. The tenth category is work.

SCORING THE PIII

The Score Sheet on page 6 of the PIII (see Appendix K) facilitates the computation of several summary indices. A patient's ratings are first summed for each dimension (intensity and frequency). The two Raw Score Sums are also converted into Percentage Scores and Average Ratings. Following the AMA *Guides'* "Pain Intensity-Frequency Grid" (1995, p. 310), these numerical indices are associated with verbal descriptors for degree of impairment. Based on a patient's scored indices of Pain Interference Intensity and Pain Interference Frequency on the PIII Score Sheet, it is possible to say that a patient reports (*intermittent, occasional, frequent,* or *constant*) pain impairment of (*minimal, mild/slight, moderate,* or *marked*) intensity.

As with most patient self-report instruments, a patient's ratings on the PIII of how much and how often pain interferes with or impairs his or her activities of daily living, are subjective and thus, subject to patient response bias. Also, very high Pain Interference Intensity and Frequency indices may be associated with tendencies toward symptom magnification or exaggeration, as may be very high ratings for certain items (e.g., items 3, 4, 5, 21, 22, 23, 24, 25, 26, 36) in the absence of a serious neurological disorder.

PSYCHOMETRIC INSTRUMENTS FOR ASSESSING PAIN BELIEFS

DEFINING PAIN BELIEFS

A growing body of evidence suggests that patients' beliefs and expectancies about pain, the causes of pain, pain treatment, self-efficacy, and coping mediate some of the relationships between pain, disability, impairment, and response to treatment (DeGood & Kiernan, 1996; DeGood & Shutty, 1992; Jensen & Karoly, 1991; Jensen, Turner, Romano, & Lawler, 1994; Shutty, DeGood, & Tuttle, 1990; Williams & Keefe, 1991; Williams, Robinson, & Geisser, 1994). *Beliefs* can be defined as "personal, evaluatively loaded cognitions, assumptions, or conceptions about the nature of certain things or about causal relationships between related things that are held with some degree of conviction." A related term is the concept of attitudes. *Attitudes* can be defined as "personal opinions and evaluatively loaded ways of perceiving and thinking about certain things that serve as dispositions to take certain types of action." Although each person's cognitions are unique, their content, shape and form are influenced by sociocultural factors such as ethnicity, family and socialization history, peer groups, the society, and significant others.

These factors are likely to influence patients' predictions and decisions, and motivate behavior. Their beliefs about self-efficacy and control over pain may at least partially determine coping efforts and adjustment (R. Anderson, Dowds, Pelletz, Edwards, & Peeters-Asdourian, 1995; Bandura, O'Leary, Taylor, Gauthier, & Gossard, 1987; DeGood & Shutty, 1992; Jensen & Karoly, 1991; Jensen, Turner, & Romano, 1991; Schiafino,

Revenson, & Gibofsky, 1991). Beliefs about the consequences of being disabled (e.g., secondary gains) may influence the occurrence of pain behaviors associated with disability as well as other expressions of disability (Feuerstein & Thebarge, 1991; Riley, Ahern, & Follick, 1988), and beliefs about illness may partially determine illness behavior (Pilowsky, 1995; Turkat & Pettegrew, 1983; Zonderman, Heft, & Costa, 1985). Beliefs and perceptions about fairness, propriety, justice, and fault may partially determine patients' experience and expression of anger and progress in treatment (DeGood & Kiernan, 1996; Fernandez & Turk, 1995). Finally, patients' beliefs about the causes of pain and its future course may partially determine coping behaviors, treatment choices, and treatment compliance (Waddell, Newton, Henderson, Somerville, & Main, 1993; Williams & Keefe, 1991; Williams et al., 1994; Williams & Thorn, 1989).

THE PAIN BELIEFS AND PERCEPTIONS INVENTORY

In an effort to assess pain patients' relevant beliefs, Williams and Thorn (1989) developed a 16-item, patient self-report questionnaire called the Pain Beliefs and Perceptions Inventory (PBPI; see Appendix L). The PBPI asks patients to record their degree of agreement or disagreement to each of 16 statements that reflect various beliefs or perceptions about their pain. The patient's responses are scored by summing and then averaging the patient's ratings for all the items on each of four factors or scales. The factors/scales are termed *Pain Mysteriousness* (Items 1, 4, 8, 14); *Pain Permanence* (Items 2, 5, 9, 12, 15); *Pain Constancy* (Items 3, 6, 10, 16); and *Self-Blame* (Items 7, 11, 13). In calculating scale scores, Items 3, 9, 12, and 15 are scored in the reverse direction, as positive scores indicate positive endorsement of negative beliefs in the pain's mysteriousness, permanence, constancy, and the patient's blameworthiness for pain. Normative means and standard deviations for the PBPI scales are provided at the bottom of the instrument. These norms are derived from Williams et al. (1994) based on a mixed sample of 213 chronic pain patients.

Research with the PBPI indicates it has promise in predicting pain treatment outcomes (Thorn & Williams, 1993; Williams et al., 1994). Patients scoring high on beliefs measuring pain permanence and constancy were reported to show poorer compliance with physical therapy and psychological treatment modalities than did other patients. Patients scoring high on the belief in pain's mysteriousness showed the greatest psychological distress (anxiety and depression symptoms), and relatively poor compliance with physical therapy, but better compliance with psychological treatment. The authors report that the dimension of self-blame was not predictive of treatment compliance in their studies but was associated with symptoms of depression. However, Williams et al. (1994) report that their sample of chronic pain patients showed limited endorsement of items measuring this dimension (the self-blame mean was −1.36). In another study with burn patients, Kiecolt-Glaser and Williams (1987) found that self-blame was associated with poorer compliance with inpatient treatment, as well as more manifest pain behavior and depression.

Our experience with the PBPI has been very positive. The test is brief and has high face validity. Pain patients accept the test and find it relevant. Like the test authors, we have found that few patients endorse the items measuring a belief in self-blame for pain, with the exception of some very depressed patients. By comparison, some patients who suffer from PTSD also tend to endorse these self-blame items. Perhaps their endorsement reflects survivor guilt or personal attributions of overresponsibility. We have also found clinically that some patients who positively endorse items measuring both pain mysteriousness and pain permanence show poor compliance with psychotherapy, as indicated by their prematurely dropping out of treatment. Also strong beliefs in pain constancy seem to be associated, in our clinical experience, with other measures of psychological distress (e.g., depression, anxiety, and overall levels of maladjustment and psychopathology). In contrast, we have found that pain patients who initially present with low scores on mysteriousness, permanence, and constancy, seem to be the most invested in physical and rehabilitative treatments for their pain.

The PBPI is a clinically useful psychological pain assessment tool that appears to tap several important dimensions highly relevant to tracking and evaluating outcomes of PMP and other pain treatments. It also appears to be uniquely useful for assessing treatment progress with post-traumatically stressed pain patients.

ADDITIONAL BELIEF ASSESSMENT MEASURES

Some other measures of pain beliefs include the Survey of Pain Attitudes (Jensen & Karoly, 1991), the Pain and Impairment Relationship Scale (Riley et al., 1988), the Chronic Pain Self-Efficacy Scale (Anderson et al., 1995), Skevington's (1990) Beliefs about Pain Control Questionnaire (BPCQ), and the Pain Coping Inventory (Eimer & Allen, 1995) which is discussed later in this chapter.

Patients' beliefs may play a key role in determining their behaviors. In one sense, beliefs can be conceptualized as construals or predictions about personally relevant events, which are put to the test by a person's behaviors and coping efforts (Kelly, 1955). Adaptive beliefs motivate coping behaviors that are positively reinforced with pain relief and lead to positive validation. Maladaptive and dysfunctional beliefs lead to punitive consequences (e.g., increased pain levels), do not produce positively reinforcing outcomes, and invalidate a person's sense of self-worth and self-esteem (e.g., lead to behaviors that trigger punitive responses from others). Therefore, the evaluation of patients in pain should incorporate some assessment of their relevant beliefs. However, because beliefs find their expression in people's behaviors, it also is important to assess relevant behaviors (e.g., coping strategies).

PAIN COPING STRATEGIES

Coping can be defined as "what people do to try to control, manage, or tolerate stressful situations, such as severe pain" (DeGood & Shutty, 1992; Eimer & Allen, 1995). The term *pain coping strategies* refers to the methods people use to manage severe pain episodes. Numerous studies have indicated that pain patients' coping strategies are related to several measures of adjustment including pain treatment outcomes (Beckham, Keefe, Caldwell, & Roedman, 1991; Brown, Nicassio, & Wallston, 1989; DeGood & Shutty, 1992; Dozois, Dobson, Wong, Hughes, & Long, 1996; Eimer & Allen, 1995; Hanson & Gerber, 1990; Hill et al., 1995; Jensen & Karoly, 1991; Jensen, Turner, & Romano, 1991; Jensen, Turner, Romano, & Karoly, 1991; Jensen, Turner, Romano, & Strom, 1995; Keefe et al., 1987; Keefe, Brown, Wallston, & Caldwell, 1989; Keefe et al., 1990a; Keefe, Crisson, Urban, & Williams, 1990b; Revenson & Felton, 1989; Rosenstiel & Keefe, 1983; Snow-Turek, Norris, & Tan, 1996; Turner & Clancy, 1986).

It makes intuitive sense that the particular methods people use to deal with severe pain episodes are related to the quality of their adjustment. Because the goal of many forms of treatment for chronic pain is management as opposed to cure, it also makes intuitive sense that the coping strategies of people in pain are related to treatment outcomes. Therefore, it is important to know what coping strategies the patient has employed and his or her views of their efficacy. Unfavorable pain treatment outcomes, marked by a lack of improvement in quality of adjustment, may be associated with certain unfavorable coping strategies.

CLASSIFYING PAIN COPING STRATEGIES: THE COPING STRATEGIES QUESTIONNAIRE

To assess coping strategies, it is necessary to have a scheme for classifying them. The most frequently used classificatory scheme has been the one developed by Rosenstiel and Keefe (1983). It is represented by seven scales or dimensions that compose their widely used 50-item patient self-report instrument, called the Coping Strategies Questionnaire (CSQ).

The CSQ (Rosenstiel & Keefe, 1983) directly addresses pain patient coping strategies. As a clinical tool, it also has excellent face validity with pain patients. It has been widely used with varied populations of pain patients in both inpatient and outpatient settings (DeGood & Shutty, 1992; Thorn & Williams, 1993). On this instrument, patients rate the frequency with which they engage in 48 coping behaviors, each of which falls under one of seven categories, or coping strategies: *diverting attention, ignoring pain sensations, increasing behavioral activities, coping self-statements, reinterpreting pain sensations, praying/hoping,* and *catastrophizing.* Two additional scales reflect patients' ratings of their perceived degree of control over pain, and their ability to decrease pain. Based on factor analytic studies, the preceding scales can be further reduced to three composite coping factors termed (a) Pain Avoidance (includes diverting attention, ignoring pain sensations, and increasing activities), (b) Conscious Cognitive Coping (includes use of coping statements and reinterpreting sensations), and (c) Self-Efficacy Beliefs (self-assessment of ability to control and decrease pain). The strategies of praying/hoping and catastrophizing appear to load on a helplessness factor (Rosenstiel & Keefe, 1983; Turner & Clancy, 1986).

Coping Strategies as Predictors of Adjustment and Treatment Outcomes

The burgeoning interest in how specific coping strategies in particular pain populations are related to quality of adjustment has led investigators to look for specific strategies associated with good and poor pain treatment outcomes (L. Anderson & Rehm, 1984; Hagglund, Haley, Reveille, & Alarcon, 1989; Hill, Niven, & Knussen, 1995; Jensen et al., 1991; Keefe et al., 1987, 1989; Turner & Clancy, 1986). The dimensions of self-efficacy beliefs and conscious cognitive coping on the CSQ have been isolated as predictive of pain severity in some studies (Hagglund et al., 1989; Parker et al., 1989), whereas, others have reported a lack of a clear association (Rosenstiel & Keefe, 1983; Spinhoven & Linssen, 1991; Turner & Clancey, 1986). In contrast, catastrophizing consistently has been associated with poorer adjustment and pain treatment outcomes (Jensen et al., 1991; Rosenstiel & Keefe, 1983; Thorn & Williams, 1993; Turner & Clancy, 1986).

In a study with phantom limb pain patients (amputees), Hill et al. (1995) reported that the relationship between coping and adjustment was primarily explained by the use of strategies within the helplessness factor of the CSQ, with catastrophizing explaining the largest proportion of the variance among measures, and increasing behavioral activities, reinterpreting pain sensations, and hoping/praying explaining smaller proportions. Their most clinically significant finding, however, was that based on the CSQ, coping strategy use was associated with increased, as opposed to decreased, levels of pain and disability. Not surprisingly, the helplessness factor (catastrophizing, praying/hoping) predicted increased pain report and greater psychosocial dysfunction, but increased behavioral activity and reinterpreting pain sensations were also positively correlated with the helplessness factor, and higher pain levels.

Although at first glance, these findings may seem counterintuitive, they may be explainable by taking into account that coping strategies are probably differentially effective for different types of pain. In fact, different pain patient populations do show varied patterns of relationship between coping strategy use, measures of adjustment, and treatment outcomes (De-Good & Shutty, 1992; Jensen, Turner, Romano, & Karoly, 1991). Low back pain patients appear to benefit with reduced pain from the use of the coping strategy of increasing activity levels (Dozois et al., 1996; Keefe et al., 1990b; Turner & Clancy, 1986), whereas amputees with phantom limb pain apparently do not benefit. Hill et al. (1995) make the point that perhaps, for their sample of amputees, the specific increased activity these patients adopted served as a physical irritant and aggravated their pain.

Clinicians need to tease apart the distinctions between which coping strategies patients employ when their pain gets bad, and which ones they perceive to work best in alleviating flare-ups. If patients report that they often use "increasing behavioral activities" when their pain flares up, it does not necessarily mean that this strategy causes increased pain or effectively reduces pain. Instead, increased pain might prompt the use of this strategy. This is an important distinction.

THE IMPORTANCE OF MULTIPLE ASSESSMENT MEASURES

These investigators' findings highlight the need to employ multiple measures in the clinical assessment of pain patients. Some measures may be better than others for tapping the relevant coping strategies in a given population. Also, the particular outcome measures employed affect the relationships between coping strategies and adjustment. Therefore, clinicians should not allow their instruments to limit the coping strategies they look at. Psychometric measures should be combined with clinical interviews and other methods to obtain the most contextually relevant picture of a patient's coping efforts, successes, and failures.

Other measures that have been developed to assess coping strategies include the Ways of Coping Questionnaire (Lazarus & Folkman, 1984) for assessing coping with stress, the Vanderbuilt Pain Management Inventory (Brown & Nicassio, 1987) for assessing active versus passive coping by chronic pain patients, the Cognitive Coping Strategies Inventory (Butler, Damarin, Beaulieu, Schwebel, & Thorn, 1989) for acute pain patients, the Chronic Pain Coping Inventory (Jensen et al., 1995), for assessing chronic pain patients' different coping responses to pain, and the Pain Coping Inventory (Eimer & Allen, 1995), which is a comprehensive pain assessment inventory discussed later in this chapter.

RISK FACTORS AND PREDICTORS OF CONTINUED PAIN AND DISABILITY

Chronic pain patients statistically show dismally poor responses to standard treatments that are typically effective with acute pain patients (Andersson, Pope, Frymoyer, & Snook, 1991; Barnes, Smith, Gatchel, & Mayer, 1989; Dworkin, Handlin, Richlin, Brand, & Vannucci, 1985; Gatchel, 1996; Hendler, 1981; Jamison, 1996; M. Jensen, 1996; Kerns & Haythornthwaite, 1988; Turk, 1996). Once pain becomes chronic, seldom can any one intervention return an individual to a prepain state. Responsiveness to pain management interventions is influenced by the patient's psychological reactions to unremitting pain and related problems over time. Therefore, selection of relevant and successful interventions depend on the accurate assessment of the person's psychological reactions to chronic pain and to previous treatments. Reasonable treatment goals such as reductions in pain intensity, decreased frequency of flare-ups, and improved levels of functionality are only reasonable if the patient agrees that they are reasonable, desirable, possible, and probable.

Reviews of the research on psychosocial and behavioral risk factors for recurrent episodes of back pain and continued disability suggest several key variables (Cairns, Mooney, & Crane, 1984; Feuerstein & Zastowny, 1996; Frederickson, Trief, Van Beveren, Yuan, & Baum, 1988; Gatchel, 1996; Linton & Bradley, 1996; Sanders, 1995b). These variables may influence patients' subjective assessments of which treatment goals are reasonable, possible, and probable. They also appear to predict patients' adjustment and pain treatment outcomes (Barnes et al., 1989; Flor & Turk, 1988; Gamsa & Vikis-Freibergs, 1991; Gatchel, 1996; Gatchel, Polatin, & Kinney, 1995; Gatchel, Polatin, & Mayer, 1996; Geisser et al., 1996; Linton & Bradley, 1996; Turk, 1996).

Job dissatisfaction is an especially relevant predictive variable in the context of work-related injuries (Bigos et al., 1991; Dworkin et al., 1985; Fordyce, 1995; Gallagher et al., 1989, 1995; Sanders, 1995b). Considering the high cost of work-injury claims, this is a critical variable (Kerr, 1993). A second predictive variable is the combined presence of low activity levels (withdrawal and avoidance) and high levels of pain behaviors, such as complaining, pain gesturing, pain posturing, drug seeking, heavy PRN (as needed) use of pain medications, and exaggerating or magnifying pain-related symptoms (Eimer & Allen, 1995; Fordyce, Shelton, & Dunmore, 1982; Keefe & Williams, 1992; Sanders, 1996; Schwartz, Slater, &

Birchler, 1990; Turk & Matyas, 1992). A third predictive variable of continued disability and diminished likelihood of return to work appears to be the cognitive factor of negative, fear-based beliefs, such as that the pain is harmful, destructive, disabling, out of control, or that increased activity will increase pain levels (Fordyce et al., 1982; Jensen, Turner, Romano, & Lawler, 1994; Vlaeyen, Kole-Snijders, Boeren, & Van Eek, 1995; Waddell et al., 1993). A fourth predictor of negative pain treatment outcome and continued disability appears to be high levels of hostility, anger, and alienation (Burns et al., 1996; Eimer & Allen, 1995; Fernandez & Turk, 1995; Kerns et al., 1994). A fifth general predictor of adjustment and treatment outcomes, as discussed earlier, is coping strategy use (Anderson & Rehm, 1984; Beckham et al., 1991; Hill et al., 1995; Holmes & Stevenson, 1990; Jensen & Karoly, 1991; Revenson & Felton, 1989; Rosenstiel & Keefe, 1983).

APPROPRIATE USE OF PSYCHOLOGICAL AND PSYCHOMETRIC TEST DATA

Caution is necessary when applying group findings reported in the literature to individual clinical assessments of chronic pain patients as well as when extrapolating findings to different patient populations. Furthermore, psychometric test data should seldom be the sole basis for predicting pain treatment outcomes. They should be supplemented by relevant, case-specific, background information derived from patient medical records, interviews and observations, and the patient's history.

Most pain patients have limited tolerance for taking a long battery of tests, and overtaxing a pain patient's tolerance may weaken the validity and consistency of the resulting data. Therefore, it is essential to select assessment tests wisely and expediently. One goal in assessment is to develop an understanding of the patient's psychological reactions to pain, and this can best be developed by collecting data from several sources. Careful observation of the patient's test-taking attitude also may yield rich information relevant to diagnostic impressions and treatment recommendations.

MEASURES OF PERSONALITY, PSYCHOPATHOLOGY, AND ADJUSTMENT

Living in constant pain is difficult and can be a major stressor. The resultingly high prevalence rates of Axis I clinical syndromes in chronic pain patients, as classified by the fourth edition of the American Psychiatric Association's *Diagnostic and Statistical Manual of Mental Disorders* (*DSM-IV*; APA, 1994) make it important to assess pain patients for comorbidity of certain common psychiatric disorders. Additionally, because personality factors appear to play a marked role in determining how patients express and manage stress or pain (Gatchel, 1996; Lazarus & Folkman, 1984; Lehrer & Woolfolk, 1993; Rudy, Turk, Kubinski, & Zaki, 1995; Turk, 1996), it is clinically advisable to assess personality traits as well. Although there is little evidence for a "pain-prone personality" (Blumer & Heilbronn, 1989; Engel, 1959; Turk & Salovey, 1984), various *DSM-IV* diagnosable, Axis II personality psychopathology may be prevalent in certain chronic pain patient populations (Gatchel, 1996; Gatchel et al., 1995; Grzesiak et al., 1996; Hendler, 1981; Love & Peck, 1987; Millon, 1995).

A TENTATIVE PERSONALITY PSYCHOPATHOLOGY TYPOLOGY FOR PAIN PATIENTS

Earlier work by Eimer (1993a, 1993b) suggested the beginnings of a simple personality psychopathology typology of chronic pain patients for clinical use in psychotherapy treatment planning. This classificatory scheme has proven useful in our clinical work and has evolved. It is helpful in sorting chronic pain patients into one or more pathognomonic categories based on prominent clinical diagnostic factors, interpersonal criteria, and personality presentations. This provides a systematic way of distinguishing between objective pain patients and psychogenic pain patients (i.e., pain patients with comorbid psychiatric disorders). The value of this typology lies in its utility for clinical assessment. There are five major groups of pathognomonic traits and characteristics each of which contains several subgroups. These groupings are not mutually exclusive; patients may fall into one or more categories and subcategories.

Pathognomonic Group I

This group includes patients who fall into one or more of the following three categories: (a) high anger, hostility, and alienation; (b) high impulsivity, aggression, and/or actual or potential dangerousness; and (c) paranoid, schizoid, and/or schizotypal personality disorder traits (*DSM-IV* Cluster A; APA, 1994).

Pathognomonic Group II

These patients fall into one or more of the following three categories: (a) hypochondriacal anxiety; (b) hysteria and histrionic personality disorder traits; and (c) self-defeating, passive aggressive, avoidant, and/or dependent personality disorder traits.

Pathognomonic Group III

These are patients who fit the *DSM-IV* clinical criteria for (a) narcissistic personality disorder; (b) borderline personality disorder; and/or

(c) antisocial personality disorder (three out of the four disorders in *DSM-IV* Cluster B).

Pathognomonic Group IV

This group includes patients who fit the clinical criteria for (a) posttraumatic stress disorder and/or (b) postconcussive syndrome.

Pathognomonic Group V

Patients in this group appear to be receiving notable secondary gains as a result of being in pain. This category would include patients whose pain may be fueling efforts at securing monetary or other compensation. Another subcategory would be patients who are the recipients of oversolicitous responses by significant others when they are demonstrating pain behaviors. Also included are patients who fit the *DSM-IV* criteria for Factitious Disorder (APA, 1994, p. 474), patients who are suspected of malingering (rare), and patients who are addicted to prescription pain medications including those who sometimes are known as "drug-seekers" who perceive pain as a ticket for receiving and/or filling another prescription for narcotics.

The preceding clinical typology has proven clinically useful because it identifies essential psychological factors, personality traits, cognitive factors, and behavioral issues that may affect patients' responses to treatment and clinicians' responses to patients. This typology guides us in our clinical workups, case conceptualization and formulation, and treatment planning. Therefore, we have found it useful to include in our initial workups several psychometric and clinical measures of psychopathology, maladjustment, and personality.

Use of the MMPI

The Minnesota Multiphasic Personality Inventory (MMPI) has been perhaps the most widely used psychological test for assessing pain patients (Bradley et al., 1992; Keefe, Lefebvre, & Beaupre, 1995; Keller & Butcher, 1991; Main & Spanswick, 1995; Sanders, 1995a; Turk & Fernandez, 1995). Because of the widespread use of the MMPI with low back pain patients and the clinical lore associated with the test, some clinicians have tended to make illegitimate and often invalid inferences from particular patterns of clinical scale and subscale elevations. Although the MMPI was not developed to assess pain patients and never has been standardized on such a population, there have been many attempts to use scales and subscales of the MMPI to predict intervention outcomes with chronic pain patients (Barnes, Gatchel, Mayer, & Barnett, 1990; Fordyce, Bigos, Battie, & Fischer, 1992; Guck, Meilman, Skultety, & Poloni, 1988; Helmes, 1994; Kleinke, 1994; Long, 1981; Love & Peck, 1987; McCreary, 1993; Watkins, O'Brien, Draugelis, & Jones, 1986). The results of many of these studies have been contradictory (Helmes, 1994). The heavy item overlap between the MMPI clinical scales and subscales as well as other problems with the test as a pain assessment instrument make it clinically invalid to base predictions about pain treatment outcomes and disability levels solely on the results of a patient's MMPI profile (Bradley, 1995; Fordyce et al., 1992; Henricks, 1987).

Another issue, discussed recently by Fishbain (1996) and Main and Spanswick (1995), is whether the MMPI measures traits or states. Given that the MMPI was originally standardized on chronic psychiatric patients, it follows that the clinical scales were seen to measure stable dispositions and psychological characteristics, and thus, attributed to traits as opposed to states. However, with populations other than chronic psychiatric patients (e.g., medical patients and pain patients), the MMPI clinical scales may be measuring psychological and physical state phenomena instead of stable dispositions and characteristics. Evidence in this regard is provided by studies that show pretreatment to posttreatment changes in pain patients' MMPI profiles (Barnes et al., 1990; Naliboff, McCreary, McArthur, Cohen, & Gottlieb, 1988; Watkins et al., 1986). It is also possible that the attendant stresses and adaptational demands of living in chronic pain can alter allegedly stable dimensions of personality functioning.

Another problem with the MMPI as a psychological pain assessment instrument is that it does not enable a clinician to reliably sort out which psychological problems are caused by a patient's physical symptoms as opposed to which psychological problems are causing or exacerbating these symptoms (Hendler, 1984). Numerous studies show that chronic pain often is associated with depression (Averill, Novy, Nelson, & Berry, 1996; Beutler et al., 1986; Blumer & Heilbronn, 1989; Brown, 1990; Dworkin & Gitlin, 1991; Haythornthwaite, Hegel, & Kerns, 1991; Kerns & Haythornthwaite, 1988; Parmelee, Katz, & Lawton, 1991; Pilowsky et al., 1977; Rudy et al., 1988; Turk et al., 1995). Depression affects not only the patient but also significant others who interact regularly with him or her (Kerns & Payne, 1996; Schwartz et al., 1990). In a progressively more dysfunctional downward spiral, depression in turn leads to reduced activity levels, increased levels of pain behavior, and further consolidation of negative and dysfunctional beliefs about pain (Ahles et al., 1987; Beutler et al., 1986; Brown, 1990; Eimer, 1989).

Pain Patients' Reactions to Taking the MMPI

In our own clinical experience, chronic pain patients show a range of reactions to the MMPI (i.e., the MMPI or MMPI-2) and various patterns of response if they complete the test. Because both the MMPI and the MMPI-2 are lengthy (566 and 567 items, respectively), and the test items tend to have poor face validity to many patients, administering either test often exacerbates their resentment and resistance to collaborating with a physician or psychotherapist. When additional tests are added to a battery that includes the MMPI, the time required to fill out forms becomes excessive for most pain patients and they tend to resent taking the test. Some pain patients begin responding inconsistently once they become frustrated; others adopt a response bias of excessive guardedness and defensiveness. Alternatively, patients may adopt a response bias of excessive symptom reporting across multiple clinical scales, especially on Scales 1 (Hypochondriasis), 2 (Depression), 3 (Hysteria), 4 (Psychopathic Deviate), 6 (Paranoia); 7 (Psychasthenia), and 8 (Schizophrenia). Lastly, because the MMPI yields no information directly relevant to pain assessment, some patients balk about the test.

MMPI Scales and Their Derivatives Associated with
Marked Maladjustment in Pain Patients

Despite all the problems with the test, in our clinical experience, given a valid MMPI profile (i.e., *L, F,* and *K* scales within a reasonable range), marked elevations on certain clinical scales and their derivative subscales often appear to be associated with severe maladjustment in pain patients and clinically associated with dismal treatment outcomes. We refer to *T*-score elevations above 80 on the following MMPI clinical scales and their derivatives (see Greene, 1991): MMPI Scale 2 (Depression) and its derivative subscales, Psychomotor Retardation, Physical Malfunctioning, Mental Dullness, and Brooding; MMPI Scale 3 (Hysteria) and its derivative subscales, Lassitude-Malaise, Denial of Social Anxiety, and Somatic Complaints; MMPI Scale 4 (Psychopathic Deviate), and its derivatives, Social Alienation and Self-Alienation; MMPI Scale 6 (Paranoia); MMPI Scale 8 (Schizophrenia) and its derivatives, Emotional Alienation and Social Alienation; and MMPI Scale 10 (Social Introversion) and its derivatives, Distrust, Discomfort with Others, and Physical-Somatic Concerns.

We also note the following patterns which are often associated with severe maladjustment, psychopathology, and disability (see Greene, 1991): (a) marked elevations in the MMPI "Wiggins Content Scales"

labeled *Manifest Hostility, Social Maladjustment,* and *Organic Symptoms;*
(b) marked elevations on the two "Tryon-Stein-Chu Cluster Scales" labeled *Resentment* and *Bodily Symptoms;* (c) marked elevations in the
MMPI Supplementary Scales labeled *Overcontrolled Hostility, Hostility,*
and *Repression-Sensitization,* and (d) marked elevations in one or more of
the MMPI Personality Disorder Scales (Greene, 1991; Morey, Waugh, &
Blashfield, 1985). There is one scale for each of the 10 *DSM-IV* personality disorders (APA, 1994): Paranoid, Schizoid, and Schizotypal (Cluster
A); Antisocial, Borderline, Histrionic, and Narcissistic (Cluster B); and
Avoidant, Dependent, and Obsessive-Compulsive (Cluster C).

We also look at the total number of items endorsed among the following groupings of Critical Items (Greene, 1991; Koss, Butcher, & Hoffmann, 1976): (a) the "Koss-Butcher Critical Items," especially within the
clusters termed Depressed-Suicidal Ideas, Mental Confusion, and Situational Stress Due to Alcoholism; (b) the "Caldwell Critical Items," within
the clusters termed Distress and Depression, and Suicidal Thoughts, and
(c) the "Lachar-Wrobel Critical Items," within the clusters termed Problematic Anger, and Somatic Symptoms. High numbers of Critical Items in
each of these groups are associated with marked psychological maladjustment in pain patients.

ASSESSING DEPRESSION AND ANXIETY

THE NEED TO ASSESS DEPRESSION

Because of the common link between pain and depression, it is essential to
thoroughly assess depression when evaluating a chronic pain patient
(Averill et al., 1996; Beutler et al., 1986; Brown, 1990; Casten, Parmelee,
Kleban, Lawton, & Katz, 1995; Dworkin & Gitlin, 1991; Haythornthwaite,
Seiber, & Kerns, 1988; Hendler, 1984; Kinder & Curtiss, 1988; Krishnan,
France, & Davidson, 1988; Rudy et al., 1988; Turner & Romano, 1984).
Along with a good clinical interview and mental status examination, most
pain clinicians use the quick and reliable 21-item Beck Depression Inven-
tory (Beck et al., 1961; A. Beck, 1987/1993; Novy, Nelson, Berry, & Averill,
1995) to obtain an objective score that measures level of depression.

The Beck Depression Inventory (BDI)

The BDI test form measures the severity of the key symptoms associated
with clinical depression including: sadness, discouragement, hopelessness,
feelings of failure and self-disappointment, self-criticism, loss of pleasure
and satisfaction, guilt and self-blame, the perception of being punished,
suicidal ideation, tearfulness, irritability, loss of interest, indecisiveness,

inertia, anergia, disturbed sleep and loss of appetite, fatigue, somatization, and loss of sex drive. Total scores on the BDI range from 0 to a maximum of 63. Total BDI scores between 9 and 15 often reflect mild overall levels of depression. Total scores ranging between 16 and 25 often reflect moderate overall levels of depression. Total scores between 25 and 34 often reflect moderate-severe levels of depression, and total scores above 34 often reflect severe levels of depression. In addition to interpreting the total BDI score, the clinician should interpret the pattern and severity of individual items endorsed in the context of a patient's history and clinical presentation.

THE NEED TO ASSESS LEVEL OF ANXIETY AND ITS COMPONENTS

Research by Waddell and his associates (Main, 1983; Main & Waddell, 1982; Waddell, Newton, Henderson, Somerville, & Main, 1993; Waddell & Turk, 1992) suggests that increased bodily awareness (or hypersensitivity to bodily sensations), as well as cognitive and affective symptoms of anxiety, constitute major aspects of psychological disturbance in low back pain patients. According to these researchers, increased somatic awareness was the most important aspect of psychological distress in their sample that was associated with pain and disability, and it "completely overshadowed other psychological measures of personality traits or fears and beliefs about illness" (Waddell & Turk, 1992, p. 29). Their research motivated the development of the Modified Somatic Perception Questionnaire for assessing level of anxious somatic preoccupation (MSPQ: Main, 1983). In a related effort, Waddell et al. (1993) developed another brief test, called the Fear-Avoidance Beliefs Questionnaire (FABQ), to assess patients' beliefs about the relationship between physical activities, work, and worsening low back pain. These investigators reported that the cognitive variable of fear-avoidance beliefs about work and physical activity was associated with work loss attributable to low back pain.

The Pain Anxiety Symptoms Scale (PASS)

Working along similar lines, McCracken and Gross (1995) developed the Pain Anxiety Symptoms Scale (PASS), a 40-item, self-report instrument for assessing four aspects or dimensions of anxiety associated with clinical pain symptoms. The four dimensions assessed are (a) *cognitive anxiety*, encompassing symptoms such as racing thoughts, agitation, and impaired concentration, (b) *fearful appraisal*, encompassing symptoms such as catastrophic thinking and apprehensive expectations, (c) *escape and avoidance*, encompassing behaviors associated with avoidance of activities for fear of making pain worse, and (d) *physiologic anxiety,* encompassing symptoms of increased somatic awareness and autonomic physiological arousal associated with pain flare-ups.

McCracken and Gross's physiologic anxiety scale on the PASS appears to assess issues similar to those on the MSPQ. Likewise, the PASS escape and avoidance scale appears to assess the same issues as the FABQ. In addition, the PASS assesses a patient's perceptions of the effects of pain on his or her cognitive efficiency and performance (i.e., cognitive anxiety), as well as a patient's tendency to think catastrophically when in pain (i.e., fearful appraisal). To date, the PASS appears to be the most comprehensive measure available of pain-related anxiety. Building on this work, McCracken (1997) recently developed the Pain Vigilance and Awareness Questionnaire (PVAQ) to assess attention to and preoccupation with pain. His study showed that anxious sensitivity and level of attention to pain are significant predictors of distress, disability, and reported pain intensity.

The Beck Anxiety Inventory (BAI)

In addition to the preceding instruments for measuring anxiety associated with pain, the 21-item Beck Anxiety Inventory (BAI: A. Beck 1990/1993) can be used as a quick assessment tool for eliciting the presence and severity of common physiological and subjective symptoms of anxiety. The BAI largely focuses on the assessment of autonomic and physiological symptoms. Some subjective aspects of anxiety are also tapped, but cognitive (apprehensive expectations and catastrophic thinking) and behavioral (avoidance) symptoms are not targeted.

The Pain Experience Scale

In another effort to measure worrying and emotionality related to living with persistent pain, Turk and Rudy (1985) developed a 19-item, self-report instrument called the Pain Experience Scale (PES). The individual items represent common negative cognitive appraisals and self-statements likely to be made by a pain sufferer during severe pain episodes. For each statement/item, patients are asked to rate on a 0-to-6 scale how frequently they experience that feeling or thought. The PES's brevity, clarity, and good face validity, make it particularly useful in pain treatment settings that require a quick screen to determine the need for further psychological intervention.

The PES is displayed in Appendix M. The ratings assigned by the patient to the items in each scale can conveniently be summed to yield summed and average scale scores for the dimensions of emotionality (13 items: 1, 3, 4, 6, 7, 9, 10, 12, 13, 15, 16, 18, 19) and worry (6 items: 2, 5, 8, 11, 14, and 17). So that a patient's scores can be compared with scale norms,

Table 3.1
Pain Experience Scale Means (Standard Deviations) for
Nine Groups of Pain Patients

		Scales	
Diagnosis	N	Emotionality	Worry
Heterogeneous chronic pain sample	500	3.74 (1.29)	4.25 (1.31)
Head, face and mouth pain	85	3.91 (1.21)	4.25 (1.27)
Cervical pain	45	3.61 (1.12)	3.93 (1.27)
Upper shoulder and upper limb pain	42	3.84 (1.33)	4.33 (1.30)
Thoracic and thoracic spine pain	25	3.49 (1.23)	4.14 (1.28)
Abdominal pain	20	4.39 (1.04)	4.71 (0.98)
Lower back pain	125	3.81 (1.28)	4.40 (1.39)
Lower limbs	75	3.57 (1.31)	4.21 (1.32)
Pelvic pain	44 (all women)	3.37 (1.38)	3.69 (1.34)
Temporomandibular pain disorders	200	2.79 (1.51)	3.20 (1.63)

Source: D. C. Turk & T. E. Rudy. (October 1985). *Pain experience: Assessing the cognitive component.* Paper presented at the Fifth Annual Meeting of the American Pain Society, Dallas, Texas. Reprinted with permission. Copyright © 1985 Dennis C. Turk.

omitted items are not included in the calculation of mean scores for each scale. Norms for different clinical pain populations obtained from the test's authors are given in Table 3.1.

The Stress Symptoms Checklist

The 38-item Stress Symptoms Checklist (SSCL) (Eimer & Allen, 1995) is another self-report instrument which was developed specifically to assess anxiety-related and stress symptoms, including symptoms of post-traumatic stress disorder associated with chronic pain. The SSCL is displayed in Appendix N–1. Patients rate the frequency with which they have experienced each of 38 listed symptoms during the past 2 weeks, on a 7-point verbal-numerical Likert scale ranging from 1 (never) to 7 (always). Several scores are then derived. Although these scores can be calculated by hand, computerized administration and scoring software is also available from CogniSyst, Inc., of Durham, North Carolina (Tel: 800–799–4654).

Scoring

First, a Total Sum of Ratings (Sum) can be computed. This is the sum of all 38 item/symptom ratings, minus a correction factor, which is the number of items on the test (i.e., 38, reduced by the number of missing entries, if any). The correction accounts for the fact that ratings of 1 indicate the complete absence of symptoms. Next, a Total Symptom Percentage (SxPct) can be computed. This is the sum of all the patient's ratings, minus the appropriate correction factor (38 if all 38 items were rated), divided by the maximum possible sum of the ratings for the rated items (228 if all 38 items were rated). The resulting quotient is then multiplied by 100. Additional summary indices can be computed, including the Percentage of Ratings > = 5, and the Percentage of Ratings > = 6. A Summary and Profiling Form is provided in Appendix N-2 for recording the computed indices and graphically plotting a patient's Total Symptom Percentage and Mean Rating for all rated items.

Table 3.2 presents normative data in the form of means, standard deviations, and percentiles for the instrument's major summary indices, based on a heterogeneous sample of 249 chronic pain patients who were referred to behavioral pain treatment programs for evaluation and treatment (Mean age = 41 years; SD = 13.8 years). Of the sample's participants, 43% were male and 57% were female; 91% of the sample reported a pain duration of at least 3 months and 70% of the sample had a pain duration of greater than 2 years. Most of the patients presented with neck pain, back pain, and headaches.

The SSCL Total Sum of Ratings (Sum) and Total Symptom Percentage (SxPct) have been used as indices for tracking treatment outcome. Also, Total Sums of Ratings and Total Symptom Percentages at the 90th percentile and above (see Table 3.2), as well as direct measures of the tendency to make extreme ratings on the checklist (e.g., high Percentages of Ratings > =6), have been used as measures of possible symptom magnification or invalidity.

Table 3.2

Stress Symptom Checklist Means, Standard Deviations, and Percentiles for Derived Measures in a Heterogeneous Sample of 249 Chronic Pain Patients

| Index | Mean | SD | Percentiles | | | | |
			10th	25th	50th	75th	90th
Sum	95.43	41.54	42	63	95	121.5	151
SxPct	42.36	18.41	18.86	28.07	42.54	54.39	66.23
Pct > = 5	35.48	23.00	5.88	15.79	34.21	52.63	68.42
Pct > = 6	23.79	20.47	2.63	7.89	18.42	35.53	52.63
SxCt5	4.38	3.13	1	2	4	6	9
SxCt6	4.67	4.19	0	1	4	7	11
SxCt7	4.27	5.59	0	1	2	6	11
PTAS Sum	39.93	23.46	13	21	37	56	72.6
PI Sum	51.18	20.53	23	35	53	67	78

Note. Sum = Total Sum of Ratings; SxPct = Total Symptom Percentage; Pct > = 5 = Percentage of Ratings > = 5; Pct > = 6 = Percentage of Ratings > = 6; SxCt5 = Number of Ratings of 5; SxCt6 = Number of Ratings of 6; SxCt7 = Number of Ratings of 7; PTAS = Posttraumatic Anxiety Symptoms; PI = Pain and Impairment.

Reliability and Validity

The 38 SSCL items were submitted to a principal components factor analysis with varimax orthogonal rotation designed to achieve simple structure. A two-factor simple structure solution was derived that accounted for 42.74% of the total variance. Table 3.3 presents the loadings of all 38 items on these factors, along with the individual items' normative means and standard deviations *(SDs)*. Significant (> 0.45) loadings are in boldface.

Factor I, labeled Posttraumatic Anxiety Symptoms (PTAS), loaded heavily with items measuring anxiety-related symptoms associated with posttraumatic stress conditions (e.g., intrusive thoughts, fear of losing control, nervous around people). Factor II, labeled *Pain and Impairment* (PI), loaded heavily with items measuring symptoms of pain, inefficiency, cognitive interference, and pain-related impairment. Based on the items with loadings of 0.50 and above on these factors, two Factor Scales were constructed. Both Factor Scales evidenced excellent internal consistency reliability based on coefficient alphas (PTAS = 0.93; PI = 0.91). A Factor Scale Score for PTAS is computed as the Sum of the Ratings for Items 3, 4, 5, 8, 10, 11, 12, 13, 17, 18, 19, 20, 25, 26, 27, 28, 29, 37, and 38, minus a correction factor of 19 (the number of items on the scale) to adjust for the 1-to-7 rating scale. A Factor Scale Score for PI is computed as the Sum of the Ratings for Items 1, 7, 8, 9, 15, 16, 22, 23, 24, 25, 27, 29, 31, 32, 33, and 34, minus a correction factor of 16 (the number of items on the scale). All items are positively loaded and none require reversal prior to summing. The Summary and Profiling Form in Appendix N-2 provides a place for recording and graphically plotting the Factor Scale Scores in the form of percentages and mean ratings. Means, standard deviations, and percentiles for each Factor Scale Score are also given in Table 3.2.

Table 3.4 presents normative data in the form of means, standard deviations, and percentiles for the instrument's major summary indices, based on a comparison sample of 48 non-patients who were teachers enrolled in a graduate teacher education stress management class (Mean age = 41 years; SD = 9.9 years). Of this non-patient sample's participants, 73% were female and 27% were male.

To statistically test whether the mean SSCL Total Sum of Ratings would be, as expected, substantially greater for the pain patient sample than for the comparison non-patient group, a 2-tailed Student t-test was conducted. The mean difference between the pain patient and non-patient groups for the SSCL Total Sum of Ratings came to 44.64 (Pain Patient Mean = 95.43; Non-patient Mean = 50.79). This difference was highly statistically significant at the .0001 level (t-value = 10.24, p < .0001).

Table 3.3
Two-Factor Solution for the Stress Symptom Checklist (SSCL):
Item Loadings, Item Means (*SD*s), and Factor Labels (*N* = 249)

	Factor	
Item No. Item Description [Means*(SD)*]	I. Posttraumatic Anxiety Symptoms (22.41%)	II. Pain and Impairment (20.33%)
1. Problems falling asleep [4.5(1.9)]	0.14	**0.53**
2. Feeling restless [4.4(1.8)]	**0.46**	0.37
3. Being easily startled [3.5(1.9)]	**0.60**	0.26
4. Afraid to be passenger in car [2.7(2.1)]	**0.65**	0.07
5. Afraid of losing control [3.3(2.0)]	**0.70**	0.24
6. Not having much appetite [3.1(1.6)]	0.37	0.20
7. Loss of efficiency [4.3(1.8)]	0.31	**0.56**
8. Periods of confusion [3.4(1.8)]	**0.50**	**0.54**
9. Trouble paying attention [3.8(1.8)]	**0.47**	**0.61**
10. Spending less time with people [3.8(1.9)]	**0.57**	0.43
11. Reliving a frightful experience [2.4(1.9)]	**0.75**	0.07
12. Worrying a lot [4.2(1.9)]	**0.52**	0.23
13. Trembling [2.5(1.7)]	**0.63**	0.23
14. Dizzy spells, faint, lightheaded [3.0(1.7)]	0.35	**0.46**
15. Feeling stiff [4.7(2.1)]	0.22	**0.51**
16. Problems staying asleep [4.5(2.1)]	0.11	**0.60**
17. Nightmares [2.5(1.7)]	**0.58**	0.29
18. Afraid of driving [2.7(2.1)]	**0.66**	0.15
19. Sad, blue, or down [4.1(1.7)]	**0.61**	0.43
20. More nervous around people [3.0(1.8)]	**0.69**	0.33
21. Eating too much [2.6(1.7)]	0.12	0.15
22. Becoming forgetful [3.9(1.9)]	0.35	**0.67**
23. More disorganized than usual [3.9(1.9)]	0.35	**0.66**
24. Losing your train of thought [4.0(1.9)]	0.41	**0.68**
25. Impatient and irritable [4.2(1.8)]	**0.52**	**0.56**
26. Intrusive thoughts [2.6(1.8)]	**0.68**	0.30
27. Loss of interest in things [3.6(1.8)]	**0.50**	**0.56**
28. Anxiety or panic attacks [2.8(1.9)]	**0.72**	0.24
29. Trouble finding words to express self [3.6(1.8)]	**0.50**	**0.50**
30. Problems being sexual because of pain [3.7(2.3)]	0.24	**0.47**
31. Feeling tired [4.8(1.9)]	0.13	**0.76**
32. Neck or shoulder pain [4.9(2.1)]	0.07	**0.58**
33. Headaches [4.3(2.1)]	0.09	**0.54**
34. Back pain [4.8(2.3)]	0.09	**0.59**
35. Stomach upset [3.1(1.6)]	0.19	**0.47**
36. Diarrhea or constipation [3.1(1.9)]	0.19	**0.46**
37. Feeling like you want to die [2.2(1.7)]	**0.57**	0.32
38. Hearing voices in your head [1.4(1.1)]	**0.51**	0.05

Table 3.4
Stress Symptom Checklist Means, Standard Deviations, and
Percentiles for a Sample of 48 Non-Patient Teachers

Index	Mean	SD	Percentiles				
			10th	25th	50th	75th	90th
Sum	50.79	23.82	20	34	47	68	88
SxPct	22.35	10.47	9	15	21	30	39
Pct > = 5	9.73	11.38	0	0	5	16	32
Pct > = 6	4.08	6.29	0	0	0	5	13
PTAS Sum	19.41	11.03	7.9	9.6	18.4	28.9	35.1
PI Sum	26.80	12.57	10.4	18.8	25	36.5	43.8

Note. Sum = Total Sum of Ratings; SxPct = Total Symptom Percentage; Pct > = 5 = Percentage of Ratings > = 5; Pct > = 6 = Percentage of Ratings > = 6; PTAS = Posttraumatic Anxiety Symptoms; PI = Pain and Impairment.

Test-Retest Reliability

To assess the SSCL's stability or test-retest reliability, we administered the test to a sub-sample of the non-patient teacher group (N = 20) a second time after 1 week. The test-retest reliability was acceptable (Pearson product-moment correlation coefficient of .67 for the SSCL Total Sum of Ratings). There was also a statistically significant change in the group mean for this sub-sample between Time 1 and Time 2 based on a 2-tailed Student t-test comparison (SSCL mean Total Sum of Ratings for Time 1 = 53.1; Time 2 = 41.8; t-value = 2.34; p < .03). This result supports the utility of the instrument as a treatment outcome measure. Time 1 was at the outset of the two weekend, 6-day stress management course; Time 2 was on the last day of the course. The course participant's stress scores went down, as hoped, after taking the stress management course.

Construct Validity

We statistically assessed the construct validity of the SSCL for this sample of 48 non-patients by calculating Pearson product-moment correlations between the SSCL and several other measures. These were: the Anxiety Symptom Questionnaire (ASQ)(Lehrer & Woolfolk, 1982), a measure of cognitive, behavioral, and somatic symptoms of anxiety; the Cognitive Error Questionnaire (CEQ)(Lefebvre, 1981), a measure of the tendency to employ cognitive distortions; and the Irrational Belief Scale (IBS)(Malouff & Schutte, 1986). The results of the correlational analysis indicate statistically significant relationships (p < .001) between the SSCL Total Sum of Ratings and the other total test scores (ASQ r = .75; CEQ r = .71; IBS r = .47).

THE ROLE OF PERSONALITY TESTS IN
THE ASSESSMENT OF PAIN PATIENTS

Personality assessment plays an important role in the evaluation of chronic pain patients because a person's adjustment and coping responses may best be understood in light of his or her personality traits. However, personality tests should not be used as a clinician's main predictors of pain treatment outcomes. Most clinical personality tests assess dimensions of psychological distress and do not enable a clinician to sort out reliably which psychological problems are caused by pain versus which psychological problems contribute to it (Gamsa, 1990; Hendler, 1984). Personality tests should be interpreted along with other more pain-relevant tests. When psychopathology is evident, it should be conceptualized from the reciprocal standpoints of (a) how it might impact the patient's adjustment to living in pain, and (b) how the stresses of living in pain might affect the psychopathology. We developed the chronic pain patient personality typology described earlier to serve as a conceptual framework for understanding personality types and responses to persistent pain.

Although extensive and formal personality testing has a more important role to play in some assessments than in others, some form of assessment is important in all pain evaluation and treatment contexts. Objectively scored personality assessment tests can be useful for evaluating comorbid psychiatric disorders and clinical syndromes based on the *DSM-IV* (APA, 1994). We have found several personality assessment tests to be clinically relevant, and less stressful for many pain patients to fill out than the lengthy MMPI. Any of the following tests may provide the clinician with helpful information for formulating psychodiagnostic impressions based on our chronic pain patient personality typology. As stated by William Osler, "It is much more important to know what sort of a patient has a disease, than what sort of disease a patient has" (Fitzhenry, 1993, p. 283).

THE MILLON CLINICAL MULTIAXIAL INVENTORIES (MCMI)

The MCMI (Millon, 1983) is a personality assessment test that was derived from Millon's theory of personality and psychopathology (Millon, 1995). As of this date, the MCMI has been revised twice and three versions have been developed—MCMI, MCMI-II, and MCMI-III. Each version was coordinated with the nosological format of the then current version of the *DSM* (APA, 1994). The MCMI can help a clinician assess both *DSM-IV* Axis I and Axis II psychiatric disorders because it has separate scales for Axis I clinical syndromes and Axis II personality disorders. In addition, the MCMI distinguishes among clinical syndromes and personality patterns in terms of their levels of psychopathological severity. The MCMI clinical scales are sorted into four major categories: (a) clinical personality patterns, (b) severe personality pathology (*DSM* Axis II personality disorders), (c) clinical syndromes, and (d) severe clinical syndromes (*DSM* Axis I psychiatric disorders). There are also several response validity indices.

The main clinical advantage of using the MCMI is that it can alert a PMP clinician to the need for further evaluation of personality and psychiatric dysfunction. High scores (moderate to severe elevations above clinical base rates) on one or more of the severe personality pathology or severe clinical syndrome scales frequently herald a poor prognosis for standard pain treatments given the presence of severe and enduring psychological distress. High scores (moderate to severe elevations above clinical base rates) on any combination of the basic clinical personality pattern scales can serve to alert a PMP clinician to the likely presence of psychological issues associated with particular types of personality dysfunction. High scores on any of the clinical syndrome scales suggest ongoing psychological distress associated with the relevant *DSM* Axis I disorders.

The MCMI (all three versions) is a relatively short test comprising 175 true/false items that are not as offensive to many pain patients as the items on the MMPI-1 and MMPI-2. The individual items do not address pain, but a scored MCMI profile is easily interpretable, and informs a clinician about the types and extent of a patient's likely psychopathology.

The Millon Behavioral Health Inventory (MBHI)

This 150-item true/false, self-administered test is also derived from Millon's theory of personality (Millon, 1995; Millon, Green, & Meagher, 1983). Computer scoring of a patient's responses yields 20 clinical scales. Eight scales measure "basic coping styles" (introversive, inhibited, cooperative, sociable, confident, forceful, respectful, and sensitive). Six scales measure "psychogenic attitudes" (chronic tension, recent stress, premorbid pessimism, future despair, social alienation, and somatic anxiety). Three scales fall into the category of "psychosomatic correlates" (allergic inclination, gastrointestinal susceptibility, and cardiovascular tendency). Finally, three additional scales fall into the category of prognostic indices (Pain Treatment Responsivity, Life Threat Reactivity, and Emotional Vulnerability).

The MBHI is a more pain-relevant test than the MMPI and MCMI (Sweet, Brewer, Hazlewood, Toye, & Paul, 1985). The individual test items have reasonable face validity to many pain patients, as they address medical and health-related issues, and the instrument was normed on a general medical population. Also, several of the MBHI clinical scales (e.g., somatic anxiety and gastrointestinal susceptibility) appear to differentiate between chronic pain patients and other medical patients with chronic illnesses as reported in one study by Richter et al. (1986). This may corroborate research findings by Waddell et al. (1993), Waddell and Turk (1992), McCracken and Gross (1995), and McCracken (1997) reported earlier. However, other studies, as summarized by Bradley et al. (1992), reportedly have failed to show reliable relationships between the MBHI Pain Treatment Responsivity Scale and documented changes on patient outcome measures following a multidisciplinary and behavioral pain treatment program. All things considered however, we have found the MBHI to be a useful test and recommend its use to obtain information about patient personality attributes and coping styles that are clinically relevant to pain treatment and management.

THE COOLIDGE AXIS II INVENTORY (CATI)

The CATI (Coolidge, 1993; Coolidge & Merwin, 1992), is a 225-item, paper-and-pencil, self-report inventory designed to assess the personality disorders classified by the *DSM-IV* (APA, 1994). The CATI items, which are answered on a 4-point, true-false, Likert scale ranging from strongly false to strongly true, have high face validity. The test profiles a patient's responses on 14 Axis II personality disorder scales, seven Axis I psychiatric disorder scales, three scales associated with hostility, and several additional scales that measure indecisiveness, maladjustment, apathy, emotional liability, introversion-extraversion, cognitive dysfunction, and personality changes due to a general medical condition.

The CATI computer-scored report provides *T*-scores (mean of 50, standard deviation of 10) and percentiles for each clinical scale. This form allows clinicians to make quantitative and qualitative comparisons that can be helpful for formulating a differential psychiatric diagnosis and evaluating indications and contraindications for particular pain treatment interventions and pain management strategies. The test appears to have acceptable psychometric properties according to several studies summarized in the test manual (Coolidge, 1993; Coolidge & Merwin, 1992). The CATI is reported to correlate well with the MCMI-II, and to demonstrate high concurrent validity with selected scales of the MMPI, the Beck Depression Inventory, and Spielberger's Trait Anxiety Score. We have found the CATI to be another useful psychometric instrument for assessing pain patients' personality traits and psychopathology. Like the MCMI, the scored CATI report is clear and easily interpreted. However, the CATI's additional scales provide information about several areas of particular relevance to understanding pain patients' adjustment and coping problems.

THE PERSONALITY ASSESSMENT INVENTORY (PAI)

This 344-item, paper-and-pencil, self-report inventory is designed to assess personality and psychopathology (Morey, 1991). The PAI items are answered on a 4-point, true-false, Likert scale ranging from *false, not at all true* to *very true*. Computer scoring of a patient's responses yields a clinical report that provides *T*-scores on 11 clinical scales (*Somatization, Anxiety, Anxiety-Related Disorders, Depression, Mania, Paranoia, Schizophrenia, Borderline Features, Antisocial Features, Alcohol Problems,* and *Drug Problems*), and their subscales. In addition, there are four validity scales, two interpersonal scales (*Dominance* and *Warmth*), and five treatment considerations scales (*Aggression, Suicidal Ideation, Stress, Nonsupport,* and *Treatment Rejection*). A completed PAI can provide a rich compendium of clinical information.

THE SYMPTOM CHECKLIST 90-REVISED

The SCL-90R is a 90-item, self-report inventory developed by Derogatis (1983) to assess nine areas of psychological disturbance common in psychiatric patients (somatization, obsessive-compulsive symptoms, interpersonal sensitivity, depression, anxiety, phobic anxiety, hostility, paranoid ideation, psychoticism). Patients rate how much each of 90 physical and psychological symptoms has distressed them over the past week on a 5-point scale ranging from *not at all* to *extremely*. The computer-scored, SCL-90R clinical report profiles responses in the form of *T*-scores on nine clinical scales corresponding to the areas of psychological disturbance. In addition, the report yields three summary measures of psychological distress which include a *Global Severity Index*. The main advantage of using the SCL-90R with pain patients is that the test is relatively brief compared with the other tests described. However, the test's factor structure appears to be quite different for chronic pain patients compared with psychiatric patients (Bradley et al., 1992). Therefore, pain patients' SCL-90R profiles may have to be interpreted differently from those of nonpain, psychiatric patients' profiles.

Our clinical experience in using the test has been that pain patients often fall into one of two groupings of SCL-90R responders: extreme symptom reporters, who report a large number of symptoms and high levels of symptom intensity on the majority of scales, and conservative or guarded symptom reporters, who report relatively few symptoms and minimal levels of intensity. Extreme symptom reporters also tend to report higher levels of functional disability and emotional distress on other measures than do conservative symptom reporters, who tend to score low on most of the clinical scales on the test. Our clinical experience appears to be similar to the results of a study with the SCL-90R reported by Jamison, Rock, and Parris (1988). They found that patients with elevated scores on a majority of SCL-90R scales tended to report higher levels of functional disability, sleep disturbance, medication use, family conflict, and emotional distress on other measures, than did patients whose scale scores fell mostly within normal limits.

The main problem in using the SCL-90R with pain patients appears to be a frequent lack of differentiation among the clinical scales. In other words, many pain patients tend to score either high or low on most of the scales. Factor analyses of the SCL-90R confirm the presence of a single factor measuring global distress (Jamison, Rock, & Parris, 1988; Schwartz & DeGood, 1983; Shutty, DeGood, & Schwartz, 1986). Nevertheless, in our clinical experience, "high" (extreme) and "low" (conservative) symptom reporters do differ in treatment prognosis: High responders tend to have a much less favorable prognosis for most pain treatments than do low responders. Additionally, several scales appear to stand out as being associated with particularly negative behavioral pain treatment outcomes: *Hostility, Paranoid Ideation,* and *Psychoticism* (measures alienation). Similar results were reported by Hendler and Kozikowski (1993). The SCL-90R appears to be most useful for alerting a PMP therapist to psychological distress factors that may complicate a patient's course of pain treatment.

THE PAIN PATIENT PROFILE

To create a brief, self-report, screening test for symptoms of psychological distress and maladjustment in chronic pain patients, Tollison and Langley (1995) developed the 44-item, Pain Patient Profile, also known as the P-3. The P-3's authors caution that the P-3 is not a diagnostic instrument. It is a tool for identifying pain patients in emotional distress who may require psychological intervention. The three clinical scales on the P-3 are Depression, Anxiety, and Somatization. Separate *T*-scores for each of these three scales are computed with reference to two separate, normative populations: other pain patients, and a community sample of non-pain, nonpatients. The test manual provides cutoffs for each normative population above which a patient's scale scores are considered to be clinically elevated. The P-3 provides overall indices of emotional distress and maladjustment in three key clinical areas. Its brevity, ease of scoring, and interpretability make the P-3 a promising screening instrument for many types of pain patients.

THE PAIN COPING INVENTORY (PCI)

This instrument assesses the key variables reported in the literature as risk factors for chronic pain-related disability and negative treatment outcomes (Eimer & Allen, 1995). The PCI is a 92-item, comprehensive, patient self-report questionnaire aimed at an eighth-grade reading level, which provides a composite measure of the following variables: pain severity, pain interference, pain coping strategies, pain-related beliefs, self-efficacy perceptions, personality dysfunction secondary to chronic pain, psychological distress, psychological maladjustment, psychological adjustment, quality of life, treatment resistance and patient alienation, and symptom magnification.

The PCI offers two modes of administration: It can be self-administered as a paper-and-pencil questionnaire, and then hand-scored or computer-scored; or it can be administered and scored on a computer. The paper-and-pencil PCI questionnaire is provided in Appendix O. The PCI is published by CogniSyst, Inc., Durham, North Carolina (Tel: 800–799–4654). A large number of scales and indices can be calculated from the PCI questionnaire. The hand scoring for the PCI outlined in this text represents the majority of these derived measures, and has largely utilized counts and sums of scale items in order to reduce computational demands and complexity. The PCI scoring software provides additional computed measures and offers features to support outcome analysis and treatment planning (Eimer & Allen, 1995).

DESCRIPTION

The questions on the PCI are organized in five sections:

1. *Section I. Degree of Distress.* The first section of the test contains 8 items (Items 1 through 8) that assess the pain's intensity or strength, its temporal pattern (continuity and duration), and two symptoms associated with posttraumatic stress syndromes (nightmares and intrusive ideation). These items are multiple choice. Each item's response options are arranged in a 7-point numerical/verbal rating scale (1–7) where higher numbers are associated with verbal descriptors reflecting greater distress.

2. *Section II. Health-Related Behaviors.* The second section of the test is entitled *Health-Related Behaviors* and contains 7 multiple-choice items (Items 9 through 15) that assess alcohol consumption, working ability, fun activities, dietary habits, junk food consumption, and exercise frequency. Response options again are arranged in a 7-point rating scale; higher numbers are associated with verbal

descriptors reflecting a greater frequency of healthful behaviors and habits, or conversely, a lesser frequency of unhealthful behaviors.

3. *Section III. Frequency of Distress.* The third section contains 18 items (Items 16 through 33) that assess activity interference, behavioral dysfunction, and psychological distress associated with pain. Responses are recorded on a 7-point rating scale from 1 (never) to 7 (always) to indicate how often each item (thought, behavioral excess or deficit, emotional reaction, or physical-sensory reaction) occurs or is experienced. Higher numerical ratings reflect a greater frequency of distress.

4. *Section IV. Coping Success.* The fourth section contains 25 items (Items 34 through 58) assessing pain coping strategies, pain relief, quality of life, and self-efficacy. Responses are recorded on a 7-point numerical/verbal rating scale to indicate how often each item (coping strategy, pain relief, state of mind) occurs or is experienced. As with Section III, the rating scale ranges from 1 (never) to 7 (always). Higher numerical ratings reflect a greater frequency of coping success.

5. *Section V. Your Beliefs.* The fifth and final section contains 34 items (Items 59 through 92) to assess a patient's beliefs about pain, pain control, self-efficacy, pain permanence, psychological factors affecting pain, other people's responses, justice/injustice and fairness, entitlement, and pain's effects. Responses are recorded on a 7-point numerical/verbal rating scale to indicate degree of disagreement or agreement with each statement. The rating scale ranges from 1 (totally disagree) to 7 (totally agree). Higher numerical ratings reflect stronger endorsement of beliefs associated with catastrophizing, hopelessness, depression, hostility, resentment, alienation, and treatment resistance.

CONTENT VALIDITY

An advantage of the PCI as a pain assessment instrument is that the individual items directly address pain and pain-related problems and thus have a high degree of face validity and relevance. The test items were constructed based on a review of the pain literature and the authors' clinical experience with the issues commonly presented by chronic pain patients. The final pool of 92 items was selected after collecting and evaluating over 500 pain patients' responses to a much larger sample of items over several revisions of the test (Eimer & Allen, 1995). Based on readability analyses, the items retained were determined to have no higher than an eighth-grade reading level. The authors report that pain patients demonstrate no significant problems understanding the test items, and had favorable responses to the current version of the test. Because of the test items' content validity, and the clarity of response options, the PCI can provide clinically relevant information just from an examination of a patient's raw responses, much like an informative, structured clinical interview. In fact, the authors suggest that the first step in interpreting the test is to examine a patient's raw responses.

SCORING AND NORMS

Paper-and-pencil scoring of the PCI is the second step for clinicians who do not have the PCI computer-scoring program. A complete PCI Summary

Table 3.5

Alpha Coefficients, Means, Standard Deviations (SD), and Percentiles for PCI Scale and Subscale Indices in the form of Summed Ratings Based on a Heterogeneous Sample of 433 Chronic Pain Patients

Index	Alpha	Mean (SD)	10th	25th	50th	75th	90th
Extreme Beliefs Frequency%	—	23.31 (20.10)	2.94	8.82	17.65	32.35	54.55
Symptom Magnification Frequency%	—	30.37 (18.86)	7.84	15.69	27.45	41.84	56.86
Global Impairment Index	0.85	384.84 (73.14)	285.2	338.1	387.32	437.92	474.72
Patient Alienation Index	0.92	123.90 (36.28)	76.84	99.45	124.1	147.56	172.04
Degree of Distress Index	0.72	36.75 (7.26)	27.44	32.00	37.68	42.00	46.00
Frequency of Distress Index	0.89	80.28 (20.18)	50.94	66.96	81.00	95.04	106.02
Physical Severity Index	0.71	44.92 (8.24)	34.02	38.97	45.00	51.03	54.99
Behavioral Interference Severity Index	0.58	66.63 (16.20)	43.96	55.02	68.04	78.96	86.94
Psychological Maladjustment Severity Index	0.93	120.16 (37.94)	68.00	93.16	121.04	146.37	166.94
Nociceptive Index	0.91	117.75 (25.22)	81.12	100.1	120.12	135.98	150.02
Catastrophizing subscale	0.84	30.89 (11.07)	16.00	23.52	31.04	38.52	45.04
Depression subscale	0.70	24.84 (8.17)	14.00	18.97	24.99	30.03	35.00
Hostility subscale	0.82	25.33 (10.10)	11.97	17.01	25.97	31.99	38.99
Paranoia and Alienation subscale	0.82	26.10 (10.61)	12.00	18.00	26.00	34.00	41.04
Psychological Coping Index	0.76	98.39 (23.83)	71.12	82.04	98.00	113.96	131.04
Healthful Behavior Index	0.36	30.61 (6.67)	21.98	25.97	31.01	35.00	38.99
Coping Success Index	0.88	85.55 (22.83)	57.00	70.00	84.00	100.00	115.00
Health-Related Behaviors Index	0.22	27.50 (5.78)	20.02	24.01	27.02	31.99	35.00
Pain Coping Index	0.86	113.12 (25.38)	81.92	95.04	112.00	128.00	146.24
Quality of Life subscale	0.84	19.03 (7.62)	8.00	14.00	19.00	25.00	29.00
Mental Conditioning subscale	0.78	15.90 (6.48)	7.98	10.98	15.00	19.02	24.00
Psychological Motivation subscale	0.57	27.56 (7.36)	18.00	22.98	28.98	33.00	36.00

Note. Each score represents the *sum of the ratings* of all of the rated items comprising that index.

and Profile Form is provided in Appendix P. This form enables a clinician to compute selected summary indices and to plot a patient's scores for comparison with the test's norms. Normative means, standard deviations, and percentiles are given on the form for the selected summary indices. This form also provides the computational formulas for each summary index, and a listing of all the items composing each selected index. Each index is computed by *summing the ratings* given to all the items making up that index. Table 3.5 displays normative data for 22 scale and subscale indices. These data consist of alpha coefficients of internal consistency reliability, means, standard deviations, and percentiles.

Normative Sample

The PCI's normative sample consisted of 433 chronic pain patients (43%, male; 57%, female; mean age = 40.8 years; SD = 12.12 years) who were referred to outpatient behavioral chronic pain treatment programs for evaluation or treatment. Ninety-two percent of the sample presented with primary pain complaints of greater than 3 months' duration. Duration of pain for the majority of patients in the sample was 2 to 3 years; 71% had pain for at least 2 years. The most common presenting pain complaints were low back and neck pain, followed by headaches. The most common pain-related diagnoses in the sample were related to lumbar and cervical discogenic disease, myofascitis (myositis), diffuse musculoskeletal pain, fibromyalgia, and chronic headaches (migraine, tension, and mixed).

EXPLANATION OF PCI INDICES

The calculation of each of the PCI indices reported in Table 3.5 is explained in this section. The majority of these indices have very good internal consistency reliability as measured by coefficient alphas ranging between 0.70 and 0.93. The exceptions are Health-Related Behaviors (0.22), Healthful Behavior (0.36), Psychological Motivation (0.57), and Behavioral Interference Severity (0.58). These four scale indices therefore should be interpreted cautiously.

PCI Invalidity Indices

The first two indices in both Table 3.5 and the Summary Form represent the test's invalidity indices. They are the Extreme Beliefs Frequency (EBF) and the Symptom Magnification Frequency (SMF). High EBF and SMF summary scores reflect a large number of extreme ratings on the test items. The EBF is equal to the total number of Section V items rated extremely (i.e., 6 or 7) and is expressed as a percentage by dividing the total number of extreme ratings by 34, the number of items in the section. The SMF is equal to the total number of items in Section I, Section III, and Section IV that were rated extremely negatively (i.e., ratings of 6 or 7 for items in Sections I and III, and ratings of 1 or 2 for items in Section IV). It also is expressed as a percentage by dividing this sum by 51, the total number of items in these three sections. High EBF and SMF scores may be associated with a tendency to magnify or exaggerate pain complaints and other symptoms.

Global Impairment Index (GII)

This index is computed as the sum of all 92 item ratings on the test keyed in the direction of greater dysfunction. Thus, all the items in Section II and Section IV are reverse-scored in computing this index. The GII, a global measure of pain-related impairment and dysfunction, is thought to measure the degree of generalization of the chronic pain condition (Eimer & Allen, 1995). Its internal consistency, as measured by coefficient alpha, is 0.85.

Patient Alienation Index (PAI)

The PAI is computed as the sum of all 34 item ratings in Section V (Your Beliefs). The PAI is a summary measure of negative cognitions and beliefs associated with anger, paranoia, mistrust, alienation, depression and treatment resistance. Its internal consistency is excellent (coefficient alpha = 0.92).

Degree and Frequency of Distress Indices

Two summary measures of pain and distress are the Degree of Distress Index (DODI) and the Frequency of Distress Index (FODI). The DODI is the sum of the 8 item ratings in Section I. The FODI is the sum of the 18 item ratings in Section III. Both scale indices have good internal consistency reliabilities (DODI alpha = 0.72; FODI alpha = 0.89).

Physical Severity Index (PSI) and Behavioral Interference Severity Index (BISI)

The PSI is a summary measure of the physical and temporal intensity of the pain (alpha = 0.71). The BISI is a summary measure of the intensity and frequency with which pain is reported to interfere with basic activities of daily living (alpha = 0.58). Items that are reverse-scored in computing these indexes have an (R) after them. The PSI is computed as the sum of Items 1–6, 32, 33, and 58(R). The BISI is computed as the sum of Items 10(R), 11(R), 17, 18, 20–26, 31, 41(R), and 45(R).

Psychological Maladjustment Severity Index (PMSI) and
Nociceptive Index (NI)

These indices are summary measures of emotional distress associated with pain. The PMSI is computed as the sum of Items 7, 8, 16, 19, 27–30, 63–66, 69, 71, 72, and 74–92. It combines measures of catastrophizing about pain, stress and anxiety, depression, hostility, paranoia, and alienation. Its alpha coefficient is excellent (0.93). The NI is computed as the sum of all the items in Section I and Section III. It also has an excellent alpha coefficient of 0.91.

Additional Emotional Distress Subscales

The PCI computer scoring program calculates 11 subscales that measure unique and important components of pain-related emotional distress. These are shown as the first 11 numbered subscales in Figure 3.1, which displays one patient's computer-scored PCI Summary Report (a detailed interpretation of these data and discussion of this patient appear later in this chapter).

Table 3.6 displays normative means, standard deviations, and percentiles for *mean ratings* on each of these 11 subscales based on the PCI's normative sample (*N* = 433). Means, standard deviations, and percentiles for summed ratings on four of these subscales—*Catastrophizing* (CAT), *Depression* (DEP), *Hostility* (HOS), and *Paranoia and Alienation* (PAR)—are also included in Table 3.5 because they are thought to measure especially important and unique components of pain-related emotional distress. CAT (alpha = 0.84) is computed as the sum of Items 74–76, 81–83, 86, and 92. DEP (alpha = 0.70) is computed as the sum of Items 16, 28, 29, 64, 71, 72, and 91. HOS (alpha = 0.82) is computed as the sum of Items 30, 65, 69, and 77–80. PAR (alpha = 0.82) is computed as the sum of Items 63, 66, 84, 85, and 87–90.

Positive Coping Indices

Several positive coping indices are also computed and recorded (see Appendix P and Table 3.5). The Psychological Coping Index, or PsyCI (alpha = 0.76), is a summary index that encompasses measures associated with adaptive coping, including perceived self-efficacy, mental or psychological conditioning, use of positive self-talk, psychological motivation, and positive quality of life. The PsyCI is computed as the sum of Items 34–39, 42–44, 46–49, 51–57, 59(R), 60(R), 61(R), 62(R), 67(R), 68(R), 70(R), and 73(R). The Healthful Behavior Index, or HBI, is a measure of positive or healthful behaviors related to good nutrition, regular exercise, and appropriate use of pain medicines. It is computed as the sum of Items 9, 12–15, 40, and 50. With an alpha reliability coefficient of only 0.36, this

Patient: A. J.   **Age:** 40   **Sex:** M   **Education:** 1 year college   **Marital Status:** Married
Type of Pain: Low back and leg pain   **Duration**: 8 years   **Injury Type**: Work-related
lifting accident
Type of Work: Blue collar-Maintenance   **Receiving Disability?** Yes   **Type?**   Workers' Comp.

Physical and Temporal Dimensions	# Crit	Ave	Physical Severity Index	81%
1 Pain Severity	3/4!	6.0+	[3, 4, 5, 6]	
2 Pain Lability	2/3!	5.0+	[32, 33, 58]	
3 Pain Continuity and Duration	2/2!	7.0+	[1, 2]	

Pain Interference	# Crit	Ave	Behavioral Interference S.I.	75%
4 Muscle Bracing/Movement Phobia	1/3	5.7+	[18, 25, 26]	
5 Sleep Disturbance	4/4	6.3+	[20, 21, 41, 45]	
6 Activity Interference/Avoidance	4/7!	5.0+	[10, 11, 17, 22, 23, 24, 31]	

Psychological Maladjustment	# Crit	Ave	Psychological Maladjustment S.I.	15%
7 Catastrophizing	1/8	2.6	[74, 75, 76, 81, 82, 83, 86, 92]	
8 Stress and Anxiety	0/4	2.3	[7, 8, 19, 27]	
9 Depression	0/7	1.7	[16, 28, 29, 64, 71, 72, 91]	
10 Hostility	0/7	1.6	[30, 65, 69, 77, 78, 79, 80]	
11 Paranoia and Alienation	0/8	1.4	[63, 66, 84, 85, 87, 88, 89, 90]	

Psychological Adjustment		Ave	Psychological Coping Index	55%
12 Perceived Self-Efficacy		4.3	[34, 39, 44, 48, 55, 59, 60, 62]	
13 Mental Conditioning		2.8	[35, 36, 38, 46, 47, 49]	
14 Positive Self-Talk		4.0	[37, 42, 51]	
15 Psychological Motivation		5.8	[43, 61, 67, 68, 70, 73]	
16 Quality of Life		4.6	[52, 53, 54, 56, 57]	

Health-Related Behaviors		Ave	Healthful Behavior Index	64%
17 Chemical Dependency		6.7	[9, 40, 50]	
18 Diet & Exercise		3.5	[12, 13, 14, 15]	

PCI Summary Indices and Scores			
Pain Coping Index		92/192	47.9%
Nociceptive Index		97/156	62.2%
Patient Alienation Index		30/204	14.7%
Global Impairment Index		227/552	41.1%
Extreme Beliefs Frequency		1/ 34	2.9%
Symptom Magnification Frequency		14/ 51	27.5%

PCI Section Summaries	Index Ave	Percentage Index	Index Name
I. Degree of Distress	5.1	68.8%	Degree of Distress Index
II. Health-Related Behaviors	3.6	42.9%	Healthy Coping Index
III. Frequency of Distress	4.6	59.3%	Frequency of Distress Index
IV. Coping Success	4.0	49.3%	Coping Success Index
V. Patient Beliefs	1.9	14.7%	Patient Alienation Index

Key to Symbols:
The symbol ! means that the critical item threshold was reached for this scale.
The symbol + means that the average scale score was > = 5.0.
The symbol − means that the average scale score was < = 2.5.

Figure 3.1   Pain Coping Inventory Computer-Scored Report

Table 3.6

Means, Standard Deviations (SD), and Percentiles for PCI Subscale Indices and Section Summary Indices in the Form of Mean Ratings Based on a Heterogeneous Sample of 433 Chronic Pain Patients

Index	Mean (SD)	Percentiles				
		10th	25th	50th	75th	90th
Physical and Temporal Dimensions						
1 Pain Severity	5.12 (0.95)	4	4.5	5.25	5.75	6.25
2 Pain Lability	4.50 (1.47)	2.33	3.67	4.67	5.67	6.33
3 Pain Continuity and Duration	5.47 (1.41)	3.5	4	6	7	7
Pain Interference						
4 Muscle Bracing/Movement Phobia	4.45 (1.64)	2	3	4.67	5.67	6.67
5 Sleep Disturbance	4.78 (1.42)	2.75	3.75	5	6	6.5
6 Activity Interference/Avoidance	4.88 (1.31)	3	4	5	5.86	6.57
Psychological Maladjustment						
7 Catastrophizing	3.86 (1.38)	2	2.94	3.88	4.82	5.63
8 Stress and Anxiety	3.26 (1.46)	1.5	2	3	4.5	5.25
9 Depression	3.55 (1.17)	2	2.71	3.57	4.29	5
10 Hostility	3.62 (1.44)	1.71	2.43	3.71	4.57	5.57
11 Paranoia and Alienation	3.26 (1.33)	1.5	2.25	3.25	4.25	5.13
Psychological Adjustment						
12 Perceived Self-Efficacy	3.37 (1.07)	2	2.63	3.38	4	4.88
13 Mental Conditioning	2.65 (1.08)	1.33	1.83	2.5	3.17	4
14 Positive Self-Talk	2.99 (1.32)	1.33	2	3	3.67	5
15 Psychological Motivation	4.59 (1.23)	3	3.83	4.83	5.5	6
16 Quality of Life	3.81 (1.52)	1.6	2.8	3.8	5	5.8
Health-Related Behaviors						
17 Chemical Dependency	4.94 (1.39)	3	3.67	5	6	6.67
18 Diet and Exercise	3.95 (1.25)	2.25	3.25	4	4.75	5.5
PCI Section Summaries						
I. Degree of Distress	4.59 (0.91)	3.43	4	4.71	5.25	5.75
II. Health-Related Behaviors	3.93 (0.83)	2.86	3.43	3.86	4.57	5
III. Frequency of Distress	4.46 (1.12)	2.83	3.72	4.5	5.28	5.89
IV. Coping Success	3.42 (0.91)	2.28	2.8	3.36	4	4.6
V. Patient Beliefs	3.64 (1.07)	2.26	2.93	3.65	4.34	5.06

Note. Each score represents the *mean of the 1-to-7 ratings* of all of the rated items composing that subscale or section index.

scale appears to have less than adequate internal consistency, and therefore should be interpreted with caution. The Coping Success Index, or CSI, is the sum of all 25 item ratings in Section IV. In contrast to the HBI, the CSI's alpha reliability is very good, at 0.88. The Health-Related Behaviors Index, or HRBI, is the sum of all of the 8 items in Section II. With a coefficient alpha of 0.22, this scale also has low internal consistency reliability and must be interpreted cautiously. The Pain Coping Index, or PCI (alpha = 0.86), is the sum of all the items in Section II and Section IV. All these adaptive coping indices are also presented in the computer-scored PCI Summary Report displayed in Figure 3.1.

Normative means, standard deviations, and percentiles for mean ratings on each of the seven adaptive coping subscales appearing as numbers 12 through 18 on the PCI computer report are also presented in Table 3.6. Table 3.6 also presents the normative mean ratings for each of the five PCI Section Summary Indices. Normative data for summed ratings are also presented in Table 3.5 for the Quality of Life (QOL), Mental Conditioning (MC), and Psychological Motivation (PsyMot) adaptive coping subscales. QOL (alpha = 0.84) comprises the sum of Items 52–54, 56, and 57. MC (alpha = 0.78) comprises the sum of Items 35, 36, 38, 46, 47, and 49. PsyMot (alpha = 0.57) comprises the sum of Items 43, 61(R), 67(R), 68(R), 70(R), and 73(R).

Results of Principal Components Factor Analysis

The 92 PCI items were submitted to a principal components factor analysis with varimax orthogonal rotation designed to achieve simple structure. A five-factor simple-structure solution was derived that accounted for 39% of the total variance. Table 3.7 presents the significant item/factor loadings.

Labels for the factors were based on the items loading highly on each factor: Factor I was labeled Alienated Depression and Hostility; Factor II, Psychological Coping and Self-Efficacy; Factor III, Physical Severity and Interference; Factor IV, General Psychological Adjustment; and Factor V, Psychological Orientation and Motivation.

Based on the items loading highest (above 0.50) on each of the preceding factors, five Factor Scales were constructed. Table 3.8 displays alpha reliability coefficients, and means, standard deviations and percentiles for the *summed ratings* of the items composing each Factor Scale. Sums were chosen to reduce computational complexity and error.

VALIDITY OF THE PAIN COPING INVENTORY

Preliminary psychometric validation of the PCI has been conducted on a number of levels and has provided evidence that the test has acceptable validity. These statistical analyses are briefly summarized here. First, as reported earlier, most of the PCI scales have acceptable internal consistency. Second, the test appears to have a stable factor structure that is replicable. The test's simple factor structure, and essential item statistics, based on an initial sample of 89 pain patients (Eimer & Allen, 1995) were

Table 3.7

Five-Factor Solution for the Pain Coping Inventory (PCI): Item Loadings and Factor Labels

Item Number and Description	Factors (Total variance accounted for by five factors = 39%)				
	I. Alienated Depression and Hostility (10.43%)	II. Psychological Coping and Self-Efficacy (6.50%)	III. Physical Severity and Interference (9.85%)	IV. General Psychological Adjustment (8.40%)	V. Psychological Orientation and Motivation (3.79%)
30. Angry about being in pain	0.45	−0.08	0.36	−0.26	0.25
63. Others blame me	0.52	0.07	−0.03	−0.06	0.00
64. Never going to get better	0.57	−0.20	0.28	0.02	−0.10
65. Angry at doctors and others	0.56	−0.11	0.20	−0.06	−0.01
66. I do not fit in anymore	0.52	0.03	0.31	−0.39	0.00
69. I've been treated unfairly	0.61	0.09	0.19	−0.15	−0.11
71. Nothing anybody can do	0.50	−0.11	0.16	−0.06	−0.35
72. Tired of going to therapy	0.42	−0.07	0.09	0.13	−0.20
74. My life is wrecked	0.48	−0.02	0.30	−0.47	−0.06
76. I'll always be in pain	0.49	−0.12	0.34	−0.18	−0.11
77. Life's treated me unfairly	0.60	−0.05	0.11	−0.39	0.00
78. Unfair I continue to suffer	0.57	0.01	−0.01	−0.26	−0.14
79. Wish others felt like I do	0.56	−0.02	0.01	−0.09	−0.10
80. Should've been helped more	0.53	−0.06	0.21	−0.11	−0.01
81. I seem to be getting worse	0.41	−0.20	0.47	−0.07	−0.02
82. Fear I'm crippled forever	0.46	−0.16	0.34	−0.18	0.06
83. I feel helpless	0.48	−0.19	0.43	−0.21	−0.09
84. People think I exaggerate	0.62	−0.06	0.00	−0.04	0.14
85. People don't believe me	0.62	−0.02	−0.03	0.00	0.10
86. Overwhelmed by problems	0.51	−0.08	0.27	−0.34	0.21
87. Doctors/others not sincere	0.63	−0.09	0.07	−0.09	−0.13
88. Hard to express my feelings	0.43	−0.03	0.10	−0.32	0.04
89. People punish me	0.64	0.02	0.00	−0.24	−0.01
90. Nobody really understands	0.65	0.03	0.17	−0.22	0.03
91. Nothing more can be done	0.59	−0.12	0.28	−0.04	−0.18
34. Gets relief without meds	0.05	0.42	−0.25	0.07	0.15
35. Cope: think of something else	0.00	0.71	−0.05	0.10	0.03
36. Cope: picture pleasant . . .	−0.04	0.78	−0.01	0.05	−0.02
37. Cope: say supportive . . .	−0.04	0.77	−0.04	0.02	−0.07
38. Cope: image pain shrinking	−0.01	0.72	−0.09	−0.10	−0.06
42. Talk self out of depression	−0.19	0.42	−0.06	0.47	−0.15
44. Reduce pain with relaxation	−0.08	0.64	−0.24	0.18	0.15
46. Cope: imagine comfort	−0.07	0.73	−0.18	0.10	0.05
47. Attend to other things	−0.17	0.43	−0.13	0.46	0.11
48. Do things that reduce pain	−0.07	0.53	−0.10	0.25	0.14
51. Cope: control acts/thoughts	−0.02	0.69	−0.15	0.27	0.01
1. My pain comes and goes	−0.01	0.08	0.58	−0.02	−0.22
2. My pain lasts	0.06	−0.11	0.57	0.13	0.01
3. In past month pain's got	0.18	−0.12	0.56	−0.02	−0.03
4. On a typical day pain is	0.08	−0.10	0.69	−0.07	−0.15
5. On a good day pain is	0.05	−0.05	0.69	−0.08	−0.27
6. On a bad day pain is	0.08	−0.14	0.62	0.02	0.07
17. Stops household activities	0.10	−0.06	0.64	−0.12	−0.02
18. Afraid to move wrong	0.25	−0.11	0.40	−0.27	0.18
20. Pain blocks falling asleep	0.00	−0.03	0.63	−0.29	−0.02
21. Pain wakes me up	0.03	−0.01	0.58	−0.35	−0.07
22. Avoid enjoyable activities	0.17	0.00	0.64	−0.23	0.01
24. Avoid being sexual	0.16	0.06	0.46	−0.47	0.05
25. Avoid movements	0.18	−0.07	0.53	−0.16	0.10
28. Feel down/discouraged	0.31	−0.07	0.54	−0.32	0.16

Table 3.7   *(Continued)*

	Factors (Total variance accounted for by five factors = 39%)				
Item Number and Description	I. Alienated Depression and Hostility (10.43%)	II. Psychological Coping and Self-Efficacy (6.50%)	III. Physical Severity and Interference (9.85%)	IV. General Psychological Adjustment (8.40%)	V. Psychological Orientation and Motivation (3.79%)
31. Prevents having a good time	0.20	0.05	**0.71**	−0.21	−0.06
32. Pain has mind of its own	0.23	−0.16	0.47	0.02	0.03
33. Pain worsens for no reason	0.13	−0.18	0.45	−0.15	0.02
41. Can get good night's sleep	0.01	0.09	−0.42	0.42	−0.03
10. I am capable of working	0.02	−0.05	−0.35	0.44	0.24
11. I do fun things	−0.20	0.07	−0.24	0.47	0.11
50. Limit use of prescriptions	−0.05	0.25	−0.07	0.41	0.09
52. My life is interesting	−0.25	0.09	−0.14	**0.66**	0.01
53. My life is full/busy	−0.19	0.06	−0.19	**0.59**	0.14
54. Consider self to be curious	−0.17	0.18	0.08	**0.54**	0.22
55. Have control over emotions	−0.24	0.17	−0.06	**0.50**	−0.31
56. I enjoy living my life	−0.33	0.02	−0.17	**0.68**	−0.11
57. Happy about life	−0.30	0.01	−0.22	**0.64**	−0.02
19. Anxiety worsens pain	0.29	0.04	0.17	−0.36	0.34
27. Stress worsens pain	0.35	0.00	0.23	−0.38	0.36
61. No point in mental . . .	0.30	−0.13	0.10	−0.12	**−0.59**
67. Don't believe mental . . .	0.01	−0.07	0.12	0.03	**−0.52**
68. Believe pain only physical	0.03	−0.03	0.14	0.11	**−0.52**
70. Unwilling to learn coping	0.27	−0.16	−0.07	−0.04	**−0.59**
73. Won't see psychologist	0.29	−0.05	−0.14	0.07	**−0.56**

Table 3.8
Pain Coping Inventory Factor-Derived Scale Score Sum Means,
Standard Deviations, and Percentiles in a Heterogeneous
Sample of Chronic Pain Patients (*N* = 433)

		Percentiles					
Scale Score	Mean (SD)	10th	25th	50th	75th	90th	Alpha
Alienated Depression and Hostility	58.38 (21.9)	30	42	59	72	88	.90
Psychological Coping and Self-Efficacy	22.59 (9.7)	11	15	22	28	37	.88
Physical Severity and Interference	67.95 (13.0)	50	59	69.7	78	83	.89
General Psychological Adjustment	23.27 (8.7)	12	17	23	30	35	.85
Psychological Orientation and Motivation	16.71 (6.5)	8	12	16	21	26	.72

Note. Alienated Depression and Hostility contains items 63–66, 69, 71, 77–80, 84–87, 89–91.
Psychological Coping and Self-Efficacy contains items 35–38, 44, 46, 48, 51.
Physical Severity and Interference contains items 1–6, 17, 20–22, 25, 28, 31.
General Psychological Adjustment contains items 52–57.
Psychological Orientation and Motivation contains items 61, 67, 68, 70, 73.

faithfully reproduced based on data collected from two totally independent, cross-validation samples of pain patients ($N = 187$, and $N = 213$).

CONSTRUCT VALIDITY

Third, preliminary determination of the PCI's construct validity was conducted by calculating Pearson product-moment correlations between the PCI and the Multidimensional Pain Inventory (MPI) based on a subsample of 80 pain patients who took both tests. The results of this correlational analysis indicate statistically significant relationships between the PCI scales/indices and the MPI indices that were predicted to correlate based on the constructs they were developed to measure. PCI indices developed to measure unique constructs were found, as expected, to have low correlations with the MPI. The important correlations are summarized here:

- *PCI Global Impairment Index.* The PCI Global Impairment Index correlated positively at the .01 significance level with MPI Pain Severity ($r = .43$) and MPI Interference ($r = .55$), and inversely with MPI Life Control ($r = -.46$) and MPI General Activity Level ($r = -.52$).
- *PCI Physical Severity Index.* The PCI Physical Severity Index correlated positively at the .01 significance level with MPI Pain Severity ($r = .55$) and MPI Interference ($r = .56$), and inversely with MPI Life Control ($r = -.46$) and MPI General Activity Level ($r = -.39$).
- *PCI Behavioral Interference Severity Index.* The PCI Behavioral Interference Severity Index correlated positively at the .01 significance level with MPI Pain Severity ($r = .55$) and MPI Interference ($r = .70$), and inversely with MPI Life Control ($r = -.32$) and MPI General Activity Level ($r = -.41$).
- *PCI Pain Coping Index and Nociceptive Index.* The PCI Pain Coping Index correlated positively at the .01 significance level with MPI Life Control ($r = .47$) and MPI General Activity Level ($r = .47$). The PCI Nociceptive Index correlated as predicted, at the same level of significance in the inverse direction with MPI Life Control ($r = -.47$) and MPI General Activity Level ($r = -.45$), and in the positive direction with MPI Pain Severity ($r = .58$), MPI Interference ($r = .72$), and MPI Affective Distress ($r = .47$).
- *PCI Factor Scales.* The PCI Physical Severity and Interference Factor Scale correlated as predicted, positively at the .01 significance level with MPI Pain Severity ($r = .64$) and MPI Interference ($r = .75$). The PCI General Psychological Adjustment Factor Scale correlated as predicted, inversely at the .01 significance level with MPI Pain Severity ($r = -.39$) and MPI Interference ($r = -.53$), and positively

with MPI Life Control ($r = .46$) and MPI General Activity Level ($r = .53$). The PCI Alienated Depression and Hostility Factor Scale correlated as predicted, positively at the .01 level with MPI Interference ($r = .41$), and inversely with MPI Life Control ($r = -.31$), Social Activities ($r = -.40$), and General Activity Level ($r = -.40$). The PCI factor scale labeled Psychological Coping and Self-Efficacy correlated as predicted, positively at the .01 level with MPI Life Control ($r = .32$). The PCI factor scale labeled Psychological Orientation and Motivation correlated inversely at the .05 significance level with MPI Household Chores ($r = -.24$), and MPI Activities Away from Home ($r = -.26$). These last two PCI factor scales appear to measure unique constructs that are not directly assessed by the MPI.

Additional construct validation of the PCI is provided by a study that examined the relationship between PCI scores and several measures of "cognitive underperformance" (Allen, Conder, Green, & Cox, 1997). A group of 93 disability claimants (mean age = 38.3 years; mean years of education = 12.2) who were evaluated as fulfilling the criteria for *DSM-IV* "Pain Disorder Associated with Psychological Factors" were administered the PCI and the Computerized Assessment of Response Bias (CARB; Allen, Conder, Green, & Cox, 1997; Allen & Cox, 1995). CARB is a forced choice visual digit recognition task for assessing patient effort and cognitive underperformance and symptom exaggeration which is easily passed by patients with verified traumatic brain injury (see Chapter 4 for a more detailed explanation). Statistically significant differences were found on a number of PCI scale means between those who passed and those who failed CARB. These mean differences were all in the expected direction. That is, pain patients who underperformed on CARB had significantly lower scores on several PCI coping measures and higher scores on several PCI measures of pain-related impairment and dysfunction. Table 3.9 displays these PCI and CARB data for the two groups.

In sum, Allen et al.'s (1997) study demonstrated a surprisingly strong association between reports of pain impairment and distress (as measured by the PCI and *DSM-IV* interview criteria) and their sample of pain disability patients' underperformance or interference with specific cognitive tasks. The pain disability compensation claimants reported by Allen et al. (1997) evidenced a 54% rate of cognitive underperformance on CARB or the Word Memory Test (WMT; Green, Allen, & Astner, 1996; discussed in Chapter 4) another measure of cognitive effort as well as rote verbal learning and memory. This was the highest CARB failure rate among the seven diagnostic groups in their sample and twice the rate for their sample as a whole.

Table 3.9
PCI Scale and Index Average Means, Standard Deviations,
and p-values (based on One-Tailed Student t-tests) for
CARB "Pass" and "Fail" Pain Patient Groups

Pain Coping Inventory Scale or Index	Pass CARB (n = 57)		Fail CARB (n = 36)		p-value (one tailed)
	Mean	SD	Main	SD	
Sleep Disturbance	4.71	1.24	5.23	1.06	.02
Activity Interference and Avoidance	4.92	1.26	5.42	1.14	.03
Stress and Anxiety	3.13	1.59	3.83	1.40	.015
Mental Conditioning	3.26	1.22	2.69	1.07	.01
Quality of Life	3.91	1.30	3.10	1.27	.002
Behavioral Interference Index	4.79	1.07	5.28	0.96	.01
Psychological Coping Index	3.74	0.93	3.42	0.66	.03
Nociceptive Index	4.53	0.88	4.90	0.93	.03
Global Impairment Index	4.08	0.85	4.40	0.64	.02
Pain Coping Index	3.79	0.81	3.39	0.71	.01
Coping Success Index	3.75	0.93	3.27	0.78	.005
Psychological Adjustment (Factor)	23.60	7.97	20.34	7.82	.03

PSYCHODIAGNOSTIC APPLICATIONS OF THE PCI

The PCI may enable a clinician to determine whether or not behavioral or psychological treatment is indicated and if so, what issues need to be addressed. The PCI can also provide a clinician with information about a patient's tendencies to exaggerate or magnify pain symptomology. It provides global indices of pain severity, pain impairment, pain generalization, psychological maladjustment, patient alienation, coping success, and psychological adjustment.

Computer Scoring of the PCI: A Case Example

The Pain Coping Inventory's full value is obtained by examining a patient's computer-scored PCI report. Figure 3.1 displays the PCI Computer-Scored Report for Alex Jones (pseudonym), a 40-year-old male patient with a history of chronic, intractable, low back and leg pain of 8 years' duration, and a history of failed back surgeries. The original onset of this patient's condition was related to a lifting accident at work. The patient was referred by his anesthesiologist and family physician for psychological evaluation, to assist in determining his suitability for implantation of a spinal cord (dorsal column) stimulator. In following the interpretation of this patient's PCI computer report, the reader may also wish to refer to Tables 3.5 and 3.6 for normative values.

Areas of Clinical Impairment

Alex Jones's PCI Computer Report (see Figure 3.1) revealed a moderately elevated level of pain severity and markedly elevated levels of pain continuity and duration of pain flare-ups compared with the PCI's normative values. His overall Physical Severity Index summed to 53 (81% expressed as a percentage). This sum places him at around the 80th percentile and approximately one standard deviation above the PCI's normative mean. This patient also scored quite highly on the *Pain Interference* subscales labeled Muscle Bracing and Movement Phobia (i.e., kinesophobia), and Sleep Disturbance. Notably, however, his score on Activity Interference/Avoidance fell within normal limits. His Behavioral Interference Severity Index was moderately elevated relative to the normative mean. His Nociceptive Index of 62.2% (sum of 123) (a summary measure of the degree and frequency of distressing symptoms) fell at around the normative mean value.

Evidence of Adaptive Coping

Mr. Jones showed no tendency on the PCI to admit to behaviors suggestive of catastrophizing about pain, or to admit to any other symptoms of psychological maladjustment. If he had, these would have been manifested by elevations on the Psychological Maladjustment subscales termed Catastrophizing, Stress and Anxiety, Depression, Hostility, and Paranoia and Alienation. His Psychological Maladjustment Severity Index summed to 65 (15% expressed as a percentage) which is markedly below the pain patient summative mean of 120.16 (42% expressed as a percentage).

Under Psychological Adjustment indices, Mr. Jones's scores were relatively high on the adaptive coping subscales labeled Perceived Self-Efficacy, Positive Self-Talk, and Psychological Motivation (above the 75th percentile). He also scored above the normative mean for the subscale termed Quality of Life. On the PCI, Chemical Dependency was not reported to be a problem. His subscale score of 3.5 for *Diet and Exercise* was on the low side. His Pain Coping Index of 47.9% (sum of 124) was significantly higher than the pain patient normative mean of 113.12 for this index.

The Absence of Clinically Significant Alienation and Hostility

This patient's score on the Patient Alienation Index (PAI), which measures treatment resistance and patient alienation was very low (Patient Alienation Index was below the 10th percentile). This may be a good sign relative to his potential for treatment compliance. However, given how low this index was (14.7%, or a summed score of 64 compared to a normative pain patient mean of 123.9), it raised the possibility that Mr. Jones might be denying psychological symptomology. This was in fact borne out to some extent, in the clinical interview.

Validity of Pain Complaints

Mr. Jones's Global Impairment Index of 41.1% (sum of 319) was significantly below the pain patient mean of 384.84 ($SD = 73.14$). Also, a tendency to make extreme ratings reflective of extreme beliefs did not appear to be a problem. His Extreme Beliefs Frequency (EBF) of 2.9% falls at the 10th percentile. This was consistent with his low score on the Patient Alienation Index. Thus, his EBF score reflects his tendency to deny feelings of alienation, resentment, and hostility. However, the extremity of his ratings of other pain-related symptoms, reflected in his Degree of Distress Index of 68.8% (summed score of 41), resulted in a Symptom Magnification Frequency of 27.5%, which falls at the 50th percentile for the test's normative population. Thus, taking into account all the above, it was considered unlikely that this patient's pain complaints were invalid or exaggerated.

Section Summary Indices

Relative to this patient's scores on the PCI's "Section Summary Indices," his Degree of Distress Index of 68.8% (summed score of 41) fell slightly below the 75th percentile, but his Frequency of Distress Index of 59.3% (summed score of 82) was right at mean level. His Coping Success Index of 49.3% (summed score of 99) was above the mean level at around the 75th percentile, and his *Health-Related Behaviors Index* of 42.9% (summed score of 25) was right at about the normative mean.

Individual Item Responses and Clinical Summary

Analysis of Mr. Jones's raw responses to the PCI items, clarified by interview with the patient, revealed the following clinically important data: He reported that he was in constant pain with no relief, that his sleep was nonrestorative and disrupted by pain, and that he suffered from a great deal of downtime. There was evident marked deconditioning and loss of physical endurance. It was apparent that pain controlled this person's activity levels, and there appeared to be a notable lack of reinforcement from leisure activities. There also was reported a strained marital relationship, but a strong relationship with his children. In clinical interview, he admitted to some mild reactive symptoms of depression.

This patient's PCI profile showed high somatization and pain severity, moderate to high overall pain interference, and minimal admission of symptoms associated with psychological maladjustment. The clinician provided the following evaluation:

REPORT OF PSYCHOLOGICAL EVALUATION

Patient Name: ___Alex Jones___   **Age (Birthdate):** _40 (02/29/56)_

Marital Status: ___Married___   **Date of Injury:** _3/9/90_

Patient's Employer: ___Janitorial Services___

Workers' Compensation Claim No.: _12345678WC_

Referring Doctor(s): ___John Smith, M.D., Department of Anesthesiology,___
Anytown Community Hospital, Anytown, New Jersey

Date of Evaluation: ___10/24/96___

Evaluation Purpose: ___Psychological screening for an implantable SCS.___

Dear Dr. Smith:

Thank you for referring your patient for psychological consultation. I saw him in consultation on 10/24/96 at your request, to assist in evaluating his suitability for spinal cord stimulator implantation (SCS). At that time, I interviewed Mr. Jones and administered several psychological and pain assessment instruments. This report summarizes my findings and documents my formal impressions.

History and Background

As you and Mr. Jones's primary care physician, Dr. Well, are both aware, your patient is a 40-year-old married man who suffered a work-related injury in March 1990 and subsequently developed chronic, persistent, severe, low back pain radiating into his left lower extremity. He underwent multiple spine surgeries, which have included laminectomies, between 1992 and 1995, but has been left with severe pain which is described as continuous and distressing. In addition to his work-related injury, your patient had also sustained prior cervical injuries in a motor vehicle accident in 1987. He also reports a history of carpal tunnel syndrome, and chronic hepatitis.

Behavioral Observations

On first presentation, I observed a tall, well nourished, white male who looked somewhat older than his stated age. He presented with an affect that can be primarily described as reserved, pleasant, and cooperative. He was noticeably in pain, demonstrating marked pain behaviors characterized by muscle bracing and guarding, frequent shifting, grimacing, and poor sitting tolerance. He ambulated into and around the office with the assistance of a cane on his right. He stated that the cane is needed given the numbness and weakness in his left leg, and the fact that the leg gives out on him. Mr. Jones described his leg pain as "strong, sharp, shooting, and constant."

Medication Use

Your patient stated that he takes various medications to "help take the edge off" of the pain. They were reported to include Ultram and Vicodan, taken every 4 hours on an as-needed basis, and Elavil (200 milligrams), taken at bedtime as prescribed by Dr. Well. Extra-strength Tylenol is also taken on an as-needed basis.

Summary of Current Living Situation and Associated Symptoms

Your patient has been married for sixteen years, and has two teenage children. He reports that he is not working because of his injuries and pain. He is receiving workers' compensation benefits. His wife is employed as a waitress, and is described as being frequently punitive with Mr. Jones. He attributes this to her resentment of his disability status. Mr. Jones does report marked impairment in his ability to perform household chores. He reports that his daily activities are controlled by pain resulting in frequent downtime. During these periods which are reported to occur two to four times a day, he lies down with a cold pack under his back, his legs elevated, and a heating pad under his neck, to relieve the pain.

Mr. Jones also reports marked symptoms of sleep disturbance due to pain, frequent headaches, and constant fatigue. However, he denies marked symptoms of depression, anxiety, or hostility. This was also borne out on psychological testing. Despite his problems, Mr. Jones stated: "I try to think positive," and "My family keeps me going." Mr. Jones told me that previous to sustaining his injuries, he worked full-time as a "maintenance mechanic" for a company that managed several professional office buildings. He also stated that he once had been very athletically active. He reported that he coached his sons' Little League baseball team; in high school, he was the Captain of the soccer and track teams; and he once played semipro men's soccer. Now, he reports that because of pain, he cannot even engage in leisure activities he once enjoyed such as hunting, camping, and fishing. He stated that although he walks every day, his walking distance is minimal due to pain (less than half a block). Standing and sitting tolerance are also reported to be markedly limited. Additionally, his limitations are worsened by "chronic fatigue syndrome" symptoms relatable to hepatitis.

Procedures Administered

Clinical Interview and Mental Status Examination; Review of Available Medical Records; Coolidge Axis II Inventory (CATI); Symptom Checklist-90 Revised (SCL-90R); Beck Depression Inventory (BDI); Pain Coping Inventory (PCI); Philadelphia Pain Questionnaire-Pain Adjective Checklist (PPQ-PAC); Multidimensional Pain Inventory (MPI); Pain Patient Profile (P-3); Pain Beliefs and Perceptions Inventory (PBPI); Hypnotic Ability and Response Profile (HARP).

Psychological Test Results

Indices of Psychopathology

On this administration of the Coolidge Axis II Personality Inventory (CATI), your patient's responses were markedly devoid of indications of personality psychopathology or psychiatric symptomology. The only elevated clinical scale on the CATI was the Schizoid Personality Trait Dimension. It was mildly to moderately elevated. This suggests that your patient sees himself as emotionally well controlled, that he denies much emotional involvement with others, that he is not easily angered, that he sees himself as independent, and that he denies feelings of jealousy, losing his temper, or having any anger problems. The CATI profile also suggests that Mr. Jones is more introverted than extroverted.

On this administration of the Symptom Checklist-90 Revised (SCL-90R), your patient's responses gave no evidence for any clinically significant symptoms of hostility, phobic anxiety, paranoia, or psychosis. However, the clinical scales measuring anxiety and depression were moderately elevated, and there was a marked elevation on the somatization scale. Also, his General Severity Index of 62 (*T*-Score), and Positive Symptom Distress Index of 66 (*T*-Score), both indicate moderate levels of global symptomatic distress. Nevertheless, these levels of symptomology are not associated with negative treatment outcomes.

Beck Depression Inventory

On the Beck Depression Inventory (BDI), your patient's BDI summary score of 14 fell within the "mild" range. On the BDI, Mr. Jones admitted to mild feelings of discouragement, guilt, irritability, thoughts of failure, self-disappointment, worrying, and self-criticism, and mild symptoms of anhedonia, inertia, anergia, insomnia, fatigue, and appetite loss. His BDI results are consistent with the other symptom indicators we have reviewed.

The Philadelphia Pain Questionnaire-Pain Adjective Checklist

On this administration of the PPQ-PAC, your patient's Total Pain Rating Index (Total PRI) came to 62%. This is right at mean levels given the test's normative data. Examination of the components of this patient's Total PRI revealed a Sensory PRI of 65% and an Affective-Evaluative PRI of 59%. Once again, both of these scores are at normative mean levels. Mr. Jones's Percentage of Words Chosen (PWC) (out of 52 words) came to 67% (35 words). For patients with low back and leg pain related to discogenic disease, this falls slightly above the 75th percentile. However, this patient's pain drawing reflected an anatomically consistent represented distribution of pain locations. His Present Pain Index was rated at 75% of maximum on a VAS, or visual analogue scale. This patient's PPQ-PAC data are taken to reflect an honest attempt to communicate the quality and intensity of his experienced pain.

The Pain Coping Inventory

On this administration of the Pain Coping Inventory (PCI), Mr. Jones's responses revealed moderately elevated levels of reported pain severity and markedly elevated levels of reported pain continuity and duration. Not surprisingly, Mr. Jones also scored highly on the PCI Pain Interference subscales labeled Muscle Bracing and Movement Phobia and Sleep Disturbance. However, evidence for adaptive coping was indicated by normatively high scores on the subscales labeled Perceived Self-Efficacy, Positive Self-Talk, and Psychological Motivation. In contrast, there was a notable absence of any admission of symptoms or attitudes reflective of psychological maladjustment. There was no evidence in this test record for hostility, paranoia, or treatment resistance or alienation.

This PCI test record indicates that your patient experiences constant pain, disrupted and nonrestorative sleep, and marked downtime. There is also marked physical deconditioning, loss of physical endurance, reduced activity levels controlled by pain and the fear of pain, and a lack of acceptable levels of reinforcement from leisure activities. There also appears to be a strained marital relationship. There are mild symptoms of depression (see BDI above), but there is a tendency to deny major symptoms of psychopathology.

Alcohol and Substance Abuse

Your patient claims that he has been abstinent since 1992. However, he admits to a history of excessive alcohol use, especially beer drinking, previous to 1992.

Pain Patient Profile

On this administration of the Pain Patient Profile (P-3), your patient scored below pain patient normative mean scores on the scales labeled Depression and Anxiety. This finding is consistent with the preceding test results. However, he showed mildy elevated (above the pain patient normative mean) scores on the scale labeled Somatization.

The Multidimensional Pain Inventory

On this administration of the Multidimensional Pain Inventory (MPI), your patient not surprisingly, had a significantly elevated T-Score for perceived Punishing Responses by his wife, and a low T-Score for perceived Distracting Responses by his wife. The MPI scales measuring Pain Severity and Interference were also mildly elevated above the normative means for low back pain patients. Also, not surprisingly, the MPI T-Scores for Affective Distress and Perceived Life Control were not clinically elevated. Interestingly, the MPI computer program, which classifies pain patients into groups based on an empirically derived taxonomy, classified Mr. Jones's profile into the "anomalous" grouping. This particular sorting means that the profile could not be fit into any of the other more well-defined pain patient categories (i.e., "adaptive coper," "dysfunctional," "interpersonally distressed," or "hybrid").

The Pain Beliefs and Perceptions Inventory

On this administration of the Pain Beliefs and Perceptions Inventory (PBPI), Mr. Jones's scores were not elevated on either of the two factors associated with the most emotional distress and poor treatment outcomes. These factors are labeled Pain Mysteriousness and Self-Blame. His scores on these two factor scales were significantly below normative pain patient means, which is a favorable prognostic sign. However, he scored above pain patient means on the factor scales measuring perceptions of Pain Constancy and Pain Permanence, with the Constancy Scale being considerably higher than the Permanence Scale. These data corroborate the other data previously reported.

Trial Therapy

I also administered to your patient in a second session, the Hypnotic Ability and Response Profile (HARP). One of the things that administration of this instrument does is assess psychological motivation and compliance. My prediction was that motivation and compliance in session would be good, based on the psychological testing I performed in the first session. This prediction was borne out. Your patient demonstrated a very favorable degree of hypnotic responsiveness and compliance with the procedure.

Diagnostic Impressions and Recommendations

Diagnoses based on the ICD-9CM are as follows:

1. 724.4 - Lumbosacral Radiculitis.

2. 724.2 - Low Back Pain Syndrome.

3. 307.89 - Chronic Pain Disorder.

Major Conclusions

There are no marked signs of psychopathology or personality dysfunction in your patient's interview and test record that would contraindicate trial implantation of a spinal cord stimulator. I believe that Mr. Jones is an acceptable candidate for the contemplated procedure. However, I do have several concerns. One concern is that there may be an underreported past history of alcohol abuse. A second concern is that there may be some tendency to deny depressive and anxiety symptoms. For example, on the BDI, Mr. Jones earned a BDI score of 14, which falls in the mild range of depression. This may be an underestimate of the severity of his depressive symptomology although Mr. Jones admits to mild feelings of discouragement, hopelessness, and self-disappointment. However, he denies having any suicidal ideation. A third concern is related to the possible effects on Mr. Jones's adjustment of his wife's reported punitive reactions. Obviously, this can be a potential sabotage factor in terms of your patient's ability to adjust to the demands of the procedure that you are considering. In terms of this man's personality profile, emotional control and compliance are obviously important issues for him, and this is probably a plus when it comes to managing and adjusting to the demands of living with a SCS. There is also evidence from my own clinical experience that patients who are as compliant as this man was with trial psychological therapy procedures such as the HARP do better in terms of their sustained adjustment to SCS than do other patients who are less compliant with trial therapy procedures.

There is no question that your patient is extremely physically disabled and impaired secondary to his pain problems. From this perspective, he is a good candidate. He definitely craves more pain relief. Furthermore, significant red flags and major contraindicators are absent. There is no evidence for psychosis, delusional thinking, major depressive disorder, current drug, alcohol, or medicine abuse, suicidality, homicidality, hostility, alienation, paranoia, or overriding secondary gains. The indications for proceeding with trial SCS definitely outweigh the contraindications; and it is my opinion that Mr. Jones is an acceptable candidate.

Once again, thank you so much for allowing me to participate in Mr. Jones's care. As always, should you feel that I might be of any further help, please do not hesitate to contact me.

Very truly yours,

_____

BRUCE N. EIMER, PH.D., ABPP, FAAPM
Licensed Clinical Psychologist

cc: Dr. Ian Well (primary care doctor)

CHAPTER 4

Treatment Planning

The only thing to know is how to use your neurosis.
—Arthur Adamov

A CLINICIAN who receives a referral from PMP must evaluate the patient's suitability for this type of pain treatment. If the patient appears to be a suitable candidate, the clinician must define the patient's target problems, determine the patient's expectations and goals, formulate and negotiate reasonable and attainable goals, and identify the most appropriate types of psychotherapy for the case (e.g., cognitive therapy, behavior therapy, desensitization therapy, memory reprocessing therapy, hypnotherapy, relaxation therapy, biofeedback therapy, supportive therapy, nondirective therapy, case management). This involves determining the most viable solution strategies (i.e., strategies for solving the defined problems and realizing the agreed-upon goals of treatment), and applicable treatment methods and modalities. A problem list needs to be drawn up, and treatment goals prioritized.

DEVELOPING A PMP TREATMENT PLAN

STEP 1. ASSESSING THE PATIENT'S UNDERSTANDING OF THE REASON FOR REFERRAL

In developing a PMP treatment plan, the clinician must first determine the patient's understanding of the reason for the referral. This involves assessing the patient's presenting complaints, and the pain evaluation and treatment context. The pain evaluation and treatment context includes the stated and actual reason for referral, the referral source, and the potential treatment setting, which encompasses any resources and obstacles to effective treatment.

118

A patient's stated reason for referral might be "to help me with my pain," whereas the unstated, underlying reason could be "to prove that I am unable to work so that I can be awarded my workers' compensation benefits." Although a patient's manifest referral source might be a treating physician, the most influential referral source (not mentioned initially) could be his or her attorney. Some obstacles to effective treatment in a busy outpatient or inpatient medical rehabilitation setting might be limited private office space; limited time available for psychotherapy; competing demands for patients' time and energy; patients with minimal energy, endurance, psychological motivation, attention spans, and cognitive persistence; attending physicians who are not psychologically oriented and who are unfamiliar with psychological interventions; and punitive or oversolicitous significant others. Some resources for effective treatment might be a patient's intelligence, curiosity, and desire to obtain relief from pain and suffering; the absence of hostility, resentment, or anger; a good family or social support system (involved significant others who are neither punitive nor oversolicitous); and psychologically oriented, treating physicians who are well educated about pain management and psychological interventions.

STEP 2. ASSESSING THE PATIENT'S EXPECTATIONS, MOTIVATIONS, AND QUALIFYING FACTORS

The clinician must next determine the patient's expectations and motivations for psychological treatment. If a patient is self-referred (as are a minority of referrals for PMP), then this is the first step in assessment. It is a necessary precursor to developing a strategy for defining the problem and formulating treatment goals. It is based on evaluating what the patient wants and needs, and is influenced by the pain evaluation and treatment context, the patient's personality type, the type of pain, associated medical and psychological problems, and any qualifying factors.

Identifying Qualifying Factors

The clinician should identify the presence or absence of the following variables that either qualify or disqualify a patient for particular types of treatment; poor intrinsic motivation, hidden agendas, pain associated with a history of trauma, significant anger and hostility, symptom magnification, self-blame, antisocial character traits, active addictions, borderline or lower intelligence, brain injury, ongoing litigation, alienation, work conflict and job dissatisfaction, physical handicaps, terminal pain, significant emotionality, current stressors, secondary gains, excessive social reinforcement for pain behaviors, unusual or bizarre perceptions of the pain, and indications of major psychological maladjustment.

Qualifying factors can sometimes operate as trump cards in favor of psychological treatment when other aspects of the clinical picture mitigate against psychological treatment.

Case Example

A 62-year-old, married patient with a left above-the-knee amputation performed 2 months previously, was referred by his physician for psychological evaluation and treatment of severe phantom limb pain. The patient had a sixth-grade education, a past history of alcohol abuse, and several, past inpatient admissions for alcohol detoxification and treatment, and was assessed to have clinically significant *DSM-IV*, Axis I psychopathology (a Dysthymic Disorder and an Adjustment Disorder with Anxious Features). On *DSM-IV*, Axis II, he also was assessed to have a Mixed/Atypical Personality Disorder with Mild to Moderate Borderline and Antisocial Personality Traits. The patient had been employed for 35 years by the same company as a welder, up until his medical problems (related to diabetic neuropathy) became disabling one year previously. He no longer worked and was currently receiving a disability pension. The patient claimed that he had been abstinent for over a year. There was no evidence of addiction to pain medications, and he had been compliant with his physicians' treatment regimens. He was also assessed to have strong intrinsic motivation to learn psychological techniques for reducing his constant pain. He had a supportive wife. His pain complaints were deemed to be objective and valid. It was determined that this patient was a good candidate for a short course of PMP emphasizing relaxation therapy, hypnotic pain relief imagery, and cognitive-behavioral strategies for stress reduction.

The second step in the treatment planning process also includes obtaining the patient's pain and treatment history. It is important to evaluate the patient's mental and psychiatric status, medical diagnoses, and relevant medical history. The clinician should administer psychological and pain assessment instruments (see Chapters 2 and 3) for obtaining descriptions of the patient's pain experience (e.g., administering a structured pain history and status interview, relevant pain adjective checklists, and rating scales) and eliciting information about the psychological effects of living with persistent pain (e.g., administering instruments that assess pain impairment and disability, pain beliefs, coping, psychopathology, and maladjustment).

Step 3. Forming a Case Conceptualization and Developing Treatment Goals

Third, it is necessary to conceptualize the case, draw up a problem priority list, and then formulate treatment goals that the clinician and the patient collaboratively will work toward attaining and solution strategies for solving the defined problems and realizing the goals. Realizing the treatment goals should help the patient get what he or she wants and needs, and result in improved adaptive functioning, pain management, and coping. Treatment methods and modalities should be based on the clinical case conceptualization, the prioritized problem list, and the agreed-upon treatment goals and solution strategies.

Our system of case conceptualization for PMP is based on seven inter-related sets of determinants that are assessed in the initial workup of the patient using the tests and assessment procedures described in Chapters 2 and 3:

1. The physical and temporal qualities of the pain.
2. The patient's associated symptoms and affective distress.
3. The patient's evaluative perceptions and pain-related beliefs.
4. The patient's behavioral states.
5. The patient's personality traits, relevant abilities, talents, and interests.
6. The patient's type and degree of personality dysfunction, psychopathology, and maladjustment.
7. The assessed validity of the patient's pain complaints.

Tailoring treatment goals and strategies to the patient requires assessing all these determinants. This is the basis for systematic treatment selection and targeted therapeutic interventions (Beutler & Clarkin, 1990; Freeman et al., 1990). These seven sets of determinants form the core of the *PMP case conceptualization*. The following section describes these case determinants as well as prototypical *treatment goals* for each determinant. These sets of determinants are not mutually exclusive.

CASE DETERMINANTS AND PROTOTYPICAL TREATMENT GOALS

Pain's Physical and Temporal Qualities

The physical and temporal qualities of the pain include the following descriptive and evaluative considerations, along with attendant treatment goals.

- Is the pain brief or of long duration? *Treatment goal:* Develop ways to make the pain more tolerable and to reduce suffering.
- Is pain frequent or infrequent? *Treatment goals:* Reduce the frequency of pain episodes. Help the patient learn ways of preventing pain flare-ups. Help the patient learn ways to cope with pain

episodes and reduce their intensity. Reduce the patient's anticipatory anxiety about having a pain flare-up. Reduce the patient's traumatic anxiety reaction to pain flare-ups.

- Is pain intermittent or continuous? *Treatment goals:* For continuous pain, help the patient learn distraction techniques for diverting attention from pain. For intermittent pain, see the goals for frequent or infrequent pain. Negotiate a behavioral contract to promote the patient's compliance with exercise quotas as opposed to "exercising to tolerance."
- Is pain of mild, moderate, or severe intensity? *Treatment goal:* Help the patient learn methods for reducing pain intensity and severity.
- Is pain localized or spread out? *Treatment goals:* Increase the patient's commitment to starting and continuing a regular physical exercise program prescribed to increase the strength, flexibility, and endurance of specific muscle groups. Reduce dysfunctional muscle bracing and guarding. Teach relaxation and energy conservation techniques.
- Is pain predictable or labile? *Treatment goals:* Help the patient learn ways of predicting, preventing, aborting, and coping with pain episodes, flare-ups, and triggers. Negotiate a behavioral contract to promote compliance with exercise quotas as opposed to "exercising to tolerance." Teach the patient "activity pacing" and help the patient begin a "graded exercise program" to "shape" increased endurance.
- Is pain anatomically consistent in its locations and distribution? *Treatment goals:* Reduce the patient's anxiety and oversensitivity to bodily sensations. Improve the patient's awareness of dysfunctional pain posturing. Utilize cognitive and desensitization procedures for reducing "movement phobia."

Assessment Procedures

The preceding determinants are assessed in the Pain History and Status Interview, the Pain Imagery Interview, the McGill Pain Questionnaire, the Philadelphia Pain Questionnaire, the PPQ-PAC, and the Pain Coping Inventory.

AFFECTIVE DISTRESS

Symptoms and states of affective distress often have to be addressed early in a PMP treatment plan. Unless a patient is affectively stabilized, pain management interventions are likely to be fruitless. Certain affective symptoms with a distinct interpersonal focus, such as hostility and alienation, present total obstacles to effective PMP, unless the therapist addresses them effectively at the outset of treatment.

- To what degree is there fatigue? *Treatment goals:* Reduce fatigue and increase endurance. Develop activity schedules and quotas. Reduce functional restrictions imposed by pain.
- How much suffering is associated with the pain? *Treatment goals:* Reduce suffering and increase pain tolerance. Teach the patient pain avoidance, symptom alteration, pain transformation, attentional diversion, and distraction techniques.
- Is there depression? *Treatment goals:* Evaluate symptoms and basis of depression. Reduce depressive symptoms. Utilize cognitive therapy and behavioral activation techniques for reducing depressive symptoms, increasing activity levels, and increasing pleasure and mastery associated with activities. Employ cognitive strategies to address the underlying cognitive basis of the patient's depression.
- Is there self-blame? *Treatment goals:* Utilize cognitive and behavioral methods for reducing self-blame and underlying tendencies to misattribute responsibility and overpersonalize events.
- Is there anger and hostility? *Treatment goals:* Utilize interpersonal and relational strategies to build the patient's level of trust and comfort in the therapeutic relationship so that pain management interventions can be introduced. Identify strategies for meeting the patient's emotional needs. Improve the patient's working relationships with other health care providers. Employ cognitive techniques to dispute beliefs fueling anger and hostility. Utilize behavioral interventions to increase the patient's behavioral control, reduce "hot" reactivity, and improve ability to cope with temper tantrum precipitants. Conduct a cognitive-behavioral analysis to disrupt the chain of events leading to blowups, or aggressive behavior. Conduct assertiveness training to reduce inappropriate responses to anger precipitants, and the patient's vulnerability to being abused and becoming abusive. This would involve (a) teaching the patient how to appropriately express disagreement, disappointment, hurts, and frustrations, and (b) teaching the patient how to say "no" to requests or demands.
- Is there alienation? *Treatment goals:* It is necessary to reduce patient alienation early in the therapeutic process because alienation breeds treatment resistance. Helping the patient notice and acknowledge similarities between self and others can reduce the sense of estrangement. Help the patient develop trust. Teach assertiveness skills. Develop strategies to help the patient meet his or her emotional needs. Help the patient develop interest in and concern for others. Help the patient normalize his or her experiences. Reduce tendencies to inappropriately and harshly judge and condemn self and others. Develop the patient's resources for acting out of kindness as opposed to resentment and anger.

- Is there anxiety? *Treatment goals:* Employ cognitive and behavioral methods to improve the patient's ability to cope with and reduce the frequency of anxiety triggers that worsen pain. Conduct an analysis of the patient's perceived threats-to-resources ratio, and increase the patient's confidence in his or her coping resources. Reduce feelings of helplessness. Teach relaxation and self-control techniques for reducing hypervigilance, autonomic arousal, and muscle bracing/guarding that increase pain and flare-ups. Reduce preoccupation with pain and other somatic symptoms.
- Assess situational and cumulative stress. *Treatment goals:* Help the patient understand the relationship between stress, psychological factors, pain, and other physical symptoms. Employ cognitive and behavioral methods to improve the patient's ability to cope with daily and situational stressors. Improve the patient's frustration tolerance.
- Is there posttraumatic stress? *Treatment goals:* Employ memory reprocessing and cognitive-affective exposure procedures to desensitize the patient to intrusive ideation associated with the original traumatic events. Employ cognitive and behavioral methods to improve the patient's ability to cope with daily and situational stressors that trigger reminders of the precipitating traumatic events and increase pain. Help the patient learn relaxation and self-control methods to reduce hypervigilance and overarousal driving autonomic dysregulation and increased pain. Identify and process emotional traumas secondary to living with chronic pain and associated with past treatments. Help the patient identify and appropriately express feelings. Emotionally process origins of the pain.
- Is there excessive emotionality? *Treatment goals:* Help the patient learn to use relaxation and self-control methods to reduce sympathetically maintained emotional reactivity. Utilize cognitive methods to decrease worrying. Desensitize excessive emotional reactions to pain.

Assessment Procedures

The preceding symptoms and states are assessed in an initial clinical interview and mental status examination, in the Pain History and Status Interview, and in the Pain Imagery Interview. They can be further assessed on the following instruments: the McGill Pain Questionnaire, the Philadelphia Pain Questionnaire, the PPQ-PAC, the Pain Coping Inventory, the Pain Experience Scale, the Pain Beliefs and Perceptions Inventory, the Pain Anxiety Symptoms Scale, the P-3, the Multidimensional Pain Inventory, the Beck Depression and Anxiety Inventories, the Symptom Checklist 90-Revised, the Coolidge Axis II Inventory, the Millon Clinical Multiaxial Inventory, the MMPI, and the Personality Assessment

Inventory. It is neither necessary nor advisable to administer all these measures. Considerations in selecting among these instruments have been discussed earlier.

EVALUATIVE PERCEPTIONS AND PAIN BELIEFS

The presence or absence, and degree of problematic pain perceptions, cognitions, and beliefs form the basis for the patient's emotional reactions and affective states discussed earlier. Cognitive, affective, and behavioral interventions for addressing the dysfunctional cognitions underlying a pain patient's emotional distress and suffering, are covered in Chapters 5 through 8. The following list categorizes these perceptions and beliefs as an aid to treatment planning.

- Pain as causing misery. *Treatment goals:* Assess, empirically examine, and dispute automatic thoughts and underlying negative beliefs that activate and maintain the experience of misery. Teach the patient to label catastrophizing thoughts and to cognitively dispute them.
- Pain as a source of punishment. *Treatment goals:* Assess, empirically examine, and dispute automatic thoughts and underlying negative beliefs that activate and maintain the experience of being punished. Assess for feelings of guilt and empirically examine their basis. Teach the patient to observe pain sensations without evaluative judgment.
- Pain as mysterious. *Treatment goals:* Provide information to educate the patient about the physical-mechanical, physiological, and psychological mechanisms that cause and maintain pain, and correct erroneous ideas. Build cognitive coping strategies.
- Pain as threatening, fearful, or frightful. *Treatment goals:* Help the patient develop a more favorable, factual perception of his or her coping resources. Empirically assess and dispute the realistic likelihood of occurrence of low probability, catastrophic, pain-related outcomes. Reduce underlying fears through the use of cognitive, affective, and behavioral desensitization methods, graduated exposure, flooding, and other behavioral techniques.
- Pain as disabling. *Treatment goals:* Assess and empirically dispute the validity of any secondary gains due to pain. Analyze the advantages and disadvantages of maintaining pain for secondary gain. Examine and compare secondary gains versus primary losses due to pain-related disability and impairment. Examine other sources of job or life dissatisfaction. Reduce behavioral withdrawal and avoidance. Gradually increase the duration, diversity, and range of the patient's daily and weekly activities.

- Pain as out of control. *Treatment goals:* Identify and dispute beliefs associated with lack of control. Motivate the patient to look for ways to increase control over reactions to pain and pain-related events. Help the patient develop positive affirmations and self-statements associated with emotional and behavioral control. Reduce anticipatory anxiety about flare-ups. Increase perceptions of resourcefulness for coping with pain-related and other adversities.
- Pain as hopeless and permanent. *Treatment goals:* Improve the patient's estimation of his or her coping resources. Identify exceptions to the patient's conclusions about pain's permanence, or the patient's lack of resourcefulness. Identify and dispute automatic thoughts associated with the conclusion that there is nothing the patient can do to obtain pain relief or prevent further deterioration in his or her condition. Reprocess with the patient any memories of temporary improvements in his or her condition. Compare the advantages with the disadvantages of feeling hopeless, and believing in pain's permanence.
- Pain as a reason to worry excessively. *Treatment goals:* Empirically examine and dispute reasons to worry. Assess and dispute cognitive distortions. Identify and reduce underlying fears through education, accurate information, cognitive correction, and cognitive and behavioral desensitization techniques. Conduct worry exposure sessions and assign worry exposure homework.

Assessment Procedures

These perceptions and beliefs are assessed in a clinical interview, in the Pain History and Status Interview and in the Pain Imagery Interview. Diagnostic tests include the McGill Pain Questionnaire, the Philadelphia Pain Questionnaire, the Pain Coping Inventory, the Pain Experience Scale, the Pain Anxiety Symptoms Scale, the Multidimensional Pain Inventory, and the Pain Beliefs and Perceptions Inventory.

BEHAVIORAL STATES

The patient's behavioral states include the presence or absence, and degree of the following problematic behavioral states along with attendant treatment goals. Some of these states can be termed "pain behaviors."

- Overreliance/dependence on narcotic analgesics. *Treatment goals:* Obtain a patient and family substance abuse history. Evaluate the possibility of an addiction problem. Assess whether the patient is abusing pain medicine. Assess whether drug tolerance is a problem. Help the patient understand the concepts of addiction, dependence, drug-seeking, tolerance, and denial. Evaluate indications for an inpatient drug detoxification or intensive, outpatient drug rehabilitation program. Obtain the patient's oral and written agreement to obtain pharmacotherapy from just one prescribing physician and one pharmacy. Work with the patient, in collaboration with one prescribing physician, to reduce reliance on as-needed (PRN) narcotic and OTC analgesics by X%. Substitute "time-contingent dosing" of narcotic analgesics in place of "pain-contingent dosing." Help the patient develop greater awareness of early, prodromal cues for impending pain flare-ups and teach the patient cognitive and behavioral coping strategies to prepare for pain flare-ups. Develop coping strategies for managing anxiety symptoms tranquilized by inappropriate drug use. Work with the patient and prescribing physician to develop criteria for deciding when it is reasonable for the patient to take an extra analgesic dose to reduce the severity of an impending pain flare-up.

- Alcohol abuse. *Treatment goals:* Obtain a substance abuse history. Assess if the patient is abusing alcohol. Obtain the patient's oral and written commitment to begin regular attendance and sponsored participation at AA meetings. Evaluate indications for admission to an inpatient alcohol detoxification program. Help patient cope with alcohol withdrawal symptoms. Identify triggers to alcohol use. Develop new coping strategies for managing triggers to drinking. Develop coping strategies for managing anxiety symptoms tranquilized by drinking.

- Unhealthy dietary habits. *Treatment goals:* Assess the patient's dietary habits. Obtain the patient's commitment to modify unhealthy habits. Identify triggers to overeating or eating junk foods. Develop new coping strategies for managing triggers to poor dietary habits. Develop coping strategies for managing anxiety symptoms tranquilized by overeating.

- Lack of exercise and physical deconditioning. *Treatment goals:* Assess the patient's compliance with previously prescribed exercise programs. Obtain the patient's commitment to work with a physician and licensed physical therapist to start a regular exercise program to improve physical conditioning. Teach and coach activity pacing and endurance shaping. Set up a behavioral reactivation program to build up activity quotas and increased daily levels of activity. Improve the patient's awareness of factors triggering overdoing it, and develop alternative pacing strategies.

- Physical impairment and disablement. *Treatment goals:* Increase motivation to become more self-reliant. Help the patient identify factors that increase vulnerability to pain-related impairment. Help the patient learn to discriminate between significant others' responses that punish versus distract attention from versus positively reinforce expressions of pain. Help the patient become more aware of how he or she expresses pain to others (i.e., interpersonal pain behaviors). Reduce behaviors and gestures that draw attention to pain, as well as complaining about pain by X%.

- Activity interference, withdrawal, and avoidance due to pain. *Treatment goals:* Reduce level of preoccupation and focus on pain and symptoms. Reduce level of functional restriction attributed to pain. Reduce family or significant others' reinforcement of pain symptoms, such as the frequency of oversolicitous behaviors. Improve coping skills for managing flare-ups. Increase the patient's ability to reduce pain severity during a flare-up. Improve the patient's awareness of vulnerability factors. Increase the patient's frequency of functional, everyday activities.

- Interpersonal conflict and distress. *Treatment goals:* Help the patient recognize the effects of his or her behavior on others. Teach self-assertion skills. Coach the patient on how to appropriately express feelings, opinions, and disagreement, and how to say no. Assess and develop functional strategies for coping with triggers to interpersonal conflict. Teach the patient skills for generating alternative solutions to interpersonal problems, testing these alternatives, and anticipating consequences. Improve the patient's social judgment.

- Dysfunctional pain coping. *Treatment goals:* Desensitize catastrophic reactions to pain sensations and flare-ups. Improve the patient's cognitive and behavioral skills for coping with continuous pain, pain exacerbations, and flare-ups.

- Excessive pain behaviors, such as complaining, muscle bracing, and guarding. *Treatment goals:* Reduce frequency of complaining about pain. Recognize adverse impact of pain behaviors on self and others. Reduce social reinforcement of dysfunctional pain behaviors. Improve postural awareness and decrease postural dypoenesis. Use biofeedback/relaxation techniques to reduce unnecessary muscle tension.

- Frequent interactions with oversolicitous significant others reinforcing pain behaviors. *Treatment goals:* Help the patient understand the effects of pain behaviors on others. Help the patient understand the disadvantages of continuing to allow significant others to do things for him or her because of pain. Work with accessible significant others to reduce unhelpful reinforcement of verbal and nonverbal pain behaviors.

- Frequent interactions with punitive significant others. *Treatment goals:* Help the patient understand how unexpressed anger worsens pain. Help the patient learn assertiveness skills. Work with accessible significant others to reduce punitive reactions to the patient. Help the patient dispute irrational beliefs about other people's responses.

- Sleep disruption and deprivation. *Treatment goals:* Begin assessment and treatment program to regulate the patient's sleep cycle. Teach the patient behavioral stimulus and response control principles of "sleep hygiene." Confer with the patient's treating physician about indications for a referral to a sleep laboratory for a nocturnal sleep study. Teach the patient relaxation techniques to use at bedtime. Evaluate factors contributing to the patient's psychophysiological sleep problems. Motivate the patient to address sleep problems by explaining connections between sleep deprivation, increased pain, and functional disability. Address irrational beliefs about sleeping.

Assessment Procedures

The preceding behavioral states can be assessed in a clinical interview, through behavioral observations, in the Pain History and Status Interview, in the Pain Imagery Interview, on the Pain Coping Inventory, the Pain Interference and Impairment Index, the Multidimensional Pain Inventory, the Illness Behavior Questionnaire; the Sickness Impact Profile, the Pain Vulnerability Checklist, and through the use of pain diaries (see Chapters 6 and 8).

PERSONALITY TRAITS

Several clinically relevant personality trait dimensions should be assessed as part of the initial patient workup.

- *Introversion versus extraversion.* Introverted patients may need a more active-directive and energetic therapist than extraverted patients.
- *Involvement and sociability versus uninvolvement and apathy.* Uninvolved, apathetic patients make tough therapy customers unless they can be persuaded to begin taking appropriate responsibility for their feelings, well-being, and therapeutic progress.
- *Trust versus mistrust.* Initially, therapy must be geared to building the patient's trust and confidence in the therapist, or else, there can be no real therapy.
- *Autonomy and assertiveness versus passivity and dependence.* The trait of dependency can be used in the service of the therapy. Dependent patients often do homework assignments. However, passivity and dependency can stand in the way of effective PMP. It is necessary to assess for passive-dependent and passive aggressive personality traits. Passive and dependent patients have to be encouraged to take responsibility for how they feel and for doing things to get better. They have to be assisted to become progressively more self-reliant

and self-assertive. As they develop coping skills and increased self-efficacy, they often gain better control over their anxiety, which can reduce pain.

- *Warmth versus coldness.* Patients who are cold and distant need to be assessed for schizoid or schizotypal traits. Sometimes it is easy to confuse distance with shyness or avoidance. The key to the differential diagnosis is the presence of suppressed or repressed emotional reactions by the avoidant individual (i.e., true shyness or avoidance), versus the absence of emotional reactions by the truly schizoid individual (i.e., true distance).

- *Pride and self-esteem versus shame and self-doubt.* Patients assessed to have substantial shame and self-doubt often benefit from assertiveness training as well as cognitive therapy. In addition, these patients may benefit from reprocessing their memories of the traumatic origins of their shame and self-doubt (see Chapter 7).

- *Impulsivity versus emotional and behavioral control.* Impulsive patients need to be assessed to understand the basis of their impulsivity. Impulsivity can be secondary to many factors: head injury; antisocial, borderline, and narcissistic personality disorders; attention deficit disorders; addictions and substance abuse disorders; mental retardation; and other cognitive disorders.

- *Calmness and patience versus impatience, nervousness, and irritability.* If impatience and nervousness are characterological *traits,* the picture will be quite different than if these qualities are *states.* Persistent pain often triggers irritability. In the latter case, self-regulation, reduced arousal, and relaxation training are in order.

- *Good humor versus seriousness.* Patients who are in serious need of help need to feel that the therapist takes them seriously. However, once good therapeutic working rapport is established, it may be possible to use therapeutic humor to dislodge rigid and inflexible beliefs and concepts.

- *Dominance and aggressiveness versus submissiveness.* As with dependency, submissiveness can be used in the service of the therapy, and so can dominance. Dominant or aggressive patients can be helped to generate their own coping solutions. A permissive approach works best. Submissive patients typically will respond well to a directive approach, which can then be used (through homework assignments) to build greater self-reliance and independence.

- *Cognitive and task persistence versus impersistence and distractibility.* It is necessary to assess the basis for a patient's apparent impersistence or distractibility. If it is secondary to pain, then learning pain management and pain reduction strategies often can help. If it is secondary to another condition such as an attention deficit disorder or a brain injury, these primary conditions have to be addressed. In

PMP, distractibility sometimes can be used to train the patient to self-distract and divert attention from the pain as a coping strategy.

- *Obsessive-compulsiveness and conscientiousness versus carelessness and negligence.* Conscientiousness and compulsiveness often are therapeutic assets. Conscientious and compulsive patients generally do their homework. However, it can be a debit if it leads a patient to obsess and worry about his or her symptoms.
- *Responsibility versus irresponsibility.* Patients must be helped to take responsibility for how they cope with their pain, as opposed to externalizing blame on, for example, their doctors, for not fixing their pain. However, overresponsibility may need to be a therapeutic target as it typically is associated with feelings of guilt and self-blame.
- *Flexibility versus rigidity.* Structure is important in doing therapy to address prioritized problems and build coping skills. However, when a patient's rigidity gets in the way of learning new pain coping strategies, the therapist must be flexible in devising creative strategies that moderate or reduce the patient's rigidity without causing alienation.

RELEVANT TALENTS AND ABILITIES

Relevant talents and abilities should be assessed:

- *Verbal intelligence.* Verbally intelligent patients are more prone to benefit from conversational and verbal therapies. As a group, they often have higher levels of education.
- *Mechanical intelligence.* With patients who have high mechanical aptitude, it often helps in therapy to use relevant visual and mechanical metaphors.
- *Vocational aptitudes, hobbies, and interests.* It is usually a good idea to devise explanations and rationales in terms that include the patient's relevant aptitudes and interests. This facilitates rapport.
- *Imagery ability.* Everyone constructs images and uses imagery. Therefore, it is important to assess a patient's dominant imagery modalities (i.e., visual, auditory, tactile-kinesthetic, olfactory) and to incorporate those modalities into therapeutic strategies and homework assignments. This can enhance rapport, amplify the effectiveness of therapeutic techniques, and ratify therapeutic phenomena. Pain patients construct and respond to internal images of their pain. Thus, PMP should help patients to develop pain replacement and relief images to counter and replace their noxious and upsetting pain images.
- *Hypnotic ability and responsiveness* (also termed hypnotizability; see Chapters 9–11). It is important to assess a pain patient's level of hypnotic ability and responsiveness. Hypnosis is an excellent modality

for pain management, but it works best when hypnotherapeutic strategies are chosen that are concordant with a patient's hypnotic talents. For patients with minimal hypnotic ability, certain hypnotic strategies can still be effective for pain management, whereas other hypnotic strategies are not likely to be effective. The more hypnotizable a patient is, the greater is the range of hypnotic strategies likely to be applicable and effective.

Assessment Procedures

Personality traits are assessed via clinical interview and history taking, mental status examination, and administration of personality assessment tests such as the Coolidge Axis II Inventory, the Millon Clinical Multiaxial Inventory, the Personality Assessment Inventory, and the Personality Adjective Check List (PACL) (Strack, 1991). The personality theorist George Kelly (1955) advises that a person's personality traits often can be assessed most directly by asking the patient to provide an open-ended self-characterization (e.g., "Please write a few short paragraphs about yourself as you might be described by a close friend, or someone who knows you very well"). In addition, or alternatively, a patient can be asked whether or not each of the preceding personality traits, or *core-role constructs* are self-descriptive (e.g., "Would you say you are 'flexible' or 'rigid'? Which are you more of? 'Conscientious or careless'"?).

Relevant talents and abilities can be assessed via administration of an intelligence test (e.g., the WAIS-R: Wechsler, 1981), a hypnotizability scale (e.g., the Hypnotic Induction Profile: Spiegel & Spiegel, 1978/1987; the Stanford Hypnotic Susceptibility Scales: Weitzenhoffer & Hilgard, 1959; the Hypnotic Ability and Response Profile: see Chapters 10 and 11), and vocational and leisure interest checklists.

PERSONALITY DYSFUNCTION AND PSYCHOPATHOLOGY

It is important to assess for the presence and degree of the following problems: personality disorder traits; a full-blown, *DSM-IV* diagnosable, personality disorder; persistent treatment resistance and alienation; hostility, anger, depression, and anxiety; and permanent impairment and disability. The personality psychopathology typology presented in Chapter 3 is useful for distinguishing between "objective" and "psychogenic" pain patients, and categorizing type and degree of personality dysfunction for treatment planning. "Objective pain patients" are responsive to brief PMP and can be treated effectively with cognitive-behavioral interventions (see Chapters 5–8) and hypnotherapy (see Chapters 9–11). However, each pathognomonic group presents unique treatment challenges.

Patients in Pathognomonic Group I (hostile, impulsive, paranoid) are not treatable with PMP unless a reliable and firm relationship is first developed, and this typically takes a long time. Strong limit-setting is essential. If these patients can be socialized for PMP, the first approach in order is cognitive-behavioral therapy (see Chapters 5–8). Cognitive and behavioral coping skills training interventions often prove most effective with these patients, once there is therapeutic rapport and they have been socialized to psychotherapy. These patients seldom respond well to pain management hypnotherapy, to strategies that involve the induction of sensory or physiological transformations (most trancework and hypnotic strategies), or to psychological uncovering or memory reprocessing strategies.

Patients in Pathognomonic Group II (Hypochondriacal, hysterical, self-defeating) are best treated with a primarily behaviorally oriented, cognitive-behavioral psychotherapy. This approach generally should precede any attempts to use hypnotherapeutic or imagery strategies, which may be perceived as paranormal or magical. Once a firm cognitive-behavioral foundation is laid, and such a patient is socialized to the psychotherapy, it may be advisable to begin employing hypnotherapeutic and imagery strategies to teach the patient additional pain coping strategies such as distraction and symptom alteration and transformation. It is advisable to reserve hypnotic and other uncovering and memory-reprocessing strategies such as EMDR for last (see Chapters 7 and 9), after a firm foundation of coping and self-regulation skills has been built. In some cases (e.g., a patient with an unstable personality or who faces many currently active stressors), it may not be advisable to employ such strategies at all.

Patients in Pathognomonic Group III (narcissistic, borderline, antisocial), in our experience, are the least treatable with PMP. It is seldom possible to do brief, time-limited, psychotherapy with these patients, who typically have other pressing manifest and hidden agendas.

Patients in Pathognomonic Group IV (PTSD) are best treated with cognitive-behavioral psychotherapy and hypnotherapy for reprocessing traumatic memories and building coping skills (see Chapters 6–9).

Finally, patients in Pathognomonic Group V (secondary gains) are best treated with cognitive-behavioral psychotherapy and hypnotherapy for the building of coping skills and for active case management.

Assessment Procedures

A patient's type and degree of personality dysfunction, psychopathology, and maladjustment are assessed via clinical interview and history taking, mental status examination, and administration of personality and psychopathology assessment tests such as the Coolidge Axis II Inventory, the Millon Clinical Multiaxial Inventory, the Personality Assessment Inventory, the MMPI, and the Symptom Checklist-90 Revised. The Pain Coping Inventory (see Chapter 3) was designed to assess (a) psychological maladjustment (via indices of catastrophizing, stress and anxiety, depression, hostility, paranoia, treatment resistance and alienation), (b) psychological adjustment (via indices of perceived self-efficacy, mental conditioning, positive self-talk, psychological motivation, quality of life), (c) tendencies toward symptom exaggeration and magnification (Extreme Beliefs Frequency, Symptom Magnification Frequency, Patient Alienation Index), (d) pain interference (Behavioral Interference Severity Index) and (e) pain impairment (Global Impairment Index). In addition, the Pain Interference and Impairment Index (see Chapter 3) was designed to measure pain interference and impairment.

PAIN SYMPTOM VALIDITY

Evaluating the validity of a patient's pain complaint refers to forming a judgment about whether the patient's complaint has an objective, unbiased, physical basis. A pain complaint that is judged to have an objective, physical basis is deemed to be valid, and a pain complaint that is judged to be unduly biased or magnified by subjective, psychological issues, or secondary gains, is deemed to be invalid. In actuality, making such a determination should be a matter of degree, not an all-or-nothing judgment. If a patient's pain complaint is magnified or unduly biased, then this information should influence treatment planning to avoid unnecessary, expensive, time-consuming, or invasive interventions. Evaluating the validity of a patient's pain complaint requires assessing a patient for (a) indications of symptom magnification or exaggeration; (b) signs of psychopathology that could motivate a person psychologically to manufacture physical symptoms and emotional distress, or adopt a sick role (e.g., a factitious disorder, or delusional disorder, as classified by the *DSM-IV*); (c) motivations to manufacture pain complaints for secondary gains, such as financial or other rewards (e.g., to collect workers' compensation benefits); and (d) indications of a stress-related psychophysiological disorder associated with increased pain (e.g., nocturnal bruxism, psychophysiological insomnia, muscle contraction or tension headaches, migraine headaches, or a somatoform disorder, as classified by the *DSM-IV*).

Tests and Procedures

  PCI Indices of Symptom Invalidity: Symptom magnification or exaggeration is assessed via several indices on the Pain Coping Inventory, as discussed in Chapter 3. Two of these are the Extreme Beliefs Frequency and the Symptom Magnification Frequency. Other signs of symptom magnification and exaggeration on the PCI include marked elevations on the Patient Alienation Index, Psychological Maladjustment Severity Index, and the Global Impairment Index. These indices, interpreted along with high scores on the Physical Severity Index and Behavioral Interference Severity Index, suggest a high likelihood of pain and symptom invalidity. Additionally, high Percentages of Extreme Ratings on the Stress Symptoms Checklist (i.e., SSCL ratings of 6 or 7) can also reflect pain symptom exaggeration.

PPQ-PAC Indices of Symptom Invalidity: Indications of symptom invalidity and pain complaint exaggeration also are obtained from six patterns of relationships among indices on the PPQ-PAC:

1. Look at the magnitude of each of the calculated Pain Rating Indices (PRIs) (Total, Sensory, Affective-Evaluative, Affective, Evaluative). The patient's PRIs are compared with the normative tables (Tables 2.5, 2.6, 2.7). PRIs above the 90th percentile are suspicious.
2. Look at the relationships between the PPQ-PAC PRIs. When a patient's Affective and Evaluative PRIs are markedly higher than that patient's Sensory PRIs, that is one sign of possible psychological magnification of the complaint of pain.
3. Look at the Total Percentage of Words Chosen (PWC). High PWCs relative to the normative data could be of some concern.
4. Qualitatively, look for the frequent selection of extreme, infrequently used pain descriptors connoting punitiveness, misery, suffering, fear, and autonomic distress (e.g., sickening, suffocating, punishing, cruel, vicious, torturing, terrifying, dreadful, miserable, agonizing, unbearable, killing, mysterious, out of control, disabling, hopeless).
5. On both the PPQ pain drawing and the patient's verbal report, look for evidence of an anatomically inconsistent distribution of pain locations.
6. Always considered highly significant when present is a patient's report of being in constant pain. Ewin (1986, 1992) has coined the term constant pain syndrome to describe cases wherein a patient denies ever having any freedom from pain—even while asleep. Such patients often have a strong psychogenic component to their pain. On the PPQ-PAC, these patients can be identified from the following indicators: (a) They indicate on Question 20 of the PPQ-Pain History and Status Questionnaire, and on Item D under PPQ-Pain Intensity Ratings and Pain Drawings, that their pain is present 100% of the time; and (b) in response to Item C under PPQ-Pain Intensity Ratings and Pain Drawings, they circle the words *continuous, constant, always there,* and *never goes away.*

Assessing Possible Response Bias: When multiple indicators of symptom invalidity, magnification, or exaggeration are found in an evaluation, this calls into question the validity of all the assessment findings. If a patient is claiming cognitive impairment as one side effect of his or her pain, then the following tests may be useful for assessing a patient's response bias toward exaggerating pain and symptom-related impairment. The Computerized Assessment of Response Bias (CARB) (Allen & Cox, 1995), and the Word Memory Test (WMT) (Green, Allen, & Astner, 1996) are two brief, computer-administered, cognitive performance tests that were designed to provide measures of patient effort and motivation. The CARB utilizes a forced-choice visual digit recognition paradigm (also known as "Explicit Alternative Testing") that has become the standard in attempts to measure feigned memory and recall deficits (Hall & Pritchard, 1996; Lezak, 1995). The WMT is based on a simple, repeated trials, verbal learning paradigm, as is exemplified by the California Verbal Learning Test (Delis, Kramer, Kaplan, & Ober, 1987) and the Verbal Paired Associates subtest of the Wechsler Memory Scale-Revised (Wechsler, 1987).

Both the CARB and the WMT can identify patients who underperform in the direction of impairment on other neuropsychological tests. The authors report very low base rates of failure in severely brain injured populations that comprise the tests' normative groups. In reality, the tasks are very easy, but the patient is not primed to think so. Therefore, poor performance below a certain level on either of these cognitive performance tests, is interpreted to reflect poor effort and motivation as opposed to a lack of true cognitive ability. However, due to the variability in test performance and the phenomenology characteristic of feigning and exaggerating patients, it is advisable to use both tests to maximize convergent validity. The WMT may be administered orally, and also provides an objective screening assessment for genuine memory impairment utilizing the same verbal paired associates word list in three additional subtests. When a patient's performance on these cognitive measures is indicative of significant response bias, poor effort, and motivation to perform well, this calls into question the validity of the patient's symptomatic complaints, and all the rest of the assessment findings. Both the CARB and the WMT can be obtained from CogniSyst, Inc., Durham, North Carolina (Tel: 800-799-4654).

The validity of a patient's pain complaints is assessed via administration of multiple measures including indices of symptom exaggeration, symptom magnification, and extreme ratings on the Pain Coping Inventory and the Stress Symptoms Checklist, indices of response bias and poor effort on cognitive symptom validity testing, high PRIs on the MPQ or PPQ-PAC, selection of infrequent or extreme words on the MPQ or PPQ-PAC, high Percentages of Words Chosen (PWCs) on the MPQ or PPQ-PAC, and an anatomically inconsistent distribution of pain locations on pain drawings and verbal report. When these invalidity indices are high, it calls into question all of a patient's symptomatic complaints. This has important treatment implications. If a patient exaggerates or feigns symptoms and deficits, treatment baselines and outcomes cannot be assessed reliably or validly. If this is the case, one question worth asking might be, What is motivating the patient in the first place?

Treatment Goals

Reasonable treatment goals would include (a) assessing the motivational factors that underlie the patient's tendencies to exaggerate symptoms and deficits, and exert poor effort on cognitive tasks; (b) helping the patient make more objective, less extreme, and less critical judgments of his or her own experiences and of other people.

"Adaptive copers" are unlikely to be motivated to expend significant energy feigning or exaggerating symptoms and deficits. They also are unlikely to be motivated to underperform on psychological, neuropsychological, and cognitive tests in an assessment situation. On the other hand, some "dysfunctional pain copers" may be motivated to prove the validity of their complaints, and in so doing, actually overdo it. Finally, some "interpersonally distressed" pain patients harbor extreme hostility and anger. Their strongly negative evaluative tendencies may lead them to make extreme judgments that are reflected in their responses to pain assessment and other psychological instruments. The following case study provides a complete Report of Psychological Pain Evaluation of a patient who presented with features of both a "dysfunctional" and "interpersonally distressed" pain coper. This case illustrates how a patient can act out his or her main problems in the context of a consultive evaluation, making it impossible to administer all the intended assessment procedures, but nevertheless, revealing a wealth of clinically important information about the patient. The following Psychological Report also illustrates a number of salient risk factors for continued pain-related impairment and disability.

Case Example: Chronic Pain with Psychological Factors

Ms. A. was a 30-year-old, divorced female (and mother of a 10-year-old) who had been referred by the Employee Health Service (EHS) of the hospital where she had worked as a Physical Therapy Assistant. The patient had injured her back in a fall at work, approximately 3 months previously, and was on partial disability, having been reassigned to a part-time, light-duty job. The Nurse Manager of the EHS was concerned about this woman's excessive use of pain medications, which had been prescribed by various physicians. In an initial phone contact, the Nurse Manager told the evaluating psychologist that the patient was depressed and was exhibiting excessive pain behaviors, and that the EHS was at a loss about how to manage the case. The Nurse Manager stated her hope that, after evaluating the patient, the psychologist would be able to provide patient management recommendations and offer some direction to her service on the case. Six initial visits were preapproved by the Hospital EHS's workers' compensation insurance carrier.

REPORT OF PSYCHOLOGICAL PAIN EVALUATION

Patient: _A.A._   **Date of Injury:** _05/06/95_

Patient Age (DOB): _30 (04/04/65)_

Occupation: _Physical therapy assistant (disabled)_

Referral Source: _B.B., R.N., EHS Nurse Manager_

Date of Evaluation: _08/12/95_   **Date of Report:** _08/13/95_

Dear Ms. B:

Thank you for referring Ms. A. for psychological consultation. I saw her on the above date for evaluation and this is a concise report of my findings and impressions.

Brief Background

Ms. A. injured her back in a fall that took place at work approximately 3 months ago, on May 6, 1995. Until then, she had been coping well despite an old back injury dating back approximately 4 years. At that earlier time, she had injured herself in a work-related lifting accident, and had been diagnosed she said, with several protruding lumbar discs and low back strain/sprain. She nevertheless recovered, given time and physical therapy, and up to the point of this recent injury, she was working full-time and going to school to earn her Associate Degree in Physical Therapy. In addition to working and being a student, Ms. A., who is divorced, is a full-time single parent of a 10-year-old daughter.

Since her fall on May 6, Ms. A. has been treating orthopedically with Dr. Fixit, who treated her for her first back injury, and Dr. Exer, a physiatrist in the hospital's rehabilitation medicine department. However, several other physicians (e.g., from the ER) have also prescribed pain medications including Tylenol with codeine, Relafen, which is a nonsteroidal anti-inflammatory drug (or NSAID), and Darvocet. She has been unable to resume full-time work, and currently is working two 4-hour days per week in Employee Health. She has also reported that she has had to quit school since hurting herself, which she states she is very depressed about.

Procedures Completed

Review of available medical records

Clinical interview and mental status examination

The Philadelphia Pain Questionnaire

Pain History and Status Form

Pain Adjective Checklist

Pain Drawing

Note: Several other pain assessment and psychodiagnostic instruments were presented, but the patient was unable to complete them.

Current Evaluation Findings

Chief Complaints. Ms. A. presented as being quite upset and depressed about her current situation. Her chief complaint is the pain and what it is doing to her life. She appeared to understand that the reason she was referred to me was "for help in dealing with the pain." She stated that her pain is *constant* and that it averages anywhere from a "6 to an 8" on a "0 to 10" pain intensity scale. It is reported as located in her low back, and described as a "grinding pressure" that spreads down both of her legs. She states that she has to lie down frequently because of the pain, which is reported to be worsened by general and repetitive activities such as sitting, standing, and walking. She cannot lift anything. She understands that she "needs to get control of her life again and deal with the pain."

Behavioral Observations and Mental Status. Ms. A.'s current mental status may be summarized as follows: She is alert and fully oriented. Appearance, personal attire, and hygiene are fine and unremarkable. She ambulated without an assistive device. She drove herself to this appointment. Her predominant mood state is characterized as moderately anxious, markedly depressed, and markedly angry. She was tearful at times. She was clearly uncomfortable about being here, and was fairly guarded.

Pain Behaviors. She both reported and evidenced several notable pain behaviors:

1. She has to lie down frequently to rest and to offset the increasing back and leg pain attendant to activities. She admits to excessive downtime, and an activity schedule that is ruled by pain. On a checklist, she checked the following activities as worsening her pain: bending, exercising, lifting, physical therapy, sitting, standing, walking, working; and the following activities as making it better: changing positions, laying down, aquatic therapy, taking medication.

2. It was evidently difficult for her to sit up straight for more than a few minutes. Because of pain, she tends to sit on her side with her legs curled up. I offered her a firm supportive chair, but she preferred to sit on the soft couch in the above position.

3. She had difficulty completing the paper-and-pencil part of this evaluation. Despite having been given ample time and opportunity to take breaks to comfort herself, she was only able to complete about one-third to one-half of the forms and questionnaires. This task made her angry. She felt that she should have been provided with these forms beforehand.

4. She stated that she cannot sleep well at night because she cannot get into a comfortable position.

5. She considers herself anywhere from 70% to 100% disabled for the following activities (*Note:* These are activities she offered and *not* from a checklist): "working out" (100%), "running-biking" (100%), "walking" with her daughter (90%), "household chores" (100%), "going to the movies" (95%), "working" (70%), "going out with friends" (90%), "skiing" (100%), "day trips" with her daughter (100%), "school activities" (70%), "going to school" (100%), and "shows" (100%). Although activities such as day trips

and shows are not in the same class as activities such as skiing, they are all rated as "100% disabled."

Medications. Ms. A. has all the previously mentioned pain medicines in her possession. She denies taking much pain medicine, but is vague about how much she does in fact ingest. In addition, she stated that she could not tolerate 25 mg of Elavil at bedtime because it made her too lethargic, and she took herself off it. Nevertheless, she stated that her pain medicine is a major source of relief (quantified by her at 80%), and her self-reported, primary pain treatment is "bed rest with heat."

Philadelphia Pain Questionnaire (PPQ) findings. On the PPQ-Pain Adjective Checklist, Ms. A's responses resulted in a very high Total Pain Rating Index of 92%. This index takes into account both affective-evaluative and sensory dimensions of her pain. She also evidenced equally very high Sensory (91.7%), Affective (91.7%), and Evaluative (92.9%) Pain Rating Indices. These were all at or above the 90th percentile relative to the test's norms. The descriptive subcategories (along with their associated Pain Rating Indices) that she chose as primarily characterizing the felt intensity of her pain experience were: affective-fatigue (average rated intensity: 100%), affective-punitive (75%), affective-fear (75%), evaluative-misery (100%), evaluative suffering (91.7%), sensory-temporal (100%), sensory-spatial (100%), sensory-punctate pressure (75%), sensory-incisive pressure (100%), sensory-additive pressure (100%), sensory-soreness (100%), and sensory-numbing (75%). All these Pain Rating Indices were markedly elevated based on the test's norms.

The primary, endorsed pain descriptors composing the preceding indices were "troublesome, tiring, exhausting, depressing, cruel, frightening, annoying, nagging, miserable, unbearable, hopeless, throbbing, spreading, stabbing, piercing, sharp, pressing, heavy, tender, sore, aching, tingling, and numb" (all individually rated very highly for intensity). On a visual analog scale, or VAS, her *Present Pain Index* was marked at 65%. She indicated that her pain is present 100% of the time (constantly).

Diagnostic Summary and Recommendations

I shall now go over my summary diagnostic impressions of Ms. A. and offer several recommendations. I discussed these with Ms. A. yesterday. My current diagnostic impressions are summarized as follows (based on the *DSM-IV*):

Axis I   1. (307.89) Chronic Pain Disorder Associated with Both Psychological Factors and a General Medical Condition.

2. (309.28) Chronic Adjustment Disorder with Mixed Anxiety and Depressed Mood.

3. (304.00) Rule out Opioid/Analgesic Dependence.

Axis II   Formal personality disorder diagnosis deferred. Rule out presence of maladaptive personality traits such as passivity and dependency.

Axis III (724.2) Low Back Pain Syndrome.

Axis IV Psychosocial problems/stressors: occupational, divorce, parenting stress, financial stress.

Axis V   Global Assessment of Functioning (with respect to psychological, occupational and social functional criteria): Current—45 out of 100 (serious symptoms and impairment in social and occupational functioning). Highest Level of Functioning in the Past Year (Estimated)—75 out of 100 (slight impairment).

1. Ms. A.'s pain condition has already become chronic (i.e., lasted for longer than 3 months), and although it is associated with a significant sprain/strain injury to her lumbosacral spine and herniation of her L4/5 discs (based on Dr. Fixit's reports), it also is associated with psychological factors that will need to be addressed, if she is to recover from the behavioral aspects of her pain condition. She appears to have a constant pain syndrome in that she reports that severe pain is present 100% of the time. This is almost always associated with psychological factors.

2. Additionally, this person suffers from a chronic adjustment disorder associated with her inability, up to this point, to accept her condition and do something constructive about it.

3. The issue of opioid dependence should be ruled out. This means determining if (a) she has reached tolerance, (b) if there is drug-seeking, (c) if she has begun to take increasing amounts of her prescribed analgesics, and (d) if there are withdrawal symptoms when she does not take opioid analgesics.

4. It is my opinion that some maladaptive personality traits may be operating that are self-defeating. These include a greater degree of passivity and dependence than is healthy. These traits, if they are present, would impede her recovery and rehabilitation.

5. Finally, Ms. A.'s Global Assessment of Functioning now, is markedly impaired (rated 45/100). Based on the information I had available, her GAF was much higher before she sustained her current injury (i.e., estimated at 75/100).

Summary

Ms. A. presents as a high risk for the development of a disabling chronic pain syndrome. Her risk factors include (1) her report of a constant pain syndrome, (2) a high frequency of pain behaviors as discussed, coupled with (3) her marked levels of depression, anxiety, and anger. These three factors constitute a poor prognostic combination. In addition, several other psychosocial and physical stressors over the past couple of years in Ms. A.'s life, have made her personal struggle harder including her divorce, a recent custody battle with her ex-husband, and an earlier injury to her knee this year sustained en route to a nursing home. In addition, Ms. A. stated that she never fully recovered from her original work-related back injury 4 years ago—that the pain had always been in the background.

Currently, Ms. A. is feeling quite alienated and depressed. She offered that she is "not suicidal" although she admitted, "I'm very upset and cry all the time." However, I do have concerns about her risk for self-destructive behavior. I was not able to conduct a thorough assessment of this in our initial session, but this does need to be followed up immediately.

I told Ms. A. that the outlook for her recovery is bleak unless she becomes willing to examine closely, in a confidential psychological counseling situation, "how she is holding herself back" from "getting beyond this current crisis and moving on with her life." She herself asked the question, I think rhetorically (it wasn't answered), "Am I holding myself back?" That she asked this question is a positive sign. However, she also feels "beaten down." If she has a victim frame of mind, this presents a poor prognosis and will have to be addressed. My point is that for Ms. A. to enable herself to recover from her current pain state, she will have to take responsibility for how she feels and what she does to cope. Up to this point in time, it is my impression that she has not taken responsibility. In fact, she stated her impression that she has "seen a 'gazillion' doctors and all they do is give me stuff for my pain. Nobody's doing anything for the pain!" Thus, up to this point, her approach to the problem has been passive, looking to doctors to take away the pain and make her better. This patient needs consistent direction and pain management, right now. I think it is imperative that she be referred immediately to a well-thought-out pain program.

One option, as you and I have already discussed, is to refer her immediately to an intensive, outpatient pain rehabilitation program (ideally interdisciplinary), such as are available through one of the University Hospitals. Alternatively, if I were to work with her, which I would be happy to do, we would need to coordinate the other aspects of her program through your office. Initially, I would consider it essential that she attend Pain Management Psychotherapy (PMP) sessions with me twice weekly, and that she start a closely supervised, graded, physical therapy program focusing primarily on active reconditioning. Thus far, she reported that the regimen of passive PT modalities had not helped. She did rate the aquatics exercise therapy as helpful (this is active as opposed to passive).

On the medicinal front, only one physician should prescribe pain medicine, with no exceptions. That physician would need to see her weekly at the outset. Consistent medical monitoring is an essential component of the program. I would recommend that the prescribing physician shift her to an exclusively time-contingent as opposed to a pain-contingent medication regimen. This is something that, if I were to be her Pain Management Psychotherapist (or PMP), I would collaborate with the prescribing physician in setting up and monitoring.

In addition, an effective Pain Management Psychotherapy (PMP) treatment plan for Ms. A. would focus on (1) sleep improvement; (2) scheduling activity quotas (a) to learn pacing, (b) to shape increased endurance, and (c) to increase positively reinforcing activities; (3) relaxation therapy; (4) cognitive therapy to alleviate depression, anger, and alienation; (5) medication-control therapy to establish time-contingent analgesic dosing; and (5) supportive therapy to decrease unhealthy levels of alienation.

Once again, thank you for giving me the opportunity of consulting. I would be happy to treat your patient if she were to present for Pain Management Psychotherapy, and I would be glad to work with you in setting up an effective pain program as suggested above.

Very truly yours,

Bruce N. Eimer, Ph.D., ABPP

SCHEMATIZING BRIEF PMP WITH
THE ARMOR MODEL

A useful algorithm for schematizing brief PMP treatment planning is spelled out by the acronym ARMOR. The "A" in ARMOR stands for Assessment. At minimum, this covers assessing a patient's experience of pain, and the patient's level of pain-related disability, depression, and anxiety. The "R" stands for Relaxation Therapy. At minimum, this involves generalized lowered arousal training, teaching basic body awareness and muscle relaxation skills (such as progressive muscle relaxation), and sleep improvement. The "M" stands for Mental Imagery Training. At minimum, this involves helping a patient generate pain replacement relief images for perceptually altering and transforming pain sensations and symptoms, and diverting attention from pain. The "O" stands for Origins Work with the pain. This involves reviewing and reprocessing core pain-related beliefs and the emotionally stressful experiences associated with their formation. The final letter "R," stands for Rehearsal of coping strategies. These include cognitive strategies such as rational responding, cognitive disputation, cognitive restructuring, self-instructional training, stress inoculation, and cognitive and imagery rehearsal.

For many patients, excessive psychopathology and maladjustment, marked psychological instability, time limitations, or obstacles associated with the treatment setting make it unfeasible to do Origins Work because it requires ample time and a stabilized patient. An appropriate Assessment is performed with every patient. Relaxation Therapy, Mental Imagery Training, and Rehearsal of coping strategies are conducted with the majority of pain patients seen.

SCHEMATIZING PMP WITH THE "BASIC ID"

A. Lazarus's (1989) model of the "BASIC ID" is also helpful in schematizing a PMP treatment plan (Eimer, 1988). First, a patient's pain problems can be broken down into "Behavioral, Affective, Sensory-Physiological, Imagery, Cognitive, Interpersonal, and Drug" categories, or modalities. The first letters of these modalities spell the acronym, "BASIC ID." Pain patients present with Behavioral deficits and excesses, Affective problems (such as depression and anxiety), Sensory-Physiological problems (e.g., pain sensations), negative Images associated with pain and suffering (e.g., daydreams, noxious images, intrusive ideation, bad dreams), Cognitive distortions and negative cognitions, Interpersonal conflicts, and problems related to the abuse of Drugs (e.g., pain medicine), and other substances. A patient's constellation of problems in each of these seven modalities comprises what can be called a "BASIC ID Modality Profile."

Second, PMP goals and methods can also be broken down into Behavioral, Affective, Sensory-Physiological, Imagery, Cognitive, Interpersonal, and Drug categories or modalities. PMP goals within each modality can be realized through the application of PMP methods and techniques from the same modality as well as from other modalities. Behavioral goals (e.g., reducing pain behaviors or improving sleep behaviors) can be attained through the application of behavioral techniques (e.g., activity scheduling, stimulus control, shaping, and operant conditioning), cognitive techniques (e.g., cognitive rehearsal, self-instructional training, reviewing advantages and disadvantages), imagery techniques (e.g., imaginal rehearsal, pain replacement imagery), sensory techniques (e.g., Relaxation Therapy), interpersonal techniques (intervening with significant others), and so on. Likewise, cognitive goals (e.g., modifying cognitive distortions and negative beliefs related to pain) can be furthered through the application of techniques from other modalities in addition to the cognitive modality (e.g., conducting behavioral experiments, keeping pain diaries, working with imagery).

Conducting a "BASIC ID Analysis"

As part of the assessment, it is often helpful to conduct a "BASIC ID Analysis" of a patient's presenting pain-related problems (Eimer, 1988; Lazarus, 1989). Constructing a Modality Profile involves asking the patient questions about each modality as it relates to the target problem. The following are some examples:

- *Behavior.* "What do you do when you are in pain? How does your behavior change?"
- *Affect.* "What emotions do you feel? Do you feel sad, angry, anxious, nervous, what?"
- *Sensations.* "How do you experience the pain? What does it feel like? Describe the sensations."
- *Imagery.* "What kinds of pictures or images flash in your mind's eye when your pain flares up?"
- *Cognition.* "What kinds of thoughts do you usually have before, during, and after a pain flare-up? What do you usually tell yourself?"
- *Interpersonal.* "Describe any typical interpersonal interactions that occur when you are in pain."
- *Drugs.* "Tell me what medicines you take, when you take them, and the dosages. Do you use any other remedies?"

A Modality Analysis Form for recording the results about each modality is provided in Appendix Q-1.

CONSTRUCTING A "MODALITY PROFILE"

By recording the patient's answers to each of the questions on the Modality Analysis Form, the therapist can construct an initial, or first-order, "Modality Profile" of a patient's pain problems. For example, starting with her behavioral modality, one patient informed us that when she felt the onset of a headache, she would stop doing whatever she was doing, go into a dark room, lie down, and apply a cold pack to her head. In turn, doing this (the behavioral modality) made her angry that she had to stop what she was doing (affective modality); her pain usually worsened anyhow (sensory modality); and she often would lie there and have intrusive flashbacks of the period in her life when she had cancer (imagery modality) while berating herself for being weak and vulnerable (cognitive modality). In addition, she worried that her husband, who was usually supportive, would nonetheless leave her (interpersonal modality), and she usually took several Extra-Strength Excedrin (drug modality).

This patient was helped to track confirmatory data between office visits with daily entries in a BASIC ID Pain Diary (see Appendix Q-2). The diary format can be a useful tool for verbally oriented patients, who can track each component of the BASIC ID for each pain flare-up or discrete pain episode (e.g., a headache). The form provides guiding questions, and the data recorded are reviewed in session with the patient as they may suggest important therapeutic targets.

The next step is to go down through each of the patient's first-order modalities (see the Modality Analysis Form) and construct a second-order BASIC ID Modality Profile for each first-order modality, or just for the ones that are relevant. The patient being discussed stated that her two predominant affective states associated with her headache problem were anger and fear. She usually felt angry about being victimized by the headaches, but she also feared that her next headache would be worse and would cripple her. When she felt very angry (affective modality), she would withdraw or snap out at her husband unintentionally (behavioral and interpersonal modalities). In contrast, when she felt anxious and fearful (affective modality), she would withdraw and cry (behavioral modality) and hope that her husband would come to reassure or rescue her (interpersonal modality). If he did not, then she would get angry (affective modality). She also realized that when she became really angry (affective modality), her pain sensations worsened. This would lead her to say things she later regretted (behavioral modality) and to think negative and distressing thoughts (cognitive modality). She stated that she was also likely to pick an argument with her husband or her mother at such times (behavioral and interpersonal modalities). In contrast, when she felt anxious and fearful (affective modality), she would cry (behavioral modality), remember the days when she had cancer (imagery modality), catastrophize about worse things happening to her (cognitive modality), withdraw, and act passively (behavioral modality), waiting to be rescued by her husband (interpersonal modality).

A BASIC ID Analysis can help in translating vague problem statements and complaints into operational terms with clear behavioral referents. This can assist a clinician in identifying (a) problems to target, (b) goals to attain, and (c) the order of priority for addressing and treating the problems. In addition, constructing first-order and second-order BASIC ID Modality Profiles can assist a clinician in conducting a functional behavioral analysis of a patient's pain complaints. This means identifying the ABC's (i.e., the "antecedents, behaviors, and consequents") or "firing order," of the components of a patient's reported problems (Lazarus, 1989). The patient in this example stated that when she felt angry but held her feelings in and did not express them in some way (antecedent), she would begin to feel headachy. Then, she would "take pills and go lie down" (behaviors). One typical consequent was that her husband would do things for her, and then she would feel "lousy" and berate herself for being "such an invalid."

PART TWO

COGNITIVE-BEHAVIORAL PAIN MANAGEMENT

CHAPTER 5

A Cognitive-Behavioral Model of Pain and Suffering

Don't defy the diagnosis, try to defy the verdict.

—Norman Cousins

GATE CONTROL THEORY AND THE COGNITIVE REVOLUTION IN PAIN MANAGEMENT

Melzack and Wall's book *The Challenge of Pain* (1982) elaborated on Melzack and Wall's (1965) "gate control theory" of pain developed 17 years earlier and primed the field of pain research for the cognitive revolution that had begun in the fields of both academic and clinical psychology. According to Melzack and Wall, within the dorsal horn of the spinal cord, a "pain gate" existed that was influenced by two types of specialized neural fibers. One type, made up of the C-fibers, was hypothesized to open the gate and permit pain sensations to ascend up the spinal cord to the brain. Conversely, the other type, the A-fibers, served to close the gate when stimulated and thereby inhibit the ascent of pain messages. Several factors were offered as explanations for the mechanisms serving to close this gate.

ESSENTIALS OF THE NEUROPHYSIOLOGICAL MODEL

The central concept in Melzack and Wall's neurophysiological and cognitive model is that all pain is a complex centrally processed event in the nervous system as opposed to being a peripherally determined unidimensional sensory phenomenon. Cortical and subcortical brain mechanisms sending messages down through descending or efferent neural pathways

149

were postulated to be operative in the perception of pain in that they modulated the ascent of pain impulses up the spinal cord. Pain sensations could be blocked at several neural levels. At the first level, counterstimulation to peripheral nerves could conceivably stimulate the faster A-fibers, which could inhibit impulses transmitted by the slower C-fibers when they interact in the dorsal horns. Similar inhibition at the dorsal horns was assumed by Shealy and his associates (Shealy, 1976) to be the basis of pain relief as a result of implantation of dorsal column spinal cord stimulators. However, as pain sensations traveled further up the spinal column, other factors were hypothesized to influence the final outcome (i.e., how pain is perceived) through their influence and action on the descending pathways. One such factor is sympathetically mediated arousal. A second factor is stimulation of serotonergic and noradrenergic neurotransmitter pathways. A third factor is stimulation of the body's production of internal or neuroendocrinologic opioids, endorphins, and enkephalins. Finally, a fourth factor comprises cognitive events.

THE ROLE OF COGNITION

According to the gate control theory, pain perception was hypothesized to be largely a cognitive event or process influenced by physiological, neurochemical, motivational, situational, contextual, affective, behavioral, attitudinal, philosophical, and informational, as well as religious and spiritual variables. However, cognitive factors were postulated to affect pain perception at all ascending neural levels of pain transmission from nociceptor input up through subcortical (i.e., thalamic) to cortical pathways. In fact, at the highest central nervous system levels (i.e., higher cortical brain centers), cognitive factors (i.e., beliefs, attitudes, expectations) were thought to play the primary role in opening or closing the pain gate. At the first level of cognitive influence, the cognitive variable of a person's conceptual constructs for classifying and discriminating nociceptive stimulation plays a first-order role. At higher levels, the cognitive variables of beliefs, attitudes, expectations, and past history are central in influencing the ascending pain messages by activating the spinal cord's descending pathways. These descending pathways either inhibit or facilitate what goes up the ascending pathways.

The perception of pain comprises three basic dimensions: the sensory-discriminative, cognitive-evaluative, and motivational-affective (Melzack, 1996; Melzack & Wall, 1965, 1982). Thus, pain experience is affected by the interaction of the cognitive and discriminative dimensions through which pain is sensed and perceived (i.e., the sensory-discriminative dimension), the primary cognitive constructs with which pain is evaluated and its implications judged (i.e., the cognitive-evaluative dimension), and the motivational forces that affect the pain sufferer's emotional reactions (i.e., the motivational-affective dimension). Mood states affect perceptions of pain qualities and pain severity directly and through the mediating variables of automatic thoughts, self-talk, activated beliefs, and underlying schema. Depressive and anxious mood states often exacerbate chronic pain:

Case Example

A 44-year-old male construction worker had sustained neck and back injuries in a fall from a scaffold on the job three years before. In addition to his chronic neck, back, and leg pain, he suffered from depressive episodes and mood swings. He would frequently ruminate about his inability to return to the "only line of work I'm good at." When his older son dropped out of college, this triggered a chain of depressive thoughts such as "my son's throwing his life away like I did" and "I'm not trained to do anything else." Concomitantly, he developed a hyperventilation syndrome and complained of not being able to catch his breath or even breathe at times. His pain level also increased as well as his intake of alcohol, and he requested that his doctor prescribe stronger pain medicine.

On the other hand, positive emotional states such as intense, pleasant, emotional involvement, absorption in an activity, the drive to accomplish something, satisfaction in an accomplishment, dedication, devotion to another person or a cause, and the feeling of gratitude can inadvertently ward off pain or decrease its felt intensity:

Case Example

A 47-year-old financial investment advisor and money manager suffered from chronic pain in his left knee related to capsulitis, chronic bilateral shoulder and arm pain related to bursitis, and chronic middle and low back pain related to degenerative changes in his thoracic and lumbar spine. He usually complained of considerable daily pain which he medicated with aspirin, acetaminophen, or ibuprofen. He called his therapist to cancel his appointment with the explanation, "I'm sitting at my desk with over $400,000 to invest and feeling great. I don't notice any of my pain and I have been so busy that I forgot to take any pain medicine since yesterday. If I think about it, I feel the pain, but at this point, I say, who cares?"

THE COGNITIVE REVOLUTION IN PAIN MANAGEMENT

Turk et al.'s (1983) book *Pain and Behavioral Medicine: A Cognitive-Behavioral Perspective* launched the cognitive revolution in pain management. Their book provided an exhaustive review of the pain and cognitive-behavior therapy literature up to that time and included a model for implementing a structured, goal-oriented, educative, short-term, cognitive-behavioral pain treatment program, aimed at teaching pain patients useful coping skills. Turk et al.'s (1983) psychoeducational curriculum for chronic pain patients is modular and amenable to individual and group administration.

In Turk et al.'s program, pain patients are provided with information about pain mechanisms and are socialized to a cognitive-behavioral model of pain management. The therapy is self-help oriented, and aimed at teaching patients skills for identifying, evaluating, and responding to their dysfunctional thoughts and beliefs using techniques for changing thinking, mood, and behavior. Patients are taught behavioral coping skills (such as pacing and shaping), cognitive coping skills (such as self-instructional training, stress inoculation training, and responding to automatic thoughts and self-talk), imagery-based coping skills (such as pain symptom-transformation imagery, attentional diversion, and distraction), interpersonal coping skills (such as assertion training), and physiological coping skills (i.e., relaxation techniques). Turk et al. provide scripts for what to say and do with patients at different stages in the treatment. They draw heavily from Meichenbaum's (1985) pioneering work on stress inoculation training and self-instructional training. Building from this foundation as well as from the cognitive therapy model of Beck, Rush, Shaw, and Emery (1979), Turk et al.'s (1983) treatment planning model was guided by the idea that it is essential to translate vague complaints into terms that are amenable to productive therapeutic intervention:

Case Example

Mrs. W. was a 36-year-old freelance journalist who had bilateral carpal tunnel syndrome of 5 years' duration. When initially seen by the first author, there was obviously marked deconditioning of both upper extremities along with notable muscular atrophy. She had been referred by another therapist to try Eye Movement Desensitization and Reprocessing (EMDR) therapy (see Chapter 7), which she had heard about and hoped might help her with her pain. Her primary goal was to overcome her deconditioning, but she realized that first she had to overcome her mental blocks, which had prevented her from making any notable progress in physical therapy and rehabilitation. Initial therapy sessions focused on a cognitive approach to identifying her negative beliefs related to her pain and her disability. After a few sessions of cognitive therapy along these lines, she came to realize, "My thinking really does affect my pain levels." She began to believe with conviction, "When I allow myself to think negatively on a consistent basis, I get depressed and/or afraid to do anything for fear of having a setback like I had three and a half years ago. I also then pay more attention to my pain, I overprotect my hands, and I hurt more. Wow, it's really amazing how your thoughts can actually make your pain worse!"

A major strength of Turk et al.'s program was its early emphasis on equipping the pain patient with strategies, or algorithms for coping with different situations associated with pain and flare-ups. Patients are coached to use positive self-statements at each phase of a pain flare-up (i.e., preparing for an anticipated flare-up; dealing with the pain; managing the worst moments of the episode, and administering self-reinforcement) and are taught how to identify and cognitively counter negative self-talk that could lead to depression. They are also coached in self-monitoring of their symptoms. Other key modules teach active imagery strategies for transforming pain symptoms into something more manageable and help patients develop distraction and attentional diversion techniques. Their program also includes psychosocial and interpersonal modules to address and modify the role of significant others in the maintenance of a patient's pain-related disability.

COGNITIVE THERAPY

Cognitive therapy is a structured, time-limited, problem-focused, goal-oriented, and educative form of psychotherapy. It is present oriented, emphasizes a collaborative therapist-patient relationship, and encourages active participation in the treatment by both therapist and patient. In cognitive therapy, patients are taught skills for identifying, evaluating, and responding to their dysfunctional thoughts and beliefs. Techniques for changing thinking, mood, and behavior are often employed (J. Beck, 1995; Beck, Freeman, & Associates, 1990; Freeman et al., 1990; Freeman & Reinecke, 1995).

THE RELEVANCE OF COGNITIVE THERAPY TO PAIN MANAGEMENT

The basic tenet of the cognitive model of emotional disorders is that people are upset not as much by the things that happen to them as by their interpretations of personal events (A. Beck, 1976; Beck, Rush, Shaw, & Emery, 1979; Ellis, 1996; Ellis & Dryden, 1987; Freeman et al., 1990). As discussed in previous chapters, this principle is especially relevant for understanding the experience of physical pain because the personal or idiosyncratic meaning of pain plays a major role in determining a person's suffering (Beecher, 1946; Melzack & Wall, 1965, 1982; Turk et al., 1983). If a person is injured in an accident and subsequently develops neck and back pain, the therapist cannot simply attribute the patient's subsequent emotional distress to his injuries and the accident but must recognize that the person's interpretation of his injuries and the accident form the core of his emotional upset and pain reactions. That is, the therapist must understand that person's thoughts and beliefs.

Most pain patients have negative thoughts related to pain. Certain stimuli are more likely than others to activate negative thinking, and persistent nociceptive input (i.e., physical pain) is one such stimulus. Constant or frequent bombardment with nociceptive stimulation obliterates a comfortable steady state, erodes homeostasis, and can block goal-oriented behaviors. Such pain can increase a person's proneness to having spontaneous or automatic, negative thoughts that, when persistent and unchallenged, tend to maintain and exacerbate pain-related emotional distress and suffering.

Cognitive therapy aimed at reducing pathogenic negative thinking is a natural remedy for alleviating psychological and emotional distress associated with persistent pain and chronic pain syndromes. Current research indicates that pain patients with clinically significant emotional disturbance and psychological maladjustment tend to entertain more pathogenically negative thinking than nondepressed and less emotionally disturbed pain patients (DeGood & Shutty, 1992; Eimer, 1989; Geisser et al., 1994; Jensen & Karoly, 1991; Jensen et al., 1994; Lefebvre, 1981; Rosenstiel & Keefe, 1983). This line of research, guided by a cognitive-behavioral model of health and adjustment, has led to the development of a number of cognitive-behavioral, chronic pain treatment programs targeting heterogeneous and specific chronic pain populations (Blanchard & Andrasik, 1985; Bradley, 1996; Catalano & Hardin, 1996; Caudill, 1995; Corey & Solomon, 1989; Hanson & Gerber, 1990; Keefe et al., 1992; Keefe & Van Horn, 1993; Marcus & Arbeiter, 1994; Nielson, Walker, & McCain, 1992; Philips & Rachman, 1996; Pilowsky, Spence, Rounsefell, Forsten, & Soda, 1995; Thorn & Williams, 1993).

BASIC ASSUMPTIONS OF THE COGNITIVE MODEL

Cognitive therapy is both a particular philosophical approach to psychotherapy and a strategic program of techniques for alleviating emotional distress. The cognitive philosophical approach forms the basis for the cognitive model of emotional disorders. It contains seven core assumptions that are briefly summarized here because of their relevance to understanding pain and psychological approaches to pain management (see J. Beck, 1995; Beck et al., 1990; Freeman & Reinecke, 1993, 1995; and Freeman et al., 1990 for extended discussions):

1. The way in which people construe or interpret events and situations determines how they will feel and behave in those situations. Drawing on the seminal work of Kelly (1955), behavior is conceptualized as a test of a person's predictions (i.e., construals). Thus, the way in which a sufferer

construes and interprets his or her pain and related personal events will determine how that person feels and behaves in reference to them.

2. Even the most passive-appearing patient is an active seeker of personal meaning, and a creator and user of information. The patient's construing of personal events enables him or her to abstract their meaning. Thus, a pain patient's responses to treatment interventions are mediated by the personal meaning he or she actively makes of them.

3. People develop, from their life experiences, idiosyncratic belief systems that guide their behavior, and these systems influence and bias their perceptions and recall of events. Personal beliefs and assumptions also influence which memories will be selectively activated by specific stimuli and events, such as pain and pain treatment. This then, makes people selectively sensitive to certain stimuli, which can become stressors if the activated memories are associated with overwhelming perceptions of threat and vulnerability. This is one explanation for why many chronic pain syndromes are associated with symptoms of posttraumatic stress disorder (Anderson & Taylor, 1995; Benedikt & Kolb, 1986; Chibnall & Duckro, 1994; Eimer, 1993a, 1993b; Geisser et al., 1996; Grzesiak et al., 1996; Haber & Roos, 1985; Harness & Donlon, 1988; Walker et al., 1988).

4. Behavior is both a test of a person's predictions as well as a source of validating data for those predictions, even when the behavior is maladaptive, and the predictions are not consistent with reality. As stated by Freeman and Reinecke (1995), "A feed-forward system is established in which the activation of maladaptive coping behaviors contributes to the maintenance of aversive environmental events and the consolidation of the belief system" (p. 1888). For example, patients who believe that their pain is mysterious, constant, and permanent are not likely to seek or comply with treatments that might otherwise explain, reduce, or alleviate the pain, thus, reducing their chances of obtaining evidence that could disconfirm those prior pain beliefs.

5. The cognitive specificity hypothesis (Freeman & Reinecke, 1995) states that specific constellations of beliefs, cognitive processes, and cognitive distortions are associated with specific clinical syndromes and disorders. For example, chronically depressed and anxious patients demonstrate certain commonalities and consistencies in their underlying schemas and views of themselves, the world, and the future, and so do chronic pain patients.

6. The cognitive model of psychotherapy holds that to be effective in reducing emotional disturbance and suffering, psychotherapy must somehow (either directly or indirectly) induce patients to examine and modify their negative and dysfunctional thinking patterns. Cognitions and emotions are two aspects of the same response. Cognitions are associated with

most emotional feelings and physical sensations (e.g., pain), and associated with most cognitions are emotional feelings and sensations. It is not a matter of which comes first. External (environmental and interpersonal) and internal (physiological and cognitive) activating events trigger cognitive (thoughts), emotional, and physiological reactions. In turn, these reactions motivate behavior. Emotional reactions, physical sensations (e.g., pain), and behaviors can trigger thoughts, and thoughts can function as activating events that in turn trigger emotional reactions, physical sensations, and particular behaviors, as well as other thoughts.

Emotional reactions and behaviors also are bound up in belief structures that are affectively and emotionally loaded. Human beings are thinking creatures who actively seek to make meaning from their environment. Therefore, the cognitive model holds that true emotional, behavioral, and experiential change cannot occur unless relevant, underlying belief structures and cognitions are addressed and changed. A major psychotherapy challenge however, is that many pain patients lack direct motivation to change their thinking or behavior. In fact, they seldom connect their suffering, which they often initially blame on their physical pain and on external events, to their thinking or behavior. In addition, impatience, irritability, low frustration tolerance, and poor sustained attention can be a problem for many chronic pain patients. Thus, cognitive therapy has to be tailored to convince these patients that there are connections between their pain experience, their thoughts, and their behaviors.

COGNITIVE THERAPY INTERVENTION TARGETS

In addition to being a particular philosophical approach to psychotherapy, cognitive therapy is a strategic program of techniques designed to alleviate emotional distress by directly modifying the dysfunctional cognitions accompanying emotional distress. *Cognitive* techniques directly address dysfunctional cognitions. *Behavioral* techniques directly target behaviors, and *affective* or *emotive* techniques directly target emotional experiences. However, cognitive techniques also address accompanying behaviors and emotional experiences, and behavioral and affective-emotive techniques also address accompanying cognitions. When a patient brings up a present or past cognition (e.g., "I can't stand to exercise," or "I thought I seriously injured myself again"), the cognitive therapist also asks what the patient is feeling or felt, and is thinking of doing, or in fact did. Likewise, when discussing a behavior, emotional feeling, or physical symptom such as pain, the cognitive therapist also asks the patient what he or she is thinking or had thought in the situation.

Cognitive change targets in Pain Management Psychotherapy (PMP) include patients' automatic thoughts, cognitive distortions, and underlying beliefs or schemas. Behavioral targets include self-regulatory, physiological behaviors (e.g., breathing patterns, postural habits, movement patterns, and muscle activity); health-related behaviors (e.g., dietary habits, exercise, and medication use); activities of daily living (e.g., activity scheduling, time-management, mastery and pleasure activities, vocational activities, sleep and self-care habits); coping behaviors (e.g., ways of coping with intense pain, relaxation methods), and interpersonal behaviors. Affective targets include the emotional states and experiences associated with particular situations, behaviors, cognitions, and physical symptoms. Physiological targets include a patient's pain and other distressing physical symptoms and sensations.

Broad psychotherapeutic goals include providing support, building and maintaining the psychotherapeutic relationship, providing relevant and timely information and education, reducing the intensity and frequency of physical and emotional symptoms, promoting cognitive awareness and insight about pathogenic thinking habits, modifying dysfunctional cognitions, modifying maladaptive behaviors, developing necessary pain coping skills, desensitizing crippling fears and anxieties, and facilitating needed emotional experiencing or reexperiencing. Many chronic pain patients have had repeated medical and surgical procedures—both traditional and nontraditional—that have failed to provide them with enduring pain relief. The oversimplified, misleading, and absolutist refrain that these patients "must learn to live with their pain" ignores the reality that they do live with their pain. The primary purpose of Pain Management Psychotherapy is to enable people with chronic and persistent pain to live a better quality of life, with less pain and suffering.

GATE CONTROL THEORY AND THE COGNITIVE MODEL

Melzack and Wall's (1965) gate control theory posited that physical, sensory-discriminative factors (pain sensations), cognitive-evaluative factors (how pain sensations are interpreted) and emotional-motivational factors, operate in concert in determining the quality and intensity of the pain experience. According to their theory, adaptive (functional or rational) cognitions and emotions can play a role in closing the pain gate on pain sensations ascending the dorsal horn of the spinal cord to the brain. Conversely, dysfunctional or maladaptive cognitions and emotions can open the pain gate.

In terms of the Cognitive Model of emotional disorders (J. Beck, 1995; Ellis, 1996; Freeman et al., 1990; Freeman & Reinecke, 1995), pain sensations can be thought of as an activating or adverse event. In Ellis's (1996) sequential and interactional, ABC model of emotional disturbance, pain sensations might be represented by the letter "A" (the initial stimulus), which stands for the activating or adverse event. Cognitive-evaluative factors, which determine how pain sensations are perceived, interpreted, and evaluated, might be represented by the letter "B," which in Ellis's and Beck's cognitive models stands for a person's beliefs. Finally, emotional-motivational factors, which determine how pain sensations are felt and experienced (the pain's quality and intensity, might be represented by the letter "C," which stands for emotional and behavioral consequences. Taking the schematic ABC model two steps further, the letter "D" can represent what a person in pain does (behavior), as a result of feeling and experiencing his or her pain in a particular way. The letter "E" can represent how a person's beliefs (B), emotional experience (C), and behaviors (D) affect his or her pain (physical effects on pain sensations and perceptions).

Case Example

A patient states that the first thing she notices when she awakens every morning is pain in her jaw and head. According to the ABC cognitive-behavioral model, this first awareness of pain can be schematized as an (A)ctivating event. When the patient is asked to recall any associated thoughts about the jaw and head pain she experienced this morning, she remembers thinking, "Today is going to be a bad day. I'm being punished again. This is terrible! I am always going to be in pain." These automatic thoughts related to her pain can be schematized as her (B)eliefs. When the patient is then asked to recall how she felt when she had these thoughts, she recollects that she felt miserable. After being helped to verbalize her emotions, she elaborates that she felt "angry, miserable, depressed, punished, and victimized." These feelings can be represented by emotional (C)onsequences. These emotional consequences in turn, lead her to (D)o the following things: take a pain pill, call in sick at work, keep the shades drawn, go back to bed, and cry. She then begins to dwell on thoughts of being a victim, and to think of herself as "cursed, defeated, and worthless." As she begins to dwell on her pain, this tends to have the (E)ffect of intensifying her headache and jaw pain.

The therapist raises the hypothesis with this patient that according to the Cognitive Model, her automatic thoughts may actually be widening the pain gate, and keeping it open longer. If this is true, some of her thoughts may be serving directly to make her pain worse (i.e., more physically intense and miserable). The therapist explains the ABC's of the cognitive model, and draws a diagram to illustrate how the pain sensations as an (A)ctivating event produce certain emotional, motivational, and behavioral (C)onsequences by way of the mediating factor of the patient's (B)eliefs. The therapist states: "At Point A, you have these pain sensations in your head and jaw. At Point B, you tell yourself, 'Today is going to be a bad day. I'm being punished again.' This is your evaluation of what you are feeling. At Point C, you feel 'angry, miserable, depressed, punished, and victimized.' Those thoughts at Point B and these feelings at Point C may make your pain experience worse than it has to be because those thoughts and feelings may be opening the pain gate in your nervous system, which lets more pain through. Does this make sense? Would you like to learn how to close the pain gate?"

Removing the "Suffering" Element from Pain

A patient's summed Pain Rating Indices on the Philadelphia Pain Questionnaire-Pain Adjective Checklist (PPQ-PAC) can give the PMP therapist a tool for helping that patient to cognitively restructure his or her understanding of the connection between pain and suffering. As discussed in Chapter 2, the PPQ-PAC Total Pain Rating Index (PRI) is the additive sum of the patient's Sensory, Affective, and Evaluative PRIs. Thus, it is a summative or additive measure of pain and suffering. Following this line of thought, the Total PRI may be reduced by diminishing or subtracting the Affective and Evaluative PRIs. A Total PRI Sum comprising only Sensory ratings will be lower than a Total PRI Sum comprising of Sensory, Affective, and Evaluative ratings. A PMP therapist can explain this simple pain arithmetic to a patient using that patient's actual PPQ-PAC PRIs to illustrate the concept.

Case Example

Your pain is composed of part pure sensation, what I call the "hurt," the "pinch," or the "sting" of pain, and part emotional suffering, what I like to call the "misery factor." This is clearly shown by your scores on the Philadelphia Pain Questionnaire-Pain Adjective Checklist. Your Total Score or Total Pain Rating Index was the additive sum of your Sensory Pain Rating Index, your Emotional Pain Rating Index, and your Evaluative Pain Rating Index. Your Sensory Pain Rating Index is a measure of how intensely you rated your pain's hurt or sting. Your Emotional and your Evaluative Pain Rating Indices are both measures of how intensely you rated the emotional upset associated with your pain. Now, here is the main point. If you could remove or strip from your pain the emotional upset, the pain sensations probably would remain, but they might feel less intense, and actually hurt less, because your Total Pain Rating Index would have lost its misery factor. Does that make sense to you? Can you see that? To put it another way, pain is part hurt and part suffering. If we can somehow remove the suffering from pain, then, in a manner of speaking, we may be able to reduce the pain. Would you like to work with me to explore different ways of reducing or removing the suffering element or misery factor from your pain? Then, we can also work together to explore different ways of reducing the hurt or the sting of your pain sensations.

THE COGNITIVE TRIAD

A basic concept in Beck's cognitive theory of depression (A. Beck, 1967, 1976; Beck, Rush, Shaw, & Emery, 1979) is the *cognitive triad*, which refers to the idea that depressed persons tend to have negative views of *themselves*, their *world* (i.e., personal events), and their *future*. In Beck's conceptualization, depressed persons' cognitions give rise to the discouraging view that the self is defective, the world is oppressive and disappointing, and the future is hopeless. Further work by Beck and associates (Freeman & Reinecke, 1995) extended this conceptualization to describe the self, world, and future views of anxious patients (Beck, Emery, & Greenberg, 1985; Freeman et al., 1990), patients with personality disorders (Beck et al., 1990; Layden, Newman, Freeman, & Byers-Morse, 1993), and substance abusers (Beck, Wright, Newman, & Liese, 1993). For example, anxious patients are observed to view themselves as vulnerable, the world as threatening and dangerous, and their future as unsure, uncertain, and fearful.

Pain Patients' Cognitive Triad

Chronic pain patients reveal the following cognitive triad:

- The self is often viewed as damaged, defective, disabled, and impaired.
- The world (personal events) is often viewed as punishing, blaming, uncaring, unfair, depriving, and disappointing.
- The future is often viewed as painful, a struggle, more disabling, deteriorating, and hopeless.

Assessing Pain Patients' Cognitive Triad

At the outset of therapy, it is often useful to ask pain patients to share their cognitions about themselves, their world, and their future. We commonly assess a pain patient's cognitive triad by asking these kinds of questions:

1. When you think about (a) your pain problem, or being in pain; (b) your pain at its worst; (c) your pain when it gets bad; (d) your pain and the problems it has caused you—what thoughts do you have about yourself? For example, how would you complete this thought? "I am . . . ?"

2. When you think about these things, what thoughts do you have about: (a) the world in general? (b) people? (c) the things that you do every day? (d) how your typical day goes? (e) the things that happen to you every day? For example, how would you complete this thought? "The world is . . . ?"
3. When you think about these things, what thoughts do you have about (a) your future? (b) what you will be doing and where you will be in one year? two years from now? three years from now? How would you complete this thought? "My future is . . . ?"

COGNITIVE DISTORTIONS

A hallmark of the Cognitive Model of emotional disorders is the concept of *cognitive distortions* (Freeman & Reinecke, 1995). This concept refers to the idea that people's perceptions, memories, and thoughts about the world are cognitive representations or constructions of reality, as opposed to being one-to-one, veridical replicas of reality. These cognitive representations or constructions carry some distortion, to a greater or lesser degree, and these distortions can be adaptive or maladaptive.

In a broad sense, representing reality with some cognitive distortion is adaptive because it allows us to selectively attend to and abstract information. This is a real asset, given the inherent limitations of our attentional capacities and our inability to process large quantities of information simultaneously. In a narrower sense, cognitive distortions can also be considered adaptive when they motivate people to think and behave in functional, goal-directed, and self-enhancing ways (e.g., calculated risk taking, acting with courage and conviction, ignoring potential obstacles and negative outcomes and concentrating on a valued goal). However, cognitive distortions can become maladaptive when they are illogical, gross oversimplifications of consensual reality that are inconsistent with consensual reality, associated with a great deal of psychic pain and discomfort, and motivate people to think and behave in nonfunctional, inefficient, and self-defeating ways.

Dysfunctional or maladaptive distortions then, represent maladaptive ways of processing information. Several authors have cataloged cognitive distortions (A. Beck, 1976; D. Burns, 1980; Freeman et al., 1990), and particular types of cognitive distortions have "become emblematic of particular styles of behaving or of certain clinical syndromes" (Freeman & Reinecke, 1995, p. 192). Individuals with specific types of psychological and physical disorders (e.g., depression, anxiety, personality disorders, chronic illnesses) distort information in certain characteristic ways that maintain the psychopathology underlying each disorder. Cognitive therapy targets people's maladaptive cognitive distortions. Three related goals of cognitive therapy are (a) to make these maladaptive distortions manifest, (b) to assist patients to recognize the negative impact of such distortions, and (c) to help patients change them.

PAIN PATIENTS' COGNITIVE DISTORTIONS

Ellis presents the hypothesis in many of his writings (Ellis & Dryden, 1987) that human irrationality and the tendency to engage in maladaptive cognitive distortions are biologically based. All human beings evidence the tendency to distort reality in the face of life's adversities. Living with chronic or persistent physical pain is a major adversity. In fact, that may be an understatement, considering the major life disruption associated with chronic pain syndromes. As with other psychological and physical disorders, people who live with the daily adversity of chronic pain evidence certain characteristic cognitive distortions. The following typical cognitive distortions of pain patients are usually associated with particular types of maladaptive behavior, or behavioral distortions, and dysfunctional emotional states. Hence they can promulgate unnecessary suffering and worsen pain.

Assessing Cognitive Distortions

Clues to the underlying presence of the cognitive distortions to be described below are provided by high total Pain Interference *Intensity* and *Frequency* scores on the Pain Interference and Impairment Index (discussed in Chapter 3). High factor scores on the Pain Beliefs and Perceptions Inventory (Willams & Thorn, 1989) and the Pain Experience Scale (Turk & Rudy, 1985) (discussed in Chapter 3) may be associated with particular cognitive distortions. Also, individual item responses and scale scores on the Pain Coping Inventory (Eimer & Allen, 1995) (discussed in Chapter 3) point to particular types of cognitive distortions. Finally, the Automatic Thoughts about Pain Questionnaire (ATPQ) (discussed in Chapter 6 and reprinted in Appendix S) was specifically developed to assess some of the cognitive distortions described below.

Dichotomous, All-or-Nothing, or Black-and-White Thinking

This distortion manifests in terms of the cognition "I am either in pain or not in pain." There are no shades of gray. Pain patients who manifest this distortion tend to be extremely sensitive to any physical indications that their pain could be worsening. This type of thinking makes it unlikely for an individual to acknowledge signs of progress. There are either good days or bad days. The black-and-white thinker sees mostly bad days, however, because most days include something that can be construed as negative (not good), which disqualifies the day from being construed as a good day. This cognitive distortion predisposes a person with persistent pain to make extreme evaluations and ratings of personal events, since there are few in-betweens. Things are either "terrible" or "great," and when it comes to events related to pain, things are invariably terrible. Concomitantly, behaviors also tend to be extreme and reactive, or reactionary resulting in avoidance, withdrawal, and overreactions to events. This thinking pattern also predisposes persons with chronic pain to engage in another common cognitive distortion, "disqualifying the positive."

Disqualifying the Positive

"So what, if I did this and this? So what if this and that happened? I'm still in pain and I still really have not accomplished anything!" These kinds of evaluative self-statements and social cognitions are made by pain patients who cannot allow themselves to acknowledge personal successes or positive events. Individuals who walk around with a kind of negative "pain halo" filter most events through that negative halo, and it prevents them from perceiving things positively and also can lead them to ignore reality. They may ignore or discount opportunities that arise or good things that happen. The result is that the individual is likely to continue to feel miserable and suffer. Pain patients who think in this manner often admit that they cannot really enjoy anything, because their pain, anger, or something else that is quite negative, always gets in the way. One patient stated, "How can I enjoy making love with my wife? I always know that I can't do it like I did before I injured my back!" This distortion can lead to anhedonia, loss of motivation, and inertia.

Selective Abstraction

This cognitive distortion is closely related to disqualifying the positive. Patients wearing negative pain halos also tend to be preoccupied with their pain, their misery, their hurt, and their suffering. Little else matters. The chronic low back pain patient mentioned earlier stated, "I've got to focus on my pain so that I don't do something to reinjure myself and make it worse. What if I move wrong, or bend, or twist too quickly, or do something without thinking? I could reherniate my disk!"

Selective abstraction can also lead a person to expect or anticipate more pain. One patient with fibromyalgia stated that he expected to feel "stiff and exhausted" when he awoke every morning. He admitted that it was hard for him to find exceptions to this self-imposed rule, (i.e., mornings when he felt good). Another patient admitted that she interpreted any little pain or untoward sensation in her head and neck as a sign of an impending migraine attack. This led her to stiffen up the muscles of her head, neck, and shoulders. It was pointed out to her that this tension could in fact precipitate a headache.

"Should" Statements

Should and have-to statements are a common companion to the other distortions. Many pain patients rigidly believe that they should and therefore must do things in certain ways. Relatedly, they often hold others and the world accountable to their rigid shoulds, have-to's, and musts as well. One chronic low back pain patient stated with conviction that he had to do things in a certain way because "I cannot and must not reinjure myself." Another patient who injured his back at work stated his belief that his employer and insurance company had treated him unfairly. However, he also believed that the poor treatment he received was unfair, and should not have happened. He believed that his employer and the insurance company "should have to" let him see a doctor of his choice, "should have to" cover his medical expenses, and "should have to" pay him his compensation benefits.

Because this patient believed that his employer and insurance company did not do what they should have to do, he continually worked himself up into an extremely rageful state whenever he was reminded of what they did not do. This made it impossible for him to engage in any productive problem solving, worsened his pain, and made him a very unpleasant patient. Another patient with "low frustration tolerance" (to be defined) often told himself, "I should not have to suffer like this. I should not have to exercise so hard, or work so hard to stay in shape, and stay out of pain." This led him to give up easily. He was unable to comply with a physical therapist's supervised exercise and reconditioning program. He tended to overdo many physical activities, which often triggered pain flare-ups and sometimes led him to reinjure himself.

Many pain patients believe that they "should be much better by now" and that they "shouldn't have any more pain." This often leads to a related cognitive distortion exemplified by the statement, "I can't stand it!"

Low Frustration Tolerance

Ellis (1996), in discussing low frustration tolerance (LFT), coined the term "I-can't-stand-it-itis." He relates it to hidden musts and shoulds, exemplified by statements such as: "Things should always be easy"; "I should not have to suffer, or work so hard"; "People should always treat me fairly"; "Things should not always be so hard"; and "Conditions should be easy or easier." Many pain patients with these beliefs tend to give up easily, and their lack of persistence often prevents them from making rehabilitative or therapeutic progress. LFT, along with should statements (its cognitive cousin), is a major cause of treatment failure with chronic pain patients.

Case Example

Dora was a 24-year-old single woman who had injured her right leg, knee, and back in a fall at work. She subsequently developed a reflex sympathetic dystrophy (RSD) syndrome affecting her right leg. She was seen by us for psychological consultation approximately 18 months after sustaining her injury, and after having seen numerous medical doctors. She described her pain as a constant "burning" that was exacerbated by almost any tactile stimulus (e.g., touch, most clothing), movement, and "stress." In addition to the allodynia and hyperalgesia in her leg, there was edema, some physical atrophy, and significant weight gain. By the time we saw her, Dora had become a very angry person. She was angry at some of the doctors who had let her down, at her former employer, and at her lawyer. She was very pessimistic about the prospects of being helped by a psychologist. History taking revealed however, that she had been a very noncompliant patient and client. She had fired her first attorney because he "did not make things happen as fast as he should have." She had not followed any of her doctors' treatment recommendations on a consistent basis. She stated that the physical therapist she had seen "hurt me too much." She believed that the professionals she had seen were "insensitive" and that physical therapy was "too hard" and caused "too much pain."

Dora was a high-strung person. One of her initial statements to us was, "I'll give you a chance because my attorney said you helped people with chronic pain, but I must tell you that I don't need psychological help. I'm not crazy!" She stated that she wanted us to help her make things the way they had been before her accident. As it turned out, she only came to see us four times. In her second, third, and fourth visits, she appeared increasingly impatient. She frequently interjected, "I can't stand talking about things that don't have to do with getting rid of this pain." She canceled several sessions last minute because she either was in "too much pain" to keep her appointment, or was "too angry" at something that happened that week. For example, she felt that one orthopedic surgeon was too "rough" when he was examining her leg. She stated that her associated thought was: "I can't stand to be touched." She told us (in her second session), "If you are going to help me, you should have done so by now." This patient was unable to overcome or temper her low frustration tolerance. Her biggest problems, from our perspective, were her anger and her unwillingness to consider entertaining, even temporarily, a new perspective. As a result, she could not commit herself to a rehabilitative treatment program.

Perfectionism

The cognitive distortion of perfectionism is closely related to low frustration tolerance. Patients with LFT also tend to believe that things should be perfect, or they are not worth doing or having at *all*. Many patients with intractable chronic pain syndromes admit to a history of perfectionism, or striving for perfection. Although this personality style is sometimes termed *overachievement*, it may be more accurately described as "overstriving." Many of these individuals have a history of striving very hard to achieve, but not achieving. They often work compulsively and suffer from stress-related burnout. Many patients diagnosed with fibro-myalgia and chronic fatigue syndrome fit this pattern. Although we es-chew the notion of a single pain-prone personality, this type of stressed-out personality or cognitive style is seen in many cases and appears to be a significant covariate with chronic pain syndromes. A likely hypothesis is that perfectionism is very stressful leading to a host of psychophysiological symptoms of autonomic (sympathetic) nervous system, noradrenergic overarousal and dysregulation, such as headaches, fatigue, muscle pain, cold extremities, anxiety, and so forth.

Common automatic thoughts among this group of people include "I can't stand to fail"; "I must succeed at all costs"; "I have to work myself to the bone so that I can succeed"; "Things never come easy for me"; and "If you don't or can't do something well, the whole thing is worthless!" The LFT these patients demonstrate is often related to the belief that "if one thing is wrong with something, then the whole thing is worthless—so give up!"

Pain-Based Emotional Reasoning (PBER)

"Because I am in pain, there must be something physically wrong!" "The fact that I am in such pain now means I will never get better!" "The pain I am in now means that I always will be in pain." "Because I am angry at you, you must have treated me unfairly, and I can't stand you." "Because I am angry that no one has been able to get rid of my pain, nobody really cares about helping me." "Because I am in such pain, I deserve to have you write another pain pill prescription for me."

The preceding statements reflect pain-based emotional reasoning (PBER). In other words, erroneous, illogical conclusions are based on the premise, "I hurt now and I am in pain." PBER is very pathogenic. It exac-erbates many pain patients' suffering by leading them to feel worse than they have to feel emotionally. It also motivates many people to act in self-defeating ways leading them to make negative predictions (to be dis-cussed), which in turn can lessen their motivation to comply with pain treatment. Like most pathogenic cognitive distortions, undisputed PBER ignores the important information (underlying premises, cognitive as-sumptions, and self-statements) beneath or behind the negative feelings and painful sensations.

Mind Reading and Personalization

These cognitive distortions are closely related to PBER. Mind reading refers to the fallacious tendency to think one can know what someone else is thinking. It is usually triggered by PBER and more likely to occur when a person in pain is feeling bad or has just experienced a disappointment. Some common examples of automatic thoughts associated with this distortion are "They want to deprive me of my benefits"; "I know they don't care"; "I know they want to do me in"; "I just know my doctor is tired of treating me." Mind reading often intensifies angry, depressed, or anxious feelings. Behaviorally, it often leads to avoidance and withdrawal. In some cases, it can lead to acting out in retaliation and anger, especially with hostile, angry, or paranoid pain patients.

Personalization refers to a person's erroneous tendency to interpret events or other people's behaviors as having been directed at him or her. People who think in this way tend to take others' actions very personally. It can also lead erroneously to self-blame if the patient assumes responsibility for an untoward event or someone else's actions. This distortion typically leads to feelings of depression, anxiety, or anger.

Case Example

One patient with intractable migraine and muscle contraction/tension headaches frequently thought to herself things like "That comment means this doctor thinks I am a hopeless case." "I should not have said that. Now he won't want to treat me since he'll know I am a bad patient." "That proves it! He won't see me for two weeks because he doesn't like to treat me." Another angry, paranoid pain patient, repeatedly attributed bureaucratic inefficiencies in his insurance company, in the workers' compensation system, in his lawyer's office, and in his doctors' offices, to the intent of making life hard for him, scamming him, or cutting off his benefits. This would get him angry and rageful, and he would sometimes make impulsive or threatening phone calls to the parties he held accountable. Finally, another patient who suffered from fibromyalgia and chronic fatigue syndrome, and who was also a victim of past sexual abuse, had a tendency to blame herself when things went wrong, or when her symptoms flared up.

Negative Prediction

The cognitive distortion of negative prediction or "fortune-telling" is also related to PBER. This distortion refers to the tendency to predict dire future consequences based on inadequate information. In the examples of PBER, negative predictions were based solely on the fact that the person was currently in pain. Some pain patients needlessly upset themselves by running a seemingly interminable chain of negative predictions and inferences in their heads.

Case Example

One low back pain patient told us: "Every time my leg pain flares up, I think the worst. For example, the other day, I was doing my back exercises, and I felt a tinge in my calf. Well, I eased up on the exercises to see if the pain in the leg would go away. It didn't. I started to worry. Movement seemed to make it worse. This had happened before, but this pain was scary. I then started to think that maybe I reinjured myself. Next, I thought that no matter what this meant, that sooner or later, I am going to end up back on the operating table again, and this time the operation won't be so successful. I'll be crippled, paralyzed from the waist down and not be able to walk. I will be in a wheelchair, and then I'll never be able to work again. I'll be in worse pain than ever, because I'll have to sit all the time. And, my heart will fail because I won't be able to do aerobic exercise." This patient went on and on (he had a good imagination!), detailing one negative prediction after another. The worst part of it was that as he thought about these things, he felt as if they were sure to happen, or worse yet, as if they had already happened.

Negative prediction is closely related to the following distortion—catastrophizing.

Catastrophizing

The term, *catastrophizing* refers to the tendency to interpret negative events as being much more negative than they really are, to the point of mentally blowing up one's interpretation of the negative consequences, way out of proportion. This distortion also frequently involves misinterpreting the probability of negative events occurring. In other words, possibilities are escalated into likely probabilities, or are treated as if they have already occurred.

Case Example

The low back and leg pain patient discussed earlier tended to catastrophize when faced with minor setbacks. He would often say to himself things like "Oh my God. That pain means I'll need another surgery!" or, "This pain is just too much for me to handle. I can't do it anymore. I can't cope anymore!" Another injured chronic neck and back pain patient became very depressed whenever he would play with his children. Playing with them triggered thoughts of "How awful it is that I cannot lift my children and wrestle with them like other fathers do." At such times, he would also start to think that he was a "bad father" because he could no longer wrestle with his children. He also worried that they would resent him for not doing with them "what every good father should do."

Catastrophizing in pain patients tends to be closely related to some of the other distortions already discussed. Most commonly, it is related to negative prediction, PBER, and LFT. Continuing with the case:

Whenever the father just described had such thoughts, he painted in his head dire images and predictions of the future. He pictured himself being divorced and lonely. He tended to catastrophize most often when he was experiencing a pain flare-up (PBER). At those times (and at other times), he tended to think, "I can't stand my life anymore. I can't stand the pain and I can't stand the adjustments I have to make in my life to live with this continual pain and to keep in shape" (LFT).

Catastrophizing has also been identified in the pain coping literature with the dysfunctional pain coping strategy of thinking the worst and letting one's negative thoughts get out of hand whenever pain flares up (Gil, Williams, Keefe, & Beckham, 1990; Jensen & Karoly, 1991; Jensen, Turner, & Romano, 1991; Jensen, Turner, Romano, & Lawler, 1994; Keefe et al., 1989; Rosenstiel & Keefe, 1983; Shutty et al., 1990; Thorn & Williams, 1993). As a pain coping strategy, it has been associated in this research literature with negative control beliefs, perceptions of poor self-efficacy, depression, emotional distress, poor adjustment, and negative coping outcomes (Jensen & Karoly, 1991).

Overgeneralization

The final cognitive distortion to be discussed is overgeneralization. We have intentionally left this one for last because it tends to be a pseudorealistic result of engaging in most of the other distortions. We say *pseudorealistic* because the unchecked use of all the other distortions can cause persistent pain to generalize into a highly dysfunctional chronic pain syndrome that negatively affects most aspects of a person's life. Therefore, overgeneralization also can be considered one of the most insidious distortions.

Pain patients often admit to thoughts such as "I'll *never* get better"; "I can't enjoy *anything* or do *anything* because of this pain"; "I'll *never* find a doctor who understands chronic pain"; "I'll *always* be in pain and I'm *always* going to suffer"; "I'm *nothing but a total failure*"; "I am a *total* pain invalid"; "I feel *worthless*"; "I *always* have to be on guard lest I move wrong and reinjure myself." The key words, in italics, are all absolutes. The main point about overgeneralization is that pain patients who continue to think in terms of the preceding cognitive distortions without vigorously disputing them (to be discussed), tend to remain stuck in a negative spiral of depressogenic thinking that keeps them from behaving more adaptively, managing their pain more successfully, and feeling better. This can lead to a state of global disability and pain impairment, which is represented by a high Global Impairment Index on the Pain Coping Inventory and high total scores on the Pain Interference and Impairment Index (discussed in Chapter 3).

SCHEMAS

The term *schemas* (or *schemata*) refers to a person's underlying beliefs and assumptions about the self and the way the world is. An individual's basic schemas provide a basis for screening, coding, and evaluating stimuli, orienting oneself psychologically in the world, categorizing and interpreting experiences, making predictions, and testing those predictions via behavior (A. Beck, 1967, 1976). According to the cognitive model of Beck and his associates, schemas are the wellsprings of a person's automatic thoughts, emotional states, and behaviors. According to Young (1990/1994), "*Early Maladaptive Schemas* refer to extremely stable and enduring themes that develop during childhood and are elaborated upon throughout an individual's lifetime. These schemas serve as templates for processing later experience" (p. 9).

Young contrasts Early Maladaptive Schemas (EMSs) with underlying assumptions. By definition, EMSs are deemed to be dysfunctional, and a basic cause of chronic psychological distress. According to Young, an EMS is an "unconditional, rigid, a priori truth" (e.g., "I am a failure"; "I am incompetent"), whereas an underlying assumption is a conditional, less rigid, "if-then" rule (e.g., "If I get attached, I'll lose the person. Therefore, avoid attachment"; "If I meet everyone's needs, people will like me, and then I'll be worthwhile"). For individuals with personality disorders, Early Maladaptive Schemas are posited to form the core of a person's self-concept and to be self-perpetuating. As such, cognitive maneuvers, or mechanisms, are hypothesized to maintain an individual's rigid EMSs. Young (1990/1994) hypothesizes that EMSs and underlying assumptions are activated, along with high levels of affect, when events in the environment occur that are relevant to a particular schema.

Persons (1989) hypothesizes that EMSs and conditional beliefs and assumptions are core, maladaptive cognitions that often constitute the underlying psychological mechanisms of overt psychological, emotional, cognitive, and behavioral problems. Her approach emphasizes the necessity of understanding these psychological mechanisms in case formulation. In our work, we have found several psychological themes or schemas to be relevant to conceptualizing the basis of pain patients' adjustment difficulties. Drawing from Persons' (1989) work, and Young's (1990/1994) extensive categorization of Early Maladaptive Schemas, these schemas are defined in the following sections. Using these definitions as a guide, a patient's basic schemas and assumptive beliefs can be formulated using a number of cognitive assessment techniques that can be implemented in a clinical interview. Some of these techniques are discussed in Chapters 6 and 7 including the "downward arrow technique"; sentence completions (e.g., "Please complete this sentence: *I am . . . ; I need . . .*"); the use of imagery; asking the patient to keep a journal to write about personal stressors; the Dysfunctional Thoughts Record; and asking a patient to verbalize automatic thoughts. Also, several published instruments have been designed to assess basic psychological schemas. The best known of these are Young's (1990/1994) Schema Questionnaire, and Weissman's Dysfunctional Attitude Scale (D. Burns, 1980; Weissman, 1980).

SCHEMAS RELATED TO AUTONOMY

Independence

The independence schema is represented by the core belief, "I don't need help. I cannot allow myself to be smothered." Patients who hold this belief and are high on the need for independence, should be given appropriate distance and autonomy in therapy. They tend to be resistant to the idea of asking for, or receiving, nonmedical help for their pain. "Dichotomous (black-and-white, "all-or-nothing") thinking (e.g., "If you help me, you smother me") is a commonly observed cognitive distortion in these patients' automatic thoughts.

Dependence

The dependence schema is represented by the core belief, "I need you. I cannot function on my own." Pain patients who hold this belief often need to be helped to develop greater independence and autonomy. They may initially want the therapist to solve their problems and give them all the solutions. They are often quite passive and can sometimes appear noncompliant with therapy homework, usually because they become anxious about doing things new or on their own, and their pain makes the going rougher. Homework assignments may often seem too difficult. Therefore, the therapist is advised to move slowly. However, if a dependent patient is also high on "need for approval," the patient may avoid doing homework in fear of getting it wrong and receiving disapproval. Low frustration tolerance (e.g., "I can't stand this. I can't do this without help"), and personalization are common.

Subjugation

The subjugation schema is represented by the core belief, "I have to meet everyone else's needs, all of the time." Patients who tend to believe this often suffer from stress-related disorders (e.g., insomnia, headaches, chronic pain). They often tend to "swallow" a lot, hold in their resentments, and suppress their negative emotions. These patients often tend to feel as if they are without choices; they are overwhelmed by their lives and stressed out. Burnout is common, and so is the operation of secondary gains from pain, which may serve as a mechanism for escaping from the demands of overcommitment and overresponsibility. "Should" statements are a common cognitive distortion in this group (e.g., "I must/have to/should take care of my significant others whenever they need me. Now, they should take care of me," or, "There is no time to take care of me"), as are personalization, and overresponsibility (e.g., "It's all my fault/responsibility").

Narcissism

As might be expected, the core belief here is "Only my needs matter." Patients who are high on narcissism tend to view others as objects who are either sources of gratification, or obstacles to getting what they want. Highly narcissistic individuals tend to externalize blame when things go wrong. Narcissistic pain patients tend to be very angry, and they are sometimes explosive, aggressive, or impulsive. Secondary gains from pain, manipulativeness, and symptom exaggeration often are operative with narcissistic pain patients. Dichotomous thinking (e.g., "You are either for me or against me"), disqualifying the positive, personalization, and selective abstraction are frequently observed cognitive distortions.

Vulnerability

Anxious pain patients who feel vulnerable typically hold the core belief, "The shoe can drop on me at any time!" and "I don't have the resources to cope." Pain is often viewed as mysterious or threatening. This schema is often associated with excessive worrying, emotionality, apprehensive expectations, vigilance, and symptoms of sympathetic arousal. Catastrophizing about pain and negative prediction are the most common cognitive distortions in this group (e.g., "This is awful! What if it is cancer?"). There is often a history of some kind of trauma.

Mistrust of Self

This schema is represented by the core belief, "I cannot trust myself." The usual implication is "Therefore, I cannot trust you and you cannot trust me either." Not surprisingly, this schema is associated with paranoia and alienation. These psychological states often breed noncompliance and treatment resistance (Eimer & Allen, 1995). Mind reading, personalization, selective abstraction (e.g., looking for and finding betrayal), and disqualifying the positive (e.g., "How can I enjoy anything being in so much pain?") are common cognitive distortions. The perception of the self having been betrayed by one's body is not uncommon in patients with chronic pain and physical illness.

Enmeshment

The schema of enmeshment is represented by the core belief, "I have no identity other than me and you." It is often associated with the schemas for dependence and subjugation. Patients who are high on this schema often have problems with setting boundaries and limits. They may evidence self-control problems, impulsive behaviors, low frustration tolerance, catastrophizing, and intolerance of being alone. They often demonstrate impersistence and problems sticking to a program. Compliance with treatment may be a problem.

SCHEMAS RELATED TO WORTHINESS

Defectiveness

The schema of defectiveness is represented by the core belief, "I am defective and/or unlovable." This schema tends to be activated by chronic pain and forms part of the core view of the self in the cognitive triad. Treatment-resistant pain breeds self-doubt. This often complicates pain treatment because it cultivates chronic hopelessness and depression. Common cognitive distortions include selective abstraction, negative labeling, should statements, overgeneralization, pain-based emotional reasoning, disqualifying the positive, and dichotomous thinking.

Social Unacceptability

This schema is represented by the core belief, "I am not acceptable." As with the defectiveness self-schema, it tends to be activated by chronic pain and forms part of the chronic pain patient's cognitive triad. It can breed alienation. Common cognitive distortions include selective abstraction, mind reading, personalization, negative labeling, should statements, overgeneralization, disqualifying the positive, and dichotomous thinking.

Incompetence

This schema is represented by the core belief, "I'm a failure and incompetent." It too, often forms part of the chronic pain patient's cognitive triad. Patients with this active schema expect to fail. They will often predict that no treatment will work with them—and patients with chronic pain tend to have plenty of evidence for this. Negative prediction, selective abstraction, disqualifying the positive, dichotomous thinking, overgeneralization, perfectionism, and negative labeling are common cognitive distortions.

Guilt and Punishment

The guilt and punishment schema is represented by the core belief, "I'm to blame when things go wrong. It's always my fault." In their cognitive triad, chronic pain patients tend to view the world as punishing. When self-blame is a consistent part of the picture, this tends to breed depression, and the belief that punishment (pain) is deserved. Personalization, overresponsibilitizing, pain-based emotional reasoning, and black-and-white thinking are common cognitive distortions. This schema is frequently associated with a history of trauma.

Shame

The shame schema is represented by the core belief, "I'm unacceptable as I am and I am shameful," and tends to be associated with the guilt and punishment schema. Patients high on this schema have trouble accepting others (this includes their therapists and doctors) as well as themselves. They often engage in denial and may repress or suppress painful psychological material. Addictions and chemical dependencies (alcohol, narcotics, and other pain medications) are not unlikely. Negative labeling, personalization, pain-based emotional reasoning, and perfectionism are common. This schema is also frequently associated with a history of trauma.

SCHEMAS RELATED TO TRUST AND CONNECTEDNESS

Emotional Deprivation

This schema is represented by the core belief, "I am very needy and I shall never get what I need." Pain patients high on this schema sometimes tend to use pain for secondary gain, for example, to gain attention, love, comfort, or emotional support. Addictions, chemical dependencies, and drug-seeking behaviors are frequently seen in this group. Low frustration tolerance, pain-based emotional reasoning, and should statements are common.

Abandonment

This schema is represented by the core belief, "If I get attached, I'll be let down and abandoned." Many chronic pain patients have a history of being let down and abandoned. Chronic pain is sometimes associated with the psychological problems of unresolved loss and grief. Pain-based emotional reasoning, negative prediction, mind reading, and personalization are common distortions.

Mistrust of Others

This schema is represented by the core belief, "If I get close, I'll be betrayed." The implication is "I can't allow myself to get close." This schema is typically associated with the mistrust of self schema, and also with paranoia and alienation. It directly gives rise to noncompliance and pain treatment resistance (Eimer & Allen, 1995). Mind reading, personalization, selective abstraction (e.g., looking for and finding betrayal), and disqualifying the positive are common cognitive distortions. This schema is frequently associated with a history of trauma.

Alienation

The core belief is "I just don't fit in. I'm different from everyone else." The alienation schema is commonly associated with the mistrust of others and mistrust of self schemas. It is exemplified by the high MMPI elevations on Scale 8 that many chronic pain patients evidence. It is also exemplified by elevated Patient Alienation Indices on the Pain Coping Inventory, and elevations on the Schizophrenia scale of the SCL-90R. It is associated with emotional distress, noncompliance, hostility, and poor pain treatment outcomes.

SCHEMAS RELATED TO LIMITS AND STANDARDS

Unrelenting Standards

The unrelenting standards schema is represented by the core belief, "I must succeed at all costs. Things must be perfect." The problem of perfectionism is associated with this schema. People with unrelenting standards may drive themselves and others unmercifully because things are never perfect enough. This schema is often associated with tendencies to be angry, hypercritical, and blaming. Patients with unrelenting standards tend to be compulsive and to feel as if little is ever good enough. Some major obstacles to pain management in this group can be their rigidity, their hyperfocused preoccupation with pain, and with finding the "right answers," and their inability to distance and self-distract from pain. Perfectionism is the most frequent distortion. Dichotomous thinking and disqualifying the positive are also common.

Entitlement

The entitlement schema is represented by the core belief, "I must get what I want when I want it. I can't stand it when I don't." This schema tends to be related to problems of low frustration tolerance and to be associated with the narcissism schema. Patients high on this schema may be impatient with themselves and others and have great difficulty delaying gratification, solving problems, and waiting for results. They have difficulty with self-control, and with setting boundaries and limits. They may evidence impulsive behaviors, should statements, low frustration tolerance, impersistence, and problems sticking to a pain rehabilitation program. Compliance with treatment may be a problem. They tend to have difficulty distancing themselves from physical pain.

PAIN-RELATED BELIEFS

A MODEL FOR THE EPIGENESIS OF PAIN BELIEFS

Cognitive therapy for pain management addresses patients' specific beliefs related to pain and suffering because these beliefs mediate coping and adjustment (DeGood & Shutty, 1992; Jensen, Turner, Romano, & Lawler, 1994; Shutty et al., 1990; Williams & Keefe, 1991). In our cognitive model, we conceptualize patients' pain beliefs to mediate between their core schemas and assumptions, and their automatic thoughts and emotional experiences. Core schemas and assumptions are the wellsprings from which a patient constructs pain beliefs based on contextual variables such as type of pain, physical and medical condition, and psychosocial and situational factors. Thus, core schemas and assumptive (B)eliefs, activated by pain and situational precipitants (Activating events), produce emotional experiences and behavioral (C)onsequences. These emotional and behavioral consequences are interpreted and evaluated. Over time, similar interpretations of recurrent experiences give rise to implicit cognitions about pain and suffering, and their psychological validity is repeatedly tested by specific behaviors. Over time, these interpretations, evaluations, and behavioral tests consolidate into specific beliefs about pain.

Given the assumption that Pain-Related Beliefs (PRBs) mediate between patients' core schemas and their automatic thoughts, PMP interventions targeting these PRBs are one point of intervention. Patients' automatic thoughts about pain, emotional experiences, and behaviors constitute other intervention targets.

CATEGORIES OF PAIN BELIEFS

As discussed in Chapter 4, chronic pain patients evidence several important categories of pain beliefs including (a) the causes of pain (mysterious vs. explainable); (b) its consequences (manageable vs. overwhelming and catastrophic); (c) its temporal pattern and intensity (e.g., intermittent, variable in intensity, constant, invariably severe); (d) its future course (permanent vs. eventually remitting); and (e) its locus of responsibility (self-blame vs. other causal or contributing factors). Research suggests that certain beliefs in each of these categories are associated with anxiety, depression, and poor responses to pain treatment (Thorn & Williams, 1993; Williams & Keefe, 1991; Williams et al., 1994; Williams & Thorn, 1989). These emotionally distressing and rehabilitatively toxic beliefs are (a) that pain's cause is mysterious, (b) that pain's temporal pattern is constant and invariably severe, (c) that pain's future course is permanent, (d) that pain's consequences are catastrophic, and (e) that the self is to blame for pain.

Beliefs about oneself in relation to others and the world (parts of the cognitive triad) mediate responses such as alienation, hostility, and either adherence or nonadherence to pain treatment. For example, the belief that others are unsympathetic and that the world has been unfair may lead to treatment resistance and alienation, hostility, and depression (Eimer & Allen, 1995). Beliefs associated with low frustration tolerance (that the pain is unmanageable and intolerable) may underlie addictions to pain medication. Beliefs about poor self-efficacy (Jensen & Karoly, 1991; Jensen, Turner, & Romano, 1991; Jensen, Turner, Romano, & Lawler, 1994) may be associated with feelings of helplessness and drug-seeking behavior. Beliefs that the consequences of pain will be catastrophic are associated with poor coping and other indices of maladjustment (Jensen & Karoly, 1991; Jensen, Turner, Romano, & Karoly, 1991; Jensen, Turner, Romano, & Lawler, 1994; Keefe et al., 1989; Rosenstiel & Keefe, 1983). Catastrophizing beliefs are also associated with higher levels of emotionality and stress response syndromes. Beliefs about the self's vulnerability and pain as a major threat are associated with worrying and anxiety (Jensen, Turner, & Romano, 1991; Jensen, Turner, Romano, & Lawler, 1994). Beliefs that pain is a form of punishment may be associated with increased suffering (Cheek, 1994; Ewin, 1986). Beliefs that pain must cause inevitable misery may be associated with increased emotional distress and physical suffering (Eimer & Allen, 1996; Ewin, 1978, 1986).

Pain beliefs can be assessed with several instruments, as discussed in Chapter 3, including the Pain Beliefs and Perceptions Inventory (Williams & Thorn, 1989), the Pain Experience Scale (Turk & Rudy, 1985), and the Pain Coping Inventory (Eimer & Allen, 1995). In Chapter 6, we cover cognitive therapy interventions for pain management, including techniques for eliciting and modifying rehabilitatively toxic automatic thoughts, cognitive distortions, and beliefs related to pain.

Implementing Cognitive Therapy for Pain Management

Nothing is more essential in the treatment of serious disease than the liberation of the patient from panic and foreboding.

—Norman Cousins

COGNITIVE RESTRUCTURING

The ultimate purpose of cognitive therapy for pain management is to promote *cognitive restructuring*, which is defined as "a basic change in a person's perspective, attitudes, beliefs, emotional reactions, and behaviors relative to an issue such as pain. It involves a reorganization of a person's thinking, modes of perceiving, and behavior relative to that issue." Cognitive PMP fosters cognitive restructuring through the strategic application of techniques that target cognitions, emotions, and behaviors. Such restructuring is a desirable and necessary objective for any pain management treatment modality. In this sense, it can be said, "All roads to pain management success with chronic pain patients lead to cognitive restructuring." One of the key cognitive restructuring goals of PMP is to promote the realization that pain management and pain relief are possible and attainable. This is contrasted with the unrealistic, one-track view that total pain alleviation is the only desirable goal or indication of pain treatment success.

Pain treatment interventions would not work without thinking making it so because pain, as demonstrated earlier, is much more than just a physical issue. Thinking can sabotage or foster the success of any pain treatment, including surgery, physical rehabilitation, and pharmacotherapy as well as psychotherapy. Ellis (1996), one of the founding fathers of cognitive therapy, concedes that some forms of noncognitive and nonrational psychotherapy (e.g., abreactive therapies, hypnosis) may be effective when they indirectly foster cognitive restructuring and produce a deep level of cognitive reorganization. He also points out, however, that the most efficient forms of psychotherapy (i.e., the cognitive-behavior therapies) directly promote cognitive restructuring and enduring cognitive reorganization, in addition to actively directing behavior change.

THE "NINE R'S" OF PMP

Earlier, we discussed the Six Dysfunctional D's of chronic pain syndromes—Distress, Deficits *(in behavioral and cognitive functioning)*, Deconditioning, Depression, Disability, and Disrupted *(sleep)*. We frequently present this metaphor to our patients along with the "Nine R's" of PMP:

1. *Reconditioning* and *Restoration* of active physical functioning to counter Deconditioning.
2. The establishment of a *Regular Routine* to counter Disability, discouragement, fatigue, inertia, setbacks, and flare-ups.
3. *Relaxation* and *Self-Regulation Therapy* to reduce Distress, anxiety, and sympathetic nervous system arousal.
4. *Reactivation therapy* to counter Deconditioning, Depression, fatigue and loss of motivation.
5. *Redirection of attention* away from pain symptoms to reduce Distress.
6. *Reducing reliance on narcotics.*
7. *Responding to, Refuting, Reframing, Reinterpreting,* and *Restructuring* negative thinking to counter Depression, Distress, and Disability.
8. *Rehearsing* pain coping strategies.
9. *Reviewing, reexperiencing,* and *reprocessing* upsetting pain-related memories and unresolved, recurrent, negative emotional experiences tied to the patient's pain problem.

PATIENT EDUCATION

A first order of business for PMP is building rapport, mutual trust, respect, and *patient education.* Good patient education lays a foundation for further building of rapport, trust, and respect. We almost always provide our patients with information about pain mechanisms in general, and about their type of pain in particular, in terms that they can understand. It is important to take the mystery out of pain through discussion and appropriate literature. Many chronic pain patients do not have enough information about why they continually hurt and believe that their pain is a mystery. Others believe that although the reasons for their continual pain have been identified, nothing further can be done. Too little information, or too much of the wrong kind of information, can be misleading and can validate the erroneous idea that one has to be in awful pain all the time.

An important consideration when imparting educational or technical information to patients is how the therapist delivers the message. Many chronic pain patients complain about having been given insensitive, condescending, and perfunctory lectures in the past that confused or scared them. *The meaning is the message.* Cold, insensitive, objectively couched, information giving often does more harm than good. Patient education had better be provided with appropriate good humor and empathy:

THERAPIST: Do you know why you are hurting all the time?

PATIENT: I have scarring from the surgeries. I had three herniated discs in my neck and back removed, my spine was compressed where the nerves run out, and my nerves were being pinched. My surgeon widened the spaces where the nerves run out. But, there is scarring left, and some instability.

THERAPIST: Has your surgeon done everything he can?

PATIENT: I think so. More surgery is not recommended.

THERAPIST: Have any of your doctors sat down and explained to you how these physical problems cause continual pain in terms that you can really understand?

PATIENT: Yes and no. Not really very well. But Doc, there's stuff messed up in there?

THERAPIST: That appears to be true. But, may I try to fill you in on some other factors that probably make your pain worse, that you may be able to learn how to change to relieve pain?

PATIENT: Sure.

THERAPIST: The scarring is probably causing the pain nerves to fire messages up your spinal column to your brain, where you think, "Ouch!"

PATIENT: Fire is right! It's fiery. Its more like, oh God this is awful. I can't bear this!

THERAPIST: Okay. But at that point, how you react, and what you do, can affect how much you hurt.

PATIENT: Are you saying it's all in my head?

THERAPIST: Absolutely not. We both know that's not true. But your head affects how you experience those messages that fire up your spinal column to your brain. I would like to get you to believe that if your doctors cannot do anything more in your spine, that we still can do something in other areas that may help to relieve that fire.

PATIENT: You mean work on my head, Doc?

THERAPIST: Well, I wouldn't put it just that way, but the idea is to use psychology to "rewire" some circuits in the "master control center," so that you can get better relief than you have been getting. Are you with me on this?

PATIENT: Yes.

THERAPIST: With certain psychological strategies, I have been able to help other patients, who were in constant pain, to retrain their nervous system to send competing messages down their spinal column that cut down on the pain messages going up.

PATIENT: Really? That sounds like a lot of hype.

THERAPIST: You mean it sounds like a bunch of baloney?

PATIENT: Well, yeh. But let's give it a good shot.

INTRODUCING THE COGNITIVE MODEL TO PATIENTS

We usually introduce the cognitive model to pain patients with some variant of the following dialogue:

THERAPIST: We all talk to ourselves. By that, I mean we communicate to ourselves silently in our head or mind just as we communicate with and talk to other people. You see, we're always communicating—with ourselves and with others. However, much of the time, when we talk to ourselves, we talk to ourselves in flashes, that is, in a quick abbreviated form, rather than in full grammatically complete sentences. So, we may not always be aware that we are talking to ourselves even when we are. Now, just as the things that we hear other people tell us can make us feel in certain ways, so too, the things we tell ourselves in our own head, that we hear ourselves saying inside, can make us feel in certain ways—scared, mad, sad, glad, content, self-satisfied, and so on. Some of the things we communicate can make us feel better—more hopeful, happier, glad, grateful, and so on; while other things we communicate make us feel worse—sadder, angrier, more scared, and so on. Can you think of some examples?

PATIENT: Sure. Like a couple of days ago, when I lost my gloves. Boy was I angry at myself! I called myself an idiot and other things as well. I guess I could've been easier on myself and I would not have felt as angry.

THERAPIST: That's a good example. Now, some messages that we tell ourselves are very basic and adaptive. They are necessary for our day-to-day survival. Can you think of some examples?

PATIENT: Like you have to eat, or, I better go to bed early tonight. I have to get up early.

THERAPIST: Good. However, other things that we tell ourselves are in reaction to the things that happen to us. Can you think of some examples?

PATIENT: Like calling myself an idiot and other names?

THERAPIST: Yes. So, when we make a mistake, we may blame ourselves and feel worse, or tell ourselves another explanation for the mistake, like it was someone else's fault and feel angry, or we may accept responsibility for our mistake and try to do better the next time. When someone else does something to us that we don't like, or makes a mistake affecting us, we again may hold ourselves accountable and feel bad, blame that other person and feel angry, or come up with some other explanation. The explanation we choose will then affect how we feel, and the actions we take—that is, what we do. Similarly, when we hurt physically and are in pain, we can tell ourselves different things.

So, let's now talk a bit about pain. When we are in pain, we can have thoughts and tell ourselves soothing and comforting things, or we can have other types of thoughts. Some thoughts that people have when they are in pain can actually make them hurt and suffer more, by frightening them or making them very angry. Can you think of some examples from your own experience?

PATIENT: Like telling myself that it's going to get worse?

THERAPIST: Yes. Exactly. You know, one patient of mine, before completing pain management therapy, used to say to himself, when his back and leg pain would begin to act up, things like: "Here we go again. Nothing has changed. It's no use trying anymore. Things just keep getting worse, so why even bother? This pain is destroying me. I can't stand it. I just can't stand doing these exercises. They're too hard and too inconvenient." And, he let these thoughts go unchecked. Because he did not come up with any rebuttals or answers, those thoughts just made him feel worse and suffer more than he needed to. Another patient of mine with neck, back, and leg pain related to an accident that had occurred at work, before therapy, used to say to himself things like "They did this to me and now they don't care, and they don't want to take care of me. I can't work, I can't drive, I can't do anything. I am a cripple, an invalid. Nobody can help me. I'm being punished." And you can imagine how those thoughts that he repeated to himself everyday made him feel.

PATIENT: Badly?

THERAPIST: Yes. Now, it's natural to have automatic negative thoughts when you are hurting. But if these negative automatic thoughts keep playing over and over and go unchecked, then they can actually make the pain feel worse, because being frightened, scared, angry, ashamed, or sad pulls down a person's strength to fight. Negative thoughts create negative feelings.

The therapist goes on to explain that strength is required to build up pain tolerance and cope with the pain. The term, *cognitive therapy,* is introduced and defined as a coping skills therapy that helps people build up their psychological resistance and immunity to negative thinking. The therapist elaborates by explaining (a) that CT teaches "verbal judo" for fighting negative self-talk, and coping strategies for reducing pain and suffering, (b) that CT is a form of self-help that must be practiced in between sessions, (c) that it helps a person become a better communicator with both self and others and (d) that CT is actually a form of "coaching"—the therapist coaches patients to coach themselves to more effectively manage unavoidable pain.

Managing the Therapeutic Relationship

The effectiveness of cognitive restructuring techniques depends on maintaining a *collaborative* working relationship with the patient. However, as discussed earlier, and in other places (Bellissimo & Tunks, 1984; Eimer, 1988, 1989; Turk et al., 1983), chronic pain patients often present in ways that can defy the implementation of effective treatment. All-or-nothing thinking may lead some patients to perceive certain doctors as either "all bad" or "all good." A physician may be seen as withholding (e.g., for refusing to write another prescription for narcotics), rejecting, callous, and insensitive; or alternatively, as the patient's last hope for redemption from a life of pain.

Extreme thinking leads many chronic pain patients to become angry and resentful of health care professionals and hypersensitive to the way things are said. The meaning many chronic patients attach to doctor visits may derive from messages with imperatives such as "You'd *better* . . . ," "You *have to* . . . ," or "You *must* learn to live with your pain," "There is nothing more that we can do for you," or "You'd better do exactly what we tell you or you will not get better!" Noncompliance with pain treatment is a frequent result.

In a collaborative therapeutic relationship, the therapist must adjust his or her degree of *active-directiveness* according to the patient's needs. With very depressed pain patients, a more active-directive stance is necessary at first. In contrast, the therapist usually must give highly passive and dependent patients greater responsibility for identifying specific problems, evaluating automatic thoughts, and developing homework assignments.

Cognitive therapy recognizes the central importance of a collaborative therapist-patient relationship in facilitating treatment compliance. As stated by Freeman and Reinecke (1995):

> The therapist is viewed as a "co-investigator"—working with patients to make sense of their experiences and emotions by exploring their thoughts,

images, and feelings with them. Guided Socratic questioning (also termed, *guided inquiry*) is often employed as a means of providing patients with an understanding of their thoughts and the ways their beliefs influence their feelings and their actions. (p. 194)

In other words, the therapist does not unquestioningly accept a patient's interpretations and reactions in relation to pain, in the interest of maintaining rapport. Through skillful questioning, humor, information giving, modeling, examples, and metaphors, the therapist encourages pain patients to examine and question their thoughts as separate objects when evaluating their *validity, functionality,* and *adaptiveness.* Dysfunctional or maladaptive thoughts related to pain are viewed as hypotheses that require empirical testing (Freeman & Reinecke, 1995).

THE TRANSFERENCE RELATIONSHIP

One other concept requires discussion because it is so ubiquitous. *Transference* refers to the tendency of most people to respond to new persons in their lives with the same ideas and expectations that guided their responses to people who played key roles at an earlier time. By activating these old ideas and expectations, or schemas, in new situations people tend to cognitively process information in old ways and repeat old behavioral response patterns that may no longer be applicable or serve an adaptive purpose. In doing so, people frequently alienate themselves further from others and maintain their interpersonal conflict and emotional distress.

Psychotherapy patients' reactions to their therapists often partially recapitulate their relationships with others. These transferred response patterns, based as they usually are on irrational beliefs, often are maladaptive and dysfunctional; they need to be examined and processed when they impede cognitive, behavioral, and emotional change, and therapeutic progress. The concepts of transference and of chronic pain are similar in that they both describe phenomena that *once might have been useful, but no longer serve an adaptive purpose.* In a sense, <u>chronic</u> pain is a relic of the past, and so is transference.

Levels of Transference

With chronic pain patients, transference may be operative on several levels. On one level, a patient can have chronic pain that does not appear to serve any adaptive purpose from a physiological or biological survival standpoint, although it may have served an adaptive purpose at one time. On a second level, patients' maladaptive schemas about doctors and health care professionals often are activated and reactivated (transferred) in the psychotherapy context. On a third level, once the therapist begins to understand a patient's socialization history and personality, it becomes apparent that the patient's Early Maladaptive Schemas are being reactivated in and out of the therapy.

Narrative Truth versus Historical Truth

It is often important conceptually to make connections between these three levels of transference. However, we generally avoid making declarative interpretations to patients about what their behavior represents because patients often experience such statements as intrusive, smug, or pretentious. In contrast, we prefer to pose tentative hypotheses to be confirmed or disconfirmed by data. This approach is more respectful, and also more realistic. The psychotherapist deals with concepts, constructs, metaphors, personal stories, and belief systems and thus must recognize the important conceptual distinction between narrative truth and historical truth (Spence, 1982). Especially in light of the controversies over the validity of recovered traumatic memories (Loftus, 1993; Ofshe & Watters, 1994; Pope & Brown, 1996) and the psychiatric epigenesis versus the "manufacture" of multiple personality disorder (Merskey, 1992), it is wise (and more adaptive) to assume that the material we process in psychotherapy is more representative of narrative truth than of historical truth.

SELF-MONITORING

Self-monitoring is a vital intervention for cognitive-behavior therapy. It involves first convincing patients of the importance of collecting data and keeping records, and then teaching them how to do it. Self-monitoring of symptoms, pain levels, and other variables is a naturalistic and contextually valid method of collecting therapy outcome data. Self-monitoring of pain levels and symptoms provides essential *pretreatment* baseline data. Self-monitoring of assigned target variables during the treatment provides a measure of patient motivation and compliance. Asking patients to collect data about their problems, symptoms, and therapy progress gives patients the opportunity to play an active role in their therapy and recovery. It also facilitates socializing patients to the cognitive-behavioral model. Regularly rating pain levels and associated factors enables patients to see that pain varies as a function of different factors and helps them discover the factors associated with variations in their pain levels.

Concurrent self-monitoring of symptoms and pain levels provides ongoing data relevant to determining whether treatment strategies are working, which enables the therapist to modify the treatment plan as necessary. In addition, self-monitoring helps patients develop greater insight and awareness about the connections between their symptoms, pain levels, and external events, and their thoughts, feelings, images, and behaviors. Finally, comparison of a patient's self-monitoring records before and after treatment, provides important "change data" for use in determining treatment efficacy. Self-monitoring is accomplished by asking patients to keep some form of symptom diary or record of their symptoms and associated phenomena of interest. We typically employ one or two of the three following recording formats.

1. The *Daily Pain and Thought Record* (DPTR) is a variant of cognitive therapy's traditional Dysfunctional Thought Record (J. Beck, 1995; Freeman et al., 1990). A blank DPTR for the reader's use is provided in Appendix R-1. After completing an initial assessment and introducing the cognitive model, we typically present *thought monitoring* through the use of the DPTR. This form allows a patient to record daily pain flare-ups, types of pain, pain levels (on a 0-to-10 scale), associated situations and activities, associated emotions and emotional intensity (rated from 0 to 10), associated automatic thoughts, rational responses, and emotional and physical outcomes.

For their initial homework assignment, patients usually just keep track of situations, type of pain, symptom intensity, and automatic thoughts. We introduce the rest of the DPTR after we have discussed *rational responding* and *cognitive disputation* in session. The "Questions to Ask Myself" section at the bottom of the DPTR prompts patients in disputing their automatic thoughts related to pain.

2. The *Pain Tracking Diary* (PTD) is a tool that enables patients to systematically collect and record data on their daily pain levels, downtime, medication use, and coping strategies. It is adapted from the form described by Thorn and Williams (1993). A blank PTD for the reader's use is provided in Appendix R-2. Patients record their pain levels (on a 0-to-10 verbal-numerical scale) and type of pain, and fill out the rest of the PTD at breakfast, lunch, dinner, and bedtime. We typically introduce patients to the Pain Tracking Diary during our initial assessment and review patients' daily PTDs at each therapy session. The therapist makes a copy for the patient's file, and the patient keeps the original. These PTDs provide pretreatment baselines and also serve as a therapy outcome measure. Patients usually are requested to keep their PTDs throughout the course of therapy.

3. The *Daily Pain Diary* (DPD) enables patients to systematically collect and record data about their daily pain levels, pain locations, pain-related situations and activities, automatic thoughts, emotional feelings, coping measures, and medication use at two-hour intervals throughout the day. A blank DPD for the reader's use is provided in Appendix H.

Pain intensity levels are recorded using Melzack's (1975) 6-point Present Pain Index (PPI). Patients can also record their distress levels on a 6-point scale. The DPD format provides more data than the other two diary formats, but it requires the patient to record entries at more frequent intervals. Therefore, many patients are more likely to keep the Pain Tracking Diary (PTD).

Patients often resist keeping journals by saying (a) "I won't have the time," (b) It will be "awkward" or "inconvenient" to carry around the forms, and (c) "Won't keeping track of my pain levels and negative thoughts make me focus even more on my pain and symptoms?" We respond by saying that (a) self-monitoring records should be simple; (b) keeping a pain diary is easy and helps patients gain control over their pain; (c) patients who keep records get better faster and become better copers; (d) keeping records helps people learn things about their pain that they never knew such as what makes it worse or better, which coping strategies work and which do not; and (e) the benefits of carrying the diary around and regularly recording in it will far outweigh any inconvenience. We also ask patients what they say to themselves whenever they first think about making a diary entry and then do not do it.

COPING STRATEGY THERAPY (CST)

Coping Strategy Therapy, or CST, is an intervention designed to help patients' evaluate their implicit pain coping strategies, and develop more effective strategies (Brown & Fromm, 1987; Thorn & Williams, 1993). A typical initial session of CST usually involves reviewing the data provided by the Pain Coping Inventory, the Coping Strategies Questionnaire, and other relevant instruments that may have been administered, such as the Pain Beliefs and Perceptions Inventory. The patient's PTD, DPTR, or DPD which are filled out in between sessions, are also reviewed. We also suggest that patients read Marcus and Arbeiter's (1994) *Freedom from Chronic Pain* after the initial evaluation. Their chapter "Coping with Pain Activating Triggers," or (PATs) (pp. 90–105) is especially relevant to CST.

At the next session, the therapist will (a) review the patient's homework and any additional test results, (b) normalize the patient's difficulties, (c) discuss the reading assignment, (d) identify and label the patient's main coping strategies, (e) suggest that the patient can have more choices and reevaluate each coping strategy's effectiveness, and (f) suggest that the patient think about trying different coping strategies. The therapist can then demonstrate several coping strategies, guide the patient in performing them, and obtain the patient's feedback. Finally, the therapist should ask the patient to practice different coping strategies for homework.

PATIENT: So, how do we begin? I want to get better, man.
THERAPIST: We begin like this: Tell me how much pain are you in now. From zero to ten.
PATIENT: About a six or seven.
THERAPIST: Do you have that bad burning in your leg?
PATIENT: That's always there, man. And also the sticking in my back, and the numbness.
THERAPIST: So, what can you do about it?
PATIENT: I don't know, man. You are the doctor.
THERAPIST: How about talking calmly to yourself? Let me demonstrate.

The session should continue with the therapist demonstrating the use of positive self talk and then asking the patient to try. The therapist coaches the patient and provides reinforcement as the patient begins to generate positive self-talk and coping alternatives. After obtaining the patient's feedback about the strategy, the therapist suggests an exercise. The therapist asks the patient to focus on a pain site (not the hardest or worst one) while the therapist guides the patient in trying out a number of different mental pain coping strategies. This exercise makes it possible to assess which coping strategies are effective and which are not for that patient. As discussed by Brown and Fromm (1987), the focus is on developing self-efficacy. The patient needs to discover what works and what does not.

The coping strategies fall into a number of categories: *distraction* (e.g., doing mental arithmetic; engaging in a pleasant fantasy; recalling a pleasant, pain-free time; thinking about engaging in a pleasant activity; consecutively refocusing on different objects in the immediate environment; refocusing attention on other sensations in different parts of the body; introducing counter stimulation to some other part of the body, such as pinching the webbing between the thumb and index finger on one hand), *direct awareness* (e.g., focusing directly and nonjudgmentally on the pain sensations; breathing slowly and deeply, and imagining directing the flow of the breath into and through the targeted pain area; following the flow of thoughts in one's stream of consciousness), *positive affirmations* (i.e., verbalizing positive and encouraging self-statements, such as telling oneself to "be strong," to "stay calm," that "I can handle the pain," that "it will pass," etc.), *relaxation* (e.g., controlled diaphragmatic breathing; progressive muscle relaxation), and *pain relief, replacement,* and *transformational imagery* (e.g., imagining the painful area becoming numb; imagining applying ice or heat to the painful area; imagining receiving an anesthetic injection to the painful area; imagining that the pain sensations are other less painful sensations; imagining that the pain is in someone else's body; imagining oneself floating; imagining oneself experiencing the pain in a different context such as while rescuing a child or fighting as a soldier in battle).

There are also additional schemes for classifying pain coping strategies such as those developed by Rosenstiel and Keefe (1983), Turk et al. (1983), Brown and Fromm (1987), and Eimer (1988, 1989). Brown and Fromm (1987) introduced the scheme of the "four As of pain control" which are Avoidance or distraction, Alleviation with imaginative suggestions, Alteration of the pain experience and the pain's meaning, and Awareness of the pain sensations and pain experience.

After each coping strategy is tried, the therapist asks if the patient was able to perform the technique and think of the pain at the same time. The therapist should also ask how each coping strategy affected the patient's pain level. The patient should be asked to give the pain a numerical rating (0–10) before, during, and after performing each coping strategy. Afterward, the therapist should ask the patient to select the most promising strategies to try for short periods each day and to record the results. Initially the patient should work with less challenging pain, rather than the most challenging pain. The therapist and patient can review this homework at the next session.

ASSESSING VULNERABILITY FACTORS AND PAIN ACTIVATING TRIGGERS

The Pain Vulnerability Checklist (PVCL) discussed earlier and displayed in Appendix F can be used to discover the factors that may make a patient vulnerable to having a pain flare-up. The following therapy dialogue also illustrates the assessment of pain activating triggers:

THERAPIST: What problem would you like to work on today?
PATIENT: These headaches that I get everyday.
THERAPIST: What gives you headaches do you think?
PATIENT: I don't know.
THERAPIST: Are there any times when your headaches are worse than at other times?
PATIENT: Well, I get the worst headaches over the weekend.
THERAPIST: Last week, you mentioned that you also get these tension headaches when you get to work. Is that right?

PATIENT: Yes. I really think going to work gives me a headache. Work is really stressful!

THERAPIST: What is most stressful about work?

PATIENT: My boss watches over me. I can never get up for air. She keeps giving me more work.

THERAPIST: What are your thoughts about that?

PATIENT: I'll never get it all done. I'll have to take work home over the weekend again. I have to work faster and faster to get the additional work done.

THERAPIST: And what feelings go along with those thoughts?

PATIENT: I'm scared I'm going to get fired and be without a job!

THERAPIST: Any other feelings about having all this work to do?

PATIENT: Yeh. No one shows any appreciation. They take me for granted.

THERAPIST: And what are your feelings about that?

PATIENT: It makes me angry!

THERAPIST: Might these things trigger your headaches when you get to work?

PATIENT: Yes. I think so.

THERAPIST: And, what about on the weekends?

PATIENT: I think people are supposed to relax on the weekends. My boss has taken over my life. I don't get paid any more. I shouldn't have to take work home, but if I don't get it done, I'll lose my job and then where will I be?

THERAPIST: Do you think that your fear of losing your job if you don't keep up and your resentment that you have to take work home trigger those weekend headaches?

PATIENT: Yes I do. I'm being exploited. There's nothing I can do about it.

Over the next few therapy sessions, we assessed this patient's automatic thoughts and beliefs associated with her fears, sense of helplessness, and anger about being exploited. We identified her cognitive distortions and disputed her irrational thoughts. We also explored options and alternatives for coping with her headache triggers.

COGNITIVE DISPUTATION

COGNITIVE DISPUTATION

Cognitive disputation is the flagship technique of cognitive therapy for pain management. The goal of cognitive disputation is to identify and challenge dysfunctional thinking associated with increased pain and emotional distress. Cognitive disputation is the process of responding to *Dysfunctional Automatic Thoughts* (DATs) to test their validity. DATs associated with pain and suffering are subjected to examination, refuted, reframed, reinterpreted, restructured, and replaced with healthier and more realistic thoughts.

FORMULATING THE TARGET PROBLEM

The Daily Pain and Thought Record (DPTR) provides an excellent format for identifying and testing Dysfunctional Automatic Thoughts (DATs) and Dysfunctional Beliefs (DBs) associated with pain. The disputation process begins by helping the patient define a target problem. Then, the ABC's of the target problem are formulated. That means identifying the *A*ctivating event or situation, the type and severity of pain, the associated emotional and behavioral *C*onsequences, and the patient's attendant thoughts and *B*eliefs:

THERAPIST: Which problem would you like to start working on?
PATIENT: My pain and stiffness.
THERAPIST: When is your pain and stiffness the most upsetting?
PATIENT: In the morning, getting dressed for work, and also on the weekend.
THERAPIST: On average, how severe is your pain in the morning on a 0-to-10 scale?
PATIENT: About a 6.
THERAPIST: And your stiffness?
PATIENT: About a 10.
THERAPIST: That's really bad!
PATIENT: Yup. It really is.
THERAPIST: What negative feelings would you say go along with the pain and the stiffness?
PATIENT: I get pretty angry. Really mad.
THERAPIST: When you feel angry and mad, what thoughts go through your mind?
PATIENT: Like I am never going to get better. It's not fair. I am a basket case.
THERAPIST: Assume for a moment that it's true that you're never going to get better. And that means what?
PATIENT: I'll have to suffer for the rest of my life! I won't be able to do the things I always dreamed of doing. I'll really be a total failure.
THERAPIST: And what do you do when you are feeling stiff and in pain in the morning?
PATIENT: I curse. I sometimes throw my clothes and I am a real drag to be around.
THERAPIST: A drag? How?
PATIENT: Well, I'll yell at my wife and my kids.

COGNITIVE RESTRUCTURING WITH "READS": THE FIVE STEPS OF COGNITIVE DISPUTATION

After the ABC's of the target problem have been formulated, and the patient's DATs and DBs have been identified, the cognitive disputation process, which is the heart of cognitive restructuring, can begin. Our conceptualization of the cognitive disputation process involves five steps. The first letters of the key words describing these steps collectively spell the acronym "READS" (Rationale for Refuting, Examination of the Evidence, Alternative Beliefs, Decatastrophization, and Steps to Solve the Problem.

- In Step 1 (R), the therapist provides the patient with an acceptable *rationale* for *responding* to and *refuting* his or her pain-related automatic thoughts and underlying beliefs.
- The goal of Step 2 (E) is to systematically *examine* and question the *evidence* supporting and refuting particular dysfunctional automatic thoughts (DATs) or dysfunctional beliefs (DBs) related to pain.
- In Step 3 (A), the therapist and patient develop *alternative*, more functional explanations or beliefs.
- Step 4 (D) is intended to *decatastrophize* the dysfunctional automatic thoughts (DATs) or dysfunctional beliefs (DBs).
- In Step 5 (S), the therapist helps the patient formulate specific, behavioral *steps* for *solving* or coping with the pain-related problem.

STEP 1. PROVIDING AN ACCEPTABLE RATIONALE FOR RESPONDING

In line with cognitive therapy's emphasis on patient-therapist collaboration, it is advisable to provide patients with an acceptable rationale for responding to and refuting DATs and DBs:

THERAPIST: So, when your pain is bad, you often have thoughts like, "I am never going to get better. Its not fair. I am a basket case. I'll have to suffer for the rest of my life! I won't be able to do the things I always dreamed of doing. I'll really be a total failure."

PATIENT: That's right.

THERAPIST: Have you ever thought of contesting these kinds of thoughts? I mean, refuting them?

PATIENT: Why?

THERAPIST: Because they are not good for you to swallow. When they come pouring on, it may be like adding gasoline to the fire!

PATIENT: Hmmm. I think I see what you mean.

THERAPIST: I mean it can be like wearing a little set of headphones while playing and replaying discouraging and defeating words over and over. Living as you do with daily pain is a real adversity. Just like a boxer who gets beat up in the ring, you need to be in shape to handle it!

PATIENT: I need to be my own coach?

THERAPIST: Exactly. You'd be best off if you are.

PATIENT: So, what do I have to learn to do?

THERAPIST: You have to learn to counterattack and refute your negative thoughts, or as we say, your dysfunctional automatic thoughts or DATs.

STEP 2. EXAMINING AND QUESTIONING THE EVIDENCE

Several cognitive techniques are employed in this step including questioning the evidence directly (e.g., "What evidence is there for the truth of that statement?"), examining the advantages and disadvantages of accepting a particular belief (e.g., "What are the advantages of accepting that thought to be true?"), assessing a patient's "idiosyncratic meaning" (e.g., "What do you mean by saying 'I was shot'?"), reassessing responsibility to refute self-blame (e.g., "Whose fault is it really? Is it fair to hold yourself to blame? Is it your job to be your own judge and jury?"), and scaling phenomena such as pain to establish shades of gray and refute all-or-nothing thinking (e.g., "Periodically rating how much pain you are in on a 0-to-10 scale may help you realize that your pain does not stay the same all the time. It varies").

QUESTIONING THE EVIDENCE

THERAPIST: Earlier, you said that thoughts go through your mind like "I am never going to get better; It's not fair; and I'm a basket case." Is that correct?

PATIENT: Uh-huh.

THERAPIST: Let's take a closer look at those dire thoughts. Okay?

PATIENT: Sure.

THERAPIST: There are actually three thoughts here. The first one is "I am never going to get better." Do you have any evidence that supports that thought?

PATIENT: Well, yes. I've had this condition (*fibromyalgia*) for nine years, and no doctor has been able to help me get rid of the condition.

THERAPIST: Those are facts. But believing that the condition is permanent. Isn't that another story? How do you know that modern medicine won't find a cure for this illness within your lifetime?

PATIENT: Well, that I don't know. But it's pretty unlikely.

THERAPIST: Okay. But I have another question. Does getting better depend on finding a cure? Haven't you told me that you've had periods that lasted where you functioned and felt much better?

PATIENT: Yes. That is true.

EXAMINING ADVANTAGES AND DISADVANTAGES

Often, it is useful to direct the discussion to a consideration of the advantages and disadvantages of believing in the DATs and DBs:

THERAPIST: And let's jump to that third thought for a second. You said, "I'm a basket case." How does repeating that thought to yourself make you feel?

PATIENT: Not so good.

THERAPIST: Does thinking "I'm a basket case" motivate you to look for reasons why you can get better?

PATIENT: No. It sure does not.

THERAPIST: During those periods when you functioned and felt better, do you think you were thinking, "I am never going to get better because I am a basket case"?

PATIENT: Nope. I was thinking positively.

THERAPIST: How about both positively and realistically?

PATIENT: Yeh. I'll buy that.

THERAPIST: And the thought, "It's not fair." Are there any advantages of going through an unfair world pining because the world is not fair?

PATIENT: Well, shouldn't people be fair?

THERAPIST: It's nice when they are. But isn't that like saying, I shouldn't have pain? I mean, where's the evidence that I shouldn't have pain? You see if you can go around and start becoming more critical about your automatic thoughts, I think you would start to feel in a better frame of mind.

PATIENT: I guess so.

THERAPIST: Doesn't this sound convincing to you?

PATIENT: Well, I've thought this way forever. What else am I going to think?

ASSESSING IDIOSYNCRATIC MEANING

It is important to assess exactly what a patient means by certain qualifying terms, such as, in the preceding example, the word, "forever":

THERAPIST: What do you mean, "forever"?

PATIENT: I mean that I have always been a negative thinker. I mean ever since I was a kid. My folks taught me how to do it really well.

THERAPIST: You've been well trained by the best in the business?

PATIENT: *(Laughs)* I guess I really have!

Many chronic pain patients characterize their pain with idiosyncratic terms that are laden with extremely stressful or even violent images reflecting their extremely stressful lives. It is important to explore exactly what patients mean and are attempting to represent with their words. Later, the therapist can suggest developing alternative *pain replacement images*. When exploring idiosyncratic meaning with such patients, or with any patients for that matter, it is important to be careful to not take your tentative understanding for granted. Tentative hypotheses about what the patient's expressions mean should be checked out with the patient for verification or further clarification.

THERAPIST: What does your pain feel like to you?

PATIENT: It feels like I'm being strangled.

THERAPIST: Can you be more specific? What do you mean that it feels like you're being strangled?

PATIENT: It feels like someone has tied a noose around my neck and is pulling on the other end.

THERAPIST: Wow. That's a violent image.

PATIENT: Everything is being thrown in my face. My life is falling apart.

THERAPIST: What do you mean by "everything is being thrown in your face"?

CLARIFY IATROGENICALLY INDUCED MEANINGS OF PAIN DESCRIPTORS

In the following example, a chronic low back pain patient who suffered from spondylolisthesis (spinal instability caused by a falling forward of two of the lumbar vertebrae), spondylomalacia (softening of the vertebrae with multiple collapsed vertebral bodies), and who had undergone 11 failed back surgeries, described her pain as feeling as if her spine was falling apart. Often, patients use terms that reflect the understanding they have derived from what doctors have told them so it is essential to ask patients to clarify what they mean. In this case, doctors had told the woman she would have to wear a brace to stabilize her spine:

THERAPIST: So, when you say your spine feels as if it is "falling apart," you mean what?

Patient: I mean it's not stable. The pain is unbearable. I can't stand up without excruciating pain. I mean I always have to be in this position (i.e., reclining).

Therapist: Jane, earlier, you also used the expression, "It feels like I'm falling over, collapsing." By that, did you mean the same thing?

Patient: Well no, not really. I meant that there's pressure on the nerves in my back, and my doctor said it's only a matter of time before it bowls me all the way over, and I won't be able to stand up, or straighten out, at all.

Assessing Idiosyncratic Meaning with Terminal Cancer Pain

In the following example, a patient with advanced lung cancer related pain described her pain experience, which was influenced by the cancer's progression and the iatrogenic effects of radiation therapy. The patient was seen at a hospice at the request of her doctor and her family. This example illustrates the importance of being exquisitely sensitive to a patient's emotional reactions. One has to watch the timing of questions. There are times when it is most respectful to reflect empathy and concern; asking for idiosyncratic meaning could be perceived as intrusive and unempathic. The therapist has to balance further inquiry with empathy and support. This approach can also be termed "just being with the patient":

Therapist: Would you tell me about the pain?

Patient: I feel like I'm strangling, smothering.

Therapist: What do you mean by that?

Patient: The radiation scalded my throat to the point where I can't even swallow water.

Therapist: What do you do?

Patient: It's hard to swallow. I've had a *(swallowing)* therapist. I have to eat ice.

Therapist: The feeling, sensation of "strangling," "smothering," please tell me what it's related to.

Patient: The cancer. It's crawling through my lungs. Choking the air out of me. Burning pain in my chest and in my throat. You can't eat or drink. This is no way to live, like this. If it weren't for the painkillers . . . I don't know *(she starts to cry).*

Therapist: Can I say "Thank God for the pain medicine?"

Patient: Yes *(meekly).*

Therapist: Are they doing a good job here helping you with the pain?

Patient: Oh yes. Before I came here *(to the hospice),* it was unbearable.

THERAPIST: Before you couldn't stand the pain and now, there's some relief?

PATIENT: *(Nods)* Yes.

THERAPIST: Do you worry about your husband?

PATIENT: Oh, yes *(starts to cry)*.

THERAPIST: What do you worry about?

PATIENT: Jack will be so lonely.

THERAPIST: I understand. Has Jack reassured you that he will be able to take care of himself?

PATIENT: Oh, yes. Jack has been wonderful.

THERAPIST: He loves you very much.

PATIENT: *(Nods, sobbing)*

THERAPIST: As a figure of speech, do you think you would be able to breathe easy knowing that Jack will be alright?

PATIENT: *(Nods, and stops sobbing)* You know Doctor, we've been married 50 years. I'm not saying its been *all* good, but we've been good to each other.

THERAPIST: Jack doesn't want to leave your side, but he strikes me as a very strong and independent man.

PATIENT: Yes. He is. He is that all right.

REASSESSING RESPONSIBILITY

After treating with numerous health care providers and not experiencing any permanent improvement, many chronic pain patients may begin to wonder whether or not they themselves are to blame for their enduring pain. The tendency to blame oneself for not getting better may be the result of the erroneous conclusion that one is not a "good enough patient," or that one is not living a healthier lifestyle because of insufficient motivation to get out of pain. Whatever its basis, self-blame is self-defeating and usually a cognitive distortion. Therefore, it is important to challenge and eradicate it.

PATIENT: Maybe I'm somewhat to blame for the way I feel. I know that I have not been doing enough to get out of pain.

THERAPIST: Wait a minute. What exactly do you mean by that?

PATIENT: I mean that I have not exercised regularly enough, and my diet could be better.

THERAPIST: How much can you do? I mean you exercise every day, you make time to stretch, you've cleaned up your diet, you go for massages, you take your supplements, you've been to physical therapy, you keep your doctor appointments, and you are also working. Aren't you being a little hard on yourself?

PATIENT: Listen, the pain is hard on me!

THERAPIST: I wonder whether the pain might become softer if you could be a little softer with yourself.

PATIENT: But what keeps running over and over again through my mind is what that nutritionist said. He said that my health is totally up to me and that staying healthy or getting back my health is hard work.

THERAPIST: I would be careful with the word "totally." Can anybody ever be totally in control of everything that happens to them?

PATIENT: No. Not really.

THERAPIST: So, do you think that it is totally healthy to believe that your health is totally up to you?

PATIENT: Maybe not if you put it that way.

THERAPIST: Might it not be healthier to believe that your health is strongly affected by the things that you yourself can control-like how you think, the feelings you create for yourself, the things that you do, and what you eat?

PATIENT: I guess so.

THERAPIST: What good does it do to blame yourself for the way you feel when you are hurting physically?

PATIENT: I guess not much good at all. It just makes me feel depressed and angry.

THERAPIST: That's right. Does it do you any good to blame yourself for not doing enough to get out of pain?

SCALING

Harboring self-blame for pain is usually a cognitive distortion involving all-or-nothing, absolutistic thinking. Therefore, it is important to teach patients how to scale their feelings and physical sensations so that they can see shades of gray.

PATIENT: When I wake up feeling really lousy, I can't help but ask myself what is it that I did yesterday that put me back in such pain? I usually conclude that I overdid something. I either ate too much, exercised too hard, or something like that.

THERAPIST: Tracking the kinds of activities that might be triggering more pain is a good idea. It is also a good idea to rate on a zero to ten scale how much you think you overate, how much you overexercised, and so on. Also, when you wake up feeling lousy and in pain, don't forget to rate how much pain you are in. Do you wake up feeling just as lousy every morning when you overate or overexercised a certain amount the night before?

PATIENT: Probably not.

THERAPIST: On every morning when you wake up in pain, is the pain always an absolute ten? Is it a nine, sometimes an eight, a five? What number is it?

STEP 3. DEVELOPING AN ALTERNATIVE, MORE FUNCTIONAL INTERPRETATION

After gathering enough evidence that does not support the DAT or DB being disputed, it is necessary to come up with an alternative, more functional thought or belief that is realistic. Some cognitive techniques that can be employed in this third step include directly asking for an alternative thought or belief (e.g., "What could you possibly think instead?" "Is there an alternative explanation or way of looking at that?"), labeling cognitive distortions, sensitively employing humor (e.g., "Is there a possible distortion or bias in your thinking about that?" "What cognitive distortion do you think is lurking behind that seemingly harmless thought?"), modeling, role-playing, and role reversal, information giving, using metaphors, and developing pain replacement imagery:

THERAPIST: So, what could you possibly think instead of "I'm never going to get better"?

PATIENT: But in a way that's right.

THERAPIST: But, haven't we already gone over the frame of mind that thought puts you in?

PATIENT: Yes. I guess we have.

THERAPIST: Do you want to see if you can start believing something more functional and realistic, instead of continuing to tell yourself such downers?

PATIENT: You mean I might actually start to feel better?

THERAPIST: That's what I'm driving at. What you tell yourself and how you feel are connected.

PATIENT: Okay. Saying "I'm never going to get better" is probably an exaggeration.

THERAPIST: When you are tired, feeling stiff, and in pain, in CAPITAL LETTERS, what might you say to yourself when you have that thought, "I'm never going to get better"?

PATIENT: I AM going to get better?

THERAPIST: You could say that. But is it believable?

PATIENT: No. Not really.

THERAPIST: Why not?

PATIENT: Because I don't feel like I am going to get better. I'm in a fog, and I am in pain.

LABELING COGNITIVE DISTORTIONS

Frequently, it is useful to point out to patients the cognitive distortions in their thinking by putting a label on the distortion and explaining it:

THERAPIST: That's a valid point. You've just described what is called "pain-based emotional reasoning" or "PBER." This means that when you are in pain, fatigued, and so on, it's really hard to believe anything but the negative, even though the negative only pulls you down more.

PATIENT: I guess it would be useful to remind myself of this when I am in that fog.

THERAPIST: Yes, indeed!

PATIENT: So, what could I say instead of I am going to or not going to get better?

THERAPIST: How do you think you'd react if I happened to be with you in spirit and you heard my voice whispering in your ear, "Think you *are* going to get better because you *can* get better, even though right *now*, you don't feel like you can believe this."

PATIENT: I think that could work! I mean it's like acknowledging how I feel, lousy, but saying to myself, look here fellow, there is hope. You can make it happen.

THERAPIST: Is it an all-or-nothing thing?

PATIENT: No, definitely not.

THERAPIST: Getting better is a process. In this case, the means equals the ends.

PAIN REPLACEMENT IMAGERY

A woman experienced neck and shoulder pain that she described as being "like someone has tied a noose around my neck and is pulling on the other end." The therapist introduced to her the coping option of developing pain replacement imagery (also termed, pain relief or pain antidote imagery) at the proper time:

THERAPIST: What do you think would happen if you pictured your neck and shoulder pain differently?

PATIENT: I don't know what you mean.

THERAPIST: What I am asking you is to consider how else you might be able to picture your neck and shoulder pain, so that you don't keep seeing it in such a violent way—as being strangled by a noose around your neck.

PATIENT: Doc, I know what you're saying. It's that I should come up with another expression, figure of speech?

THERAPIST: Well, yes. I just wonder if you could get some deserved relief by consciously making an effort to bring to mind a less violent picture of what is going on in your body?

PATIENT: I can try *(laughs)*.

THERAPIST: *(laughs)* Maybe I can get you to cut the rope. Then we can untie the noose.

DEVELOPING PAIN REPLACEMENT IMAGERY FOR CANCER PAIN

In the earlier example of the patient with cancer pain, she had described feeling as if the cancer was crawling through her lungs. "Choking the air out of me. Burning pain in my chest and in my throat. You can't eat or drink." Using therapeutic touch and a simple concentration and relaxation exercise, the therapist worked with this patient to develop "replacement imagery" that could provide an alternative picture:

THERAPIST: Would you consider doing a little "pain-killing exercise" with me that may help you to feel more comfortable?

PATIENT: Yes. I will.

THERAPIST: It involves using a little imagination to picture something that could kill the cancer cells in your lungs and stop them from choking you . . . stop them from burning and suffocating you . . . stop them from crawling through your lungs. How does that sound to you?

PATIENT: Okay.

THERAPIST: Good. I also would like you to remember that you and I can change any images that come up for you at any time. That's the beauty of imagination. Does that make sense?

PATIENT: Yes *(and nods)*.

THERAPIST: May I hold and stroke your hand? *(Patient nods in agreement)* Okay. Then, it helps to first get as relaxed as possible. So, just concentrate on your left hand, while I gently hold your hand and stroke it. *(Therapist begins to stroke the patient's hand, and then gently and rhythmically to sway the hand and forearm, bent at the elbow, back and forth and around)* Let's just take a few minutes to settle back into a nice relaxed state. Does that feel good? Just nod if it does. You don't have to talk now. *(Patient nods)* Concentrate on your hand . . . Can you count along with me? *(Patient nods)* Good. Now I am going to watch your breathing, and count each breath out loud. Please count with me to yourself. Okay? *(Patient nods and Therapist starts counting out loud as he continues to gently work with her left hand)*

PATIENT: *(Begins to become anxious and breathing becomes labored)* Oh, oh. Oh God. I can't breathe. It's choking me again!

THERAPIST: Ellen, it's all right. You got a little nervous because of what you have been through. It's okay. That's understandable. Ellen, just try to relax your body, and I'd like you to keep your attention on your hand too, the hand I am holding, and swaying. Is that okay? *(Ellen nods)* Good. *(The patient begins to calm down and relax)* Very good. That's it. Very good. Just R–E–L–A–X for now . . .

PATIENT: I am better, more relaxed now.

THERAPIST: Now Ellen, would you be willing to bring to your mind a picture of something capable of killing those cancer cells? *(Patient nods)* Good. Think about it and nod when you have such a picture. *(Patient nods)* Good. Very good. Please tell me the picture.

PATIENT: I see like an oxygen tank that has in it oxygen and also a powerful cancer killer. I'm inhaling the oxygen, deep into my lungs . . .

THERAPIST: Is the oxygen cool?

PATIENT: Yes. Cool and soothing.

THERAPIST: Go on. Tell me what you imagine next.

PATIENT: I can imagine the cancer-killing gas mixed with the cool oxygen engulfing the crawling cancer cells and smothering, crushing them.

THERAPIST: Good. You feel cool oxygen and imagine the cancer-killing gas engulfing the crawling cancer cells and killing them dead in their tracks. Maybe opening up the air passage ways. And then what happens?

PATIENT: And then, I don't know . . .

THERAPIST: Can you work with this image for a little while? Stay with it? *(Therapist keeps encouraging and swaying her arm. Patient nods).* You're doing great. Just stay relaxed.

PATIENT: Uh, I feel . . . like, I'm trying to imagine the forced air rushing in and cleaning out the debris, blowing out the debris with my breath . . .

THERAPIST: Good. And can you . . . stay relaxed? . . . Can you imagine the air passages in your lungs being cleaned out? The medicine in the oxygen, opening up the passages, healing inflammation, soreness, getting rid of a lot of debris, engulfing and killing the cancer?

PATIENT: Yes. I am more relaxed now. Doctor, whatever we did, I am more relaxed.

THERAPIST: Good. I'm really glad to see that.

STEP 4. DECATASTROPHIZING THE DYSFUNCTIONAL BELIEF

The term *decatastrophizing* refers to the technique of helping patients realize that a situation or an anticipated event is really not as awful as they thought or imagined. This technique is especially relevant to Pain Management Psychotherapy because catastrophizing is a maladaptive coping strategy associated with pain and depression (Geisser et al., 1994; Lefebvre, 1981; Rosenstiel & Keefe, 1983; Sullivan & D'Eon, 1990). After developing an alternative, more functional explanation or belief, it is important to help the patient identify and respond to any underlying beliefs that the situation is unsolvable, overwhelming, or awful. If such beliefs are present and not addressed, they are likely to block the cognitive disputation and restructuring process. In that event, the new, more functional interpretation of the situation is unlikely to feel acceptable to the patient. Therefore, Step 4 involves assisting the patient to decatastrophize the dysfunctional thought or belief. As pointed out by Freeman and Reinecke (1995), patients are helped to "evaluate whether they are *overestimating* the nature of a situation. Patients can be helped to see that the consequences of their life actions (and pain) are not 'all or nothing', and thereby, are less catastrophic" (p. 200): The following fibromyalgia patient explores this possibility:

PATIENT: Dr. Eimer, but what if I can't get myself to do this? What if I'm really in bad shape and just let myself get carried away with the negative thinking because I'm in such a fog and in such a prison of stiffness and so much pain?

THERAPIST: Okay, so what if that's what happens?

PATIENT: I'll stay miserable?

THERAPIST: And if tomorrow you succumb to "pain-based emotional reasoning" or PBER, so what's the worst that can happen?

PATIENT: I'll have a miserable day?

THERAPIST: And if that came to pass, what would be so terrible?

PATIENT: I guess I'd survive.

THERAPIST: I guess you would.

PATIENT: And if I give in to the negative stuff, and keep going on with I am a failure, I guess the worst that can happen is I'll feel like a failure until I straighten out my thinking. Right?

THERAPIST: That's right. Okay, but what if you have a bad week. A really bad week, let's say this week. What's the worst that can happen?

PATIENT: I'll have a bad week. I'll be less efficient, more tired, stiff, and a real goose.

THERAPIST: A goose? What do you mean?

PATIENT: Cooked. Just feathered and cooked *(laughs)*.

THERAPIST: *(laughs too)* What's the worst thing about having a really bad week?

PATIENT: I guess I won't be so productive.

Fantasized Consequences

It is sometimes useful to guide a patient to fantasize or imagine the worst coming to pass. Supervising such an exercise in the office can achieve several purposes. First, it is an exposure to the dreaded situation. Repeated exposure can habituate anxiety and reduce fear. Second, countering avoidance tendencies by preventing an avoidance response can begin to restructure the belief that avoidance is a necessary behavior. Imagining the worst can also lead a patient to realize that the worst possible scenario is really not so bad and can be managed. It can also uncover other irrational beliefs as well as other revealing insights. Then the therapist can work with the patient to dispute those beliefs, to assess realistic threats and dangers, and to develop coping strategies, should the worst come to pass. The working man with fibromyalgia illustrates this exercise:

THERAPIST: You know, I'd like to suggest we do a little exercise now. Have you ever heard of the old game show called *Truth or Consequences?* Well, this little exercise is called "Fantasized Consequences."

PATIENT: Okay.

THERAPIST: To do this exercise, you start describing to me your own fantasy of the worst possible thing that you can imagine happening.

PATIENT: Yeh? And then what?

THERAPIST: Well, you describe it to me as if it is really happening right now, as if you're going through it now. Be big about it and tell me what images or pictures come up for you and what feelings and thoughts come up.

PATIENT: I do this all the time!

THERAPIST: Yup. I know! Good point!

PATIENT: Okay. I'm waking up, and . . . Oh God, do I feel beat. I mean I can't move. I have this important meeting at work this morning, and I woke up late. I can't get out of bed. I feel like I have the flu. I hurt all over. I start to try to get going, but, I just can't do it. The shower feels too cold. The back and legs hurt. I can't move my head. I have a splitting headache. My gums hurt when I brush my teeth. Shit, I'm out of mouthwash. My hair is dirty and I have to wash it, but my scalp hurts. Then the phone rings. It's my lawyer. He wants to change the time of our appointment to prepare for the deposition. That's it! I can't take this. I'm thinking this.

THERAPIST: Stop. What other thoughts are running through your mind?

PATIENT: I can't stand being like this. I am going to have to go on disability again.

THERAPIST: What can you do at this point?

PATIENT: I don't know. I'm feeling so miserable.

THERAPIST: Have you ever felt like this before?

PATIENT: Yes.

THERAPIST: And, what happened? How did it turn out?

PATIENT: It's damned inconvenient, but I got through it.

THERAPIST: You survived?

PATIENT: Yeh, I survived.

STEP 5. FORMULATING STEPS TO COPE WITH OR SOLVE THE PROBLEM

After clearing away a self-defeating thought or belief and establishing the validity of an alternative cognition, it is often necessary to formulate a concrete strategy for coping with the situation or solving the problem. The therapist and patient should list specific cognitive and behavioral coping options and then evaluate their viability by anticipating the likely consequences of their use. This step may also involve additional cognitive and imagery techniques including *imaginal rehearsal* (e.g., "Can you imagine, really see yourself, doing that? Bring it up and then run it through your mind from 'A to Z.' Signal me when you've done so, and we can then talk about it. If at any point you get stuck, signal me by lifting your right index finger, and we can talk about where you're stuck and what to do about it"); *turning adversity to advantage;* use of the *Automatic Thoughts about Pain Questionnaire* (ATPQ) (to be discussed); "Self-Instructional Training" (SIT) (Meichenbaum, 1985); *pain replacement imagery, distraction* and *attentional diversion, thought stopping; role playing; role reversal; therapist modeling; guided practice;* and *graded exposure.* Again, drawing on the transcript of the patient with fibromyalgia:

THERAPIST: What did you do to cope?

PATIENT: One time I called in sick. Another time I woke up and felt like this, I called in and said I'm sick and running late. Another time, I rushed, rushed, rushed, and stayed very miserable all day.

THERAPIST: What can you do now?

PATIENT: I don't know?

THERAPIST: Well, what's the main problem here?

PATIENT: How I feel physically, and my head is not feeling good. I'm cognitively impaired and in pain!

THERAPIST: Can you accept that this is how you feel and be gentle with yourself?

PATIENT: That's a joke! You mean give in to it?

THERAPIST: I mean acknowledge the main problem, which is you feel ill and you have this important meeting that it doesn't look like you are going to get to on time.

PATIENT: Oh. Okay. Hmmm. I don't know. I guess if I died they would have to do without me.

THERAPIST: Can they wait for you if you call in and explain the situation?

PATIENT: I guess they'll have no choice!

THERAPIST: Can you picture yourself calling in? You dial the office and when the receptionist answers, you ask for your boss. Your transferred to the boss's office. The boss's secretary gets on the phone and you say?

PATIENT: Debbie, I woke up feeling ill this morning. I'm on my way, but I will be an hour late. I will apologize to the clients when I get there.

THERAPIST: Good! How does that feel?

PATIENT: I think I can do it!

THERAPIST: But how does it feel to handle it that way?

PATIENT: Quite good. It's good for the self-esteem.

THERAPIST: And I'll bet it doesn't make the pain any worse?

PATIENT: Nope. It does not.

THERAPIST: So, how bad does the day turn out to be?

PATIENT: Not as bad as it could have. But what if I am fired? It happens too many times.

THERAPIST: What if you *are* fired? Then what?

PATIENT: I guess I'd start looking for another position. Maybe I'd consider going on disability. Maybe I'd collect my unemployment and rest for a while.

THERAPIST: All things that are manageable. Not so bad, huh?

PATIENT: No, not bad enough to put a gun to my head for.

TURNING ADVERSITY TO ADVANTAGE

This technique refers to the cognitive maneuver of reframing an adverse situation such as a pain flare-up (an "A" in the ABC cognitive model) as an opportunity to test out or practice new pain coping skills:

THERAPIST: What if you have a really bad morning tomorrow?

PATIENT: I guess I'll try to do what we've talked about.

THERAPIST: Is it possible for you to think about another "bad morning" as an opportunity to put what we've been talking about to the test?

PATIENT: Well, I don't know. You mean want it to happen like that?

THERAPIST: Well yes and no. More like when you have your next bad morning, whenever that is, tomorrow or the next day, put it in perspective.

PATIENT: Like say to myself, here's an opportunity to practice coping differently?

THERAPIST: Yes. Using the techniques we've been talking about.

PATIENT: Okay. I think I can see it that way. Hmmm. That's a good way to take it. But you know, I have so many negative thoughts about my condition. We can't cover them all here.

THERAPIST: *(Repeats Patient's last statement)* Does that imply that there's no use bothering?

PATIENT: Yes. That's another self-defeating, negative thought isn't it?

THERAPIST: "So, there's no use bothering." Yes. That is quite a potentially defeating DAT.

PATIENT: Well, it is true!

SCALING

The therapist asks the patient to scale his degree of belief in the last DAT:

THERAPIST: So, you believe it how much on a scale of zero to six, where zero is "completely false" and six is "completely true"?

PATIENT: I guess about a "six."

THERAPIST: It feels completely true?

PATIENT: Yup.

THERAPIST: Okay. How do you think such a thought as "DAT" will affect you when you have it tomorrow morning while in the midst of a pain and stiffness, "fibrofog" bout?

PATIENT: *(Laughs)* It'll probably cook me good!

THERAPIST: I'd tend to agree with you about "DAT."

PATIENT: *(Laughs)* So seriously, what can I do? We're back to square one, aren't we?

THERAPIST: "Back to square one." What type of distortion is "DAT"?

PATIENT: Throwing everything out the window? The baby with the bathwater?

THERAPIST: Sure disqualifies all we've covered that's hopeful and positive, doesn't it?

PATIENT: It does.

USING THE DPTR AND THE AUTOMATIC THOUGHTS ABOUT PAIN QUESTIONNAIRE (ATPQ)

At this point, the therapist decides to reemphasize the importance of using the Daily Pain and Thought Record (DPTR) to track, rate, and evaluate DATs. He also introduces the ATPQ, which is a 45-item checklist of automatic thoughts about pain (displayed in Appendix S):

THERAPIST: Let me suggest something. Continue to track, rate, and evaluate your DATs about pain with your Daily Pain and Thought Record. Do you need any more of them?

PATIENT: *(Patient nods)*

THERAPIST: I'll give you a few more. Also, take a look at this. *(Therapist hands Patient three copies of the Automatic Thoughts about Pain Questionnaire or ATPQ)* There are 45 typical dysfunctional automatic thoughts or "DATs" about pain on this checklist. You can use this checklist in two ways. One is to look at it when you're down. It can help you to decode what your automatic thoughts are. Then, you can write them down on your Daily Pain and Thought Record. Second, you can go through and answer the entire questionnaire a couple of times this week, to identify how often you are thinking certain DATs about your pain, and how true they feel. Does that sound like a useful assignment?

PATIENT: Yes, it does.

MENTAL REHEARSAL AND SELF-INSTRUCTIONAL TRAINING

A major psychological obstacle to pain management is lack of preparedness for handling pain flare-ups. Some patients describe pain that comes on suddenly and is unrelenting. Other patients in continuous pain may experience an exhaustion of their psychological and physical resources for coping. Nonpreparedness and fatigue increase the likelihood of impulsive and maladaptive coping behaviors. This is where the technique known as *Self-Instructional Training* (SIT) can be useful.

First described by Meichenbaum (1977) as a method for teaching impulsive children to "stop and think" before they act out, SIT has been subsequently applied to the areas of stress and anxiety management (Meichenbaum, 1985) and pain management (Turk et al., 1983). SIT is a simple and readily understandable "mental rehearsal" method that involves using *covert self-statements* to guide oneself through a difficult situation, such as an intense pain experience. These self-statements are meant to be positively motivating. They remind and encourage a person in rising pain to employ effective coping techniques, guide him or her through the most challenging moments of the pain experience, and self-reinforce the person for having persisted once the worst pain has subsided.

THE FOUR PHASES OF SIT

Employing SIT to cope with constant or recurrent pain, or other repetitive, stressful experiences, has four phases. This is how we explain it to patients:

Phase 1 of Self-Instructional Training, or Stress Inoculation Training as we also call it (SIT for short), involves preparing yourself for your oncoming or anticipated stressful experience. This first phase involves reminding yourself of the coping techniques that you can employ as the stress and pain begin to mount. This phase also involves feeding yourself encouraging but realistic thoughts that put you on the right track. What can you say to yourself at this point *(wait for the patient to answer)?*

During Phase 2, after the pain has come on, you begin to employ appropriate coping techniques such as controlling your breathing, relaxing your muscles, talking to yourself in an encouraging way, distracting yourself in some way, and thinking of something that takes your mind off the pain. The pain has gotten bad and you need to handle it! And, you will! What can you say to yourself to help you cope once the pain comes on *(wait for an answer)?*

Now, during Phase 3 of SIT, when the situation begins to turn downright ugly—when the pain is at its worst—you need to be ready to employ your most powerful coping techniques. During this phase, you want to feed yourself your most powerful self-talk, to keep you on the right track, so you can get through the storm or the fire, as it were, successfully. This is when things are at their *worst,* and you want to be at your *best!* By best, I mean, psychologically at your strongest, so you have your needed edge. What can you say to remind yourself to use your most powerful coping strategies? When the pain is at its worst, what can you say that will get you through it?

Finally, Phase 4. Thank God for that fourth phase, which marks your being over the hump. The worst is over. At this point, you want to remind yourself that you got through the pain, and you want to give yourself credit that you handled it well. You coped! You managed it! What can you say to yourself to give yourself credit for handling the situation well?

Training the Pain Patient in SIT

Initially, in the SIT training process, these self-statements, or "self-talk" are verbalized aloud. To promote internalization, they are gradually faded from overt verbalization, through quieter subvocalization, to covert thought without overt verbalization. The goal is that the patient be able to self-administer appropriate self-statements intentionally and covertly whenever similar stressful and painful situations arise again. However, it is perfectly acceptable for a person to vocalize appropriate self-instructions overtly in especially challenging and stressful situations where added emphasis and intensity are needed. It's like having an energetic, forceful coach and a loud troupe of cheerleaders at the sidelines to help in one's pain management.

Effectively training a pain patient to use this self-management technique involves four steps. In Step 1, the therapist introduces a rationale for how SIT can be beneficial. Step 2 requires that the therapist role-play to model how the patient can actually use the technique. In Step 3, the therapist coaches the patient in practicing the technique. This step also involves troubleshooting and processing actual as well as anticipated difficulties in using the technique. The therapist provides the patient with reinforcing feedback throughout the process and also elicits the patient's feedback. Step 4 involves assigned practice of the technique for homework.

Case Example

Tom (introduced in Chapter 1) was 81 years old, married, and retired. He suffered from advanced metastatic prostate cancer and a severe post-radiotherapy pain syndrome marked by hematuria (bloody urine), progressively worsening perineal and rectal pain, burning pain in the scrotum and penis, and proctitis (rectal inflammation, irritation, and pain). Despite regular, around-the-clock dosing with sustained-release morphine compounds, his breakthrough pain was agonizing. The sharp, burning, pressing pain made it extremely difficult for him to sit. When the pain became severe, Tom would tell his wife that he wanted to die. We worked with Tom and his wife over the course of five sessions until Tom was admitted into a hospice for palliative care, where more aggressive pharmacotherapeutic pain management was implemented. SIT was included as part of the agenda of several of these counseling sessions:

THERAPIST: How are you feeling today Tom?

PATIENT: Oh, the same. I can't sit comfortably. The pain in my rectum gets so bad.

WIFE: He can't find a place for himself *(She starts to cry slightly).*

THERAPIST: *(stays on track)* Tom, what is your pain level right now from 0 to 10?

PATIENT: Oh, about a 3.

THERAPIST: That's not too bad?

PATIENT: No. Right now, it's tolerable.

THERAPIST: *(begins by trying to establish a rationale for introducing SIT)* Tom, what can you say to prepare yourself when you know your pain is coming on or getting worse? What can you say to yourself to get ready for it?

PATIENT: Dr. Eimer, when the pain starts to get so bad, there is nothing I can say to make it hurt less.

THERAPIST: I do understand. But, you told me before that the pain comes on like an avalanche. Is that right? *(Patient nods)* Avalanches bury you because you have no time to get out of the way. Avalanches catch people unprepared, and they can't get out of the way fast enough, right? *(Patient nods in agreement)* Is it possible that even though your pain is going to come on at times like an avalanche, that maybe you can do something to get out of the way to lessen its destructive impact?

WIFE: If you could teach him that, that would be wonderful.

PATIENT: That's very clever. I am open to learn whatever you can teach me to do that, to get out of the way.

THERAPIST: Well, there's this psychological technique, which we call Stress Inoculation Training that may help you to sort of inoculate yourself against some of the pain.

PATIENT: Like a shot?

THERAPIST: Like a psychological shot of strength—of strong, psychological pain medicine.

PATIENT: Okay?

THERAPIST: *(Role-play and demonstration)* I have arthritis. When I wake up on a bad day, I usually ask myself, "Your pain seems like it is going to be bad today. What can you do starting now, to prepare for it, so you can handle it with the least amount of interference?" Tom, what can you say to yourself, and maybe even ask Sally to say to you, to prepare to handle that rectal pain? As bad as it can get?

PATIENT: I don't know. I guess I can tell myself that I have stood it before, so, I can do it again now.

THERAPIST: Good. That's one thing. I'm going to write this down. Sally, is there anything else you could say to Tom that might help him prepare to handle the pain?

WIFE: I guess I could say, "Darling, I'm with you. I'm by your side. I'll do whatever it takes."

THERAPIST: Okay. Those are good. Let's write them down. *(Therapist writes the preceding preparatory statements down, as does Sally)*.

PATIENT: I can remind myself to take slow deep breaths. I can also get the donut pillow *(a donut-shaped foam pillow for reducing pressure on the rectum when sitting)*.

THERAPIST: Now Tom, as the pain begins to rise, what else can you say and do?

PATIENT: I have to remain positive.

THERAPIST: Yes. That's true. In fact, that's something we should write down. Can you tell yourself that? "I have to remain positive" *(Patient nods in agreement)*.

PATIENT: I have to take my mind away somehow from the pain.

THERAPIST: Yes. Good point.

WIFE: Maybe he can think about fishing? He finds it so relaxing.

DISTRACTION

At this point, the therapeutic conversation touches on the important coping strategy of *distraction,* or *attentional diversion.* As with anxiety and panic disorder patients (Beck, Emery, & Greenberg, 1985; Freeman et al., 1990), distraction and attentional diversion can be an excellent coping strategy for pain patients. That one can get some relief by taking one's mind off the pain is a rational, intuitively simple idea to understand, and thing to do. It also is potentially validating of an important *decatastrophizing belief:* The pain is *not* going to get worse and the consequences are *not* going to be catastrophic if one does not remain continually preoccupied with the pain. It is all right to take a break! Thus, successful experimentation with the coping technique of distraction can lead to important cognitive restructuring:

THERAPIST: Is there a particular fishing image that is especially absorbing and soothing? Something that will be good for distracting you from the rising pain?

PATIENT: Yes. I have several in mind.

THERAPIST: You do? That's good. Let's write them down. What's number one?

PATIENT: Standing on the pier. The wind is blowing fresh saltwater air. I can smell the fish. There are other fishermen lined up on the pier.

THERAPIST: I hope it's a sunny day? *(laughs)*

PATIENT: Pretty sunny, but with big cotton puff clouds. *(He smiles)*

WIFE: Tom used to go out in the rain! *(Everyone laughs)*

THERAPIST: So far, we have *(reads his notes):* "stay calm, be positive, tell myself that I have stood it before, so, I can do it again now, take slow deep breaths, take my mind off the pain, and think of fishing." Good. Now during the third phase of the pain, when it is at its worst, you need to remind yourself to use your strongest coping strategy. This is when you'll need all the strength you can muster. When you are feeling the worst, in a sense, you want to be psychologically at your strongest. What can you tell yourself?

PATIENT: I can get through this?

WIFE: I'm at your side.

THERAPIST: I know you are. *(Therapist rubs Sally's and Tom's hands)*

PATIENT: I have to keep breathing.

THERAPIST: That will help. Good. What else?

PATIENT: There's a storm at sea. There's lightning and thunder. I can watch the storm from the comfort of some shelter.

THERAPIST: Okay. Yes. That is a good image. Also, what about your pain medicines? You do take regular doses, right?

PATIENT: Yes.

THERAPIST: Can you tell yourself that the last dose you took will be kicking in?

PATIENT: *(Shakes head)* Well . . .

THERAPIST: And if it's not enough to cover you, can you take a supplemental dose, on an as needed basis?

PATIENT: That should work.

WIFE: Doctor gave us these also for that purpose. *(Wife shows Therapist pill vial)*

THERAPIST: Okay. Good. (*Writes down important points*) Now, the last phase is realizing that you got through the pain. That you made it over the hump again—you coped. It's usually a good idea to give yourself credit for having handled the rise in pain.

WIFE: Tom has always handled pain well. He really has. Now he says he wants to die!

THERAPIST: I'm sure that it's true that Tom always handled pain well. But this is not easy. It's very hard.

PATIENT: So, guess I got to try this on my own? See if I can do it. See if it works.

THERAPIST: It usually takes some practice. Like a pair of walking shoes, you have to break them in. At first they may feel stiff. The most important thing from my point of view, is that you are not too hard on yourself. What you are going through is not easy.

PATIENT: (*starts to cry. Wife puts her hand out to him*) I've always done my job, my homework.

THERAPIST: What you're both going through is very hard. The stress inoculation steps we've gone over, they're meant to give you a psychological edge or boost. They do help. But, Tom, please, give yourself credit for how well you've coped, handled everything up to this point. Sally has borne witness and attests to this fact.

WIFE: Thank you, Doctor.

THERAPIST: Oh, you're both welcome. And, I thank both of you for having such open minds and being such eager and cooperative learners.

PRACTICAL ISSUES

THE IMPORTANCE OF STRUCTURE

Our approach to Pain Management Psychotherapy emphasizes the importance of "structure." Depressed, chronic pain patients frequently lack structure in their lives and that can be a big part of their problems—the pain often takes over their lives. Building on a collaborative therapeutic relationship, we try to gently socialize patients from the outset of treatment to expect therapy sessions to be structured and to have an *agenda*. This is not to say that if a patient needs to ventilate and feel heard, we always discourage this in favor of doing structured, cognitive therapy. We acknowledge the importance of flexibility and of occasionally just being with a patient in the interest of what might be termed, "relationship healing." This is especially important when working with cancer pain patients. Our primary conceptual and procedural framework, however, is a cognitive-behavioral one, and when we listen to any patient, we attend to the connections between their physical sensations (e.g., pain), emotions, behaviors, thoughts, and underlying beliefs.

TAKING SESSION NOTES

For the benefit of both the patient and ourselves, we often take notes during the session. This makes it easy for us to make connections between things that have been brought up at different points and facilitates summarizing the session.

SESSION STRUCTURE

We typically schedule 45- to 50-minute sessions. We usually schedule double or "extended" sessions (i.e., 90 to 100 minutes) for doing memory uncovering, review, and reprocessing work (see Chapters 7 and 9). A typical 45- to 50-minute Pain Management Psychotherapy session usually follows the structure described in this section. We open the session by saying: "How are you? Tell me how you have been since our last session." As the patient responds, we note the patient's agenda, subjective complaints, presenting problems, predominant symptoms, current level of functioning, and mental status. After allowing about 5 minutes for the patient to bring us up to date and give us feedback about the previous session, we inquire about the patient's homework, if he or she has not already told us about it. We jot down the data regarding the patient's adherence to the homework assignment, as well as any homework-related problems.

After about 10 minutes into the session, we usually shift to setting up the session's goals and therapeutic agenda. We ask the patient, "What would you like to work on today?" "What do you want to put on today's session agenda?" We negotiate the contents of the agenda and problems to target, based on our case conceptualization, our therapeutic objectives, the patient's preferences, and a realistic assessment of the material that can be covered in the time available. It is our job to gauge what we can and cannot achieve in the scheduled time.

The middle 25 to 30 minutes of the session are devoted to performing specific clinical interventions, and implementing therapeutic strategies and procedures, based on our established agenda. As part of our job as therapist/coach, we are ever mindful of time limitations and try to keep ourselves, the patient, and the session on track so that we can cover all the items on the agenda.

We always aim to set aside about 10 minutes at the end of the session to summarize what we have discussed and obtain the patient's feedback. We typically ask patients to summarize the session in their own words and to tell us what was helpful and not helpful, what they liked and did not like. At this point, we either summarize the homework (if previously assigned), or assign new homework. We take this time to make sure that every patient understands the rationale for the homework, and exactly what is expected. We also record on our notepad, or on a Pain Management Psychotherapy Progress Note form (PN), the clinical outcomes of the session's interventions, any additional problems addressed, and any special problems arising in the session (e.g., poor collaboration, resistance to adhere to the session agenda, homework noncompliance, hostility, interpersonal issues between patient and therapist, transference issues).

PMP PROGRESS NOTES

For the reader's convenient clinical use, two blank PMP Progress Note (PN) forms appear in Appendix T. Progress Note 1 is organized as a Session Summary Checklist. It covers the practical in-session issues previously discussed. Progress Note 2 is an open-ended variation of the much used "SOAP" note format. Each PN form has its advantages. Typically, we write notes on the open-ended SOAP form during or immediately after a session. On the other hand, the Session Summary Checklist provides a convenient, quick, and efficient vehicle for checking off and summarizing important information about a session.

The open-ended PMP Progress Note form provides space for the therapist to record the following data:

1. The procedures administered using the American Medical Association's (1997) *Current Procedural Terminology* (CPT) codes.
2. The results of any tests, evaluation, or outcome measures administered, including several average weekly pain ratings.
3. The patient's *Subjective* complaints, presenting problems, agenda, and adherence to the previous session's homework.
4. The *Objectives* and goals of the session.
5. An *Abstract* of the session's focal points (session highlights, problems addressed, clinical interventions, results of procedures employed, and assessment of clinical outcomes).
6. *Assignments* for patient homework.
7. The therapist's *Plan* for the following sessions.

AVERAGE WEEKLY PAIN RATINGS

The patient's average weekly pain ratings are obtained and recorded on the PMP Progress Note 2 using several quickly administered, pain rating

Patient name: _____   Today's date: _____

1. Visual Analogue Scale—Pain Intensity Line:

Please make an "x" on the line below to show *how bad* your pain has been on the average or overall this week.

NO PAIN ├───────────────────────────────────────┤ WORST POSSIBLE PAIN

2. Present Pain Index—Verbal Description:

Check the *one* word below that best describes how bad your pain has been on the average or overall this week.

____ 0. None   ____ 1. Weak   ____ 2. Moderate   ____ 3. Severe   ____ 4. Excruciating

3. Percentage Pain Relief:

Please circle the percentage relief your pain treatment has provided you on the average or overall this week.

0%   10%   20%   30%   40%   50%   60%   70%   80%   90%   100% relief

4. Subjective Units of Distress ("SUDs"):

Please circle the number that shows how emotionally distressed you have been on the average or overall this past week.

(not at all)   0   1   2   3   4   5   6   7   8   9   10   (worst possible distress)

5. Pain Disability Rating:

Please circle the number that shows how much your pain has disabled you overall this week. A "0" means that you have *not been disabled by pain at all* this week. A "10" means that *all of your usual activities have been totally disrupted or prevented* by your pain this week.

(no disability)   0   1   2   3   4   5   6   7   8   9   10   (totally disabled by pain)

Figure 6.1   Global Pain Rating Scales

scale measures. These *Global Pain Rating Scales* (GPRS) are presented in Figure 6.1. They allow the patient to rate pain, pain relief, emotional distress, and pain disability. The GPRS can be administered orally by the clinician, or in paper-and-pencil form. The patient's GPRS ratings are recorded on PMP Progress Note 2 in the spaces provided in the section, "Results of Any Tests, Evaluation, or Outcome Measures Administered" (see Appendix T).

1. The patient's *Visual Analogue Scale* (VAS) average pain rating for the past week is recorded in the designated space on the PN. Note that this rating is obtained by asking the patient to place an "X" on a 100 millimeter pain intensity line. This is presented to the patient as Item 1 on the GPRS. The VAS numerical rating equals the number of millimeters from the beginning of the line where the X is marked (e.g., an X marked at 66 mm would equal a score of 66). Then, the patient's VAS rating for the current

week is compared with the patient's VAS rating for the previous week, and the change is recorded on the PN in the space provided. Following Poulain, Langlade, and Goldberg (1977), the difference or change is assigned a numerical score depending on whether the VAS rating has increased (2), decreased (0), or remained the same (1).

2. The number representing the patient's current week's *Present Pain Index* (Verbal Description of the pain, and Item 2 on the GPRS) is recorded on the PN in the space provided.

3. The patient's rating of the *Percentage Pain Relief* obtained on the average over the past week from treatment (GPRS Item 3) is recorded on the PN in the designated space.

4. Following Poulain, Langlade, and Goldberg (1997), a summative or composite *Global Pain Score* (GPS) (range: 0–10) is computed as the sum of the numerical scores for Items 1, 2, and 3. The patient's GPS for the week is recorded on the PN in the designated space.

5. The patient's self-rating of the average *Subjective Units of Distress* (SUDs) experienced over the past week (GPRS Item 4) is recorded on the PN. Note that this is a rating of emotional distress, as distinguished from physical or pure pain.

6. The patient's self-rating of global pain disability for the week (GPRS Item 5) is recorded.

The global pain ratings provide simply and easily obtained data for measuring and charting pain treatment progress. By collecting these data at the beginning of every PMP session, the therapist socializes the patient to the idea of measuring and scaling his or her pain experience. This helps to focus the session and keep it pain-relevant; it can also help in combating all-or-nothing thinking.

CHAPTER 7

Reprocessing Pain Beliefs and Stressful Experiences

The body never lies.

—Martha Graham

A PERSON'S *core schemas* about self and the world (parts of the cognitive triad) are activated by and interact with stressful events such as persistent pain to give rise to domain-specific beliefs (e.g., pain-related beliefs). According to our cognitive model, a person's core schemas and domain-specific beliefs, activated by external events (environmental stressors, other people's behavior) and internal events (physiology, pain, illness, activating cognitions, the person's behavior) are the wellsprings of that person's automatic thoughts and emotional distress. Interventions with pain patients targeting these domain-specific beliefs and core schemas are implemented at different points in cognitive therapy.

Underlying beliefs are frequently uncovered and addressed during the cognitive disputation process. Some of the cognitive techniques discussed in Chapter 6—idiosyncratic meaning, questioning the evidence, rational responding, Socratic questioning, replacement imagery, reassessing responsibility, decatastrophizing, fantasized consequences—frequently bring up core beliefs. However, effective PMP is seldom complete without examining, reviewing, and reprocessing some of the psychologically influential past experiences that contributed to the consolidation of emotionally charged core schemas and pain-related beliefs (Anderson & Hines, 1994; Anderson & Taylor, 1995; Ciccone & Lenzi, 1994; Eimer, 1993a, 1993b). To effectively change such beliefs, it is often necessary to induce the emotional experiences associated and stored with the targeted

218

beliefs. Until we explore a patient's beliefs and related memories in the course of psychotherapy, we can only speculate about what types of episodic memories are stored with particular beliefs.

TRAUMATIC MEMORIES AND CORE BELIEFS

Many pain patients have traumatic memories related to their pain, past pain treatments, and influential, or touchstone events that preceded or occurred at the time of onset of their pain (Anderson & Taylor, 1995; Ciccone & Lenzi, 1994; Eimer, 1993a, 1993b; Engel, 1959; Grzesiak et al., 1996; Harness & Donlon, 1988; Pilowsky, 1985; Walker et al., 1988). As part of our initial workup, we assess any trauma history. As we begin to conduct PMP with cognitive techniques such as those discussed earlier, we begin to elicit a patient's irrational beliefs along with other cognitions such as automatic thoughts and cognitive distortions. We target for possible modification any dysfunctional or irrational beliefs that appear to be causing significant emotional disturbance and maladaptive behavior, as well as beliefs that may be blocking cognitive, behavioral, or emotional progress. When we encounter evidence of emotionally charged past experiences that contributed to targeted, pain-relevant beliefs, we often guide a patient to review and reprocess those experiences (Eimer, 1993a, 1993b).

PAIN BELIEF ASSESSMENT INSTRUMENTS

Several of the pain belief assessment instruments previously described (e.g., the Pain Coping Inventory, Pain Beliefs and Perceptions Inventory, Pain Experience Scale) can be useful as starting points for discussing a patient's relevant beliefs, and for motivating a patient to explore the factors associated with increased pain:

THERAPIST: Earlier you checked on the Pain Coping Inventory that you strongly believe that people punish you or treat you unfairly and that you also believe that nobody really understands what you are going through. Is that right?

PATIENT: Yes. It is.

THERAPIST: How do you think those two beliefs that you hold make you feel?

PATIENT: Pretty angry.

THERAPIST: And how do you think the anger affects your pain?

PATIENT: Does it make it worse?

THERAPIST: It does for some people I've worked with, but I really don't know yet if this is also true for you. So, what do you say we work together to find out?

PATIENT: That's why I'm here.
THERAPIST: Great.

SENTENCE COMPLETIONS

Incomplete sentence stems are a useful tool for abstracting underlying themes and schemas. The therapist looks for the common themes:

THERAPIST: What did you say earlier about physical therapy?
PATIENT: The therapist hurts me!
THERAPIST: I think that you also said, like all the rest of those doctors and therapists, what?
PATIENT: What? He's just like the rest of them. He don't care about me. He just wants to bill.
THERAPIST: You also said that he, the physical therapist, did not . . . ? Did not, what?
PATIENT: Oh yeh, he didn't listen to me. Nobody listens to ME, man! You know?
THERAPIST: Nobody? What about me? Am I "chopped liver"?
PATIENT: No, man. But you're the only one.
THERAPIST: I am . . . ? Complete this incomplete sentence. I am what?
PATIENT: A nice guy. You seem to care.
THERAPIST: I am . . . ? What?
PATIENT: An exception, man.
THERAPIST: And, everyone else in the world is . . . ? What?
PATIENT: Out to get what they can off you! Nobody cares about you.
THERAPIST: The world is . . . ?
PATIENT: Dangerous, man! Dangerous!

USING IMAGERY TO DISCOVER HIDDEN BELIEFS

Just as words often evoke associated images and mental pictures, images and mental pictures can provide a vehicle for uncovering or discovering underlying beliefs:

PATIENT: I feel like I can't go on. I can't stand the pain no more. I want to shoot myself!
THERAPIST: When you think, "I feel like I can't go on, I can't stand the pain no more, I want to shoot myself!" what image or mental picture comes up for you?
PATIENT: I just don't see myself handling anything. I see myself suffering.
THERAPIST: What do you see yourself doing?

PATIENT: I mean I see myself busting things up. Busting the wall out of frustration. Screaming in pain, and no one hears me. No one hears me!

THERAPIST: I hear you.

PATIENT: You are about the only one.

THERAPIST: So, if I were to take a picture, a snapshot of you, busting the wall, screaming in pain, with no one hearing you, what might the caption underneath the picture read? What might it say about you as a person?

PATIENT: It would have to say, "He's a good person, but he's a *LOSER*. Nobody cares about this guy and he's at the end of his rope."

THERAPIST: If there were some background pictures that came before this picture, that led up to it, what might they show?

PATIENT: They'd show me asking for help and not getting it. Begging to be heard and no one takes me seriously.

THERAPIST: And what thoughts about yourself does that bring to your mind?

PATIENT: That people think I'm worthless.

THERAPIST: Do you think you're worthless?

PATIENT: Sometimes.

WRITING IN A JOURNAL

For patients who are so inclined (many are not), we suggest or encourage them to keep a journal. Writing in a journal about daily stressors, key thoughts, significant events, and pain coping, can be an excellent method for uncovering or discovering one's core beliefs and assumptions. One patient wrote:

> When I first saw Dr. Eimer, I thought that cognitive therapy could not do anything for my pain. I was very skeptical. Therapy is just talk. Right? Wrong! I've always kept a journal at different times in my life, but I never thought that the journal could provide clues about how the way I see the world could affect how much pain I have! Pain is just physical. Right? Wrong again! Therapy helped me to see that my attitude affects how I feel. Specifically, my beliefs. Now that I have learned a lot about my underlying beliefs, I can accept that they do affect me in many ways, including my behavior, how I feel and how much pain I have.
>
> After our last therapy session, while writing in this journal, I came to a major realization about the 5-month period two and a half years ago, when I started to make *real progress*. My insight was that what was different about how I felt during that period was what I believed! I believed that whenever I had a pain flare-up, that it wasn't catastrophic! I told myself that it was because I was deconditioned and that it was "good pain" (if it had not gone up more than 2 or 3 from where I was at baseline). I accepted

it. If it went up more than 3 notches from baseline, then I considered that I probably overdid it. Up until now, ever since I lost that progress, I considered everything a catastrophe, as I have always basically done in my life! I was too afraid of pain. Now, I say to myself: "A little pain is my friend." I tell myself, when I feel a twinge of pain, that "I'm just deconditioned" and "without any pain, there can be no gain!" I now monitor my tendency to overdo things. I don't believe it any more that it is good to overdo things like I used to.

The "Downward Arrow" Technique or "Inference Chaining"

The vertical or *downward arrow technique,* also known as "guided association" or "guided discovery" (Freeman et al., 1990; Freeman & Reinecke, 1995), involves working with a patient to connect ideas, thoughts, and images by means of Socratic questioning and inference chaining (Dryden & DiGiuseppe, 1990). The technique entails asking patients, for purposes of the procedure, to assume that the worst has occurred. Then, the therapist guides patients in discovering the themes or schemas underlying their automatic thoughts through a sequence of questions, such as "If that were true, what would it mean?" and "If that were true, then what?" "What would happen then?" In this manner, patients can be helped to explore their underlying beliefs and the significance they see in situations and events:

PATIENT: If I can't get back to the way I was before the accident, I'm not going to be able to go on.

THERAPIST: Let's assume for a moment the worst, that you are going to remain like this. If that were true, what would that mean?

PATIENT: What would that mean? Listen, man, I want to have my life back you know! I don't want to go on living like this.

THERAPIST: Saying, "I don't want to live like this" is quite different from saying, "I'm not going to be able to go on," isn't it?

PATIENT: Yes, it is.

THERAPIST: But, let's assume that things remain as they are now. You wake up with headaches, neck, and back pain. You don't sleep well at night. It takes you hours to get going in the morning. You are not able to go back to your line of work. You continue to have a weak memory. So, what would happen then?

PATIENT: My wife might divorce me!

THERAPIST: Okay, assume she divorces you. And then what?

PATIENT: Then what? I want a wife you know!

THERAPIST: I know you want to stay married. But, let's say, just for argument's sake, she decides she wants out. Then what?

PATIENT: I'll be alone. I'll be lonely. I'll never find another woman like her who'll put up with me.

THERAPIST: And what would that mean for you?

PATIENT: What would that mean for me? It would mean that my father was right all along. I'll never amount to anything. I'm really a failure. Good for no one, destined to live alone, just like my cousin.

THERAPIST: And that would mean? Just take it a little further.

PATIENT: Further? God, further is nowhere. I'd be nowhere. A nobody. Then people really would say, hey, this guy is a poor soul. He probably once thought he had a life, but he was just fooling himself. He could have never amounted to anything worthwhile. Then, I'd never be admired. I'd really be a failure!

WRITING AN ALTERNATIVE
ASSUMPTION OR BELIEF

Once patients identify some of their core operating beliefs and basic guiding assumptions, the therapist can help them formulate alternative beliefs. One way to do this is to guide the patient, in session, to produce written alternatives. Then, for homework, they can test these rewritten beliefs against the available evidence:

THERAPIST: It sounds like you've been operating on the assumption that you've been fooling people, that underneath your exterior act, you still basically are a failure. Is that accurate?

PATIENT: I really think it is.

THERAPIST: What if you were to adopt an alternative belief such as I have always been very good at making favorable impressions? That I can present myself in a positive and successful light, and that I'm basically likable? What would that mean if you really believed that?

PATIENT: Man! I guess if I really believed that, then I'd feel different.

THERAPIST: How would you feel?

PATIENT: Like I'd have more hope that things could get better. I'd probably be able to bounce back in time.

THERAPIST: Bounce back from your injuries?

PATIENT: Hmmn. Get positive about rehab. Not be so hard on myself.

THERAPIST: Would you be willing to do something with this for homework?

PATIENT: What? What are you thinking?

THERAPIST: I'm thinking of asking you, for homework, to take this new belief home with you on paper. Let's finish writing it out here. Then, I think it would be a good idea for you to take this piece of paper home, and do a bit of research on this belief. Gather evidence for and against this belief. Set aside a section in your homework notebook and make two columns on a page. In Column A, record experiences that support this new belief, and in Column B, write down experiences that don't support it. How does that sound to you? Does it sound like you will do this?

PATIENT: Yes it does.

FIXED-ROLE THERAPY

Kelly (1955), working as a personal construct therapist, developed a belief change technique that he called *Fixed Role Therapy*. Basically, the technique involves asking a patient to set aside a specific time period during which he or she will act as if a desired feeling or belief were present, even when it is not. This cognitive-emotive-behavioral technique is based on the assumption that a person who waits for feelings or beliefs to change before acting differently probably is going to have a long wait! One is more likely to feel or believe differently as a result of acting differently than the other way around. Actually, as discussed earlier, all three variables—beliefs, emotions, and behaviors—go hand in hand. When the preceding patient returned a few sessions later, the therapist obtained feedback about his Fixed-Role-Therapy homework assigned the week before:

THERAPIST: How did your homework go?

PATIENT: It was interesting. I didn't want to do it at first and resisted for the first few days. But then I had a really bad day on Thursday. I really felt hateful and angry. I had yelled at the lady at the insurance company, and at my lawyer. I really lost control. But then, I said to myself: The weekend's coming up. Try the damned homework with the wife and the kids, and the in-laws. Dr. Eimer said, "You don't have to believe it. Just act as if you believe it, and get some data. See how it goes." So, I did just that on Friday and Saturday, and on Sunday I reverted back.

THERAPIST: And then what happened?

PATIENT: Well, you know on Friday night, I really felt different by acting as if I was good at making favorable impressions and that I present myself in a positive and successful light, that I'm really likable. I found myself thinking that it's not a matter of hiding something inside, the feeling of being a failure, being a phony on the outside, or whatever. I really like people and enjoy being nice! Now on Sunday, I woke up in a lot of pain and my wife yelled at me for something.

THERAPIST: So, what happened?

PATIENT: So, I blew up. But, after things calmed down, I thought about it, and realized that it's not an all-or-nothing thing, like I'm either a failure and a phony, or a success and a likable guy. I mean, I thought, I'm human. I have lapses. I can act in a certain way and if the result is positive, hey, then maybe it means it is possible to have good stuff happen!

THERAPIST: What if the result is negative?

PATIENT: Well didn't you say a few weeks ago that I should also collect evidence for and against the belief that I'm supposed to act as if I'm likable, and I enjoy being likable, and I'm good at it?

THERAPIST: Yes that was the assignment.

PATIENT: So, I think I've learned that it's possible for me to be both. If the pain is really bad, God, I have a choice. I can be likable, or miserable. But underneath, even if I act miserable because I feel that way because of the pain, it still doesn't mean I'm a total failure or loser! Damned forever!

INDUCING DISSONANCE

Conflict is ubiquitous in chronic pain patients. A frequent source of conflict is the discrepancy between current levels of functionality and prepain level of functionality, prepain self-perceptions, and prepain beliefs. Another frequent source of conflict is the discrepancy between a pain sufferer's current level of functionality and other people's directly and indirectly expressed beliefs about that pain sufferer's appropriate level of functionality. There is bound to be anxiety when there is conflict between what a patient believes, what he or she actually does, feedback from others, and how the person subsequently feels. This anxiety can motivate the person to somehow resolve the discrepancy, or *cognitive dissonance* (Festinger, 1957).

Many people attempt to reduce cognitive dissonance in maladaptive ways. Pain sufferers, motivated as they are to avoid further pain and anxiety, often seek to escape through oversedation with pain medications. Other pain sufferers avoid activities, social involvements, and vocational activities that they enjoyed when in good health. Some chronic pain sufferers, in an attempt to reduce their dissonance by changing their beliefs, adopt maladaptive, pain-related beliefs about themselves, the world, and their future (Beck's cognitive triad) that are consistent with their behaviors and how badly they feel.

Interestingly, a therapist can often induce further dissonance by highlighting these conflicts. Because many pain patients have adopted maladaptive beliefs in concert with maladaptive behaviors to reduce cognitive dissonance, the therapist usually must induce dissonance to motivate and assist the patient to resolve the dissonance in an adaptive way. This technique often can effectively induce positive self-motivation to make healthy cognitive or behavioral changes:

THERAPIST: You said before that you don't believe there is any way that I can help you since I can't "get rid of your pain." But tell me. Do you believe I am likely to be less helpful or more helpful than the three surgeons who did your last seven operations, and whom you say left you in worse pain than before?

PATIENT: They lied to me.

THERAPIST: Do you expect me to lie to you?

PATIENT: If you do, I'm out of here. You'll be the last psychologist I'll ever see.

THERAPIST: But do you expect me to lie to you?

PATIENT: I don't really know.

THERAPIST: Do you hear me saying that I promise you I will "get rid of your pain"?

PATIENT: No.

THERAPIST: Did the surgeons who lied to you promise that after each surgery your pain would be gone?

PATIENT: Yes. Otherwise, why would I go under the knife?

THERAPIST: So, you would not submit to the knife again even if you were promised that the operation would take away your pain, once and for all?

PATIENT: No, I guess if there was a good chance that another operation, if they said that it would take the pain away, I'd think about going through with it.

THERAPIST: You mean you'd submit to the risks of surgery again, even though the previous surgeons broke their promises?

PATIENT: Well, if I had no other options?

THERAPIST: Isn't this, working with me, another option?

PATIENT: Well, yeh. But it's just talk.

THERAPIST: What's the risk of just talking?

PATIENT: None really.

THERAPIST: So, if you gain nothing, what will you have risked losing?

PATIENT: Nothing really. Just my time.

THERAPIST: Is your time something you'd be willing to gamble with in order to get better pain relief?

PATIENT: Well, yes, when you put it that way.

THERAPIST: Do you think I am lying to you?

PATIENT: Not right now.

THERAPIST: And what will you have lost if you come to the conclusion in three sessions or so, that I lied to you?

PATIENT: Just my time.

THERAPIST: Are you willing, once and for all, to take the time to learn how you can manage your pain?

PATIENT: I think you got me.

THERAPIST: I don't want to get you, or lie to you. I want to teach you how to manage your pain. But, hear me well. I am not promising anything other than that I will give you all of my attention while we are together and use my knowledge, the best I know how, to help you find relief. Does that sound fair?

PATIENT: Yes. Yes it does. I really can't ask for more. Let's go for it.

HELPING PATIENTS DEVELOP POSITIVE SELF-MOTIVATION

Chronic pain patients often lack direct self-motivation to change their cognitions or behavior. In some cases, patients fail to see a direct connection between their thoughts, their behaviors, and their pain. Patients may not see the benefits of changing their thoughts or behaviors, or secondary gains may be associated with them. In other cases, patients' motivations to change are blocked by fears about the consequences, certain "blocking beliefs," or doubts that change is even possible. Often, positive motivation is dampened by directly or indirectly expressed feelings of anger and resentment. PMP therapists need to help patients develop positive self-motivation to make healthy changes in their thinking and their behavior. Often, this involves confronting the ubiquitous and controversial issue of excessive reliance on narcotics and other pain medications:

PATIENT: I know I should get off those pills (hydromorphone/Dilaudid and oxycodone/Percocet). They really are not doing me any good in the long run.

THERAPIST: But you said a few minutes ago, that a thought that keeps running through your mind is "Why bother? I'm going to be in constant pain, probably forever, anyway. So I might as well get some immediate relief." Is that correct?

PATIENT: Yeh. That's what I do think.

THERAPIST: So, from what you keep telling yourself, you believe that there's really no point to trying to get off those pain pills. Is that right?

PATIENT: That is the truth Doc.

THERAPIST: Suppose there were some legitimate reasons why it is worth bothering to get off of the pills? Do you think it would make a difference?

PATIENT: I don't know.

THERAPIST: Are there any good reasons for bothering? That you can see pretty easily?

PATIENT: Well, I guess I would be less groggy. I wouldn't be as sleepy. I probably wouldn't have gotten into those other accidents if I wasn't so soused. I'd be awake when my kids get home from school.

THERAPIST: Those sound like some good reasons to bother. Don't you think so?

PATIENT: (Nods) Yup.

THERAPIST: I mean, you wake up one morning, feeling groggy, out of it, and in pain. You roll out of bed. You head to the medicine cabinet, or wherever you keep your pain pills, and you find that you ran out. I mean, there's none left in the house! Then what do you do?

PATIENT: Get panicky. Maybe head for the liquor cabinet? Make some frantic phone calls to see if I can get a refill?

THERAPIST: I mean, man, is that any way to live?

PATIENT: It ain't good, but what's the alternative? I usually feel lousy and in pain.

THERAPIST: Do you think those pills help you to stand on your own two feet? Can anything ever change as long as you continue to eat such large quantities of pain pills regularly?

PATIENT: Nope. Not likely, man.

THERAPIST: Do you have any idea how you would feel if you overcame your excessive reliance on the pain pills?

PATIENT: But I'm in constant pain!

THERAPIST: But, do you have any idea how it would feel to not be groggy at 12 noon? To be able to talk with your kids when they get home from school? Maybe make them something to eat, help them do their homework?

PATIENT: No. Man, I'm so screwed up!

THERAPIST: Does it help to say that to yourself?

PATIENT: I'm usually pretty angry with myself.

THERAPIST: And when you feel angry with yourself, does that make you want to bother?

PATIENT: Usually no.

THERAPIST: What's going through your mind about wanting to bother right now?

PATIENT: You know Doc, right now I actually feel that it is worth bothering.

THERAPIST: What do you mean?

PATIENT: I mean that right now at this moment, I really don't feel good about what I've become. (*Starts to cry*) I mean, I had a life once, you know? That accident and this damn pain took it away!

THERAPIST: So, is it worth bothering to get your life back, or to rebuild a new life?

PATIENT: When you put it that way, the answer is definitely yes!

THERAPIST: So, where do you want to start?

PATIENT: You want me to say, let's start by stopping the pain medicine, right?

THERAPIST: How about we work together with Dr. D. (Patient's physician) to create a plan to wean you off of all of that pain medication?

PATIENT: I think we should bother.

THERAPIST: Well, okay. Let's get started.

ALEXITHYMIA, EMOTIONAL ILLITERACY, AND SOMATIC HYPERRESPONSIVENESS

The concept of *alexithymia* was introduced by Sifneos (1973) to explain observed restrictions in a person's ability to label and communicate affective and emotional experiences. This phenomenon is characteristic of many chronic pain patients (Blumer & Heilbronn, 1989; Engel, 1959; Grzesiak et al., 1996). The term *emotional repression* has been also used (Gamsa, 1994; Gamsa & Vikis-Freibergs, 1991; Grzesiak et al., 1996), but it really refers to a different concept, derived from the psychoanalytic perspective, which is that the emotional experience is warded out of awareness because it is nonconsciously perceived as threatening.

The term *emotional illiteracy* refers to the idea that persons who can be characterized as being alexithymic, may lack the vocabulary and perhaps even the concepts that would enable them to discern, construe, and discriminate varied emotional states. Without the requisite concepts and vocabulary, their emotional experiencing understandably would be impoverished. Finally, the term *somatic hyperresponsiveness* refers to the nonconscious expression of emotional arousal through the body, by many persons who lack the verbal-linguistic concepts to construe and interpret their arousal. The character, Festus, in the movie and long-running television serial *The Addams Family* illustrates caricaturishly, better than words can tell, the tendency to tense up, or brace up the entire body, as a nonverbal expression of emotional arousal. That character lacked the words to label and describe his feelings.

A patient who is emotionally illiterate, alexithymic, and hence somatically hyperresponsive could be at risk for developing chronic musculoskeletal tension and autonomic/sympathetic hyperarousal. All three concepts have been raised and revisited over the years by investigators of the concept of "pain-proneness" (Blumer & Heilbronn, 1989; Engel, 1959; Grzesiak et al., 1996; Sifneos, 1973). Related ideas that have been raised concern the possibility that pain-prone individuals may be pathologically self-reliant and "ergomanic," engaging in relentless activities and self-sacrifice (Gamsa, 1994; Grzesiak et al., 1996).

Although more research is needed, the phenomena associated with these concepts are frequently observed in patients suffering from chronic pain, addictions, and chronic posttraumatic stress disorder. It is reasonable to speculate whether psychotherapy directed toward remediating such emotional restriction could facilitate recovery from being in chronic pain. Certainly, cognitive therapy deals with the whole issue of integrating thoughts and feelings and helps patients become aware of their feelings, and their connection to their thoughts.

Another relatively new method of cognitive psychotherapy that can help patients to work out the connections between their thoughts, feelings, images, and physical sensations is Eye Movement Desensitization and Reprocessing (EMDR; Shapiro, 1995). The following sections provide a brief overview of the EMDR procedure as well as a review and description of its applications in PMP. Therapists who are interested in using EMDR in a clinical setting are advised to read *Eye Movement Desensitization and Reprocessing: Basic Principles, Protocols, and Procedures* (Shapiro, 1995) and to take formal EMDR training. Our guiding assumptions are as follows:

- Chronic, treatment-resistant pain often produces chronically negative and impaired mood.
- Persistent and rigid avoidance and inhibition of the negative images, cognitions, and feelings associated with chronically impaired mood and chronic pain can be maladaptive and unhealthy. It may produce and maintain intrusive images, anxious ruminations, negative cognitions, and maladaptive behaviors. It may also lead to a gradual erosion of self-esteem.
- The effort required to (a) persist in inhibiting the expression of this material and (b) cope with the guilt, shame, or anger that may result from its inappropriate or unwelcomed expression can be very stressful. Cumulatively, this stress may result in a chronic state of excessive physiological arousal or exhaustion (Pennebaker, 1989, 1993).
- Repeated, guided volitional exposure to distressing images, memories, and cognitions (a) may counter their avoidance and (b) may be necessary for their emotional processing (Kelley, Lumley, & Leisen, 1997; Pennebaker, 1989, 1997).
- Volitional emotional processing of this material to a point of resolution may yield (a) improvements in physical symptoms and (b) better

subjective, emotional, behavioral, and physical health (Greenberg & Stone, 1992; Kelley, Lumley, & Leisen, 1997; Pennebaker, 1989, 1997).

These assumptions are validated by a recent study with rheumatoid arthritis patients that investigated the effects of verbal disclosure and emotional processing of stressful events on their pain, physical and affective dysfunction, and joint condition (Kelley, Lumley, & Leisen, 1997). This study concluded that although disclosure and emotional processing resulted in immediate increases in negative mood, this was temporary. After 3 months, patients who verbally disclosed and emotionally processed their stressful events evidenced less emotional disturbance and better physical functioning than did a control group.

EYE MOVEMENT DESENSITIZATION AND REPROCESSING ("EMDR") THERAPY

EMDR was originally developed by Francine Shapiro between 1987 and 1989 to treat people suffering from posttraumatic stress disorder (Shapiro, 1989a, 1989b, 1995). It is a procedure in which the central component is the generation of rhythmic, back-and-forth, saccadic eye movements by the patient as the patient is helped to concentrate on a specific, troubling memory to be desensitized.

The therapist structures and sets up the eye movement procedure by first helping the patient to construct an *imaginal representation* of a troubling memory. This mental image is maintained while the patient is guided in eliciting a presently held, maladaptive, *negative self-referencing belief,* or *Negative Cognition* (NC) about the remembered incident. Next, an alternative, *positive self-referencing belief,* or *Positive Cognition* (PC) about the remembered incident is elicited, along with the patient's degree of belief in the Positive Cognition. The patient is asked to rate his or her degree of belief on a 1-to-7 scale termed the *Validity of Cognition* (VoC) scale. Then, the patient is helped to verbalize his or her current negative emotions and rate their intensity on a 0-to-10 Subjective Units of Distress (SUDs) scale. The patient is also asked to report any associated bodily sensations felt while thinking of the troubling memory, the image, and the negative self-referencing belief. Finally, the patient is asked to hold all of the above in mind while simultaneously tracking the therapist's index and middle finger as they are moved rapidly back and forth from side to side in sets of anywhere from 10 to 50 or more saccades or finger sweeps.

After each set of therapist-directed eye movements, the patient is asked to share with the therapist "what came up." The main therapeutic goals are (a) to eliminate the "negative emotional charge" associated with the remembered, troubling incident, and (b) to replace the Negative Cognition with a more functional and adaptive self-belief by (c) repeatedly pairing the Positive Cognition (PC) with the targeted memory after the original negative emotional reactions have been desensitized and largely alleviated. At that point, the patient is guided to hold the memory of the troubling incident in mind along with the PC as the therapist directs repeated sets of patient eye movements. The specific objectives of the EMDR procedure are to bring the "negative emotional charge" associated with the remembered, troubling incident (i.e., the SUDs) down to a level of 0 or 1, and the felt validity of the Positive Cognition (VoC) up to a 6 or 7 level of confidence.

Since 1990, there has been a virtual explosion of published research on psychotherapy for trauma and PTSD (Figley & Carbonell, 1995; Meichenbaum, 1994; van der Kolk, McFarlane, & Weisaeth, 1996), and EMDR has received a relatively large amount of attention. Numerous published case studies and several controlled studies have attested to the clinical efficacy of EMDR for treating acute and chonic PTSD, as well as other psychological and psychophysiological disorders (Boudewyns et al., 1993; Goldstein & Feske, 1994; Kleinknecht, 1992, 1993; Levin et al., 1994; Lipke & Botkin, 1992; Marquis, 1991; McCann, 1992; Vaughan et al., 1995; Wilson, Tinker, & Becker, 1994; Wolpe & Abrams, 1991). This has sparked efforts to dismantle the efficient components of the method to understand how EMDR effects cognitive and emotional changes in traumatized individuals (Boudewyns et al., 1993; DeBell & Jones, 1997; Levin et al., 1994; Renfrey & Spates, 1994; Sanderson & Carpenter, 1992; Vaughan et al., 1995). These reports have also generated thoughtful and sometimes forceful critiques of the evidence supporting the utility and efficacy of the method (DeBell & Jones, 1997; Herbert & Mueser, 1992; Lohr et al., 1992).

From our perspective, Eye Movement and Desensitization and Reprocessing is a structured, cognitive, emotive, imaginal, and behavioral technique. It is useful for assisting a patient to remember, review, emotionally reprocess, verbally disclose, reframe, and cognitively restructure stressful experiences that were instrumental in forming, consolidating, or activating dysfunctional assumptions, core beliefs or Early Maladaptive Schemas. These assumptions, beliefs, and schemas may be currently relevant to understanding a patient's maladaptive coping.

EMDR APPLICATIONS FOR
PAIN MANAGEMENT PSYCHOTHERAPY

We have found that the EMDR technique may be clinically useful in a number of ways in PMP:

1. EMDR may enable a patient to tell his or her story of pain and to process its emotional and cognitive components. This pain-related information complex would include (a) the circumstances surrounding the onset of the pain; (b) the primary losses and secondary gains resulting from the patient's condition; (c) the person's experiences as a pain patient, and his or her pain treatment history; (d) feelings of guilt and beliefs about having self-blame for pain; (e) the patient's representative alienating experiences of being let down, rejected, shamed, punished, abandoned, or condemned by others or the system (e.g., family members, friends, associates, insurance companies, employers, doctors, attorneys); (f) the patient's fears of what the future will bring; and (g) the patient's pain-related images and pain relief images.

2. EMDR may assist a patient to recognize the automatic negative self-talk associated with his or her pain and to generate adaptive, alternative positive cognitions. For example, EMDR could be used to reprocess a patient's memories of being in pain and anticipating the pain getting much worse, along with all the associated negative self-talk.

3. Where there is a history of trauma, EMDR can assist a patient to reprocess the traumatic memories and related, intrusive PTSD symptomatology. Unprocessed and unmetabolized traumatic memories often generate much cognitive and emotional interference and may be associated with the perpetuation of persistent pain states (Cheek, 1965, 1994; Eimer, 1993a, 1993b; Elliot, 1996; Ewin, 1978, 1986, 1992; Geisser et al., 1996; Harness & Donlon, 1988; Muse, 1986). Such material needs to be reviewed, reprocessed, reframed, and restructured so it can be put into a different, more adaptive perspective.

4. EMDR may enable a patient to rehearse employing pain replacement imagery and pain coping strategies. The expectation of invoking adaptive pain relief images and using functional pain coping strategies can then be strengthened or installed with the rhythmic, back-and-forth eye movements (Eimer, 1993a, 1993b; Shapiro, 1995).

5. EMDR may enable a patient to practice sustaining *focused volitional awareness* of the current physical pain sensations. The PMP therapist may use this structured form of *pain exposure therapy* to help the patient build increased pain tolerance.

EMDR—AN INTEGRATIVE TECHNIQUE

One thing that appears to set EMDR apart from other cognitive-behavioral methods is that it combines a number of psychotherapeutic paradigms into one, tightly structured procedure. These paradigms are imaginal and graded exposure, flooding and abreactive work, systematic

desensitization, psychophysiological self-regulation therapy, body awareness work, cognitive restructuring, and cognitive psychodynamics. To
date, we know of no formal or controlled outcome studies on the efficacy
of EMDR therapy with pain patients, and thus such applications must at
this point remain clinically anecdotal.

There has been speculation that eye movements may have pain ameliorating effects (Hekmat, Groth, & Rogers, 1994). Our experience has been
that pain patients who focus on their pain sensations while doing directed eye movements sometimes report an increase in felt pain intensity
during the exposure sessions. For many pain patients, this can be a negative experience. However, it can often be therapeutically transformed into
a positive experience if the PMP therapist successfully encourages the patient to stay with and process the cognitive and emotive material that
comes up. The experience may then provide a therapeutic window for
helping the patient develop a greater awareness and understanding of the
feelings and core beliefs associated with the pain. Temporarily increasing
pain intensity with stronger focusing and awareness can also function as
a therapeutic pain challenge by providing the PMP therapist with an excellent opportunity for coaching the patient in the use of pain coping
strategies.

Installation of Pain Replacement Imagery and Imaginal Rehearsal of Coping Strategies

The EMDR technique provides a methodology for strengthening or in-
stalling, positive cognitions. After a troubling memory and its associated
negative self-referencing cognitions have been adequately processed, the
patient does the eye movements while thinking about the appropriate
Positive Cognition (PC) and the target memory with which it is to be associated. Similarly, pain replacement images (PRIs) can be strengthened
or installed with eye movements to counter a patient's noxious pain images (NPIs). Also, a patient's confidence and emotional resolve to employ
desirable pain coping strategies during a severe pain flare-up can be
strengthened and installed by having the patient do eye movements
while thinking about (or mentally rehearsing) himself or herself employing the desired coping strategies in vivo. When self-doubts and negative
automatic thoughts arise during this mental rehearsal process, they too
can be targeted with the eye movements and reprocessed:

THERAPIST: Can you bring to mind an image, or picture, or snapshot of
your pain?

PATIENT: Yeh. I see a sharp knife stuck in my back, and a hand twisting it in further. I also see an electric shocker sending current down my left leg.

THERAPIST: Okay. That's pretty vivid. Can you also bring to mind an alternative image associated with pain relief? Something that would be nice to replace those painful images with?

PATIENT: I don't know. Not really.

THERAPIST: Okay. Just think about it and see what comes up. (*Therapist conducts a set of 25 back-and-forth eye movements.*) Okay. Take a deep breath. Now blank it out and let it go. What comes up for you?

PATIENT: Yes. Wow! I see a hand removing that knife! And I see a switch or dial on the electric shocker being switched to another channel. Instead of shock, it is sending out soothing ultrasound waves.

THERAPIST: How vivid or clear are these images of relief for you?

PATIENT: Pretty clear.

THERAPIST: Good. Now let's see if we can strengthen these more comfortable, pain replacement images. So, hold these replacement images of relief in mind. Think of them, and just follow my fingers. (*A set of about 20 to 25 back-and-forth eye movements is conducted.*) Okay. Good. Now, take a deep breath. Blank it out and let it go. Good. Tell me what comes up for you now.

PATIENT: Well, I guess that the image got a bit stronger. It also changed a bit. I imagined getting a nice, gentle therapeutic massage. I also imagined the application of a cool, soothing compress to the area.

THERAPIST: Very good. Now, earlier we talked about how else you could act, instead of getting panicky and catastrophizing, the next time you have a flare-up of that stinging, burning leg pain. Do you recall?

PATIENT: Yes I do.

THERAPIST: Can you imagine yourself now, having a flare-up, let's say tomorrow, and you start acting in that better, noncatastrophic mode?

PATIENT: Hmmn. It's fuzzy.

THERAPIST: Okay. Then think of it, however you can get it right now. Hold it in mind and follow my fingers. (*Therapist conducts an eye movement set.*) Now, blank it out and take a deep breath. Let it go. What comes up?

PATIENT: It's clearer. I can see myself doing it!

THERAPIST: Let's do a few more sets of eye movements to see if we can strengthen it somewhat more. Okay? So, bring it to mind. Think of it. (*Conducts another set of eye movements.*) Deep breath. Blow it out. What do you get now?

PATIENT: It's still about the same, but I thought of the fact that I probably will think of something stupid, but frightful, that usually gets me all riled up.

THERAPIST: What's that?

PATIENT: That I really am fooling myself with all this therapy stuff. That I need something that I do not have and probably can't get, because of the type of person I am. And maybe I really can't change!

THERAPIST: Which you take to mean?

PATIENT: That I'm a hopeless case! That I am not really like anyone you've ever treated. That I'm much worse off! And that's why I'm in so much pain, even though they can't verify it with any of their medical tests!

THERAPIST: Let's process that. Think of that and follow.

A COGNITIVE-BEHAVIORAL PAIN EXPOSURE THERAPY PROTOCOL INCORPORATING EMDR

EMDR is a means of reprocessing and restructuring the cognitive-evaluative, affective-motivational, and sensory-discriminative components of the chronic pain experience. The technique may be especially useful for addressing the misery and suffering dimensions of pain, and the attendant cognitive interference factors that frequently obstruct adaptive pain coping strategies. We have developed a brief, Cognitive-Behavioral Pain Exposure Therapy protocol incorporating EMDR that can be successfully implemented in anywhere from 12 to 15 sessions. This step-by-step PMP protocol is summarized in Figure 7.1 and described in this section. The central therapeutic ingredients are (a) patient education, (b) cognitive therapy for reframing the patient's maladaptive interpretations of the pain sensations, (c) Pain Exposure Therapy using EMDR, and (d) Coping Strategy Training. The two main goals of the protocol are to help the patient build pain tolerance and learn to think about (medically evaluated and treated) chronic pain as a "false alarm," if it is medically appropriate to do so. It is ill-advised to employ this model without medical clearance to view the chronic pain as a false alarm. Therefore, it is important to work closely with the patient's treating physicians: *Pain that has not been medically evaluated should NOT be treated this way!*

STEP 1. ASSESSMENT

Initial assessment usually takes up the first and second sessions. Figure 7.1 lists our standard assessment procedures and instruments. The

I. ASSESSMENT: Administer Pain History and Status Interview, Pain Coping Inventory (PCI), McGill or Philadelphia Pain Questionnaire (MPQ or PPQ), Beck Depression Inventory (BDI), Stress Symptoms Checklist (SSCL), Symptom Checklist 90-Revised (SCL-90R), and a personality test such as the Coolidge Axis II Inventory (CATI), or Personality Assessment Inventory (PAI). Assign use of a Pain Diary, such as Daily Pain Diary (DPD) or Pain Tracking Diary (PTD).

II. PATIENT EDUCATION: 1. Chronic pain can be thought of as a "false alarm." It may need to be turned down or ignored. "Smart Questions": Is your pain a helpful reminder not to overdo it? If yes, do you need such a loud alarm? 2. Teach Patient (a) distinctions between pure pain sensations and emotional distress about pain, and (b) how to rate pain intensity (from 0 to 10) and emotional distress using the Subjective Units of Distress or SUDs scale (from 0 to 10). 3. Assign relevant reading. 4. Keep and review pain diaries.

III. DEVELOP ALTERNATE INTERPRETATION OF THE PAIN SENSATIONS: 1. "Smart Questions": If the pain is not a false alarm, what is it? If it does not mean there is something wrong, what does it mean? Are there other ways you can alert yourself if something is wrong? 2. Use the Daily Pain & Thought Record (DPTR) to respond to Dysfunctional Automatic Thoughts (DATs) about pain in different triggering situations. 3. Keep and review pain diaries.

IV. ASSESS HYPNOTIC ABILITY. TEACH APPROPRIATE RELAXATION/ SELF-CONTROL TECHNIQUE: Administer the Hypnotic Ability and Response Profile (HARP).

V. EXPOSURE THERAPY TO LEARN TO IGNORE FALSE ALARMS AND BUILD PAIN TOLERANCE: Rationale: We want to help you learn to discriminate between pure pain sensations and your emotional distress about the pain. We may not be able to reduce the pure pain sensations, but we can reduce suffering, distress, and misery. This in turn may decrease the sensations. We also want to help you (a) build greater pain tolerance, (b) learn to ignore "false alarms" so you can focus on practicing pain coping strategies, and (c) improve your mental conditioning and toughness.

The EMDR Direct Pain Exposure Protocol:

1. Have patient rate pure pain intensity (0–10), then label and rate emotional distress (i.e., SUDs: 0–10).

2. Have patient focus on the pain sensations and describe them. Then, have Patient re-rate pure pain and SUDs.

3. Help Patient generate a target Negative Cognition (NC). Have Patient rate its felt validity (VoNC) (1 to 7). Ask Patient "Smart Questions": What does the way the pain feels right now mean about the pain? What does the pain mean to you? What does it mean or say about you? About the world and how it operates? What does it mean about your future? What are you afraid might

(continued)

Figure 7.1 Cognitive-Behavioral Pain Exposure Therapy Protocol Using EMDR

happen? If this were so, what is the worst that could happen? What images/ memories do you get when you think about your pain? Are you imagining something that might happen or remembering something that did?

4. Help Patient generate an alternative Positive Cognition (PC). Have Patient rate its felt validity (VoPC) (1 to 7). Ask "Smart Questions": If you really believed this idea (the PC) instead of that other idea (the NC), how do you think it would affect your pain level? How do you think holding that new belief would affect your level of emotional distress?

5. Help Patient identify and label type of affective distress experienced. Ask patient to rate present Subjective Units of Distress (SUDs level: from 0 to 10), and pain level (from 0 to 10).

6. Help Patient identify any additional physical sensations he or she is presently experiencing.

7. Implement direct exposure with Eye Movements (EMs) to desensitize Patient's pain-related distress. Ask Patient to think about simultaneously: pure pain sensations + target NC + affective distress. Carry on exposure with EM sets until: Patient's SUDs level decreases to 0 or 1, and VoNC reaches 1. Check VoNC, SUDs, and pain level every other EM set.

8. Install the PC. Ask Patient to think about simultaneously: pure pain sensations + PC. Carry on direct exposure with EM sets until the VoPC goes up to 6 or 7, as appropriate. After each installation set, check pain level and VoPC.

9. Assign for homework (HW) scheduled, self-directed, volitional pain awareness sitting sessions during which the patient is to focus on the pain, and describe his or her pain sensations and DATs out loud. Prescribe gradual increases in the duration of sitting focusing sessions. Patient is to note experiences, pain, and distress levels on the DPTR and pain diary.

VI. IMPLEMENT COPING STRATEGY TRAINING FOR PAIN CONTROL (the 4 A's of pain management):

1. Awareness strategy training: Begun in Step V. Continue volitional pain awareness training.

2. Avoidance strategy training: Teach strategies such as "taking a mini-vacation from pain," and distraction techniques.

3. Alleviation strategy training: Teach imagery, relaxation, and self-hypnotic techniques for decreasing the felt intensity of pain and filtering the hurt out of the pain.

4. Alteration strategy training: Teach imagery and self-hypnotic techniques to transform perceptions of pain.

VII. REASSESS: Readminister all assessment instruments. Review DPTRs and diaries.

Figure 7.1   *(Continued)*

patient is also taught daily self-assessment or self-monitoring using a pain diary such as the Daily Pain Diary (DPD) or Pain Tracking Diary (PTD).

Step 2. Education

Patient education is usually begun in the second or third session. The key points to communicate to the patient are (a) chronic pain may be thought of as a false alarm, and (b) an important distinction should be made between *pain sensations*, or "pure pain," and *emotional distress about pain*. It is conveyed that when pain, like a false alarm, has outlived its signal value (signaling function), it may need to be turned down or ignored. It is cautioned, however, that pain may not be a completely false alarm if it still serves as a healthy reminder not to overdo it and not to ignore physical deconditioning or true physical problems requiring treatment. The patient is asked to continue to record and review relevant data in the pain diaries. Relevant reading is also assigned, such as *Freedom from Chronic Pain* by Marcus and Arbeiter (1984), or *Managing Pain before It Manages You* by Caudill (1995).

Step 3. Development of Alternate Interpretations

The patient uses the Cognitive Therapy Daily Pain and Thought Record (DPTR) to identify and dispute Dysfunctional Automatic Thoughts (DATs) about pain in different triggering situations. The PMP therapist works with the patient to develop alternative interpretations that allow a more adaptive response. This step usually begins in the third session and continues throughout the therapy.

Step 4. Assessment of Hypnotic Ability

The therapist assesses the patient's hypnotic ability and responsiveness to design the most appropriate relaxation or self-hypnotic pain and anxiety management technique for the patient's self-directed use. We use the Hypnotic Ability and Response Profile (HARP) (Eimer & Oster, 1996) for this purpose. The HARP is covered in Chapters 10 and 11. This step is generally implemented in the fourth or fifth session.

Step 5. Exposure Therapy

The therapist introduces and administers EMDR as a form of *direct exposure therapy* to pure pain sensations and pain-related emotional distress. We generally introduce and administer the EMDR procedure between the sixth and ninth sessions. We convey to patients that although we may not be able to attain a major or permanent reduction in pain sensations, we nevertheless can often reduce the distress and misery component. This in turn may decrease the pain's subjectively felt intensity. Our goal is to help the patient learn to ignore false alarms so that he or she can focus on employing adaptive pain coping strategies. Otherwise, there may be too much cognitive interference to using coping strategies. We want to help the patient build greater *pain tolerance* and improve his or her mental conditioning and toughness.

The EMDR Direct Pain Exposure Protocol

The following protocol may be conducted over several sessions:

1. Have the patient rate the intensity of the pain on a 0-to-10 scale. Then, ask the patient to label how the pain makes him or her feel, and to rate his or her emotional distress on a 0-to-10 Subjective Units of Distress (SUDs) scale.

2. Have the patient focus intently on the pain sensations and describe them. After doing this, the patient should rerate the pain and SUDs.

3. Use *guided inquiry* to help the patient come up with several "hot," self-referencing Negative Cognitions (NCs) that summarize what the pain means to the patient and what it means about the patient. The hottest NC, which carries the most emotional charge and best summarizes the pain's idiosyncratic meaning, is selected as the target NC. Then, the patient's degree of belief in this target ("how true it feels," termed the *Validity of Negative Cognition* [VoNC]) is rated on a 1-to-7 scale. Questions for eliciting hot NCs are given in Figure 7.1.

4. Help the patient generate an alternative Positive Cognition that reframes the pain's meaning and summarizes it in a more functionally adaptive way. The patient then rates this replacement cognition's felt validity on a 1-to-7 Validity of Positive Cognition (VoPC) scale and answers the following questions: (a) If you really strongly believed this idea (the PC) instead of that other idea (the NC), how do you think it would affect your pain level? (b) How do you think having this new belief would affect your emotional distress?

5. The patient once again identifies and labels his or her affective distress, and rates its intensity on a 0-to-10 SUDs scale. The patient is also asked to rerate his or her pain level.

6. The patient is asked to become aware of and verbalize any additional physical sensations he or she is experiencing at the moment.

7. The therapist implements the patient's direct exposure to the preceding target material to desensitize the patient's pain-related distress. The patient is asked to simultaneously think about the pure pain sensations, the target NC, and the affective distress (emotional and physical)

experienced about this material. While the patient holds this material in mind, Eye Movement (EM) sets are conducted. After every other set of 20 to 30 saccadic eye movements, the therapist checks the NC's felt validity (VoNC) and the patient's pain and SUDs levels. This direct pain exposure/desensitization step in the protocol is continued until the patient's SUDs level decreases to 0 or 1, and the VoNC goes down to around 1, or to as close to 1 as is considered reasonable.

The therapist-directed eye movements (EMs) provide rapid, alternating, bilateral (left-right) sensory stimulation that appears to catalyze the processing and reprocessing of the targeted information and help maintain the patient's focus on it. Most patients readily accept the EMs. Occasionally, we have also used *bilateral auditory stimulation* fed through headphones in an alternating pattern into the patient's right and left ears, and some patients prefer this technique. We conjecture that these patients may find auditory stimulation more facilitative than Eye Movement stimulation for inward somatic focusing. However, EMs are easier for the therapist to direct and pace and require no equipment. Furthermore, most pain patients can be taught how to perform self-directed EMs as part of their homework assignments for mental rehearsal of coping strategies and direct pain exposure sitting sessions (see Step 9).

8. It is necessary to "install" or strengthen the alternative PC once the formerly hot NC has lost its emotional charge, and the SUDs level has been substantially brought down. The therapist then conducts EM sets while the patient focuses simultaneously on the pure pain sensations, any triggering situational circumstances, and the PC. After each installation set (15 to 30 saccades), the patient is asked to check his or her pain level and the felt VoPC. Focusing on and reprocessing of this material is continued until the VoPC goes up to a 6 or a 7, as is clinically appropriate.

9. In between EMDR office sessions, *direct exposure homework* is assigned that requires the patient to schedule self-directed, volitional pain awareness sitting sessions, usually two per day. Patient is instructed to use the time to focus on the pain, verbally describe the pain sensations to himself or herself, and verbalize any DATs that come up. After each session, the patient records his or her experience, pure pain intensity, emotional distress level, and DATs on the DPTR and pain diary forms. These focusing sessions help expand the patient's volitional awareness, improve his or her mental toughness and mental conditioning, and increase pain tolerance.

Note that a *behavioral shaping* or *graded task assignment* approach is taken. The amount of time initially assigned for sitting and inwardly focusing is always determined in collaboration with the patient. This initial baseline duration must be within the patient's initial level of tolerance. The sitting and focusing duration is gradually increased from baseline as is clinically and medically appropriate. *Caution:* The clinician should obtain medical clearance for the patient before conducting this protocol. No patient should be instructed to sit for longer than is tolerable for his or her physical-medical pathology, as evaluated by a physician.

In preparation for the direct exposure, focused awareness homework, the therapist instructs the patient and coaches the patient to employ slow, controlled, deep diaphragmatic or abdominal breathing as a coping strategy, even when the pain's intensity rises. The patient is educated to expect a subjective increase in intensity during the exercise since the patient will be focusing directly on the pain. The patient will in all likelihood have already experienced this in the office during the EMDR procedure. The patient is instructed to target one painful area at a time and is coached how to (a) imagine opening up around and through the targeted painful area, (b) relax the entire target area, (c) imagine directing his or her breath through the target area, and (d) imagine displacing the pain with the breath to another part of the body such as the abdomen, from where it can be blown out of the body with the breath.

Some pain patients may also benefit from doing self-directed EMs during these homework sessions. Patients are generally taught several alternative, self-directed, bilateral stimulation methods:

1. The patient stares at a wall using the wall's left and right corners as endpoints, and keeps his or her head steady while moving his or her eyes back and forth, from left to right between these two endpoints.

2. (a) The patient places the right hand palm down and flat on the right leg, and the left hand palm down and flat on the left leg, or (b) places both hands flat and palms down on a table, and (c) raises the right and left index fingers in alternating fashion while the eyes move back and forth, from left to right, between each alternatingly raised index finger.

3. Another method is to gently tap one's left and right temples in alternating fashion with the right and left index fingers, or index and middle fingers, so that an audible tapping sound can be heard, and a tactile-kinesthetic sensation of gentle tapping can be felt. This is called the temporal tap.

Step VI. Coping Strategy Training

This training generally takes place formally between the 9th and 12th sessions. Following Brown and Fromm (1987), we introduce the metaphor of the "Four A's" of self-directed pain management. The first *A*, "Awareness strategies," has already been initiated with EMDR and the direct exposure, somatic focusing homework. We may also teach the patient additional direct awareness coping strategies, such as (a) studying pure pain sensations objectively, without emotional interference, for increasing periods of time; (b) opening up into and around the painful areas, using acceptance, direct awareness, and controlled, deep diaphragmatic or abdominal breathing, as discussed; and (c) observing the automatic thoughts and images that arise in one's stream of consciousness.

The second *A*, "Avoidance strategies," involves teaching the patient self-directed, cognitive and imaginal distraction techniques. Techniques that fall into this class are covered in Chapters 8 through 11.

The third *A*, "Alleviation strategies," involves teaching the patient self-directed cognitive, imaginal, relaxation, biofeedback, and self-hypnosis techniques for directly reducing the pain's subjectively felt intensity. One example is Stress Inoculation and Self-Instructional Training, which was covered earlier. Alleviation strategies are also discussed in Chapters 8 through 11.

The fourth *A*, "Alteration strategies," involves teaching the patient self-directed cognitive, imaginal, relaxation, and self-hypnotic techniques for transforming the perception of pain. Formidable pain descriptors identified earlier on the MPQ or PPQ Pain Adjective Checklist may be transformed into less onerous ones. For example, it may be suggested that the patient imagine a burning pain turning into an itch, or imagine pain in one area of the body being displaced into another area that is less bothersome or ominous. Alteration strategies are more fully covered in Chapters 9 through 11.

The patient may mentally rehearse the use of coping strategies in each of the preceding categories and conducting a series of EMs may strengthen or install confidence in their employment.

Step VII. Reevaluation

The therapist reevaluates the patient employing the same instruments that were administered in the initial assessment. This allows for the assessment and quantification of changes in the patient's functional, behavioral, psychological, and pain status that can be attributed to the treatment.

Summary

The clinical applications of EMDR in PMP are thought-provoking, exciting, and promising. However, to date, no formal or controlled studies have been conducted. Whether the emotional processing, reexperiencing, and self-disclosure facilitated by EMDR can be forged into positive pain

PAIN MANAGEMENT PSYCHOTHERAPY PROGRESS NOTE

PATIENT: **Z. A.**   DATE: July 14, 1997

CHECK PROCEDURES/S (CPT): _X_ Extended psychotherapy-90842
____ Psychotherapy-90844   ____ Biofeedback training-90901
____ Psychol. tests-96100   ____ Psych Diag Interview Exam-90801
____ Patient educational supplies-99071   ____ Psychophysiological Therapy-90876

RESULTS OF ANY TESTS, EVALUATION, OR OUTCOME MEASURES ADMINISTERED—
Visual Analogue Scale Pain Rating (VAS: 0–100) $VAS_{this\ week}$ = _40_
$VAS_{last\ week}$ = _65_ VAS_{change} = _X_ 0 (decreased pain)
____ 1 (no change in pain level)   ____ 2 (increased pain)
Present Pain Index$_{week's\ ave.}$ = _2_   PPI = 0 (none)   1 (weak)   X2 (moderate)
3 (severe)   4 (excruciating)
Percent Pain Relief$_{this\ week}$ = ____ 0(100%)   ____ 1(80–99%)   ____ 2(50–79%)
_31%_ 3(30–49%)   ____ 4(0–29%)
Global Pain Score (GPS: 0–10)$_{this\ week}$ = _5_   SUDs (0–10)$_{this\ week}$ = _2.5_
Pain Disability Rating$_{this\ week}$ = $0_{(no\ disability)}$ – $10_{(all\ usual\ activities\ have\ been\ totally\ disrupted\ by\ pain)}$ = 4

SUBJECTIVE COMPLAINTS, PRESENTING PROBLEMS, PATIENT'S AGENDA, AND PREVIOUS SESSION'S HW—
1. Pt reported on his experiences this week with the self-directed exposure homework (HW) which involved sitting for 15 minutes 2x/day focusing his awareness on the pain, describing the pain sensations, rating pure pain and emotional distress about pain (0 to 10) every 5 minutes, verbalizing his dysfunctional automatic thoughts (DATs), and recording his pain sensations, pain images, DATs, and pain levels on his Daily Pain and Thought Records (DPTR). 2. What came up for Pt. were his resentments about his wife's NOT understanding "what he goes through" and doubting the validity of his pain. 3. We also addressed Pt's current fears, some of which were brought up in his HW awareness exercises.

OBJECTIVES AND GOALS OF SESSION—1. Assess outcomes of last session's EMDR desensitization protocol, review self-directed pain exposure HW and Pt's DPTRs. 2. Address negative cognitions that have interfered with Patient's compliance w/treatment. 3. Continue with EMDR desensitization of catastrophic reactions to pain. 4. Continue to build readiness to use adaptive pain coping strategies, and decrease "cognitive interferences" to their employment.

ABSTRACT OF SESSION'S FOCAL POINTS—Procedures: 1. Therapeutic conversation. 2. Review of Homework. 3. Discussion of medication issue. 4. Used DPTR and "cognitive model" to analyze the DATs associated with brief episode of depression on Saturday. 5. Did short EMDR set to reinforce positive insights & pain desensitization outcomes.
Summary. 1. Pt. reported pain levels were down this week (see above). Self-directed HW exposure sessions helped him to see what makes him depressed and enraged, AND helped him to feel the distinctions between pure pain (rated) and his misery or emotional distress about pain (rated separately). 2. Pt. ventilated about his resentment that he is no longer the breadwinner, about how he misses working for a living, and the detrimental effects on him of being dependent and disabled. Reminisced about his memory of being a workaholic before he got injured. Had frank discussion about the Catch-22 of waiting for Insurance Co. to settle/commute his claim—Pt. wants to be able to return to a vocational avenue he can physically handle—perhaps start up and own a small business in his area (i.e., tree cutting or carpentry) and administering it, hiring the physical labor, procuring the business, etc. But, he feels he will need Ins Co to settle so he has capital to start up.

Figure 7.2   PMP Exposure Therapy Progress Note for Z. A.

Understandably, Pt. fears Ins Co. will either consider him as too disabled to use a settlement constructively to start up his own business, OR that they will consider him as NOT being disabled given his motivation, and that they will try to cut him off. 3. Pt. reported he made appt. with Psychiatrist to whom I referred him (for 7/28) in order to re-assess his medications. He also stated that he has begun to take his Elavil regularly as I suggested (and was Rx'd) every night at around 6 PM. This he stated has not resulted in his awakening groggy and oversedated in the following AM. Up until now, he was taking the medication sporadically. 4. Pt. reported the positive therapeutic realization that he can be partially distracted from his pain when he's having a good time socializing with friends, although he remains aware that the pain is still there.

ASSIGNMENTS FOR PATIENT HOMEWORK—Same HW assigned.

PLAN FOR FOLLOWING SESSIONS—We shall meet again in one week. Plan next session to re-address Pain Coping Strategy Training using the "4 A's" model. We shall begin discussing plans for preparation for trial SCS—anticipated that Pt will be ready for hospital procedure in about 2 months (around late Sept. or early Oct.).

BRUCE N. EIMER, PH.D., ABPP

Figure 7.2 *(Continued)*

rehabilitation outcomes remains a topic of much interest that merits future investigation. However, if it is true that restrictions in the pain sufferer's ability to label and communicate affective and emotional experiences, contribute to the maintenance of chronic pain states, then EMDR may provide a mechanism for remediating this deficiency.

The following therapeutic conversation took place with a patient during the session immediately following the first administration of the EMDR Direct Pain Exposure Protocol. The patient is a 35-year-old, male, chronic low back pain patient who was not working, and who was receiving workers' compensation. He was being seen for a course of brief "Pre-Implant Psychotherapy" as part of the screening process for Spinal Cord Stimulator implantation (Williams, 1996b). This segment of the transcript illustrates how the EMDR protocol may facilitate the disclosure and emotional processing of important thoughts and feelings that otherwise might have remained unacknowledged, denied, concealed, inhibited, or suppressed. A PMP Progress Note summarizing this particular session is displayed in Figure 7.2.

THERAPIST: So, tell me how your pain exposure sitting sessions have been, and what you have learned.

PATIENT: It got easier and easier. Like quicker for me to be able to bring myself to that state, feeling depressed, you know, and everything. But, it was time to stop and let go of it. It got easier for me just to blow it off too. I mean, the first couple of times, it made me think for a lot of hours afterward. I'd keep going back and thinking. Besides my pain, it brought back other things, but it got easier to blow off.

THERAPIST: Did things change as the week went on?

PATIENT: Yes. Toward the end of the week, it got to be, you know, where you get to that point where I didn't feel as depressed about it. I didn't feel as bad, and then, I could just snap out of it right away.

THERAPIST: Do you mean when you were doing the sitting, or when you would be going about your business during the day and suddenly find yourself overtaken by depressed feelings?

PATIENT: Well, both really. If I got depressed during the day, I'd think about things and move my eyes back and forth like we did here. But the "sits" you know, made me think about a lot of things I hadn't thought about in years.

THERAPIST: So, are you saying that you found yourself getting into up-setting feelings and thoughts about your pain, but that the more you did those "sits," the easier it became to blow it off?

PATIENT: Yeah. Like I said, the first couple of days it stayed with me, the thoughts stayed with me for hours. But after that, when I blew it away, it was gone.

THERAPIST: Do you feel any lighter? Have you felt somewhat less disturbed by the pain?

PATIENT: Yes. I guess somewhat. I guess it's helped me to maybe accept myself a little bit more. You know what I mean?

THERAPIST: Yes I do.

PATIENT: Cause I really thought about a lot of things. It brought back a lot of other things besides my pain. Things fighting for each other's attention in my eye. I think it worked somewhat. It made me feel freer of it. It's hard to put into words, but at the same time, I would have thought that it would have been harder for me to get depressed. But you know, it wasn't. I could just jump to that state real quick, you know what I mean?

THERAPIST: Yes. I think I do. So, this exercise helped you realize that it's really easy for you to get depressed about your pain, and also that you can blow it off?

PATIENT: Yeah, but like I said, there are other things that came in with it too.

THERAPIST: Such as?

PATIENT: Well, it made me become aware, I mean, like, I've been thinking about, my main thing is I've always been what you would call the "provider" for my family. Now, my wife brings in more money than I do! The other part is my kids, not being able to physically do things with them. And I also miss working. I mean, I was a workaholic before I got hurt. Now, I hear it from my wife all the time, "You know you're on a big vacation, you don't do anything!" You know, it's not my choice to be like this!

THERAPIST: And does all that make you angry?

PATIENT: You bet it does!

THERAPIST: Do you remember what I told you last week was the main reason to do this exercise, here in the office, and the "sits" twice a day at home?

PATIENT: To realize that I have the pain, and it's there, but to try to realize that I can overcome it.

THERAPIST: Yes. That's it precisely. And also, to help you build pain tolerance and stop running in fear from the pain.

PATIENT: So, you said, I can learn how to cope with it better.

THERAPIST: Yes.

PATIENT: Yeah, I was going to say, my pain level has been down. I have noticed my pain level has been less lately. I mean, I haven't been in as much pain, you know?

THERAPIST: Yes. I hear what you are telling me and I am glad to hear it, but not surprised.

CHAPTER 8

Behavior Therapy for Pain Management

I enjoy convalescence. It is the part that makes the illness worthwhile.
—George Bernard Shaw

BEHAVIORAL INTERVENTIONS directly address the problem of promoting compliance with pain treatment. Because noncompliance is a major problem that often depotentiates the efficacy of treatments for pain patients (Meichenbaum & Turk, 1987; Turk et al., 1983), behavioral interventions are an essential component of PMP. Pain management therapies that ignore behavioral issues are doomed to fail. Although this is a strong statement, it generally holds true: In a sense, behavioral interventions are the glue that hold everything else together.

Fordyce (1976, 1988) contributed greatly to the field of pain management by elucidating the role of operant behavioral conditioning principles in the genesis and maintenance of pain behavior problems. These principles not only appear to govern the natural history of such problems, but also provide effective guidelines for formulating a behavioral cure. As in all good therapy, however, the pain management therapist must be consistent and persistent in applying operant and respondent conditioning techniques, and cognitive therapy techniques as well, in the remediation of pain behavior problems. By "consistent," we mean (a) having an adequate cognitive-behavioral and psychophysiological conceptualization of the case, and understanding of the patient's physical and medical problems, (b) providing the patient with clear rationales and definitive instructions that are adequately broken down into implementable steps, (c) sticking to the principles of the program, and (d) not vacillating by shifting the focus or the ground rules arbitrarily. By "persistent," we mean that the therapist must be diligent in following up on problems with patients, and conscientious in not giving up. This involves determining the reasons for noncompliance, and addressing them to promote compliance.

BEHAVIORAL EXCESSES AND DEFICITS

The mainstay of the behavioral approach is the targeting of operationally defined indices of behavior for assessment and modification. Behavioral excesses as well as deficiencies are targeted for intervention (Fordyce, 1976, 1988; A. Lazarus, 1989; O'Donohue & Krasner, 1995; Spiegler, 1983; Wolpe, 1990). Excesses (also termed, positive behavioral symptoms) would include behavioral habits that occur frequently enough to be deemed maladaptive. Behavioral deficits (also termed, negative behavioral symptoms) would include adaptive behaviors that are in short supply (such as coping strategies), as well as avoided behaviors that are considered healthy and necessary to successful adaptation (such as being employed and working). PMP targets behavioral excesses for reduction or elimination, and for replacement by more adaptive behaviors. Likewise, behavioral deficits are targeted for remediation through shaping and positive reinforcement procedures.

PAIN BEHAVIORS AND WELL BEHAVIORS

The term *pain behaviors* refers to maladaptive or dysfunctional behaviors in response to pain that are associated with continued pain and disability (Keefe & Williams, 1992; Pilowsky, 1995; Sanders, 1996; Turk & Matyas, 1992). In contrast, the term *well behaviors* refers to adaptive or functional behaviors in response to pain that are associated with diminished pain and disability. Both pain behaviors and well behaviors can either be overt or covert. *Overt pain behaviors* are externally observable behaviors that indicate the person emitting the behaviors is in pain.

Positive and Negative Behavioral Symptoms

Overt pain behaviors can be sorted into two categories: *positive* and *negative* behavioral symptoms of pain. Common examples of positive behavioral symptoms (behavioral excesses) are (a) *nonverbal pain behaviors* such as limping, grimacing, moaning, rubbing parts of the body that hurt, muscle guarding and bracing, stiffening, movement avoidance, pacing, screaming, and crying; (b) *addictive behaviors* defined as seeking and using pain medicine or other substances for purposes other than pain relief such as to tranquilize anxiety; and (c) *verbal pain behaviors* such as complaining about pain; making statements communicating hopelessness, helplessness, depression, anger, fear, anxiety, and other indications of emotional distress or suffering; and making excessive requests for assistance. Common examples of negative behavioral symptoms (behavioral deficits) are lying down, reclining, or sleeping excessively (termed downtime); avoidance of activities; withdrawal; cognitive problems such as concentration difficulties and forgetfulness; loss of libido; inertia; loss of motivation; and not working.

Conversely, overt well behaviors are functional, externally observable, cognitive, and emotional responses to pain that are not "ruled by pain." This category would include following an activity schedule, using pain medicine on a time-contingent as opposed to a pain-contingent basis, following sleep hygiene principles, and exercising or working according to a predetermined and realistic quota, rather than on the basis of one's momentary pain tolerance.

Covert pain behaviors are internally emitted by the person in pain and, hence, usually nonobservable by others. These include dysfunctional automatic thoughts and negative self-talk associated with depression, anxiety, fear, and anger; morbid images and daydreams (e.g., intrusive recollections and visions of oneself being helpless, in agony, becoming worse); bad dreams and nightmares; excessive awareness of and preoccupation with pain sensations; and internal physiological events, such as actual pain sensations, sympathetic nervous system responses associated with autonomic hyperarousal, and emotional perceptions of anxiety, fear, sadness, and anger. Conversely, covert well behaviors are functional, internal, cognitive, emotional, and physiological responses to pain.

Assessing Pain Behaviors

Evaluation of a pain patient is not complete without including an assessment of pain behaviors. This almost always involves obtaining the patient's perceptions of his or her behavioral responses to pain. Frequently, significant others who know the patient well are also interviewed with the patient's permission. Following Sander's (1996) "basic indications for operant conditioning effects in chronic pain patients" (p. 118), we ask questions to determine (a) whether the patient exhibits overt pain behaviors; (b) if so, whether overt pain behavior is related to time of day, particular situations or places, persons present, or particular activities; (c) whether overt pain behaviors are acknowledged and responded to by others, and if so, by whom and how; (d) whether overt pain behaviors are followed by positive or negative reinforcers, or punitive responses, and if so, what they are; (e) whether overt pain behaviors reflect symptom exaggeration or magnification; and (f) whether the patient associates increased pain with increased activity and returning to work.

INTERVIEW ABOUT PAIN BEHAVIORS

We typically interview the patient about pain behaviors. If there are significant others, and we have the patient's permission to talk with them, we ask them variants of the same questions. The following standard questions can identify areas of behavioral dysfunction:

- Do you know the present cause or causes of your pain? What do you think they are? What is maintaining your pain problem? Why do you think you continue to have pain?
- At what time of day is your pain the worst?
- How does movement affect your pain?
- Do certain activities make your pain worse? How about better? What are these activities?
- How does exercise affect your pain?
- Do you ever require an assistive device to walk? What? How often? When?
- Do you ever ask others for help because your pain prevents you from doing something on your own? What do you ask for help doing? How often? Whom do you ask? How do they respond to your request?
- How do you think other people treat you? How do you feel about this? Do people show you as much respect as you would like? If not, why not?
- Do other people know you are in pain? How do they know this? Do you tell them? Or, do they see it?
- Do you have any limitations as a result of your chronic pain? What are they?
- Can you work? If not, why not?
- Do you ever complain about your condition? How often? To whom? How do they usually respond?
- How often do you lie down each day because of pain? How long do you lie down or rest? How do you feel after you get up compared with the way you feel before resting?
- What medications do you take for pain? What are the doses? How often do you take each medication?
- Do you take pain medicine at fixed times each day, or do you take it based on when you need it?
- Who prescribes your pain medication?

- Where do you fill your prescriptions for pain medicine?
- Has anyone ever said to you that you take too much pain medicine?
- Have any doctors ever refused to treat you because they thought you took too much pain medicine?
- Have you ever been treated in a hospital or clinic for addiction to pain medicine? For addiction to other drugs? For abusing alcohol? Have you ever gone to a doctor just to get a pain medicine prescription?
- Have you ever been unable to get out of bed or wake up because you were on heavy pain medicine?
- Has anyone ever said to you that you seem drunk, out of it, or punchy? Who? When? Were you on a lot of pain medicine at the time? If so, what was the name of the medicine? How much were you taking?
- Do you believe that you have a problem with taking too much pain medicine? Does anyone else feel you have a problem with taking too much pain medicine?
- Would you say that you are very afraid of moving wrong and re-injuring yourself?
- Financially, are you doing better now, by not working, or would you do better financially if you went back to work?

BEHAVIORAL PROBLEMS OF
CHRONIC PAIN PATIENTS

The failure to reduce pain behaviors is usually associated with the failure to restore a patient's functionality. Because a patient's functionality is measured in terms of appropriate, adaptive, and functional behaviors, PMP should include interventions aimed at increasing the frequency of such behaviors. Behavioral principles and techniques are applicable across a wide range of PMP and rehabilitative interventions. Several common behavioral problems, however, require the focused implementation of behavioral techniques, along with the application of other modalities, such as cognitive therapy and hypnotherapy. These problems fall under the Six Dysfunctional D's of chronic pain: (a) deconditioning, (b) disability, job dissatisfaction, and work dysfunction, (c) depression, (d) other types of emotional distress (e.g., anger, hostility, anxiety), (e) disturbed sleep, and (f) deficient cognitive and behavioral skills (e.g., cognitive deficiencies in attention and memory, deficient social and assertiveness skills). When there are strong reasons to suspect opioid drug-seeking compelled by motives other than pain relief (e.g., to experience the drug's psychic effects), then this becomes a "Seventh D" that must be addressed.

The balance of this chapter is devoted to discussing the management of behavior problems in the context of PMP *coaching principles.*

MANAGING THE USE OF ANALGESICS FOR PAIN MANAGEMENT

There continues to be much resistance among physicians to prescribing opioids to chronic pain patients because of the widespread fear that patients will abuse these drugs and become drug-dependent (S. Hill, 1987; Twycross, 1994). Yet, there is little evidence that chronic pain patients who do not have a prior history of drug abuse, are prone to becoming addicted if strong opioids are responsibly prescribed for analgesic purposes (Portenoy & Foley, 1986; Porter & Jick, 1980; Twycross, 1994). In fact, studies reveal that long-term use of opioids for pain relief is not associated with the development of psychological dependence (Portenoy & Foley, 1986; Twycross, 1994). The terms *psychologically dependent* and addiction are used synonymously. As quoted by Twycross (1994), based on the World Health Organization's (1969) definition, both terms refer to "behavioral and other responses that always include a compulsion to take the drug on a continuous or periodic basis in order to experience its psychic effects, and sometimes to avoid the discomfort of its absence. Tolerance may or may not be present" (p. 947).

Drug abuse appears to be much more strongly related to factors such as underlying personality and social environment (Millon, 1995), as opposed to the seeking of relief from pain (Twycross, 1994). Unless there is strong evidence to the contrary in a particular case, it appears to be more clinically useful to conceptualize the problem of opioid drug-seeking by chronic pain patients as a problem stemming from poor pain control, as opposed to being a symptom of an addictive personality disorder. The primary reason that most pain patients seek analgesic medications is for pain relief.

This book is not an appropriate place to discuss the controversies, procedural issues, and guidelines pertaining to prescribing analgesic medications for pain patients. Several comprehensive sources include Portenoy (1996b), Portenoy and Kanner (1996b), Portenoy and Payne (1992), and Twycross (1994). Several points need to be made here, however, to serve as basic clinical guidelines for nonphysician PMP therapists whose patients present with problems related to opioids and nonopioid adjuvant analgesics. The guidelines in the following sections are derived from Portenoy (1996b), the other sources cited earlier and from our clinical experience.

CONFERRING WITH THE PATIENT'S PHYSICIAN

Ethical and professional standards require that the nonphysician psychotherapist defer to a patient's treating physicians when it comes to the pharmacological management of their pain. It is both unethical and unprofessional for the nonphysician therapist to advise patients about the use of pharmaceuticals without conferring closely with their treating and prescribing physicians.

PAIN PATIENTS WITH A PREEXISTENT SUBSTANCE ABUSE DISORDER

Patients with dual diagnoses (e.g., a psychiatric disorder and a substance abuse disorder, or a chronic pain syndrome and an addictive disorder) are usually harder and more complicated to treat than patients with a single diagnosis. Chronic pain patients with a preexisting substance abuse disorder frequently present as opioid drug-seekers. The therapist needs to clinically conceptualize the factors motivating the drug-seeking for each case. Frequently, such patients are motivated by factors other than pain relief, and the pain problem just makes matters worse. Effective treatment of these patients falls within the domain of addictions psychiatry and medicine.

If the primary problem is addiction, pain medicine is likely to be abused. Pharmacologically oriented pain management specialists such as Portenoy (1996b) suggest that comorbid personality/character pathology probably is a contraindication for the use of opioids for pain management. As discussed in Chapter 4, however, there may be particular qualifying factors for opioid therapy that should be acknowledged. Our general experience has been that pain management is unlikely to be effective until such individuals are actively in recovery from their addictive disorders.

When we assess a new pain management referral that falls into this category, we usually recommend that an evaluation also be conducted by a psychiatrist specializing in addictions. Often, the first course of action is to admit the patient into an inpatient, physician-directed, detoxification program. On discharge, a definitive program of intensive, outpatient addictions treatment should be in place. Treatment should guide the person through the phases of recovery and emphasize relapse prevention and maintenance strategies (Marlatt & Gordon, 1985). It is also essential for the patient to actively participate in an appropriate, ongoing recovery program such as a Twelve Step or Rational Recovery group (Ellis, McInerney, DiGiuseppe, & Yeager, 1988). PMP can be incorporated into the primary addictions treatment program, once the patient is well on the way in recovery.

Drug Tolerance

Current consensus among pain pharmacologists is that the problem of drug tolerance in chronic pain patients has been overestimated (Twycross, 1994). In fact, there is evidence that tolerance to the adverse side effects of opioids used in the management of certain chronic pain conditions (e.g., cancer pain) develops more readily than does tolerance to analgesia (Bruera, Macmillan, Hanson, & MacDonald, 1989; Twycross, 1994).

Obtaining the Patient's Informed Consent

When a pain patient is deemed an appropriate candidate for opioid pain management, it is advisable to require that the patient give informed consent before the initiation of opioid therapy (Portenoy, 1996b). Responsible opioid pain management demands that only one physician and pharmacy write and fill the prescriptions. It is sometimes a good idea to formulate a written contract to be signed by the patient and the key members of the patient's pain management team (e.g., prescribing physician, treating physicians, physical therapist, and psychotherapist) (Portenoy, 1996b). A patient's misinformation also needs to be corrected at the outset of opioid pain therapy. Patients should be helped to understand what the likely side effects and risks of continued use of opioids can be (e.g., some cognitive impairment, particular physical side effects, likelihood of physical dependence for pain relief but low risk of true addiction).

Fixed-Interval Dosing

The consensus among experts (Portenoy, 1996b; Portenoy & Foley, 1986; Twycross, 1994) is that in cases of continuous or frequently recurring pain, opioids should be administered on a fixed time-interval dosing basis for maximum pain management effectiveness. PMP therapists often see patients who are using both opioids and nonopioid adjuvant analgesics on an as-needed (PRN) basis. This is considered maladaptive because "as needed" means that consumption of the medication is pain contingent. If there is pain behavior, there is pain medication. If there is no pain behavior, there is no medication. This in effect tends to reinforce pain behavior, whereas an important pain treatment goal is to reduce its frequency. Removing major sources of reinforcement for pain behavior is one means of doing this. Therefore, pain medicine should not be pain behavior contingent. The adaptive alternative is fixed-interval dosing. Another advantage of fixed-interval dosing is that it maximizes continuous blood levels of the analgesic and therefore tends to dampen pain before it flares up.

If a patient is using opioids and/or nonopioid adjuvant analgesics on an as-needed basis, the psychotherapist should discuss with the patient the advisability of conferring with the prescribing physician. With the patient's consent, it is usually expeditious for the psychotherapist to discuss the matter on the telephone with the prescribing physician. Then, based on the outcome of that conversation, it is usually recommended that the patient set up an appointment with the prescribing physician to agree on and make necessary adjustments in the writing and use of the prescriptions.

ABERRANT DRUG-RELATED BEHAVIORS

If there is ever new evidence suggestive of "aberrant drug-related behaviors that raise concern about the potential for addiction" (Portenoy, 1996b, p. 257), it requires the immediate attention of the prescribing physician and the dispensing pharmacy. These behaviors include the concurrent abuse of alcohol or any illicit recreational drugs, borrowing or stealing drugs from others, forging prescriptions, repeatedly escalating doses on one's own, "losing" prescriptions, seeking prescriptions from sources other than the agreed primary source, drug-hoarding, and an apparent deterioration in the patient's functionality. Responsible opioid therapy in the face of any of these is impossible. Additional red flags are repeated visits to hospital emergency rooms for pain medication, multiple indications of noncompliance with pain therapies, and nonnegotiable resistance by the patient to recommended adjustments or changes in the therapy. Again, *each case should be evaluated on an individual basis by the patient's prescribing physician.*

PERIODIC ASSESSMENTS OF MENTAL AND FUNCTIONAL STATUS

The nonphysician PMP therapist can perform an important function by conducting periodic assessments of the pain patient's mental and functional status. Patients receiving ongoing opioid pain management therapy should be regularly assessed to evaluate (a) degree of analgesia or comfort derived from the drug therapy; (b) drug side effects, such as cognitive interference, lassitude, and fatigue; (c) physical and psychosocial functional status; and (d) aberrant behaviors (Portenoy, 1996b).

Degree of Analgesia

Analgesia effectiveness is easily evaluated with the Pain Tracking Diary and the Daily Pain and Thought Record. In the therapist's office, visual analogue and numerical pain ratings can be obtained by having the patient fill out the Global Pain Rating Scales at each visit (see Chapter 6). Periodically the patient can also fill out one or two of the following instruments: the PPQ-PAC, the Brief Pain Status Questionnaire, the SF-MPQ, the original MPQ, the P-3, or the PCI.

Drug Side Effects

Drug side effects such as cognitive interference are easily evaluated by examining the patient's mental status (discussed in Chapter 2), and interviewing significant others. In addition, cognitive and neuropsychological screening tests can be useful for evaluating percepto-motor functioning (e.g., the Bender Visual Motor Gestalt Test), sustained attention, reaction time, and vigilance (e.g., a Continuous Performance Test, or the Speech-Sounds Perception Test and Seashore Rhythm Test of the Halstead-Reitan Neuropsychological Test Battery), and memory (e.g., the California Verbal Learning Test or the Wechsler Memory Scale). The interested reader should refer to Lezak (1995) for a review of these measures and other alternatives.

Physical and Psychosocial Functional Status

Physical and psychosocial functional status is best assessed via clinical interview, mental status examination, behavioral observation, and interviewing significant others. In addition, instruments such as the Pain Interference and Impairment Index, the Multidimensional Pain Inventory, the Illness Behavior Questionnaire, the Pain Experience Scale, the Pain Coping Inventory, and the Job Dissatisfaction Index (to be discussed) can be useful.

THE PAINKILLER TRAP

Portenoy (1996b) states the following primary consideration: "The guidelines [for opioid pain management] highlight the need to consider concurrent treatments and continue a therapeutic focus on functional restoration. Opioid therapy is not a substitute for a comprehensive pain management approach that incorporates psychologic and rehabilitative therapies" (p. 268). We have already mentioned the most noticeable side effects of opioids (i.e., cognitive impairments, sedation, fatigue). Other potential physical side effects are nausea, vomiting, pruritus, urinary retention, constipation, hypotension, and respiratory depression (Twycross, 1994). Adjuvant pain-relievers such as nonsteroidal antiinflammatory drugs (NSAIDs), acetominaphen, and aspirin compounds can cause gastrointestinal side effects and analgesic rebound pain, especially in chronic headache patients (Schoenen & de Noordhout, 1995). In cases of analgesic rebound pain, medically supervised withdrawal from the analgesic drug is usually necessary and requires a brief inpatient stay.

Behavioral Guidelines for Cutting Back

There are several useful guidelines for helping nonaddicted and non-drug-abusing pain patients cut back on both opioid and nonopioid pain medications:

1. The nonphysician pain management psychotherapist should always work in conjunction with the patient's prescribing and treating physician.
2. It is usually best to delay cutting back on pain medicine until the patient has learned some effective pain coping strategies, anxiety management skills, and relaxation and self-regulation methods, as discussed elsewhere in this book. This criterion can be measured through patient self-report, reports of significant others, and examination of the patient's diaries. For example, on the PTD, pain levels ought to be somewhat lower, and there ought to be some evidence of the successful application of pain coping strategies. On the DPTR, we look for evidence that the patient can identify and dispute dysfunctional automatic thoughts.
3. Working in conjunction with the prescribing physician, once all the above considerations have been addressed, we recommend a program of graded reduction in the doses taken of the drug targeted for weaning. Once again, referring to the tool of bibliotherapy, we recommend that patients read Marcus and Arbeiter (1994). They recommend that patients gradually wean themselves from the target drug following the "20 percent rule":

Case Example

Julie, who suffered from chronic back, neck, and headache pain, agreed to comply with a graded program of reduction in her excessive use of Tylenol with codeine. She was using anywhere from two to three tablets of Tylenol with codeine every 3 to 4 hours. Her prescription read two tablets every 4 to 6 hours as needed. In collaboration with her prescribing physician, we agreed on the following drug weaning protocol: (1) She agreed to stick to the prescription as written for the first week, but on a fixed time-interval dosing pattern (i.e., two tablets every 4 to 6 hours—two tablets at wakeup, two tablets at lunchtime, two before dinner, and two at bedtime). (2) For the second week, she was to take one and a half tablets at regular 4- to 6-hour intervals. (3) The third week, she was to cut down her intake to one tablet at regular 4- to 6-hour intervals. (4) At the fourth week, she was to cut down to a half tablet every 6 hours. (5) The fifth week she was to take a half tablet every 8 to 10 hours. (6) The sixth week she was to take a half tablet at the same time just once a day. (7) By the seventh week, she was to be "Tylenol with codeine free." Her physician also began her on the NSAID Naprosyn 375 mg, to be taken with food twice a day, and he prescribed an initial low dose (10 mg) of the antidepressant Elavil at bedtime. Julie successfully completed the drug-weaning program. In working with her, we had her record her pain levels, medication use, coping strategies, uptime activities, and downtime in her Pain Tracking Diary and Activity Schedule. She also recorded her pain levels, emotional symptoms, negative automatic thoughts and her cognitive disputations in her Daily Pain and Thought Record. These data records were reviewed during each PMP session.

4. "Pain cocktailing" and dose fading strategies can help patients decrease their reliance on pain medications (Fordyce, 1976). Following Fordyce (1976), the term *pain cocktail* refers to an orally consumed liquid preparation containing a mixture of active pain medication and nonactive ingredients. On an inpatient pain treatment unit, a pain cocktail would be administered on a fixed-interval schedule as opposed to on an as-needed basis (e.g., at three fixed times each day). Over an adequate period of time, the potency or concentration of the active analgesic ingredients would be faded or decreased. Evidence of withdrawal symptoms may indicate a too rapid decrease. The pain cocktail concept can also be implemented on an outpatient basis under a knowledgable prescribing physician's direction. All other nonemergency pain treatment interventions for "old pain" are also administered on a planned, time-contingent as opposed to an unplanned, pain-contingent basis. Any acute occurrences of new pain are appropriately medically evaluated and treated.

On an outpatient basis, the pain cocktail might consist of a fixed number of pills taken at regular intervals during the day. These pills might include an opioid analgesic, an antidepressant, nonopioid adjuvant analgesics (e.g., a NSAID, muscle relaxant, acetaminophen, or aspirin compounds), and perhaps, vitamin and mineral supplements. The idea is to work out a specific plan, under one prescribing physician's direction, for gradually reducing the doses of painkillers administered at each daily fixed interval. This closely and carefully, medically supervised graded reduction needs to be carried out over a long enough time period to minimize untoward physical withdrawal effects. In addition to a graded reduction in analgesic doses, the fixed time intervals between doses can also be gradually increased, so as to effect a graded decrease in *fixed number of doses.* The concept is similar to the nicotine fading procedure often used for treating cigarette smokers that involves systematically directing them to smoke cigarette brands containing less and less nicotine, until they finally "kick the habit" (Fox, 1985). The success of the graded reduction program depends on: (a) adequate patient motivation; (b) the absence of a true addictive disorder; (c) the absence of a serious characterological or personality disorder; (d) a collaborative working relationship with the patient; and (e) a collaborative relationship with one prescribing, involved physician.

THE PROBLEM OF DISTURBED SLEEP

Disrupted and disturbed sleep patterns are very common in pain patients. The relationship between disturbed sleep and pain is a reciprocal one. Pain often makes it difficult for an individual to fall asleep and stay asleep. On the other hand, a nonrestorative pattern of sleep deprivation can lead to mental and physical fatigue, muscle fatigue, the development of muscle tender points, more pain, feelings of malaise, depression, loss of cognitive efficiency, and cognitive impairment (McCain, 1995). It is therefore important to assess pain patient's sleep problems and to devise strategies for improving the restorative properties of their sleep. Borrowing a metaphor from Corey and Solomon (1989), sleeping with severe pain can be like trying to sleep on a "bed of thorns." It is certainly "no bed of roses."

Corey and Solomon (1989) describe an excellent program for retraining healthy sleep behavior patterns based on stimulus control and response control principles. We frequently apply these principles successfully to retrain sleep-deprived pain patients by using the following steps:

1. Establish with the patient a *regular wake-up time* in the morning.
2. Explain to the patient the importance of "waiting until you are sleepy before going to bed" (Corey & Solomon, 1989, p. 156). The rationale is provided that the bed and the bedroom should be treated as discriminative stimuli that set the occasion for only two specific responses—sleeping or sex. A corollary to this principle is the idea that the bedroom should be a discriminative stimulus for relaxing responses only (e.g., reading, watching television).
3. Explain to the patient why he or she should *stop trying to fall asleep.* This makes intuitive sense to most patients. The rationale is that certain things have to come spontaneously, and that they do when a person is relaxed and not trying to make them happen. Sleep happens to be one such phenomenon. People who have sleep

onset insomnia often err by "trying to fall asleep." Rather than inducing sleep, this often results in their becoming more anxious and uptight. To circumvent this, Corey and Solomon (1989) suggest that a person lie awake in bed for no more than one half-hour. It is recommended that if the individual is unable to fall asleep by the end of that time period, then he or she should get out of bed, leave the bedroom, and do something soothing and relaxing in another part of his or her living quarters. When the individual begins to feel sleepy and ready to go to bed again, he or she should return to bed. However, once again, if sleeplessness recurs, the individual should not lie in bed awake, trying to fall asleep for more than 30 minutes. This principle should be observed at any time during the night if the patient awakens and is unable to return to sleep.

4. To augment the program, equip the patient with a soothing relaxation technique to employ while lying in bed or just before retiring. We often make for patients in session a hypnotic relaxation/sleep tape. These tapes are personalized based on patient input and feedback. We consider our tape a success when a patient reports that he or she never gets to listen to an entire side of the tape because he or she always falls asleep on it! Our basic guidelines for making a relaxation/sleep tape are to incorporate comforting, soothing, and personalized images and words, delivered and trailing off in a low, drowsy, dreamy, hypnotic, monotone. It is important to deliver suggestions on the tape in a permissive fashion. Sleep problems are usually associated with cognitive distortions such as absolute thinking and harsh internal demands. On the tape, we usually incorporate slow counting down (e.g., starting from one hundred), interspersed with positive, individualized suggestions that are intended to be both distracting and comforting. If our tape is a bit boring, that is okay too, as this is likely to make it work better (i.e., put the patient to sleep). Sometimes, we add soothing background music if a patient thinks it will make the tape more sedating.

A basic script for recording such a tape is provided in Appendix U. Although this script can and should be individualized, the fundamental sequential components or stages of the script are (a) an *introduction* that presents a permissive mind-set or framework; (b) a section that guides the listener to begin *settling inward,* and that acknowledges the presence of painful sensations; (c) a section suggesting that the listener bring to mind an image of a calming and *safe place.* In this section, *counting backward* from one hundred, for deepening the listener's absorption and relaxation is begun; (d) a section that gently guides the listener to think of *pain relief imagery,* as the counting down is continued; (e) a section delivering permissive suggestions that the listener *listen to his or her own body;* (f) a section delivering permissive suggestions to cease *self-punishment;* and (g) a final section delivering appropriate *positive and supportive suggestions.*

5. Further drawing on stimulus and response control principles, it is important to persuade the patient not to plan on taking naps during the day. This does not preclude taking regular and planned breaks to perform relaxation techniques such as guided imagery, progressive muscle relaxation, meditation, and self-hypnosis. The rationale is that napping tends to further disrupt normal sleep patterns and make it more difficult to sleep through the night.

6. Explain to the patient the important role of physical exercise and activity in the maintenance of a balanced sleep-wake cycle. We advise patients to experiment with the best times of day for them to exercise. As pointed out by Corey and Solomon (1989), patients who are invigorated by physical exercise should not exercise for several hours before retiring for the night.

JOB DISSATISFACTION

Job dissatisfaction is at the top of the list of risk factors for failure to return to work. This is intuitively obvious. Work-injured low back pain patients who are not back to work after a year or more are not likely to return to their preinjury jobs (Fordyce, 1995). Interestingly, compensation for lost work is not a sole predictor of rate of recovery from injury or rate of return to work (Beals, 1984; Lancourt & Kettelhut, 1992). A work-injured pain patient's *degree of perceived control* over his or her work situation and *degree of job satisfaction* appear to be important mediators of an injured worker's likelihood of return to work (Beals, 1984; Fordyce, 1995; Lancourt & Kettelhut, 1992; Yelin, 1986). The key outcome predictive question is not only whether a disabled pain patient resumes his or her former job or occupation, but also whether that patient returns to some form of functional work, where the term "functional" is defined from the patient's perspective. Unfortunately, but understandably, many disabled pain patients are reluctant to admit to any return to functionality given their fears of repercussions such as the loss of compensation and benefits. However, in order to fully evaluate pain treatment effectiveness, future outcome studies must find ways to address this concern. In addition, the absence of depression, anger and hostility, extreme fear of pain, avoidant behaviors, symptom magnification and exaggeration, and positive evidence of adequate compliance with physical exercise and reconditioning regimens are associated with positive rehabilitation outcomes and return to functionality (Bigos et al., 1991; Gatchel, 1994; Gatchel, Polatin, & Kinney, 1995; Gatchel, Polatin, & Mayer, 1996; Hazard, Haugh, Green, & Jones, 1994).

WORK DYSFUNCTION

Pain-related work dysfunction usually arises from the interaction of several factors (Bigos et al., 1991; Feuerstein & Zastowny, 1996; Fordyce, 1995; Linton & Bradley, 1996; Sanders, 1995b). Unless these factors are accurately assessed and then addressed, efforts at remediating this complex problem are unlikely to be successful. Work dysfunction is highly prevalent in this country. For someone who has been dissatisfied with his or her job, chronic pain may make that job more of a challenge, and possibly aversive. Many individuals with chronic pain who are vocationally challenged, may face further adversity as a result of their employer's unwillingness to make job modifications to accommodate their pain problem or disability.

ASSESSING JOB DISSATISFACTION

Given the centrality of job dissatisfaction in the matrix of pain complaints, work dysfunction, and disability claims, the assessment of job dissatisfaction is an essential part of the disability examination process. Therefore, we have developed a clinical self-report checklist that can assist a clinician in evaluating a disabled pain patient's job dissatisfaction. The Job Dissatisfaction Index (JDI) is a measure in development. It is displayed in Appendix V. The purpose of this 32-item questionnaire is to enable the clinician to assess how a patient feels about his or her *last* or *present* job. The JDI can be given as a structured interview, but typically it is administered as a self-report checklist to the patient who is asked to answer each question by circling either YES or NO. Some YES/NO questions are followed by questions that ask the respondent to explain his or her answer.

The JDI contains questions that assess the person's current work status, the worker's perceptions of his or her current level of disability, perceptions of financial equity, perceptions of job security, interpersonal problems on the job, perceptions of the fairness of the worker's treatment and whether justice was done, job enjoyment and pride in one's work, and perceptions of the adequacy of the worker's training, motivations, and feelings.

The JDI is useful in the assessment of work dysfunction, especially in workers' compensation cases and as part of disability and vocational evaluations. The JDI may predict the likelihood of a pain patient's return to work. The following clinical guidelines are helpful in interpreting the patient's pattern of responses on the JDI:

1. For coding purposes, a "yes" response is coded as a "1" and a "no" is coded as a "2." The code column gives the number (1 or 2) of the clinically work dysfunctional or clinical response for each item. The clinician circles the number in the code column for each item for which the dysfunctional response was selected.

2. The number of circled codes are added up (not the actual numbers). This sum gives the total number of items answered in a way that reflects job dissatisfaction. When more than half of the 32 items are answered in this direction, we have found that job satisfaction is low and dissatisfaction is high. This seems to correlate clinically with a dimmer likelihood of return to work.

3. An additional consideration are "Yes and No" responses to the items. These indecisive responses reflect the presence of dissatisfaction and reservations. For clinical purposes, such "on the fence" responses are coded as reflecting job dissatisfaction. They are included in the total sum of items indicating job dissatisfaction.

4. We also look at the patient's response to item 22. The question reads:

   Are there any days in which you are absolutely unable to attend work?
   Yes   No

   If yes, how many days per week? _____ *per month?* _____
   Why are you absolutely unable to attend work on these days? _____

   The answers to these questions have differing significance depending on the job. Generally speaking, however, the less time flexibility and tolerance for missed days there are in a position, the more significance this item will have.

EMPLOYER AND EMPLOYEE ACCOUNTABILITY

The evaluation of work dysfunction should include assessing both employer and employee accountability and responsibility. Job analyses are a necessary component of a comprehensive vocational assessment. Too often, a job analysis is not done, or if it is, it excludes the resources within the workplace for making appropriate job modifications.

A BIOPSYCHOSOCIAL PERSPECTIVE

The assessment of work dysfunction should proceed from a biopsychosocial perspective (Gatchel, 1996; Turk, 1996) that includes a periodic psychiatric and psychological examination. The intervals between assessments should be based on the unique factors of each case: type of work, work setting, resources within the work setting for modifying the job or work environment to accommodate the patient's needs, job security, level of training required for the job, and the patient's level of job satisfaction and work history. The assessment should also include an evaluation of the patient's injury, physical pathology, and chronic pain, duration of time out of work, motivation to return to work, and secondary gains likely to be operative. Additionally, a patient's physical and cognitive work capacities, and support systems in place, need to be assessed and factored into the return-to-work equation. The longer an injured worker remains out of work and is receiving disability payments, the dimmer are the chances of his or her returning to work (Fordyce, 1995; Sanders, 1995b).

PMP for pain-related work dysfunction typically needs to address the preceding systemic complex of factors. Vocational retraining often focuses narrowly on checklist cataloging of general vocational preferences, sometimes followed by training for a specific job. Perhaps more than with any other facet of psychosocial therapy, work dysfunction can benefit from a team or network approach. First, taking a thorough history of the patient's work problems is in order. Second, the reality factors cited earlier need to be addressed using a case management approach incorporating behavioral and systemic interventions. Behavioral contingency contracting plays an important role. Psychological as well as economic, interpersonal, and physical factors need to be considered along with pre- and postpain job dissatisfaction. When pain becomes an apparent "easy out," it is essential to deal with the loaded issue of secondary gains. Cognitive distortions require using cognitive therapy techniques, whereas emotional traumas related to work, pain, suffering, and disability respond to an integrated combination of cognitive therapy and memory review, reexperiencing, and reprocessing techniques (such as EMDR, as discussed in Chapter 7).

BEHAVIORAL COACHING PRINCIPLES

Behavioral principles of effective coaching (as in athletic disciplines and sports medicine) are highly applicable to PMP and pain rehabilitation.

THE PREMACK PRINCIPLE

The main idea of the "Premack Principle" (Hilgard & Bower, 1966; Premack, 1959), is to enhance positive motivation to engage in an initially undesirable, nonreinforcing activity (such as exercise) by rewarding such engagement with the opportunity to engage in an alternative, desirable, positively reinforcing activity. In other words, "for any pair of responses the more probable one will reinforce the less probable one" (McGlynn, 1985, p. 166).

Case Example

Jim suffered from chronic low back pain, leg pain, and fibromyalgia. He had been diagnosed as having several bulging lumbar discs. His orthopedic surgeon recommended a conservative course of treatment (i.e., a physical therapist supervised home exercise program), which he stated offered Jim the best chance of avoiding back surgery. However, Jim never seemed to be able to find the time to do his exercises, and he remained severely deconditioned. Recently, Jim told his pain management psychotherapist that his pain was getting worse again. Consultation with the orthopedist yielded the recommendation to "get going" on the exercise program. Because of Jim's lack of motivation, the pain management therapist suggested the following plan: Eating was a "high-frequency behavior" for Jim, who loved to eat and especially enjoyed ice cream. So, the therapist recommended that Jim make "eating ice cream" contingent on completing a set of his back exercises.

SUCCESSIVE APPROXIMATION AND SHAPING

Using the principle of successive approximation, or shaping, the patient gradually develops a desirable level of intensity, duration, and frequency of a target behavior or activity. Aiming to reach a behavioral criterion all at once is both unrealistic and foolish and smacks of all-or-nothing thinking. Many chronic pain patients are severely deconditioned. Therefore, an effective pain rehabilitation program assures progress by utilizing a shaping strategy, whereby each small step moves the patient closer and closer to the eventual goal. In setting up a behavioral reactivation or physical rehabilitation program, pain patients, many of whom are immobilized by anxiety and depression, should not be pushed to do too much at once.

Case Example

In Jim's case, Jim's PMP therapist conferred with Jim's physical therapist to design a home exercise program that could be built up gradually. Initially, Jim agreed to start a flexibility and strength training exercise program by coming three times a week to the gym at the physical therapist's office. For the first couple of weeks, no home exercises were assigned. Then, beginning in the third week, Jim was instructed to do certain exercises at home, on the days that he did not go to the gym. The intensity level, the number of repetitions, and the number of sets of each exercise, were very gradually increased. Once Jim mastered the assigned exercises and reached a desired performance criterion, additional, more demanding strengthening, flexibility, and aerobic exercises were added.

THE PACING PRINCIPLE

Pacing refers to the need for pain sufferers to regulate and remain in control of the frequency, intensity, and duration of their energy-expending activities. Everyone has limitations on the energy they have to expend on different activities; chronic pain patients may have smaller reserves than others. Coping with daily pain uses up energy. Perhaps as a reaction to their energy limitations, perhaps as a result of all-or-nothing and black-and-white thinking, many chronic pain sufferers tend to vacillate between avoidant withdrawal and overexertion. Although such behavior often reflects the desire of pain sufferers to make up for lost time and accomplish something, it is usually dysfunctional because it can lead to exhaustion, pain flare-ups, or reinjury. Coaching patients to pace themselves requires teaching the related principle of flexibility, frustration, and ambiguity tolerance.

FLEXIBILITY, FRUSTRATION, AND AMBIGUITY TOLERANCE

The goal of this coaching principle is to promote the patient's acceptance that "it pays to be flexible" (in more ways than one). Pain patients who tend to vacillate between total inactivity and doing too much can profit when they learn how to tolerate the frustration of not finishing an important task. It is a human tendency to want to complete that which is incomplete. Human beings generally seek to achieve stability and certainty wherever there is ambiguity. However, learning to tolerate ambiguity can be adaptive.

Pain patients with an obsessive-compulsive bent may find this notion goes against their grain. When energy is in short supply, however, conservation is essential, and it is not always possible to accomplish everything that was intended in an allotted time period. Positively motivated persons with chronic pain will often tell themselves that they can accomplish "just a little more" in a given day. When this turns out to be a cognitive distortion, the feeling of being overwhelmed can trigger a pain flare-up. Therefore, the therapist must coach pain patients to assess realistically how much they can do in an hour, in a day, and so on.

Having pain patients keep an Activity Schedule (Freeman et al., 1990; Freeman & Reinecke, 1995) can help them practice and test out new self-pacing skills that are taught and coached in session. It can also increase a patient's positive reinforcement from pleasant activities. However, the

Activity Schedule (including "pain," "pleasure," and "mastery" ratings) needs to be realistic.

Patients are coached in planning their days and their week using a standard Activity Schedule form (Freeman et al., 1990). A blank form is provided in Appendix W. They are asked to schedule a short but fixed block of time (around 20 minutes), at the end of each week, to plan their following week. The therapist also should suggest that patients schedule 10 to 15 minutes at the end of each day for planning the details of the following day, and for reviewing how that day went. During their day, after they complete each activity, they are asked to check that activity off on the Activity Schedule, or write it in, and to rate that activity on several 0-to-10 scales (see Appendix W).

Reactivation Therapy Outcome Measures

These data, recorded on the Activity Schedule, provide several useful behavioral reactivation therapy outcome measures for the therapist to track and share with the patient when appropriate. The treatment goal is for each of the following measures to go up: (a) compliance versus noncompliance with the task assignment; (b) average daily and weekly pleasure ratings; (c) average daily and weekly mastery ratings; (d) average daily and weekly number of activities rated above 7 on pleasure; (e) average daily and weekly number of activities rated above 7 for mastery; (f) average daily and weekly number of hours filled with pleasurable activities; and (g) average daily and weekly number of hours filled with mastery activities.

Shaping Uptime and Reducing Downtime

By recording their pain levels four times daily in their Pain Tracking Diary, patients can establish their average daily baseline pain. By recording the amount of time spent lying down or reclining because of pain or fatigue, patients can establish their average daily downtime. To assist patients to learn how to pace themselves effectively, and to help them shape a healthier, more active lifestyle that is not contingent on pain, we follow the suggestions of several pain management authors (Caudill, 1995; Corey & Solomon, 1989) and ask patients to record several additional ratings on their Activity Schedule including their "preactivity baseline pain level" (BP), which is defined as a person's starting pain level when beginning a potentially pain triggering activity. Patients record a baseline pain number from 0 to 10 in that activity's box before they start a potentially pain-triggering activity (e.g., BP = 3).

Next, patients are instructed that as soon as they note their baseline pain rising more than 2 points while they are engaging in the pain-triggering activity, they are to stop the activity and record their increased pain level, or "new pain" in the activity box as well as the exact amount of uptime they engaged in the activity. They are then told to break from the activity and not return to it until their pain level returns to its original baseline. This downtime is also recorded in the appropriate box on their Activity Schedule. These data provide several additional behavioral reactivation therapy outcome measures for the therapist to track: (a) average uptime and average total daily uptime (*goal:* to increase); (b) average downtime and average total daily downtime (*goal:* to decrease); (c) The average ratio of uptime to downtime (*goal:* to increase); (d) average number of mastery and pleasure activities completed without downtime (*goal:* to increase); (e) average baseline pain levels (*goal:* to decrease); (f) instances of pain rising 1 or 2 points above baseline; (g) instances of pain rising 3 points above baseline; and (h) instances of pain rising more than 3 points above baseline (*goal:* to decrease).

Discriminating between Hurt and Harm

Our two main goals are (a) to help patients learn to discriminate between *hurt* and *harm,* and (b) to help patients divorce their activities from being controlled by pain. Our first goal is attained by coaching patients to "listen to their bodies" and attend to minimal or prepain cues. A small increase in pain during many activities (a minimal or prepain cue of a 1- or 2-point rise in pain, in some cases, on a 0-to-10 pain scale) is to be expected, and is not typically a sign of harm. In general, however, when pain rises more than 2 points while performing a pain-activating activity, it is usually wise to stop, because it may be a warning sign of overexertion. It is usually better to build up, or shape, one's endurance gradually (the amount of time and intensity with which one can perform an activity) than to attempt to build it up bullishly by ignoring marked increases from baseline pain levels (pain rising more than 3 points above baseline). We often tell patients, "Bullishness often turns into foolishness when it leads to reinjury."

Self-Pacing and Shaping Steps for Divorcing Activities from Pain

Frequently, we realize our second goal by coaching patients to comply with the following self-pacing and shaping steps:

1. The patient is instructed to stop an activity when he or she experiences pain rising 3 or more points above baseline.
2. The patient is told to break from the activity until the pain returns to its preactivity baseline.
3. At that point, the patient resumes the activity, but is to cut it back by one-quarter, one-third, or one-half (i.e., cut back time, intensity, speed, weight—whatever is relevant), so that resumption of the activity is unlikely to trigger another rise in pain.

4. The patient paces himself or herself by doing the activity at the easier, below-baseline level and is instructed to maintain the same pace for the next few times he or she engages in that activity. The idea is to complete the activity without having to stop because of pain and to gradually build up or "shape up" the activity's difficulty level.
5. The patient confers with us to formulate an exact shaping plan for gradually building up to and beyond the baseline activity level that originally triggered the 3-point or more rise in pain. This plan should not trigger more than a 1- or 2-point rise in pain at each step (i.e., if the patient cuts back enough and then builds up gradually enough). Recall that the goal is to enable the patient to perform the activity without an associated increase in pain.

Caveats and Problems

Because patients report variable responses to the shaping and pacing strategy, it is important to follow this protocol on an individual case basis; the numbers are not written in stone. It is best to apply the principles, but to adapt the actual amount of increased pain from baseline to signal the intentional shift to downtime, the amount to cut back, and the speed or pace of building up to each patient. Many patients cannot do anything without experiencing a marked (3 points or more) increase in pain. We typically handle this by markedly scaling back the initial intensity and duration of these patients' activities, and shaping up in very small increments. This strategy requires an excellent therapeutic relationship to provide enough leverage for the intensive coaching needed. Although the therapist has to be consistent, it is also important to retain flexibility with difficult, fearful, and avoidant patients who evidence marked movement phobia and fears of reinjury (i.e., kinesophobia). Still, one of the biggest obstacles is patient impatience, which is often a reflection of cognitive distortions.

A related problem is that many patients have difficulty quitting when they are in the middle of an activity, even when their pain levels rise the requisite 3 points or more. It is important that patients understand the necessity of recording their pain levels so that they can pace themselves. Patients' cognitive distortions, revealed in self-talk such as "must do's," "absolute demands," and all-or-nothing thinking, drive them to overdo activities. These patients often believe that tiny, "baby steps" are not worth taking at all. They want to see marked improvement immediately or they tend to disqualify everything. Therefore, cognitive distortions need to be corrected to make any real progress.

As stated by Corey and Solomon (1989, p. 69), the purpose of a behavioral shaping and pacing reactivation program is not to finish each and every activity, but rather to "re-program the pain system." The goal is to dissociate activity from pain. As discussed earlier, relative to cutting back on painkillers, we want patients to become comfortable with working to a fixed schedule as opposed to working to tolerance. Because many patients markedly resist changing their activity behavior, it is necessary to guide them to discover what they are telling themselves that prevents them from pacing and prioritizing their activities. Also, we often suggest that patients consider the costs of such thinking and behavior:

PATIENT: So, yesterday, my wife and I were going to go to dinner.

THERAPIST: What time was it?

PATIENT: It was around 6:00. I had a pretty full day. I had exercised for an hour in the afternoon, I had taken my kids shopping to buy a present for the twins' birthday party, and I had accomplished a few other things during the day. Well, my wife tells me to take a shower, after she took one. Mind you, the baby-sitter had already arrived. And, I told her that if I showered, number one, it would take me a while, since I was tired, even though I had meditated and napped for an hour. And two, I told her that if I had to shower, I would be too tired to go out. Then boy, did she flip out at me!

THERAPIST: Did you shower?

PATIENT: No!

THERAPIST: Did you two go to dinner?

PATIENT: Yes.

THERAPIST: Do you think you did too much on Saturday?

PATIENT: Yes!

THERAPIST: How can you perhaps better pace yourself next Saturday?

PATIENT: Not try to fit so much in during the day, if I know I have to go out at night!

THERAPIST: What were you thinking as you were doing one activity after the other during the day?

PATIENT: Boy, am I getting a lot done today!

THERAPIST: That desire is understandable. But what was the cost?

PATIENT: I exhausted myself to the point where I was too tired to take a shower!

THERAPIST: And really to go out with your wife!

PATIENT: But what can I say to myself to pace myself better when I am so driven during the day?

THERAPIST: That might be a good thing for you to experiment with for homework. You might write your self-talk on your activity schedule, or on your Daily Pain and Thought Record. Next week, let's review what you have discovered that seems to be the best way to tell yourself to slow down and pace yourself. How does that sound to you?

REWARDS AND PENALTIES

There are two parts to the principle of "positive reinforcement" or "rewards and penalties." The first part is that behaviors that are positively reinforced or rewarded are more likely to recur. The second part is that given the necessary motivation, *self-punishment* in the form of an appropriate, self-administered penalty can effectively promote a patient's compliance with therapy homework. The Premack Principle discussed earlier represents the use of positive reward or reinforcement. Patients are coached to reward themselves for sticking to the program. For example, one patient agreed to reward himself by putting aside a couple of dollars at the end of each day that he kept his pacing and activity schedule. On the other hand, he agreed to *penalize* himself for each day he did not keep his pacing and activity schedule by taking twice that amount and putting it in an envelope destined to be donated to a cause he detested.

Much research has shown that people in general, and pain patients in particular, respond most favorably when their well-intended, honest attempts to learn something new or cope are framed or reframed in a favorable light. People in general, and pain patients in particular, respond more positively to the perception of success than they do to negative feedback, censure, and criticism (Arena & Blanchard, 1996; Blanchard, Kim, Hermann, & Steffek, 1993; Holroyd et al., 1984). The implications of this finding are:

> Give your patients plenty of positive feedback. Reframe lapses, noncompliance, setbacks, and adversities as advantages. They can be reframed as opportunities to learn something useful. Reframe most patient behavior as basically well-intentioned, although possibly irrational, misdirected, or inefficient. Turn adversity into advantage.

THE PERSISTENCE PRINCIPLE

Persistence refers to the idea that the PMP therapist needs to model patience, tenacity, perseverance, determination, and resolve, which are qualities that we want the pain patient to adopt in working toward successful rehabilitation and recovery. People who suffer from treatment-resistant, persistent pain states understandably feel like giving up at times. The therapist needs to acknowledge this in an understanding and empathic manner. However, it is also essential to convey that because pain is persistent, so must be the patient and the therapist. Persistence and perseverance are promoted when the therapist, in working with patients, ardently and consistently follows the five principles described previously: (a) Premack Principle, (b) Successive Approximation/Shaping, (c) Pacing, (d) Flexibility/Frustration Tolerance/Ambiguity Tolerance,

(e) Positive Reinforcement/Rewards and Penalties, and employs the cognitive model through the frequent use of cognitive disputation and rational responding.

The Principle of Observational Learning

The old adage that "children learn more from what they see and hear their parents do than from what their parents say," exemplifies the social learning principle of *observational learning* (Bandura, 1986). This principle refers to "the learning that occurs from the observation of others" (Matson, 1985). This powerful principle is directly applicable to the therapist-patient interaction in PMP. A related corollary is the social psychology principle that people are more apt to imitate models that are respected as having high status and perceived as being similar to them (Bandura, 1986). Certainly, therapists and health care professionals with academic degrees are often accorded high status in light of their assumed education, training, and professional skills. Relative to the similarity factor, we often suggest to our supervisees and trainees, that timely and judicious sharing of information about one's own battles with pain or physical illness may help build rapport. Telling patients stories about other people with similar problems who have been helped to manage their pain instills hope and counters hopelessness.

Training patients to use effective pain coping strategies requires that the therapist take a hands-on approach that includes *direct modeling, participant modeling,* and *guided practice.* As we use the term, direct modeling refers to the practice of plainly and explicitly demonstrating to a patient how to implement specific coping strategies. Participant modeling refers to the use of physical prompting and tactile contact with the patient to train particular responses that successively approximate the desired goal response. Finally, guided practice refers to coaching a patient to shape successively closer approximations of the desired goal response. This involves alternating between direct modeling of a particular behavior, participant modeling, patient practice, and the therapist's contingent provision of feedback to the patient.

The importance of observational learning is apparent in the implementation of biofeedback and relaxation therapies. When training a patient to reduce his or her autonomic arousal, the therapist needs to be an at-ease model of calm, effortlessness, and composure, which is the ideal goal state intended for the patient. Thus, before conducting a biofeedback or relaxation training session with a pain patient, the therapist ought to use his or her own biofeedback self-regulation skills to get focused and calm. In contrast, if the therapist is unfocused, distracted, or nervous, the patient will pick this up, and it is likely to impede the relaxation therapy.

Controlled Diaphragmatic Breathing Training

The principle of observational learning is illustrated in the following example of *controlled diaphragmatic breathing training*, along with shaping, successive approximation, and the strategic use of corrective feedback and positive reinforcement:

PATIENT: Doctor, what can you teach me to help me better manage my pain?

THERAPIST: I suggest that we start with a simple physical exercise, in the form of a healthy breathing technique that you can use to relax and reduce your pain. You can watch me doing this form of breathing now.

The therapist begins to demonstrate diaphragmatic or abdominal breathing with one hand placed on his abdomen, or belly, and the other hand on his chest. He demonstrates "hand on belly" pushing outward or rising up and away from the body as he inhales and his belly "inflates." He then demonstrates "hand on belly" pushing inward or falling into the body as he exhales and his belly "deflates."

THERAPIST: Would you like to try this?

PATIENT: Sure.

THERAPIST: Position your hands like mine and just breathe. (*Patient positions hands*) Okay, place your feet flat on the floor. Now, as you breathe in and out, notice how much movement you feel and see where your hands are. Feel and watch your hands. Most of the movement is coming from where?

PATIENT: From my chest.

THERAPIST: That's exactly right. That is the way most of us normally breathe. Now the form of breathing in this exercise is the opposite of that. Instead of your chest doing most of the work, it should be your belly or abdomen. Like this (*Therapist demonstrates*). You p—u—l—l the air down into your lungs by expanding your stomach as you inhale. Then, you p—u—s—h the used air up and out of your lungs by pushing in with your abdominal muscles as you breathe out.

The therapist allows the patient to do this for about a minute and then asks the patient to stop, take a break, and relax. The therapist asks the patient about the exercise and then continues:

THERAPIST: Now, let me suggest an image that you might hold in your mind that can help you make your tummy rise and fall a bit more easily and effortlessly. Imagine that there is a big colorful beach ball in your belly. As you inhale through your nose, imagine that you are inflating this beach ball through a long air tube that starts in your nostrils where the air valve is. Imagine that this air tube travels all the way down through your throat and chest into your belly, where the ball is. Pull the air down into that inflating beach ball in your belly. In your mind, as you inhale, follow the flow of air down your air tube from your nostrils as the air is pulled down into your lungs by the pressure of the inflating ball in your belly. Can you get such an image?

If the patient cannot visualize the image, the therapist should work with the patient to generate an alternative image. If visual imagery does not work at all, then the therapist should rely on tactile and kinesthetic props such as having the patient place his or her hands on the belly and chest, having the patient recline in a supine or semisupine position, or by placing an object, such as a book or a pillow, on the patient's stomach. Then, the patient can be instructed to try and make the object on his or her belly slightly rise with each inhalation, and fall with each exhalation. The therapist can set the pace and rhythm of inhalation/exhalation cycles by counting in the following fashion: *inhale—one, two, and exhale—one, two; inhale—one, two, and exhale—one, two;* and so on. As the patient begins to get the knack of this form of breathing, the therapist can lengthen the inhalation and exhalation counts to shape a slower and deeper breathing pattern (i.e., to decrease the number of breaths per minute). However, the therapist must take care to proceed slowly, and to provide abundant positive verbal reinforcement and immediate, corrective verbal, visual, and tactile-kinesthetic feedback to the patient. The therapist should also reassure, inform, and educate anxious patients.

The therapist goes on to convey to the patient the importance of regular but brief daily practice sessions. Initially, it is suggested that the patient limit each practice session to three sets of four inhalation/exhalation cycles per set to avoid straining the diaphragm and abdominal muscles. The patient is instructed to separate each set with about a half-minute to a minute of rest. During the rest periods, the patient should become absorbed in a pleasant image such as watching the ocean waves at the beach or feeling "waves of relaxation" washing over him or her. Initially, each breathing session will require about 5 minutes. The therapist instructs the patient to practice six times per day. As with any physical exercise, the number of repetitions in each set should be *gradually* increased to *shape* increased strength and endurance. As the number of repetitions per set are increased, so will the time required to do the exercise. Therefore, as the practice sessions become lengthier, the number of practice sessions per day should be cut down. The final training goal is for the patient to be able to do 20 continuous minutes of controlled diaphragmatic breathing, with perhaps one or two short rest breaks during the 20-minute session, at least once a day and ideally twice per day.

The Generalization of Training Principle

Generalization of skills training or *transfer of training* involves designing ways to promote the application or transfer of skills learned in the office and practiced in ideal circumstances, to the less than ideal daily situations that the patient encounters naturalistically.

For example, in biofeedback-assisted relaxation training, initially, patients are given the opportunity to close their eyes and recline on a comfortable chair in a quiet, dimly lit room, perhaps even with soothing background music, if this is appealing to the patient and promotes relaxation. However, as relaxation and self-regulation skills are developed, the patient gradually is encouraged to perform the self-regulation procedures in the office, under circumstances that more closely approximate the real world. The patient may be asked to sit up, then to sit in a hard chair, and finally to practice the procedures standing up. Also, lights may be turned on, eyes are usually open, and distracting sounds may be introduced. Additional stressors may be introduced, such as asking the patient to perform mental arithmetic or think of current problems while being coached simultaneously to perform an appropriate self-regulation or low arousal relaxation technique. Correspondingly, once the patient has mastered the skills in ideal circumstances, the patient is then instructed, in between sessions, to begin practicing the skills in less than ideal circumstances, "on the go," in the office, while driving, stopped at a traffic light (with the eyes open, of course), when in pain and under stress, and so on.

Cue-Controlled, Pain Management Coping Strategy Training

This training involves teaching pain patients to control their anxiety in response to pain by performing a specific, well-rehearsed coping strategy in response to a privately produced signal or *cue* (McGlynn, 1985). This facilitates generalization of self-regulation coping strategies to varied settings because the cue, which is "portable," takes on the properties of a "pain-relieving trigger." In session, after patients have attained a relaxed muscular state, they are instructed to pair this state with a self-selected, appropriate *cue-word* or *cue-phrase* such as "easy," "comfortable," "let go," "just be," "pain-free," or "stay calm." The procedure involves repeatedly pairing the verbal cue (which is subvocalized or privately rehearsed by the patient) with a physical response that is under the patient's voluntary control (e.g., each controlled exhalation that comes with taking slow, deep breaths). Alternatively, a nonverbal cue, such as a pleasant or relaxing image, can be employed in place of, or in addition to, a verbal cue.

For example, one patient paired her controlled deep breathing (inhalations and exhalations) with an image of the waves and the surf washing out (paired with inhalation) and washing in (paired with exhalation) at the beach. Another patient initially paired a pain-relieving replacement image of "bathing in the cool, soothing deep blue water of a country pond" with the physical coping responses of stretching, controlled deep breathing, and a 12-muscle-group progressive relaxation sequence. Over the course of seven sessions, the progressive relaxation sequence was reduced to 3 muscle groups. By the eighth PMP session, the patient reported that just bringing up the pain replacement image, taking a stretch, and taking several slow deep breaths, served to calm him and reduce his anxiety in response to several frequent pain-activating triggers.

Finally, coping skills should be well learned in ideal circumstances before implementing generalization training. The desired endpoint is to help patients learn to employ relevant and effective coping strategies whenever pain-activating trigger situations occur.

OPERANT CONDITIONING

The behavioral principle of *operant conditioning*, as stated by Sanders (1996), "asserts that all overt behavioral responses are significantly influenced by their consequences and the surrounding context in which they are emitted" (p. 112). This is highly evident with chronic pain patients. Overt and covert pain behaviors are influenced by contextual variables that include internal, activating events and consequential events (thoughts, images, memories, and physiological events) and external, activating events and consequential events (the situational and interpersonal context, interpersonal "triggers," other people's reactions, situational expectations and demands, etc.). Likewise, "well behaviors" (functional and adaptive coping behaviors) are also influenced by these contingencies.

Interpersonal Feedback Contingencies

Overt pain behaviors are what other people witness when they come into contact with a pain sufferer. The interpersonal feedback that is contingent on the occurrence of these behaviors in turn influences the pain sufferer's future responses. Other people's responses can serve as positive or negative reinforcers, as punishment, or aversive stimuli, or as discriminitive stimuli or stimulus cues for either pain behaviors or well behaviors. For example significant others can act in an oversolicitous, punitive, distracting, or supportive manner. These responses can be measured in several ways including paper-and-pencil questionnaires, self-report inventories that evaluate the patient's perceptions, (e.g., the Multidimensional Pain Inventory: Rudy, 1989; Turk & Rudy, 1992), interviewing the patient, interviewing significant others, direct observation, and asking patients and/or significant others to keep pain diaries (Keefe & Williams, 1992).

Positively reinforcing interpersonal feedback or circumstances, such as with solicitous responses or financial compensation, increases the probability that associated pain behaviors will recur. In other words, when a pain sufferer's behaviors lead to the procurement of desirable or pleasant stimuli (i.e., positive reinforcers), then those behaviors are strengthened, or positively reinforced. On the other hand, negative reinforcers are behaviors or events that serve to remove, or enable the pain sufferer to escape from, aversive or punitive stimuli. They too increase the probability of recurrence of the pain sufferer's associated behaviors.

As discussed by Sanders (1996), the use of a cane by a back pain patient can serve as a negative reinforcer if it reduces pain and the risk of falling, associated with ambulation. Thus, the cane is more likely to be used in the future. Likewise, a spouses's repeated assistance of a low back pain patient with activities of daily living, such as dressing or bathing, can serve as a powerful negative reinforcer by temporarily helping to reduce pain:

THERAPIST: Does your wife help you at all with dressing or bathing?

PATIENT: With dressing she does. When I wake up, or before bed, when I am feeling stiff and tired, I often ask my wife to put my socks and shoes on, or to take them off. I ask her for help because it is painful for me to bend to do these things. On a number of occasions I injured myself bending to put my socks and shoes on.

THERAPIST: Do you think that it is a good idea to ask your wife for help with this?

PATIENT: Yes. I do. I hate being this way, but I am in pain.

THERAPIST: Do you think that your wife helping you get dressed when you can do it without her help really helps you get better in the long run?

PATIENT: Probably not in the long run. It's just in the short run. It helps me avoid the stress and the pain of stretching and bending to put my shoes and socks on.

EXTINCTION OR NONREINFORCEMENT

The principle of *extinction*, or *nonreinforcement* is central to the application of the principle of operant conditioning with chronic pain patients. The premise is that ignored behaviors (i.e., not reinforced) eventually will diminish, become extinct, or be extinguished. Pain behaviors, as discussed, are frequently reinforced by well-meaning significant others, such as a patient's spouse. It is often important to assess others' responses to a patient's pain behaviors. Chronic pain patient-spouse behavioral interactions may predict patient disability (Romano et al., 1995).

Functional Analysis of Significant Others' Responses to Pain Behaviors

Operant approaches to PMP (Fordyce, 1976; Fordyce, Roberts, & Sternbach, 1985; Keefe, 1994; Keefe & Dunsmore, 1992; Roberts, 1986; Sanders, 1996) emphasize the importance of performing functional behavioral analyses at the outset of therapy and periodically throughout its course. This involves assessing the antecedents and consequents of targeted, operationally defined problems, followed by the development and implementation of a treatment plan.

For example, if excessive complaining and pain gesturing (e.g., groaning, rubbing the sore spot, avoiding movement, muscle bracing, or verbal complaining about pain) are targeted for modification, the operant behavior therapist would recommend (a) ignoring these behaviors to extinguish them, and (b) selectively delivering positive reinforcement for agreed-on replacement behaviors considered adaptive (e.g., standing up straight, sitting for more than 10 minutes without pain posturing or complaining, bending to pick something up, lifting light packages, maintaining a positive affect).

The operant behavior therapist would also want to work with the pain patient's significant others (usually family members) to coach them to carry out the program. The most frequent reason behavior programs fail is lack of follow-through and generalization in the patient's everyday home environment (Sanders, 1996; Spiegler, 1983; Wolpe, 1990). However, it often is a challenge to modify the resistance of significant others who regularly come into contact with the patient.

Fordyce stresses teaching a pain patient's significant others to ignore the patient's pain complaints and to restrain themselves from being oversolicitous and helpful (Fordyce, 1976; Fordyce et al., 1985). The rationale offered is that the only way the patient can be rehabilitated (i.e., returned to functionality) is to do more and more things for himself or herself without assistance. Significant others are seen to err on the side of either doing too much for the pain patient in response to the pain sufferer's pain gestures, or to err on the side of being punitive and hostile. In fact, in clinical situations, we often see these two reaction tendencies occurring side by side as significant others vacillate between feelings of guilt for not doing enough to help their loved one (and hence, becoming overresponsible and oversolicitous), and feelings of anger and resentment for doing too much and carrying all the burdens (and hence, becoming punitive, undergiving, and hostile).

In Fordyce's operant-behavioral approach, significant others are routinely coached to develop their awareness of the natural tendency to vacillate between these extremes. They learn to inhibit their responses (or not respond) to the triggers to becoming oversolicitous or overhelpful, and to self-reinforce their responses to the cues for being supportive and encouraging of the pain patient's responsibility and autonomy. The pain patient is helped to see that he or she is subject to these contingencies and changes as well. Thus, the pain patient learns to anticipate these behavioral tendencies and to recognize the ones that reinforce helplessness and pain posturing as well as those that reinforce functionality and resourcefulness. The pain patient is coached to engage in behaviors that reduce the probability of responding to significant others' oversolicitousness or to significant others' punitiveness, and that increase the probability of initiating self-directed and self-efficacious responses.

A possible trap that inadvertently can result from the teaching of an operant-behavioral approach is the unintentional encouragement of all-or-nothing thinking. We emphasize that rational responses by significant others to the person in persistent pain preclude black-and-white polarized thinking. It is important to coach significant others and the pain patient to see shades of gray. It is our position that it is often better to scale behaviors and experiences, than it is to categorize them as either wholly appropriate or inappropriate.

A major problem with pain is that it is largely a subjective experience. Other people cannot see a person's pain or quantify its severity in the same way that they can see and quantify the severity of an obvious physical limitation, disability, or deformity such as a paralysis, paraplegia, and so forth. The only outward indications of pain are what the person communicates either verbally, gesturally, or in movement patterns. Thus, nonreinforcement of pain behaviors can conceivably be misapplied as a result of gross insensitivity. In fact, pain behaviors inadvertently can be reinforced by an angry, resentful, or chastising spouse, or significant other. However, resentment just breeds more resentment. Very frequently, therapeutic intervention needs to be directed at encouraging a compromise between the harsh demands of an angry spouse and the reflexive tendency of the pain sufferer to perpetuate disablement through withdrawal and avoidance:

Case Example

A 39-year-old married man who suffered from ankylosing spondylitis and myofascial pain syndrome told his therapist that his wife was insensitive to his pain. He admitted that his wife carried more than her share of responsibility for the performance of household duties which she was quite vocal in communicating. However, he stated that whenever he tried to take a more active part in performing certain household chores such as taking out the trash, his wife would make disparaging and critical comments such as that he was too slow, too inefficient, or just plain lazy. This made him angry and he would then retaliate by cutting back again and "laying low." He stated, "If she does not show me any appreciation, then I might as well just not do anything!" She stated, "I just can't imagine that my husband's pain is so bad that he cannot help around the house more than he does, which is nothing." The therapist asked her if she would be willing to "try out what it feels like to be more understanding as after all you cannot possibly feel your husband's pain nor would he want you to." She softened up and the therapist added, "but just enough so as not to encourage him not to do anything—moderation is the key here." The therapist suggested to his patient, "You're just going to have to make an effort to do a certain predetermined amount irrespective of pain, that is, if you want to improve the quality of your marriage—oh, and it will help with your pain also. Your pain has to learn that it's not the boss—you are."

THE PUNISHMENT PRINCIPLE

Pain and punishment are often used synonymously, because pain, by definition, is unpleasant or aversive. Thus, pain often serves to punish (or decrease the future probability of recurrence of) behaviors that precede its occurrence. In the example under the heading "Interpersonal Feedback Contingencies" of the patient whose wife helped him put on his socks and shoes, pain, occurring contingent on the patient's attempts to put on his socks and shoes without assistance, served as a punishment for putting his shoes and socks on by himself. It therefore reduced the probability of his doing it himself the next time. In this case, not attempting to do it himself the next time and asking his wife for help were negatively reinforcing by facilitating the avoidance of more pain. The main treatment implication of this principle is to modify the operants that lead to pain by applying the principles of pacing *and* shaping, along with the other behavioral, cognitive, and educational principles described earlier.

Punishment and Negative Reinforcement

It is clinically significant that the occurrence of pain typically serves as a punitive stimulus, whereas pain's removal typically serves as a negative reinforcer. Pain as a punitive stimulus can have biologically adaptive value by warning a person of the potential for reinjury and can thus serve to prevent it by inducing the person to cease the pain-producing, potentially injurious behavior. However, this adaptive role mostly applies to acute pain. With chronic pain, the behaviors that are mostly punished (i.e., suppressed) are adaptive behaviors. In the preceding example, the patient's independent dressing behaviors were suppressed by pain. On the other hand, with chronic pain, behaviors associated with the removal or avoidance of pain (such as the patient's asking his wife to put on his shoes and socks) are negatively reinforced, and therefore strengthened.

These negatively reinforced pain behaviors are often dysfunctional and maladaptive because they typically lead to *psychosocially* punitive consequences (e.g., censure, loss of admiration and respect, disrespect, loss of self-esteem, interpersonal conflict, disability). Note that *punishment* can refer either to the presentation of an aversive stimulus (e.g., interpersonal conflict, censure, and reprimand) or to removal of a desirable stimulus (e.g., loss of admiration and respect, loss of money, esteem, and loss of interpersonal harmony).

Exercise and Deconditioning

Another example of the reciprocal roles played by punishment and negative reinforcement in the maintenance of a chronic pain syndrome is observed in the pervasive problem of physical deconditioning. Pain patients frequently avoid regular exercise because, at least initially, it often leads to more pain. In other words, exercise can be punishing in the short run. Consequently, the avoidance of exercise can serve as a negative reinforcer in that it briefly spares a patient from excess pain (although not in the long run). One goal of the PMP therapist, working in tandem with the patient's treating physician and a physical therapist, should be to promote physical reconditioning by positively reinforcing regular exercise. This can be managed by employing the operant behavioral concepts of extinction, shaping, successive approximation, and pacing, along with cognitive restructuring. An excellent and highly motivating chapter on pain rehabilitation exercises, entitled "Relaxing and Strengthening Your Body," is contained in Marcus and Arbeiter's (1994) book, *Freedom from Chronic Pain*, which is often prescribed reading for patients. For example:

THERAPIST: I understand you hate to do your back exercises?

PATIENT: They take up too much time, and frankly, I often hurt too much to do them!

THERAPIST: Did you ever think of the possibility that it also hurts too much NOT to do them?

PATIENT: Yes. But, it takes so much energy to do exercises regularly, and I often overdo them.

THERAPIST: Yes. That is a danger. Tell me, when you overdo your exercises, is it usually because you do them too fast, because you're impatient to get them all done?

PATIENT: Yes. That's definitely it!

THERAPIST: What usually goes through your mind when you decide that it is time again to do your assigned physical therapy exercises?

The therapist should assess the patient's automatic negative thoughts and beliefs about exercise and help the patient dispute them by suggesting that (a) a regular routine of exercise can reverse the negative effects of physical deconditioning and help the patient stay out of pain, and (b) it helps to believe that exercise and movement are good for you and will make you feel better. The therapist also stresses the importance of being committed to exercising, having a dedicated time and place to exercise, and wearing comfortable clothing. It is also important to convey the need to be aware of any tendency to engage in pain behaviors that can dilute the beneficial effects of exercise or sabotage the intent to do them in the first place. These include making excuses not to exercise, mismanaging time, complaining, moaning, and bracing and guarding muscles. Finally, the therapist should stress concentrating on the exercises while exercising, and rationally responding to negative automatic thoughts.

Determining the Causes of Patient Noncompliance

Another behavioral principle of effective PMP is that it is essential to determine the exact causes of patient noncompliance with the treatment. For example, it is important to know whether the main reason a patient did not do the therapy homework, or is not making therapeutic progress, is because he or she holds certain blocking beliefs, still lacks the requisite skills, cannot cope with the attendant anxiety, or has significant others who are reinforcing the opposite responses. Often, assessment reveals that it is a combination of these things. On other occasions, the problem may largely be due to one or two factors.

A particularly problematic area where both skill deficits and blocking, dysfunctional beliefs usually operate in concert, has to do with anger, hostility and aggressive behavior evidenced by some chronic pain patients. Unless these problems are effectively addressed, PMP as well as other rehabilitative therapies is usually headed for failure (Burns et al., 1996; Fernandez & Turk, 1995; Hendler, 1981; Kerns, Rosenberg, & Jacob, 1994; Kinder & Curtiss, 1988). It has been our experience that many chronic pain patients can benefit from some form of assertiveness training. Frequently, patients reduce their destructive, hostile and aggressive behavior when they recognize that it is usually easier, more effective, and more comfortable to behave assertively when faced with an interpersonally imposed obstacle or frustration.

ASSERTIVENESS TRAINING

Assertiveness, as opposed to aggressiveness or hostility, can be defined as the ability to stand up for oneself in an argument, defend one's position, and protect one's rights without losing control. Assertiveness means being able to say no, make one's preferences and decisions clear about matters of direct concern, and express one's feelings or disagreement in a clear and appropriate manner. It also involves being able to set limits and make choices about what one will do or not do in the context of an interpersonal interaction. Many pain patients lack skills that would allow them to do these things. For detailed descriptions of assertiveness training techniques, see Bower and Bower (1991) and Catalano and Hardin (1996).

There is an apparent relationship between chronic pain and the traits of *alexithymia, emotional illiteracy,* and *somatic hyperresponsiveness* (Blumer & Heilbronn, 1989; Engel, 1959; Grzesiak, 1996; Sternbach, 1974). It may be that many chronic pain sufferers who lack assertiveness skills, and hence the ability to express their disagreement or register their disapproval through appropriate social channels, express their disagreement and disapproval somatically, through their bodies. It is not possible at this stage of our knowledge to claim without reservation that assertiveness deficits are a causal factor for some forms of chronic pain. However, it is indisputable that living with the limitations imposed by many chronic pain states can expose a person to potential conflicts with other people and institutions with competing interests. Therefore, assessing a pain patient's assertiveness skills and improving them if they are deficient are behavioral treatment priorities. Deficits in assertiveness skills could be partly responsible for the prevalence of anger and hostility evidenced by many chronic pain patients. Thus, assertiveness training (AT) could help to reduce the problems of impulsive, hostile, aggressive, acting out behavior evidenced by some chronic pain patients. For example:

THERAPIST: How are you doing?

PATIENT: Terrible. I was ready to punch out my physical therapist the other day.

THERAPIST: What happened?

PATIENT: He hurt me. He kept making me do those exercises until I screamed out in pain. And then he still said, "Come on, if you want to get better, you are going to work harder!"

THERAPIST: You say "he made you" do exercises? I think you mean that he asked you to do some exercises, which you began to do. Sounds like when you began to hurt, you possibly didn't say anything until the point where you could no longer tolerate it. Is that true?

PATIENT: No. I told him I couldn't do them!

THERAPIST: At what point? Before you started to do them, or after you started doing them, and got to the point where you hurt too much?

PATIENT: Before I started.

THERAPIST: So, then you began to do them anyway. Why didn't you just stop when you felt it hurt too much?

PATIENT: I didn't know what to say!

THERAPIST: How about saying, "I'm in a lot of pain now, I want to stop"?

PATIENT: I guess.

THERAPIST: Would that have worked?

PATIENT: Probably.

THERAPIST: Let's role-play together to try it out. I'll make believe I'm George (*the physical therapist*) and you play yourself. Make believe you are in the physical therapist's office now. "Okay, Thomas, I'd like you to do two sets of ten repetitions of this exercise."

PATIENT: I'll start now.

THERAPIST: Okay.

PATIENT: (*After a minute*) "I can't do this!"

THERAPIST: "Why not?" (*as the physical therapist, George*)

PATIENT: "It hurts too much."

THERAPIST: "Okay, let's make it easier. Stop the exercise." (*as George*). Was that too hard, to express yourself and notify George that you want to stop?

PATIENT: Nope.

THERAPIST: Good. You spoke up. You set a limit and said "no more"! That's called assertiveness, or standing up for yourself before you get to the point where you feel like a victim and then want to kill!

RESPONDENT AND COVERT CONDITIONING APPROACHES

Respondent or covert conditioning approaches to chronic pain target internal behaviors such as mental images, self-talk, and feeling states (Cautela & Kearney, 1986; Spiegler, 1983; Wolpe, 1990). Emphasizing a stimulus-response or classical conditioning framework, this translates operationally into modifying the internal stimulus triggers to dysfunctional and disabling pain states. A list of covert conditioning techniques (McMullin, 1986) would include teaching the pain patient how to employ covert extinction, covert positive reinforcement, covert desensitization, covert avoidance, covert escape conditioning or negative reinforcement, and covert aversive conditioning or self-administered punishment to modify covert stimulus triggers and responses to persistent or recurring pain.

Covert conditioning approaches to chronic pain emphasize treating internal or covert thoughts and images as behaviors. An internal functional analysis of these covert behavioral events precedes any intervention. Then, specific covert behaviors (i.e., thoughts or images) determined to fall into a stimulus-response chain of covert and overt events are targeted for modification. The following covert conditioning techniques are usually employed in combination. As in the operant conditioning paradigm, one technique (e.g., covert negative reinforcement: stopping a thought or behavior) often immediately leads to another technique (e.g., positive reinforcement: starting another thought or behavior).

COVERT REINFORCEMENT

Covert negative reinforcement or *escape conditioning* includes thought-stopping and redirection of attention to positive thoughts or images. *Covert positive reinforcement* includes (a) self-praise for engaging in a desired behavior; (b) "changing the channel" on an undesirable thought or aversive image by thinking of something else; and (c) thinking of rewarding and pleasant thoughts or images contingent on engaging in a desirable behavior, such as emptying the trash or not complaining about pain for an hour.

COVERT EXTINCTION

Covert extinction includes the application of practical techniques to break the chain of negative behavioral events that follow a pain-related thought or image. Whenever the pain patient catches himself or herself thinking a negative thought related to pain, he or she should be coached to ignore it and to refocus on whatever he or she was previously doing or thinking.

COVERT RECIPROCAL INHIBITION, COUNTERCONDITIONING, AND SYSTEMATIC DESENSITIZATION

Following the pioneering work of Wolpe (1990) on *reciprocal inhibition* and *systematic desensitization,* the pain patient is taught to pair an aversive stimulus (e.g., thinking about pain) with a pleasant stimulus (e.g., a relaxing or comforting image). In this paradigm, thinking about pain might be conceptualized as an unwanted conditioned stimulus that produces undesirable conditioned responses such as depression and withdrawal. As soon as the patient catches himself or herself needlessly thinking about pain (negative conditioned stimuli), he or she is coached to shift the focus to a stronger, pleasant thought, image, or activity (the desired conditioned stimulus) that produces a desired conditioned response (e.g., relaxation, calm, self-efficacy feelings). The stronger, desired conditioned stimulus is paired repeatedly with the weaker, negative conditioned stimulus. Theoretically, eventually, the negative conditioned stimulus (pain thoughts) will elicit the desired conditioned response (e.g., relaxation, calm, self-efficacy feelings or a neutral state).

In the traditional systematic desensitization approach pioneered by Wolpe, a hierarchy of anxiety-provoking images or thoughts from least upsetting (bottom of the hierarchy) to most upsetting (top of the hierarchy) is first constructed. Items are then rated and ranked based on a 0-to-10 or 0-to-100 scale of subjective units of disturbance (SUDs). Then, the counterconditioning process is carried out starting at the bottom of the hierarchy with the least anxiety-provoking stimulus (lowest SUDs rating) and proceeding up the hierarchy. At each step of the desensitization ladder, the patient is asked to imagine the thought connected to that step on the ladder. The thought is then paired with the counterconditioning reciprocally inhibitory response (e.g., relaxation, a pleasant replacement image). The pairing procedure is continued until the patient reports that the SUDs level has gone down to 0, indicating that the thought is no longer anxiety-provoking, or upsetting. The therapist continues to move the patient up through each of the steps of the desensitization hierarchy or ladder in this manner. The clinical application of covert reciprocal inhibition and counterconditioning is illustrated in the following example:

Case Example

Mr. D. was a 29-year-old married man who had sustained severe neck, back, and leg injuries 4 years before in a motor vehicle accident. The accident left him in severe and constant pain, along with a marked rage problem. His rages frequently resulted from minor frustrations such as an insensitive comment by someone or a feeling of being victimized. Mr. D. was not receptive to formal relaxation training or to the application of a formal hypnosis induction given his emotional lability, restlessness, anxiety, and irritability. He was receptive to "talk therapy" and therapeutic conversation, and had good rapport with his therapist. They agreed that when his pain flared up, so did his temper, and that when he acted out, while it gave him a temporary feeling of tension release, it actually reinforced his severe pain. Mr. D. agreed to listen when his therapist offered to show him another way to release tension and reduce pain.

The therapist modeled the following sequence: Whenever Mr. D. felt frustrated for whatever reason, he should complete the sentence, "I am mad because . . ." Then, he should complete the sentence, "I want to . . ." (usually do something destructive), "but I want pain-relief more." He was instructed to say this to himself even if he did not feel it was true. This man knew right from wrong and it was agreed that even if the statement did not seem true, he still needed to restrain himself from acting out. He was also told to "change the channel" to something pleasant after he said the statements to himself (covert positive reinforcement). At that point, he was instructed to praise himself for having good control and to also say to himself, "If I can control my rage, then I can control this (expletive) pain!"

There is considerable overlap between respondent or covert conditioning approaches and operant approaches to PMP. The covert respondent approaches incorporate operants as well. It is also apparent that cognition plays a major role in the chain of behaviors targeted by both operant and respondent behavioral intervention paradigms. No one approach can accomplish all that needs to be accomplished for the successful rehabilitation of a chronic pain patient. An informed integration of techniques and constructive integration of theoretical models is necessary to make meaningful advances in the treatment of something as complex and multidimensional as chronic pain. The multidimensional and multifactorial nature of the problem necessitates what A. Lazarus (1989) terms "technical eclecticism."

PART THREE

HYPNO-BEHAVIORAL PAIN MANAGEMENT

CHAPTER 9

Hypno-Behavioral Pain Management Psychotherapy Strategies

The point of therapy is to get unhooked, not to thrash around on how you got hooked.

—Maryanne Walters

THE APPLICABILITY OF HYPNOSIS TO PAIN MANAGEMENT

The construct of *hypnosis* is used to represent both a particular state of consciousness and the method employed for inducing such a state. In many ways, the construct is quite elusive, given the abundance of myths and misconceptions about hypnosis. There are several excellent scholarly sources that review the current state of research and knowledge on the neurophysiology and phenomenology of hypnosis (Cheek, 1994; Edmonston, 1986; Hilgard & Hilgard, 1994; Rhue, Lynn, & Kirsch, 1993; Rossi, 1993; H. Spiegel & D. Spiegel, 1978/1987; Weitzenhoffer, 1989a, 1989b). This chapter covers what is clinically relevant for our purposes: how therapeutic hypnosis can induce a greater responsiveness and receptivity to pain management strategies and interventions.

Definitions of Hypnotherapy and Hypno-Behavioral PMP

Hypnotherapy may be defined as "the clinical application of hypnosis for the therapeutic purpose of inducing a controlled state of dissociation." Such a state may be termed a "therapeutic hypnotic state" or "therapeutic trance." *Hypno-Behavioral Pain Management Psychotherapy,* (Hypno-Behavioral PMP) may be defined as "the therapeutic utilization of trance induction techniques, along with cognitive and behavioral strategies, for purposes of improving a patient's self-management of pain and coping."

Like any state of consciousness, the actual hypnotic state of consciousness is difficult to measure and objectify. However, the consensus is that the hypnotic state of consciousness differs from the waking state in several ways (Cheek, 1994; Edmonston, 1986; Hilgard & Hilgard, 1994; H. Spiegel & D. Spiegel, 1978/1987; Weitzenhoffer, 1989a, 1989b):

1. The hypnotic state, or therapeutic trance, is a mental state of (a) sustained responsive concentration, (b) focused imagination, and (c) heightened receptivity to acceptable suggestions.
2. The patient entering a hypnotic state, or in a hypnotic state, collaborates with the therapist and freely complies with the therapist's instructions, directives, and suggestions, as long as they are acceptable.
3. The patient in a hypnotic state experiences acceptable, suggested sensations, perceptions, and positive cognitions associated with his or her targeted therapeutic goals.
4. The hypnotized individual experiences some degree of involuntariness in his or her responses to hypnotic suggestions. It may seem as if responses to suggestions occur on their own, as opposed to their being deliberate, completely voluntary, and effortful.
5. The hypnotized individual can be described as being in a state of "parallel awareness" (H. Spiegel & D. Spiegel, 1978/1987), being able to process information effortlessly on a number of levels simultaneously. This state of consciousness may be labeled *controlled dissociation* in the service of the therapy. It is marked by "the ability to be here and there at the same time" (H. Spiegel, personal communication, 1996).
6. Logically inconsistent or contradictory ideas may be experienced simultaneously without the same level of dissonance that might be experienced in a waking, nonhypnotic state.
7. An individual in a hypnotic state is usually physically relaxed, while being mentally alert and focused.

These features of the hypnotic state make hypnosis valuable as a tool for inducing temporary relief from persistent pain. In contrast to a hypnotic state, a persistent pain state usually impedes information processing because of the person's preoccupation with pain and fear of pain worsening. Perceptions tend to be infected with negative and critical thinking, and the flow of attention is usually restricted to pain-related events. When in pain, many people are minimally receptive to positive suggestions and ideas, and are relatively incapable of envisioning themselves in a manner that promotes comfort. Pain is often perceived as permanent, continuous, or mysterious.

The Induction of Hypnosis

The therapeutic induction of a hypnotic state usually involves some sort of ceremony or ritual for inducing an alteration in consciousness from whatever is an individual's typical state of mind and mood, to a different, relaxed, imagination-dominated state. When a hypnotic induction is administered to one person by another person, it is termed *heterohypnosis.* Self-administered induction is termed *autohypnosis* or *self-hypnosis.*

Hypnosis is as natural a phenomenon as is paying attention. A person "shifts into it" (H. Spiegel, personal communication, 1996). That is one of the things that makes it effective for pain management. In a therapeutic context, a hypnotic state can be induced in a receptive, attentive patient who is capable of sustaining a "ribbon of concentration" (H. Spiegel, personal communication, 1996; H. Spiegel & D. Spiegel, 1978/1987). Therapeutic hypnosis is not coercive. It is a guided phenomenon and must be distinguished from other unethical ways to induce a trance state. As discussed by H. Spiegel and D. Spiegel (1978/1987), it is possible to induce an antitherapeutic state of trance via *seduction* or *coercion.* For example, fright and fear can coerce an individual into a trance state, and trauma can catapult an individual into such a state. However, this is not anything like the therapeutic trance, which is never induced with seduction, fright, or coercion.

In a therapeutic context, you cannot make a patient enter a hypnotic state, just as you cannot make a person pay attention or make a person believe something that is unbelievable. However, patients who are willing and able to enter a state of hypnosis can realize an effective temporary escape from pain. The extent of pain relief depends on a willing patient's hypnotic ability, and how he or she uses that ability. The real advantage of hypnosis for pain relief is that a hypnotic state is as natural and as potentially healing as a state of sleep—although hypnosis is not sleep. In a hypnotic state, ideas that are imagined (e.g., sensations and perceptions of comfort and pain relief) may feel more or less real. Perceptions are not forced or pressured. Just as in a deep sleep, within which the events of a dream feel real, during hypnosis a receptive person is likely to experience his or her thoughts and imagination as genuine and tangible. Thus, what a person wishes he or she could experience (i.e., pain relief, perceptions associated with comfort) can feel more real in a hypnotic state than when imagined in a usual state of consciousness. Moreover, contradictory perceptions and ideas can be experienced more easily and without dissonance.

HYPNOTIC CAPACITY

A number of prominent investigators (Hilgard & Hilgard, 1994; H. Spiegel & D. Spiegel, 1978/1987; Weitzenhoffer, 1989a) have spent their careers researching individual differences in hypnotic capacities and abilities. People with average or greater hypnotic capacity are receptive to the induction of hypnosis if they perceive it to be in their best interest. In the appropriate context, the greater a person's hypnotic capacity is, the more receptive he or she is likely to be to induction. Also, the greater a person's capacity, the more capable that person will be of experiencing the range of hypnotic phenomena.

Many writers have equated hypnotic capacity with *depth* of hypnosis (Edmonston, 1986; Erickson, 1952; Field, 1965; Weitzenhoffer, 1989a). However, there is no consensus in the literature on methods for operationalizing and measuring depth of hypnosis. The term depth, in this context, is a metaphor. In practice, hypnotic depth is inferred from the range of phenomena a hypnotized person demonstrates or internally experiences. The more difficult it is to experience a hypnotic phenomenon, the more depth of hypnosis it requires. Hypnoanalgesia (diminished pain) is scaled as being more difficult than other hypnotic phenomena such as relaxation, vivid imagination and visualization, eye fatigue, eye closure, muscle catalepsy (marked heaviness and physical inertia), and sensations such as lightness or floating. Hypnoanesthesia (complete absence of all sensation) is scaled as being even more difficult. A minority of patients with persistent pain can be trained with hypnosis to experience complete relief from their pain. Nevertheless, under the right circumstances and with appropriate motivation, most pain patients can be helped to experience some degree of hypnoanalgesia through the induction of other contributory hypnotic phenomena.

A person's receptivity to utilizing hypnosis as a window of opportunity for pain relief depends on factors such as motivation, beliefs, and hypnotic capacity. *Motivation* refers to how important it is to the person to achieve pain relief. Some important related questions are, How important is it to the individual to learn new ways to manage pain? How hard is the individual willing to work at it? *Beliefs* include the persons expectations and convictions about the cause of the pain and about what can help manage or reduce it. *Hypnotic capacity* and *hypnotic ability* refer to a person's ability to (a) achieve a state of hypnosis, (b) experience a range of hypnotic phenomena, (c) learn and use self-hypnosis, and (d) be receptive and responsive to hypnotic suggestion. These terms are often used interchangeably with the term *hypnotizability*. These factors should be assessed before formulating a PMP treatment plan.

HYPNOTIC STRATEGIES FOR PAIN CONTROL

In the context of PMP, a therapeutic strategy is what a PMP therapist does to achieve a therapeutic goal related to pain management. As discussed in the preceding chapters, pain management involves a wide range of therapeutic strategies. Most PMP strategies can be implemented without hypnosis. However, some are more easily implemented with hypnotherapy. As a general rule, we usually start with the simplest and most direct strategies and then move on to more complex strategies based on a patient's response. The specific strategies and combinations of strategies selected are based on our case formulation and treatment goals.

Directed clinical hypnosis can facilitate PMP strategies that involve imagery and controlled breathing to achieve relaxation, distraction, escape from pain, alteration of pain sensations, transformation of pain perceptions, and hypno-analgesia. It can also facilitate PMP strategies employing cognitive coping statements to bolster patient motivation and counter demoralization as well as pain control strategies employing cognitive disputation to restructure negative thinking patterns associated with pain. Hypno-behavioral strategies can enhance mental rehearsal of adaptive ways of coping with pain. Finally, hypno-behavioral strategies incorporating techniques of age regression, memory recall, and memory reconstruction may augment cognitive restructuring of psychological issues associated with the perpetuation of old emotional wounds. Particular strategies may be employed to desensitize and reprocess affect-laden memories associated with persistent pain.

CAUTIONS AND CONTRAINDICATIONS IN THE USE OF HYPNO-BEHAVIORAL PMP

Although hypnosis is worth a try in most clinical pain management situations, it should be used cautiously or may be in fact contraindicated for (a) situations in which pain is a symptom of an as yet untreated, medically treatable physical condition; (b) patients with severe psychiatric illness, or who experience intense feelings of heightened anxiety under hypnosis; (c) patients involved in ongoing litigation; and (d) patients with low or no hypnotizability.

SITUATIONS IN WHICH PAIN IS A SYMPTOM OF A MEDICALLY TREATABLE PHYSICAL CONDITION

Hypnosis should never be used to mask or suppress pain that has a medically treatable, physical cause. Therefore, it would be a poor decision to proceed with hypnosis to treat pain that has not been worked up medically. This is not to imply that hypnosis is inappropriate for patients with medically evaluated and medically treatable pain. In such cases, hypnosis can often be an adjuvant pain management modality to facilitate a patient's coping. However, the pain should be respected as an informative signal of the status of the underlying nociceptive process. Our basic position is that even when all medical workups have come up with negative findings, pain usually serves some purpose and should be respected as an informative signal. The PMP therapist should formulate a plan to address that purpose, as it is understood, in a way that relieves unnecessary pain and suffering.

Hypnotic strategies may help a patient filter the hurt and suffering out of the pain sensations. It is therapeutic (a) to distinguish between the minimum pain necessary to provide informative feedback and excessive, unnecessary pain, and then (b) to factor this distinction into the formulation of hypno-behavioral pain management strategies. It is usually naive and may be risky to suggest that all pain will diminish permanently. Hypno-behavioral strategies should be formulated to diminish unnecessary pain and restructure patients' perceptions of their pain as continuous, permanent, mysterious, and excruciating.

PSYCHIATRIC ISSUES

The PMP clinician should always evaluate the likelihood of various diagnosis and case-specific negative reactions before assuming that hypnosis for pain management could work. Hypno-Behavioral PMP would seldom be considered applicable or safe in cases characterized by marked paranoia, active delusions, explosive tendencies, severe acting out, antisocial behavior, marked memory or concentration problems, severe identity confusion, marked histrionic or manipulative tendencies, and active substance abuse.

DISSOCIATIVE DISORDERS

Workers in the treatment of dissociative disorders (Horevitz, 1993; Kluft, 1982) report that hypnosis is a viable modality for working with patients who have dissociative identity disorder (DID), or multiple personality disorder (MPD). These patients dissociate naturally in the service of their psychopathology. Correspondingly, hypnotic strategies are indispensable in redirecting these dissociative tendencies toward integration and recovery. If a pain patient turns out on formal assessment to be suffering from a *DSM-IV* diagnosable, Axis I dissociative disorder, the clinician should not use hypnosis for pain management if he or she does not know how to work with a dissociative patient. If at all possible, the clinician should refer the patient to someone else who does. However, hypnosis would not be contraindicated if the clinician knows how to work with dissociative pathology. In that case, the clinician should be able to formulate the patient's pain complaints in light of the overall clinical picture.

Forensic and Legal Issues

Clinicians see a significant percentage of pain patients who attribute their pain to a personal injury that has involved them in ongoing litigation (e.g., injuries in motor vehicle accidents, work-related accidents, personal mishaps, and personal assaults). When working with these patients, the clinician should be mindful that legal pitfalls in the use of hypnosis (Scheflin & Shapiro, 1989) can potentially jeopardize the legal acceptability of a plaintiff's testimony in court. The greatest risks are incurred where hypnosis is used to assist in the recall and reprocessing of traumatic memories. Hypnotically "refreshed" memories have been ruled inadmissible as evidence in a number of court cases (Scheflin & Shapiro, 1989).

It is necessary to obtain the patient's informed consent about the legal risks before using hypnosis in a personal injury case. Scheflin and Shapiro (1989) advise, "Before attempting any actual hypnosis, the therapist must again carefully inform the client as to potential loss of legal rights if hypnosis is undertaken. It is prudent to offer the client alternatives to hypnosis . . ." (p. 235). It has been our experience that personal injury patients appreciate being able to make an informed decision about any treatment modality that has the potential of jeopardizing their case. While some patients decline hypnosis immediately when presented with this information, most choose to confer with their attorneys and/or family members before making a decision.

Low or No Hypnotizability

Assuming that hypnosis is indicated, what should the clinician do if the patient's hypnotizability tests poor or nonexistent? The best answer is that the clinician should not be deterred in using viable psychological pain control strategies. Many imagery and relaxation strategies can still be employed without the formal use of hypnosis. Then too, there are many cognitive and behavioral PMP strategies to consider employing. Additionally, electronic or computerized biofeedback therapy is a useful tool for teaching relaxation and self-control techniques to pain patients who cannot benefit from hypnosis. Several excellent clinical biofeedback primers (Arena & Blanchard, 1996), and comprehensive biofeedback practitioner guides are available (Cram, 1986; Cram & Associates, 1990; Schwartz & Associates, 1995).

CLASSIFYING HYPNOTHERAPEUTIC PAIN MANAGEMENT STRATEGIES

From a practical clinical standpoint, hypnotic or hypnotherapeutic pain management strategies can be classified along a dimension of *coping-supportive* versus *uncovering-exploratory*. Coping-supportive hypnotherapeutic strategies are direct, suggestive, cognitive, and imagery interventions such as *relaxation training, guided pain-relief imagery,* and other *symptom-transformative* methods designed to relieve pain and ameliorate suffering.

Uncovering-exploratory hypnotherapeutic strategies include interventions designed to uncover and reprocess underlying emotional factors associated with persistent pain (Cheek, 1994). These methods aim to identify personal historical antecedents related to the pain patient's present mental and physical state. These reconstructed antecedents are then reframed in a more adaptive context. A number of uncovering-exploratory hypnotic pain therapy strategies are described later in this chapter.

STRATEGIES FOR ALTERING PAIN SENSATIONS AND SYMPTOMS

Distraction

Distraction, or attentional diversion, is perhaps the most direct, simple, and intuitively sensible pain control strategy. It involves helping the patient learn to refocus attention away from the pain and onto something else. This strategy can encompass a wide range of distractions that are incompatible with the continued experience of severe pain. Patients can be taught to divert their attention externally or internally in fantasy. *External* diversion includes studying one's surroundings and concentrating or meditating on some external focus point. *Internal or fantasy* diversion includes mentally going to one's favorite place, to any place where one feels comfortable and safe, and remembering what it feels like to perform a pleasant activity. Alternatively, a patient might imagine that he or she is somebody else admired. The patient might fantasize how that admired person would handle a similar pain state. Additionally, a patient might fantasize transforming the contextual circumstances into something dramatic, such as being one's favorite undercover operative, or detective hero, recovering from a bullet wound.

PAIN DISPLACEMENT

Pain displacement is perhaps less intuitive but nevertheless, simple and straightforward. It involves imagining a similar or different sensation in a different part of one's body where it is less painful or distressing. For example, one man with severe low back pain would make a tight fist and squeeze it whenever his pain got bad. Erickson (1980) often suggested that patients work with the idea of displacing pain sensations into less threatening places in their body. In the context of working with a cancer patient who, for example, was understandably worried about metasteses in his body and internal organs, Erickson might suggest something like the following: "Suppose you had all that body pain right here in your left hand. You are not going to worry about that. It isn't going to hurt half as much as the pain in your body" (Erickson, 1980, p. 317).

SYMPTOM SUBSTITUTION

Symptom substitution involves imaginally substituting for the pain something else that is similar but that hurts much less or is of lesser intensity. For example, a burning pain might be imaginally transformed into an itch. Erickson (1980, 1986) advocated working with, fragmenting, and transforming pain sensations. He would often ask pain patients to consider reconstruing their pain in less noxious, emotionally distressing, and destructive terms. For example, he might suggest: "'This short, cutting, stabbing, blinding pain of yours, could you make that into dull, heavy pain?' In the hypnotic state, subjects are open to ideas. *They like to examine ideas in terms of their memories, their learnings, their conditionings and all of the various experiential learnings of life*" (Erickson, 1980, p. 318).

IMAGINATIVE TRANSFORMATION OF A PAINFUL SYMPTOM'S CAUSE

The imagined cause and signal value (or informative purpose) of a painful symptom can be reinterpreted and imaginatively transformed into something less destructive, more benign, and hence more acceptable. For example, the imagined cause and reason for continual burning neuralgic pain which at first a patient takes to signify continuing nerve damage and destruction might be reframed; it can be reinterpreted as a symptom (or informative signal) of overstimulated nerves, oxygen-depleted and inflamed tissues, and muscles in chronic spasm. This interpretation is more benign and probably more medically accurate as well. It can also provide clues for developing fitting symptom alleviation strategies and congruent pain relief images. An important caveat in the use of this strategy and in the use of hypnosis in general is that the pain has been adequately worked up medically. Hypnosis is not and must never be utilized as a substitute for appropriate medical treatment. Hypnotic pain control strategies should be used as adjuncts to appropriate medical treatment.

Case Example

A 74-year-old man was referred for treatment to help him cope with postherpetic neuralgia burning pain in his mid-thoracic area. At first, he was helped through direct hypnotic suggestion to transform his impressions of the burning sensation into the perception of an itch which he found much less bothersome (i.e., symptom substitution). He could then very gently rub a soothing balm on the itchy area and realize some relief, or he could just ignore the itch. After some "working through," he also accepted the explanatory reframe that the burning and itch indicated that the nerves to the painful area had been overstimulated and the surrounding tissues deprived of oxygen. This reinterpretation suggested certain pain alleviation strategies: (a) the wearing of a neoprene-type pressure binder over the painful area to stimulate the lower threshold, faster A-fibers which could "close the pain gate" by inhibiting the transmission of pain messages up the spinal cord by the higher threshold, slower C-fibers (Irving & Wallace, 1997; Melzack & Wall, 1965, 1982), (b) the application of a soothing balm to the painful area, (c) the use of relaxation techniques and relaxing images to calm the overstimulated nerves, (d) deep, slow, controlled diaphragmatic breathing while imagining breathing through the painful area to restore oxygen to the tissues, and (e) the evocation of pain relief and antidote images of reduced inflammatory response, bolstered antiviral immune function, and regional blockade of the irritated nerves with intradermal and epidural injections of anesthetic agents. The patient's physician was willing to support this palliative reinterpretation of the patient's painful symptoms and psychological treatment strategy. As a result, the patient was able to successfully transform his interpretation of the originally highly distressing burning symptoms into less destructive, more benign and acceptable signals of healing.

HYPNOANALGESIA

Hypnoanalgesia means using hypnotic suggestion to induce the perception of a decrease in pain magnitude or intensity. Suggestions can be verbal as in "your discomfort will diminish more and more over the next ten minutes," tactile-kinesthetic as in "imagine that your arm is surrounded by a block of ice" (e.g., for burning pain) or visual as in "imagine the redness and swelling diminishing."

GLOVE ANALGESIA AND ANESTHESIA

In glove analgesia or anesthesia, the therapist first suggests analgesia or anesthesia in one of the patient's hands. It is called *glove anesthesia* because the sensory feeling induced is one of numbness as in having a thick glove on the hand. Then, the feeling of numbness is transferred or displaced to the part of the body that hurts by physically placing the numbed hand on the painful body part. The patient is then directed to rub the painful body part with the numbed hand while thinking and imagining that the numbness will flow from the hand into the painful body part. If the patient cannot reach the painful body part, this is not a problem. The numbed hand is placed on an accessible spot and it is suggested that the numbness will flow into the targeted painful area.

PATTERN INTERRUPTION

This term refers to the strategy of interrupting and disrupting the patient's automatic response pattern to pain so as to modify the patient's current sensory perception and interpretation of the pain. Pattern interruption may involve the introduction of discrepant information that scrambles or rearranges the elements of the patient's perception and/or interpretation of pain. It might involve suggesting that the patient do something differently, alter a well-established ritual, or add or delete a step in a sequence of coping strategies.

SYMPTOM REINTERPRETATION AND REFRAMING

A therapist may suggest to a patient or guide a patient to develop an alternate interpretation or different meaning for the pain. Symptom reinterpretation and reframing focus less on a pain symptom's assumed physical cause and more on the implications and meaning of the pain condition. For example, one patient was in the habit of thinking and saying, "I am cursed" and "I'm the one who is always punished, this damn pain proves it!" The therapist asked him if he ever thought differently. He answered with a resounding "no!" The therapist then asked him if he liked his job. His answer was another resounding "no!" The therapist then suggested that because he was out on temporary disability because of the pain, perhaps his pain was "in some sense, the gift you have been waiting for that can let you take a break from the job you hate and spend some time figuring out just what you might want to do with the rest of your life." The patient readily agreed with this reinterpretation of his current pain condition.

TIME DISTORTION

With this technique, the therapist suggests either that time spent in pain is speeding up or time spent in between pain episodes is slowing down.

NONJUDGMENTAL FOCUS OF AWARENESS

This exposure-based coping strategy refers to concentrating directly and objectively on the current pain sensations. It is usually suggested that this strategy be employed when the pain becomes intense. Typically, there is a tendency to catastrophize when the pain gets bad. Negative thinking and negative emotional states exacerbate pain. By objectively focusing just on the physical pain sensations with an intentional inhibition of emotional reactivity, the patient often will experience temporary pain intensification followed by a drop in the pain's intensity. When using this strategy, the therapist should also coach the patient to breathe deeply and slowly.

DELIBERATELY INCREASING PAIN INTENSITY

A related strategy that is also exposure-based is to deliberately intensify the pain sensations. By doing this, the patient can often be brought to the experiential realization, "If I can temporarily increase the pain, then it is somewhat under my control and I can therefore temporarily decrease it." Temporarily holding the breath, and breathing rapidly and shallowly also tend to intensify pain.

THERAPEUTIC PAIN RELIEF IMAGERY

One of the simplest, most direct, and often most effective pain management strategies is to teach the patient to evoke pain relief images when pain worsens. As part of our initial workup, we routinely ask patients to describe their idiosyncratic images of their pain (see the Pain Imagery Interview). We then redirect them to come up with images associated with comfort, relief, healing, rehabilitation, and pain management. Before treatment, most patients readily admit that when in severe pain, they do not naturally think of pain relief images. In fact, the directness and sensibility of this strategy almost makes it appear too simple and naive. However, when the strategy is discussed in the context of facilitating distraction from pain and replacing suffering and hurting with thoughts and images associated with comfortable feelings, it usually starts to make more sense to the patient. The efficacy of imagery as a PMP strategy appears to be enhanced when combined with hypnosis. The hypnotic modality facilitates relaxation, receptivity, and suggestibility. Table 9.1 presents some classes of imagery that have popular appeal and efficacy for inducing pain relief.

A CONTROL PANEL OF LIGHT SWITCHES

An excellent technique described by LeCron (1964) involves suggesting that the patient visualize a row of light switches with a different colored

Table 9.1
Classes of Pain Relief Imagery

Symptom Alteration Imagery
   Images of pain shrinking, expanding, or diffusing; symptom substitution and transformation; symptom displacement; symptom diminution; numbness, anesthesia, and analgesia; idiosyncratic pain relief images

Attentional Diversion
   Thinking of a favorite place; studying one's surroundings; visualizing a flower or a lit candle; meditation on a focus point image

"Healing Lights" and "Neutralizing Spirals of Energy"
   A healing "colored light stream" that neutralizes pain and physical hurt (Shapiro, 1995); "body lights" imagery of the feelings in different parts of the body (Rossi & Cheek, 1988); an energy spiral reversing and neutralizing the energy channels associated with the pain (Shapiro, 1995)

Technology Metaphors
   An electronic panel of controls that can switch pain on and off (Lecron, 1964); electronic dials to change the pain's intensity and other attributes; a pain meter or pain thermometer/barometer; computer file metaphors; a file cabinet for storing pain associated with different times and different activities; a three-paneled movie or video screen (Spiegel & Spiegel, 1978/1987)

Nature Images
   Floating clouds; running water; storms; the beach; the ocean; floating in water

"Inner advisor" Imagery (Bresler, 1979)
   A wise, all-knowing inner advisor; an internal boardroom with a board of advisors; an internal protector; favorite hero imagery

Time-Travel Imagery
   Age regression and age progression; visualization of the self pain-free or before the condition developed; visualization of the self pain-free and healthy in the future

light bulb above each switch; each switch goes to a different part of the patient's body. The clinician then says:

> Imagine that you are now turning off the switch that controls the sensations in your *(insert: target area of pain)*. What color is that switch? That switch is connected to your *(target area)* and sends nervous impulses from your brain down to that part of you and from that part of you back up to your brain. Now, when you imagine turning that switch off, you can see that the *(insert: color)* light above the switch goes out, or it may just grow dimmer. Which it does, does not really matter. Now, you may or may not immediately have a sensation of numbness or diminished sensation in your *(targeted area of pain)*. The important thing is to experience this anesthesia or diminished discomfort at an unconscious or inner level. What is also important, is that you take the time to practice this exercise because by doing so you are conditioning your inner mind to be less sensitive to the pain in *(insert: targeted pain area)*. The more you practice this exercise, the better you will become at using it to diminish your discomfort in your *(insert: target area)*. Your success in using this exercise will also depend on your mental attitude. Doubts on your part will only impede your ability to get it to work and to get relief. Skepticism prevents self-suggestion from taking root, while positive belief promotes your ability to accomplish something worthwhile such as what you have come here looking for—which is help so that you can get relief from your pain.

ROSSI AND CHEEK'S "BODY LIGHTS" IMAGERY

Rossi and Cheek (1988) developed an elegant hypno-exploratory imagery technique for relieving painful symptoms. The following is a step-by-step adaptation of their approach:

1. The first step in the process is to instruct the patient how to establish ideomotor finger signals (discussed below). A *yes* finger, a *no* finger, and an *I'm not ready to know consciously yet* finger are established.
2. Next, the patient is asked to imagine standing in front of a full length mirror and seeing tiny colored lights in different parts of his or her body. It is suggested that the colors represent physical sensations including pain and that the *yes* finger will lift when the patient can see the total picture.
3. The patient is then asked to scan the entire picture and to report what the colors of each light represent.

4. Next, the patient is asked to select the least painful body part to do some therapeutic work. The therapist says: *Let your inner mind go back to a time when that body light stood for comfort* (flexibility, agility, strength, etc.). *Your yes finger will lift when you are back at that time.* The therapist waits for the yes finger to signal and then says: *Now, shift forward in time to the first moment when the light that now stands for pain took the place of the light that stood for comfort. Your yes finger will lift when you arrive at that moment. When you are there, please tell me your age and what is going on.* The therapist waits for the finger signal and for the patient to verbally respond.

5. The therapist then asks: *Is there any good reason now why you have to continue having pain in that body part?* The therapist waits for the patient to reply verbally or to signal with the fingers. If the patient answers *yes,* it is important to explore the patient's reasons.

6. If the patient answers *no,* the therapist asks: *Now that you are aware of what is happening, is your inner mind willing to let you turn off that pain and continue the healing process?*

7. If the patient answers that his or her inner mind is *not* willing to allow the pain to be turned off, the therapist and patient need to explore the factors that stand in the way of pain relief. The therapist should also ask: *Is your inner mind willing to let you <u>turn down</u> that pain and continue to heal?*

8. If the patient answers that his or her inner mind *is* willing to allow the pain to be turned *off* or *down,* the therapist should ask the patient to imagine a future time when the patient will no longer be suffering from pain in that body part. It is then suggested: *When you are there, your <u>yes</u> finger will lift and you will see the month, day, and year as though written on a chalkboard right in front of you.*

9. It is suggested that the patient practice orienting to that future time and rehearse imagining the associated sensations.

10. The above steps are repeated for other more painful body parts so that the patient gradually works his or her way up a hierarchy of increasingly painful body parts.

COGNITIVE HYPNOTHERAPEUTIC PAIN CONTROL STRATEGIES

POSITIVE SELF-SUGGESTION, COPING SELF-STATEMENTS, AND POSITIVE AFFIRMATIONS

Positive self-talk or self-instructional training can help a patient get through difficult periods when pain worsens and becomes intense. The technique of self-instructional training (also termed stress inoculation training) (Turk et al., 1983) discussed in Chapter 6 can also be used with hypnosis.

Patients are helped to construct a list of relevant coping statements to help them cope with pain-related crises. Patients can prepare cue-cards with positive coping statements written on them for each stage of a crisis situation. The added value of hypnosis is that it can help a patient rehearse positive coping statements and suggestions mentally as preparation for challenging pain-related situations. Furthermore, the hypnotic modality makes it easy to deliver to the patient cues for coping in the form of postinduction or posthypnotic suggestions. In hypnosis, the patient can be guided through each stage of an anticipated pain flare-up while being prompted to mentally repeat relevant positive coping suggestions.

After a hypnotic state has been induced, the therapist can deliver the following suggestions for rehearsing the stress inoculation steps:

Self-hypnosis helps you enter a mind-set in which you are receptive to rehearsing how you are going to cope when your pain gets bad and when your pain starts to challenge your inner strength and mental toughness. So, you will now be able to cope, or have something to fight back with, when you feel the pain beginning to worsen. As soon as you notice that the pain is beginning to go up, you can tell yourself something like: I am now going to get ready to deal with this. I can handle this. I have coped with it before. This time it will be easier for me to manage. I shall be okay. I can listen to what my body is telling me. Then, as the pain begins to get stronger, you too can get stronger as you tell yourself: I am doing fine. I shall not let the pain get the best of me. There are plenty of things that I can do to make this tolerable. I can do my deep breathing. I can just notice the sensations. I can shift my attention elsewhere. I can go into self-hypnosis. I can filter the hurt out of the pain. I can make comforting pictures in my mind. When the pain is at its worst, you can be at your strongest. You will be able to remind yourself of the following things: This is a temporary problem. I am handling this. I will continue to breathe comfortably. I can stand this. I am my own best friend. I can continue to coach myself through this. This pain will pass. I will only have as much pain as necessary. No pain need last forever. I will not let negative thinking get the better of me. Keep talking to myself. I can stick with the task. Just notice the sensations while I breathe through them. Finally, when the pain flare-up begins to subside, you can remember to give yourself credit for coping and staying in control. You can tell yourself things like, I did it! I remained strong. I coped well. I stuck to my plan. I used my coping skills well. You can feel good about yourself. It will be easier next time. You have a coping plan in place.

COGNITIVE DISPUTATION

Cognitive disputation of negative automatic thoughts, as discussed in Chapter 6, is another cognitive strategy that can be used very effectively in Hypno-Behavioral PMP. While a patient is in a hypnotic state, the patient can be guided to rehearse the steps in cognitive disputation. For example:

> As soon as you become aware that you are thinking *(insert: one of your patient's negative thoughts related to pain),* you will immediately counter that nonsense with *(insert: a rational response associated with coping). Or,* as soon as you notice yourself beginning to feel discouraged or depleted (or: angry, helpless, hopeless, panicky, and so forth), your first step will be to ask yourself: What just went through my mind? What was I just thinking? And, you will see what comes up. Then, your second step will be to evaluate the thoughts that came up.
>
> You will do this by asking yourself: Is that thought realistic? Does it really make sense? What disadvantages are there of thinking that way? Will that type of thinking help me? What does that type of thinking do to my pain? And again, you will see what answers come to you. Then, your third step will be to fix your thinking by asking yourself something like: What is a more realistic thought about that? What makes more sense? What can I think instead that won't make me hurt or suffer even more? Then again, you will wait and see what comes to mind. You will already know how to respond to your automatic negative thoughts and keep them at bay. And, the more that you practice this exercise, the easier it will become for you to talk sense to yourself and to fix your negative thinking. Most importantly, you will realize that it is hogwash to blame yourself for having negative thoughts. As a human being, it is perfectly natural to have automatic negative thoughts. Your only responsibility to yourself is to stay committed to catching your negative thoughts so that these poisonous ideas don't add misery to the pain.

HYPNOTIC UNCOVERING, EXPLORATORY, AND REPROCESSING STRATEGIES

The central assumption of the cognitive approach to pain management is that uncontested negative thinking about pain in the present forms the basis for excessive emotional distress (suffering) about persistent pain.

No causal assumptions about pain being psychologically based are considered necessary. However, practitioners acknowledge that negative thinking breeds anxiety, depression, and anger, which makes pain worse.

This perspective is often challenged by practitioners of a very different school of thought who frequently suspect persistent pain to be the outcome of discrete or cumulative psychological trauma (Cheek, 1994; Ewin, 1986; LeCron, 1964; Rossi & Cheek, 1988; Watkins, 1992). These practitioners criticize the cognitive perspective as being both too narrow and too shallow. Cognitive therapy is seen as addressing only one aspect of the problem and simply skimming the psychological surface. It is argued that unless the emotional factors maintaining persistent pain are insightfully addressed (i.e., unconscious factors), the pain will remain persistent. These emotional factors, such as unresolved grief, repressed anger, self-blame, self-punishment, repressed fears, and "negative imprints," are posited as frequently lying at the root of persistent pain syndromes. Given their assumptions about psychological causality, this dynamically and insight oriented, psychosomatic school of practitioners emphasizes hypnotically assisted memory recall, reconstruction and reprocessing strategies in the treatment of persistent pain. Hypnosis is induced to explore the past for emotionally charged precipitants of chronic, persistent pain syndromes. Old memories are thus recalled, reexamined, reprocessed, and reconstructed.

THE CONSTANT PAIN SYNDROME

Ewin (1986, 1992) has coined the term "constant pain syndrome" to characterize persistent pain states manifesting the following triad of factors. They are: (a) a presenting complaint of pain that never goes away, (b) mental disorientation, and (c) the fear of death. The second and third factors have to be associated with the circumstances of the pain's original onset. Ewin theorizes that continued and constant pain may subconsciously serve to reassure an affected individual that he or she did not die in the pain-precipitating traumatic event. Thus, the pain may serve an essential psychodynamic function: It may symbolize life. According to Ewin (1986, 1992), the first step in diagnosing a constant pain syndrome is to ask the patient if there ever has been a time when he or she was completely free of pain since the pain problem began. If the patient answers no, and also denies ever having been free of pain while asleep, then according to Ewin, it is likely that the patient's pain is psychogenic and related to a constant pain syndrome.

Ewin's creative, hypnoanalytical approach to working with such patients encompasses the following steps:

1. A focused, relaxed state is induced.
2. The patient is regressed (age regression is discussed later in the chapter) to the traumatic event which precipitated the pain and/or injury.
3. The patient is guided in reviewing the precipitating event and helped to accept the value of the pain at the time. It is pointed out that the pain helped the patient know that he or she was alive at the time, but that the pain is no longer needed for that purpose, because there are many other reliable ways for the patient to know that he or she is alive now.
4. The patient is asked whether he or she would be willing to spend a few minutes in trance without pain or with less pain. If the patient is willing to do this and reports that the pain diminished or was completely gone, then this success is validated, and its major significance is pointed out (i.e., the patient was able to diminish the pain and remain alive).

Ewin's methodology usually involves first instructing the patient to respond to questions and suggestions using ideomotor finger signals (discussed later), and then presenting the following questions and suggestions to the patient:

1. "Would it be all right with you to go back in time and review the experience of what first caused your pain and what that experience meant to you?" If the answer is "yes," then the patient is asked to review the memories and to indicate with a finger signal when he or she has completed the review. If the patient answers "No," this resistance should be explored.

2. If the patient reviews the material, upon the patient's finger signal, he or she is asked, "Are you afraid that you are going to die?" If the answer is "no," other themes are explored. If the answer is "yes," then this theme is explored, and the patient is told, "The danger and the threat to your life have passed. You have survived and your life is no longer threatened. We know this don't we?" The patient is asked to confirm this fact with an ideomotor signal. If the patient cannot, then the reasons are explored.

3. If the patient can confirm this, then the patient is asked: "Does the deepest part of your mind know that you did survive and that you are fully alive?" If the patient answers "no," then the reasons for that answer must be thoroughly explored. However, if the patient answers "yes," then the therapist may suggest: "Your pain and suffering have served a useful purpose—they let you know that you were alive, that you did not die.

Your pain and suffering helped you survive, and you did survive. You are alive. But now, that experience is all over. Do you know and really believe that it is all over?" Again, the therapist waits or an ideomotor answer. If the answer is "no," then further exploration is necessary to determine why the patient does not feel that the experience is over and safety is still an issue.

4. If the answer is "yes," then the therapist may move on and ask the patient: "Now that you know you are fully alive, that the experience is completely over and you survived, do you still need that constant pain to prove that you are fully alive?" A "no" response may lead the therapist to make the following point: "Since you don't need that constant pain anymore to prove that you are alive, and since you came here for help in getting rid of your pain, would it be all right with you to just let that pain go?

Ewin (1986, 1992) makes the point that often, there will be an understandable resistance to letting the pain go since the pain may have symbolically served as a psychological life support system up to that point. This may need to be acknowledged and the patient's reticence to give up his or her pain may need to be validated. At the same time, however, Ewin urges that the therapist also validate the patient's self-efficacy, especially if the pain increases as it often does. In that event, Ewin suggests that the therapist communicate to the patient the paradoxical idea that *it is wonderful that you have discovered how to take control of your pain as evidenced by your making it worse! This is an excellent sign because if you can make the pain worse, then you have control over it, and that means you can also make it better! Would you like to make it better now?*

5. If the patient signals "yes," then the patient may be asked to cut it down by a certain amount (e.g., *"Would you like to cut it in half?"*). The patient can be helped to progressively fractionate the pain.

6. Ewin (1986) also recommends that the therapist ask the following question: *"Would it be all right to have one minute of being completely free of pain, realizing it is better to be alive* without *pain than to be alive* with *pain?"* (p. 285). Then, if the patient can switch the pain off for one minute, it may be suggested that whenever he or she is ready, the patient will be able to turn the pain off for two minutes and then for progressively longer periods. However, if the patient signals "no" to either of the above questions, then further exploration of the psychological factors at play is indicated.

7. Other suggestions that are consistent with Ewin's approach to be delivered at the appropriate time include:

- "You no longer need all that pain and all that suffering to let you know that you are alive. You only need to have as much pain as is necessary to keep you informed about what you have to keep doing to recover from your injuries." This suggestion places the pain into a realistic perspective.

- "No pain need last forever." This suggestion dispels the negative idea held by many pain patients that their pain is permanent and that their suffering will be endless.
- "Perhaps you have suffered more than enough. It is time to let yourself off the hook. No person should serve as both his own judge and jury." This suggestion is intended to enhance the patient's motivation to issue himself or herself a pardon, and absolve himself or herself of guilt and self-blame.
- "Perhaps it is time to forgive *(insert name of the person or entity blamed for the patient's condition).* You are the one who is suffering and miserable, not they. Holding on to anger (or blame) only intensifies your suffering and pain. It is enough." This suggestion is intended to release destructive anger.

A Note about Memory Work

We live with our memories. Our memories help define how we perceive ourselves, what we believe, how we act, and therefore how others perceive us. Memory work, or the reworking of memories, often constitutes an important part of psychotherapy. A rational approach to memory work should not typically look for recovered memories to be accurate or true reflections (or images) of what in fact happened. Rather, memories are *reconstructions*, as opposed to being exact replicas of past reality. Human memory, by its very nature, contains distortions (Loftus, 1993; Pope & Brown, 1996; Schacter, 1996; Scheflin & Shapiro, 1989). Memories of pain and suffering, for example, are colored by contextual, affective, motivational, and cognitive factors (Thorn & Williams, 1993). Therefore, what is important for PMP therapists to address is not only whether or not events occurred, but the psychological significance of a patient's present memories.

Hypnoprojective Techniques

The strategies of age regression, emotional re-experiencing or revivification of past events, and reframing of the past are often facilitated with hypnoprojective techniques. These techniques utilize hypnosis and imagery to capture and portray a patient's inner representations of a targeted problem or problematic situation onto some imaginary medium such as a movie screen. These projected images can then be discussed, processed, and modified.

Age regression refers to the strategy of suggesting that the patient remember back to an earlier time just before pain became a persistent problem. Once old material is brought up, various things can be done with it. One option is to encourage the patient to reexperience the affect and emotions associated with events that occurred at that earlier time. This strategy may also be termed *emotional reliving* or *revivification*. The patient is then usually helped to change the inner scripts associated with these revivified past events. This strategy is called *rescripting* or *reprocessing*. Eye Movement Desensitization and Reprocessing (EMDR) is a reprocessing strategy for desensitizing excessive, negative emotional reactions associated with dysfunctional, pain-related beliefs.

The therapist using hypnotic memory recall, reconstruction, and reprocessing strategies might first suggest to the patient, "Imagine taking a trip back in time, back through the years to when you were without chronic pain." The patient might then be guided to focus on the desirable and adaptive aspects of life back then while it is suggested that positive feelings be brought back into the present. The therapist might also suggest that the hypnotized patient go back to a time just before the pain became a problem. Events and factors active then that could have made the patient vulnerable to becoming a chronic pain patient might then be explored. Disturbing memories brought up might be reframed to construct more livable psychological implications (see discussion below of David Cheek's work). With chronic benign pain, using *age progression*, the therapist might suggest, "Imagine a time in the future when you no longer have this pain problem." Prospective situations and events might then be mentally rehearsed so that potential trouble spots can be discussed and desensitized.

THE SPLIT-SCREEN TECHNIQUE

The *split-screen technique* is a projective imagery technique described by H. Spiegel and D. Spiegel (1978/1987) for the treatment of posttraumatic stress. It fits well within this class of memory recall and reconstruction strategies for resolving chronic pain issues. The patient is guided to visualize a movie or video screen divided into three panels. On the center panel, the patient views himself or herself in a particular problematic situation. As the patient views this panel, he or she is instructed to project all negative feelings onto the left panel. Conversely, all positive feelings and potential solutions to the problem are to be projected onto the right panel. Finally, when some resolution to the problem is felt, the panels are merged back into a single screenplay of the situation. The procedure is directed toward generating helpful insights for resolving the problem and coping with the problematic situation in the present and the future:

Case Example

An 84-year-old man with advanced prostate cancer was seen for a consultation at the request of his son. A urostomy had been performed several months earlier to seal off the man's cancer-ravaged bladder with the goal of stopping his hematuria and total urinary incontinence. Despite this procedure, the genito-urinary bleeding persisted along with marked bladder spasm and pain. Antispasmodics had no effect and the patient also had a bad reaction to an antidepressant. When first seen, the man was very depressed, had stopped eating, and said that he wanted to die. He was described by his wife and son as having been "a fighter all of his life." His current mental state was seen as understandable, but they wanted to know if anything psychological could be done to reverse his depression and lessen his suffering.

The patient was willing and cooperative. His primary goal was to be rid of the painful bladder spasm. No formal induction was employed. He was asked to visualize a three-paneled movie screen. He was then asked to project onto the center panel a picture of his bladder, prostate, and kidneys. As he watched this imaginary panel, the first thing he saw was "a bloody mess of cancer cells eating away inside my bladder." He was asked to project this image onto the left panel. What was left on the center panel was a picture of his father who had been killed in the Nazi Holocaust. He then remembered the last words his father had said to him before he as a young man had left his family to seek his fortune. His father's words were: "Life is hard, but suffering makes it harder. Do we need to add suffering to a life that is already so hard? Always remember: Only you can stop your own suffering. Nobody else can make you suffer or make you stop suffering. Not even your father or mother can do this for you. Only you can do this." After he related these moving words to the therapist, it was suggested that he project this image of his father and those words onto the right panel. On the center panel now was left a picture of a calm and quiescent bladder, a cancer-ridden prostate gland, and a pair of healthy kidneys.

The patient next was asked if he could imagine starving the cancer cells of their nutrient-rich blood flow. The therapist suggested: "Study the left panel. Visualize depriving those cancer cells of their nourishment. See if you can starve those cancer cells so that there is no blood supply feeding them. He stated that he imagined seeing little tourniquets being tightly tied around the blood vessels feeding into the bladder and prostrate gland. As he worked with this image for awhile, he reported visualizing the inner lining of the bladder beginning to lose its deep red color, and beginning to shrink. He was asked to project this image onto the right-hand panel.

The patient stated that he felt like something important had just happened, but that he was not sure what it was. He also felt a warm feeling in his bladder that seemed to mask or dampen the spasmodic pain. The therapist received a telephone call a few days later from the man's wife. She stated that she didn't know what the therapist had done, but her husband seemed much more at peace and that he certainly was in much less pain. She stated that he had slept more continuously and comfortably over the past few nights and that both of them were grateful to be able to get some sleep again.

AN IDEOMOTOR EXPLORATORY STRATEGY FOR ALLEVIATING PERSISTENT PAIN

Perhaps no other medical practitioner has been as tenacious and active in researching hypnotic strategies for treating chronic and persistent pain states than David Cheek (Cheek, 1965, 1994; Cheek & LeCron, 1968; Rossi & Cheek, 1988). As a practicing obstetrician-gynecologist, he pioneered the use of ideomotor techniques in the investigation of psychological factors underlying persistent pain states.

Ideomotor Responses

The term *ideomotor response* refers to the expression of thoughts in the form of an automatic, largely nonvolitional motor response. In a nonclinical context, agreement (yes) and disagreement (no) are often communicated nonverbally through implicitly understood head nods. In the clinical hypnotherapeutic context, explicit ideomotor finger signals are set up formally with the patient before exploring factors underlying the patient's presenting somatic complaints.

Finger signals for "yes," "no," and "I 'm not ready to know consciously yet" are established (Cheek, 1994; Rossi & Cheek, 1988). The therapist then facilitates the patient's inner exploration by asking about factors that could underlie the patient's symptomatic complaints. The patient uses the finger signals to answer the questions. The purpose of having the patient respond with ideomotor signals as opposed to giving exclusively verbal responses is to bypass conscious, verbal censorship. Ideomotor signals provide direct access to the patient's most immediate emotional responses and evaluations of emotionally loaded material. This material often underlies persistent somatic problems such as chronic pain (Cheek, 1994; Rossi, 1993). The patient should be seated and one hand or the other should be selected for the work. That hand and arm can rest palm down on the patient's lap, on an armrest, or the hand and forearm can be propped up on the elbow.

Establishing Ideomotor Finger Signals

Ideomotor finger signals are set up in the following way:

> The therapist says: "The innerpart of your mind frequently knows what you may not remember or even know consciously. So that you can easily answer yes, no, or otherwise, to tell me what your inner mind knows

and what you are experiencing, we are going to let your fingers do the talking." The therapist strokes the patient's fingers to promote the patient's sensory awareness, and says: "Just as with head nods, we will need one finger to signify yes, one to signify no, and one to signify, I'm not ready to know consciously yet. So, I'd like you to concentrate on that hand. Think the word *yes, yes, yes* repeatedly and wonder which finger your inner mind will select to signal yes. One of the fingers on that hand will soon lift or twitch as a sign that your inner mind has selected that finger to be your yes finger." The therapist waits until a finger lifts signifying that this will be the yes finger, and then says: "Very good. Now, think *no, no, no.* Another finger on that hand will soon lift or twitch as a sign that your inner mind has selected that finger to be your no finger." The therapist waits for a finger to lift, and then says: "Good. Now sometimes your inner mind is just not ready to let you know something consciously. So, concentrate on your fingers and just wonder which finger your inner mind will select to signal 'I'm not ready to know consciously yet.'" The therapist waits for a finger to lift, and then says: "Good. This then is your yes finger (Therapist strokes the designated 'yes' finger), this is your no finger (strokes designated 'no' finger), and this one is your I'm-not-ready-to-know-consciously-yet finger (strokes designated finger)."

This modality of communication is used to explore the emotional underpinnings of the presenting pain and somatic symptoms. As this ideomotor exploration proceeds, yes responses are always taken to the next deeper level. No responses are also explored and never ignored. I'm-not-ready-to-know-consciously-yet responses are interpreted as psychological resistance to further exploration of the material.

CHEEK AND ROSSI'S STRATEGY

Cheek and Rossi (Cheek, 1994; Rossi & Cheek, 1988) developed a systematic method of using ideomotor or "ideodynamic" exploration to uncover and then modify emotional factors associated with persistent pain states. The steps are as follows:

1. *Determining a patient's willingness to be helped.* First, using ideomotor signaling, the patient is asked whether or not he or she is willing to be helped with the presenting problem. Given a yes response, the patient next is asked using the finger signals, whether or not he or she is willing to explore how the pain initially started.

2. *Exploring the pain's origins.* For example, the clinician says to the patient: "I'd like you to go back in time to when you were well, right before

your pain became a problem. Your yes finger will lift to signal when you are there." The therapist waits for a finger signal, and then proceeds. "I'd like you to review what is happening (Note the use of the present tense) that is going to cause this pain to become a problem for you. This may be related to something somebody important to you will say or do; this may be related to the distress of another person; or this may be related to a bad experience of some kind that will imprint the notion that you will have to live with this pain. (Patient's name), please review what is happening and tell me if any of these things is going to be true for you and if any of these things is going to make your pain become a problem for you." The therapist waits for a signal, and then says to the patient: "(Name), please tell me what is happening."

3. *Orienting to the moment the pain began.* Next, the patient is directed to go forward to the first moment the pain was experienced. The clinician says: "(Name), please go forward to the first moment you begin to experience this pain. Are you awake or asleep at this time? Can you tell me (Name) what is happening that is making this pain so important to you, (Name)? Is it something somebody who is very important to you is saying or doing? Is it something that someone has already said? Is it something that you are thinking? Please review what is happening and then tell me what it is." This material is reviewed as deeply and as thoroughly as possible.

4. *Establishing the patient's expectancy about a cure.* After completing this review, the patient is asked: "(Name), now that you know all of this, do you believe that you and I can work together to: get you well, help you learn to manage this pain, reduce your suffering with this condition, or find a cure for your pain? (Therapist chooses which of these possibilities to ask.)

5. *Exploring potential obstacles to getting well.* Whether the patient's signaled answer is "yes" or "no," the clinician next orients the patient to the first moment when this judgment is made. The clinician asks: "(Name), Is there anything that I don't know that is getting in the way of your getting well? (Name), please tell me what it is." The therapist waits for an answer, and then says to the patient: "(Name), you can talk to me. Tell me what it is." This material is then thoroughly reviewed with the goal of working out a resolution so that a cure or solution to the problem is considered possible and extraordinarily painful symptoms are no longer psychologically necessary.

6. *Practicing turning the pain off unconsciously.* The patient is then instructed: "(Name), I'd like you to see if you can turn off *some* or *all* of that pain at an unconscious level. Let your 'yes' finger lift when you have accomplished this." The clinician watches the patient closely while waiting for an ideomotor response. The clinician then asks: "I

wonder if you can tell me when you know consciously that *some* or *all* of the pain is gone."

7. *Strengthening the patient's self-efficacy.* The patient's sense of control and self-efficacy over the pain are then strengthened. If the patient achieves some reported reduction in pain intensity, he or she is then asked: "(Name), I wonder whether you can turn the pain back on again. This time I'd like you to temporarily make it twice as strong as it was earlier. I want you to do this temporarily because it is often helpful to know how to turn up pain so that you can then turn it down or turn if off. Our bodies often are more easily convinced that we can control pain when we first see that we can turn pain up. You know, it's just like adjusting the volume control on a TV set. It's that easy.

8. *Assigning and rehearsing a cue-word or postinduction signal.* A postinduction signal for pain control is then established. The clinician says: (Name), it is often helpful to come up with a special word, thought, image, or signal that can turn down or turn off unnecessary pain. I wonder if you can come up with such a signal now. Tell me what it is if you like when you discover it." Next, the use of this pain-control cue is rehearsed several times. However, to avoid disappointment, the patient is told: "But, please try to avoid using this signal on your own until we know that it is going to be successful."

9. *Orienting to the future.* The patient is then asked to orient forward to a future time when he or she is free of pain, or is coping well. The patient is told that his or her "yes" finger will lift when he or she locks onto such a time. Also at that point, a date is obtained from the patient.

10. *Self-hypnosis instruction.* Lastly, the patient is trained in self-hypnosis, and suggestions for pain relief that include the postinduction pain-control cue are incorporated in the self-hypnosis exercise. It is important that the patient be taught how to induce total relaxation for a brief period (two to three minutes). The patient is told to induce self-hypnosis for two to three minutes, four times a day—before each meal, and at bedtime. As pointed out by Cheek (1994) and Rossi and Cheek (1988), if a time limit on the exercise is not set, many patients end up feeling that too much time is being wasted doing the exercises.

LECRON'S "SEVEN KEYS"

David Cheek and Leslie LeCron developed a model of seven "psychosomatic keys" to persistent pain complaints that have no identifiable physical cause (Cheek, 1994; Cheek & LeCron, 1968; LeCron, 1964). The PMP therapist sees many chronic pain cases that fit in this category or into the related category of pain complaints that are out of proportion to the objective physical findings. This model serves well in guiding an ideomotor exploration of the psychological factors associated with or underlying persistent pain states. The seven psychosomatic keys are Conflicts; Organ language; Motivational factors; Past experience; Associations and identifications with personally significant people; Self-punishment; and Self-suggestions, or imprints. For ease of identification, we have arranged these seven keys to spell the acronym, "COMPASS." We have also added three concepts: (a) Under Motivational factors, we have added Meaning, (b) under Self-punishment, we have added Self-blame, (c) under Self-suggestion/imprint we have added Self-talk.

We explain each of the seven keys in the following section and also provide examples of the questions we typically ask pain patients. In practice, we may not explore these seven keys in the order given here, but rely on clinical considerations and hypotheses in a given case. When there is little basis for hypothesizing which factors carry the most weight, we usually start with the "past experience" key.

THE SEVEN KEYS DEFINED

CONFLICTS

The term *Conflicts* refers to internal dissension where there are competing values, motivations, necessities, or demands within the patient as well as disagreements and disharmonies between the patient and other people or external agencies. The patient's persistent pain may provide an interim solution to this persistent internal conflict. To investigate this, the patient enters a state of hypnosis and is asked to respond to the following questions using ideomotor finger signals: "Using your fingers to answer, is your pain in some way related to a conflict that you have or a problem that you have making some sort of decision?" If the patient's "yes" finger lifts, the therapist should say: "Please tell me what this conflict is." If the patient indicates that he or she is not aware of what it is, the therapist should then suggest: "Just think of it and when something comes to mind, your 'yes' finger will lift."

When the patient's "yes" finger lifts, the patient is asked: "Please tell me what came up for you." In this way, the patient is helped to gradually uncover the conflict. In most cases, however, when a patient's "yes" finger indicates the existence of conflict or indecisiveness, the patient is able to say what the conflict is. If the patient's "no" finger lifts in response to the original conflict question, then the therapist should move on to another key.

ORGAN LANGUAGE

The term *Organ language* refers to the theory that negative emotional states can be converted into or expressed as physical symptoms (Cheek,

1994; Cheek & LeCron, 1968; LeCron, 1964; Rossi, 1993). Disgust can be converted into or expressed as upper gastrointestinal pain as in "swallowing it." Anger and rage can be expressed as lower gastrointestinal pain as in "being all eaten up inside" or "stomaching it." Fear can be expressed as back pain and stiffness as in "I'm being held back" and "being rigid and unbending." To investigate this, the patient in a state of hypnosis, can be asked to respond to the following questions with the ideomotor finger signals: "Is your pain symbolic or representative of something else? In other words, is the pain in some way a physical expression of an underlying situation that can also be expressed as a figure of speech such as: it bugs you, you're being held back, you're being eaten up inside, you can't stomach something, it's a real headache, and so forth?" If the patient's "yes" finger lifts, the therapist should say: "Tell me what the pain represents." The therapist should then say: "Tell me how you feel about this," and the issue should be explored. If the "no" finger lifts, the therapist should move on to another key factor.

MEANING AND MOTIVATIONAL FACTORS

Meaning refers to the pain patient's personal interpretation of the significance of the pain sensations. To assess this, the patient is asked the following questions: "What do you make of it when your pain gets worse? What does it mean to you when your pain flares up? What do you think about? What do you usually attribute a pain flare-up to?"

In a hypnotic state, the patient is then asked to respond to the following questions with ideomotor finger signals: "Can you recall the last time your pain flared up and you thought about it like this?" Given a "yes" response, the patient is asked if it would be all right to return to that incident now. If the patient answers "yes" again, then he or she is assisted in recalling the incident in as much detail as is possible. The patient is told: "Please return to that incident as if it is happening now. I will make sure that you remain safe and that nothing happens to you." When the patient indicates by lifting a "yes" finger that he or she has regressed back to the incident, he or she is asked: "Now, please tell me everything that is happening." The incident is then processed.

The therapist also may ask, "Tell me what is going through your mind in relation to this situation. Tell me what you are telling yourself. Tell me what you are thinking about. Is there something that you are afraid of? Tell me what it is. Are you afraid that this flare-up means that you are going to get worse? Are you afraid that this flare-up means that you are not going to get better? Are you holding yourself to blame for this pain flare-up? Do you feel that you caused it in some way? Do you feel that you caused it by doing something that you should not have done? Do you feel that you caused it by not doing something that you should have done? Is there another less upsetting way to think about this flare-up? How would you prefer to think about this situation that will help you cope with it better? Run through this situation again holding this new thought in mind. Then tell me what your experience is. How does it feel now?" The material that comes up is explored and processed.

Given a "no" response (that the patient cannot recall the last time the pain flared up and he or she thought about it like this), the patient is asked if it would be okay to imagine the pain flaring up and thinking about it in the aforementioned negative way. The explanation is given that this is an exercise that will help to inoculate the patient against such an eventuality. If the patient agrees, then the clinician assists the patient in imagining such an incident in as much detail as possible. The material that comes up is then explored and processed.

The term *Motivational factors* refers to the underlying reasons for the way the patient chooses to cope with pain. This concept assumes that the patient makes a choice (which may or may not be a conscious choice). Motivational factors also include the secondary benefits (gains) of complaining about pain. To investigate these possibilities, the patient is asked to respond to the following questions with ideomotor finger signals: "Is your pain in some way a chance for you to get some benefits that you would not otherwise get without your pain? If the "yes" finger lifts, the patient should be asked: "Please tell me what these benefits are." The issues that come up should then be explored.

If the "no" finger lifts, or the "yes" finger lifts but the patient cannot say what the benefits are, then the following question is asked: "Is there any good reason for you to continue to cope with your pain in the exact way that you have been coping with it without making any changes?" If the answer is "yes," ask the patient: "What is the reason?" If the answer is "no," ask: Then, is there any good reason why you cannot learn to handle the pain in a different and perhaps healthier way?" The therapist continues to process with the patient the material that comes up.

PAST EXPERIENCE

The term *Past experience* refers to earlier events that might have laid the foundation or wellsprings for the development of the patient's persistent pain complaints. It also refers to past events that were proximate in time and possibly associated psychologically with the pain's onset and development. To investigate this possibility, the patient is asked: "Is your pain in some way related to a past experience of any kind? or Is there an upsetting past experience associated with the pain?"

If the answer is "yes," the patient is asked a series of questions to determine how old he or she was when this experience occurred. For example:

"Did this experience happen before you were 20 years old? Before you were 16 years old? Between the ages of 17 and 19?" Then, questions are asked to identify the type of experience it was. For example: "Was it an accident? Was it related to an illness? Did it happen inside or outside? Was anyone else around? Were you hurt? Was anyone else hurt?"

Next, the patient is asked if it would be all right to return to that incident now. If "yes," the patient is helped to recall the incident in as much detail as is possible. The patient is told: "Please return to that incident as if it were happening now. I will make sure that you remain safe and that nothing happens to you." When the patient indicates by lifting a "yes" finger that he or she has regressed back to the incident, he or she is asked: "Now, please tell me everything that is happening." The incident is then processed.

Other questions that are asked include: "Does this incident have something to do with your present pain?" If the answer is "yes," then the therapist should say: "There is a reason for this. When a thought comes to you about what the connection is, you will tell me what it is." The material that comes up is further explored and processed.

If the answer is "no," that the pain is not associated with some past experience, then the therapist should move on to investigating another key.

ASSOCIATIONS AND IDENTIFICATIONS

Associations and identifications refer to a perceived connection with a personally significant figure from the past or present who suffered from a similar problem. To investigate this possibility the patient is asked to respond to the following questions with ideomotor finger signals: "Is there anyone else that you know or are close to who suffered in a similar way?" If the answer is "yes," the therapist asks: "Tell me who this person is." The therapist next asks: "Is there a connection between your suffering and this person's suffering?" If the answer is "yes," this connection is processed. The therapist may say something like: "There is a reason for this. A thought will now come to you as to what the connection is." The material that comes up is then further processed. The therapist moves on to another key if the patient initially answers "no," he or she does not know anyone who similarly suffered, or indicates that there is no connection between his or her pain and that other person's suffering.

SELF-BLAME AND SELF-PUNISHMENT

Self-blame refers to the idea of blaming oneself or holding oneself responsible for having a chronic pain syndrome. It implies the notion of guilt, which means that the individual believes that he or she made a choice to think or act in a way that transgressed some rule. As a consequence of this implied transgression, the condition developed. The patient may feel guilty about not having done something that "should" have been done or about having done something that "should not" have been done. Typically the notion of guilt is connected to the belief that punishment is deserved.

These ideas of self-blame, guilt, and being deserving of punishment also imply that the patient is serving as both his or her own judge and jury. That is, the patient has found himself or herself guilty of some crime and in addition has set the sentence—a particular punishment, such as continuing to suffer in pain. To investigate these possibilities, the patient can be asked: "Do you blame yourself when your pain gets worse?" "Do you tend to blame yourself for not getting better?" "Do you feel guilty about something?" "Is your pain somehow connected to a punishment you have sentenced yourself to endure?" "Have you judged yourself guilty of some misdoing that is deserving of such punishment?" "Are you perhaps serving as both your own judge and jury?" "Have you also sentenced yourself to be punished for some crime or wrongdoing you feel you have committed?"

"Yes" answers to any of these questions with the ideomotor finger signals are followed up with further inquiries about the circumstances under which such imagined transgressions occurred and so forth. This material is then processed with the goal of reframing the imagined blameworthy actions or transgressions in ways that can be seen as more innocent and not deserving of retribution.

SELF-SUGGESTION, IMPRINTS, AND SELF-TALK

The last key is termed *Self-suggestion,* or *self-talk.* Cheek and LeCron (1968) used the term *imprint* to refer to the same concept. The concept is that sometimes chronic pain partially results from the continuing influence of strong beliefs formed earlier in the patient's life when he or she was receptive and suggestible. To investigate this possibility, the patient can be asked the following questions: "Did you ever hear anyone say that you had better learn to live with this pain?" If the answer is "yes," then the when, who, what, and where of the circumstances in which this was first heard are explored. The material is reprocessed to reframe and dislodge the implications and corollaries of this belief. Such implications often include the corollary beliefs, "without pain I will die," and "I cannot live without this pain" (Ewin, 1986, 1992). If the answer is "no," then the therapist should move on to the question: "What do you usually tell yourself when your pain gets bad?" The beliefs underlying these self-statements are then pursued and the circumstances under which these beliefs were acquired are recalled and processed. Questions that assist such exploration and reprocessing include: "Is this somehow related to something that you heard somebody else say?" and "When did you first start to believe this? Do you recall the situation that gave rise to this belief? Please remember it now."

RATIONALE AND PROCEDURAL ISSUES

Ideomotor questioning guided by the seven keys can promote insight into the psychological and emotional underpinnings of persistent pain states. Usually, it also brings up affectively loaded material that needs to be worked through, desensitized, and reprocessed. The process can often induce a light-to-medium hypnotic state without any formal induction, if the patient is receptive. However, this is not always the case. Therefore, it is generally advisable to induce a relaxing state of hypnosis before proceeding so that the patient is more relaxed, at ease, and receptive. Then, ideomotor finger signals are set up as described earlier.

Before the clinician begins the exploration, he or she should ask the patient the following question: *"(Patient name), is it all right for you to know what psychological factors are underlying your pain?"* If the patient answers "yes," the clinician/therapist can begin the exploration with the seven keys. However, if the answer is "no," then the patient may not feel ready to face, process, or talk about his or her underlying issues. In that case, the following questions may be asked via ideomotor finger signaling: *"If we can carefully step around the roadblock to knowing what psychological factors are underlying your pain, would you be willing to proceed? This barrier has a reason for being. I wish to show no disrespect for it. So, could we possibly go around this barrier, and then return to it at some later time, if it is needed?"* This line of ideomotor questioning may defuse the patient's initial resistance to proceeding.

If we are ready to proceed with ideomotor exploration and processing, we typically begin investigating the past experience key first.

CHAPTER 10

Inducing Hypnosis and Assessing Hypnotic Ability and Responsiveness

There is no so wretched and coarse a soul wherein some particular
faculty is not seen to shine.

Montaigne

MOST OF the hypnotic strategies described earlier can be applied without a formal induction. In fact, Cheek (1994) expresses the view that individuals enter a hypnotic state naturally when they focus their attention on remembering the temporal sequence of behaviors, emotions, sensations, images, and cognitions associated with a personally significant past event. However, a formal induction, as long as it is relatively brief, has several uses. First, it tests the patient's hypnotic ability and responsiveness to hypnotic strategies and suggestions for pain relief. Second, for patients with even low-to-moderate hypnotizability, a brief formal induction sets the stage for the hypnotic strategies previously described by encouraging a receptive frame of mind. Third, a formal induction introduces a ceremonial aspect to the clinical pain management situation (H. Spiegel & D. Spiegel, 1978/1987). This is important because it separates hypnotic strategies from other aspects of the clinical interaction with the patient. Rituals and ceremonies play an important healing role in most cultures.

DEFINING HYPNOTIC RESPONSIVENESS
AND HYPNOTIZABILITY

People vary in their responsiveness to hypnotic interventions. In turn, their hypnotic responsiveness will affect how much they are likely to benefit from the use of hypnosis for pain management. Some patients cannot be trained to use self-hypnosis for pain relief. Others may benefit minimally, and still others may benefit significantly. To be most therapeutically effective, the methods of hypnosis employed and the self-hypnosis exercises created for a patient should match the patient's type and level of motivation, relevant beliefs, and individual Hypnotic Ability and Response Profile (HARP). A person's Hypnotic Ability and Response Profile, which we use synonymously with the term *hypnotizability* refers to a person's hypnotic potential or aptitude, as reflected in his or her assessed level of subjective, physiological, and physical responsiveness to hypnotic suggestions.

THE SPIEGEL HYPNOTIC
INDUCTION PROFILE

H. Spiegel and D. Spiegel (1978/1987) developed a portable and clinically practical method for assessing a patient's hypnotizability, or Hypnotic Ability and Response Profile, which they labeled the "Hypnotic Induction Profile" (HIP). The HIP is brief to administer (7 to 10 minutes for the experienced clinician), and yields a wealth of clinical data on a patient's responsiveness to an actual hypnotic induction. The HIP is a trial treatment and diagnostic procedure that provides the clinician and patient with the opportunity to observe how the patient responds to an actual hypnotic induction and the teaching of a simple self-hypnosis method. A structured occasion is created for the patient to enter, experience, and exit a therapeutic trance.

Despite the brevity, elegance, rich theoretical foundation, and clinical promise of the HIP, frequently it is not a clinically revealing procedure with pain patients. According to H. Spiegel and D. Spiegel (1978/1987; H. Spiegel, personal communication, 1996), the HIP has to be administered quickly for the hypnotic interaction to flow continuously and smoothly in building up momentum. This necessitates adopting a rather authoritarian, directive, businesslike manner that can alienate many patients. In addition, many pain patients get "left behind" if the clinician moves too fast with the hypnotizability assessment procedure. In fact, the HIP, administered as recommended by its authors, does not pace many patients adequately and thus fails to construct a collaborative therapeutic context.

We find it counterproductive to move too fast in an induction, and authoritarian procedures seldom work well with pain patients. Because the Spiegels' HIP, administered as recommended by its authors, does not adequately pace the patient and often fails to build good rapport, a more permissive procedure is needed to assess some of the hypnotic phenomena measured by the HIP, as well as other important hypnotic phenomena. Like the HIP, the procedure should induce hypnosis and produce a clinically valid picture, or profile, of the patient's hypnotic abilities and responsiveness.

THE HYPNOTIC ABILITY AND RESPONSE PROFILE (HARP)

To this end, we have developed the *Hypnotic Ability and Response Profile*, (HARP; Eimer & Oster, 1996), partially inspired by the theoretically rich, pioneering work of H. Spiegel and D. Spiegel (1978/1987). The HARP has been designed to be more permissive than the HIP, to be easier to administer and score, to assess additional hypnotic phenomena, and to be more comprehensive. Also, in situations where the entire HARP cannot be given, portions of it can be administered. In contrast, the HIP must be given in its entirety. When only portions of the HARP are administered, a useful picture of the patient's hypnotic abilities and responsiveness can still be obtained. The HARP does take more time to administer than does the HIP (anywhere from approximately 25 to 35 minutes for the HARP as compared 7 to 10 minutes for the HIP).

Like the HIP, the HARP samples the entire process of entering, experiencing, and exiting a hypnotic state. The HARP was designed to be interactive and behaviorally oriented, and to be useful in assessing pain patients' hypnotic abilities and responsiveness, and motivating them to learn psychological pain coping strategies. The HARP provides data about how a clinician can hypno-behaviorally work with a patient by testing a patient's ability to (a) follow instructions, (b) participate in a collaborative relationship with the clinician on the shared task of induction, (c) focus, sustain, and redirect attention, (d) concentrate effortlessly, (e) let go and relax, (f) exercise imagination, (g) respond to acceptable suggestions, and (h) experience subtle sensory-perceptual and sensory-motor alterations. These factors compose the essence of hypnosis, and are all directly relevant to PMP.

The HARP, which is an instrument in development, is presented step by step in its entirety in this chapter. We also present preliminary validation data on the HARP's psychometric properties based on a pilot study with 17 participants. Although the HARP is a new clinical procedure, portions of it, such as the "eye-roll sign," and "signaled arm levitation," were inspired by Herbert and David Spiegel's (1978/1987) Hypnotic Induction Profile (HIP).*

Before describing the HARP, it is necessary to stress that clinical hypnosis is much more than the skillful implementation of techniques. Among other things, it is a therapeutic relationship. For the hypnotic ceremony to be effective, both parties to it need to be comfortable and secure in their relationship. A patient with excellent hypnotic capacity may be responsive with one clinician and unresponsive with another. Therefore, what we are measuring in effect is more than pure hypnotic capacity: We are measuring the extent to which a patient's hypnotic potential is realized in the context of a particular relationship.

ASSESSING BELIEFS ABOUT HYPNOSIS AND ORIENTING THE PATIENT TO HYPNOSIS

Hypnosis is not for everyone just as there is no therapy that is appropriate for everyone. It is the clinician's job to assess the patient to determine the modalities that are fitting. We should not force the patient to fit the treatment. The treatment must fit the patient. When patients present with negative beliefs about hypnosis, it may not be appropriate to proceed with hypnosis. For some patients, hypnosis flies in the face of their religious beliefs.

The nice thing about using hypnosis for pain management is that it is relatively risk-free. It is physically noninvasive. The only risks are psychological. The most common iatrogenic negative psychological effects are for a patient to have second thoughts or increased anxiety due to misconceptions about hypnosis or unspoken objections. If a patient construes being hypnotized as a sign of mental or moral weakness, then he or she is likely to resist some or all of the therapist's hypnotic suggestions. Similarly, a patient who fears losing control if hypnotized is likely to resist the therapist's suggestions. When such patients do experience hypnotic phenomena, they are likely to feel apprehensive and anxious. It is therefore important to assess a patient's beliefs about hypnosis before proceeding. Discussing these preconceived ideas and clarifying misconceptions can reduce resistance and strengthen compliance.

Before formally assessing a patient's hypnotizability, it is often helpful to enable the patient to communicate his or her beliefs and expectations

---

Note. Portions of the HARP were adapted with permission from the Hypnotic Induction Profile (HIP) appearing in *Trance and Treatment: Clinical Uses of Hypnosis,* by Herbert Spiegel and David Spiegel. Excerpts from HIP/Table 10-1A/Text Excerpts from *Trance and Treatment* by Herbert Spiegel, M.D. and David Spiegel, M.D. Copyright © 1978 by Herbert Spiegel, M.D. and David Spiegel, M.D. Reprinted by permission of BasicBooks, a division of HarperCollins Publishers, Inc.

about hypnosis through some form of checklist. For this purpose, we have developed the *Hypnosis Beliefs Questionnaire (HBQ)*, which follows and expands on earlier work by Heller (1996). It is displayed in Table 10.1. The HBQ surveys the patient's degree of agreement with 32 belief statements about hypnosis. This brief survey is administered to the patient and then reviewed by the clinician prior to utilizing hypnosis. It is then discussed briefly with the patient. If the patient's responses indicate serious misconceptions, unrealistic expectations, apprehensions, religious contraindications, reservations, or philosophical disagreements that cannot be corrected through informed educative discussion, then we do not proceed with hypnosis.

Items 1, 2, 3, 4, 5, 7, 15, and 22 on the HBQ represent belief statements associated with favorable responses to hypnosis. Items 23 through 32 represent self-evaluation statements regarding personal traits, abilities, behaviors, values, and preferences that may be associated with favorable responses to hypnosis (Bates, 1993; Coe, 1993; Tellegen & Atkinson, 1974). Items 6, 8 through 14, and 16 through 21 represent belief statements that may be associated with unfavorable responses to hypnosis. Summed scores can be calculated for each of these 3 sets of items. High scores for the first 2 sets of HBQ items suggest that a patient's beliefs and expectations may be favorable for proceeding with hypnotic methods of treatment. However, high scores on the third set of items suggest that a patient's beliefs and expectations are likely to be problematic from the standpoint of employing hypnosis. The highly rated items in this third set should be discussed thoroughly before proceeding to use hypnosis.

Before proceeding with the HARP or any other induction for the first time, we make sure that the patient understands that hypnosis involves a collaborative relationship between the therapist and patient. We emphasize that to attain the maximum therapeutic benefit from hypnosis, the patient needs to accept the ideas and imagine the things suggested by the therapist. We also discuss the importance of paying attention in a relaxed, effortless way and staying awake because hypnosis is not sleep.

If proceeding with hypnosis is indicated, then we typically explain what hypnosis is and what it is not. We briefly define hypnosis in terms understandable to the patient. We point out that (a) hypnosis is not sleep, and (b) that it also is not about one person exerting authoritarian control over another. We make sure to dispel the myth that persons can be hypnotized so deeply that they may not be able to come back out of hypnosis. We emphasize that to the contrary, hypnosis is about increasing one's self-control and ability to self-regulate one's experience and reactions to aversive events such as pain.

We usually state that all hypnosis is self-hypnosis and that the therapist/hypnotist is really a guide and facilitator. We point out that people vary in their hypnotic ability and responsiveness but that most people

Table 10.1

Hypnosis Beliefs Questionnaire

Rate how much you agree with each statement below by circling a number on the following rating scale:

0–totally disagree   1–strongly disagree   2–mildly disagree   3–neutral
4–mildly agree   5–strongly agree   6–totally agree

Beliefs about Hypnosis	Rate Agreement
1. I will be a good hypnotic subject.	0 1 2 3 4 5 6
2. I am very suggestible.	0 1 2 3 4 5 6
3. Hypnosis will benefit me.	0 1 2 3 4 5 6
4. I have an excellent imagination.	0 1 2 3 4 5 6
5. I can pay attention and concentrate well.	0 1 2 3 4 5 6
6. Hypnosis is similar to sleep.	0 1 2 3 4 5 6
7. Anyone can be hypnotized as long as they don't resist.	0 1 2 3 4 5 6
8. I am afraid of losing control if I let myself be hypnotized.	0 1 2 3 4 5 6
9. I am too strong-willed to let myself be hypnotized.	0 1 2 3 4 5 6
10. I am afraid to let myself be hypnotized.	0 1 2 3 4 5 6
11. I'm afraid that I will do something stupid if I let myself be hypnotized.	0 1 2 3 4 5 6
12. I won't be able to relax enough to let myself be hypnotized.	0 1 2 3 4 5 6
13. I am afraid of going crazy if I let myself be hypnotized.	0 1 2 3 4 5 6
14. I am afraid of getting stuck in hypnosis.	0 1 2 3 4 5 6
15. I want to learn how to use self-hypnosis.	0 1 2 3 4 5 6
16. It is hard for me to trust other people.	0 1 2 3 4 5 6
17. I really don't expect hypnosis to work for me.	0 1 2 3 4 5 6
18. I will need to be hypnotized very deeply to attain my goals.	0 1 2 3 4 5 6
19. Only weak-minded people can be hypnotized.	0 1 2 3 4 5 6
20. Letting myself be hypnotized would be against my religion.	0 1 2 3 4 5 6
21. Submitting to hypnosis is a sign of moral weakness.	0 1 2 3 4 5 6
22. Hypnotic ability can be increased through training.	0 1 2 3 4 5 6
23. I can become so absorbed in an activity that I'll lose awareness of my surroundings.	0 1 2 3 4 5 6
24. I can recall some experiences so vividly that it almost feels as if I am there.	0 1 2 3 4 5 6
25. I am a very sensitive person.	0 1 2 3 4 5 6
26. I am an introverted person.	0 1 2 3 4 5 6
27. I often place greater value on how I feel about things than on thinking things through logically.	0 1 2 3 4 5 6
28. I can be very happy left to myself for hours with a good book.	0 1 2 3 4 5 6
29. As a child, I spent hours at a time playing by myself with my toys or daydreaming.	0 1 2 3 4 5 6
30. I am artistic.	0 1 2 3 4 5 6
31. I generally prefer to spend time by myself than in a group with other people.	0 1 2 3 4 5 6
32. I love to watch movies.	0 1 2 3 4 5 6

Note. Some of the items on this questionnaire were adapted with permission from the Hypnosis Belief Survey. Copyright © 1994 Robert F. Heller, Ed.D.

who are positively motivated can be hypnotized and can learn self-hypnosis. We explain that it is a myth that gullible people are most easily hypnotized. In contrast, hypnotic ability is correlated with the ability to pay attention and think flexibly. We also state that a person does not have to be in a deep trance to reach therapeutic goals and that those who benefit most from hypnosis are people with strong motivation. We make clear that the patient will always retain the ability to accept suggestions and images that fit and reject or ignore those that do not. We are careful to inform the patient that the hypnotic induction procedure we wish to use (i.e., the HARP) will require some touching and stroking of the patient's hands and arms. Some patients are uncomfortable with being touched. If this is the case, then we have to consider an alternative hypnotic induction procedure.

Assessing Hypnotizability with the HARP

As the reader studies the following step-by-step instructions for administering and scoring the HARP, he or she should refer to Appendix X, which presents the complete step-by-step HARP administration script in the form of a clinical recording/scoring booklet. Note that portions of the HARP are adapted with permission from Herbert and David Spiegel's Hypnotic Induction Profile appearing in *Trance and Treatment: Clinical Uses of Hypnosis* (copyright, 1978, HarperCollins Publishers). As with all the instruments included in the Appendixes, the reader has permission to photocopy the HARP scoring booklet for his or her personal clinical use. The HARP should be administered verbatim from this script and the patient's responses should be recorded and scored in the booklet. The clinician begins by filling out the demographic section of the HARP Test Battery Data Summary cover page.

Administration and Scoring of the HARP

Step 1: Positioning and Preparation of the Patient

The first step in the HARP is to make sure that the patient is favorably positioned for the procedure. The patient should be comfortably seated in a chair that has armrests. The chair's armrests should be wide enough to provide adequate support for the entire arm. A comfortable but firm reclining chair is best. The patient may be seated upright or in a reclining position. We allow the patient to choose. Both arms should be resting on the armrests. The clinician should be seated at the patient's *left* side. The clinician should then verbalize the script for Step 1 given in Appendix X.

Step 2: Administering the Hand-Clasp Test

Following H. Spiegel and D. Spiegel (1978/1987, p. 127), before beginning the formal assessment of the patient's hypnotizability with the HARP, we administer the "hand-clasp test." We first determine the patient's handedness by asking which hand he or she uses to write and to hammer a nail, eat with a spoon, carry a suitcase, and swing a tennis racket or baseball bat. We also ascertain whether the patient's handedness was switched as a child. If the patient's handedness was switched as a child, we consider the patient's true handedness to be that which existed before it was retrained or switched. If the patient is left-handed, we do not proceed with the hand-clasp test.

For a right-handed dominant patient, we next ask the patient to clasp his or her hands together in front of his or her chest, interlocking the fingers, with one thumb on top of the other. We then note which thumb is spontaneously positioned on top of the other thumb. The thumb positioned on top is considered the dominant or "top thumb." The Spiegels' (1978/1987) clinical research suggests that for right-handed dominant people, crossed thumb dominance on the hand-clasp test (i.e., the left thumb positioned on top of the right thumb) often is associated with greater hypnotic ability and responsiveness.

The Spiegels' interpretive neuropsychological explanation of this phenomenon is that right-handed people who show crossed or left-thumb dominance may have an innate preference for right hemispheric activation or cerebral functioning. Because hypnosis is thought to involve stimulation of the brain's right cerebral hemisphere and an inhibition on some level of the brain's left hemisphere, the Spiegels postulate that this phenomenon may signify greater hypnotic capacity. This phenomenon is limited to "right-handers." However, there is some limited clinical evidence from our own work that left-handers also have an innate preference for right hemispheric activation and functioning which may be associated with greater hypnotizability.

Step 3: The Eye-Roll Sign. Entering Hypnosis

The third step in the HARP procedure is to assess the patient's *eye-roll*. The eye-roll sign is thought to provide a measure of the patient's natural or biological hypnotic capacity (H. Spiegel & D. Spiegel, 1978/1987, pp. 335–355). It indexes how much white remains below the eyeballs when a person rolls his or her eyes up as far as possible and simultaneously closes the eyelids. The amount of white remaining visible when a person rolls up the eyes in an up-gaze or while closing the eyelids is commonly associated in implicit psychology with how momentarily entranced a person is. For example, people are seen to gaze up or roll up their eyes in momentary dismay, ecstasy, shock, disorientation, and so forth. Our procedure makes sense and is easy to do.

Instructions. The clinician verbalizes to the patient the script for Step 3 provided in Appendix X.

Scoring.   As the patient complies with these directives, the clinician notes how much white or sclera remains visible between the lower eyelid and the lower border of the iris. A score of 0, 1, 2, 3, or 4 is assigned with 0 representing no sclera and 4 representing maximum sclera. The greater the observed eye-roll and the larger the numerical score assigned, the greater inherent potential capacity for experiencing hypnosis the patient is inferred to have. A score of 0 is coded when there is no sclera (white) visible. A score of 1 is assigned when a very little sclera remains visible. A score of 2 is coded when the sclera showing goes up to about the imaginary horizontal midline of the eyes. A score of 3 is coded when the sclera rises somewhat above the midline of the eyes. Finally, a score of 4 is coded when the visible sclera rises far above the midline and the iris disappears up and into the upper eyelid. The line-drawn eye diagrams in Figure 10.1 illustrate each eye-roll score.

At this point, the clinician has one measure of the patient's natural, biological capacity or potential to experience trance. The greater the numerical score, the greater the potential. Following the administration of

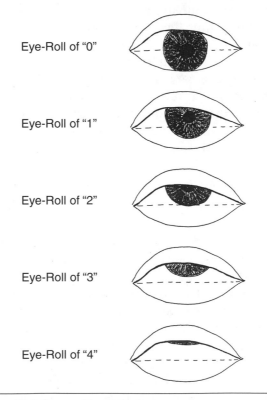

Eye-Roll of "0"

Eye-Roll of "1"

Eye-Roll of "2"

Eye-Roll of "3"

Eye-Roll of "4"

Figure 10.1   Eye-Roll Scores Illustrated

this assessment and hypnosis "entry" measure, a series of interactive tests and exercises are administered for assessing the patient's hypnotic responsiveness.

An Alternative Hypnotic Entry Procedure for Patients Who Lack Intact Ocular-Motor Ability

If a patient does not have intact ocular-motor ability and mobility, it is impossible to use the eye-roll index, and the clinician must select a different entry procedure. One alternative is simply to instruct the patient to close his or her eyes and focus all of his or her attention on the eyes. Then suggestions are delivered for eye catalepsy and relaxation. Suggestions for eye closure and relaxing the eyes leading to eye fatigue or catalepsy can provide a simple, effective, and quick hypnosis entry procedure (Edmonston, 1986; Schafer, 1996).

> Close your eyes, and just rest back and relax. Now, take a deep breath and hold it. Hold. That's right, Now, breathe out all the way, and allow your eyes to completely relax. Let your eyelids remain closed and concentrate all of your attention on your eyes. Concentrate on relaxing your eyes, more so, and more so. Allow yourself to experience your eyes as so relaxed that they just want to remain closed, because they just do not feel like opening. When you feel that your eyes are so relaxed that they just want to remain closed because they just do not feel like opening, spread that deep relaxation over your entire body, and allow your body to experience a pleasant floating sensation.

The next two steps involve the administration of suggestions for furthering or deepening the patient's experience of floating sensations and relaxation. In Steps 4 and 5, the clinician also tests the patient's ability to produce a suggested ideomotor response in the form of a finger signal.

Step 4: Give Suggestions for Relaxation and Floating

The clinician verbalizes the script for Step 4 and performs the procedure described.

Scoring. The clinician should assign a score of 1 if the index finger lifts. If the index finger does not lift, a score of 0 should be assigned and marked on the HARP script and scoring sheet.

Step 5: Deepen the Relaxation through Counting

The clinician then verbalizes the script for Step 5 to help the patient deepen the relaxed feelings and performs the procedure described.

Scoring. The clinician should assign a score of 1 if the index finger lifts. If the index finger does not lift, a score of 0 should be assigned and marked on the HARP script and scoring sheet.

Step 6: Induce Arm Levitation

The clinician verbalizes suggestions for arm levitation. *Arm levitation* is defined as "the experience of the targeted arm involuntarily lifting or floating up, in response to a cue, specified in an earlier verbal suggestion."

Clinical Significance.   This step tests the patient's ability to respond to a suggested sensory-perceptual alteration (arm lightness and floating) and suggested sensory-motor phenomenon (arm levitation). If the patient does not have intact use of either of his or her arms, this item in the HARP naturally cannot be administered. Performing this step, however, provides a valuable experience directly relevant to pain management because the patient discovers his or her own responsiveness to therapeutic suggestion and undergoes an alteration in his or her usual perceptions of voluntary control. Given an adequate rationale and debriefing about this experience, a pain patient can be helped to see that it is possible to shift attention in such a way as to effect a real change in physiology. This can be a valuable lesson in socializing a patient to psychological methods of pain management. The clinician verbalizes the script and follows the procedure for Step 6.

On the word *ready* the clinician should stroke the patient's left middle finger with his or her index and middle fingers. The clinician should stroke the back of the patient's left hand and arm in one continuous motion from the middle finger all the way up to the elbow and then wait and observe the patient's response.

Scoring.   Scoring of the patient's arm levitation response is based on the number of reinforcements needed to induce the patient's left arm to lift up. The scores range from a 4 which is coded if the arm levitation happens right away without any reinforcements, down to a 0, which is coded if the upward movement of the arm just does not happen at all. In this instance, the patient is instructed "Let's just put it up there like this."

First Reinforcement.   If within 5 to 10 seconds after stroking the patient's hand and arm, nothing happens, a score of 4 cannot be assigned, and the clinician should give the first reinforcement. This reinforcement is both tactile and verbal. The tactile part is accomplished by encircling the patient's wrist subtly and giving the left arm a gentle boost to prompt the suggested arm levitation. Then, the verbal prompt (first reinforcement) is delivered. If the arm levitates all the way up, the clinician should assign a levitation score of 3.

Second Reinforcement.   If within 5 to 10 seconds after administering the first reinforcement, nothing happens, the clinician should give the second reinforcement. If the left arm now levitates all the way up, the clinician should assign an arm levitation score of 2.

Third Reinforcement.   If after 10 seconds, the patient's left arm still has not lifted into a fully upright position, bent at the elbow, the clinician should give the third reinforcement. Again, the clinician provides another tactile prompt by subtly encircling the patient's left wrist and giving the arm a small boost. If the left arm now levitates all the way up, the clinician should assign an arm levitation score of 1.

Fourth Reinforcement. If a fourth reinforcement is required after 10 seconds to get the arm all the way up, then a score of 0 is assigned. The clinician should manually place the patient's arm into an upright position and state:

Let's just put it up there like this.

Step 7: Test the Lightness-Heaviness of the Left Arm While Positioning It and Administer a Postinduction Suggestion for Signaled Levitation

The clinician should now manually position the patient's left arm in an upright position, bent at the elbow with the left hand flexed loosely forward, and verbalize the script for Step 7.

Scoring. The clinician scores this item by evaluating whether the patient's arm is *light* and *loose* or relatively *heavy* and *resistant.* If the arm and hand are light and loose, score a 1. If the arm is relatively heavy and resistant, score a 0 for this item. A light and loose arm indicates a relaxed patient who is responsive to this part of the HARP. Conversely, a heavy and resistant arm can be indicative of a lack of cooperation and responsiveness, negativism and oppositionality to the procedure, anxiety, or some other source of resistance to cooperating fully and responding to the clinician's suggestions.

Step 8: Administer a Postinduction Suggestion for Restoring Normal Bodily Sensations

At this print, it is necessary to give the patient a future signal for restoring normal sensations later—after the completion of the formal induction ceremony and hypnotic exercises. The clinician verbalizes a postinduction restoration suggestion which, at later points in the HARP is repeated twice.

Step 9: Administer Postinduction Suggestions for Self-Hypnosis

The clinician instructs the patient on three simple steps for practicing self-hypnosis in the future.

Step 10: Countdown to End The Formal Induction

The clinician counts down from three to one to end the formal induction.

In the next three steps, the clinician assesses the patient's sensations and perceptions to determine whether or not the patient is experiencing desirable alterations in sensation. The patient is asked the following questions:

Step 11: Assess for Comfort in the Upright Arm

The clinician first asks: "Is your left arm comfortable?" A "yes" answer (the desired answer), is assigned a score of 1 and a "no" answer is assigned a score of 0.

Step 12: Assess for Tingling Sensations

Next, the clinician asks:

(a) Tell me what sensations you are experiencing in your left arm and hand and (b) Are you aware of any tingling sensations?

A "yes" answer to the second question, which is the desired answer from the standpoint of experiencing hypnotically induced altered sensations, receives a score of 1. A "no" answer receives a score of 0.

Step 13: Assess for Sensations of Physical Dissociation

Finally, the clinician asks the following two questions:

(a) Does your left hand feel as if it is not as much a part of your body as your right hand? (b) Does your left hand feel as connected to your left wrist as your right hand feels connected to the right wrist?

A "yes" answer to the first question, which indicates that the hand is perceived in a physically detached or dissociated way, is scored a 1, and a "no" answer is scored a 0. A "yes" answer to the second question however, is scored a 0, whereas a "no" answer, which signifies sensations of dissociation in the left, hypnotized hand, is scored a 1. However, the total score possible for this item is 1 if the answers to either or both questions earn a score of 1, or 0, if the answer to neither question earns a score of 1.

The desired answers from the standpoint of the patient's experiencing hypnosis are (a) yes, the upright arm is comfortable, (b) yes, there is tingling in the levitated arm, and (c) no, the upright hand does not feel as connected to the wrist as does the other hand. If the patient answers "no" to the first question (the arm is uncomfortable), you are unlikely to find the patient responsive to the rest of the procedure. A negative answer to the second question (no tingling at all) is also a harbinger, although less so, of subsequent unresponsiveness. A "yes" to the third question (no physical sense of dissociation: the left hand does feel as connected to the left wrist as the right hand feels connected to the right wrist) is also an indication that the patient is unlikely to be very responsive to the rest of the procedure.

This third question taps the sensory phenomenon of dissociation. In this context, dissociation refers to the physical experience of distance or of one part of the body feeling removed from the rest of the body; in this case, the levitated hand feels separate. The response of dissociating from parts of the body that are in pain is obviously a valuable skill for a person in pain to learn. That is why dissociation is considered important.

Step 14: Test the Patient's Responsiveness to the Signal for Arm Levitation

Whether or not the patient reports the desired alterations in sensory perception in the previously described steps, the clinician now moves on to this step to test the patient's responsiveness to the earlier postinduction suggestion (Step 7) for signaled arm levitation (arm floating upward). The clinician first orients the patient by saying: "Now watch this." Then, the clinician gently lowers the patient's left hand to the armrest and waits to see what happens next. If the hand and arm immediately begin to float back upward without the need for any verbal reinforcements, then this item receives a maximum score of 4.

Scoring. Scores range from 4 down to 0 based on the number of verbal reinforcements required to prompt the arm to lift up. Tactile reinforcements are not applied.

First Verbal Reinforcement. A score of 3 is assigned if just *one* verbal reinforcement is needed to prompt a complete floating upward of the hand and arm. That is, if after 5 to 10 seconds, the left arm does not begin to lift up, the clinician says: "Now turn your head, look at your left hand and see what is going to happen." The clinician then waits and obviously watches the left hand. If after another 5 to 10 seconds, the hand does not begin or continue the process of lifting up, a *second* verbal reinforcement is given.

Second Verbal Reinforcement. A score of 2 is assigned if after the following verbal reinforcement, the patient's left hand lifts all the way up into an upright, bent-at-the-elbow position. The clinician says:

> In your mind, see your hand as if it was a big, colorful, hot-air balloon. As the air gets hotter, and the balloon becomes larger, it, and your hand, gently float upward.

After verbalizing this *second* prompt, the clinician again waits and watches the patient's left hand for another 5 to 10 seconds. If after another 5 to 10 seconds, the hand still does not begin or continue the process of lifting up, a *third* verbal reinforcement is given.

Third Verbal Reinforcement. A score of 1 is assigned if after the following verbal reinforcement, the patient's left hand finally lifts all the way up into an upright, bent-at-the-elbow position. The clinician says: "See your hand being that large, colorful, hot-air balloon, floating off, taking off into the sky." After verbalizing this *third* prompt, the clinician again waits and watches the patient's left hand for another 5 to 10 seconds. If after another 5 to 10 seconds, the hand still does not begin or continue the process of lifting up, a *fourth* verbal reinforcement is given. If a fourth verbal reinforcement has to be given, then the patient is assigned a score of 0 for this signaled levitation test.

Fourth Verbal Reinforcement.   The clinician says:

> That's fine. See yourself as if you were a large, white, fluffy cloud, floating and drifting upward and through the sky. Your hand is the cloud, your whole body is the cloud, floating upward peacefully and comfortably. Pretend. Just put your arm back up there.

After delivering the fourth verbal reinforcement, it is significant whether the patient puts the arm back up on his or her own, and if so, when. Some patients lift up their arm before being told, "Pretend. Just put your arm back up there." Others do so afterward. Still others require that the clinician physically help the patient position his or her left hand and arm into the upright, bent-at-the-elbow position it was in before.

Clinical Significance and Interpretation.   Patients who have strong motivation to respond positively to hypnosis for pain control usually do well on signaled levitation. In fact, based on our pilot data set ($N = 17$), signaled levitation statistically correlated 0.81 with the HARP Total Score, 0.71 with the patient's perception of the depth of hypnosis attained (HARP item 23G), 0.82 with the patient's self-evaluation as a "good hypnosis subject" (HARP item 23C), and 0.71 with the patient's evaluation of the degree of involuntariness, automaticity, and spontaneity of the entire experience (HARP item 23K) (all at the $p < .01$ significance level). In our clinical experience, a positive response to the signaled levitation item is also usually associated with a positive response to the previous three items on the HARP (Steps 11 through 13). Based on our pilot data set, signaled levitation statistically correlated 0.51 (at the $p < .01$ significance level) with both arm comfort and physical dissociation. It also statistically correlated very highly with both ideomotor finger signaling items in Step 4 ($r = 0.81$, $p < .01$) and Step 5 ($r = 0.82$, $p < .01$), the initial induction of arm levitation in Step 6 ($r = 0.86$, $p < .01$), and the test for arm lightness in Step 7 ($r = 0.69$, $p < .01$). However, the correlation of signaled levitation with the eye-roll sign (Step 3) was not statistically significant ($r = 0.33$). In clinical practice, we see different patterns of relationship between patients' scores on the eye-roll (Step 3) and their response to signaled levitation (Step 14).

Hypnosis helps to establish a response set, such that contingent on certain cues (e.g., signaled levitation), the patient involuntarily or automatically initiates a particular behavior. Compared with poor responders to signaled levitation, and to the next item, control difference, good responders, typically have an easier time utilizing self-hypnosis strategies for pain management. They are also typically more successful in their efforts.

Step 15: Assess for the Perception of a Control Difference between Arms

The clinician checks to determine whether the patient's response to signaled levitation actually *feels real* to the patient. That is, does the patient actually experience a difference in control in the levitated (dissociated) arm and hand compared with the other arm and hand. To assess the patient's perception of *control difference* between his or her arms, the clinician verbalizes the script for Step 15:

Script.

As your arm remains in this upright position, raise your right hand all the way up. Good, lower your right hand back down. (1) Are you aware of any difference in sensation in your right hand going up compared with your left? (2) For example, does one arm feel lighter or heavier?

The desired response to these two questions is "Yes, there is a difference in sensation." If the patient answers "yes," the clinician should ask this next question:

(3) Which arm feels lighter?

The desired answer to this question is, "The left, levitated arm feels lighter." After obtaining an answer to the *third* question, the clinician should ask the following two questions:

(4) Is there any difference in your sense of control in one arm compared with the other? (5) In which arm do you feel more control?

If the answer to the *first* question was "no," the clinician should skip the third question, and ask the fourth and fifth questions. The desired response to the fourth question is "Yes, there is a felt difference in control in one arm compared with the other." We hope that more control is felt by the patient in the right arm compared with the left, levitated arm. This is what is meant by a perceived control difference, or as H. Spiegel and D. Spiegel (1978/1987) term it, a perceived "control differential."

Scoring for the Control Difference. This item is assigned a score of 2, 1, or 0 depending on the patient's answers to the preceding questions.

A Score of 2. A score of 2 is assigned if a definite difference in control between the arms is felt. That is, the patient's answers to the first two "difference in sensation" questions are that there is a definite difference in sensation. The patient's answer to the third question that goes along with these is that the left, levitated arm feels lighter. The patient's answers to the fourth and fifth questions are that there is a control difference between the two arms, with less control felt in the left arm as compared with the right arm.

A Score of 1. If a bit of probing is necessary before the patient concedes that maybe there is a little bit of difference in control between the two arms with there being a little more control in the right arm, then a score of 1 is assigned.

A Score of 0. Finally, a score of 0 is assigned if the patient absolutely insists that no difference in control between the two arms is felt.

If the patient showed some degree of signaled levitation of the arm that was stroked (in Step 14), but on questioning (in Step 15), does not perceive any control difference between the two arms, then this may indicate several things. (a) One possibility is that the arm's levitation did not feel real to the patient. (b) Another possibility is that the patient made the arm go up as opposed to experiencing it as involuntary. (c) A third possibility is that the patient initially experienced something and then lost it. None of these possibilities suggests an adequate enough response to hypnosis to be very therapeutically useful. The patient in either case is judged to be unable to sustain enough responsive concentration for experiencing hypnosis and responding to hypnotic suggestion. Somehow the patient's "ribbon of concentration" (Spiegel & Spiegel, 1978/1987) was broken.

Step 16A: Special Place Imagery

The clinician reintroduces a brief induction ceremony by instructing the patient that he or she is going to count to three, and that by the count of three, the patient's eyelids will once again close. The clinician then suggests that the patient will return to a pleasant, relaxed state and participate in another exercise involving some parallel awareness (dissociation), visualization, and imagination. The clinician then verbalizes open-ended, permissive suggestions for the patient to imagine a "very special, important place." Following this open-ended guided imagery, the clinician instructs the patient that he or she is going to count down to one. The clinician suggests that by the count of one, the patient's eyelids will open, as the patient remains "fully alert from the neck on up, and deeply relaxed and hypnotized from the neck on down." The clinician administers this step by verbalizing the script for Step 16A.

Clinical Rationale. Later, the clinician will inquire about the patient's imagery experience. The purpose of this exercise in Step 16A is to assess the patient's responsiveness to guided imagery and ability to utilize pleasant imagery modalities. This exercise also sets the stage for Step 16C, which assesses the extent to which analgesia can be induced hypnotically. This assessment is directly relevant to formulating a PMP treatment plan. It is important to learn what types of imagery come easily to the patient and what types of imagery are more difficult for the patient to invoke. These data can later guide the clinician in designing individualized self-hypnosis exercises for the patient, with the patient's collaboration.

Step 16B: Repeat Postinduction Suggestion for Restoring Normal Sensation

This is the first repetition of the postinduction suggestion given in Step 8, for restoring normal sensations with a specific tactile cue. The clinician tells the patient that on the administration of the physical cue, normal sensations will be restored to the left arm, and that as the clinician counts backward slowly from 10, the patient's usual sensations and control will be restored in the rest of the patient's body (see script for Step 16B).

Step 16C: Induce Hypnoanalgesia

The clinician attempts to induce *hypnoanalgesia.* In Step 16E, following a second repetition of the suggestion for restoring normal sensations (Step 16D), the clinician assesses the patient's responsiveness to this attempted hypnotic induction of analgesia. This assessment of the patient's ability to experience hypnoanalgesia is directly relevant to formulating a PMP treatment plan. It is important to learn how well the patient can respond to direct suggestions of pain diminution. If the patient proves to be a good responder, then this strategy can be incorporated into the hypnotic pain treatment plan and into the design of individualized self-hypnosis exercises (see script for Step 16C).

Step 16D: Repeat Postinduction Suggestion for Restoring Normal Sensation

This is the second repetition of the same postinduction suggestion given in Steps 8 and 16B, for restoring normal sensations with a specific tactile cue. Thus, the suggestion for restoring normal sensations is given three times in all.

Step 16E: Test Hypnoanalgesia

The clinician assesses the patient's responsiveness to the attempted hypnotic induction of analgesia in Step 16C. The test hypnoanalgesia script is as follows: "And now, I'd like to show you how well you are able to do this exercise. Watch the top of your left hand." The clinician firmly pinches a small fold of skin on top of the patient's left hand, holds on to the skinfold, and asks: "How does that feel?" The clinician then asks: "Is it painful?" (refer to Item 16E-1 of the HARP recording form in Appendix X).

Scoring.   If the patient answers "Yes," then a 0 is scored for Item 16E-1. If the answer is "no," then a 1 is scored. The clinician next asks: "Do you feel me touching your hand?" For this item (refer to Item 16E-2), a "yes" receives a score of 0, and a "no" receives a score of 1. The clinician next asks: "Do you feel pressure but no pain?" (refer to Item 16E-3) If the patient's response indicates that that part of the hand is completely numb, then a score of 2 is assigned. If pressure but no pain is felt, a score of 1 is assigned, and if pain is felt, 0 is assigned. Finally, the clinician asks: "What else do you feel?" The patient's answers are all recorded on the HARP recording form.

Interpretation.   Responses indicative of hypnoanalgesia are (a) that the patient does not feel any pain in the pinched skinfold or hand, (b) that the patient in fact does not feel any touch sensation at all (hypnoanesthesia: This is rare and associated with high hypnotic ability), and (c) that the patient feels some pressure but no pain (hypnoanalgesia).

Further Script, Scoring, and Interpretation.   Next, the clinician pinches the skinfold even harder and then asks: "How does it feel now?" The clinician then repeats the exact sequence of questions asked previously, and records the patient's answers on the HARP recording form (refer to Items 16E-4, 16E-5, and 16E-6 on the HARP recording form in Appendix X). Responses to Items 16E-4 through 16E-6 are interpreted identically to responses to Items 16E-1 through 16E-3. Finally, the clinician, while still holding the pinched skinfold, pinches yet a bit harder while shaking the patient's hand to the right and left. The clinician then repeats the same sequence of questions a second time and records the patient's responses on the HARP recording form (refer to Items 16E-7, 16E-8, and 16E-9 on the HARP recording form in Appendix X).

Step 16F: Testing for a Nociceptive Difference between Hands

The clinician tests for an experienced *nociceptive difference* between the hypnotized left hand and the nonhypnotized right hand. The clinician says: "Now, look at your other hand and tell me how this feels." Then, the clinician, with the patient's right hand on the armrest, firmly pinches a skinfold on top of the right hand. The clinician then asks: "How does that feel? Is it painful?" Next, the clinician pinches the left hand at the same time as he or she continues to pinch the right hand.

Scoring and Interpretation.   The clinician hopes that the patient reports that the pinched, nonhypnotized right hand feels painful compared with the pinched hypnotized left hand. Therefore, a score of 1 is assigned for Item 16F-1 if the patient answers that pinching the right hand feels more painful than pinching the left. One is looking for evidence of a nociceptive difference between the two hands. In line with this, one also expects the responsive patient to answer "yes" to Question 16F-2, "Do you feel me touching your right hand?" Therefore, a "yes" response to this question is scored 1, and a "no" response is scored 0. To the next question (Item 16F-3), "In your right hand, do you feel pressure but no pain," a "yes" response (i.e., "I feel just pressure") is scored 0, and a "no" response ("I feel pain") is scored a 1 because the patient is expected to feel both pain and pressure in the pinched, nonhypnotized, right hand. Finally, the clinician asks: "What else do you feel?" He or she then records the patient's answer on the HARP recording form. The clinician then releases the skinfolds and says: "Very good. You did fine." That marks the end of the test for hypnoanalgesia.

Step 17: Administer the Signal for Restoring Normal Sensations

The clinician administers and tests the patient's responsiveness to the *restoration signal* that had been suggested three times earlier in the HARP. The procedure is given under Item 17 in the HARP script.

Scoring.   A score of 3 is assigned if the patient reports that both the control difference between the arms has remitted, and normal sensation and control have returned in the rest of the body. If the patient reports that the control difference has not remitted and normal sensation and control have not returned in the rest of his or her body, the procedure for administering the restoration signal is repeated. A score of 2 is assigned if both the control difference between the arms remits and normal sensation and control return in the rest of the body at this point. If not, the restoration procedure has to be repeated a second time. A score of 1 is assigned if normal sensations are restored after this second repetition. If normal sensations are still not restored, a score of 0 is assigned for this item, and the clinician must work with the patient to restore normal sensation.

Patients who score 0 on the restoration signal tend to be suggestible but also willful, obstinate, and inflexible. Often their willfulness and obstinacy can be perceived or present as oppositionality. Such persons are often intensely affected by the things that happen to them such as pain or the things that other people say and do. For therapeutic relationship management purposes, the therapist should avoid coming on too strong (e.g., being too forceful, dogmatic, opinionated, or argumentative) as these patients often have these traits.

Step 18: Test for Amnesia to the Restoration Signal

The clinician assesses whether the patient has any idea why the difference in control between the two arms has remitted. This is a test for *amnesia* to the restoration signal. It is clinically important because it can convince a skeptical patient of the value of hypnosis. The clinician follows the procedure for Step 18 (see HARP script).

In the domain of pain, the primary value of *hypnoamnesia* is its direct relevance to selecting a strategy for pain management. Memories of past pain as well as worries and fears of future pain often intensify present pain (Eimer, 1988, 1989, 1993a, 1993b; Erickson, 1986; Thorn & Williams, 1993). If a patient who demonstrates some level of hypnoamnesia is convinced of its value for diminishing suffering associated with pain, then this hypnotic phenomenon can be utilized therapeutically. Pain patients who have amnesia for the restoration signal tend to be able to use the pain management strategies of time distortion and dissociating (or dis-associating) from their pain. When channeled appropriately, these strategies can be adaptive. Interestingly, amnesia for the restoration signal (Step 18) correlates at the markedly significant magnitude of 0.94 with hypnoanalgesia (i.e., sum of the "absence of pain" Items: 16E-1, 16E-3, 16E-4, 16E-6, 16E-7, 16E-9) in our sample.

Debriefing about the Experience of Hypnosis. After the patient has regained normal sensations in the hand, arm, and rest of the body, the HARP is formally completed. At this point, the clinician should begin to debrief the patient, inquiring about aspects of the patient's hypnotic experience.

Step 19: Check for the Experience of Floating and Lightness

The clinician asks the patient if he or she experienced sensations of *floating* or *lightness* in the levitating left arm, hand, and the rest of the body as the hand lifted upward (see script).

Scoring. A score of 2 is assigned if the patient reports that a sensation of floating or lightness was felt in the levitating left arm, and in other parts of body as well. A score of 1 is assigned if the patient reports a sensation of floating or lightness only in the levitated arm. Finally, a score of 0 is assigned if the patient reports feeling no sensations of floating or lightness at all, or that he or she lifted the arm volitionally, not involuntarily.

Interpretation. This item, like the items "tingling sensations" (Step 12), "physical dissociation" (Step 13), and "control difference" (Step 15), taps whether the patient is able to experience and sustain a suggested alteration in sensation (i.e., floating or lightness sensations). This type of responsiveness is directly relevant to pain management. The mainstay of the hypnotic and suggestive treatment of pain is the introduction and discovery of alternative ways to reexperience and diminish the perception of pain.

Step 20: Check for the Experience of Involuntariness

In this step, we check for the experience of *involuntariness* as the patient's arm was lifting up. H. Spiegel and D. Spiegel (1978/1987) assert that this experience is a central defining quality of the hypnotic experience. The experience of involuntariness contrasts with deliberately or effortfully trying to make something happen, which is not hypnosis (see script). A score of 1 is assigned if the patient answers that it felt as if the arm went up on its own. A score of 0 indicates the patient felt as if he or she volitionally put it up.

Step 21: Check for Amnesia and the Experience of Relaxation

The clinician follows the procedure given in the script for Step 21.

Step 22: Assess the Patient's "Special Place" Imagery Experience

At this point, the clinician follows the script for Step 22 to systematically assesses the types of imagery the patient invoked during the Special Place Imagery exercise (Step 16A). This inquiry provides data concerning the patient's degree of absorption in the experience and preferred imagery modalities.

Step 23: Debrief the Patient

Finally, the clinician conducts a general debriefing regarding the patient's overall hypnotic experience. The clinician asks the questions provided in the script for Step 23.

Step 24: Summary Debriefing Script

This is the last step in the formal administration of the HARP. At this time, the clinician should go through with the patient all of the points provided in the script for Step 24 to help put the entire hypnotic experience into a useful, therapeutic perspective.

Step 25: Design for the Patient an Individualized Self-Hypnosis Exercise

The clinician should teach the patient an individualized, simple, and brief (3, 4, or 5-step), self-hypnosis exercise incorporating the hypnotic phenomena that (a) the patient reported experiencing as most pleasant, easy, and spontaneous, and (b) were associated with high scores on the HARP. Clinically relevant pain relief and self-management suggestions are also incorporated in the exercise. The clinician may use the checklist of assessed hypnotic phenomena under HARP Item 25 to number in sequence the items to comprise the patient's self-hypnosis exercise.

SUMMARIZING THE HARP DATA

Based on the initial version of the HARP employed in our pilot study, which is described in the following section, there were a total of 44 item categories. All of these categories contained one item with the exception of the three item categories under the Hypnoanalgesia Scale (Scale VIII, see HARP Summary Sheet) each of which contained more than one item. A patient's total scores for each of the 44 categories were summed to yield a Total HARP score ranging from 0 to 86. The patient's scores on all of these items were recorded and summarized on the HARP Summary Sheet contained in the HARP Record Booklet (see Appendix X). However, based on clinical, theoretical, and statistical analyses of these data, some of the HARP items were modified. The resulting instrument, given in its entirety in Appendix X, contains 45 item categories. As in the original pilot version of the instrument, only the three item categories that assess hypnoanalgesia (i.e., absence of pain: 6 items; anesthesia: 3 items; nociceptive difference between hands: 3 items) contain multiple items. Also, as with the pilot version, a Total HARP score is computed as the sum of a patient's total scores for all 45 categories. Total HARP scores on the current version of the instrument can range from 0 to 100.

On the HARP Summary Sheet (see Appendix X), the 45 HARP scored item categories, consisting of a total of 54 individually administered and scored items, are sorted into Scales I through VIII. A patient's scores on each of the 45 scored item categories should be recorded in their proper place on the HARP Summary Sheet. There is also a place at the bottom of the summary form to record the patient's Total HARP score. The individual scales are labeled *Patient's Repose* (Scale I: 1 scored item; Does the patient start out "calm" or "restless"? Score range = 0–1), *Hand-Clasp test* (Scale II: 1 scored item; Score range = 0–1), the *Eye-Roll sign* (Scale III: 1 scored item; Score range = 0–4), *Ideomotor Responsiveness and Compliance* (Scale IV: 7 scored items; Score range = 0–16), *Subjective Response to Suggestions* (Scale V: 21 scored items; Score range = 0–34), *Amnesia* (Scale VI: 4 scored items; Score range = 0–7), *Imagery Responses and Ability* (Scale VII: 7 scored items; Score range = 0–22), and *Hypnoanalgesia* (Scale VIII: 3 scored item categories, containing a total of 12 scored items; Score range = 0–15).

Based on our pilot validation sample, coefficient alpha internal consistencies were computed for the five scales containing more than one item or item category (this excluded Scales I through III). Excellent internal consistency reliability scores were obtained for Scale IV (Ideomotor alpha = 0.87), Scale V (Subjective Responses alpha = 0.86), and Scale VII (Imagery Responses alpha = 0.75). Alphas for Scale VI (Amnesia alpha = 0.38) and Scale VIII (Hypnoanalgesia alpha = 0.55) were not quite as high. Thus, the theoretically constructed HARP scales do appear, statistically and empirically, to form true scales based on these preliminary data. Finally, the measured alpha internal consistency of the entire HARP, based on all 45 item categories (and all 54 scored items) came to 0.74, revealing that the test as a whole has good properties of internal consistency.

PRELIMINARY PSYCHOMETRIC DATA ON THE HARP

SAMPLE

Preliminary psychometric data on the HARP have been obtained and analyzed based on a pilot sample of 17 subjects who were recruited at a professional psychology graduate training program. The sample comprised 6 patients recruited at the program's psychological clinic, and 11 nonpatients who were graduate student volunteers (mean age = 42.8 years; SD = 11.5 years). There were 10 males and 7 females in this pilot sample.

INSTRUMENTS ADMINISTERED

Patients were administered the following procedures as part of the HARP pilot study: the HARP, the Stanford Hypnotic Clinical Scale (SHCS) (Hilgard & Hilgard, 1994), the Spiegel AOD Personality Inventory (H. Spiegel & D. Spiegel, 1978/1987), the Personality Adjective Checklist (PACL) (Strack, 1991), and the Symptom Checklist-90 Revised (SCL-90R) (Derogatis, 1983). Nonpatients received the same battery of procedures with the exception of the SCL-90R. The HARP Test Battery Data Summary sheet used in the pilot study constitutes the HARP cover sheet given in Appendix X. Order of administration of the HARP and the SHCS was counterbalanced. Student *t*-tests were conducted to determine if there were any order effects on Total HARP and SHCS scores. None of the resulting *t*-values were statistically significant at even the .80 level (2-tail probabilities). None of the resulting *F*-ratios were statistically significant at even the .20 level (2-tail probabilities). Thus, the effect of order was not significant on either Total HARP scores or SHCS scores.

The Stanford Hypnotic Clinical Scale (SHCS)

The SHCS is a well validated, brief, clinical instrument for assessing hypnotic ability and responsiveness (Hilgard & Hilgard, 1994). Five items make up the scale. They are (a) moving hands together (an ideomotor item), (b) hypnotic dreaming, (c) hypnotic age regression, (d) posthypnotic suggestion, and (e) posthypnotic amnesia. Total scores on the SHCS can range from 0 to 5. Total scores of 0 to 1 are considered evidence of "low hypnotic responsiveness," total scores of 2 to 3 are considered evidence of "medium hypnotic responsiveness," and total scores of 4 and 5 are considered evidence of "high hypnotic responsiveness." Because the SHCS is an established instrument with known clinical and psychometric properties, it was chosen as a measure against which to validate our new instrument.

Our overall clinical experience with the SHCS has been positive. Patients generally respond favorably to the test. Given the nature of the five items on the test, the Stanford tends to induce a relatively deep, private, internal hypnotic experience. However, given our orientation as active-directive, interactive, PMP therapists (most pain patients need their therapists to have such an orientation), we needed a hypnotic assessment procedure that also was more active, interactive, and behavioral. This led us to develop the HARP. The HARP assesses a wider range of hypnotic phenomena than does the Stanford and is also more interactive and behaviorally oriented. After administering the HARP to a pain patient, a clinician will have gathered a wealth of data relevant to understanding how he or she may be able to work hypno-behaviorally or otherwise with that patient to achieve favorable pain management outcomes.

The Spiegel AOD Personality Inventory

The Apollonian-Odyssean-Dionysian Personality Inventory (AOD Inventory) was developed by the Spiegels (1978/1987) as a measure of personality styles thought to relate to hypnotizability. The Spiegels basically conceptualized three "personality styles," or "types," characterized by unique cognitive, affective, and coping styles. On one extreme of a continuum, *Apollonians* were seen to be cognitively, intellectually, and logically oriented, predominantly left-brained, and the least hypnotizable. On the other extreme, *Dionysians* were seen to be intuitive, feeling-oriented, guided by their hearts much more than by their heads, predominantly right-brained, and the most hypnotizable. *Odysseans* were seen to be in between the two, having combinations of both styles, with less well-defined preferences. They were also postulated to fall in between the other two extreme styles in terms of hypnotizability.

The AOD Inventory contains 10 straightforward questions meant to measure these styles by asking about such issues as time and space perception, interpersonal control, personal values, trust proneness, preferred learning style, and perceptions of responsibility. For each question, a patient's response is classified as reflecting one of the three styles. The AOD Inventory is adapted and reproduced in Appendix Y. It is scored by calculating the number and percentage of a patient's responses falling into each of the three response style categories (Apollonian, Odyssean, and Dionysian). Also, a Total AOD score (range = 10 to 30) is calculated in the following manner. Each response category (A, O, & D) is assigned a constant numerical value (A=1, 0=2, D=3). Dionysian (D) responses are assigned the highest numerical value (3) to reflect that they represent the most right-brained orientation. Then, the number of responses falling into each category is multiplied by that category's numerical value to yield a numerical score for that category. The numerical products for each category are then summed to yield the Total AOD score.

The AOD is a theoretically interesting, clinical test. Based on our pilot data, the Odyssean percentage correlated highly negatively (–0.65) with the Total HARP score and the SHCS (–0.67). Also, the Dionysian percentage correlated moderately positively (0.53) with both the Total HARP score and the SHCS, as well as with the Hand-Clasp test (0.50). However, the correlations of the Apollonian percentage were not significant.

The Personality Adjective Checklist (PACL)

The Personality Adjective Checklist, or PACL, (Strack, 1991) is a 153-item personality adjective checklist based on Theodore Millon's theory of personality styles (Millon, 1995). The primary purpose of the test is not to measure psychopathology, but rather to measure variation in normal, or nonpathological personality traits. Therefore, the PACL was a good choice for measuring personality styles in our nonpatient sample of subjects, as well as in our patient sample.

On the PACL, subjects and patients are simply asked to check off all the words that are descriptive of them. The resulting data is computer-scored to yield *T*-scores on nine personality dimensions operationalized as scales. These nine scales are labeled: *Introversive* (Scale 1), *Inhibited* (Scale 2), *Cooperative* (Scale 3), *Sociable* (Scale 4), *Confident* (Scale 5), *Forceful* (Scale 6), *Respectful* (Scale 7), *Sensitive* (Scale 8), and *Personality Psychopathology Indicator* (PI: Scale 9). The ninth scale (PI) is interpreted to be an indicator of potential personality problems and pathology.

The Symptom Checklist-90 Revised (SCL-90R) (Derogatis, 1983) was administered only to our patient subjects ($N = 6$). Given the missing SCL-90R data on our nonpatient subjects, we did not include the SCL-90R in these analyses.

Pilot Data Analysis Results

A one-way repeated measures ANOVA was conducted with the Total HARP score as the dependent variable, and patients' scores on the SHCS (scores of either 1, 2, 3, 4, or 5) as the independent variable. The results of this analysis were statistically significant (F ratio = 6.29, $p < .002$) indicating a statistically significant, positive relationship between patients' performance on the HARP and their performance on the well-established SHCS. In fact, the Pearson Product-Moment correlation coefficient between total performance scores on the 2 hypnosis tests came to 0.84 ($p < .01$). Thus, the HARP correlates very highly with the Stanford scale.

Table 10.2 presents means, standard deviations, and percentiles for HARP Scale summary scores (III through VIII), the Total HARP score (range: 0 to 86), the SHCS (range: 0 to 5), and the A, O, and D percentages, from our pilot sample data set ($N = 17$).

Table 10.2

Means, Standard Deviations, and Percentiles for HARP Scale
Summary Indices, the SHCS, and AOD Percentages
Based on a Pilot Sample of 17 Subjects

		Percentiles				
Index	Mean (SD)	10th	25th	50th	75th	90th
HARP Scale Indices						
III. Eye-Roll	2.24 (1.39)	0	1	3	3	4
IV. Ideomotor Responsiveness	10.53 (5.99)	0	5	13	14.5	16
V. Subjective Response to Suggestions	22.65 (10.11)	9	13	27	31	32
VI. Amnesia	3.29 (1.83)	0	3	4	4	6
VII. Imagery Ability	6.00 (2.21)	3	5	6	8	8
VIII. Hypnoanalgesia	8.88 (4.21)	1	8	9	11.5	15
Total HARP Score	55.18 (21.81)	20	42	65	70	75
Stanford Hypnotic Clinical Scale	3.41 (1.62)	1	1.5	4	5	5
AOD Inventory Indices						
Apollonian Percentage	32.35 (20.16)	10	20	30	45	60
Odyssean Percentage	46.47 (23.17)	20	25	50	65	80
Dionysian Percentage	21.17 (19.65)	0	10	10	35	50

Note. Portions of the HARP were adapted with permission from the Hypnotic Induction Profile (HIP) appearing in *Trance and Treatment: Clinical Uses of Hypnosis,* by Herbert Spiegel and David Spiegel. Excerpts from HIP/Table 10-1A/Text Excerpts from *Trance and Treatment* by Herbert Spiegel, M.D. and David Spiegel, M.D. Copyright © 1978 by Herbert Spiegel, M.D. and David Spiegel, M.D. Reprinted by permission of BasicBooks, a division of HarperCollins Publishers, Inc.

Table 10.3 presents correlations between the major variables in our pilot study on the HARP. Examination of Table 10.3 reveals several clinically interesting patterns of relationships between the measures analyzed that are worth noting. First, all of the HARP scales, with the exception of the Eye-Roll sign, correlate highly positively at the 0.01 significance level with the Total HARP score, and the Stanford Hypnotic Clinical Scale (SHCS). Interestingly, the Hand-Clasp test (Item/Scale II on the HARP) correlates more highly than does the Eye-Roll (Item/Scale III on the HARP) with all the other HARP scales. Second, the Total HARP score correlates highly (0.84, $p < .01$) with the SHCS, which is a well-validated and established measure of hypnotic ability and responsiveness. Third, the HARP Hypnoanalgesia scale (VIII) correlates highly significantly ($r = 0.81, p < .01$) with the HARP Amnesia scale (VI). This empirical relationship suggests that hypnotically induced amnesia (the ability to forget) may be a clinically important variable when it comes to learning hypnotic pain relief (analgesia) strategies.

Table 10.3
Correlations of Selected HARP Scale Scores and Other
Measures Based on a Pilot Sample of 17 Subjects

SCORE	HARP-T	Clasp	ER	IMR	Subj	Amn	Imag	Analg	SHCS	A	O	D
HARP-T	1	0.57*	0.44	0.91**	0.96**	0.71**	0.81**	0.62**	0.84**	0.23	-0.65**	0.53*
Clasp	0.57*	1	0.27	0.58*	0.61**	0.04	0.44	0.20	0.58*	-0.05	-0.38	0.50*
ER	0.44	0.27	1	0.31	0.49*	0.19	0.39	0.04	0.34	0.02	-0.15	0.15
IMR	0.91**	0.58*	0.31	1	0.86**	0.56*	0.63**	0.46	0.84**	0.17	-0.55*	0.47
Subj	0.96**	0.61**	0.49	0.86**	1	0.56	0.82	0.39	0.81	0.19	-0.63	0.55
Amn	0.71**	0.04	0.19	0.56*	0.56*	1	0.45	0.81**	0.63**	0.23	-0.55*	0.41
Imag	0.81**	0.44	0.39	0.63**	0.82**	0.45	1	0.42	0.59*	0.41	-0.59*	0.27
Analg	0.62**	0.20	0.04	0.46	0.39	0.81**	0.42	1	0.47	0.19	-0.43	0.30
SHCS	0.84**	0.58*	0.34	0.84**	0.81**	0.63**	0.59*	0.47	1	0.26	-0.67**	0.53*
A	0.23	-0.05	0.02	0.17	0.19	0.23	0.41	0.19	0.26	1	-0.60*	-0.32
O	-0.65**	-0.38	-0.15	-0.55*	-0.63**	-0.55*	-0.59*	-0.43	-0.67**	-0.60*	1	-0.32
D	0.53*	0.50*	0.15	0.47	0.55*	0.41	0.27	0.30	0.53*	-0.32	-0.32	1
Inhib	0.05	0.06	-0.29	0.08	0.06	0.19	-0.18	0.09	0.05	-0.57*	-0.13	0.72**
Cooper	0.46	0.10	0.00	0.66**	0.40	0.46	0.11	0.20	0.53*	0.14	-0.18	0.06
Confid	0.28	0.27	0.34	0.09	0.40	-0.09	0.56*	-0.04	0.24	0.43	-0.29	-0.11
Respon	0.14	0.07	0.06	0.27	0.06	0.04	0.24	0.00	0.31	0.63**	-0.32	-0.27
Sensit	-0.16	-0.13	-0.13	-0.18	-0.17	-0.03	-0.31	0.07	-0.33	-0.59*	0.10	0.47
PI	-0.12	0.03	-0.15	-0.14	-0.12	-0.09	-0.23	0.07	-0.28	-0.69**	0.26	0.41

HARP-T = Total HARP score. Clasp = Hand-Clasp test (Scale II). ER = Eye-Roll (Scale III). IMR = Ideomotor Responsiveness and Compliance (Scale IV). Subj = Subjective Response to Suggestions (Scale V). Amn = Amnesia (Scale VI). Imag = Imagery Responses and Ability (Scale VII). Analg = Hypnoanalgesia (Scale VIII). SHCS = Stanford Hypnotic Clinical Scale. A = Apollonian Style. O = Odyssean Style. D = Dionysian Style. PACL Scales: Inhib = Inhibited. Cooper = Cooperative. Confid = Confident. Respon = Responsible. Sensit = Sensitive. PI = Personality Psychopathology Indicator.
Note. * = $p < .05$ significance level. ** = $p < .01$ significance level.
Note. Portions of the HARP were adapted with permission from the Hypnotic Induction Profile (HIP) appearing in *Trance and Treatment: Clinical Uses of Hypnosis,* by Herbert Spiegel and David Spiegel. Excerpts from HIP/Table 10-1A/Text Excerpts from *Trance and Treatment* by Herbert Spiegel, M.D. and David Spiegel, M.D. Copyright © 1978 by Herbert Spiegel, M.D. and David Spiegel, M.D. Reprinted by permission of BasicBooks, a division of HarperCollins Publishers, Inc.

Imagery ability (HARP Scale VII) also correlates highly ($r = 0.82$) with patients' Subjective Response to Suggestion (HARP Scale V), and with patients' Ideomotor Responsiveness and Compliance (HARP Scale IV) ($r = 0.63$, $p < .01$). Subjective Response to Suggestion correlates very highly with Ideomotor Responsiveness and Compliance ($r = 0.86$, $p < .01$). Interestingly, the Odyssean and Dionysian Scales on the Spiegel AOD Inventory correlate significantly (Odyssean $r = -0.65$; Dionysian $r = 0.53$), albeit in opposite directions with the Total HARP score, and with the individual HARP scales.

Certain personality traits measured by the PACL have strong correlations with certain other measures. *Inhibition* correlates significantly negatively (-0.57) with the Apollonian scale, and highly positively (0.72) with the Dionysian scale on the AOD Inventory. *Cooperativeness* not surprisingly, correlates highly (0.66) with the HARP Ideomotor Responsiveness and Compliance Scale, and with the SHCS (0.53). *Confidence* correlates strongly with the HARP Imagery scale (0.56), and *Responsibility* correlates strongly with the AOD Apollonian scale (0.63). Finally, *Sensitivity,* and the *Pathology Indicator* correlate strongly negatively with the AOD Apollonian scale (-0.59 and -0.69).

Table 10.4

Correlations of Selected HARP Items with HARP Scale
Scores Based on a Pilot Sample of 17 Subjects

SCORE	HARP-T	Clasp	ER	IMR	Subj	Amn	Imag	Analg	SHCS	A	O	D
Clasp	0.57*	1	0.27	0.58*	0.61**	0.04	0.44	0.20	0.58*	−0.05	−0.38	0.50*
ER	0.44	0.27	1	0.31	0.49*	0.19	0.39	0.04	0.34	0.02	−0.15	0.15
Init Lev	0.80**	0.64**	0.24	0.90**	0.82**	0.30	0.63**	0.25	0.79**	0.07	−0.51*	0.53*
Signal Lev	0.81**	0.52*	0.33	0.92**	0.76**	0.50*	0.59*	0.35	0.85**	0.21	−0.50*	0.38
CD	0.77**	0.27	0.23	0.73**	0.70**	0.59*	0.55*	0.60*	0.57*	0.19	−0.32	0.18
Restore	0.75**	0.56*	0.10	0.82**	0.64**	0.56*	0.33	0.66**	0.63**	0.02	−0.49*	0.55*

HARP-T = Total HARP score. Clasp = Hand Clasp test (Scale II, Item 2). ER = Eye-Roll (Scale III, Item 3). IMR = Ideomotor Responsiveness and Compliance (Scale IV). Subj = Subjective Response to Suggestions (Scale V). Amn = Amnesia (Scale VI). Imag = Imagery Responses and Ability (Scale VII). Analg = Hypnoanalgesia (Scale VIII). SHCS = Stanford Hypnotic Clinical Scale. A = Apollonian Style. O = Odyssean Style. D = Dionysian Style. Init Lev = Initial arm levitation induction (Item 6). Signal Lev = Signaled arm levitation (Item 14). CD = Control difference (Item 15). Restore = Response to restoration signal (Item 17).
Note. * = p < .05 significance level. ** = p < .01 significance level.
Note. Portions of the HARP were adapted with permission from the Hypnotic Induction Profile (HIP) appearing in *Trance and Treatment: Clinical Uses of Hypnosis*, by Herbert Spiegel and David Spiegel. Excerpts from HIP/Table 10-1A/Text Excerpts from *Trance and Treatment* by Herbert Spiegel, M.D. and David Spiegel, M.D. Copyright © 1978 by Herbert Spiegel, M.D. and David Spiegel, M.D. Reprinted by permission of BasicBooks, a division of HarperCollins Publishers, Inc.

Finally, we report on the other HARP items (in addition to the eye-roll) that were adapted from the Spiegel Hypnotic Induction Profile. These items are *initial arm levitation* (Item/Step 6), *signaled arm levitation* (Item/Step 14), the *control difference* (Item/Step 15), and response to the *restoration signal* (Item/Step 17). The data show that all four measures correlate above 0.75 at the .01 significance level with the Total HARP score. Interestingly, all four measures also correlate highly positively with most of the HARP scales with the exception of the Eye-Roll scale. Also, the signaled levitation item does not correlate significantly with the Hypnoanalgesia scale, the initial levitation item does not correlate significantly with either the Amnesia or Hypnoanalgesia scales, and the restoration signal item does not correlate significantly with the HARP Imagery scale. Table 10.4 displays all these correlations.

CHAPTER 11

Using the Hypnotic Ability and Response Profile (HARP) Strategically

Everyone must row with the oars he has.

English Proverb

ANALYZING AND INTERPRETING THE PATIENT'S HYPNOTIC ABILITY AND TEACHING SELF-HYPNOSIS

The clinician's analysis and interpretation of a patient's HARP protocol should guide the formulation of the hypno-behavioral portion of the PMP treatment plan. Table 11.1 summarizes recommended imagery and hypno-behavioral suggestion strategies based on level of hypnotic ability as measured by the HARP.

PATIENTS WITH LOW HYPNOTIC ABILITY AND RESPONSIVENESS

Patients who earn Total HARP scores between 0 and 24, HARP Ideomotor Responsiveness scores (Scale IV) between 0 and 5, and HARP Subjective Response to Suggestion scores (Scale V) between 0 and 10 may be categorized as demonstrating "low hypnotic ability and responsiveness." Typically, such patients tend to respond minimally to the attempted induction of levitation and to signaled levitation. Generally, they fail to experience any control difference between their arms on the HARP. They also seldom experience floating and lightness, and are more likely to show arm heaviness and resistance. They almost never report experiencing involuntariness in their ideomotor responses to suggestion.

Table 11.1

Recommended Pain Management Imagery and Suggestion Strategies
by Level of Hypnotic Ability as Measured by the HARP

HARP Index	Low Hypnotic Ability	Medium Hypnotic Ability	High Hypnotic Ability
HARP Total	0 to 24	25 to 70	71 to 100
SCALE V— Subjective Response to Suggestions	0 to 10	11 to 24	25 to 34
SCALE IV— Ideomotor Responsiveness	0 to 5	6 to 12	13 to 16
Patient Qualities	Reluctant to give up control; have to work hardest; low suggestibility; rely more on logic; require explanations; take longer to be convinced; critical; once convinced, stick to beliefs; no ideomotor finger signals; do not respond much to deepening strategies such as counting; unable to experience floating; more likely to have arm heaviness and resistance than lightness; no hypnoamnesia; do not experience involuntariness. Show mostly Apollonian (cognitively oriented) traits on the AOD Personality Inventory.	Willingness to relinquish control depends on trust, rapport, and mood—so does suggestibility and ease of going into trance. Medium suggestibility; rely on both logic and emotions; memory recall and reconstruction may induce trance; less likely to experience revivification but may abreact; some hypnoanalgesia; can benefit from deepening strategies. May experience some involuntariness and hypnoamnesia. May experience floating sensations in arm. Show combination of Apollonian and Dionysian (emotion-focused) traits on the AOD Personality Inventory.	Willing to give up control; go into trance with the greatest of ease; highly suggestible; rely most on feelings; do not require explanations; easily convinced but suggestions do not stick; can be fickle; good ideomotor finger signals; memory recall and reconstruction induces trance; likely to experience revivification in age regression and to abreact; respond to deepening strategies such as counting; demonstrate crossed thumb dominance on hand-clasp test; able to experience floating in entire body; hypnoamnesia; experience involuntariness. Show predominance of Dionysian (emotion-focused) traits on the AOD Personality Inventory.

Table 11.1　*(Continued)*

HARP Index	Low Hypnotic Ability	Medium Hypnotic Ability	High Hypnotic Ability
Imagery and Suggestions	Do not use the term *hypnosis*. Use *relaxation, imagery, self-control, self-regulation, autogenics*. It is best to present patients with a menu of strategies from which to select. Permissiveness works best. Respond best to *physical distraction and refocusing* and *activity imagery*. Physical props (e.g., ice bags) can work but they need to be applied longer. Use *open-focus* work, EMG biofeedback, progressive muscle relaxation, meditation, the relaxation response, pleasant imagery, and favorite places. Respond well to *cognitive-evaluative* and *self-instructional* strategies. Often have difficulty imaging. Lazarus's BASIC I.D. modality profile can be useful in designing suggestions. So can use of the gate control theory and the "ABCs" of rational-emotive behavior theory for designing suggestions. Memory recall and reconstruction least likely to "implant" ideas.	Give choices. Be permissive. Length of induction often affects level of relaxation attained and degree of "letting go." Thus, some may need longer induction. Use terms like *self-suggestion* and *self-hypnosis.* Respond well to short periods devoted to visualization of pain relief imagery, replacement images, sensory transformation, and verbal and visual metaphors. Respond well to focus on pain "submodalities" and changing them (e.g., size, shape, color). Respond well to physical props (such as ice on painful area) to strengthen pain relief imagery. The props can then be faded. Respond well to suggestion to *filter the hurt out of the pain.* Respond to *autogenic training, hand-warming,* and *thermal biofeedback.* Develop suggestions based on a BASIC I.D. modality profile. Can use *ideomotor finger signals.* Respond well to combination of *cognitive-evaluative, sensory-transformational,* and *motivational-affective* strategies.	Perform short inductions. Tell the patient what to feel. Least need to be permissive. A *directive approach* can work well. Respond well to direct suggestions of analgesia, anesthesia, numbness, and pain diminution. Basically any imagery can work. Easily establish *dual* or *parallel awareness—dissociation potential* is high. Respond well to *thermal and skin conductance biofeedback.* Also respond to *time distortion* techniques such as *time-telescoping.* Memory recall and reconstruction most likely to "implant" ideas. Need to proceed with utmost caution here. Respond well to ideomotor finger signaling, suggestions for amnesia, floating and physical dissociation. Respond best to sensory-transformational and motivational-affective strategies.

In fact, they generally fail to respond to the ideomotor finger signaling items whatsoever. In contrast, they tend to report that all their responses feel deliberate and voluntary.

These patients also do not usually respond positively to hypnotic strategies, such as counting, to deepen relaxation. They typically remember most of what was said to them and seldom show a talent for hypnoamnesia. They tend to show mostly Apollonian (cognitively oriented) traits on the Spiegel AOD Personality Inventory. Such patients are usually reluctant to give up control and hypnotic self-suggestion strategies often turn into control issues. If such a patient happens to be highly motivated to employ hypnosis for pain management, he or she will have to work very hard at using hypnosis. It just does not come easily. These patients are minimally suggestible. They rely more on logic than on intuition when learning something new and tend to be critical thinkers. Thus, they may take longer to be convinced of new ideas than do more hypnotically responsive persons. However, once convinced of something, patients with low hypnotizability tend to stick to their beliefs.

Imagery and Suggestions for Patients with Low Hypnotic Ability and Responsiveness

With these patients, who tend to be skeptical, it is often advisable to avoid the term hypnosis and use other terms instead, such as *relaxation, imagery, self-control, self-regulation,* and *autogenic training.* It is best to present the patient with a menu of pain management strategies from which to select. A permissive style generally has the most favorable outcome. These patients generally respond best to pain management strategies that employ *physical distraction* and *refocusing* (e.g., rubbing or pinching another part of the body to self-distract from the pain) and *activity imagery* (e.g., imaging oneself engaging in pleasant, vigorous, or involving activities). Sometimes actual physical props (e.g., an ice bag) help these patients more vividly imagine pain-relief images. These patients also generally respond well to *open-focus* work (Fritz & Fehmi, 1982), EMG biofeedback training, progressive muscle relaxation, meditation training, learning Benson's (1975) relaxation response, and pleasant imagery, such as recalling favorite places.

Cognitive-evaluative strategies such as cognitive therapy, rational-emotive therapy, multimodal cognitive-behavioral therapy, stress inoculation and self-instructional training, goal setting, and coping strategy therapy also tend to be a good fit. Many of these patients report that they have difficulty imaging, especially in the visual modality. A. Lazarus's (1989) "BASIC ID modality profile" can often prove useful in gathering information for designing suggestions. The basic model of Melzack and Wall's

(1965) gate control theory interpreted along the lines of the "ABC's" of Ellis's (1993, 1996) rational-emotive behavior therapy can also be useful in designing suggestions. Finally, these patients often can benefit from EMDR therapy as discussed in Chapter 7. Memory recall and reconstruction strategies are least likely to result in "implanted" ideas in these patients, compared with more suggestible (i.e., hypnotizable) patients.

Teaching Self-Hypnosis

When constructing a self-hypnosis pain management exercise for these patients, we usually find it best to call the exercise something other than self-hypnosis. We typically use one of the alternative terms mentioned earlier, such as self-control or relaxation imagery training. As with all patients, the construction of the exercise is individualized by incorporating hypnotic phenomena that the patient reported he or she experienced as pleasant, easy, and spontaneous. Clinically relevant suggestions and images are incorporated into the final exercise.

We generally develop, with the patient's collaboration, a simple, 4-step self-control or relaxation/imagery exercise which we teach, then model, and then have the patient practice with us. The first step usually involves *eye-closure and taking a few deep breaths* (as opposed to doing an eye-roll). The second step usually contains some *progressive muscle relaxation imagery.* The third step usually entails *counting to 5 or 10* to increase the patient's absorption and level of relaxation. It may also entail thinking about something pleasant, comforting, or heartwarming. Finally, the fourth step typically includes individualized suggestions and images tailored to counter the patient's unique problems and take into account his or her relevant psychodynamics. We refer to the patient's HARP profile to develop those hypnotic phenomena that he or she was able to experience:

> Earlier, we went through a number of different exercises to find out what kinds of relaxation and imagery might work for you, to help you distract yourself from your pain. You seemed to respond well to some things, and not respond very much to other things. This is important information for both of us to have. Now, I would like to see if we can use this important information to create a self-control exercise that you can practice on your own, for distracting yourself from some of your pain. I would like to suggest the following exercise for you to practice on your own. I would like to first go through the steps with you. There are four simple steps in the exercise I am going to show you. Then, I'd like to give you a chance to try it out with me. It would be best if you can keep an open mind about this exercise, because you may or may not feel much of a difference today. I would like to request of you that you agree

to give this exercise a chance, by practicing it several times a day, between now and your next visit with me. If you agree to do this, I am sure that you will experience it as helpful in relieving your pain. Most people with your type of problem, and your style of response on the exercises we just did together, find that the more they practice the following exercise, the more beneficial and easier it becomes. Here is your self-control exercise.

First, you take a few minutes for yourself and get comfortable. You close your eyes, and just rest back and relax. Then, take several slow, deep breaths, and imagine that you are breathing away tension, each time you exhale. Let your eyelids stay closed for the entire exercise. Focus all of your attention on your eyes. Experience your eyes as so relaxed that they simply do not feel like opening. When you know that your eyes are so relaxed that they just do not feel like opening, spread that relaxation over your entire body. Second, starting in your jaw and moving down your body, scan each part of your body for tension and stress, and release it. Just let it go. Mentally move down through your neck, shoulders, arms, hands, chest, abdomen, back, buttocks, hips, thighs, legs, and feet. Experience each part of your body that you scan as becoming more and more relaxed, loose, and limp. When you know that a part of your body is as relaxed as you can make it, then continue on to the next part of your body, spreading that relaxation over your entire body. Third, you might find that counting slowly to 10 helps you to further your relaxation along, to deepen your experience of relaxation. If so, begin counting slowly to 10. You might also find that bringing to mind a pleasant memory, something comforting, or heartwarming, helps you to relax more and more. On the other hand, you might find that imagining yourself actively engaged in some pleasant, perhaps vigorous activity, helps to nicely distract you from the pain for a little while. Whatever works is just fine. Everybody has their favorite distractions and daydreams.

Finally, the fourth step in your exercise is to bring to mind the idea that there is no one, right way to get relief from pain. Each person is different, and so is each person's pain. The interesting thing about this is that each person's favorite form of relief will be different also. The important thing is that you do something to actively distract yourself from the pain. So, as you actively concentrate on spreading feelings of relaxation throughout your body, counting numbers, imagining pleasant activities, or whatever, you can also meditate on the idea that the sensation of pain can only be experienced as it is interpreted. What this means is that you first feel the sensation of pain at point "A." Then, you interpret it, explain it to yourself, comprehend it, or make a comment to yourself about it, at point "B." Finally, you experience it, perceive it, and endure it, at point "C," based on how you comprehend and understand it. The goal of coming up with a self-control exercise for managing your pain is to make your pain more endurable, more tolerable.

You can stay with your sensations of pain in the present, and ride the wave of the pain, or distract yourself as best you can, by bringing to mind something else. But, when you worry about future pain or disturb yourself by remembering past pain, this actually can intensify the pain you have in the present. So it is better to stay in the present or think about something else that is pleasant. It is very important to just do something. Yet, on the other hand, sometimes doing nothing at all is doing something. By actively making a choice of how you will cope, you are doing something, and that will help you to find relief and feel better.

At this point, the clinician may offer additional ideas and suggestions for the patient to think about, based on the patient's unique pain, personality, and hypnotic response profile.

PATIENTS WITH MEDIUM HYPNOTIC ABILITY AND RESPONSIVENESS

Patients who earn Total HARP scores between 25 and 70, HARP Ideomotor Responsiveness scores (Scale IV) between 6 and 12, and HARP Subjective Response to Suggestion scores (Scale V) between 11 and 24, may be categorized as demonstrating "medium hypnotic ability and responsiveness." Typically, such patients tend to have signaled levitation responses of around 2, with partial control difference scores of 1. Many do experience floating and lightness, and also respond favorably to the ideomotor finger signaling items.

Generally, the willingness of patients with medium hypnotic ability to relinquish control depends on the factors of trust, rapport, and mood state, as does their suggestibility, and ease of going into trance. They tend to rely on both logic and emotions in making choices and processing and evaluating new ideas. Compared with persons with low hypnotic ability, these patients are more likely to enter a hypnotic state when absorbed in memory recall and reconstruction. Although they are less likely than "high hypnotic ability patients" to experience *revivification,* they still may have abreactions when recalling emotionally pregnant material.

Unlike those with low hypnotic ability, these patients may evidence some hypnoamnesia, and may experience some involuntariness in their response to ideomotor suggestions such as arm levitation and ideomotor finger signaling. On arm levitation, they are likely to experience some floating sensations, which may be localized in the levitating arm as opposed to being spread throughout the body. People with medium hypnotic ability usually can benefit from hypnotic deepening strategies, such as counting and deepening imagery. These patients typically show a combination of Apollonian (logical, cognitively oriented) and Dionysian (emotion-focused, intuitive) traits on the Spiegel AOD Personality Inventory.

Imagery and Suggestions for Patients with Medium-Grade Hypnotizability

With medium hypnotic ability patients, it is usually best to be permissive and to give choices when performing hypnotic inductions. The length of an induction often affects the level of relaxation attained and the degree of the patient's ability to experience a sense of really "letting go" (i.e., letting whatever happens happen, and accepting it, without self-criticism or exerting conscious, deliberate effort). Therefore, some medium ability patients will need long inductions, whereas some will still do well with short inductions. Also, at different times, depending on mood and the interpersonal context, the same patient may require a longer or a shorter induction, to enter and experience hypnotic trance.

With these patients, it is usually acceptable to use the terms self-suggestion and self-hypnosis. These patients respond well to self-hypnosis exercises devoted to focused visualization that involve short periods repeated throughout the day. They can be taught to perform focused visualization of pain-relief imagery and pain replacement images, and to practice sensory transformation exercises. They benefit from coaching that incorporates individualized verbal and visual metaphors associated with competence, coping, and pain relief. They can also use ideomotor finger signals.

These patients usually respond well to an imagery and cognitive focus on working with pain submodalities (e.g., the pain's imagined size, shape, color). Thus, it might be suggested that the patient first focus on becoming aware of the pain's basic qualities, and then imagine changing some of them (e.g., concentrating the pain into a smaller area, changing its shape, its color). These patients also typically respond well to the use of actual physical props (such as ice on a painful area, as the patient is imagining "icy cold sensations"). The props can eventually be faded, but they are helpful in reinforcing and strengthening the patient's imagery.

Patients with medium hypnotic ability tend to respond well to the suggestion to filter the hurt out of the pain. Good results are also frequently obtained by employing the techniques of autogenic training (Norris & Fahrion, 1993), and EMG/muscle tension and thermal/skin temperature biofeedback training (Arena & Blanchard, 1996; Schwartz & Associates,

1995; Wickramasekera, 1988). These patients respond well to a multi-modal combination of *cognitive, sensory transformational,* and *motivation enhancement* strategies. Also, it is often helpful to construct with the patient a BASIC ID modality profile, as discussed in Chapter 4. This can provide much useful data for constructing therapeutic suggestions.

Teaching Self-Hypnosis

When developing a self-hypnosis pain management exercise for patients with medium hypnotic ability, it is usually acceptable to call the exercise *self-hypnosis training.* As with all patients, the construction of the exercise is individualized. We incorporate hypnotic phenomena that the patient reported he or she experienced as pleasant, easy, and spontaneous on the HARP. Clinically relevant suggestions and images are incorporated into the final exercise. We usually create a simple, 4- to 5-step self-hypnosis exercise, with the patient's collaborative input. This exercise is taught, modeled by the clinician, and then practiced by the patient, while the clinician provides coaching:

> Earlier, I suggested that you will be able to go into relaxing self-hypnosis in the future, by practicing a few simple steps. These steps follow from the exercises we have done here today. I am going to go over these steps with you now. By practicing this self-hypnosis exercise, you'll find that it becomes easier and easier to filter the hurt out of your pain, as you make yourself relaxed and inwardly focused. The steps are as follows: First, you cast your eyes upward to the top of your head. Then, while looking upward, you slowly close your eyelids, take a deep breath and hold it. Second, you breathe out all the way, and as you release the tension, you relax your eyes, and let your eyelids remain closed. Third, you allow yourself to experience a pleasant sense of relaxation throughout your body. Imagine spreading pleasant sensations of relaxation, floating, lightness, or whatever other sensations feel good, over your entire body, from your head down to your toes, while you slowly and silently count to ten. Fourth, as you are counting to ten, concentrate on letting your body feel more and more relaxed, and also imagine sensations of lightness and floating spreading through one of your arms. Let one arm or the other feel light and airy. Imagine that arm to feel like a hot-air balloon, and let it float all the way upward. Your elbow will bend, allowing your forearm to float upward into an upright position, just as it did here. Fifth, as you concentrate on these sensations of floating and relaxation in your arm and in the rest of your body, you can meditate on the following: *Insert individualized suggestions and images and say:* Take a few minutes to absorb yourself in these ideas and images.

These suggestions are developed to counter the patient's specific problems and take into account his or her relevant psychodynamics. We refer to the patient's HARP profile to develop and incorporate those hypnotic phenomena that the patient was able to experience.

The procedure is terminated by saying:

> When you are ready to exit this pleasant state of self-hypnosis, at five, get ready. At four, with your eyelids closed, cast your eyes upward. At three, open your eyelids. At two, with your eyelids open, relax your eyes and look at your arm that has been floating. Finally, at one, make a fist, then relax your hand, and bring your arm back down onto the armrest or your lap. Take a few deep breaths as all your normal sensations are restored in your arm and in the rest of your body. You will remain relaxed, but alert, and all parts of your body will regain their normal sensations of control, but you will retain those pleasant sensations that will help you to continue to filter the hurt out of your pain.

PATIENTS WITH HIGH HYPNOTIC ABILITY AND RESPONSIVENESS

Patients who earn Total HARP scores between 71 and 100, HARP Ideomotor Responsiveness scores (Scale IV) between 13 and 16, and HARP Subjective Response to Suggestion scores (Scale V) between 25 and 34, may be categorized as demonstrating "high hypnotic ability and responsiveness." Patients with high hypnotic ability frequently score in the 3-to-4 range on the eye-roll, and they tend to have good initial levitation and signaled levitation responses of 3 to 4. They also show definitive control difference scores of 2, and typically, earn scores of 2 for floating and lightness on HARP Item 19; they tend to experience floating and lightness in other parts of their body, in addition to their left arm. They respond favorably to the ideomotor finger signaling items, earning a 1 on each of these HARP items (Items 4 and 5). Also, they often demonstrate crossed thumb dominance on the hand-clasp test. Interestingly, our data show that crossed thumb dominance, in right-handers, is more predictive of a range of hypnotic responsiveness than is the eye-roll.

Generally, highly hypnotizable patients are willing to relinquish control, are highly suggestible, and achieve a hypnotic state (i.e., trance), "with the greatest of ease" (H. Spiegel, personal communication, 1996). They tend to rely on their emotions and intuition in making choices and processing and evaluating new ideas. Compared with persons who have low and medium hypnotic ability, high hypnotizables typically do not require cognitively oriented, logically based rationales and explanations.

They are typically willing to accept instructions from a professional authority figure. In fact, they are usually easily subject to social influence. However, because of this quality, suggestions often do not stick. Thus, they may appear to change their minds easily. Low and medium hypnotizables are not as easily convinced, but when they finally change their mind about something, the change tends to be maintained.

Highly hypnotizable patients show a prevalence of Dionysian (emotion-focused, intuitive, interpersonally influenced) traits on the Spiegel AOD Personality Inventory (H. Spiegel & D. Spiegel, 1978/1987). With high hypnotizables, involvement in memory recall and reconstruction is highly likely to induce trance, and these patients tend to experience revivification. When recalling negative emotionally pregnant material, they are likely to have abreactions. Compared with low and medium hypnotizables, high hypnotizables are also likely to show significant hypnoamnesia. They also typically report the experience of involuntariness in their response to ideomotor suggestions, such as arm levitation and ideomotor finger signaling. While high hypnotizables can usually benefit from hypnotic deepening strategies, such as counting and deepening imagery, extensive deepening strategies and long induction ceremonies are often unnecessary. These patients can go into trance quickly and easily, and are usually receptive to brief induction strategies.

Imagery and Suggestions for Patients with High Hypnotic Ability

It is usually best to tell the patient what he or she will feel during the induction of hypnosis. Compared with low- and medium-grade hypnotizables, there is less need to be permissive in delivering hypnotic suggestions and induction instructions. A more directive approach tends to be most efficacious. Patients with high hypnotic ability usually respond well to direct suggestions for analgesia, anesthesia, numbness, and pain diminution. They also respond well to ideomotor finger signaling techniques, and suggestions for amnesia, floating, and physical dissociation. However, they also respond well to many other varieties of imagery, such as sensory-transformational strategies. These patients have a high potential for controlled dissociation (i.e., hypnosis). It is relatively easy to help them achieve a mental state of parallel awareness (i.e., physically being in one place, while experientially being somewhere else, at the same time, in a controlled manner, for a therapeutic purpose). Therefore, these patients also typically respond well to time distortion techniques, such as making an hour of pain seem like a few minutes, or refocusing attention on the periods of time in between bad episodes of pain.

Other hypnoassistive techniques to which these patients respond well include *thermal, skin-conductance, heart rate,* and *surface EMG biofeedback.*

The use of these biofeedback procedures, as external aides to hypnosis, is discussed later in this chapter.

Teaching Self-Hypnosis

As with all patients, the construction of a self-hypnosis exercise for a highly hypnotizable patient is individualized. We incorporate hypnotic phenomena that the patient reported he or she experienced as especially pleasant, enjoyable, and easy on the HARP. Clinically relevant suggestions and images are incorporated into the exercise:

> Earlier, I suggested that you will be able to go into relaxing self-hypnosis in the future, by practicing a few simple steps. These steps follow from the exercises we have done here today. I am going to go over these steps with you now. By practicing this self-hypnosis exercise, you'll find that it becomes easier and easier to replace your pain with numbness, or with some other less unpleasant sensation. You will easily make yourself feel relaxed and be inwardly focused. The steps for your exercise are as follows: First, you cast your eyes upward to the top of your head. Then, while looking upward, you close your eyelids, take a deep breath and hold it. Second, you breathe out all the way, and as you release the tension, you relax your eyes, and let your eyelids remain closed. Third, you relax your entire body and imagine yourself floating, while you slowly and silently count to ten. Concentrate on letting your body feel more and more relaxed. Fourth, as you concentrate on this imaginary sensation of floating and continue counting, you also concentrate on letting your left or right hand float upward. Imagine sensations of lightness and floating, spreading through the arm that will float upward. Let that arm feel light and airy. Imagine that arm to feel like a hot-air balloon, and let it float all the way upward. Your elbow will bend, allowing your forearm to float upward into an upright position, just as it did here. Fifth, as you concentrate on these sensations of floating and relaxation in your arm and in the rest of your body, you can meditate on the following ideas and images. Take a few minutes to absorb yourself in these ideas and images.

At this point, the clinician should insert suggestions and images tailored to counter the patient's unique problems and take into account his or her relevant psychodynamics. We refer to the patient's HARP profile to develop and incorporate those hypnotic phenomena that were most salient for the patient. We are also guided by the imagery and suggestions that typically work with high-grade hypnotic ability patients:

Then, you may focus on the following things: Begin to feel sensations of numbness *(or suggest spreading sensations associated with the patient's personal image of pain relief)* spreading into your *(refer to the area that hurts)* and replacing the hurt associated with the feeling of *(insert the patient's idiosyncratic pain description)*. You will be glad to experience this numbness *(or insert the patient's pain relief descriptors)* in place of the pain. Each time you do your exercise, you will be improving your ability to communicate with your body through the power of your inner mind. Your body will appreciate this positive attention that you are learning to give it. As you continue to practice communicating with your body through the power of your inner mind, you will get better at informing your body about how you want it to behave. You will get better at speaking the language of your body and you will better understand your pain. As you get better at speaking the language of your body, you also will develop more control over your body through the power of your inner mind. This will mean that you will no longer need to suffer with that *(insert type of pain)*. You will be able to safely and comfortably live without that *(insert the patient's worst descriptor of the pain)*. You will only need to feel the tiniest sensation of discomfort in *(refer to the area that hurts)* so that you remain aware of what you need to do to protect your *(refer to the area that hurts)*, to take care of your *(refer to the area that hurts)*, to help the rest of your body remain healthy, to get stronger, and *(insert if appropriate: to stay out of the hospital and off narcotics)*. You will also get better and better at telling your body how to increase those sensations of *(insert the patient's pain relief imagery and descriptors)* in place of those sensations of *(insert the patient's worst pain descriptors)*.

Then the clinician administers the following suggestions for exiting self-hypnosis:

When you are ready to exit this pleasant state of self-hypnosis, at five, get ready. At four, with your eyelids closed cast your eyes upward. At three, open your eyelids. At two, with your eyelids open, relax your eyes and look at your arm that has been floating. Finally, at one, make a tight fist, then relax your hand, and bring your arm back down onto the armrest or your lap. Take a few deep breaths as all your normal sensations are restored in your arm and in the rest of your body. You will remain relaxed, but alert, and all parts of your body will regain their normal sensations of control, but you will retain those pleasant sensations that help you continue to diminish and numb the pain. Then, you get ready to resume your activities . . . always feeling glad that you did your exercise, and always feeling better about yourself. It is also important to note the amount of pain relief that you feel at the conclusion of the exercise. You will feel better after doing your exercise. You will be able to repeat your self-hypnosis exercise anytime on your own as we did before. To review: At one, you cast up your eyes, close your eyelids, and take a deep breath. At two, you breathe out all the way, releasing tension as you do. At three, you relax your entire body, and imagine yourself floating. At four, you let one arm float upward like a balloon. At five, you meditate on the ideas we went over. I will also write them down so that you can take them with you. Then, when you are ready to exit this pleasant state of self-hypnosis, you count in reverse, from five down to one. At one, you make a tight fist with the hand that is floating, relax the hand, and then bring the arm down. You will feel relaxed, alert, comfortable, and all normal sensations will have returned into your arm, and the rest of your body.

ADDITIONAL IMAGERY AND SUGGESTIONS FOR PATIENTS WITH MEDIUM TO HIGH HYPNOTIC ABILITY

The following types of imagery and suggestions are suitable for medium and high hypnotic ability patients.

IMAGERY FOR MEASURING SUBJECTIVE ANALGESIA

Visualize a thermometer that takes or measures your pain. It is called a pain meter. The bottom mark or bulb on this pain meter/thermometer reads zero, which registers no pain. The top mark reads ten, which registers the worst pain you can imagine. When you are able to see this pain meter, your "yes" finger will lift. Are you able to see this pain meter now? Tell me, what number is it registering? *Wait for the patient to respond and then say:* When the meter registers a lower number that is noticeably more comfortable, your "yes" finger will lift.

SUGGESTING A MENU OF GOALS AND STRATEGIES FOR PAIN RELIEF

The clinician says, after instructing the patient in self-hypnosis:

In this pleasant, relaxed state of self-hypnosis, you can talk with your body about ways to effectively reduce your pain. You want to filter the hurt out of whatever is causing those pain sensations. You want to diminish those pain sensations. To do this, you can use an effective strategy that you have determined beforehand. . . . Your strategy might be to replace the pain with numbness or coolness, or to replace the pain with that feeling that you associate with the most pain relief. . . . Your strategy might be to remind yourself of these positive thoughts: *Insert positive suggestions that fit (see Table 11.2).* Your strategy might be to imagine a colored stream of light in your favorite color associated with healing, directing itself throughout your body and especially where you most need it. . . . Your strategy might be to distract yourself in some way from the pain. . . . Your strategy might be to float off or go to your favorite place, such as a beach, the mountains, or your own special safe hideaway, either by yourself or to be with someone or something you really like. . . . Or, you might just come up with a new positive coping thought to tell yourself and your body at any time. . . . Your strategy might be to recall all of the vitality and strength that you had at an earlier time in your life and enjoy those feelings now. . . . Or, you might decide to think about someone you admire and whom you would enjoy being like. You might enjoy thinking about how that person copes with life's adversities, and how that person would cope with pain such as yours.

Give the Patient a Chance to Try Some Strategies Out

The clinician says:

Now, you can take a few minutes to reflect on these ideas. I'd like you to do this now, to see which of the ideas that I have just suggested seem to work for you. Run through these ideas in your mind. Try some of them out right now. When you are ready to tell me what works, or what doesn't, your "yes" finger will lift. *(Wait for the patient's "yes" finger to lift. Then go on.)* Now, please tell me what you are experiencing.

Further Debriefing about Hypnosis

The clinician can say, before concluding the self-hypnosis training something like the following:

You see, this is what it is like to practice self-hypnosis. It is a method for communicating with your body and telling your body how you would like it to feel and behave. It is a state of relaxed concentration in which your body is most receptive to positive suggestions. It is also a way of being "here and there" at the same time. While part of you is physically here, mentally listening to me, aware of your pain, at the same time, another part of you can be someplace else, mentally enjoying itself, distancing you from the pain. Hypnosis is a state in which your mind

Table 11.2

Positive Cognitions and Suggestions for Pain Relief and Coping

I. *Suggestions Associated with Improving Frustration Tolerance*
1. I can manage this pain. I can handle this.
2. I can live without all this pain.
3. I don't have to suffer even though the pain is there.
4. I'm going to survive and cope with this.
5. Life can be hard and life can be pleasant. I can remember times when things went well and life felt good. Life can be joyful.
6. I can make time for myself to relax.
7. I can still enjoy things.
8. I can deal with/stand/handle/cope with this.
9. Easy does it. A little bit at a time, I am mastering my pain.
10. I can stand pain.
11. I can control my behavior for my own good.

II. *Suggestions for Replacing Helplessness and Victimization with Resource-fulness and Self-Efficacy*
12. I can do things to ease how much I hurt.
13. This is really going to work!
14. I can manage my pain by controlling my thoughts and behavior.
15. I have choices. I have power.
16. I can do something to help myself. There's always something that I can do.
17. I can talk to myself positively.
18. I can start where I am and give myself credit for beginning.
19. I can control this pain.
20. I can cope or manage. I can take care of myself.
21. I can do things for myself.
22. I can take care of myself. I'm fine as I am. I can believe in myself. I can take positive actions to feel healthier.
23. Work is good for me.
24. I can rebuild my life. I can recover what I have lost.
25. I can always do something to get relief.
26. My body is learning to be more receptive to my own thoughts.
27. I can make comforting pictures in my mind to ease my pain.

III. *Suggestions for Replacing Perceptions of Pain Constancy with Perceptions of Pain Variability*
28. My pain varies in intensity although it is always with me.
29. There are times when I'm pain-free.
30. I can feel comfortable at times.
31. I am getting better. I can be healthier. I'm getting stronger.
32. I can spread the comfort from one part of my body to any other.
33. I can filter the hurt out of the pain.
34. My pain changes. The sensations go up and down.

Table 11.2   *(Continued)*

IV. *Suggestions for Replacing Perceived Pain Permanence with Perceived Pain Temporality*

   35. Things can be done to relieve my pain. There is a cure for my suffering.

   36. My pain is a temporary problem.

   37. I am getting better.

   38. I have other things to live for.

   39. I can be comfortable.

   40. I can enjoy living with comfort as well as occasional pain.

   41. I can get rid of unwanted thoughts and keep positive thoughts.

   42. Everyday I can do a little bit more, more and more.

   43. Everyday it gets better and better.

V. *Suggestions for Replacing Hostility and Alienation with Feelings of Gratitude and Acceptance of Reality*

   44. I can learn to love again.

   45. I understand myself.

   46. I can wait and see if I can trust you. Some people can be trusted.

   47. I shouldn't expect too much from people.

   48. I can learn to get along with my pain. I can befriend my pain.

   49. My pain is part of me. I am learning to relate to it and understand it.

   50. I am going to enjoy my life once again or for the first time in my life.

   51. I accept my pain.

VI. *Suggestions for Replacing Perceptions of Pain Mysteriousness with Perceptions of Pain Being Understandable*

   52. I understand some things about my pain.

   53. I can listen to what my body is telling me.

   54. I understand my pain. I know quite a lot about my pain.

   55. I have been able to get some understanding of why I am in pain.

VII. *Suggestions for Transforming Self-Blame and Devaluation into Self-Acceptance and Appropriate Responsibility*

   56. I'm okay as I am. I'm okay even with this pain.

   57. I accept myself even though I have this pain.

   58. I am managing the best I can.

   59. I am doing the best that I can to manage my symptoms.

   60. I have good intentions. I'm doing the best I can to manage my condition.

   61. I can find rewards in my life.

   62. I am all right as I am. I can start to see myself coping.

   63. I am deserving of pain relief.

   64. I now have faith in my ability to heal myself.

   65. I am a lot more than my pain.

   66. I can choose to look at this *objectively* or to feel it at a deeper level.

   67. I deserve to be comfortable.

   68. I accept myself *with* my pain and I accept myself *without* my pain.

   69. This condition/pain is not my fault. I am not to blame.

Note. The seven categories under which these positive cognitions for pain relief and coping are sorted are not mutually exclusive. They are overlapping. We have simply grouped them for heuristic purposes.

can attend to more than one thing at the same time. This means that while your mind is attending to gifting your body with helpful suggestions for pain relief, it can also be attending to other things. You can hear what is going on around you and could respond appropriately if you had to, but you'll want to stay in this state of relaxed concentration to finish the exercise. This state of awareness, which we call hypnosis, is a state that will be easy for you to enter and use for managing your pain. It is not sleep. It is a shifting of your attention that is within your control. This is why we also call it "self-hypnosis," or "self-control training." In "self-hypnosis," although you feel very relaxed, you are still awake. You are always in control. When you get ready to resume your activities, after practicing your self-hypnosis exercise, you will always feel glad that you did your exercise. You will feel better about yourself. At the end of your exercise, you will also want to note the amount of pain relief that you feel because you will feel better after doing your exercise.

SUMMARY OF PAIN MANAGEMENT STRATEGIES GUIDED BY HYPNOTIC ABILITY LEVEL

The purpose of assessing a pain patient's hypnotic ability is to predict which pain management strategies will be most effective. Refer to Table 11.1 for a summary of pain management imagery and hypno-suggestive strategies arranged according to level of assessed hypnotic ability.

H. Spiegel and D. Spiegel (1978/1987) point out that low hypnotizable persons on their hypnotizability scale (i.e., Grades 0 through 1.5 on the Spiegel HIP) respond most favorably to pain management techniques that emphasize distraction. Therefore, they recommend that when working with low hypnotizable patients, the clinician offer strategies for developing sensations that compete with pain. These would include the use of physical props and strategies that involve the patient in active relaxation, imagery, and generation of alternative sensory stimulation. An example of the latter would be suggesting that the patient rub or pinch another area of his or her body when the pain gets bad. H. Spiegel and D. Spiegel (1978/1987) also advise that to promote patient compliance, a clear cognitive rationale should be provided with each suggested pain management strategy. The key point is that patients with low hypnotizability should be told what to do, taught how to do it, and given a reason for doing it. An explanation should be given for every pain management strategy that is taught. Low hypnotizables should also be presented with multiple alternative pain control strategies from which they can choose what feels and works best. A permissive approach seems to be most effective with this group.

For patients with medium hypnotic ability (i.e., Grades 2 through 3 "intact profiles" on the Spiegel HIP), H. Spiegel and D. Spiegel (1978/ 1987) recommend that the therapist and patient develop individualized pain relief imagery strategies. The Spiegels use the term "intact profile" when a patient's eye-roll and control differential scores are greater than zero, and the patient evidences a complete signalled arm levitation after the third reinforcement or before. The patient might be asked to imagine changing the temperature of the painful body part (e.g., changing a sensation of heat into an impression of coolness), or to imagine the area being anesthetized. The key point is to replace noxious pain images and sensations with alternative images and sensations associated with pain relief. For this group, the Spiegels advocate using more of a combination of direct suggestion, along with cognitive strategies, explanation, and education. According to the Spiegels, mid-range hypnotizable patients should be told what to do, what will happen when they do it, and given a reason for doing it. It is also efficacious to present multiple alternative pain control strategies to this group. A combination of permissiveness and directness seems to work best.

For highly hypnotizable patients (Grades 3.5 and above on the Spiegel HIP), the Spiegels recommend placing the greatest emphasis on administering direct suggestions for symptom transformation, physical dissociation from the pain, and pain diminution. These patients should be told what to do and what will happen when they do it. It is not as necessary to provide a cognitive rationale for each strategy given this group's heightened level of suggestibility. For the same reason, these patients generally respond well to one or two pain relief strategies. Hence, fewer alternatives need be provided, and a direct approach often works well.

ALTERNATIVE HYPNOTIC INDUCTIONS

As mentioned earlier, there are patients with whom we cannot perform the HARP procedure due to physical limitations such as ocular-motor problems or restricted use of their upper extremities. In these cases, we must use other induction procedures. Each of the following alternative methods is relatively simple and places few performance demands on a patient. These methods can be useful with patients who earn very low hypnotic ability scores on the HARP and are appropriate bedside induction procedures with frail, physically impaired, or agitated pain patients, in hospital or nursing facility settings. In such cases, the patient may be very weak or in a highly anxious or agitated state, secondary to an episode of excruciating pain. These methods can also be useful in a "pain emergency situation," or crisis, when medicine does not seem to be working.

The Pen-Drop Induction

The *pen-drop technique* was described by Cheek (1994, pp. 31–32). Essentially the clinician verbalizes something like the following: "Please hold this pen between your thumb and index finger just like this." The clinician positions the pen between the thumb and index finger of the patient's non-dominant hand, and then says: "I am going to ask that you allow your fingers to pull apart as soon as you are able to remember how your other arm would feel if you had been sleeping on it for a few hours during the night. As soon as you are able to remember that numb, pins-and-needles sensation, allow your fingers to pull apart." Until the pen drops, the clinician should talk about sleeping on that arm and not realizing it because one is asleep, and sleeping and not being aware of the pins and needles until one somehow decides to wake up. As soon as the pen drops, the clinician should positively reinforce the patient (e.g., "very good"), and then say, "You give orders to your subconscious mind when you are in hypnosis, and then you wait for an indication that your order has been followed. That is what just happened, free of any effort. Hypnosis is easy, free of any effort." The clinician then continues by providing appropriate deepening suggestions, followed by specific therapeutic suggestions that address the patient's problems.

Eye Focusing, Fatigue, Closure, and Catalepsy Methods

Eye focusing, eye fatigue, eye closure, and eye catalepsy induction methods have been described by numerous authors in the hypnosis literature (Edmonston, 1986; Hammond, 1988; LeCron, 1964; Schafer, 1996; Weitzenhoffer, 1989a). Earlier, in describing Step 3 of the HARP, we introduced our version of this method as "an alternative hypnotic entry procedure for patients who lack intact ocular-motor ability." This method is adaptable for working with weak, physically impaired, highly anxious, or agitated pain patients, who are being seen at bedside in a hospital or nursing facility. It also can be useful for working with a patient who is having a pain emergency. When working with a pain emergency patient who is highly anxious or agitated secondary to excruciating pain, it is necessary to work very quickly. The immediate goal is to redirect the patient's attention away from the severe pain and onto something soothing and absorbing. To succeed in shifting the patient's attention away from severe pain, the induction method has to be simple, brief, soothing, and relatively free of mental or physical performance demands.

INTERNAL FOCUSING AND PHYSIOLOGICAL RELAXATION INDUCTION

This method can also be useful in working with weak, physically impaired, highly anxious, or agitated pain patients, and patients who are being seen at bedside. It meets all the previously identified requirements for working with patients who are having a pain emergency. In essence, this induction is a biofeedback technique, without biofeedback equipment. It redirects the patient's attention away from the severe pain onto his or her own breathing or pulse pattern. Through gentle encouragement and calming suggestions, the patient is helped to stay focused on his or her internal physiological processes, and to "turn down the switch" on his or her sympathetic nervous system hyperarousal (i.e., by slowing down heart rate and respiration rate). This process often succeeds in shifting a patient's attention away from severe pain.

Typically, we first ask for permission to check the patient's pulse. While we hold the patient's wrist, we ask the patient to effortlessly and easily concentrate on his or her breathing. We then place the patient's other hand on his or her abdomen. We suggest that as the patient concentrates on breathing, his or her eyes will soon close and the breathing and pulse rate will slow down. It is suggested that the patient will become very relaxed and enter a pleasant state of hypnosis.

> Your pulse and your breathing will continue to settle down into a slow, even and relaxed pattern, more and more relaxed . . . more and more even and regular . . . easy and restful. *(Observe the patient closely for signs of physical relaxation and slowing and evening of the breathing.)* . . . In the future, each time you want to go into self-hypnosis, and when it is appropriate to do so, you can concentrate on slowing your breathing or slowing your pulse, and you may start relaxing all of the muscles in your body. When you give yourself the signal to enter this state so that you can perform an exercise for pain relief, your mind will shift to concentrating on your breathing or your pulse and to relaxing all of your muscles from the top of your head all the way down your body to the bottoms of your feet. Your attention will then easily flow along with your breathing, as your breathing and pulse slow down, and you will feel more and more relaxed as a wave of relaxation gently washes down through all of the muscles in your body. Finally, when you are ready to exit from your self-hypnosis, you will count to yourself up to five, and at the number five, you will open your eyes feeling awake, alert, refreshed,

and comfortable. After you have counted yourself awake and opened your eyes, the exercise is over. Each time you do your exercise in self-hypnosis, you will feel better at the end of your exercise.

SOME EXTERNAL AIDS TO HYPNOSIS

MUSIC

Some pain patients do not respond favorably to formal hypnotic induction procedures. They might be too distractible. However, many patients who do not respond favorably to formal inductions, do respond positively to informal inductions augmented by certain external aids. Music is a modality that works for many patients. The right kind of music can have relaxing effects and function as an excellent focus point for distraction from pain and hurting. Depending on the patient, music can form the centerpiece of an informal induction or it can be played in the background. Many patients are encouraged to relax to music in a meditative sort of way, just enjoying and following the music. They are instructed that when disturbing thoughts or pain intrude, they should just acknowledge the disturbance and refocus attention back on the music. We usually play music that is flowing and dreamy. There are many excellent "New Age," modern jazz, and classical compositions that fit the bill. The patient is then encouraged to do this at home.

RELAXATION AND SELF-HYPNOSIS TAPES

Most of the time, we also find it helpful to make patients audiocassette tapes containing their self-hypnosis instructions and relevant suggestions for pain control. Our clinician-made tapes are always focused and individualized. We seldom use prerecorded tapes, as they rarely tap into where the patient is at the time. We follow two principles in making patients individualized self-hypnosis tapes: (a) to make the tapes brief, as patients generally do not make time to listen to tapes lasting over 20 minutes; and (b) to record material that gives the patient the opportunity to practice the hypnotic strategies covered in the session.

METRONOMES

A handy, inexpensive external aid to hypnosis is the metronome. Like heart rate, it can be used to gently pace and guide a patient into a relaxed state:

As you listen to the beat of the metronome, you will gradually become more and more relaxed. You will find it interesting that as the beat slows down, you'll find yourself slowing down, relaxing more and more *(the clinician adjusts the beat of the metronome to pace his or her suggestions and observations of the patient)* . . . gently shifting into a more relaxed and comfortable state of being right now. And, its almost as if the beat of this little metronome is pacing the rhythm of your pulse, . . . the pace of your breathing, . . . getting slower, more even, . . . more regular *(the clinician continues to adjust the beat of the metronome to pace suggestions and observations of the patient).*

ONE-SESSION HYPNO-BEHAVIORAL PAIN MANAGEMENT PSYCHOTHERAPY

Most of the previously described techniques and strategies can be used regardless of whether contact with a pain patient is brief and time limited, as in *one-session therapy,* or extended, as in ongoing psychotherapy. However, in single-session therapy, the evaluation and treatment must be performed within the same session. There also needs to be some sense of completeness to the session such that the patient feels the chief problem was addressed and some solution was offered. In many medical settings, there is pressure to offer some solution-oriented intervention in the first session even if follow-up sessions are scheduled. Additionally, in many managed care settings, one or two sessions are all that are initially authorized. To meet these demands, we present an algorithm for evaluating and treating a pain patient that can fit within a one-session therapy framework. However, the following steps can easily be extended over more than one session.

PHASE I. ASSESSMENT

Step 1

Ask the patient to describe the physical quality and location of the pain. Determine whether the pain is continuous or intermittent. Diagnose whether there is a constant pain syndrome (Ewin, 1986, 1992) by asking the patient in a waking state, "Since this started, has there ever been *any* time when you were completely free of pain?" and "What about when you were asleep?" (Ewin, 1986, p. 283). If the patient answers "no" to both questions, then it is likely that the patient has a psychogenic constant pain syndrome. Also, ask the patient, "What percentage of the time is your pain present, from 0 to 100 percent of the time? Patients who have a "constant pain syndrome" will answer 100% of the time.

If the pain is intermittent or episodic, determine how often the pain gets bad or flares up. Obtain pain ratings for "usual pain" during at least five different times during the day (e.g., in the early morning, mid-morning, noon, mid-afternoon, late afternoon, evening, and late evening). Also, administer, score, and interpret the Philadelphia Pain Questionnaire-Pain Adjective Checklist (PPQ-PAC).

Step 2

Assess pain-activating triggers and precipitants. Assess pain relievers. Determine if pain activating triggers are avoidable. Determine how accessible pain relievers are.

Step 3

Elicit the patient's idiosyncratic, personal images of the pain as well as the idiosyncratic meaning he or she attributes to pain flare-ups. Elicit the main negative thoughts or beliefs that the patient associates with most occurrences of pain. For example: "There is something very wrong with me," "I can't stand this," "I am an invalid," "I am always in pain," and "I am always going to be in pain." If the patient has a constant pain syndrome, determine the patient's understanding about why there is never any relief from pain. Develop several alternative central positive thoughts that are preferable. For example: "I can cope with this pain and still enjoy my life," "I can handle this," "There are times when I am pain-free," and "I will someday be pain-free, or learn to master my pain." It is important to formulate concrete and realistic positive cognitions.

PHASE II. INTERVENTION

Step 4

Help the patient think about and create an image of a "personal, happy place." Develop a list of liked activities. Determine the patient's "favorite color associated with healing." Elicit pain relief images and pain replacement images. Also, identify one or more healthy role models with whom the patient can identify.

Step 5

Administer the HARP or the Spiegel HIP to assess hypnotic ability and responsiveness. Utilize the patient's assessed hypnotic abilities and strengths to induce hypnosis and create a self-hypnosis exercise that incorporates some of the following strategies:

- Teach controlled, deep breathing.
- Establish ideomotor finger signals.
- Establish an arm levitation.

- Develop the patient's awareness of the ever-present tension between "pain" and "no pain." Introduce the distinction or discrimination between "pain on" and "pain off" sensations. Help the patient to perceive that there can be relief in between the pain sensations. Emphasize the times when the pain is not present, or less intense. Also, administer suggestions for opening up and relaxing into the pain sensations.
- Develop a pure pain awareness strategy. Following Ewin (1978, 1986), tell the patient that when suffering is removed, "pure pain" does not really hurt so much: (a) Explain that the Total Pain Rating Index on the PPQ-PAC is the "additive sum" of the Sensory, Affective, and Evaluative Pain Rating Indices; (b) point out that the Total Pain Rating Index *minus* the Affective, and Evaluative Pain Rating Indices would leave a pure Sensory Pain Rating Index; (c) suggest that the pain measured by the Sensory Pain Rating Index would be much easier to tolerate than the Total Pain Rating Index because the Affective and Evaluative components that intensify the suffering component of pain would be removed; (d) give examples of pain minus the suffering (e.g., drawing blood from a vein for a blood test when the patient is not squeamish about needles); (e) ask the patient, "Would it be all right for you to experience a small amount of pure pain as long as it is at a tolerable level?" and have the patient answer with ideomotor finger signals while in trance; (f) if the patient gives permission, suggest that the patient focus solely on the "pure pain sensations" without evaluating them. For example, the therapist might say:

  > Take two minutes to just attend to the pure pain sensations of *(insert the relevant sensory descriptors obtained earlier in interview and from the PPQ-PAC)* in your *(insert the relevant body part)*. Breathe into those pure sensations and notice what you feel. Just observe the sensations in a passive and detached sort of way, almost as if you were studying those sensations like a scientist gathering data to write an objective report.

- Debrief with the patient about the resulting pain experience.
- Suggest strategies for avoiding or softening the impact of pain activating triggers and maximizing the utilization of pain relievers. Create posthypnotic cues to remind the patient to attend to pain relievers. If the pure pain awareness strategy lessened the pain's subjective intensity, suggest that the patient use that strategy when practicing self-hypnosis.
- Develop the image of a healing colored light stream shining or beaming into the painful areas and spreading relaxation and comfort

throughout the body. Combine this imagery with the patient's favorite pain relief images. Suggest replacement images for transforming the patient's pain images into pain relief images. Suggest images for filtering the hurt and suffering out of the pain. Suggest antidote images and healing words to soften the sensory, affective, and evaluative pain descriptors rated most intensely by the patient earlier on the PPQ-PAC.

- Validate the patient's commitment to the process of managing the pain. Obtain the patient's agreement to process associated emotional/suffering factors at another time, when appropriate.
- Evoke the image of the patient's healthy role model. Have the patient visualize himself or herself coping as would this healthy role model. Suggest that the patient visualize mastery and pleasure experiences. Suggest that the patient visualize coping with pain activating triggers and precipitants.
- Suggest that the patient "forgive" himself or herself for being less than perfect. Create positive suggestions and affirmations:

  "I let go of . . . ; I release myself from . . . ; I deserve to be pain-free, but I am still okay even with this pain; No pain need last forever; This pain once had value to me because it let me know that I was alive (or protected me from further injury). Now I have other ways of knowing that I am alive (or protecting myself from further injury). Therefore, I no longer need this pain to tell me I am alive. I can live without this pain; I accept myself even with this pain. I only need as much pain as is necessary to protect me from further injury.

- Evoke the patient's central positive cognitions, and reframe the central negative cognitions.
- Direct the patient to think about or escape to his or her "personal, happy place" as a way of dissociating in a controlled manner from the pain sensations.

Step 6

Bring the patient out of hypnosis and debrief. Elicit the patient's feedback and reactions. Summarize and conclude the session.

BIOFEEDBACK-ASSISTED PAIN MANAGEMENT PSYCHOTHERAPY

During the induction of hypnosis, physiological monitoring of a patient with a biofeedback instrument can be useful as an external pacer for shaping the patient's responsiveness to suggestions. Biofeedback involves connecting the patient to an electronic instrument that provides continuous information about the activity of specific physiological functions. The most commonly monitored physiological modalities are muscle tension, peripheral skin temperature, electrical skin conductance, heart rate or pulse, and respiration rate. Electronic biofeedback instruments transform a raw physiological signal into an electronic signal. This electronic signal is then amplified and displayed in the form of a visible and/or audible stimulus such as a changing tone, a light bar, or a moving line on a computer screen. Biofeedback can facilitate physiological relearning of healthier cognitive and behavioral response patterns to pain and stress. It can also serve as a helpful convincer that actual physiological changes are taking place during hypnotic treatment because it yields objective evidence of the ongoing connection between a patient's mental processes and his or her physiological state. It is the therapist's job to assist the patient to process this data.

Initially, many pain patients are skeptical of the claim that there is a connection between what they are thinking, what they are feeling, and what is going on in their body. When successful, hypnotic treatment enables many patients to experience these connections. However, many patients, especially those with low hypnotic ability, are not very responsive to hypnosis. Such patients can often benefit from the inclusion of biofeedback therapy as an external aid to hypno-behavioral PMP. In comparison, highly hypnotizable patients may experience biofeedback signals as an interference.

Biofeedback therapy in this context is not a separate treatment. It adds a mechanistic and technological quality to the hypnotic treatment that is useful for many patients, but it is not the electronic instrumentation that is the essential ingredient. In fact, when we first introduce biofeedback, we tell patients, "The machines will not do anything but register and display what you are doing in your body. We will use this feedback to help you adjust your inner strategy and increase your self-control." Even when biofeedback is used, the essential therapeutic ingredient continues to be the quality of the relationship between therapist and patient. What is most important is what the clinician says and does and how the patient perceives and processes it.

There is a hypnotic potential to being connected to a machine that gives you instantaneous and continual feedback on your internal physiology. However, the therapist needs to advance this hypnotherapeutic potential by inducing in the patient a curious, internally focused, but permissive frame of mind. With or without electronic biofeedback, the patient should be encouraged to discover his or her own potential to modify his or her internal, subjective experience. What biofeedback adds is a technological mirror or observational window, to validate or ratify the strategy the patient is using to achieve a desired state.

Biological feedback supplies corrective information. When the feedback indicates that a patient is realizing the desired physiological outcome (e.g., lowering muscle tension, raising skin temperature, decreasing heart rate, lowering skin conductance), the clinician should positively reinforce this achievement. When the feedback indicates that a patient is not physiologically progressing, the clinician may want to coach the patient to modify his or her internal strategy, or the clinician may simply choose to encourage the patient to relax and stay focused. Using this technological mirror can inspire patients to adopt an open-minded, experimental attitude. The therapist fosters this attitude with appropriate suggestions:

> Just take as much time as you need to get comfortable. Enjoy playing with the equipment. By that, I mean you have a window in front of you into your internal physiological workings, moment-by-moment. Take some time and discover how you can affect that tone (or moving line, light bar, etc.). That tone reflects the activity of your facial muscles (or your current finger temperature, sweat gland activity, etc.). As you allow yourself to relax and to think about relaxing things, you will notice that the tone (or light bar, moving line, etc.) will also change. See what makes it go up and see what makes it go down. Play with it for a little while and have some fun. It's pleasant and relaxing. . . . What I am asking you to do is to just go inside for a few minutes and relax. While you are focusing on doing this, you will start to discover some connections between what you are thinking and imagining, in other words what you have on your mind, and the feedback from the machine. The machine neither does anything to you nor puts anything into you. It just simply and elegantly registers what you are doing and internally experiencing and feeds back to us this important information.

The PMP therapist's hypnotic role is to help the patient stay focused and positively motivated. The therapist offers verbal feedback about the machine's feedback and continually relates this feedback to what the patient is thinking and doing. The therapist also offers permissive suggestions to deepen relaxation, strengthen the patient's focus of concentration, and link these things to an expected reduction in the patient's symptoms. The rationale for monitoring any of the preceding physiological indices is that they are associated with the body's moment-by-moment reactions to stress. Therefore, they provide objective measures of the extent to which a person is relaxed and at ease versus upset and tense. Patients can learn which signals from the electronic biofeedback instrument represent desirable changes in any one or more physiological indices. Then, those signals can serve as evidence of success and positive reinforcers when the patient responds in such a way as to produce those signals.

Biofeedback equipment today is relatively inexpensive and easily available. The following sections provide brief overviews of the five most easily employed and readily available psychophysiological modalities: respiration, heart rate or pulse, peripheral skin temperature, electrical skin conductance, and muscle tension (surface EMG). For more extensive and technical treatments of this vast subject, the reader is referred to a number of excellent sources (Arena & Blanchard, 1996; Basmajian, 1989; Cram, 1986; Cram & Associates, 1990; Norris & Fahrion, 1993; Schwartz & Associates, 1995).

BREATHING RETRAINING

Certain modalities of biofeedback are universally applicable to all psychophysiological dysregulation syndromes, including chronic pain, whereas other modalities are more disorder-specific (Arena & Blanchard, 1996; Gatchel & Blanchard, 1993). For example, breathing retraining with or without respiration monitoring is an intervention that is universally applicable (M. Schwartz, 1995). Learning to breathe from the diaphragm and to control one's breathing is directly associated with increased control of autonomic nervous system arousal. Deep, slow, controlled diaphragmatic breathing is associated with lowered arousal and parasympathetic nervous system activation and is applicable in the treatment of most pain disorders, including pain-related anxiety states (see Chapter 8).

HEART RATE

Pulse rate and rhythm are measures of autonomic and sympathetic nervous system arousal in most people when they are not engaged in a physical activity. Persons who are physically healthy typically have a strong, slow, and even pulse at rest (under 75 beats per minute) and an even slower pulse when deeply relaxed. The pulse can be monitored manually. However, a simple electronic pulse-meter can give both the therapist and patient continuous auditory and visual feedback on heart rate. The signals are usually emitted as pulse beeps along with a corresponding digital read out. Autonomic arousal triggers an instantaneous rise in heart rate in most individuals. Using an electronic pulse-meter, the patient and clinician can follow moment-by-moment changes in the patient's pulse rate and rhythm. The clinician can use this shared feedback to pace the patient's current level of physiological arousal, validate the patient's responses to suggestions, and shape these responses:

If the patient's heart rate is high but steady, the clinician can suggest:

> Just continue to relax. Take it easy. You're doing great. Just breathe nice and easy. Slowly and deeply. Eventually, those beeps will start to slow down. Even and steady. Slow and even . . . in concert with your breathing, slow it down a bit. Very good.

If the patient starts to get anxious and the heart rate goes up and becomes irregular, the clinician can suggest:

> It's natural to feel a little anxious at first. After all, who could believe that your heart rate can be so suggestible. Yet it is. And, before you know it, it can help you to slow down a bit and have a bit of rest from all of that stress and discomfort. Listen to how steady and strong your pulse is. So sensitive and responsive to how you feel and what you do. It's such an ideal source of feedback to help you adjust and turn down the tension. So, in a little while, as you settle down and get a little more comfortable, only a little bit, those tones will also settle . . . that's right, a bit more even and regular . . . in concert with your breathing.

The most important thing is for the therapist to be encouraging and to build confidence. As the patient's heart rate slows down, the clinician can validate this autonomic response by saying something like the following:

> Very good. More even, more regular, slower . . . steady . . . a nice even pace, getting more relaxed, deeper relaxed, and as you continue to develop your ability to regulate your pulse, so too, you will gain better, improved control over your pain and other symptoms.

The clinician can use the heart-rate biofeedback selectively to validate desired responses and to ratify hypnotic phenomena.

SKIN CONDUCTANCE RESPONSE BIOFEEDBACK

Skin conductance response biofeedback (SCR), monitors the electrical activity or electrical conductivity of the skin. This measure is very sensitive. The skin's electrical activity (conductance) tends to increase sharply and suddenly as soon as a person anticipates being stressed. It also rises sharply in many individuals while they are in distress. Spikes or sharp rises in electrical skin conductance are therefore associated in most people with fear states, pain states, anger states, shock, and surprise. For most people, skin conductance reflects moment-by-moment changes in their emotional state of arousal, or sympathetic nervous system activity. Because this measure is very sensitive, it can also reflect subtle changes in a person's emotional state and arousal level.

SCR biofeedback can serve as a useful adjunctive modality in desensitization therapy. Applied to PMP, the therapist can coach a patient to focus on pain sensations while simultaneously maintaining a low state of autonomic arousal as monitored with SCR biofeedback. The patient is coached to minimize skin conductance reactivity despite pain, and the therapist suggests that as the patient learns to reduce skin conductance reactivity, he or she will be developing a greater capacity to manage the pain. In this way, the patient can be psychophysiologically desensitized to the pain sensations.

One SCR biofeedback strategy we use frequently is to suggest that the patient focus all of his or her attention on the pain and simultaneously bring up his or her worst thoughts about the condition. We give examples such as "This pain is killing me," "I can't stand this," "I feel like I want to die when the pain gets so bad," "What if it gets much worse?" If there is a rise in SCR activity, we point this out. We normalize this physiological response by stating, "It is normal to get upset about those types of thoughts but it also makes the experience of being in pain worse." We then suggest that the patient think something else that is more positive but still realistic. We again give the patient some examples: "I can stand this. In fact I can handle this and cope quite well," "When the pain gets worse, there are things I can do to help me manage the situation," "I do not have to fear this pain." We also simultaneously redirect the patient to stay focused on his or her present physical sensations and emotional experience.

This method can also desensitize a patient to upsetting thoughts associated with different situations and activities restricted by pain. This can be done by guiding the patient through the preceding steps while he or she pictures these situations and thinks the upsetting thoughts. Sometimes, we ask the patient to talk through the situation out loud if we believe the patient will otherwise avoid thinking about it. If arousal is heightened during this imaginal exposure, we coach the patient in a relaxation or self-control technique to help lower the arousal. The goal is for the SCR levels to go down. With repeated exposure trials, this is what usually happens. Patients who are physiologically hyperreactive responders are good candidates for the use of this biofeedback modality. Whenever there appears to be a strongly reactive emotional component underlying a patient's persistent pain state, this biofeedback modality should also be considered.

THERMAL BIOFEEDBACK

Thermal or peripheral skin temperature biofeedback can be used in a similar way. The moment-by-moment monitoring of finger temperature also provides a window into the activity of the sympathetic nervous system because changes in peripheral blood flow reflect changes in that system. Higher finger temperature (reflecting increased peripheral blood flow) is associated with increased relaxation and lowered sympathetic arousal. Warm hands are associated with relaxation, safety, security, well-being, and freedom from suffering. Hence, patients are coached to generate thoughts and images that can help them to warm their hands.

Research with migraine headache patients has revealed that hand-warming can be an effective strategy for developing increased control over the symptoms that precipitate recurrent headaches (Arena & Blanchard, 1996; Blanchard & Andrasik, 1985). Many migraine and tension headache patients can learn to use hand-warming as a first-order response to the prodromata of an impending headache episode. In many cases, this can ward off a headache, or at least lessen its severity. Typically, we suggest initially that patients generate their own idiosyncratic thoughts and images to help them warm their hands. We help patients enrich and vivify their images, and we introduce additional images that fit with patients' preferred activities, pleasant places, and enjoyable experiences. We also suggest certain popular generic images for patients to try out. Some popular generic images associated with hand-warming include lying on a beach on a sunny day, being in a hot tub or taking a warm bubble bath, placing one's hands over a warm, crackling fireplace or on a warm window pane heated by the sun's rays, wearing warm electric gloves, and feeling the fingers pulse as blood flows into the hands.

In terms of the mechanics of biofeedback-assisted coaching, we reinforce most positive responses and generally ignore nonresponses (no change in hand temperature) and contrary responses (hand-cooling). When patients are unable to increase their hand temperature and appear to be struggling with reversing a contrary response trend (hand-cooling), we nonetheless offer encouragement and normalize the patient's experience. Often, we are working with perfectionistic individuals who tend to be hard on themselves. This may make it difficult for them to relax, be spontaneous, and let go, a tendency that can block a person from responding to hypnosis:

> Very often patients like yourself who are very positively motivated to learn this technique first rapidly develop the skill of cooling their hands before they develop the skill of warming the hands. This is how it should be and this is okay. So, please give yourself permission to delight in discovering what will happen next. . . . Will your hands continue to cool or will they just stay at their present temperature? Or, will they decide to warm up just a little? I just want you to know that whatever they decide to do, whatever happens is all right. Nothing is "supposed to" happen in this process of physiological learning and

discovery. The point is to discover what your body is capable of, and our bodies are capable of some pretty amazing and wonderful things that will lead you to a more healthy and pain-free state as long as you stick with this.

As shown by Blanchard et al. (1993), Holroyd et al. (1984), and Arena and Blanchard (1996), the "perception of success" is a key variable in determining the efficacy of self-regulatory therapies for chronic pain disorders such as migraine and tension headaches. Therefore, it is important to liberally administer permissive suggestions that help patients feel at ease by taking away performance demands. Success can be defined in this context as helping the patient explore a range of responses and capabilities, have fun, stay in the present, and adopt an open-minded, experimental attitude. With this approach, the patient begins to relax, and contrary or nonresponse trends usually reverse.

SURFACE ELECTROMYOGRAPHIC (SEMG) BIOFEEDBACK

Surface electromyographic biofeedback (EMG) targeting muscle groups associated with the patient's response to pain is another useful adjunctive clinical treatment modality (Arena & Blanchard, 1996; Cram, 1986; Cram & Associates, 1990). The central rationale for EMG biofeedback training is to identify muscle groups that are excessively active (tense) because continuously tensed or contracted muscles can produce spasm and increased pain. It is not uncommon for patients to involuntarily tense certain muscles when they are in pain or encountering stress. In fact, with many chronic pain patients, tensing muscles becomes habitual so that it occurs even in the absence of external stress. This is often observed as muscle bracing and guarding.

The chief strategy in the use of EMG biofeedback with chronic pain patients is to retrain dysfunctionally overactive muscles by coaching the patient to lower the surface EMG readings (measured in microvolts) associated with the targeted muscles. This is essentially a behavioral shaping process utilizing both operant and respondent conditioning learning principles along with patient education. The most common muscle site monitored for general relaxation, lowered arousal, and stress reduction training is the forehead or frontalis muscles. These muscles usually are reactive to most types of stress. Therefore, attention to relaxing these muscles often can help induce a general relaxation or quieting response. Also, as suggested by Wickramasekera (1988), an untrained patient's ability to rapidly lower his or her frontalis EMG appears to be associated with level of hypnotic ability. Therefore, frontalis EMG monitoring may provide another means of assessing hypnotic ability.

When we use EMG biofeedback, we usually start by targeting the frontalis muscles. Our initial goal is for the patient to demonstrate the ability to lower frontalis muscle activity to below three microvolts (using a "narrow band pass") and to maintain that low level of arousal during the training period. We then typically target the muscles associated with the patient's pain syndrome. Biofeedback training of these muscles is guided by our psychophysiological assessment findings. It is usually important to conduct a surface EMG muscle scan to identify the "hot" (i.e., reactive) muscles (Cram, 1986; Cram & Associates, 1990). In some cases, the appropriate goal is to work with a patient to lower the muscle activity readings (e.g., in the lumbar paraspinal muscles for a low back pain patient or in the head, facial, neck, and shoulder muscles of a headache patient). In other cases, the appropriate goal is to achieve a better balance between the same muscles on the right and left sides of the body (Arena & Blanchard, 1996; Basmajian, 1989; Cram, 1986; Cram & Associates, 1990).

We usually introduce EMG biofeedback as a high-tech tool for accelerating muscle relearning and retraining. We orient new patients by hooking them up to the biofeedback equipment and letting them experience the feedback while we discuss how biofeedback works and how it can help remediate problems. For example, a headache patient who was referred for biofeedback therapy and hypnosis by his physician was initially connected to a computerized surface EMG biofeedback instrument using a frontalis hookup, and oriented as follows:

THERAPIST: Pain creates stress in both the body and the mind. As you know, the emotional and mental stress of living with almost continual headaches is depression and anxiety about having another worse headache. But, I wonder if most people know what the physical counterpart of this stress is. What do you think it is? (Therapist waits for the patient to respond and then validates the patient's contribution)

PATIENT: High blood pressure?

THERAPIST: Yes. That is one very common symptom of stress. But in your case, and in the case of many folks who suffer from continual headaches, the physical counterpart is muscle tension. Muscle tension leads to muscle spasm. So what happens, is that first you have pain, then, in response to pain, your muscles tighten or brace up. Prolonged muscle bracing and tightening can then lead to a state where the muscles become "hyper" and stay locked up and contracted. We call this "spasm," and muscle spasm makes the original pain worse. So, it adds pain on top of pain. Now, the obvious solution is to reduce muscle spasm. But how?

PATIENT: Relax the muscles?

THERAPIST: Yes. But, unfortunately, very often, you may not even be aware that the muscles are tense or even in spasm. You may have become so used to having tightened muscles that it starts to feel normal. But, I can assure you, it is not normal. Normal muscles have the ability to tense, flex, and contract when you choose to use them and they have the ability to relax and stretch when they are not in use. But, it is just not necessary to flex and contract all of your muscles all at the same time, and it certainly is not necessary to continually flex those particular muscles that are causing your pain. They desperately need a break. They desperately need to be allowed to relax. Now, where does biofeedback fit in?

PATIENT: It helps you learn to relax those muscles that are tense? That you may not know are tense?

THERAPIST: Exactly. The line that you see moving across the computer screen right now represents your muscle activity. Your head pain is partly due to too much of this activity. In other words, too much of this muscle activity can cause muscle spasm. Muscle spasm can in turn cause headaches, or make them worse, and make them last longer. So, if you can learn what it takes to make this excessive muscle activity go down, then this line on the screen will start to move downward. . . . And as this line begins to move downward, the intensity, the duration, and the frequency of your headaches may also go downward or decrease. In other words, you will learn to reduce the spasm. As you learn to do this, and as you get good at this, you will begin to have more control over your body's responses to everyday stress. That is what your doctor referred you to us to learn.

PATIENT: How will biofeedback exactly help me to do this? To learn this?

THERAPIST: You will learn to control that moving line on the screen by what you are thinking and imagining, and also, by how you sit, your posture, how you move, how you breathe, and so on. This will help you learn how to cope better with stress, and by learning this, you will gain control over your medical symptoms. So, by learning how to control the line on this screen, you will learn how to reduce your pain, and in the process, you will develop much greater awareness and control over your body and how it reacts to stress. By learning some very simple, natural, and pleasant exercises here in the office and practicing them everyday, you will inoculate yourself against unnecessary stress in your life that can cause more pain. First, you will learn these stress reduction and self-control techniques in this neutral, relatively stress-free environment. Next, you will get the opportunity to practice them at home. Eventually, as you develop the ability to control these muscles and to relax, you will be able to apply these techniques when you are confronted with stress at work. You will develop skill in identifying where there is unnecessary tension in your body, and in releasing that tension, so that your muscles can rest and recover. You will actually be able to look forward to handling your stress when it happens at work, and leaving it there! Then you will not end up taking it home with you, and you will be able to anticipate having stress-free and headache-free weekends!

Epilogue

Pain has an element of blank;
It cannot recollect
When it began, or if there were
A day when it was not
It has no future but itself,
Its infinite realms contain
Its past, enlightened to perceive
New periods of pain.

Emily Dickinson

THE FOREGOING chapters constitute a framework and technology for conducting Pain Management Psychotherapy. However, as anyone who has worked with patients knows, people do not always fit textbook descriptions, nor are they frequently ready to collaborate with a psychotherapist to "get better." As researched by Prochaska, DiClemente, and Norcross (1992), there are stages of readiness to change, or at least collaborate with a health care professional, to modify a given problematic behavior. We have yet to schematize stages of readiness to learn pain management skills in chronic pain patients (M. Jensen, 1996). However, one issue that remains a source of conflict is the dialectic between *pain treatment* and *pain management*.

The fact is that many chronic pain patients believe in the former and not in the latter. The controversy over the long-term use of opioids for pain management figures prominently in this debate. We often hear patients say that what they are searching for is a "pain doctor" who specializes in "pain treatment" (as opposed to pain management). Physicians who are willing to prescribe and medically supervise the long-term use of opioids are usually classified in the pain treatment category. What this implies is the belief that such physicians are willing to do something for the pain patient to give the patient pain relief, whereas physicians who do not emphasize long-term opioid treatment in their practices are not.

This is not the place to get into the debate about the long-term use of opioids for the management of "intractable" pain syndromes. Pharmacological pain treatment, like psychotherapy for pain management (PMP), should be conducted by a specialist in the area. Different pain syndromes respond differently to different classes of therapeutic drugs, and each case has to be evaluated individually. For example, there are clear indications for opioid pharmacotherapy in the palliative treatment and management of cancer pain. What is relevant here is the conflict or dialectic between pain treatment and pain management. The term pain treatment often implies a passive patient, as opposed to the term pain management, which requires a more active patient. Actually, these contrasting implications serve little good. When it comes to chronic pain, the patient qualities that are desirable from the standpoint of achieving positive treatment outcomes are *activity* and *responsibility*. "Good" (positive) pain treatment outcomes depend on "good" (defined as *effective*) pain management. Effective pain management in turn, depends on patients assuming an active, responsible, collaborative role in their treatment.

In the context of treating posttraumatic stress disorder, Shapiro (1995) employed the concepts of safety, responsibility, and choice to develop a model for "cognitively interweaving" adaptive information into a traumatized patient's information-processing system. The therapeutic objective of the cognitive interweave process, according to Shapiro, is to catalyze an adaptive transformation of the patient's pathogenic perspective on the original traumatic events. Taking each cognitive interweave concept in turn, a traumatized patient first must feel *safe,* before any further psychologically reorganizing work (i.e., true cognitive restructuring) can take place. For example, if a perpetrator is still out there, and has the potential to "revictimize" the victim, it makes little sense to work toward "insightful psychological transformation" when basic safety is still the issue. First things must come first. A patient first needs to work on the practical issue of maximizing his or her safety and security. There is a basic, natural hierarchy of human needs, as Maslow (1967) argued 30 years ago. Biological survival comes before psychological issues. It is the therapist's job to assist patients to prioritize their target problems.

In the case of trauma patients, after the issue of safety is resolved, it makes sense to move on to process, or reprocess, the issue of *responsibility* as it relates to the notion of who actually was responsible (or to blame) for the traumatic event. In recovering from a traumatic experience, patients need to be assisted to move beyond self-blame, so that they can move on to the next level of recovery, which is termed *choice.* At this level of reprocessing, patients can be assisted to realize that they have choices now, although they might not have had choices at the time of the trauma. Obviously, this distinction is unlikely to make much therapeutic sense if the patient is still not resolved on the first issue of safety, due to the continued threat of the original perpetrator.

In PMP, several concepts also are indispensable for cognitively interweaving adaptive information into a pain patient's information-processing system. Effective processing of these concepts can assist in catalyzing an adaptive transformation of the patient's pathogenic perspective on his or her pain. Unless the following concepts are processed on some significant level, effective pain management usually cannot take place: These concepts are safety, responsibility, choice, coping, and management.

SAFETY

The concept of *safety* should be the first priority in the context of PMP, just as it must be in trauma treatment. Pain patients need to know that everything possible has been done medically to control any physical or bodily perpetrator associated with their pain problem. This means assuring that proper medical workups have been done before proceeding with PMP. It also means collaborating whenever possible with an informed treating physician. The concept of safety in the PMP context extends to giving a pain patient access to palliative treatments such as opioid pharmacotherapy when it is medically appropriate. It also involves helping a patient to believe and feel that he or she is understood and cared about. Developing therapeutic rapport means creating a safe place in which to do PMP.

The concept of safety also relates to whether a patient feels that it is safe to give up his or her pain. As discussed earlier, it is important to assess the pain's idiosyncratic and symbolic meaning to a patient. Ewin (1978, 1986, 1992) developed the idea of the constant pain syndrome to characterize traumatized pain patients who, on a deep inner level, may be vigilantly holding on to their pain because they do not feel it is safe to let it go. If the pain originated in an incident in which the patient became disoriented and feared imminent death, the pain may have come to represent life itself. Earlier, we described Ewin's hypnoanalytic approach for working with such patients to help them move beyond being stuck with their pain as their only symbol of having survived. However, the circumstances need not be so life threatening or dramatic for a patient to feel unsafe about giving up his or her chronic pain. For example, if notable secondary gains are connected to remaining in pain (e.g., a paycheck, or the avoidance of returning to an aversive job), then a patient understandably may not feel safe about giving up the pain. Another example would be a patient's belief that the pain signifies a potentially life threatening, but as yet, undiagnosed physical problem. In such a case, the patient understandably might not want to squelch the pain which could be the only indication of the dreaded, life-threatening condition (e.g., cancer, nerve damage, or imminent paralysis).

The main point is that unless a patient feels safe about giving up his or her pain to get better, PMP is unlikely to proceed. Thus, the PMP therapist's first task is to assess and address the safety issue, and to help the patient feel safe.

RESPONSIBILITY

After the safety issue, the next essential is *responsibility*. Patients need to take responsibility for managing their pain. After hearing numerous health professionals say "You have to learn to live with the pain," there had better come a time (preferably sooner than later) when a pain sufferer becomes ready to adopt an attitude that says *it is my responsibility to help myself*. This does not mean ceasing to seek professional and supportive help. It does mean, as stated in the American Chronic Pain Association's informational brochure (ACPA, 1993, p. 2), that an adaptive course for a pain sufferer to follow, philosophically and behaviorally, includes performing the following behaviors: (a) Make an honest and sincere effort to be involved in your own recovery, (b) become aware of what your needs are and how to meet them, (c) know your limitations, (d) take an active part in your recovery through pain management skills, and (e) follow your doctor's advice.

The ACPA's first-order philosophy emphasizes not dwelling on or talking repeatedly about pain symptoms. PMP clinicians need to assist patients to distinguish between assuming healthy responsibility for one's own pain management and shouldering unhealthy responsibility, which equates with "over-responsibilitizing" and pathogenic self-blame. Assuming healthy responsibility means accepting one's ability to make choices about the steps one will take to achieve more effective pain management. It presumes and requires assertiveness and the willingness to take calculated actions. It also presumes the ability to consider and weigh the potential costs and risks versus the benefits of alternative courses of action, and the willingness to make decisions and follow through with them. The chronic pain sufferer ultimately has to accept that only he or she has the responsibility and the right to make choices about his or her avenues for pain management. Thus, the next order of business, after responsibility, is choice.

CHOICE

Within the realm of pain management, *to choose* presumes the at least implicit knowledge that there are choices, and that one has the right and the ability to choose among alternative courses of pain management. Often, pain patients who are alienated, depressed, and hostile, do not acknowledge that they have choices. Patients who view their pain as mysterious and permanent may believe that they lack viable choices. Patients who view their pain as constant may feel too overwhelmed to make choices. All of these patients may not yet feel it is safe to be rid of, or reduce, the pain. In addition, patients who harbor marked self-blame for pain may be too depressed and angry at themselves to even consider making choices. It is the PMP therapist's job to assist patients to process and cognitively restructure such pathogenic attitudes and beliefs. These beliefs are usually associated with failed treatment outcomes. That is why PMP is a necessary adjuvant to the medical treatment of pain.

COPING

Next on the agenda is *coping*. All patients cope whether they acknowledge that they do or not. The central issues are (a) what are the main coping strategies that a person employs? and (b) how well are they working? Following the ACPA's key principles, which include making an honest and sincere effort to be involved in one's own recovery, and taking an active role through the employment of pain management skills, requires patients to take a close look at their coping strategies and their efficacy. That has been a primary focus of this book. That is one of the main missions of PMP. This is not simply a matter of asking whether a pain patient is coping well. It is a matter of carefully analyzing a patient's existent coping strategies and styles, evaluating their effectiveness, improving on them, and developing new coping strategies for the painful situations that have been identified.

PAIN MANAGEMENT

The ultimate order of business is *pain management*. Once a pain patient is assisted by his or her PMP therapist or physician (a) to feel legitimately understood, and cared about *(empathy)*, (b) to feel *safe* in all the important ways discussed earlier, (c) to accept that it is he or she who is accountable to help himself or herself to pain management *(responsibility)*, (d) to understand that he or she has the ultimate responsibility of deciding among alternative pain management options *(choice)*, and (e) to evaluate his or her existent coping strategies, and perhaps to develop new ones *(coping)*, then that patient will be ready for effective pain management. Once again, drawing on Prochaska et al.'s (1992) model of stages in the readiness to change, PMP therapists and physicians often receive and treat patients who are not yet ready to learn pain management skills.

STAGES OF READINESS FOR PAIN MANAGEMENT

Some patients may want a "silver bullet" for their pain. They may still solely be seeking pain treatment. At this stage, the idea of learning pain management skills is likely to be a foreign one. Alternatively, some patients may intend to learn how to better manage their pain, but they do not yet feel safe enough, or ready, to accept responsibility for a more active role; they can be termed "comtemplative," (Prochaska et al., 1992). Still other patients may be prepared to accept responsibility and to adopt a more active role, but they may yet lack the ability to make viable choices. Their anxiety, alienation, depression, or hostility may stand in their way, and they may be holding on to negative beliefs that can impede successful pain rehabilitation. They may also lack prerequisite cognitive and behavioral skills, which can be taught and coached by a PMP therapist.

It is the role of the PMP therapist to evaluate every new patient's stage and readiness to learn pain management skills. Many pain treatment failures may reflect a mismatch between the patient's stage of readiness and the therapist's expectations that could have been averted if pain specialists systematically assessed patients' stages of readiness to change. A pain patient who is not yet even ready to contemplate learning self-management skills for pain control (i.e., is at the "precontemplative" stage), is unlikely to respond favorably to training in pain management skills. After participating in a systematic, initial psychological assessment, such a patient deserves a clear and unambiguous test interpretation and feedback session. The patient should be informed about the psychologist's impressions. Good patient education often entails providing honest and unambiguous feedback. This may include sharing with the patient the PMP clinician's impressions about the patient's stage of readiness for pain management.

There are techniques and strategies for enhancing motivation to change or to learn new things (M. Jensen, 1996). It could be well worth the effort for clinicians who work with pain patients and specialize in pain management to familiarize themselves with motivation enhancement strategies, whatever their primary health care discipline. Unless pain patients can be adequately helped to recognize the full nature and extent of their pain-related problems, and to express concerns about how they are managing these problems, effective Pain Management Psychotherapy is unlikely to take place. Essentially, this entire book has also been about this task. Its central importance underscored our decision to highlight it as we bring this book to closure. Despite the huge impact that pain can have on a pain sufferer's life, little accomplishments can add up to big successes. The clinician must keep in mind the big picture while setting attainable goals in therapy.

As we were nearing completion of this book, we became aware of a body of programmatic research on a system of self-control techniques and emotional self-management interventions for reversing the effects of chronic stress on the autonomic nervous system (Childre, 1994, 1996; McCraty, Atkinson, Tiller, Rein, & Watkins, 1995; Rein, McCraty, & Atkinson, 1995; Research Overview, 1997; Rozman, Whitaker, Beckman, & Jones, 1995). This ongoing work conducted at the Institute of Heart-Math located in Boulder Creek, California, has produced evidence that regular practice of these techniques may modulate pain signals and perception through their physiological effect on afferent vagal input to the brain (McCraty et al., 1995; Research Overview, 1997). The basic techniques are relatively easy to learn and teach and are described by Childre (1994, 1996). One of the main techniques, "Freeze-Frame"© (Childre, 1994), can be practiced whenever a person experiences any personal vulnerability factors for increased pain and stress (as identified on prior assessment with the Pain Vulnerability Checklist, see Chapter 2 and Appendix F). The five steps of "Freeze-Frame" may help generate renewed strength, positive motivation, courage, and confidence for coping more effectively with the stressor or pain, thus shortcircuiting a stress response and offsetting more pain.

The Freeze-Frame steps are described in detail by Childre (1994). We have created the mnemonic TORAH to help recall the abbreviated steps. They are (a) Take a **T**ime-out. Freeze-Frame your negative automatic reaction to the stressful situation; (b) **O**rient your attention to your physical heart area and away from your stressor, increased pain, racing mind, or emotional distress. For 10 seconds or more, keep your attention focused on your heart area, breathe slowly but naturally, and imagine breathing in and out through your heart; (c) **R**ecall a heart-warming feeling associated with a positive emotional experience and try to re-experience it, while continuing to focus on your heart; (d) **A**sk your heart, as you continue to focus inward, for a better, more efficient way to cope with the stressor; (e) **H**ear how your heart and body respond. Listen for a better answer to the problem.

Another technique, termed "Cut-Through" (Childre, 1996), may also be practiced to cut-through the cognitive distortions and emotional distress associated with pain and stressful situations—what Childre terms "overcare." The goal of this technique is to transform the unbalanced, energy-draining extremes of overcare into the energy-conserving middle ground of balanced care so that stressful reactions and increased pain become opportunities for personal empowerment and greater self-efficacy. Pain may then be reinterpreted as a signal to focus inwardly and "go deeper in the heart to find balance and intelligent understanding" (Childre, 1996, p. 42).

Both of these techniques hold promise as practical, easily learned methods for responding to pain vulnerability factors with increased attention to the connection between bodily processes and emotional experiencing. Psychophysiological outcome research on the effects of regular practice of these and related techniques on pain levels, adaptive functionality, mental health, medical symptoms, and autonomic nervous system functioning will hopefully be conducted in the future.

In closing, we are reminded of some wise words composed long ago but as true today as they were then. Henry David Thoreau said, "Things do not change, we do." Eleanor Roosevelt said, "You gain strength, courage and confidence by every experience in which you really stop to look fear in the face. You are able to say, 'I lived through this horror. I can take the next thing that comes along.' You must do the one thing that you think you cannot do." Similarly, in managing chronic pain, each small success can build on a previous accomplishment and lead to a new accomplishment. It is also important to acknowledge, however, that it takes a lot of ongoing motivating, strength, courage, and regularly renewed confidence to cope well with the major adversity that is chronic pain. The importance of bringing together heart and mind is proclaimed in the old Jewish adage, "Our faith does not close its eyes to tragedy and does not deny that we human beings shall never possess the everlastingness of stone, the silent perduring quality of the mountain peak, but we have other gifts, conscious minds, aspiring hearts, far-visioned souls." (Jewish Book of Remembrance.)

APPENDIX A
New Patient Information

Date: _____ Social Sec. No.: _____

Patient First Name: _____ Middle: _____ Last Name: _____

Street Address: _____

Birth Date: _____ Age: _____ Sex: _____

Home Phone: _____ Business Phone: _____

Occupation: _____ Patient's Employer: _____

Address: _____

Marital Status (Circle) S M W D Separated __ Spouse's Name: _____

Emergency Contact with Phone No.: _____

Address: _____

═══

Insurance Information

Medicare No.: _____ Effective Date: _____ Part A __ Part B __

Blue Cross/Blue Shield

Subscriber: _____ Relationship to Patient: _____

Group No.: _____ Identification No: _____

Private/HMO/Other Insurance   Subscriber: _____

Name of Insurance: _____ Relationship to Patient: _____

Insurance Address: _____ Phone No.: _____

ID No.: _____ Referral No.: _____

═══

Workers Compensation or Auto Accident

Name of Insurance: _____ Claim No.: _____

Insurance Address: _____ Phone No.: _____

Address/Adjuster: _____

Date of Injury: _____

═══

Family Physician

Name: _____ Address: _____

Phone No.: _____ Do you wish a report sent? __Yes __ No

Who referred you to our office? _____

═══

Attorney Information

Attorney's Name: _____ Address: _____

Phone No.: _____ Do you wish a report sent? __Yes __ No

Signed Authorizations and Informed Consents

Patient Name: _____ Date: _____

Authorization to Release My Medical Records

I _____ authorize that Dr. _____ release medical and psychological records of my evaluations and treatment to the following: __

_____

Signed and Agreed: _____ Date: _____

Authorization to Receive My Medical Records

I _____ authorize that Dr. _____ receive medical and psychological records of my evaluations and treatment at/with: _____

_____

I wish these medical/psychological records to be sent to Dr. _____

Signed and Agreed: _____ Date: _____

Authorization to Bill Insurance and for Payment

I _____ authorize that Dr. _____ bill my insurance company for psychological services rendered to me. I also authorize my insurance carrier to make payment to Dr. _____ for services rendered to me for evaluation and treatment of my condition related to the medical or psychiatric diagnoses appearing on my insurance claim form and/or statement/bill. I authorize Dr. _____ to furnish my insurance company with medical and other information about me (e.g., evaluation reports, treatment notes) that is required for processing my claim for medical benefits to be paid. I realize that I am financially responsible for all insurance deductibles and co-payments, as well as for services to which I consent that are not covered by insurance.

Signed and Agreed: _____ Date: _____

Informed Consent to Evaluation and Treatment

I _____ agree that this authorization shall also serve as my informed consent to psychological evaluation and treatment.

Signed and Agreed: _____ Date: _____

Authorization to Use Copies of This Document and Term of This Authorization

I _____ also permit a copy of this entire authorization to be used in place of the original. This entire authorization will remain in effect until revoked by me in writing.

Signed and Agreed: _____ Date: _____

The Philadelphia Pain Questionnaire

INSTRUCTIONS: This questionnaire is designed to help you describe your pain so that your doctor can have a better understanding of your pain condition. This questionnaire has 7 pages. Please answer all of the questions on each page. The first 4 pages cover your *pain's history and current status.* Pages 5 and 6 contain a *pain adjective checklist* to help you describe the qualities your pain has. On page 7, you are asked to make several ratings showing the *intensity of your present pain,* and to *complete a picture* showing *where* you have pain.

Today's Date: _____ Patient Name: _____

1. Patient's Social Security No.: _____ 2. Birthdate: _____ 3. Age: ___
2. Gender: ___ Male ___ Female 5. Your Primary Doctor's Name: _____
3. Who referred you to our office? _____
4. Why were you referred to our office? _____
5. What is the purpose of your visit? _____
6. What is your primary problem for which you are seeking help? _____
   _____

10. How do you think your life will be different if you are successful in solving this problem? _____
    _____

11. Do you suffer from pain? _____ Yes _____ No   From what kind of pain do you suffer? Describe your pain. _____

12. Write a #1 next to your primary area of pain, and a #2, #3, etc. next to your secondary sites of pain.
___ head/face/mouth ___ neck ___ shoulders/upper arms ___ lower arms
___ hands/fingers ___ abdomen/stomach ___ chest ___ upper back ___ mid-back
___ low back ___ upper legs ___ lower legs ___ feet ___ pelvis ___ buttocks
___ hips ___ anal area ___ genital area ___ Other: _____

13. Using the "0 to 10" SCALE below, rate the *strength* or *intensity* of your pain for each area you marked above. Record a number rating on the line next to each area or site of your pain below.

  No Pain   Worst Pain Imaginable
  0   1   2   3   4   5   6   7   8   9   10
___ head/face/mouth ___ neck ___ shoulders/upper arms ___ lower arms
___ hands/fingers ___ abdomen/stomach ___ chest ___ upper back ___ mid-back
___ low back ___ upper legs ___ lower legs ___ feet ___ pelvis ___ buttocks
___ hips ___ anal area ___ genital area ___ Other: _____

14. Number of years of formal education: _____ (e.g., high school graduate = 12 years; 2 yrs college or Associates Degree = 14 yrs; Bachelors Degree = 16 yrs; Masters Degree = 18 yrs)

15. Marital Status: ___ Married ___ Living w/ someone ___ Single Separated ___ Divorced ___ Widowed

16. Ethnic Background: ___ White ___ Black ___ Hispanic ___ Asian Native American ___ Other

17. What do you think is the primary cause for your pain? (Write #1 next to the "primary cause, #2, #3, and so on, next to any secondary causes, and write in the specific cause/s if you can)

___ motor vehicle accident ___ a fall ___ a lifting accident ___ arthritis: _____
___ moving wrong ___ an assault ___ cancer: _____
___ a chronic illness: _____ ___ a repetitive strain injury: _____
___ an infectious disease: _____ ___ diabetes
___ pulmonary disease: _____ ___ an inflammatory disease: _____
___ herniated disc ___ cardiac disease ___ a degenerative condition: _____
___ a metabolic condition: _____ ___ unknown cause
___ Other Known Cause: _____

18. Please explain the causes for your pain that you have marked above:

_____

19. What is/are your primary medical diagnosis or diagnoses? _____

_____

20. What percentage of time are you in pain?_____ Please circle the % of time you are in pain below.

% Time in Pain = 0%   10%   20%   30%   40%   50%   60%   70%   80%   90%   100%

21. Is pain due to a work-related accident? ___ Yes ___ No   22. Date pain started? Month/Yr: _____

23. How long have you had the pain? Months/Yrs:

24. Are you working now? ___ Yes ___ No   25. If not, why not?

26. If yes, how many hours/week?_____   27. What type of work do or did you do?

28. Are you receiving disability? ___ Yes ___ No   29. Is an application planned? ___ Yes ___ No

30. Are you involved in a lawsuit related to your pain? ___ Yes ___ No
Attorney's name: _____

31. List all medications you are currently taking below.

Medication Name   Dosage (mg.)   No. times per day? Taking for what?

_____   _____   _____   _____
_____   _____   _____   _____
_____   _____   _____   _____
_____   _____   _____   _____

32. Did the cause of your pain include a head injury or concussion?
___ Yes ___ No

33. How many surgeries have you had to correct the cause of your pain?

Date   Type of Surgery

_____   _____
_____   _____
_____   _____
_____   _____

34. List the types of medical & other treatments you've had for your primary and secondary pain problems.

Date   Type of Treatment and Rendered By Whom?

_____   _____

_____   _____

_____   _____

_____   _____

35. Rate the strength of your primary pain on the following scale for each situation or time below:

No Pain   Worst Pain Imaginable

0   1   2   3   4   5   6   7   8   9   10

A. pain now ____   B. least pain this week ____   C. worst pain this week ____

D. usual level of pain ____   E. pain in the early morning ____

F. pain at breakfast ____   G. pain in mid-morning ____   H. pain at noon ____

I. pain in the mid-afternoon ____   J. pain in the late afternoon ____

K. pain in the early evening ____   L. pain at dinnertime ____

M. pain in the late evening ____   N. pain at bedtime ____   O. pain at work ____

36. What kinds of things ease or relieve your pain? Be specific. _____

_____

37. What kinds of things make your pain worse? Be specific. _____

_____

38. Below, list the kinds of things you used to do or enjoy that *now your pain prevents you from doing*. Next to each item or activity, record a *percentage* (0 to 100%) to show how much your pain *disables* or *stops you* from doing that activity.

% Disabled = 0%   10%   20%   30%   40%   50%   60%   70%   80%   90%   100%

Activity   Percentage   Activity   Percentage   Activity   Percentage

_____   _____   _____

_____   _____   _____

_____   _____   _____

_____   _____   _____

39. Circle a percentage below to show how much your pain disables you overall.

% Disabled = 0%   10%   20%   30%   40%   50%   60%   70%   80%   90%   100%

40. At what time/s of the day is your pain the worst?_____   The least?_____

41. For this past week, circle how much relief your pain medication has given you.

% Pain Relief = 0%   10%   20%   30%   40%   50%   60%   70%   80%   90%   100%

42. Currently, what is your primary pain treatment? _____

_____

For this past week, circle how much relief your primary pain treatment has given you.

% Pain Relief = 0%   10%   20%   30%   40%   50%   60%   70%   80%   90%   100%

43. Please tell us about any previous psychiatric or psychological treatment. __

_____

_____

44. Have you been experiencing any problems in your ability to remember things? ___ Yes ___ No

45. What have you been forgetting? _____

46. Have you been experiencing any problems understanding what you read? ___ Yes ___ No

47. Have you been experiencing any problems in your ability to concentrate on things? ___ Yes ___ No

48. Have there been any marked changes in your mood, personality, or behavior? ___ Yes ___ No

49. If *yes*, please describe these mood or personality changes. _____

_____

_____

50. Have there been any marked changes in your handwriting? ___ Yes ___ No

51. Have you been experiencing any problems calculating figures or handling money? ___ Yes ___ No

52. If *yes*, please describe these problems. _____

_____

_____

53. Have you experienced any changes in your ability to speak or understand others? ___ Yes ___ No

54. If *yes*, please describe these changes. _____

_____

_____

55. Are you able to do household chores? ___ Yes ___ No

56. Circle a percentage below to show how much your pain disables you from doing household chores.

% Disabled = 0%   10%   20%   30%   40%   50%   60%   70%   80%   90%   100%

57. Please explain your answers. _____

_____

_____

58. What is your regular type of work? _____

59. Are you able to do your regular type of work, or go to work? ___ Yes ___ No

60. Circle a percentage to show how much your pain disables you from doing your regular type of work.

% Disabled = 0%   10%   20%   30%   40%   50%   60%   70%   80%   90%   100%

61. Please explain your answers. _____

_____

_____

62. Medical History: Mark an X next to each medical problem you've had/have. Mark XX next to your main problems.

___ alcoholism
___ cancer
___ stomach problems
___ heart murmur
___ jaundice
___ herpes zoster
___ lung disease
___ depression
___ frequent colds
___ herniated disc
___ fibromyalgia
___ tension headaches
___ other urinary problem(s)
___ venereal disease
___ rheumatic fever
___ multiple sclerosis
___ hernias
___ gas/cramps/ indigestion
___ weakness or paralysis
___ pneumonia
___ a head injury
___ ringing in the ears
___ insomnia
___ double vision
___ severe appetite change
___ loss of smell or taste
___ anemia

___ diabetes
___ colitis
___ mitral valve prolapse
___ liver disease
___ oral herpes
___ emphysema
___ nightmares
___ chronic fatigue
___ fractures
___ other arthritis
___ migraine headaches
___ gynecologic problems
___ stroke
___ low blood sugar
___ lupus
___ hemorrhoids
___ shaking/tremor
___ trouble remembering
___ sickle cell anemia
___ menstrual problems
___ frequent heartburn
___ frequent diarrhea
___ blackouts
___ major weight change
___ loss of coordination
___ asthma
___ drug addiction
___ diverticulitis

___ heart disease
___ hepatitis
___ genital herpes
___ hearing problem
___ panic attacks
___ osteoarthritis
___ esophagitis
___ AIDS or HIV +
___ cluster headaches
___ thyroid problems
___ serious injuries
___ obesity
___ anxiety & nervousness
___ constipation
___ fainting spells
___ trouble concentrating
___ hemophilia
___ endometriosis
___ psychiatric problems
___ near death experience
___ loss of balance
___ numbness
___ severe nausea
___ allergies/hay fever
___ epilepsy/ seizures/ convulsions
___ irritable bowel syndrome
___ heart attack

___ high blood pressure/ hypertension
___ kidney disease
___ eye problems
___ skin problems
___ rheumatoid arthritis
___ repetitive strain injury
___ sinus problems
___ frequent urinary infections
___ ulcers
___ tuberculosis
___ glaucoma
___ cold/freezing hands or feet
___ foot problems
___ dizziness/ lightheaded
___ attention deficit disorder
___ coronary artery disease
___ history of physical or sexual abuse
___ serious infections
___ blurred vision
___ unable to use your hands
___ pins and needles sensation
___ Other: _____

63. Have any therapists taught you methods to relax when you get tense?
____ Yes ____ No

64. What relaxation methods do you use? _____

_____

_____

_____

65. Do you use any of these relaxation methods regularly when you get tense?
____ Yes ____ No

PPQ PAIN ADJECTIVE CHECKLIST

Patient Name: _____ Date: _____

INSTRUCTIONS FOR SECTION I: Please mark an X next to the qualities that your pain has. For those qualities you have marked, please show how much of that quality your pain has, how bad that quality is, or how well that quality describes your pain, by marking an X under (1) "a little bit," (2) "somewhat," (3) "quite a bit," or (4) "very much/a lot."

Pain Quality	(1) A Little Bit	(2) Somewhat	(3) Quite A Bit	(4) Very Much/ A Lot	
_____ 1. troublesome	_____	_____	_____	_____	
_____ 2. tiring	_____	_____	_____	_____	
_____ 3. exhausting	_____	_____	_____	_____	
_____ 4. depressing	_____	_____	_____	_____	aFa _____
_____ 5. sickening	_____	_____	_____	_____	
_____ 6. nauseating	_____	_____	_____	_____	
_____ 7. suffocating	_____	_____	_____	_____	aAu _____
_____ 8. punishing	_____	_____	_____	_____	
_____ 9. cruel	_____	_____	_____	_____	
_____ 10. vicious	_____	_____	_____	_____	
_____ 11. torturing	_____	_____	_____	_____	aPu _____
_____ 12. fearful	_____	_____	_____	_____	
_____ 13. frightening	_____	_____	_____	_____	
_____ 14. terrifying	_____	_____	_____	_____	
_____ 15. dreadful	_____	_____	_____	_____	aFe _____
_____ 16. annoying	_____	_____	_____	_____	
_____ 17. nagging	_____	_____	_____	_____	
_____ 18. miserable	_____	_____	_____	_____	eMi _____
_____ 19. intense	_____	_____	_____	_____	
_____ 20. agonizing	_____	_____	_____	_____	
_____ 21. unbearable	_____	_____	_____	_____	
_____ 22. killing	_____	_____	_____	_____	eSu _____
_____ 23. mysterious	_____	_____	_____	_____	
_____ 24. out of control	_____	_____	_____	_____	
_____ 25. disabling	_____	_____	_____	_____	
_____ 26. hopeless	_____	_____	_____	_____	eMs _____

A–E: Sum Rating _____   Percent of Max _____   Average _____

A: Sum Rating _____   Percent of Max _____   Average _____

E: Sum Rating _____   Percent of Max _____   Average _____

Note. Some of the items/adjectives on this checklist are adapted with permission from the McGill Pain Questionnaire. Copyright © 1975 Ronald Melzack, Ph.D.

INSTRUCTIONS FOR SECTION II: Please mark an X next to the qualities that your pain has. For those qualities you have marked, please show how much of that quality your pain has, how bad that quality is, or how well that quality describes your pain, by marking an X under (1) "a little bit," (2) "somewhat," (3) "quite a bit," or (4) "very much/a lot."

Pain Quality	(1) A Little Bit	(2) Somewhat	(3) Quite A Bit	(4) Very Much/ A Lot	
___ 27. throbbing	___	___	___	___	
___ 28. pounding	___	___	___	___	sTe ___
___ 29. spreading	___	___	___	___	
___ 30. splitting	___	___	___	___	
___ 31. shooting	___	___	___	___	sSp ___
___ 32. piercing	___	___	___	___	
___ 33. stabbing	___	___	___	___	sPP ___
___ 34. sharp	___	___	___	___	
___ 35. cutting	___	___	___	___	sIP ___
___ 36. tight	___	___	___	___	
___ 37. pinching	___	___	___	___	
___ 38. squeezing	___	___	___	___	
___ 39. cramping	___	___	___	___	sCP ___
___ 40. tugging	___	___	___	___	
___ 41. pulling	___	___	___	___	sTP ___
___ 42. hot-burning	___	___	___	___	
___ 43. stinging	___	___	___	___	sHo ___
___ 44. pressing	___	___	___	___	
___ 45. heavy	___	___	___	___	sAP ___
___ 46. tender	___	___	___	___	
___ 47. sore	___	___	___	___	
___ 48. gnawing	___	___	___	___	
___ 49. aching	___	___	___	___	sSo ___
___ 50. tingling	___	___	___	___	
___ 51. numb	___	___	___	___	
___ 52. cold-freezing	___	___	___	___	sCo ___
___ Other: ___	___	___	___	___	
___ Other: ___	___	___	___	___	

S: Sum Rating ___   Percent of Max ___   Average ___

TOT: Sum Rating ___   Percent of Max ___   Average ___

Note. Some of the items/adjectives on this checklist are adapted with permission from the McGill Pain Questionnaire. Copyright © 1975 Ronald Melzack, Ph.D.

PPQ PAIN INTENSITY RATINGS AND PAIN DRAWINGS

A. Pain Intensity Line: Make an "x" on the line below to show *how bad* your pain is *now*.

NO |——| WORST
PAIN   POSSIBLE PAIN

B. Present Pain Intensity: Check the *one* word below that best describes your present pain.

＿＿0. No pain ＿＿1. Mild ＿＿2. Discomforting ＿＿3. Distressing
＿＿4. Horrible ＿＿5. Excruciating

C. Temporal Quality of Your Pain: Please circle all of the words below that describe your pain.

Brief   Comes and goes   Continuous   Constant   Always there
Never goes away   Appears and disappears   Intermittent

D. Percentage of Time in Pain: Please circle the percentage (%) of time you are in pain.

0%   10%   20%   30%   40%   50%   60%   70%   80%   90%   100%

E. Pain Drawing: On the front and rear views of the human figure below, show the areas on your body where you have pain by drawing in the following symbols: "xxx" for pain; "lll" for pins & needles; and "000" for numbness.

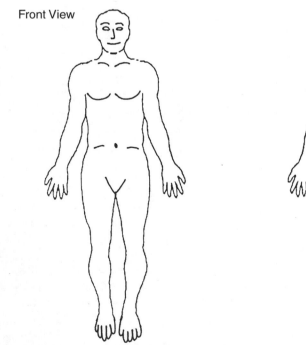

Front View   Rear View

F. For up to 6 areas on your body where you marked that you have pain above, choose up to 3 words from the Pain Adjective Checklist that best describe the pain in each area you marked. Number each area on the figures above.

Most painful area: 1. ——————————   ——————————   ——————————

                          2. ——————————   ——————————   ——————————

                          3. ——————————   ——————————   ——————————

                          4. ——————————   ——————————   ——————————

                          5. ——————————   ——————————   ——————————

Least painful area: 6. ——————————   ——————————   ——————————

Note. Items A, B, and C are adapted with permission from the McGill Pain Questionnaire. Copyright © 1975 Ronald Melzack, Ph.D.

APPENDIX D
Brief Pain Status Questionnaire

Patient Name: _____ Date: _____

INSTRUCTIONS: Please fill out this questionnaire based on how you have been feeling this week.

1. Do you suffer from pain? _____ Yes _____ No From what kind of pain do you suffer? Describe your pain. _____

   _____

2. What percentage of time are you in pain? _____ Please circle the % of time you are in pain below.

   % Time in Pain = 0% 10% 20% 30% 40% 50% 60% 70% 80% 90% 100%

3. Write a #1 next to your primary area of pain, and a #2, #3, etc. next to your secondary sites of pain.

   ___ head/face/mouth ___ neck ___ shoulders/upper arms ___ lower arms
   ___ hands/fingers ___ abdomen/stomach ___ chest ___ upper back ___ mid-back
   ___ low back ___ upper legs ___ lower legs ___ feet ___ pelvis ___ buttocks
   ___ hips ___ anal area ___ genital area ___ Other: _____

4. Using the "0 to 10" scale below, rate the *strength* or *intensity* of your pain for each area you marked above. Record a number rating on the line next to each area or site of your pain below.

   No Pain   Worst Pain Imaginable
   0   1   2   3   4   5   6   7   8   9   10

   ___ head/face/mouth ___ neck ___ shoulders/upper arms ___ lower arms
   ___ hands/fingers ___ abdomen/stomach ___ chest ___ upper back ___ mid-back
   ___ low back ___ upper legs ___ lower legs ___ feet ___ pelvis ___ buttocks
   ___ hips ___ anal area ___ genital area ___ Other: _____

5. List all medications you are currently taking below.

   Medication Name   Dosage (mg.)   No. times per day? Taking for what?

   _____   _____   _____   _____

   _____   _____   _____   _____

   _____   _____   _____   _____

   _____   _____   _____   _____

6. Are you working now? _____ Yes _____ No   7. If yes, how many hours/week? _____

8. Rate the strength of your primary pain on the following scale for each situation or time below:

   No Pain   Worst Pain Imaginable
   0   1   2   3   4   5   6   7   8   9   10

   A. pain now _____   B. least pain this week _____   C. worst pain this week _____
   D. usual level of pain _____   E. pain in the early morning _____
   F. pain at breakfast _____   G. pain in mid-morning _____   H. pain at noon _____
   I. pain in the mid-afternoon _____   J. pain in the late afternoon _____
   K. pain in the early evening _____   L. pain at dinnertime _____
   M. pain in the late evening _____   N. pain at bedtime _____   O. pain at work _____

9. What kinds of things ease or relieve your pain? Be specific. _____

_____

10. What kinds of things make your pain worse? Be specific. _____

_____

11. Below, list the kinds of things you used to do or enjoy that now your pain prevents you from doing. Next to each item or activity, record a percentage (0 to 100%) to show how much your pain disables/stops you from doing that activity.

% Disabled = 0%   10%   20%   30%   40%   50%   60%   70%   80%   90%   100%

Activity	Percentage	Activity	Percentage	Activity	Percentage
_____	_____	_____	_____	_____	_____
_____	_____	_____	_____	_____	_____
_____	_____	_____	_____	_____	_____
_____	_____	_____	_____	_____	_____

12. Circle a percentage below to show how much your pain disables you overall.

% Disabled = 0%   10%   20%   30%   40%   50%   60%   70%   80%   90%   100%

13. Are you able to do household chores? ____ Yes   ____ No

14. Circle a percentage below to show how much your pain disables you from doing household chores.

% Disabled = 0%   10%   20%   30%   40%   50%   60%   70%   80%   90%   100%

15. Are you able to do your regular type of work, or go to work? ____ Yes ____ No

16. Circle a percentage to show how much your pain disables you from doing your regular type of work.

% Disabled = 0%   10%   20%   30%   40%   50%   60%   70%   80%   90%   100%

17. At what time/s of the day is your pain the worst? _____

   The least? _____

18. For this past week, circle how much relief your pain medication has given you.

% Pain Relief = 0%   10%   20%   30%   40%   50%   60%   70%   80%   90%   100%

19. Currently, what is your primary pain treatment?

20. For this past week, circle how much relief your primary pain treatment has given you.

% Pain Relief = 0%   10%   20%   30%   40%   50%   60%   70%   80%   90%   100%

21. Please check the one word that best describes your present pain.

   ____ It's brief   ____ It comes and goes   ____ It is constant. It's always there.

22. Please make an "X" on the line below to show *how bad* your pain is *right now*.

NO |———| WORST
PAIN   POSSIBLE PAIN

23. Have any therapists taught you methods to relax when you get tense?
   ____ Yes ____ No

24. What relaxation methods do you use? _____

25. Do you use any of these relaxation methods regularly when you get tense?
   ____ Yes ____ No

The Pain Imagery Interview

Presenting Complaint
  1. What is the reason you are here today?
  2. How do you wish to be helped?

Pain Experience
  3. Please describe what your pain is like.
  4. Where in your body do you experience the pain? Where does it start? Does it travel?
  5. Does your pain penetrate deeply like a stomachache, or is it more on the surface near your skin?

Pain Onset
  6. How did your pain begin?
  7. When did your pain start?
  8. How long have you had this pain?
  9. What do you think caused the pain?

Pain Imagery
  10. What does your pain feel like?
  11. What do you imagine your pain to be when it gets bad? If you could take a photograph of your pain, what might it look like? Where is it located?

Pain Relief Factors and Imagery
  12. What seems to make your pain feel better? What seems to take it away or bring relief?
  13. If you could take a photograph of what brings you relief, what would it look like?
  14. What seems to prevent or block you from having the pain relief you want?
  15. What do you think might get rid of this obstacle to obtaining the relief you want?
  16. What have you done to lessen your pain?

Pain Triggers
  17. What seems to make your pain get worse?
  18. How often does your pain get worse?
  19. When and where does your pain get worse?
  20. Does it seem to get worse when you are doing certain things, or are around certain people?

Projective Questions
  21. What are some of the different ways in which your pain affects you?
  22. How would your life be different without this pain?
  23. What could you do that you are not doing now, if you did not have this problem?
  24. What do you think caused the pain in the first place?
  25. Why do you think the pain has not gone away or been alleviated by now?

Pain Severity and Pain Interference

26. How *bad* is your pain right now on a "0" to "10" Pain Meter (0 = no pain, 10 = worst pain imaginable)?
27. How *bad* is your pain at its worst on this "0" to "10" Pain Meter (0 = no pain, 10 = worst pain imaginable)?
28. At its least?
29. How does your pain interfere with your life?
30. How was your life different before you had this pain condition?
31. What kinds of things does your pain condition prevent you from doing now?

Negative Cognitions

32. Think of your pain right now. What *negative thoughts* about yourself come to mind?
33. What *negative thoughts* do you *usually* get when you think about your pain?

Positive Cognitions

34. What *positive thought* do you think might help you get relief from your pain?

Belief in Positive Cognition

35. How true does that positive thought feel to you right now (1 = does not feel true at all, 7 = feels completely true)?

Primary Losses

36. What have you *lost* as a result of being in this condition?

Alternative Complaints

37. How has being in this condition *complicated* your life?
38. What other symptoms have you had since your accident/injury/pain began?
39. What would you say are the *big three stressors* in your life right now?

Work and Disability

40. How has your condition affected your ability to work? Are you working now? When did you last work?
41. Were you working before this condition started?
42. How does your condition affect your ability to do household chores?

Social Support

43. With whom do you live?
44. How do they treat you?
45. Does anyone treat you differently when you are in pain? How so?

Associated Emotions

46. What are you most afraid of?
47. What was the most anxious, fearful experience of your life?
48. What was the saddest, most depressing experience of your life?
49. What has been one of the happiest experiences of your life?
50. What has been one of your proudest moments?
51. What are you most ashamed of?

Past Occurrences and Vulnerabilities

52. Has anything like this ever happened to you in the past, before your present problems began?
53. What was your childhood like?
54. Was your childhood happy or sad? Please explain.
55. As a child or teenager, did you ever suffer any major trauma?
56. As an adult, have you ever suffered any major trauma (besides your current condition)?
57. As a child or teenager, were you ever abused or sexually molested?

Secondary Gains

58. Is there anything that you have already gained, or stand to gain, because of this condition (accident/pain/injury)?
59. What are some of the OTHER (secondary) benefits that may come to you because of your condition (pain)?

Previous Treatment

60. Who else have you gone to for treatment of your pain problem? How much did each one help on a scale of 0% to 100%?

More Pain Imagery

61. Picture your pain at its worst. What is it like? What do you see? How vivid is the picture on a 0 to 10 scale with 10 being most vivid?
62. Picture your pain at its least. What is it like? What do you see? How vivid is the picture?
63. Picture what makes your pain worse. What is it like? What do you see? How vivid is the picture?

More Pain Relief Imagery

64. Picture what brings you pain relief. What is it like? What do you see? How vivid is the picture?
65. Picture yourself being pain free. What is it like? What do you see? How vivid is the picture?
66. On a scale of "0" to "100" percent, how pain free can you picture yourself?
67. What is the picture like? What do you see? How vivid is the picture?

Coping

68. How have you been coping?
68A. What kinds of things do you do to cope when the pain gets bad?

Projective Coping Question

69. What do you think you could do to *make friends with* your pain?

Motivation Question

70. On a scale of "0" to "100%," how motivated are you to do everything you can within your power, to get relief from your pain?
71. How motivated are you to work really hard to learn to better manage your pain condition?

Improvement Ratings

72. How much pain relief have you gotten since starting therapy (0 . . . 100%)?
73. How much better do you feel (0 . . . 100%)?

Additional Questions

74. Is there anything you want to say more about?
75. Is there anything else you want to say that is relevant to your problem?
76. How do you feel now, at this moment, about your purpose for being here?
77. Do you have any other thoughts about how you would like me to be of help to you?

The Pain Vulnerability Checklist

Patient Name: _____ Date: _____

INSTRUCTIONS: The purpose of this checklist is to discover the things that make you vulnerable to having a flare-up of your pain. By knowing these things, we can then help you to modify some of your reactions to situations and behaviors that typically lead to a pain flare-up. This may help you prevent a pain flare-up or lower its severity.

So, please read each item below. For each item, first, circle a number that tells how many days over this past week you *felt* or *did* that item. Then, circle a number that tells *how vulnerable* you believe that item made you to having a pain flare-up.

	Over the past 7 days, how many days have you *felt* or *done* the things below?	How vulnerable to having your pain flare up did this make you? 0 = not at all vulnerable 1 = a little vulnerable 2 = quite a bit vulnerable 3 = very vulnerable
	Number of Days?	**How Vulnerable?**
1. You worried a lot about something important to you	0 1 2 3 4 5 6 7	0 1 2 3
2. You worried a lot about your health	0 1 2 3 4 5 6 7	0 1 2 3
3. You punished yourself over something you felt guilty about	0 1 2 3 4 5 6 7	0 1 2 3
4. You tried to punish someone else for something you think they did wrong	0 1 2 3 4 5 6 7	0 1 2 3
5. You yelled at someone over something annoying to you	0 1 2 3 4 5 6 7	0 1 2 3
6. You felt embarrassed about something	0 1 2 3 4 5 6 7	0 1 2 3
7. You felt ashamed about something	0 1 2 3 4 5 6 7	0 1 2 3
8. You were overly responsible	0 1 2 3 4 5 6 7	0 1 2 3
9. You accepted blame for something that was not your fault	0 1 2 3 4 5 6 7	0 1 2 3
10. You felt guilty about something	0 1 2 3 4 5 6 7	0 1 2 3
11. You dwelled on negative thoughts about yourself	0 1 2 3 4 5 6 7	0 1 2 3
12. You had a temper tantrum over something that did not go your way	0 1 2 3 4 5 6 7	0 1 2 3
13. You got very angry over something	0 1 2 3 4 5 6 7	0 1 2 3
14. You got very anxious or nervous about something	0 1 2 3 4 5 6 7	0 1 2 3
15. You did not eat enough	0 1 2 3 4 5 6 7	0 1 2 3
16. You ate too much	0 1 2 3 4 5 6 7	0 1 2 3

Patient Name: _____ Date: _____

	Over the past 7 days, how many days have you *felt* or *done* the things below?	How vulnerable to having your pain flare up did this make you? 0 = not at all vulnerable 1 = a little vulnerable 2 = quite a bit vulnerable 3 = very vulnerable
	Number of Days?	**How Vulnerable?**
17. You ate junk food	0 1 2 3 4 5 6 7	0 1 2 3
18. You did not sleep enough	0 1 2 3 4 5 6 7	0 1 2 3
19. You slept too much	0 1 2 3 4 5 6 7	0 1 2 3
20. You had very restless or disturbed sleep	0 1 2 3 4 5 6 7	0 1 2 3
21. You dwelled on the loss of something very important to you	0 1 2 3 4 5 6 7	0 1 2 3
22. You worked too much or too hard	0 1 2 3 4 5 6 7	0 1 2 3
23. You did not work enough	0 1 2 3 4 5 6 7	0 1 2 3
24. You did not eat regular meals	0 1 2 3 4 5 6 7	0 1 2 3
25. You stayed up unusually late	0 1 2 3 4 5 6 7	0 1 2 3
26. You went to bed unusually early	0 1 2 3 4 5 6 7	0 1 2 3
27. You did not get enough physical exercise	0 1 2 3 4 5 6 7	0 1 2 3
28. You woke up much earlier than usual	0 1 2 3 4 5 6 7	0 1 2 3
29. You slept much later than usual	0 1 2 3 4 5 6 7	0 1 2 3
30. You were overly critical of yourself	0 1 2 3 4 5 6 7	0 1 2 3
31. You did not stand up for yourself in a situation	0 1 2 3 4 5 6 7	0 1 2 3
32. You said "yes" when you really meant "no"	0 1 2 3 4 5 6 7	0 1 2 3
33. You bottled up your feelings in a tense situation	0 1 2 3 4 5 6 7	0 1 2 3
34. You had recurring thoughts about something traumatic or very upsetting to you	0 1 2 3 4 5 6 7	0 1 2 3
35. You ate something that disagreed with you	0 1 2 3 4 5 6 7	0 1 2 3
36. You felt very hurried or pressured over something	0 1 2 3 4 5 6 7	0 1 2 3
37. You did not go to work	0 1 2 3 4 5 6 7	0 1 2 3
38. You overdid some physical activity and overexerted yourself	0 1 2 3 4 5 6 7	0 1 2 3
39. You argued with your spouse or with your significant other	0 1 2 3 4 5 6 7	0 1 2 3

Patient Name: _____ Date: _____

Over the past 7 days, how
many days have you *felt* or
done the things below?

	Number of Days?	How Vulnerable?
40. You bent or moved wrong	0 1 2 3 4 5 6 7	0 1 2 3
41. You lifted something wrong or too heavy for you	0 1 2 3 4 5 6 7	0 1 2 3
42. You felt unable to make a decision about something	0 1 2 3 4 5 6 7	0 1 2 3
43. You did not pace yourself	0 1 2 3 4 5 6 7	0 1 2 3
44. You worried a lot about there being something seriously wrong with you	0 1 2 3 4 5 6 7	0 1 2 3
45. You tried to control something that is uncontrollable	0 1 2 3 4 5 6 7	0 1 2 3
46. You avoided taking responsibility for something that you were probably responsible for	0 1 2 3 4 5 6 7	0 1 2 3
47. You drank any kind of alcoholic beverage	0 1 2 3 4 5 6 7	0 1 2 3
48. You felt very hateful toward someone	0 1 2 3 4 5 6 7	0 1 2 3
49. You felt taken advantage of	0 1 2 3 4 5 6 7	0 1 2 3
50. You told a lie	0 1 2 3 4 5 6 7	0 1 2 3
51. You made an excuse for refusing to do something, instead of being honest and saying you just did not want to do it	0 1 2 3 4 5 6 7	0 1 2 3
52. You were insincere with someone or manipulative	0 1 2 3 4 5 6 7	0 1 2 3
53. You got depressed	0 1 2 3 4 5 6 7	0 1 2 3
54. You tried too hard to get or accomplish something	0 1 2 3 4 5 6 7	0 1 2 3
55. You intentionally were mean or tried to hurt someone	0 1 2 3 4 5 6 7	0 1 2 3
56. You felt resentful or jealous of someone	0 1 2 3 4 5 6 7	0 1 2 3
57. You were overly demanding of yourself	0 1 2 3 4 5 6 7	0 1 2 3
58. You were overly demanding of someone else	0 1 2 3 4 5 6 7	0 1 2 3

Patient Name: _____ Date: _____

	Over the past 7 days, how many days have you *felt* or *done* the things below?	How vulnerable to having your pain flare up did this make you? 0 = not at all vulnerable 1 = a little vulnerable 2 = quite a bit vulnerable 3 = very vulnerable
	Number of Days?	**How Vulnerable?**
59. You were feeling very hurried or pressured to get something done	0 1 2 3 4 5 6 7	0 1 2 3
60. You were feeling very bored	0 1 2 3 4 5 6 7	0 1 2 3
61. You felt like a failure	0 1 2 3 4 5 6 7	0 1 2 3
62. You felt like doing harm to someone	0 1 2 3 4 5 6 7	0 1 2 3
63. You got quite angry and felt like there was no way to express it	0 1 2 3 4 5 6 7	0 1 2 3
64. You felt quite angry and took it out on someone	0 1 2 3 4 5 6 7	0 1 2 3
65. You spent too much time reading	0 1 2 3 4 5 6 7	0 1 2 3
66. You spent too much time typing at a computer keyboard	0 1 2 3 4 5 6 7	0 1 2 3
67. You spent too much time lying in bed	0 1 2 3 4 5 6 7	0 1 2 3
68. You spent too much time sitting	0 1 2 3 4 5 6 7	0 1 2 3
69. You acted or felt very competitive	0 1 2 3 4 5 6 7	0 1 2 3
70. You pushed yourself too hard in some way	0 1 2 3 4 5 6 7	0 1 2 3
71. You stood on your feet too much	0 1 2 3 4 5 6 7	0 1 2 3
72. You felt preoccupied with a stressful situation	0 1 2 3 4 5 6 7	0 1 2 3
73. You let yourself remain preoccupied with your pain	0 1 2 3 4 5 6 7	0 1 2 3
74. You did something you did not want to do, even though you did not have to do it	0 1 2 3 4 5 6 7	0 1 2 3
75. You got angry at what you thought to be ignorant people	0 1 2 3 4 5 6 7	0 1 2 3
76. You dwelled on some trivial and unimportant annoyances	0 1 2 3 4 5 6 7	0 1 2 3
77. You smoked more than you usually do	0 1 2 3 4 5 6 7	0 1 2 3
78. You felt worthless	0 1 2 3 4 5 6 7	0 1 2 3
79. You spent too much time watching television	0 1 2 3 4 5 6 7	0 1 2 3
80. You used your pain as an excuse to get out of doing something	0 1 2 3 4 5 6 7	0 1 2 3

Patient Name: _____ Date: _____

	Over the past 7 days, how many days have you *felt* or *done* the things below?	How vulnerable to having your pain flare up did this make you? 0 = not at all vulnerable 1 = a little vulnerable 2 = quite a bit vulnerable 3 = very vulnerable
	Number of Days?	How Vulnerable?
81. You drank coffee	0 1 2 3 4 5 6 7	0 1 2 3
82. You drank some caffeinated beverage other than coffee	0 1 2 3 4 5 6 7	0 1 2 3
83. You did not exercise at all	0 1 2 3 4 5 6 7	0 1 2 3
84. You exercised too much	0 1 2 3 4 5 6 7	0 1 2 3
85. You did not plan your day	0 1 2 3 4 5 6 7	0 1 2 3
86. Other? _____	0 1 2 3 4 5 6 7	0 1 2 3
87. Other? _____	0 1 2 3 4 5 6 7	0 1 2 3
88. Other? _____	0 1 2 3 4 5 6 7	0 1 2 3
89. Other? _____	0 1 2 3 4 5 6 7	0 1 2 3
90. Other? _____	0 1 2 3 4 5 6 7	0 1 2 3

APPENDIX G-1
The Geriatric Pain Assessment Interview

Patient _____ Date _____ Rm No. _____ Facility _____

Original Admission Date _____ No. Years in Facility _____ Ethnicity _____

Age _____ Birthdate _____ Sex _____ Education _____ Marital Status ___

Former Occupation _____ Physician _____

Reason for Being in Nursing Home _____

Medical and Psychiatric Diagnoses _____

_____

_____

Medication	Dose	How Often	Medication	Dose	How Often
_____	____	_____	_____	____	_____
_____	____	_____	_____	____	_____
_____	____	_____	_____	____	_____

Reason for Psychology Consultation: _____

Type of Pain: _____Time Since Onset: _____

The Temporal Pattern of the Pain

1. Is your pain constant? Are you always in pain?   Yes (1)   No (0)
2. Are there ever times when you are pain free?   Yes (0)   No (1)
3. Does your pain change on you?   Yes (0)   No (1)
4. Does your pain come and go?   Yes (0)   No (1)
5. Does your pain get worse and then better, worse   Yes (0)   No (1)
   and then better, and so on?
6. Does your pain always stay the same?   Yes (1)   No (0)
6a. How long does the pain last? _____

The Pain's Severity

7. Is the pain mild?   Yes (0)   No (1)
8. Is the pain uncomfortable?   Yes (0)   No (1)
9. Is the pain very uncomfortable?   Yes (1)   No (0)
10. Is the pain distressing?   Yes (1)   No (0)
11. Is the pain horrible?   Yes (1)   No (0)
12. Can you ever ignore the pain?   Yes (0)   No (1)
12a. What is the least amount of pain you ever have (0–10)? _____
12b. What is the worst it gets (0–10)? _____
12c. How bad is it now? (0–10)? _____

The Pain's Spatial Pattern and Distribution

13. Does the pain stay in one spot?   Yes (0)   No (1)
14. Does the pain spread?   Yes (1)   No (0)
14a. Describe the location and distribution of the pain. _____

Page 1 Column Sums _____   _____

Patient Name: _____ Date: _____

Description of the Pain
15. Is the pain a hot or burning pain?   Yes (1)   No (0)
16. Is it a sharp or stabbing pain?   Yes (1)   No (0)
17. Is it a dull aching pain?   Yes (1)   No (0)
18. Is it a throbbing or pounding pain?   Yes (1)   No (0)
18a. How else would you describe the pain?

Pain Triggers
19. Does it hurt you more when you move?   Yes (1)   No (0)
20. Does sitting for awhile make the pain worse?   Yes (1)   No (0)
21. Does it hurt more when you get up?   Yes (1)   No (0)
22. Does it hurt when you are lying in bed?   Yes (1)   No (0)
23. Do you know what else makes the pain worse?   Yes (0)   No (1)

Pain Relievers
24. Do you know what makes the pain better? More   Yes (0)   No (1)
     tolerable? What lessens the pain?
25. Does taking pills or medicine help?   Yes (0)   No (1)
26. Can you sleep at night?   Yes (0)   No (1)
27. Do you get relief when you are asleep?   Yes (0)   No (1)
28. Do you have trouble falling asleep at night?   Yes (1)   No (0)
29. Do you have trouble staying asleep at night?   Yes (1)   No (0)
30. Can you nap during the day?   Yes (0)   No (1)
31. Are the nurses who take care of you able to do   Yes (0)   No (1)
     anything to lessen the pain?
31a. What can they do to lessen the pain? _____
32. Is there anything that you can do to lessen the pain   Yes (0)   No (1)
     and get relief?
32a. What can you do to lessen the pain? _____
32b. What do you do to cope when the pain gets bad? _____

Emotional Consequences of Pain
33. Does the pain get so bad that you just want to die?   Yes (1)   No (0)
34. Do you feel there is anything that I/we can do to   Yes (0)   No (1)
     lessen your pain and give you relief?
34a. What do you think I/we can do to help you?
35. Do you have an appetite?   Yes (0)   No (1)
36. Do you think a lot about your pain getting worse?   Yes (1)   No (0)
37. Are you depressed because of this pain?   Yes (1)   No (0)
38. Are you irritable when you are in pain?   Yes (1)   No (0)
39. Are you impatient when you are in pain?   Yes (1)   No (0)
40. Are you afraid the pain is going to get worse?   Yes (1)   No (0)
41. Does the pain drive you crazy?   Yes (1)   No (0)
42. Do you worry when you are in pain?   Yes (1)   No (0)
42a. What do you worry about? _____

Page 2 Column Sums _____   _____

Patient Name: _____ Date: _____

43.	Do you ever feel disappointed in yourself for giving in to the pain?	Yes (1)	No (0)
44.	Do you blame yourself when you are in pain?	Yes (1)	No (0)
45.	Do you feel that your life is still worth living?	Yes (0)	No (1)
46.	Do you feel sorry for yourself when you are in pain?	Yes (1)	No (0)
47.	Can you think of other things besides your pain?	Yes (0)	No (1)
40.	Do you think that it is hard to do anything at all when you have pain?	Yes (1)	No (0)
49.	Are you afraid that there might be something seriously wrong that they are not telling you?	Yes (1)	No (0)
50.	Are you bothered by unwanted thoughts when you are in pain?	Yes (1)	No (0)
50a.	What are some of these thoughts? _____		

_____

Page 3 Column Sums _____   _____

Patient Name: _____ Date: _____

SCORING PROFILE FORM FOR THE GERIATRIC
PAIN ASSESSMENT INTERVIEW

Category	Raw Score	Percentage	Graphic Profile (Higher Scores Mean a Greater Pain Problem)
Total Score (53 scored items)	____ /80	____ %	0 10 20 30 40 50 60 70 80 90 100
Temporal Pattern (items 1–6)	____ /6	____ %	0 10 20 30 40 50 60 70 80 90 100
Pain Severity (items 7–12 plus the sum of the ratings for items 12a–c)	____ /36	____ %	0 10 20 30 40 50 60 70 80 90 100
Spatial Pattern (items 13 and 14)	____ /2	____ %	0 10 20 30 40 50 60 70 80 90 100
Pain Description (items 15–18)	____ /4	____ %	0 10 20 30 40 50 60 70 80 90 100
Pain Triggers (items 19 -23)	____ /5	____ %	0 10 20 30 40 50 60 70 80 90 100
Pain Relievers (items 24–31, 32)	____ /9	____ %	0 10 20 30 40 50 60 70 80 90 100
Emotional Consequents (items 33, 34, 35–42, 43–50)	____ /18	____ %	0 10 20 30 40 50 60 70 80 90 100

Comments:

APPENDIX G-2
Report of Psychological Evaluation Conducted in
Hospital or Residential Care Facility

Patient: ———————— Evaluation Date: ———— Birthdate/Age: ——
Room No.: ——— Date of Admission: ——— Referring Physician: ———
Insurance Information: ———————— Nearest Relatives: ————

BACKGROUND INFORMATION:

Reason for admission: Medical and psychiatric diagnoses:

Reason for referral: Current physical limitations:

Pertinent life history:

PROCEDURES ADMINISTERED:

Recent Stressors; Precipitating Events; Problem Behaviors; Current Symptoms:

Mental Status and Interpersonal Behavior *(report on all that are relevant)*—(a) orientation; (b) ability to communicate; (c) response to attention; (d) affect & mood; (e) behavior; (f) attitude and manner; (g) speech, language, & comprehension; (h) complaints and perceptions; (i) predominant thought content; (j) Patient's fears if determinable; (k) judgment & insight; (l) preserved cognitive skills; (m) cognitive deficiencies; (n) pain complaints or problems; (o) adjustment to living in SNF; (p) test results:

DIAGNOSTIC IMPRESSIONS:

(continued)

REPORT OF PSYCHOLOGICAL EVALUATION RE: _____

RECOMMENDATIONS AND TREATMENT PLAN:

Current Symptoms/Problems That Are the Focus of Treatment	Treatment Goals	Treatment Modalities

Date _____   Clinical Psychologist _____

Name: _____ Today's Date: _____

INSTRUCTIONS: Rate your *pain's intensity* every *two* hours by recording a number in the appropriate column to indicate: **0 = no pain; 1 = mild pain; 2 = discomforting pain; 3 = distressing pain; 4 = horrible pain; or 5 = excruciating pain.** Each time you rate your pain, record your *pain location/s,* the *situation* or *activity,* your *automatic thoughts,* and *coping measures.* In the column marked *Pain Medications,* record the *names, dosage,* and *# tablets taken* for every drug you take for your pain. To rate your *emotional distress,* record a number under your pain rating (e.g., 4/3) to indicate: **0 = not at all distressed; 1 = just a little distressed; 2 = more than a little distressed; 3 = quite a bit distressed; 4 = distressed a lot; 5 = terribly distressed.**

Time	0	1	2	3	4	5	Pain Location/s	Situation and Activity	Automatic Thoughts	Emotional Feelings	Coping Measures	Pain Medications
6 AM												
8 AM												
10 AM												
12 PM												
2 PM												
4 PM												
6 PM												
8 PM												
10 PM												
12 AM												
2 AM												
4 AM												

Note. The 0 to 5 verbal-numerical pain intensity scale on this form is adapted with permission from the McGill Pain Questionnaire. Copyright © 1975 Ronald Melzack, Ph.D.

APPENDIX I
PPQ Pain Adjective Checklist—Oral Administration Version

Patient Name: _____ Date: _____

<u>Oral Administration—General Instructions.</u> The examiner introduces the purpose of the PPQ as follows: I am going to ask you some questions because I want to learn from you what your pain is like - what it feels like to you. I want you to be able to describe your pain to me and also to tell me how intense, how bad, or how strong it is. Nobody can know exactly what someone else's pain feels like, but if you answer the following questions, at least I can get a better idea of what your pain feels like to you and how bad it is. Is that all right with you? If the patient indicates, "Yes, it is all right," then the examiner should say: Good. Then let's begin.

<u>Marking Pain Locations.</u> The examiner should begin by asking the patient to indicate where the pain is felt. The examiner says: Please tell me or show me where you have pain, starting with where your pain is the worst. The examiner may want to facilitate this by asking the patient to shade in or mark Xs on a figure drawing (front and rear views). The examiner can ask the patient to indicate for each pain location: Do you feel the pain near the surface of your skin or deep, below your skin?

Pain Locations: _____

<u>Administering the PPQ Adjective Checklist—Sections I and II.</u> The examiner should begin administering the 52 PPQ items in numbered order, beginning with item #1 ("troublesome"). The format for administering each item is given below. The appropriate descriptor is inserted in the blanks.

        Is your pain _____? How _____ is your pain?
        Is it "a little bit" _____? Is it "somewhat" _____?
        Is it "quite a bit" _____? Or, is it "very much/a lot" _____?

The items should be administered in the numerical order in which they appear. All 52 items should be administered. Do not skip or omit any items! If the patient affirms that his or her pain is characterized by a given descriptor, then, the examiner should mark an "X" next to that descriptor's number and ask the patient to rate the intensity of that descriptor. The examiner should also mark an "X" to record the patient's intensity rating for each relevant descriptor. If the patient denies that his or her pain is characterized by a given descriptor, then, the examiner should move on to the next descriptor.

<u>Oral Administration Instructions for Section III</u>

A. Next, the examiner says to the patient: Please tell me how bad your pain is right now by giving your pain a number from "0 to 100." "Zero" means that right now you have no pain, and "100" means that right now your pain is 100% bad, or as bad as it could be. How bad is your pain right now?

    Present Pain Index (0–100) = _____

B. If the patient is currently in pain, ask the following questions and underline the patient's selections: Right now, is your pain Mild? Is it Discomforting? Distressing? Horrible? Or, Excruciating? If the patient is not currently in pain, ask: When you are in pain, is it usually Mild? Discomforting? Distressing? Horrible? Or, Excruciating?

C. The examiner then asks: Is your pain brief? Does it come and go? Or, is it constant?

Note. Adapted with permission from the McGill Pain Questionnaire. Copyright © 1975 Ronald Melzack.

426

APPENDIX J
PPQ-PAC Scoring and Profile Form

PATIENT_____ DATE_____ DOB_____/AGE_____ SEX_____ MARITAL_____ ETHNICITY_____

EDUCATION_____ OCCUPATION_____ WORKING: __Yes __No LITIGATION: __Yes __No DISABILITY: __Yes __NO

PAIN SITE_____ CAUSE OF PAIN_____ PAIN DURATION_____

Where "_N_" = # items selected and rated: S = Sensory   A = Affective   E = Evaluative   A-E = Affective-Evaluative

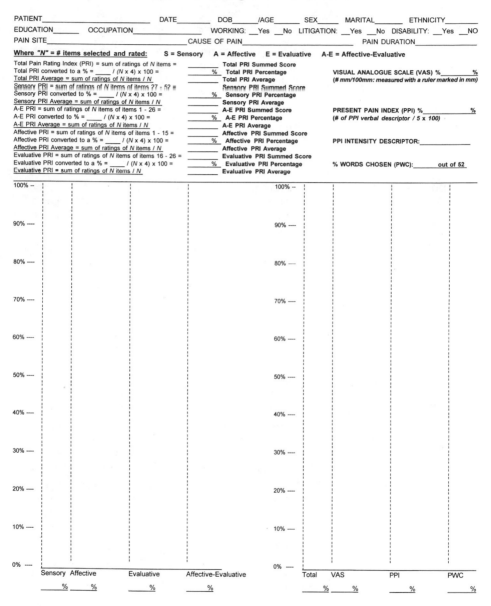

Total Pain Rating Index (PRI) = sum of ratings of _N_ items =   _____   **Total PRI Summed Score**

Total PRI converted to a % = ____ / (_N_ x 4) x 100 =   ____%   **Total PRI Percentage**   VISUAL ANALOGUE SCALE (VAS) %_____%

Total PRI Average = sum of ratings of _N_ items / _N_   _____   **Total PRI Average**   *(# mm/100mm: measured with a ruler marked in mm)*

Sensory PRI = sum of ratings of _N_ items of items 27 - 52 =   _____   **Sensory PRI Summed Score**

Sensory PRI converted to % = ____ / (_N_ x 4) x 100 =   ____%   **Sensory PRI Percentage**

Sensory PRI Average = sum of ratings of _N_ items / _N_   _____   **Sensory PRI Average**

A-E PRI = sum of ratings of _N_ items of items 1 - 26 =   _____   **A-E PRI Summed Score**   PRESENT PAIN INDEX (PPI) %_____%

A-E PRI converted to % = ____ / (_N_ x 4) x 100 =   ____%   **A-E PRI Percentage**   *(# of PPI verbal descriptor / 5 x 100)*

A-E PRI Average = sum of ratings of _N_ items / _N_   _____   **A-E PRI Average**

Affective PRI = sum of ratings of _N_ items of items 1 - 15 =   _____   **Affective PRI Summed Score**

Affective PRI converted to a % = ____ / (_N_ x 4) x 100 =   ____%   **Affective PRI Percentage**   PPI INTENSITY DESCRIPTOR:_____

Affective PRI Average = sum of ratings of _N_ items / _N_   _____   **Affective PRI Average**

Evaluative PRI = sum of ratings of _N_ items of items 16 - 26 =   _____   **Evaluative PRI Summed Score**

Evaluative PRI converted to a % = ____ / (_N_ x 4) x 100 =   ____%   **Evaluative PRI Percentage**   % WORDS CHOSEN (PWC):_____ out of 52

Evaluative PRI Average = sum of ratings of _N_ items / _N_   _____   **Evaluative PRI Average**

427

Pain Interference and Impairment Index

Patient: _____ Date: _____

INSTRUCTIONS: For each activity below, circle the number of the response that shows how much and how often pain interferes with that activity. Record your responses for every activity. Do not skip any items.

Does Pain Interfere with . . .	How Much?	How Often?
1. Bathing independently?	0. not at all 1. slightly 2. a lot 3. it stops me completely	0. less than 25% of the time 1. 25% to 50% of the time 2. 51% to 75% of the time 3. 76% to 100% of the time
2. Dressing independently?	0. not at all 1. slightly 2. a lot 3. it stops me completely	0. less than 25% of the time 1. 25% to 50% of the time 2. 51% to 75% of the time 3. 76% to 100% of the time
3. Eating?	0. not at all 1. slightly 2. a lot 3. it stops me completely	0. less than 25% of the time 1. 25% to 50% of the time 2. 51% to 75% of the time 3. 76% to 100% of the time
4. Using the toilet independently?	0. not at all 1. slightly 2. a lot 3. it stops me completely	0. less than 25% of the time 1. 25% to 50% of the time 2. 51% to 75% of the time 3. 76% to 100% of the time
5. Speaking?	0. not at all 1. slightly 2. a lot 3. it stops me completely	0. less than 25% of the time 1. 25% to 50% of the time 2. 51% to 75% of the time 3. 76% to 100% of the time
6. Writing?	0. not at all 1. slightly 2. a lot 3. it stops me completely	0. less than 25% of the time 1. 25% to 50% of the time 2. 51% to 75% of the time 3. 76% to 100% of the time
7. Using a keyboard?	0. not at all 1. slightly 2. a lot 3. it stops me completely	0. less than 25% of the time 1. 25% to 50% of the time 2. 51% to 75% of the time 3. 76% to 100% of the time
8. Standing?	0. not at all 1. slightly 2. a lot 3. it stops me completely	0. less than 25% of the time 1. 25% to 50% of the time 2. 51% to 75% of the time 3. 76% to 100% of the time
9. Sitting?	0. not at all 1. slightly 2. a lot 3. it stops me completely	0. less than 25% of the time 1. 25% to 50% of the time 2. 51% to 75% of the time 3. 76% to 100% of the time
10. Laying down?	0. not at all 1. slightly 2. a lot 3. it stops me completely	0. less than 25% of the time 1. 25% to 50% of the time 2. 51% to 75% of the time 3. 76% to 100% of the time

Does Pain Interfere with . . .	How Much?	How Often?
11. Walking?	0. not at all 1. slightly 2. a lot 3. it stops me completely	0. less than 25% of the time 1. 25% to 50% of the time 2. 51% to 75% of the time 3. 76% to 100% of the time
12. Bending?	0. not at all 1. slightly 2. a lot 3. it stops me completely	0. less than 25% of the time 1. 25% to 50% of the time 2. 51% to 75% of the time 3. 76% to 100% of the time
13. Reaching for things?	0. not at all 1. slightly 2. a lot 3. it stops me completely	0. less than 25% of the time 1. 25% to 50% of the time 2. 51% to 75% of the time 3. 76% to 100% of the time
14. Stooping or squatting?	0. not at all 1. slightly 2. a lot 3. it stops me completely	0. less than 25% of the time 1. 25% to 50% of the time 2. 51% to 75% of the time 3. 76% to 100% of the time
15. Twisting?	0. not at all 1. slightly 2. a lot 3. it stops me completely	0. less than 25% of the time 1. 25% to 50% of the time 2. 51% to 75% of the time 3. 76% to 100% of the time
16. Carrying things?	0. not at all 1. slightly 2. a lot 3. it stops me completely	0. less than 25% of the time 1. 25% to 50% of the time 2. 51% to 75% of the time 3. 76% to 100% of the time
17. Lifting things?	0. not at all 1. slightly 2. a lot 3. it stops me completely	0. less than 25% of the time 1. 25% to 50% of the time 2. 51% to 75% of the time 3. 76% to 100% of the time
18. Pushing or pulling things?	0. not at all 1. slightly 2. a lot 3. it stops me completely	0. less than 25% of the time 1. 25% to 50% of the time 2. 51% to 75% of the time 3. 76% to 100% of the time
19. Climbing stairs?	0. not at all 1. slightly 2. a lot 3. it stops me completely	0. less than 25% of the time 1. 25% to 50% of the time 2. 51% to 75% of the time 3. 76% to 100% of the time
20. Exercising?	0. not at all 1. slightly 2. a lot 3. it stops me completely	0. less than 25% of the time 1. 25% to 50% of the time 2. 51% to 75% of the time 3. 76% to 100% of the time
21. Feeling things with your hands?	0. not at all 1. slightly 2. a lot 3. it stops me completely	0. less than 25% of the time 1. 25% to 50% of the time 2. 51% to 75% of the time 3. 76% to 100% of the time
22. Seeing?	0. not at all 1. slightly 2. a lot 3. it stops me completely	0. less than 25% of the time 1. 25% to 50% of the time 2. 51% to 75% of the time 3. 76% to 100% of the time
23. Hearing?	0. not at all 1. slightly 2. a lot 3. it stops me completely	0. less than 25% of the time 1. 25% to 50% of the time 2. 51% to 75% of the time 3. 76% to 100% of the time

Does Pain Interfere with . . .	How Much?	How Often?
24. Smelling?	0. not at all 1. slightly 2. a lot 3. it stops me completely	0. less than 25% of the time 1. 25% to 50% of the time 2. 51% to 75% of the time 3. 76% to 100% of the time
25. Grasping things with your hands?	0. not at all 1. slightly 2. a lot 3. it stops me completely	0. less than 25% of the time 1. 25% to 50% of the time 2. 51% to 75% of the time 3. 76% to 100% of the time
26. Holding things with your hands?	0. not at all 1. slightly 2. a lot 3. it stops me completely	0. less than 25% of the time 1. 25% to 50% of the time 2. 51% to 75% of the time 3. 76% to 100% of the time
27. Riding in a car?	0. not at all 1. slightly 2. a lot 3. it stops me completely	0. less than 25% of the time 1. 25% to 50% of the time 2. 51% to 75% of the time 3. 76% to 100% of the time
28. Driving?	0. not at all 1. slightly 2. a lot 3. it stops me completely	0. less than 25% of the time 1. 25% to 50% of the time 2. 51% to 75% of the time 3. 76% to 100% of the time
29. Traveling by bus or train	0. not at all 1. slightly 2. a lot 3. it stops me completely	0. less than 25% of the time 1. 25% to 50% of the time 2. 51% to 75% of the time 3. 76% to 100% of the time
30. Having desired sexual activity	0. not at all 1. slightly 2. a lot 3. it stops me completely	0. less than 25% of the time 1. 25% to 50% of the time 2. 51% to 75% of the time 3. 76% to 100% of the time
31. Having restful sleep?	0. not at all 1. slightly 2. a lot 3. it stops me completely	0. less than 25% of the time 1. 25% to 50% of the time 2. 51% to 75% of the time 3. 76% to 100% of the time
32. Participating in a hobby you used to enjoy?	0. not at all 1. slightly 2. a lot 3. it stops me completely	0. less than 25% of the time 1. 25% to 50% of the time 2. 51% to 75% of the time 3. 76% to 100% of the time
33. Participating in an athletic activity you used to do on a regular basis	0. not at all 1. slightly 2. a lot 3. it stops me completely	0. less than 25% of the time 1. 25% to 50% of the time 2. 51% to 75% of the time 3. 76% to 100% of the time
34. Going out socially?	0. not at all 1. slightly 2. a lot 3. it stops me completely	0. less than 25% of the time 1. 25% to 50% of the time 2. 51% to 75% of the time 3. 76% to 100% of the time
35. Working at your previous or current job?	0. not at all 1. slightly 2. a lot 3. it stops me completely	0. less than 25% of the time 1. 25% to 50% of the time 2. 51% to 75% of the time 3. 76% to 100% of the time
36. Doing any kind of work?	0. not at all 1. slightly 2. a lot 3. it stops me completely	0. less than 25% of the time 1. 25% to 50% of the time 2. 51% to 75% of the time 3. 76% to 100% of the time

PIII SCORE SHEET

Patient: _____ Date: _____

Pain Interference *Intensity* Ratings – Raw Score Sum = _____

Pain Interference *Frequency* Ratings – Raw Score Sum = _____

Pain Interference *Intensity* – Percentage [(sum of ratings/108) × 100] = _____

Pain Interference *Frequency* – Percentage [(sum of ratings/108) × 100] =

Pain Interference *Intensity* – Raw Score Average [sum of ratings/36] = _____

Pain Interference *Frequency* – Raw Score Average [sum of ratings/36] = _____

Pain impairment categories for Pain Interference *Intensity* – Percentage:

    <25% = Minimal   25% to 50% = Mild/Slight

    51% to 75% = Moderate   76% to 100% = Marked

Pain impairment categories for Pain Interference *Frequency* – Percentage:

    <25% = Intermittent   25% to 50% = Occasional

    51% to 75% = Frequent   76% to 100% = Constant

Pain impairment categories for Pain Interference *Intensity* – Raw Score Average:

    0. 00 to 0.50 = Minimal   0.51 to 1.50 = Mild/Slight

    1.51 to 2.50 = Moderate   2.51 to 3.00 = Marked

Pain impairment categories for Pain Interference *Frequency* – Raw Score Average:

    0. 00 to 0.50 = Intermittent   0.51 to 1.50 = Occasional

    1.51 to 2.50 = Frequent   2.51 to 3.00 = Constant

Pain Beliefs and Perceptions Inventory

Patient: _____ Date: _____

Indicate how much you agree or disagree with each statement below about your pain. If you strongly disagree, circle –2. If you disagree, circle –1. If you agree, circle 1. If you strongly agree, circle 2.

Rate Degree of Agreement

–2	–1	1	2	1. No one's been able to tell me exactly why I'm in pain.
–2	–1	1	2	2. I used to think my pain was curable, but now I'm not so sure.
–2	–1	1	2	3. There are times when I am pain free.
–2	–1	1	2	4. My pain is confusing to me.
–2	–1	1	2	5. My pain is here to stay.
–2	–1	1	2	6. I am continuously in pain.
–2	–1	1	2	7. If I am in pain, it is my own fault.
–2	–1	1	2	8. I don't know enough about my pain.
–2	–1	1	2	9. My pain is a temporary problem in my life.
–2	–1	1	2	10. It seems like I wake up with pain and I go to sleep with pain.
–2	–1	1	2	11. I am the cause of my pain.
–2	–1	1	2	12. There is a cure for my pain.
–2	–1	1	2	13. I blame myself if I am in pain.
–2	–1	1	2	14. I can't figure out why I'm in pain.
–2	–1	1	2	15. Someday I'll be 100% pain-free again.
–2	–1	1	2	16. My pain varies in intensity but is always with me.

For the Clinician's Use:

PM = 1 ____ + 4 ____ + 8 ____ + 14 ____ = ____ / 4 = ____ (PM: M = .29/SD = 1.15)

PP = 2 ____ + 5 ____ + 9 ____ + 12 ____ + 15 ____ = ____ / 5 = ____ (PP: M = .45/SD = .89)

PC = 3 ____ + 6 ____ + 10 ____ + 16 ____ = ____ / 4 = ____ (PC: M = .82/SD = 1.01)

SB = 7 ____ + 11 ____ + 13 ____ = ____ / 3 = ____ (SB: M = –1.36/SD = .75)

Note. Items 3, 9, 12, and 15 are reverse scored. Reproduced with permission. Copyright © 1989 David A. Williams & Beverly E. Thorn.

Pain Experience Scale

Name: _____ Date: _____

Many people report having certain thoughts and feelings related to flare-ups of their physical pain. We would like to know how often you experience some of these thoughts and feelings when your pain flares up. So, please read each statement below and then circle a number from 0 to 6 where 0 means *you never feel that way* and 6 means *you feel that way very often*.

EM   WO

( )   ___   1. I feel frustrated. (never) 0 1 2 3 4 5 6 (very often)

___   ( )   2. I think about my pain getting worse. (never) 0 1 2 3 4 5 6 (very often)

( )   ___   3. I feel irritable. (never) 0 1 2 3 4 5 6 (very often)

( )   ___   4. I am depressed because of my pain. (never) 0 1 2 3 4 5 6 (very often)

___   ( )   5. I wonder what it would be like to never have any pain. (never) 0 1 2 3 4 5 6 (very often)

( )   ___   6. I feel angry. (never) 0 1 2 3 4 5 6 (very often)

( )   ___   7. I feel overwhelmed. (never) 0 1 2 3 4 5 6 (very often)

___   ( )   8. I feel afraid that my pain will get worse. (never) 0 1 2 3 4 5 6 (very often)

( )   ___   9. I think, "This pain is driving me crazy." (never) 0 1 2 3 4 5 6 (very often)

( )   ___   10. I feel impatient with everybody. (never) 0 1 2 3 4 5 6 (very often)

___   ( )   11. I worry about my family. (never) 0 1 2 3 4 5 6 (very often)

( )   ___   12. I think about whether life is worth living. (never) 0 1 2 3 4 5 6 (very often)

( )   ___   13. I feel anxious. (never) 0 1 2 3 4 5 6 (very often)

___   ( )   14. I feel disappointed with myself for giving in to the pain. (never) 0 1 2 3 4 5 6 (very often)

( )   ___   15. I feel everyone is getting on my nerves. (never) 0 1 2 3 4 5 6 (very often)

( )   ___   16. I think, "It's so hard to do anything when I have pain." (never) 0 1 2 3 4 5 6 (very often)

___   ( )   17. I wonder how long this will last. (never) 0 1 2 3 4 5 6 (very often)

( )   ___   18. I think of nothing other than my pain. (never) 0 1 2 3 4 5 6 (very often)

( )   ___   19. I feel sorry for myself. (never) 0 1 2 3 4 5 6 (very often)

___   ___   SUMS   ___   ___   AVERAGES
EM   WO   EM   WO
                           /13   /6

Note. Reprinted with permission from Turk and Rudy (1985). Copyright © 1985 Dennis C. Turk.

APPENDIX N-1
The Stress Symptoms Checklist

Name: _____ Date: _____ Date of Birth: __/__/__ Age: _____

Sex: ____ M ____ F   Marital Status: ____ never married   ____ married

____ living with someone   ____ separated   ____ divorced   ____ widowed

Level of Education: _____ Occupation: _____

Working now? ____ Yes ____ No   Currently on disability? ____ Yes ____ No

INSTRUCTIONS: For each symptom below, circle the number that shows how often you have had that symptom over the past 2 weeks. Please use the following scale to rate *every* symptom:

    1 = never 2 = very seldom 3 = sometimes 4 = half the time

    5 = often 6 = very often 7 = always

No.	Symptom		
1.	Problems falling asleep		1 2 3 4 5 6 7
2.	Feeling restless		1 2 3 4 5 6 7
3.	Being easily startled		1 2 3 4 5 6 7
4.	Afraid of being a passenger in a car		1 2 3 4 5 6 7
5.	Afraid of losing control		1 2 3 4 5 6 7
6.	Not having much of an appetite		1 2 3 4 5 6 7
7.	Loss of efficiency		1 2 3 4 5 6 7
8.	Having periods of confusion		1 2 3 4 5 6 7
9.	Having trouble paying attention		1 2 3 4 5 6 7
10.	Spending less time with people (i.e., family and friends)		1 2 3 4 5 6 7
11.	Reliving a frightful experience over and over		1 2 3 4 5 6 7
12.	Worrying a lot		1 2 3 4 5 6 7
13.	Trembling		1 2 3 4 5 6 7
14.	Having dizzy spells, feeling faint or lightheaded		1 2 3 4 5 6 7
15.	Feeling stiff		1 2 3 4 5 6 7
16.	Having problems staying asleep		1 2 3 4 5 6 7
17.	Having nightmares		1 2 3 4 5 6 7
18.	Being afraid of driving		1 2 3 4 5 6 7
19.	Feeling sad, blue, discouraged, or down		1 2 3 4 5 6 7
20.	Feeling more nervous around people		1 2 3 4 5 6 7
21.	Eating too much		1 2 3 4 5 6 7
22.	Becoming forgetful		1 2 3 4 5 6 7
23.	Being much more disorganized than usual		1 2 3 4 5 6 7
24.	Easily losing your train of thought		1 2 3 4 5 6 7
25.	Feeling impatient and irritable		1 2 3 4 5 6 7
26.	Having intrusive thoughts you cannot control		1 2 3 4 5 6 7
27.	Loss of interest in things		1 2 3 4 5 6 7
28.	Having anxiety or panic attacks		1 2 3 4 5 6 7
29.	Having trouble finding words to express yourself		1 2 3 4 5 6 7

INSTRUCTIONS: For each symptom below, circle the number that shows how often you have had that symptom over the past 2 weeks. Please use the following scale to rate *every* symptom:

1 = never   2 = very seldom   3 = sometimes   4 = half the time
5 = often   6 = very often   7 = always

No.	Symptom							
30.	Having problems being sexually intimate because of pain	1	2	3	4	5	6	7
31.	Feeling tired	1	2	3	4	5	6	7
32.	Neck or shoulder pain	1	2	3	4	5	6	7
33.	Headaches	1	2	3	4	5	6	7
34.	Back pain	1	2	3	4	5	6	7
35.	Stomach upset	1	2	3	4	5	6	7
36.	Diarrhea or constipation	1	2	3	4	5	6	7
37.	Feeling like you want to die	1	2	3	4	5	6	7
38.	Hearing voices in your head when nobody else is around	1	2	3	4	5	6	7

The Stress Symptoms Checklist—Summary and Profile Form

Patient _____ Date _____ DOB _____ /Age ____

Sex _____ Marital _____ Ethnic Background _____

Education _____ Occupation _____ Working: ____ Yes ____ No

Litigation: ____ Yes ____ No   On Disability: ____ Yes ____ No

Pain Site _____ Cause of Pain _____ Pain Duration _____

Symptom Percentage Scores   Symptom Mean Rating Scores

```
100% _____

 90% _____

 80% _____

 70% _____        7 _____

 60% _____        6 _____

 50% _____        5 _____

 40% _____        4 _____

 30% _____        3 _____

 20% _____        2 _____

 10% _____        1 _____

  0% _____          _____
```

| Total SxPct | Posttraumatic Anxiety | Pain & Impairment | Total Mean Rating | Posttraumatic Anxiety | Pain & Impairment |

SSCL Indices:

| | Scale I: Posttraumatic | |
Entire Test	*Anxiety Sxs*	*Scale II: Pain and Impairment*
Total Sum of Ratings _____	Total Sum of Ratings _____	Total Sum of Ratings _____
Total Symptom Percentage ___	Total Symptom Percentage ___	Total Symptom Percentage ___
Percent of Ratings > = 5 _____	Percent of Ratings > = 5 _____	Percent of Ratings > = 5 _____
Percent of Ratings > = 6 _____	Percent of Ratings > = 6 _____	Percent of Ratings > = 6 _____

The Pain Coping Inventory

Name: _____ Date: _____ Date of Birth: ___ / ___ / ___ Age: _____

Sex: _____ M _____ F   Marital Status: _____ never married _____ married

_____ living with someone _____ separated _____ divorced _____ widowed

Level of Education: _____ Occupation: _____

Working now? _____ Yes _____ No   Currently on disability? _____ Yes _____ No

How long have you had your pain? _____

Currently in a lawsuit? _____ Yes _____ No   Cause of your pain? _____

Pain sites: Please name all the parts of your body where your pain is located.

_____

_____

Please describe what your pain feels like. _____

_____

Please check the *one* word below that best describes your *present pain.*	Is your pain ? (Please check just one line)
0 No Pain _____	_____ Brief
1 Mild _____	_____ On and off. It comes and goes.
2 Discomforting _____	_____ Constant. It's there all the time.
3 Distressing _____	
4 Horrible _____	
5 Excruciating _____	

Please make an "X" on the line below to show *how bad* your pain is *right now.*

NO ├───┤ WORST
PAIN   POSSIBLE PAIN

Instructions for Section I.

Degree of Distress (Items 1–8):
For each item below, please circle
the *one* number that best applies
to you. Please answer every item.
Do not leave any blank.

Section I Sum = _____

Section I Average = (Sum of ____)/8 = _____

Section I Percentage = (Sum of ____ −8 = ____)/48

---

1. My pain comes and goes
   1 - several times a month
   2 - 1 to 3 times a week
   3 - 4 to 5 times a week
   4 - on a daily basis
   5 - several times per day
   6 - on an hourly basis
   7 - NO! Its always there

2. When my pain comes on, it usually
   lasts for up to
   1 - several minutes
   2 - half-hour to an hour
   3 - several hours or more
   4 - a half a day
   5 - a full day
   6 - several days or more
   7 - a week or more

Name: _____   Date: _____

3. Over the past month, my pain has gotten
   1 - completely better
   2 - much better
   3 - slightly better
   4 - about the same
   5 - slightly worse
   6 - much worse
   7 - Awful! I can't stand it anymore

4. On a "typical day," my pain is
   1 - completely gone or absent
   2 - very mild and easily ignored
   3 - mild but still can be ignored
   4 - annoying and hard to ignore
   5 - uncomfortable, limits what I do
   6 - very uncomfortable and limiting
   7 - excruciating and disabling

5. On a "good day," my pain is
   1 - completely gone or absent
   2 - very mild and easily ignored
   3 - mild but still can be ignored
   4 - annoying and hard to ignore
   5 - uncomfortable, limits what I do
   6 - very uncomfortable and limiting
   7 - excruciating and disabling

6. On a "bad day," my pain is
   1 - completely gone or absent
   2 - very mild and easily ignored
   3 - mild but still can be ignored
   4 - annoying and hard to ignore
   5 - uncomfortable, limits what I do
   6 - very uncomfortable and limiting
   7 - excruciating and disabling

7. I have bad dreams or nightmares
   1 - never
   2 - one night a month
   3 - 2 to 3 nights a month
   4 - one night a week
   5 - 2 to 3 nights a week
   6 - 4 to 5 nights a week
   7 - every night

8. I relive a bad experience from the past
   1 - never
   2 - one night a month
   3 - 2 to 3 days a month
   4 - one day a week
   5 - 2 to 3 days a week
   6 - 4 to 5 days a week
   7 - every day

Instructions for Section II.

Health-Related Behaviors (Items 9–15): For each item below, circle the number of the *one* response that best describes *how often* you do that behavior. Please answer every item. Do not leave any blank.

Section II Sum = _____

Section II Average = (Sum of ___)/7 = _____

Section II Percentage = (Sum of ___ −7 = ___)/42

---

9. My consumption of alcoholic beverages (beer, wine, or liquor) comes to
   1 - 4 or more drinks per day
   2 - 2–3 drinks per day
   3 - one drink per day
   4 - 3–4 drinks per week
   5 - 1–2 drinks a week
   6 - 1–3 drinks a month
   7 - I do not drink at all

10. At the present time, I am capable of working
   1 - not at all at this time
   2 - up to 5 hours per week
   3 - 6 to 10 hours per week
   4 - 11 to 20 hours per week
   5 - 21 to 30 hours per week
   6 - 31 to 35 hours per week
   7 - full-time (40 hours)

Name: _____ Date: _____

11. I do fun things
   1 - never
   2 - once a month
   3 - 2 to 3 times a month
   4 - once per week
   5 - 2 to 3 times a week
   6 - 4 to 5 times a week
   7 - every day

12. I do stretching exercises
   1 - less than once a week
   2 - one day a week
   3 - twice a week
   4 - three times a week
   5 - 4 to 5 times a week
   6 - once every day
   7 - twice or more per day

13. I do aerobic exercises (e.g., walking, jogging, cycling, swimming, treadmill)
   1 - less than once a week
   2 - one day a week
   3 - twice a week
   4 - three times a week
   5 - four to five times a week
   6 - once every day
   7 - twice every day

14. I drink cans, cups, or bottles of beverages with caffeine (like coffee, colas, teas)
   1 - four or more a day
   2 - two to three cups per day
   3 - one cup or can every day
   4 - three to four per week
   5 - one to two per week
   6 - one to three per month
   7 - rarely or never

15. I eat "junk food" (e.g., cakes, sweets, fried foods, fast foods)
   1 - four or more times a day
   2 - two to three times a day
   3 - once every day
   4 - three to four times a week
   5 - one to two times a week
   6 - one to three times a month
   7 - rarely or never

Instructions for Section III.

Frequency of Distress (Items 16–33): For each item, circle the number that shows *how often* that item is true for you. Please answer every item. Do not leave any blank.

Section III Sum = _____

Section III Average = (Sum of _____)/18 =

Section III Percentage = (Sum of _____ − 18 = _____)/108

---

1 = never   2 = very seldom   3 = sometimes   4 = half the time
5 = often   6 = very often   7 = always

No.	Item							
16.	When my pain gets really bad, I can't stand it and I don't want to go on living.	1	2	3	4	5	6	7
17.	My pain stops me from doing things around the house.	1	2	3	4	5	6	7
18.	I am afraid that if I move wrong, I will reinjure myself or get worse.	1	2	3	4	5	6	7
		1	2	3	4	5	6	7
19.	My anxiety or nervous condition worsens my pain.	1	2	3	4	5	6	7
20.	My pain keeps me from falling asleep at night.	1	2	3	4	5	6	7
21.	My pain wakes me up at night and I cannot get back to sleep.	1	2	3	4	5	6	7

Name: _____ Date: _____

1 = never   2 = very seldom   3 = sometimes   4 = half the time
5 = often   6 = very often   7 = always

No.	Item							
22.	I avoid doing things I used to enjoy because of my condition.	1	2	3	4	5	6	7
23.	I stay away from people I used to like because of my condition.	1	2	3	4	5	6	7
24.	I avoid being sexual or intimate because of my condition.	1	2	3	4	5	6	7
25.	I avoid moving in certain ways for fear of making my pain worse.	1	2	3	4	5	6	7
26.	My muscles tense up for no good reason in different situations.	1	2	3	4	5	6	7
27.	I am under a lot of stress which seems to make my pain worse.	1	2	3	4	5	6	7
28.	I feel down and discouraged about not being able to do what I used to do, because of pain.	1	2	3	4	5	6	7
29.	I blame myself for not getting better.	1	2	3	4	5	6	7
30.	I feel angry about being in pain.	1	2	3	4	5	6	7
31.	My pain stops me from having a good time or doing things I used to enjoy.	1	2	3	4	5	6	7
32.	My pain has a mind of its own.	1	2	3	4	5	6	7
33.	My pain seems to get worse or come on for no reason at all.	1	2	3	4	5	6	7

THIS IS THE END OF SECTION III.
PLEASE GO ON TO SECTION IV ON THE NEXT PAGE.

Name: _____ Date: _____

Instructions for Section IV.

Coping Success (Items 34–58): For each item, circle the number that shows *how often* that item is true for you. Please answer every item. Do not leave any blank.

Section IV Sum = _____

Section IV Average = $\dfrac{\text{(Sum of \quad)}}{25} =$ _____

Section IV Percentage = (Sum of ___ $-25 =$ ___)/150

1 = never   2 = very seldom   3 = sometimes   4 = half the time
5 = often   6 = very often   7 = always

No.	Item							
34.	Without taking medication, I can do something to get pain relief.	1	2	3	4	5	6	7
35.	When my pain gets bad, I cope by thinking of something other than the pain.	1	2	3	4	5	6	7
36.	When my pain gets bad, I cope by picturing pleasant things, feelings, or sensations.	1	2	3	4	5	6	7
37.	When my pain gets bad, I cope by saying supportive things to myself.	1	2	3	4	5	6	7
38.	When my pain gets bad, I cope by imagining my pain shrinking or becoming weaker.	1	2	3	4	5	6	7
39.	I cope well with my pain.	1	2	3	4	5	6	7
40.	I limit my use of over-the-counter nonprescription pain relievers.	1	2	3	4	5	6	7
41.	I am able to get a good night's sleep.	1	2	3	4	5	6	7
42.	I talk myself out of becoming too depressed about my condition.	1	2	3	4	5	6	7
43.	I do relaxation exercises to reduce my pain.	1	2	3	4	5	6	7
44.	I reduce my pain with some form of mental or physical relaxation.	1	2	3	4	5	6	7
45.	I get relief from pain when I am sleeping.	1	2	3	4	5	6	7
46.	When my pain gets bad, I cope by imagining comfortable and pleasant sensations.	1	2	3	4	5	6	7
47.	I pay attention to other things besides pain.	1	2	3	4	5	6	7
48.	I do things that ease or reduce my pain.	1	2	3	4	5	6	7
49.	When my pain gets bad, I cope by concentrating directly on my pain.	1	2	3	4	5	6	7
50.	I limit my use of prescription pain medicine.	1	2	3	4	5	6	7
51.	I cope with pain by controlling my behavior and my thoughts	1	2	3	4	5	6	7
52.	My life is interesting.	1	2	3	4	5	6	7
53.	My life is full or busy.	1	2	3	4	5	6	7
54.	I consider myself to be curious about things.	1	2	3	4	5	6	7

Name: _____ Date: _____

1 = never   2 = very seldom   3 = sometimes   4 = half the time
5 = often   6 = very often   7 = always

No.	Item							
55.	I have control over my emotions.	1	2	3	4	5	6	7
56.	I enjoy living my life.	1	2	3	4	5	6	7
57.	I am happy about how my life is going.	1	2	3	4	5	6	7
58.	I know what will bring on or worsen my pain.	1	2	3	4	5	6	7

Instructions for Section V.

Your Beliefs (Items 59–92):   Section V Sum = _____
For each statement below, circle
the *one* number that shows how   Section V Average = (Sum of _____)/34 = _____
much you agree or disagree with
that statement. Please answer   Section V Percentage = (Sum of _____ − 34 = _____)/204
every item. Do not leave any blank.

1 = totally disagree   2 = strongly disagree   3 = mildly disagree
4 = neutral   5 = mildly agree   6 = strongly agree   7 = totally agree

No.	Item							
59.	I have no control over this pain.	1	2	3	4	5	6	7
60.	Nothing I do makes a real difference with my pain.	1	2	3	4	5	6	7
61.	I do not see any point in learning mental coping techniques to help manage my pain.	1	2	3	4	5	6	7
62.	My pain stays the same no matter what I do.	1	2	3	4	5	6	7
63.	Other people such as doctors, family, or friends blame me for not getting better.	1	2	3	4	5	6	7
64.	I believe that I am never going to get better.	1	2	3	4	5	6	7
65.	I am angry at doctors and others for telling me they could help me when they really could not.	1 2 3 4 5 6 7 1	2	3	4	5	6	7
66.	I do not feel like I fit in anymore because of my condition.	1	2	3	4	5	6	7
67.	I do not believe that there are mental issues that affect my pain.	1	2	3	4	5	6	7
68.	I believe my pain is only a physical issue.	1	2	3	4	5	6	7
69.	I believe I have been treated unfairly because of my condition.	1	2	3	4	5	6	7
70.	I am not willing to learn mental coping techniques to help better manage my pain.	1	2	3	4	5	6	7
71.	I believe that there is nothing that anybody can do about this pain.	1	2	3	4	5	6	7
72.	I am tired of going to therapy of any kind.	1	2	3	4	5	6	7

Name: _____ Date: _____

1 = totally disagree   2 = strongly disagree   3 = mildly disagree
4 = neutral   5 = mildly agree   6 = strongly agree   7 = totally agree

No.	Item	
73.	I am not willing to work with a psychologist to learn to cope with my pain.	1 2 3 4 5 6 7
74.	My life is completely wrecked.	1 2 3 4 5 6 7
75.	I am a total invalid.	1 2 3 4 5 6 7
76.	I can see now that I will always be in pain.	1 2 3 4 5 6 7
77.	Life has treated me much more unfairly than it has treated most people.	1 2 3 4 5 6 7
78.	It is unfair that I continue to suffer while other people are not suffering.	1 2 3 4 5 6 7
79.	I wish other people could spend time in my shoes and feel like I do.	1 2 3 4 5 6 7
80.	I should have been helped more by now.	1 2 3 4 5 6 7
81.	I seem to be getting worse.	1 2 3 4 5 6 7
82.	Whenever my pain gets worse, I fear I am going to be crippled forever.	1 2 3 4 5 6 7
83.	I feel helpless because there is nothing I can do that will make a real difference.	1 2 3 4 5 6 7
84.	People think that I exaggerate or lie about my symptoms.	1 2 3 4 5 6 7
85.	People do not believe that my pain is real.	1 2 3 4 5 6 7
86.	I am overwhelmed by my problems.	1 2 3 4 5 6 7
87.	Doctors and others are not sincere and do not really care about me.	1 2 3 4 5 6 7
88.	It is difficult to express my feelings.	1 2 3 4 5 6 7
89.	People punish me or treat me unfairly.	1 2 3 4 5 6 7
90.	Nobody really understands what I am going through.	1 2 3 4 5 6 7
91.	People really believe that nothing more can be done for my pain and that I have to learn to live with it.	1 2 3 4 5 6 7
92.	My doctor is my last resort and my hope for a better life.	1 2 3 4 5 6 7

APPENDIX P
PCI Summary and Profile Form

Patient _____ Birthdate _____ Education _____

Test Admin. Date _____ Type of Pain _____

Medical Dx _____ Pain Duration in Yrs/Mons _____

Index	Mean (SD)	Percentiles				
		10th	25th	50th	75th	90th
EBF% Norms:	23.31 (20.10)	2.94	8.82	17.65	32.35	54.55
Patient EBF%:	_____	_____	_____	_____	_____	_____
SMF% Norms:	30.37 (18.86)	7.84	15.69	27.45	41.84	56.86
Patient SMF%:	_____	_____	_____	_____	_____	_____
GII Norms:	384.84 (73.14)	285.2	338.1	387.32	437.92	474.72
Patient GII:	_____	_____	_____	_____	_____	_____
PAI Norms:	123.90 (36.28)	76.84	99.45	124.1	147.56	172.04
Patient PAI:	_____	_____	_____	_____	_____	_____
DODI Norms:	36.75 (7.26)	27.44	32	37.68	42	46
Patient DODI:	_____	_____	_____	_____	_____	_____
FODI Norms:	80.28 (20.18)	50.94	66.96	81	95.04	106.02
Patient FODI:	_____	_____	_____	_____	_____	_____
CSI Norms:	85.55 (22.83)	57	70	84	100	115
Patient CSI:	_____	_____	_____	_____	_____	_____
HRBI Norms:	27.50 (5.78)	20.02	24.01	27.02	31.99	35
Patient HRBI:	_____	_____	_____	_____	_____	_____
PSI Norms:	44.92 (8.24)	34.02	38.97	45.00	51.03	54.99
Patient PSI:	_____	_____	_____	_____	_____	_____
BISI Norms:	66.63 (16.20)	43.96	55.02	68.04	78.96	86.94
Patient BISI:	_____	_____	_____	_____	_____	_____
PMSI Norms:	120.16 (37.94)	68.00	93.16	121.04	146.37	166.94
Patient PMSI:	_____	_____	_____	_____	_____	_____
PsyCI Norms:	98.39 (23.83)	71.12	82.04	98.00	113.96	131.04
Patient PsyCI:	_____	_____	_____	_____	_____	_____
HBI Norms:	30.61 (6.67)	21.98	25.97	31.01	35.00	38.99
Patient HBI:	_____	_____	_____	_____	_____	_____
PCI Norms:	113.12 (25.38)	81.92	95.04	112.00	128.00	146.24
Patient PCI:	_____	_____	_____	_____	_____	_____
NI Norms:	117.75 (25.22)	81.12	100.1	120.12	135.98	150.02
Patient NI:	_____	_____	_____	_____	_____	_____
CAT Norms:	30.89 (11.07)	16.00	23.52	31.04	38.52	45.04
Patient CAT:	_____	_____	_____	_____	_____	_____
DEP Norms:	24.84 (8.17)	14.00	18.97	24.99	30.03	35.00
Patient DEP:	_____	_____	_____	_____	_____	_____
QOL Norms:	19.03 (7.62)	8.00	14.00	19.00	25.00	29.00
Patient QOL:	_____	_____	_____	_____	_____	_____

444

Index	Mean (SD)	Percentiles				
		10th	25th	50th	75th	90th
MC Norms:	15.90 (6.48)	7.98	10.98	15.00	19.02	24.00
Patient MC:	_____					
HOS Norms:	25.33 (10.10)	11.97	17.01	25.97	31.99	38.99
Patient HOS:	_____	_____	_____	_____	_____	_____
PAR Norms:	26.10 (10.61)	12.00	18.00	26.00	34.00	41.04
Patient PAR:	_____	_____	_____	_____	_____	_____
PsyMot Norms:	27.56 (7.36)	18.00	22.98	28.98	33.00	36.00
Patient PsyMot:	_____	_____	_____	_____	_____	_____

Notes.

1. Means, Standard Deviations (SDs), and Percentiles are based on a heterogeneous sample of 433 chronic pain patients.

2. EBF% stands for *Extreme Beliefs Frequency Percentage,* and is the total number of Section V (Your Beliefs) items rated 6 or 7, divided by the total number of items in that section (i.e., 34) expressed as percentage. SMF% stands for *Symptom Magnification Frequency Percentage,* and is the total number of items in Section I (Degree of Distress), Section III (Frequency of Distress), and Section IV (Coping Success) rated extremely negatively (i.e., ratings of 6 or 7 for items in Sections I and III, and ratings of 1 or 2 for items in Section IV), divided by the total number of items in those 3 sections combined (i.e., 51).

3. GII stands for *Global Impairment Index,* and is the sum of all 92 item ratings on the test keyed in the direction of greater dysfunction. Thus, all of the items in Section II (Health-Related Behaviors) and Section IV (Coping Success) are *reverse-scored.* PAI stands for *Patient Alienation Index,* and is the sum of all 34 item ratings in Section V (Your Beliefs). DODI stands for *Degree of Distress Index,* and is the sum of the all 8 item ratings in Section I (Degree of Distress). FODI stands for *Frequency of Distress Index,* and is the sum of all 18 item ratings in Section III (Frequency of Distress). CSI stands for *Coping Success Index,* and is the sum of all 25 item ratings in Section IV (Coping Success). HRBI stands for *Health-Related Behaviors Index,* and is the sum of all 7 item ratings in Section II (Health-Related Behaviors).

4. An (R) next to any of the item numbers below means that the item is *Reverse-scored.* PSI stands for *Physical Severity Index,* and is the sum of items: 1–6, 32, 33, and 58(R). BISI stands for *Behavioral Interference Severity Index,* and is the sum of items: 10(R), 11(R), 17, 18, 20–26, 31, 41(R), and 45(R). PMSI stands for *Psychological Maladjustment Severity Index,* and is the sum of items: 7, 8, 16, 19, 27–30, 63–66, 69, 71, 72, and 74–92. PsyCI stands for *Psychological Coping Index,* and is the sum of items: 34–39, 42–44, 46–49, 51–57, 59(R), 60(R), 61(R), 62(R), 67(R), 68(R), 70(R), and 73(R). HBI stands for *Healthful Behavior Index,* and is the sum of items 9, 12–15, 40, and 50. PCI stands for *Pain Coping Index,* and is the sum of all the items in Section II (Health-Related Behaviors) and Section IV (Coping Success). NI stands for *Nociceptive Index,* and is the sum of all the items in Section I (Degree of Distress) and Section III (Frequency of Distress). CAT stands for *Catastrophizing Index,* and is the sum of items: 74–76, 81–83, 86, and 92. DEP stands for *Depression Index,* and is the sum of items: 16, 28, 29, 64, 71, 72, and 91. QOL stands for *Quality of Life Index,* and is the sum of items: 52–54, 56, and 57. MC stands for *Mental Conditioning Index,* and is the sum of items: 35, 36, 38, 46, 47, and 49. HOS stands for *Hostility Index,* and is the sum of items: 30, 65, 69, and 77–80. PAR stands for *Paranoia and Alienation Index,* and is the sum of items: 63, 66, 84, 85, and 87–90. PsyMot stands for *Psychological Motivation Index,* and is the sum of items: 43, 61(R), 67(R), 68(R), 70(R), and 73(R).

APPENDIX Q-1
Basic ID Modality Analysis Form

Patient: _____ Date: _____

Target Problem: _____

Behaviors—*What do you do when* . . .
　When you do that, . . .

　　Affect - _____

　　Sensations - _____

　　Images - _____

　　Cognitions - _____

　　Interpersonal - _____

　　Drugs -_____

Affect—*What emotions do you feel when* . . .
　When you feel that way, . . .

　　Behaviors - _____

　　Sensations - _____

　　Images - _____

　　Cognitions - _____

　　Interpersonal - _____

　　Drugs -_____

Sensations —*How do you experience* . . . *Describe the sensations. What does it feel like?*
　When you have those sensatiions, . . .

　　Behaviors - _____

　　Affect - _____

　　Images - _____

　　Cognitions - _____

　　Interpersonal - _____

　　Drugs - _____

Images—*What kinds of images flash in your mind's eye when* . . .
　When you have those images, . . .

　　Behaviors - _____

　　Affect - _____

　　Sensations - _____

　　Cognitions - _____

446

Interpersonal - _____

Drugs - _____

Cognitions—*Thoughts before, during, and after . . .*
When you have those thoughts, . . .

Behaviors - _____

Affect - _____

Sensations - _____

Images - _____

Interpersonal - _____

Drugs - _____

Interpersonal—*Typical interpersonal interactions when . . .*
When you have those interactions, . . .

Behaviors - _____

Affect - _____

Sensations - _____

Images - _____

Cognitions - _____

Drugs - _____

Drugs—*What medicines do you take? When? At what dosages?*
When you take those medicines, . . .

Behaviors - _____

Affect - _____

Sensations - _____

Images - _____

Cognitions - _____

Interpersonal - _____

Name: _____

APPENDIX Q-2
Basic ID Pain Diary

Date/Time * What is the situation? * Rate Pain Level on a "0–10" scale	Behavior * What do you do when you are in pain? * How does your behavior change when in pain?	Emotions-Feelings * What emotions do you feel? * Do you feel sad, angry, anxious, afraid, depressed, etc.?	Sensations * How do you experience the pain? * What does the pain feel like? * Describe the sensations	Images/Mental Pictures * What kinds of pictures or images flash in your mind's eye?	Cognitions/Thoughts * What kinds of thoughts do you have? * What do you tell yourself?	Interpersonal * Describe any interpersonal interactions that occur when you are in pain.	Drugs * List any meds you take, when you take them, and the dosage. * Any other remedies?

APPENDIX R-1
Daily Pain and Thought Record

Name:_____

Date and Time	Situation and Type of Pain Briefly describe the situation and the type of pain experienced	Emotions(s) Rate 0–10 Pain Level Rate 0–10	Automatic Thoughts(s) What went through my mind? What am I telling myself? Rate degree of belief in each thought from 0 to 100%	Rational Thought(s)* Another way to think about it? Rate degree of belief in new thought(s) [0 to 100%] Coping Behaviors	Outcome Re-rate emotions & pain now

Technique	Questions to Ask Myself*
Personal meaning	What does this situation mean to me (or about me)? Is there another way to look at it?
Question the evidence	How do I know this? What's the evidence? On what basis do I draw this conclusion?
Alternative explanation	Is there another explanation? Is there another way to look at this situation?
Rational responsibility	Whose fault is it really? Do I deserve blame here?
Decatastrophizing	What if it were true? So then what? What is the worst that could happen? The probability is?

Technique	Questions to Ask Myself*
Pros and cons	What are the "advantages and disadvantages" of thinking/acting like this?
Adversity-to-advantage	How might this situation be used to my advantage? What can I learn from this?
Cognitive distortion	What's the possible distortion in my thinking? (*e.g.,* all or nothing thinking; mind reading; emotional reasoning; personalizing; overgeneralizing; catastrophizing; "shoulding on myself"; objectifying the subjective; unfair comparison; disqualifying the positive; perfectionism; selective abstraction; externalizing my self-worth; fallacies of: total control, magical change, rationalizing worrying, "head in the sand"; "fair world"; "having to be right"; "heaven's reward."
Stress Inoculation	What can I tell myself to help me cope and get through this?
Imagined consequences	Play it out in my mind to the end. And then what? And then what?
Relief/antidote imagery	What images can I picture in my mind to make it feel better?
Imaginal rehearsal	Can I mentally rehearse a more positive, desirable outcome?
Distraction	How can I distract myself from the pain?
Identification of voices	Who is talking inside me? Whose voice is that?
Scaling	Rate the degree of distress from 0 to 100% or from 0 to 10.
Helper role	What would I tell someone else who was going through the same thing?

APPENDIX R-2
Pain Tracking Diary

Name _____ Dates Rated _____

Circle the number that best describes your pain level at breakfast, lunch, dinner, and bedtime.

Pain Levels and Primary Type of Pain Being Tracked _____

0 = no pain
1 = very weak pain
2 = weak pain
3 = mild pain
4 = mild to moderate pain
5 = moderate pain

6 = moderate to strong pain
7 = strong pain
8 = very strong pain
9 = very, very intense pain
10 = excruciating, unbearable pain

Day of the Week _____   Date _____

Breakfast	0	1	2	3	4	5	6	7	8	9	10
Lunch	0	1	2	3	4	5	6	7	8	9	10
Dinner	0	1	2	3	4	5	6	7	8	9	10
Bedtime	0	1	2	3	4	5	6	7	8	9	10

How much time did you spend lying down or in bed today because of pain or fatigue? _____

Name of Medication	No. Taken	Milligram Dose	Time Taken

What coping methods did you use today? _____

Day of the Week _____   Date _____

Breakfast	0	1	2	3	4	5	6	7	8	9	10
Lunch	0	1	2	3	4	5	6	7	8	9	10
Dinner	0	1	2	3	4	5	6	7	8	9	10
Bedtime	0	1	2	3	4	5	6	7	8	9	10

How much time did you spend lying down or in bed today because of pain or fatigue? _____

Name of Medication	No. Taken	Milligram Dose	Time Taken

What coping methods did you use today? _____

451

0 = no pain
1 = very weak pain
2 = weak pain
3 = mild pain
4 = mild to moderate pain
5 = moderate pain

6 = moderate to strong pain
7 = strong pain
8 = very strong pain
9 = very, very intense pain
10 = excruciating, unbearable pain

Day of the Week _____   Date _____

Breakfast	0	1	2	3	4	5	6	7	8	9	10
Lunch	0	1	2	3	4	5	6	7	8	9	10
Dinner	0	1	2	3	4	5	6	7	8	9	10
Bedtime	0	1	2	3	4	5	6	7	8	9	10

How much time did you spend lying down or in bed today because of pain or fatigue? _____

Name of Medication	No. Taken	Milligram Dose	Time Taken

What coping methods did you use today? _____

Day of the Week _____   Date _____

Breakfast	0	1	2	3	4	5	6	7	8	9	10
Lunch	0	1	2	3	4	5	6	7	8	9	10
Dinner	0	1	2	3	4	5	6	7	8	9	10
Bedtime	0	1	2	3	4	5	6	7	8	9	10

How much time did you spend lying down or in bed today because of pain or fatigue? _____

Name of Medication	No. Taken	Milligram Dose	Time Taken

What coping methods did you use today? _____

Note. Adapted with permission. Copyright © 1993 Beverly E. Thorn, Ph.D.

Automatic Thoughts about Pain Questionnaire (ATPQ)

Name: _____ Birthdate (Age): _____ Date: _____

Type of Pain: _____ Cause of Pain: _____

How Long Since Pain First Started: _____

INSTRUCTIONS: For each thought below, circle a number on the "How Often Scale" to show how often you think that thought when you are in pain. Then, circle a number on the "How True Does It Feel Scale" to show how true that thought feels when you are in pain. There are 45 thoughts on this questionnaire. Please circle two (2) numbers for every thought.

How Often Scale:	0	1	2	3	4	5	6
	Never think that			Sometimes think that			Always think that
How True Does It Feel Scale:	0	1	2	3	4	5	6
	Completely false						Completely true

When you are in pain, *how often* do you think . . . and *how true* does it feel?

	How often?	How true does it feel?
1. There is nothing I can do.	0 1 2 3 4 5 6	0 1 2 3 4 5 6
2. Its no use to bother working hard to prevent pain flare-ups.	0 1 2 3 4 5 6	0 1 2 3 4 5 6
3. Nothing I do will make a difference.	0 1 2 3 4 5 6	0 1 2 3 4 5 6
4. I will always be in pain.	0 1 2 3 4 5 6	0 1 2 3 4 5 6
5. The pain will never end.	0 1 2 3 4 5 6	0 1 2 3 4 5 6
6. I can't function like this.	0 1 2 3 4 5 6	0 1 2 3 4 5 6
7. Nothing I do makes a difference.	0 1 2 3 4 5 6	0 1 2 3 4 5 6
8. Nothing I did up until now has made a difference.	0 1 2 3 4 5 6	0 1 2 3 4 5 6
9. I am back to square one again.	0 1 2 3 4 5 6	0 1 2 3 4 5 6
10. It's too hard trying to stay in shape to prevent pain flare-ups. I'll never succeed.	0 1 2 3 4 5 6	0 1 2 3 4 5 6
11. This is horrible.	0 1 2 3 4 5 6	0 1 2 3 4 5 6
12. I can't stand this.	0 1 2 3 4 5 6	0 1 2 3 4 5 6
13. This is intolerable.	0 1 2 3 4 5 6	0 1 2 3 4 5 6
14. I just can't function like this.	0 1 2 3 4 5 6	0 1 2 3 4 5 6
15. I'm being punished.	0 1 2 3 4 5 6	0 1 2 3 4 5 6
16. Its all my fault.	0 1 2 3 4 5 6	0 1 2 3 4 5 6
17. I did this to myself.	0 1 2 3 4 5 6	0 1 2 3 4 5 6
18. I don't deserve this.	0 1 2 3 4 5 6	0 1 2 3 4 5 6
19. I'm a cripple.	0 1 2 3 4 5 6	0 1 2 3 4 5 6
20. I'm a weak person.	0 1 2 3 4 5 6	0 1 2 3 4 5 6
21. This means I'm going to be crippled.	0 1 2 3 4 5 6	0 1 2 3 4 5 6
22. This is going to be a bad or horrible flare-up.	0 1 2 3 4 5 6	0 1 2 3 4 5 6
23. This is it—the big one.	0 1 2 3 4 5 6	0 1 2 3 4 5 6
24. I am going to be disabled.	0 1 2 3 4 5 6	0 1 2 3 4 5 6
25. Nobody knows the real reason I am in pain.	0 1 2 3 4 5 6	0 1 2 3 4 5 6

How Often Scale:	0	1	2	3	4	5	6
	Never think that			Sometimes think that			Always think that
How True Does It Feel Scale:	0 Completely false	1	2	3	4	5	6 Completely true

When you are in pain, *how often* do you think . . . and *how true* does it feel?

	How often?	How true does it feel?
26. The problems causing my pain are too complex and hidden for any doctors to discover and correct.	0 1 2 3 4 5 6	0 1 2 3 4 5 6
27. My pain is a mystery to everyone.	0 1 2 3 4 5 6	0 1 2 3 4 5 6
28. I am always in pain.	0 1 2 3 4 5 6	0 1 2 3 4 5 6
29. Nothing ever changes.	0 1 2 3 4 5 6	0 1 2 3 4 5 6
30. Nobody cares.	0 1 2 3 4 5 6	0 1 2 3 4 5 6
31. People should only know what it feels like to be in my body.	0 1 2 3 4 5 6	0 1 2 3 4 5 6
32. They deserve to be in pain. I don't!	0 1 2 3 4 5 6	0 1 2 3 4 5 6
33. This is just not fair and therefore, it should not be so.	0 1 2 3 4 5 6	0 1 2 3 4 5 6
34. My life will be ruined.	0 1 2 3 4 5 6	0 1 2 3 4 5 6
35. I can't handle this. I can't cope.	0 1 2 3 4 5 6	0 1 2 3 4 5 6
36. I'll never be able to go back to work.	0 1 2 3 4 5 6	0 1 2 3 4 5 6
37. It is no use trying anymore.	0 1 2 3 4 5 6	0 1 2 3 4 5 6
38. Things just keep getting worse.	0 1 2 3 4 5 6	0 1 2 3 4 5 6
39. I may have overdone it. I need to lie in bed.	0 1 2 3 4 5 6	0 1 2 3 4 5 6
40. The pain is destroying me.	0 1 2 3 4 5 6	0 1 2 3 4 5 6
41. Oh my God! I know the pain I just felt means I've done something terrible to my body!	0 1 2 3 4 5 6	0 1 2 3 4 5 6
42. If I keep doing this activity, I know I'll ruin myself physically. I'd better quit right now.	0 1 2 3 4 5 6	0 1 2 3 4 5 6
43. Why should I have to keep working so hard at not being in pain? No one else I know has to.	0 1 2 3 4 5 6	0 1 2 3 4 5 6
44. Staying with the program is too hard. It's just too inconvenient.	0 1 2 3 4 5 6	0 1 2 3 4 5 6
45. I just can't stand doing these exercises.	0 1 2 3 4 5 6	0 1 2 3 4 5 6

Automatic Thought Categories:
Hopelessness, helplessness, and pain permanence (items 1–6, 35, 37)
Disqualifying the positive (items 7–10, 38)
Pain intolerance and catastrophizing (items 11–14, 40, 43, 44, 45)
Punishment and self-blame (items 15–18)
Overgeneralization and negative labeling (items 19–20)
Negative prediction, worry, threat, and fear (items 21–24, 34, 36, 39, 41, 42)
Pain mysteriousness (items 25–27)
Constancy (items 28–29)
Alienation and hostility (items 30–33)

Pain Management Psychotherapy Progress Note—
Session Summary Checklist

Patient: _____ Date: _____ Session No.: _____

Procedures/s (CPT): ___Ext psychotherapy-90842 ___Psychotherapy-90844
___Biofeedback tx-90900 ___Psych tests-96100
___Psych diag int exam-90801 ___Neurobehavioral status exam-96115
___Psychophysiologic tx-90876 ___Pt. educ. supplies-99071

Objective Scores: _____ Medications: _____

1. PT's current functioning, chief complaints, subjective presentation, predominant symptoms and agenda:

___problems sleeping ___loss of appetite ___suicidal ideation ___paranoia
___fatigue ___specific worries or fears: _____
___concentration difficulties ___loss of mental efficiency
___loss of physical efficiency ___phobic avoidance:
___pain/other physical sxs: _____
___interpersonal conflict ___depressed ___angry ___lack of motivation
___anxiety ___posttraumatic sxs:

2. Patient's adherence to previous session's homework (HW):

3. Therapist's objectives, agreed-upon session agenda, targeted problems:

___pain management ___anxiety reduction ___mood management
___anger management ___reduce phobic avoidance:
___reduce worrying ___improve self-esteem ___increase assertiveness
___improve ability to relax ___reduce negative thinking
___diminish social withdrawal/increase activity levels ___sleep improvement
___increase frustration tolerance ___activity pacing
___reduce hyperventilation ___desensitize fears ___reduce posttraumatic sxs
___expand affective responsiveness
___improve self-control ___improve concentration/memory
___reduce muscle bracing ___improve coping skills
___time/stress management ___safe processing of traumatic memories
___improve judgment ___remediate behavioral deficits
___increase stimulus control thru contingency management
___teach the "12 step" philosophy ___eliminate behavioral excesses
___feedback/educational material ___conflict resolution ___reduce depression
___control panic ___reduce performance anxiety

4. Clinical interventions, strategies, and techniques employed in this session:

____clinical interview ____mental status exam ____supportive psychotherapy_____
   ____biofeedback therapy _____
____relaxation training ____therapeutic imagery ____therapeutic conversation
   ____empathic listening ____identifying and releasing of affect
____advantages/disadvantages ____decision therapy ____emotional reprocessing
   ____ideomotor techniques ____graded exposure ____guided discovery
____downward arrow technique ____examining the evidence ____cognitive therapy
   ____rational-emotive therapy ____hypnotherapy
____play therapy ____parent counseling ____rehearsal of coping techniques
   ____EMDR ____therapeutic modeling ____cognitive restructuring
____social skills training ____assertiveness training ____behavioral desensitization
   ____graded in vivo exposure ____graded imaginal exposure
____problem solving ____guided inquiry ____graded task assignment
   ____activity scheduling ____stimulus control therapy
   ____provision of test feedback
____information/education ____provision of educational materials→ ____booklets
   ____audio cassette/s ____distraction training/attentional refocusing
____pain management training ____chronic pain therapy
   ____anxiety management training ____anger management training
   ____self-control training
____cognitive disputation ____contingency management
   ____behavior/habit modification ____mood elevation and control techniques
____respiratory control training ____cognitive rehabilitation therapy
   ____ICPS training ____crisis counseling ____critical incident stress debriefing

---

5. Clinical outcomes, additional problems addressed, and/or special problems
   arising in session:

____Pt. did HW ____Pt. did *not* do HW ____Interpersonal issues bet therapist and
   patient arose ____Pt. expressed hopelessness about continuing therapy
____Pt. relapsed ____Pt. expressed anger toward therapist ____Pt. regressed
____Interventions were successful ____Collaboration was: ____excellent
   ____good ____fair ____poor ____Pt. improved ____No change
____Teamwork was not possible

---

6. Homework assigned today and goals for next session:

Clinician's/Therapist's Signature

Pain Management Psychotherapy Progress Note

Patient: _____ Date: _____

Check Procedures/S (CPT): ___Extended psychotherapy-90842
___Psychotherapy-90844   ___Biofeedback training-90901
___Psychol. tests-96100   ___Psych Diag Interview Exam-90801
   Patient educational supplies-99071   Psychophysiological Therapy-90876

Results of Any Tests, Evaluation, or Outcome Measures Administered—

Visual Analogue Scale Pain Rating (VAS: 0–100) $VAS_{this\ week}$ = ___ $VAS_{last\ week}$ = ___
VAS_{change} = ___ 0 decreased pain ___ 1 no change in pain level ___ 2 increased pain
Present Pain Index$_{week's\ ave.}$ = ___   PPI = 0 (none) 1 (weak) 2 (moderate) 3 (severe) 4 (excruciating)
Percent Pain Relief$_{this\ week}$ = ___ 0 (100%) ___ 1 (80–99%) ___ 2 (50–79%)
   ___ 3 (30–49%) ___ 4 (0–29%)
Global Pain Score (GPS: 0–10)$_{this\ week}$ = _____   SUDs (0–10)$_{this\ week}$ = _____
Pain Disability
Rating$_{this\ week}$ = $0_{(no\ disability)} - 10_{(all\ usual\ activities\ have\ been\ totally\ disrupted\ by\ pain)}$ = _____

Subjective Complaints, Presenting Problems, Patient's Agenda, and Previous Session's HW—

Objectives and Goals of Session—

Abstract of Session's Focal Points (problems addressed, interventions, outcomes)—

Assignments for Patient Homework—

Plan for Following Sessions—

Clinician's/Therapist's Signature

APPENDIX U
Hypnotic Relaxation/Sleep Tape Script

1. *Introduction.* Hello. The purpose of this tape is to guide you through a healing meditation that will help you to fall asleep comfortably, easily and effortlessly. You may already have some idea about what you would like to hear, or you may not . . . These suggestions can be like a compass that sets you in the right direction . . . offering opportunities for discovering soothing images and finding a safe, peaceful place that is restful and comforting. Now, the important idea here is that whatever comes up for you . . . is just fine. That's right. Nothing h-a-s to happen. Whatever comes up for you is just fine. It's important to open up to your own ideas and feelings . . . And, if I don't say something exactly in the way that you want to hear it, then by all means give yourself permission to hear it in the way that will make you most comfortable . . . and please feel perfectly comfortable about saying it to yourself in the way you would most like to hear it . . . And remember that whatever you experience is just fine.

2. *Settling Inward.* First, it is important to settle inward. So, begin by finding a comfortable position in which to lie or sit, and quietly begin to focus on your breathing. Find a safe place in your mind where you can go while you breathe slowly and deeply. Pay attention to the rhythm of your breathing, the rising and falling of your chest . . . Let yourself take slow, deep, even breaths . . . breathing in . . . and . . . breathing o-u-t . . . And it is a good idea if you happen to notice now how much you hurt, that before we continue with this exercise, you acknowledge the painful sensations that are there. Don't try to suppress the sensations. So, how strong is your pain right now? Can you imagine a thermometer with the bulb at the bottom being no pain, a zero, and the mark on the top of the crystal being the most pain, a ten? And how high is your pain now on this painometer?

3. *Safe Place Imagery and Counting Down.* Now, you might also want to imagine being in a safe and pleasant place where you can be yourself, maybe be by yourself, or just be with someone special, and feel secure, comfortable, and relaxed. And this can enhance your meditation. And, while you think of such a place, I hope you can allow your mind to wander off to somewhere pleasant, as I begin to count slowly down from one hundred. Now, you may want to silently count down along with me, or not. Or, visualize each number floating in front of you as if on a puffy white cloud across a powder blue sky . . . floating across the horizon . . . Or perhaps, watch as each number is written on a blackboard, and then erased, and then, replaced by the next number, and so on, and so on . . . Whatever feels most comfortable is best. But please continue to notice your breathing, and I hope that by now it is noticeably slower, . . . deeper, easier, and more regular . . . 100 . . . 99 . . . on to 90 . . . (Move on to the *Pain Relief Imagery*).

4. *Pain Relief Imagery.* Now, I would like you to identify for yourself what your pain feels like in the primary area where you hurt. So, I'd like to invite you to take a few deep breaths and concentrate on your pain. Let any image come to mind that can tell you something about your particular pain condition. What does it usually feel like? Now, if you think about that image, or picture, or feelings that represent your pain, can you think of some of the situations, behaviors, or activities that make you feel more comfortable? . . . Usually pain comes and goes. Sometimes it pulsates, or throbs, or stings, or pinches, or aches, or feels heavy, or pulls, or draws, or presses, or tugs, and so on. Most people can find some

relief underneath or between their sensations of pain and one way to do this is to open up around the area that hurts. So, breathe deeply and move your breath in and around your primary pain area. Allow the natural wisdom and language of your own body to guide you and for the time being, let yourself open up to your pain and to any objections you may have to this process. I am just asking you to meditate on your pain, around and underneath your pain, and to notice the subtle changes. Concentrate on your pain. Now, taking another few deep breaths, let another image come up for you that stands for relief or soothing. So, scan inside as you breathe deeply and see if you can bring up an image of relief, something that can take your pain away or lessen it. Allow such an image to completely subsume and absorb the image of your pain. Concentrate on this for awhile and continue to breathe deeply. What comes up? Now, imagine seeing that image through a lens of your favorite color that you associate with healing, and flood the areas that hurt with a light beam of this healing color as you breathe into it, and along with it. . . Eighty-nine . . . 88 . . . 87 . . . 86 . . . 85 . . . 84 . . . 83 . . . 82 . . . 81 . . . 80 . . . (On to O*rgan Language* script)

5. *Organ Language.* Can you listen to your body and try to understand what your body is trying to tell you in its own "body language"? You want to be rid of your pain. Perhaps your pain has caused you to lose sight of what had been important to you once. But perhaps your unconscious mind has found other ways to find meaning and rewards in your life despite your suffering. So, think of this. If you are still awake now, give yourself permission right now to postpone dwelling on any past upsetting experiences that may come up, or trying to solve any problems right now. Perhaps you can put your problematic thoughts away for now in some confidential and safe place until another time when it is appropriate and safe to deal with them. For right now, I wonder if you can give yourself permission to sleep on it . . . . It also is quite important to come up with a healthy role model of how you want to be. Try to see yourself coping and once again, reclaiming mastery over your life and your pain. Start right now to see yourself coping and mastering the pain triggers that you earlier identified and for right now, substitute pleasure for your pain and your pain triggers. It's perfectly all right to think about pleasurable, soothing, pleasant, absorbing activities and to imagine what you can do for yourself or even what you would like to get somebody else to do for you. And, can you visualize somebody you admire right now? How would that person handle a problem such as yours, physical pain? 79 . . . 78 . . . count down to . . . 70 (On to *Self-Punishment*).

6. *Self-Punishment.* Now it is also important if you want relief now to stop punishing yourself if you have been in any way and to forgive yourself for being human and making mistakes. Try and tell yourself right now, whether or not you believe it, that you deserve comfort and to live with noticeably less pain than you have been living with. And you do deserve to fall asleep and enjoy a pleasant night's rest, so that you can wake up at the same time that you have decided to wake up every morning, feeling rested, refreshed, and restored . . . So say to yourself, "I let go of whatever it is that has been tying me to more pain in my life than I need." And, give yourself permission to sleep through the night tonight, so that you will wake up in the morning at the time you have decided or set, feeling rested and refreshed, feeling restored and healed from a night's sleep having had pleasant and comforting dreams . . . Sixty-nine . . . 68 . . . 67 . . . 66 . . . 65 . . . 64 . . . 63 . . . 62 . . . 61 . . . 60 . . . (On to *Positive Suggestions* script).

7. *Positive Suggestions.* Now, play and replay in your mind any positive words, or thoughts that you would like to hear right now. Free yourself for right now of any objections that you don't need. You deserve to be comfortable, pain free, and to sleep peacefully tonight so that you wake up in the morning feeling restored. Let yourself become aware now of any negative suggestions you tend to replay in your mind that could be making your pain worse and kindly replace those with positive self-talk to strengthen your relief, lessen your pain, and increase your confidence that you can be the master of your condition, cope with your condition, and manage your pain. So, for now, I'd like to invite you to bring up any of these positive coping thoughts to mind, or not. Install or imprint the one which is most right now into your brain by hearing it, seeing it, and breathing into it. Lastly, I suggest that you continue to meditate on that healing colored light stream, noticing what happens to the shape and the space of your primary pain as you direct that light stream to permeate, and spread, and penetrate deeply into and throughout the area that hurts. . . Fifty-nine . . . 58 . . . 57 . . . 56 . . . 55 . . . 54 . . . 53 . . . 52 . . . 51 . . . 50 . . . Now, quietly blank your mind again for the next few minutes and allow yourself a space in which to appreciate any pain relief you may have gotten, and to fall asleep . . . The more that you work with these images and thoughts as well as the physical sensations that we have identified, the more control you will develop over your pain sensations, the more mastery you will experience, and the better you will sleep tonight, and every night, even though you may have some pain . . . Your sleep will be d-e-e-p-e-r, . . . much d-e-e-p-e-r, . . . and you will feel much more restored and refreshed when you wake up in the morning after you have a good night's sleep. You will sleep deeply and comfortably all night long, and wake up at the time you have set in the morning feeling refreshed, restored, and renewed . . . Ready to begin a new day, in the morning, with a lot of good positive energy to do the things you need to do, and also with plenty of energy to manage your pain tomorrow . . . Forty-nine . . . 48 . . . 47 . . . 46 . . . 45 . . . 44 . . . 43 . . . 42 . . . 41 . . . 40 . . . Sleep well now. Have a good comfortable night's sleep.

Job Dissatisfaction Index

Name: _____ Age _____ Birthdate _____ Today's Date: _____

Please tell us the last job you held: _____

When did you last work? Are you on disability? Yes   No

If yes, why are you on disability?: _____

INSTRUCTIONS: The purpose of this 32-item questionnaire is to enable you to inform us about how you feel about your last or present job. So, please answer each question by circling either yes or no. Try to choose either yes or no, unless you just cannot say yes or no to the question because your answer is really yes *and* no. In that case, you may circle *both* yes *and* no.

		Answer		Code
Work Status	1. Are you working now?	Yes	No	2
	2. If no, do you expect to be back to work soon?	Yes	No	2
Financial	3. Were/are you fairly paid for the job you did?	Yes	No	2
Job Security	4. Is/was your job secure?	Yes	No	2
	5. Do/did you fear a loss of job security?	Yes	No	1
	6. Were there a lot of changes going on at work?	Yes	No	1
	7. If yes, were you able to handle them well?	Yes	No	2
Personal	8. Were you in conflict with your boss or supervisor at work?	Yes	No	1
	9. Did you have any problems with your boss or supervisor on the job?	Yes	No	1
Justice	10. Do you feel you were treated unfairly by your boss, supervisor, company, or the system?	Yes	No	1
	11. Do you feel you were taken advantage of?	Yes	No	1
Enjoyment	12. Did you enjoy your job?	Yes	No	2
Pride	13. Did you look forward to going to work?	Yes	No	2
	14. Did you like the atmosphere at your workplace?	Yes	No	2
	15. Did you feel pride in your work?	Yes	No	2
Training	16. Are/were you adequately trained for the job you did?	Yes	No	2
	17. Was your job too difficult for you?	Yes	No	1
	18. Was your job too easy or boring?	Yes	No	1
	19. Were you overworked or was your job too demanding?	Yes	No	1
Disability	20. Can you still do your job? If not, why not? _____	Yes	No	2
	21. Could you do it if certain changes were made for you at your job? What changes or modifications would need to be made? _____	Yes	No	2

Name: _____ Date: _____

		Answer		Code

22. Are there any days in which you are absolutely unable to attend work? Yes No 1

If yes, how many days per week?_____ per month?_____

Why are you absolutely unable to attend work on these days? _____

_____

_____

Motivation 23. Do you want to go back to work? Yes No 2

24. Do you want to return to your last job? Yes No 2

25. Would you like to begin a different job? Yes No 1

26. Would you like to change careers? Yes No 1

27. Do you want to stop working period? Yes No 1

Costs 28. Do you earn almost as much or more now on Yes No 1
Benefits Workers' Compensation or Disability as you did when you were working?

29. Does it pay you financially to go back to work? Yes No 2

Feelings 30. Are you angry about the way you have been Yes No 1
treated by your employer or the system since your injury?

31. Are you angry about the way you were treated Yes No 1
by your employer or the system before you became injured?

32. Is it worth it to you to attempt to go back Yes No 2
to work?

APPENDIX W
My Activity Schedule for the Week of: _____

Name: _____

For each hour record: Activity engaged in; Baseline Pain (BP = ?) from 0 to 10; New Pain (NP = ?) from 0 to 10; Mastery (M = ?) from 0 to 10; Enjoyment (E = ?) from 0 to 10; Uptime (U = ?) in minutes; Downtime (D = ?) in minutes. For example—11AM: treadmill, BP = 3, NP = 6, M = 5, E = 9, U = 20, D = 10.

Days:	Mon	Tues	Wed	Thurs	Fri	Sat	Sun
1 AM to 6 AM							
7 AM							
8 AM							
9 AM							
10 AM							
11 AM							
12 PM							
1 PM							
2 PM							
3 PM							
4 PM							
5 PM							
6 PM							
7 PM							
8 PM							
9 PM							
10 PM							
11 PM							
12 AM							

Hypnotic Ability and Response Profile (HARP)
Test Battery Data Sumary

Patient: _____ HARP Date: _____ Birthdate: _____ Gender: 1. M 2. F

Race: ___1. White, Non-Hispanic ___2. African-American ___3. Hispanic
___4. Asian ___5. Native American ___6. Other

Marital Status: ___1. Single ___2. Married ___3. Divorced
___4. Separated ___5. Other Yrs. of Educ.: _____

Handedness: 1. R 2. L List Medications: _____

Work Status: ___1. Working F/T ___2. Working P/T ___3. Disabled
___4. Retired ___5. Student F/T ___6. Other

___1. Student ___2. Patient ___3. Other Occupation: 1. Blue collar
2. Professional 3. Clerical 4. Unskilled 5. Student 6. Other

Total Household Income: 1. less than 20,000/yr. 2. 21,000–50,000
3. 51,000–75,000 4. 76,000–100,000 5. more than 100,000

Counterbalance Version: 1. HARP → SHCS 2. SHCS → HARP

SHCS: Low (0–1) Medium (2–3) High (4–5) Total No.:

AOD Personality Inventory: A____% O____% D____% Total AOD_____/30
(1 × No. ___) (2 × No. ___) (3 × No. ___)

HARP Response
Cluster Scores: I. Repose____/1 II. Hand Clasp____/1 III. Eye Roll____/4
IV. Ideomotor Responsiveness & Compliance____/16
V. Subjective Response to Suggestions____/34 VI. Amnesia____/7
VII. Imagery Responses & Ability____/22 VIII. Hypno-Analgesia____/15
TOTAL HARP SCORE_____/100

SCL-90R T-Scores:
1. Somatization____ 2. O-C____ 3. Interpersonal Sensitivity____
4. Depression____ 5. Anxiety____ 6. Hostility____ 7. Phobic Anx____
8. Paranoia____ 9. Psychoticism____
GSI____ PSDI____ PST____

PACL T-Scores:
1. Introversive____ 2. Inhibited____ 3. Cooperative____ 4. Sociable____
5. Confident____ 6. Forceful____ 7. Respectful____ 8. Sensitive____
9. Personal Problems____

DSM-IV DX:
Axis I: _____ 0. None 1. GAD 2. Adjustment dis 3. Panic dis
4. Phobia 5. PTSD 6. OCD 7. Depressive dis
8. Bipolar dis 9. Tic dis 10. Pain dis 11. Somatization dis
12. Hypochondriasis 13. Conversion dis 14. DDNOS
15. MPD 16. Sleep dis 17. Sexual dysfunction
18. Substance abuse dis 19. Eating dis
20. Impulse control dis 21. Psychotic dis

Axis II: _____ 0. None   1. PD-NOS   2. Antisocial   3. Borderline
4. Narciss   5. Histrionic   6. Dependent   7. O-C
8. Avoidant   9. Schizotypal   10. Schizoid   11. PaPD

Axis III: 0. None   1. Chronic pain syndrome   2. Other: _____

Axis V (GAF: 0–100) _____

Comments/Observations:

Note. Portions of the HARP were adapted with permission from the Hypnotic Induction Profile (HIP) appearing in *Trance and Treatment: Clinical Uses of Hypnosis,* by Herbert Spiegel and David Spiegel. Excerpts from HIP/Table 10-1A/Text Excerpts from *Trance and Treatment* by Herbert Spiegel, M.D. and David Spiegel, M.D. Copyright © 1978 by Herbert Spiegel, M.D. and David Spiegel, M.D. Reprinted by permission of BasicBooks, a division of HarperCollins Publishers, Inc.

Patient: _____   Date: _____

1. POSITION AND PREPARE THE PATIENT:

Patient should be sitting up with head supported, looking straight ahead, both arms on armrests and feet flat or up. Okay to touch patient?   Yes   No
Appearance: Calm/still (1)   Restless/fidgety/fitful (0)

Soon we shall begin your hypnosis experience. I will be offering a number of suggestions for you to experience. You may experience some of them, while others you may not. People vary greatly in how they experience and respond to hypnosis. Our goal today is for both of us to learn how you respond. Unless I ask you to do otherwise, please listen carefully, and allow yourself to respond to what you are feeling. Try not to make things happen. Just let things happen. And please feel free to move around at any time to adjust your level of comfort. Should you at any time need to change your position, get up, or stretch, you may do so. Do you have any other questions before we begin?

2. ADMINISTER THE HAND-CLASP TEST (to right-handers only):

Handedness: Left   Right
Dominant thumb: Left   Right
   Crossed thumb dominance: Yes (1)   No (0)

3. ASSESS THE PATIENT'S EYE-ROLL:

1. Cast your eyes upward, toward your eyebrows. Now, roll your eyes toward the top of your head as if you were looking out the top of your head.
2. While looking upward, allow your eyelids to close. As your eyelids remain closed, continue to look upward.
3. Take a deep breath and hold it. Hold. That's right.
4. Breathe out all the way, allow your eyes to completely relax, and let your eyelids remain closed. Allow your body to experience a pleasant floating sensation.

ER Score: 4   3   2   1   0

4. GIVE SUGGESTIONS FOR RELAXATION AND FLOATING:

You might experience a pleasant floating sensation. Some people experience floating down through the bottom of the chair, others experience a floating upward, out of the chair. As you experience this floating sensation, it can feel pleasant and comfortable and it will help you feel completely relaxed. As you experience this comfortable sensation of floating, allow this finger to float upward as well (Examiner gently strokes the patient's left index finger from the nail up to the knuckle. Examiner waits for the finger signal and verbally reinforces the patient's response). This can be your signal to me that you are experiencing this floating sensation. As you continue to experience your floating sensation, focus your attention on your eyes. Continue to focus on relaxing your eyes, more so, and more so. Experience your eyes as so relaxed that they simply do not feel like opening. When you feel that your eyes are so relaxed that they just do not feel like opening, spread that deep relaxation over your entire body as you continue to enjoy the feeling of floating.

   Ideomotor finger response: Yes (1)   No (0)

5. DEEPEN RELAXATION THROUGH COUNTING:

As you continue to focus on spreading your relaxation and floating, I am going to count to 10 and when I say "10," allow yourself to feel twice as relaxed and twice as comfortable as you were before. Very deeply relaxed and very comfortable. When you feel twice as relaxed, and twice as comfortable, allow this finger to lift up as a signal to me that you feel pleasantly relaxed and comfortable (Examiner strokes Patient's left index finger from the nail up to the knuckle, begins counting, waits for the finger signal, and reinforces the patient's responses). One . . . two . . . three . . . four . . . ten . . .

Ideomotor finger response: Yes (1)   No (0)

6. INDUCE ARM LEVITATION:

While you continue to focus on your floating experience and these pleasant feelings of relaxation and comfort, I am now going to focus on your left hand (Place hand on Pt's left wrist). Soon, I shall stroke your middle finger. After I do, movement sensations will develop, and these movement sensations will spread causing your left hand, to feel light and airy. Your elbow will bend, allowing your forearm to float upward into an upright position, just as if your hand was a large, colorful, hot-air balloon. *Ready.*

ARM LEVITATION SCORING IS BASED ON THE NUMBER OF REINFORCEMENTS NEEDED:

(4) - Stroke middle finger and back of hand up to elbow.

(3) - (First reinforcement) First your middle finger, then the others begin to become lighter and float upward. While the tiny movements in your fingers and hand spread, your elbow bends and it allows your forearm to float upward as well. (Examiner subtly encircles Patient's wrist and gives it a gentle boost)

(2) - (Second reinforcement) In your mind, see your hand as if it was a big, colorful, hot-air balloon. As the air gets hotter, and the balloon becomes larger, it, and your hand, gently float upwards.

(1) - (Third reinforcement) See your hand being that large, colorful, hot air balloon, floating off, taking off into the sky. Let me help it along. (Again, subtly encircle wrist and give arm a small boost)

(0) - (Fourth reinforcement: Manually place the arm up) Let's just put it up there like this.

Initial Arm Levitation Score: 4   3   2   1   0

7. TEST LIGHTNESS/HEAVINESS OF THE LEFT ARM WHILE POSITIONING IT AND GIVE A POSTINDUCTION SUGGESTION FOR SIGNALED LEVITATION:

As I position your arm like so (Examiner positions patient's forearm upright, bent at the elbow, with the hand flexed forward), you'll find your arm remains in this upright position. Your arm will remain in this position, even when your eyes are open. In fact, your arm will remain in this position no matter what I do or say. Even after I push your arm down to the armrest, it will float back up into this position. You may even be amused or surprised when you see this happen. (Is arm light & loose (1) or heavy & resistant (0)?)

Arm lightness score: light & loose (1)   heavy & resistant (0)

8. GIVE A POSTINDUCTION SUGGESTION FOR RESTORING NORMAL SENSATION:

Later, when I touch your elbow, as I am doing now, and then when I stroke your arm and hand, your arm and hand will return to it's normal position and sensation. Then, as I count backward slowly from 10, you will feel that your usual sensation and control will return throughout your body. Your entire body will return to its normal sensation and sense of control. In fact, after I do this, you will come completely out of hypnosis and be totally awake.

9. GIVE POSTHYPNOTIC SUGGESTIONS FOR SELF-HYPNOSIS:

In the future, you'll find you can go into relaxing self-hypnosis by just practicing a few simple steps. First, you roll your eyes upward. Second, you take a deep breath, and close your eyes. Third, you let that breath out, and relax your eyes and your body. You will find yourself relaxed and inwardly focused. Each time you practice your self-hypnosis exercise, you will find it to be easier and easier. In a little while, I'll demonstrate these steps and let you practice so that you will remember them.

10. COUNTDOWN TO END THE FORMAL INDUCTION:

Now, I am going to count down from three to one. At three, get ready, at one, open your eyes, and let your arm remain in this upright position. Three, get ready, two, with your eyelids closed roll up your eyes, one, open your eyelids.

11. SCORE FOR COMFORT IN THE UPRIGHT ARM:

Is your left arm comfortable? Yes (1)   No (0)

12. ASSESS FOR TINGLING SENSATIONS:

(12a) Tell me what sensations you are experiencing in your left arm and hand.

(12b) Are you aware of any tingling sensations?

Score for tingling sensations: Yes (1)   No (0)

13. ASSESS FOR THE SENSATION OF PHYSICAL DISSOCIATION:

(13a) Does your left hand feel as if it is not as much a part of your body as your right hand? Yes (dissociative response)   No

(13b) Does your left hand feel as connected to your left wrist as your right hand feels connected to the right wrist? Yes   No (dissociative response)

Score for physical dissociation: Present (1)   Absent (0)

14. TEST THE PATIENT'S RESPONSIVENESS TO THE SIGNAL FOR ARM LEVITATION: SIGNALED LEVITATION SCORING IS BASED ON THE NUMBER OF REINFORCEMENTS NEEDED:

(4) - (No reinforcements) Now watch this (Place hand down onto armrest).

(3) - (First reinforcement) Now turn your head, look at your left hand and see what is going to happen.

(2) - (Second reinforcement) In your mind, see your hand as if it was a big, colorful, hot-air balloon. As the air gets hotter, and the balloon becomes larger, it, and your hand, gently float upward.

(1) - (Third reinforcement) See your hand being that large, colorful, hot-air balloon, floating off, taking off into the sky.

(0) - (Fourth reinforcement) That's fine. See yourself as if you were a large, white, fluffy cloud, floating and drifting upward and through the sky. Your hand is the cloud, your whole body is the cloud, floating upward peacefully and comfortably. Pretend. Just put your arm back up there.

(Examiner helps Patient position the hand and arm in former upright position)

Signaled Levitation Score: 4   3   2   1   0

15. ASSESS FOR THE PERCEPTION OF A CONTROL DIFFERENCE BETWEEN ARMS:

As your arm remains in this upright position, raise your right hand all the way up. Good, lower your right hand back down. (1) Are you aware of any difference in sensation in your right hand going up compared to your left? Yes   No

(2) For example, does one arm feel lighter or heavier? Yes   No

(3) Which arm feels lighter? __Left Lighter   __Right Lighter   __Both the Same

(4) Is there any difference in your sense of control in one arm as compared with the other? Yes   No   (5) In which arm do you feel more control? _____

__Right Has More Control   __Left Has More Control   __Both the Same

    2   - definite difference in control; left has less control
    1   - a little bit of difference in control felt
    0   - absolutely no difference felt

Control Difference Score: 2   1   0

16A. SPECIAL PLACE IMAGERY:

Now, I'm going to count to three. When I say the number three, your eyelids will gently close all the way down and you will return to the pleasant hypnotic experience of a few moments ago. Examiner begins to count. One .. two . . . three . . . close . . . There is one last exercise I'd like to do before we stop for today. While one part of your mind continues to focus on your left hand and arm, I'd like another part of your mind to help you imagine a very special, important place. It may be a place you've been to before and would like to go to again, or it may be a place you've read or dreamed about and would like to visit. It is your special place. Allow yourself to begin to see clearly the images associated with that place. See the colors, the shapes, the textures, and the shades associated with that place. As you begin to experience your place, you will become more relaxed and more comfortable, and go deeper into your experience. You may actually place yourself there and sense yourelf as being completely in the experience.

As you can see your place, you might begin to hear sounds associated with that place. It might be the sounds of the breeze blowing past your ears, or the sounds of water lapping on the shore. Different people experience different sensations. You might experience all of the sensations I describe or only one or two. Its your experience and your experience is the correct one. As you see the sights and relax, you hear the sounds and relax. Also, imagine smelling the smells associated with this place and relax. Maybe you can taste tastes associated with this place. You see the sights and relax, you may hear the sounds and relax, you may taste the tastes and relax. Maybe you can smell smells associated with this place and relax. Maybe you can feel feelings associated with your place. Those can be either emotional feelings or physical feelings. You may see the sights, hear the sounds, smell the smells, taste the tastes, and feel the feelings associated with your place, and you become more and more involved in your experience.

In a little while, I will ask you to tell me about this experience so you'll be able to remember it clearly. But first, I am going to count down again from three to one. On the number one, you may let your eyes open. Like before, your body, from the neck on down will remain deeply relaxed and comfortable, and feel as if it is completely asleep. From the neck on up, you will feel as if you are relaxed but fully alert. Three, get ready, two with your eyelids closed roll up your eyes, and one, let your eyes open, remaining deeply hypnotized from the neck on down and feeling as if you are fully alert from the neck on up.

16B. REPEAT POSTINDUCTION SUGGESTION FOR RESTORING NORMAL SENSATION:

Later, when I touch your elbow, as I did earlier, and then when I stroke your arm and hand, your arm and hand will return to its normal position and sensation. Then, as I count backwards slowly from 10, you will feel that your usual sensation and control will return throughout your body. Your entire body will return to its normal sensation and sense of control. In fact, after I do this, you will come completely out of hypnosis and be totally awake.

16C. INDUCE HYPNOANALGESIA:

With your left hand and arm remaining in this upright position, I'd like you to look at your left hand. Focus your attention on it. As deeply relaxed and asleep as your whole body is from your neck down, as deeply relaxed and asleep as your left hand is, I'd like you to allow this area here to become numb (With his or her middle and index fingers, the examiner gently strokes in a continuous circular motion an oval area on top of Patient's hand, between the wrist and the knuckles, and between the first and third knuckles). All sensation within this area will fade further away, further than the dull sensation in the rest of your hand (Examiner continues to gently encircle suggested area). The absence of feeling, the dullness, the numbness, in the circle becomes more so than in the rest of your left hand. It's as if you had an injection of novocaine, like you may have had in the dentist's office, in this area. As a matter of fact, that dull feeling continues to move down through your hand, from the top of your hand (Examiner still encircling area) on down through your hand and all the way down into the palm of your hand (Examiner now encircles the same area on the palm without turning the hand over). Your hand can feel so dull, without feeling, that you could have surgery in this area, without chemical anesthetic.

16D. REPEAT SUGGESTION FOR RESTORING NORMAL SENSATION A SECOND TIME:

Later, when I touch your elbow, as I did earlier, and then when I stroke your arm and hand, your arm and hand will return to it's normal position and sensation. Then, as I count backward slowly from 10, you will feel that your usual sensation and control will return throughout your body. Your entire body will return to its normal sensation and sense of control. In fact, after I do this, you will come completely out of hypnosis and be totally awake.

16E. TEST HYPNOANALGESIA:

And now, I'd like to show you how well you are able to do this exercise. Watch the top of your left hand (Examiner gently pinches a small fold of skin on top of patient's hand and holds the skinfold). How does that feel?

(16E-1) Is it painful? Yes (0)   No (1)
(16E-2) Do you feel me touching your hand? Yes (0)   No (1)
(16E-3) Do you feel pressure but no pain? What else do you feel?

(0) No. I feel pain   (1) Yes. Just feel pressure   (2) It's numb, no feeling

(Examiner pinches harder) How does it feel now?

(16E-4) Is it painful? Yes (0)   No (1)
(16E-5) Do you feel me touching your hand? Yes (0)   No (1)
(16E-6) Do you feel pressure but no pain? What else do you feel?

(0) No. I feel pain   (1) Yes. Just feel pressure   (2) It's numb, no feeling

(Examiner, still holding the pinched skinfold, pinches still harder, and shakes left hand right and left.)
E. asks: How does this feel?

(16E-7) Is it painful? Yes (0)   No (1)
(16E-8) Do you feel me touching your hand? Yes (0)   No (1)
(16E-9) Do you feel pressure but no pain? What else do you feel?

(0) No. I feel pain   (1) Yes. Just feel pressure   (2) It's numb, no feeling

(Examiner releases skinfold)

16F. TEST NOCICEPTIVE DIFFERENCE BETWEEN HANDS:

Now, look at your other hand and tell me how this feels (Examiner, with Patient's right hand on the armrest, lightly to moderately pinches a skinfold on top of hand). How does that feel?

(16F-1) Is it painful? (Then Examiner pinches the left hand at the same time as he or she continues to pinch the right hand.) Which hand hurts more when I pinch it? Your right or your left? Left (0)   Right (1)
(16F-2) Do you feel me touching your right hand? No (0)   Yes (1)
(16F-3) In your right hand, do you feel pressure but no pain? What else do you feel?   (0) Yes. I feel just pressure   (1) No. I feel pain

(Examiner releases skinfolds)
Very good. You did fine.

17. ADMINISTER THE SIGNAL FOR RESTORING NORMAL SENSATIONS:

Now note this. (Physically apply the "restoration signal" by performing the following steps in rapid succession in order to establish a smooth flow):

(1) First, touch the patient's left elbow with your right hand, and with your left hand, place the patient's left arm down onto the armrest.

(2) Using your left hand, quickly pat the patient's left hand.

(3) With your left hand, briefly rub the patient's left elbow, to punctuate the application of the restoration signal.

(4) With your left hand, stroke the patient's left arm from the elbow down to the hand in the opposite direction from the initial induction, and then press down on the patient's left hand to punctuate the termination of the restoration signal.

(5) (Then, verbally direct the patient as follows:) Make a fist, and now relax your hand. Move your body. Stretch. Take a deep breath. Now relax. Before there was a difference between the forearms.

Are you aware of any change in sensation in your arms now? Yes   No

Is the difference in control between your two forearms totally gone? Yes   No
Is the control in your forearms becoming equal? Yes   No

Now, I am going to count backward slowly from 10. (Start counting) 10. . . 9 . . . Tell me when you feel that your usual sensation and control has returned throughout your body. . . 8 . . . (Go to "0").

Has your usual sensation and control returned to the rest of your body from your neck on down? Yes   No

_____ Score a 3, if control difference between arms totally remits. Patient reports that usual sensation and control has returned to the rest of the body.

(If the control difference does not totally remit, and normal sensations have not returned in the rest of the patient's body, then, place the patient's left hand and arm back up in the previous position, and repeat the restoration signal as described. Then, say the following:)

Make a fist, and now relax your hand. Move your body. Stretch. Take a deep breath. Now relax. Before there was a difference between the forearms.

Are you aware of any change in sensation now? Yes   No

Is the difference in control between your two forearms totally gone? Yes   No

Is the control in your forearms becoming equal? Yes   No

Now, once again, I am going to count backward slowly from 10. (Start counting) 10 . . 9 . . . Tell me when you feel that your usual sensation and control has returned throughout your body. . . 8 . . . (Go to "0").

Has your usual sensation and control returned to the rest of your body from your neck on down? Yes   No

_____ Score a 2, if the control difference now totally remits.

(If the control difference still does not remit, along with a complete return of normal sensations throughout the body, repeat the restoration signal once again. Then say the following:) With your left hand, make a fist a few times. Now open it. Now, make a fist with both of your hands at the same time. Raise both of your hands up a few times. Move your body. Stretch. Take a deep breath. Now relax. Now, one more time, I am going to count backwards slowly from 10. (Start counting) 10 . . . 9 . . . Tell me when the control in both your arms is equal, and tell me when you feel that your usual sensation and control has returned throughout your body. . 8 . . (Go to "0").

Are you aware of any change in sensation now? Yes   No

Is the difference in control between your two forearms gone? Yes   No

Is the control in your forearms becoming equal? Yes   No

Has your usual sensation and control returned to the rest of your body from your neck on down? Yes   No

_____ Score a 1, if the control difference now totally remits.

_____ Score a 0, if the control difference still does not remit.

(If at this point, the control difference still has not remitted, and normal sensations have not completely been restored, additional work with the patient will be required to correct for the inappropriately sustained control difference and altered sensations.)

Score Response to Restoration Signal: 3   2   1   0

18. TEST FOR AMNESIA TO THE RESTORATION SIGNAL:

Is the control difference between your arms gone, and has the rest of your body regained its normal sensation? Yes   No   Do you have any idea why? Yes   No

Tell me why you think the difference in control in your arms is gone and the rest of your body has regained normal sensation.

    4   - Patient has no idea why normal sensations were restored

    3   - Patient knows you said or did something, but cannot remember what

    2   - Patient associates backward counting with restoration of sensations

    1   - Patient recalls the arm being touched and stroked

    0   - Patient recalls prior verbal suggestions for restoration of sensations

Score Amnesia to Restoration Signal: 4   3   2   1   0

19. CHECK FOR THE EXPERIENCE OF FLOATING AND LIGHTNESS:

When your left arm lifted up before, did you get a feeling of floating or lightness in that hand and arm? Yes   No

Were you aware of any similar sensations of floating or lightness in any other parts of your body? Yes   No

Where else in your body did you experience these feelings?

    Score for Floating and Lightness: 2   1   0

    2   - Floating sensations reported in arm and in other body parts

    1   - Floating sensations just reported in the left arm or hand

    0   - Patient did not have these sensations

20. CHECK FOR EXPERIENCE OF INVOLUNTARINESS:

Did you sense your arm was going up on its own? Or, did you feel as if you were just putting it up there?

FELT LIKE IT WENT ON ITS OWN (1)   FELT LIKE PATIENT PUT IT UP (0)

    Score Involuntariness: 1   0

21. CHECK FOR AMNESIA AND THE EXPERIENCE OF RELAXATION:

Earlier, I asked you to make your eyes so relaxed and comfortable that they just would not feel like opening.

    (21A)   Do you remember me suggesting that to you earlier?

              Score for Amnesia to Relaxed Eyes Suggestion:

                  Yes (0)   No (1 - Amnesia)

    (21B)   Were you able to get your eyes so relaxed and comfortable that they just did not want to open?

              Score for Response to Relaxed Eyes Suggestion:

                  Yes Experienced (1)   No (0)

Earlier, I asked you to spread the relaxation over your entire body as you focused on letting your body float.

    (21C)   Do you remember me suggesting that to you earlier?

              Score Amnesia to Spreading Relaxation Suggestion:

                  Yes (0)   No (1 - Amnesia)

(21D)   Do you recall experiencing feelings of relaxation and comfort spreading over your entire body?
Score Response to Spreading Relaxation Suggestion:
Experienced (1)   No (0)

(21E)   Do you recall experiencing a sensation of floating, floating down through the chair, or upward?
Score Response to Floating Suggestion:
Yes downward (2)   upward (1)   Not (0)

Earlier, I counted to 10 and I suggested that by the count of "10," you would feel twice as relaxed and comfortable. Deeply relaxed and very comfortable.

(21F)   Do you remember me counting and suggesting that to you earlier?
Score Amnesia to Counting/Deepening Suggestion:
Yes (0)   No (1 - Amnesia)

(21G)   Do you recall becoming noticeably more deeply relaxed and comfortable?
Score Response to Counting/Deepening Suggestion:
Yes (1)   No (0)

22. ASSESS THE PATIENT'S "SPECIAL PLACE" IMAGERY EXPERIENCE:

A moment ago I asked you to imagine some things. Please explain for me your experience with the imagination exercise.

(22A)   SCORE ABSORPTION:
Did it feel as if you were really there, or did it feel as if you were just thinking about being there while you were sitting here?
Score 4 - Felt as if really in the experience. Almost forgot where he/she was.
Score 3 - Felt as if really in the experience, but knew where he/she was.
Score 2 - Mostly felt as if there. At times, felt as if just thinking of it.
Score 1 - Mostly felt as if just thinking of it. At times, felt as if there.
Score 0 - Felt as if just thinking about it.   _

(22B)   VISUAL IMAGERY:
Did you experience visual imagery? Yes (1)   No (0)
What did you see?
Did you see colors? Yes (1)   No (0)
Did you see different shapes and sizes? Yes (1)   No (0)

(22B)   SCORE VISUAL "SPECIAL PLACE" IMAGERY:
Were the visual images clear? Yes   No   How clear or vivid were they?
Score 2 - Images very clear
Score 1 - Images somewhat clear
Score 0 - Images not clear
Total Visual Imagery Score: 5   4   3   2   1   0

(22C)   SCORE AUDITORY "SPECIAL PLACE" IMAGERY:

Did you experience any sounds associated with that place?
Yes (1)   No (0)

What were they?

Were the sounds clear or distinct? Yes   No   How clear or distinct were they?

Score 2 - Sounds very clear
Score 1 - Sounds somewhat clear
Score 0 - Sounds not clear

Total Auditory Imagery Score: 3   2   1   0

(22D)   SCORE OLFACTORY IMAGERY:

Did you smell anything associated with that place? Yes (1)   No (0)

What did you smell?

Were the smells clear or distinct? Yes   No   How clear or distinct were they?

Score 2 - Smells very distinct
Score 1 - Smells somewhat distinct
Score 0 - Smells not distinct

Total Olfactory Imagery Score: 3   2   1   0

(22E)   GUSTATORY IMAGERY:

Did you taste any tastes associated with that place? Yes (1)   No (0)

What were they?

Score Gustatory "Special Place" Imagery: 1   0

(22F)   EMOTIONAL FEELINGS:

Did you experience emotional feelings associated with that place? Yes (1)   No (0) What were they?

Were the emotional feelings clear or distinct? Yes   No How clear or distinct?

Score 2 - Emotions very clear and distinct
Score 1 - Emotions somewhat clear and distinct
Score 0 - Emotions not clear or distinct

Total Emotional Feelings Score: 3   2   1   0

(22G)   SENSORY FEELINGS OR PHYSICAL SENSATIONS:

Any physical feelings or sensations? Yes (1)   No (0)

What were they?

Were the physical sensations clear or distinct? Yes   No How clear or distinct?

Score 2 - Sensations very clear and distinct
Score 1 - Sensations somewhat clear and distinct
Score 0 - Sensations not clear or distinct

Total Physical Sensations Score: 3   2   1   0

23. DEBRIEF THE PATIENT:

(23A)   Overall what was this experience like for you? What did you especially like about the experience? What didn't you like? (NOT SCORED)

(23B)   Was it pleasant? Yes (1)   No (0)
        Was it relaxing? Yes (1)   No (0)
        Score Evaluation as "Pleasant and Relaxing Experience":
        2   1   0

(23C)   Do you feel that you were a good hypnotic subject?
        Score Self-Evaluation as a "Good Subject":
        Yes good (1)   Not good (0)

(23D)   Were you at all distracted during the procedure? Yes   No   If so, how much? (Answers implying "a lot" are scored "0." Everything else is scored "1")
        Score "Self-Rated Distractibility":
        1 (not so much)   0 ("distracted a lot")

(23E)   Did you get absorbed in aspects of the experience? If so, what?
        Score "Self-Rated Absorption":
        Yes absorbed (1)   Not absorbed (0)

(23F)   Do you think you were hypnotized?
        Score "Hypnotized Perception" (Yes/Not)
        Yes hypnotized (1)   Not (0)

(23G)   On a scale of 1–10, with 10 being very deeply hypnotized, how would you rate your degree of being hypnotized?
        Score Self-Rated Degree of "Depth":
        10 9 8 7 6 5 4 3 2 1

(23H)   Do you think that you went into a deep trance?
        Score "Depth" Yes/No
        Deep Yes (2)   moderately (1)   Not deep (0)

(23I)   Are you at all disappointed in your experience? Tell me about it.
        Score "Disappointment" Yes/No
        Disappointed Yes (0)   Not disappointed (1)

(23J)   Were you able to experience many of the things I suggested? What do you especially remember experiencing?
        Score "Perceived Hypnotic Responsiveness" (Y/N)
        Yes experienced (1)   No (0)

(23K)   Did you get the feeling that things were happening spontaneously and automatically? What were they?
        Score "Perceived Involuntariness":
        Yes experienced (1)   Not experienced (0)

(23L) Did you at any point feel as if you were here listening to me and at the same time that you were somewhere else?

Score "Subjective Feeling of Dissociation":
Yes experienced (1)   Not (0)

(23M) Would you like to learn to practice self-hypnosis on your own?

Score "Desire to Learn Self Hypnosis": Yes (1)   No (0)

24 SUMMARY DEBRIEFING:

You see, this is what it is like to experience hypnosis. It is a shifting of your attention into a pleasant state of relaxed, easy concentration. Your imagination is working, but it is focused. You are responsive to suggestion but you do not have to try to make anything happen. You can let go and just let whatever happens happen. In fact, there can be a pleasant element of surprise in that you discover a difference in sensation in your body. For example, I did not tell you that there would be a difference in control between your two arms. You discovered this for yourself. I suggested that your left arm would feel light and airy, and float up like a balloon. You responded to this suggestion and then you discovered the difference in sensation between your right and left arms. You freely complied with my suggestions and discovered the difference in how you felt on your own. Part of your mind was focused on my suggestions, and at the same time, another part of your mind was focused on how you felt. Hypnosis is a pleasant combination of easy, effortless concentration, and an attitude of self-discovery and pleasant surprise. This is coupled with your willingness to allow yourself to freely respond to acceptable suggestions. These qualities distinguish the state of hypnosis from the waking state. And these qualities make hypnosis an excellent tool for relieving pain. Hypnosis helps you to be in more than one place at the same time easily, without any effort. You can be aware of your pain, and at the same time, still follow along with some easy suggestions, while discovering a difference in sensation. It is this difference in your sensation, your openness to positive suggestion, and your flexibility in redirecting your attention, that can bring you real pain relief.

25. DESIGN FOR THE PATIENT AN INDIVIDUALIZED SELF-HYPNOSIS EXERCISE:

Teach the patient a simple three-, four-, five-, or six-step self-hypnosis exercise. Individualize it by incorporating the hypnotic phenomena that the patient reported he/she experienced and that were pleasant, easy, and spontaneous. Insert clinically relevant suggestions. Use the checklist of hypnotic phenomena below by numbering in sequence the items to comprise the patient's self-hypnosis exercise.

_____ Hand-clasp

_____ Eye-roll and deep breath

_____ Eye closure, relaxed eyes perception, and eye catalepsy

_____ Floating and lightness

_____ Spreading of relaxation

_____ Counting to deepen relaxation

_____ Ideomotor finger signals

_____ Arm/hand levitation

____Physical dissociation

____Parallel awareness

____Perception/experience of involuntariness and spontaneity

____Amnesia

____Absorption

____Subjective experience of hypnotic depth

____Self-evaluation as a hypnosis subject

____Pleasant and vivid visual imagery

____Pleasant and vivid auditory imagery

____Pleasant and vivid tactile-kinesthetic imagery

____Pleasant olfactory imagery

____Pleasant gustatory imagery

____Pleasant and distinct emotional feelings

____Pleasant and distinct physical sensations

____Hypnoanalgesia

____Strong desire/motivation

____Response to posthypnotic cues

____Relaxed breathing

THE HYPNOTIC ABILITY AND RESPONSE
PROFILE SUMMARY SHEET

Patient: _____ Date: _____

Score   Scale

_____   I. PATIENT'S REPOSE (item 1):
Calm/still (1)   Restless/fidgety/fitful (0)

_____   II. HAND-CLASP TEST (item 2):
Handedness: Left   Right
Dominant thumb: Left   Right
Crossed thumb dominance (for right-handers only): Yes (1) No (0)

_____   III. EYE-ROLL SIGN (item 3):
Score: 4   3   2   1   0

_____   IV. IDEOMOTOR RESPONSIVENESS AND COMPLIANCE (max = 16):
_____ Ideomotor finger response (item 4: 0–1)
_____ Ideomotor finger response (item 5: 0–1)
_____ Initial arm levitation (item 6: 0–4)
_____ Arm lightness (item 7: 0–1)
_____ Signalled levitation (item 14: 0–4)
_____ Control difference (item 15: 0–2)
_____ Response to "restoration signal" (item 17: 0–3)
(Note: There is no scoring for items 8, 9, and 10)

_____   V. SUBJECTIVE RESPONSE TO SUGGESTIONS (max = 34):
_____ Arm comfort (item 11: 0–1)
_____ Tingling sensations (item 12: 0–1)
_____ Physical dissociation (item 13: 0–1)
_____ Floating and lightness (item 19: 0–2)
_____ Involuntariness (item 20: 0–1)
_____ Relaxed eyes perception (item 21B: 0–1)
_____ Spreading relaxation perception (item 21D: 0–1)
_____ Floating downward/upward perception (item 21E: 0–2) Which?
_____ Relaxation deepened with counting (item 21G: 0–1)
_____ Pleasant and relaxing experience (item 23B: 0–2)
_____ Self-evaluation as "hypnotic subject" (item 23C: 0–1)
_____ Distractibility (item 23D: 0[a lot]–1)
_____ Absorption (item 23E: 0–1)
_____ Hypnotized - Yes/No (item 23F: 0–1)
_____ Perception of degree of hypnosis (item 23G: 0–10)
_____ Perception of "hypnotic depth" (item 23H: 0–2)
_____ Disappointment - Yes/No (item 23I: 0–1)
_____ Perceived extent of hypnotic responsiveness (item 23J: 0–1)
_____ Involuntariness (item 23K: 0–1)

_____ Subjective feeling of "dissociation (item 23L: 0–1)

_____ Desire/motivation to practice self-hypnosis (item 23M: 0–1)

(Note: Item 23A is not scored)

_____ VI. AMNESIA (max = 7):

_____ Amnesia for "restoration signal" (item 18: 0–4)

_____ Amnesia for "relaxed eyes suggestion" (item 21A: 0–1)

_____ Amnesia for "spreading relaxation suggestion" (item 21C: 0–1)

_____ Amnesia for "counting relaxation to 10" (item 21F: 0–1)

_____ VII. IMAGERY RESPONSES AND ABILITY (max = 22):

_____ Absorption (item 22A: 0–4)

_____ Visual "special place" imagery (item 22B: 0–5)

_____ Auditory "special place" imagery (item 22C: 0–3)

_____ Olfactory "special place" imagery (item 22D: 0–3)

_____ Gustatory "special place" imagery (item 22E: 0–1)

_____ Emotional feelings assoc. w/ "special place" (item 22F: 0–3)

_____ Physical feelings/sensations assoc. w/ "special place:
(item 22G: 0–3)

_____ VIII. HYPNOANALGESIA (max = 15):

_____ Absence of pain (items 16E-1, 16E-3, 16E-4, 16E-6, 16E-7,
16E-9: 0–9)

_____ Anesthesia (items 16E-2, 16E-5, 16E-8: 0–3)

_____ Nociceptive difference bet. hands (items 16F-1, 16F-2, 16F-3:
0–3)

(Note: Items 16A through 16D are not scored)

_____ TOTAL HYPNOTIC ABILITY AND RESPONSIVENESS SCORE
(Range: 0–100)

The Spiegel Apollonian-Odyssean-Dionysian Personality Inventory

Patient Name: _____ Date: _____

1. SPACE AWARENESS: As you concentrate on watching a movie or play, do you get so absorbed in what is going on that you lose awareness of where you are?

    No = A   Not that much = O   Yes = D

    If yes, ask: Do you ever get so absorbed that when the show ends you are surprised to realize it was just a movie or a play? Yes = DD   No = D

2. TIME PERCEPTION: As you perceive time, do you focus more on the present, the past and the future, or all three about equally?

    Past and/or future = A   All three = O   The present = D

3. MYTH-BELIEF CONSTELLATION (HEAD vs. HEART): The French philosopher Pascal once said: "The heart has a mind which the brain does not understand." He said that there are two kinds of mind, the "heart-mind" and the "brain-mind." Which of these two minds do you give priority to?

    Brain or mind = A   Both = O   Heart = D

4. INTERPERSONAL CONTROL: As you relate to most people, do you prefer to control the interaction or do you prefer to let the other person take over if they wish?

    Control interaction = A   Both or it depends = O   Give control to other = D

5. TRUST PRONENESS: In your tendency to trust other people, where would you place yourself on a scale of below average—average—above average?

    Below average = A   Average = O   Above average or high = D

6. CRITICAL APPRAISAL AND LEARNING STYLE: As you are learning something new, do you tend to critically judge it as you are learning it, or do you accept it, absorb it, and perhaps critically evaluate it at a later time?

    Immediately judge = A   Both/varied = O   Suspends judgment = D

7. RESPONSIBILITY: As you sense you responsibility for what you do, where do you place yourself on a scale of below average—average—above average?

    Above average = A   Average/moderate = O   Below average/low = D

8. PREFERRED MODE OF CONTACT: If you are learning something new, and you know that it can be learned equally well and safely by either seeing it or touching it, what is your preference—to see it or to touch it?

    See it = A   Both valued equally = O   Touch it = D

9. PROCESSING: When you come up with a new idea, there are two parts to it. One is to dream the idea up. The other part is to figure out how to do it and make it work. Which part gives you greater fulfillment and satisfaction?

    Figure out how to do it = A   It varies/both = O   Dream it up = D

10. WRITING VALUE: As you come up with or work out a new idea, is it necessary to write notes or do you feel your way through without writing?

    Rely on notes = A   Minimal/some writing = O   Without taking notes = D

    % A = _____   % O = _____   % D = _____
    A = Apollonian   O = Odyssean   D = Dionysian

References

Adams, R. L., Parsons, O. A., Culbertson, J. L., & Nixon, S. J. (Eds.). (1996). *Neuropsychology for clinical practice: Etiology, assessment, and treatment of common neurological disorders.* Washington, DC: American Psychological Association.

Ahles, T. M., Yunus, M. B., & Masi, A. C. (1987). Is chronic pain a variant of depressive disease? The case of primary fibromyalgia syndrome. *Pain, 29,* 105–111.

Allen, L. M., Conder, R. L., Green, W. P., & Cox, D. R. (1997). *CARB '97 Computerized assessment of reponse bias manual.* Durham, NC: CogniSyst.

Allen, L. M., & Cox, D. R. (1995). *Computerized assessment of response bias manual* (Rev. ed.). Durham, NC: CogniSyst.

American Chronic Pain Association. (1993). *Help and hope* (Informational brochure). Rocklin, CA: Author.

American Medical Association. (1995). Pain. In T. C. Doege & T. P. Houston (Eds.), *Guides to the evaluation of permanent impairment* (4th ed., pp. 303–314). Chicago: Author.

American Medical Association. (1997). *Physicians' current procedural terminology: CPT 97.* Chicago: Author.

American Pain Society. (1992). *Principles of analgesic use in the treatment of acute pain and cancer pain.* Skokie, IL: Author.

American Psychiatric Association. (1994). *Diagnostic and statistical manual of mental disorders* (4th ed.). Washington, DC: Author.

Anderson, D. A., & Hines, R. H. (1994). Attachment and pain. In R. C. Grzesiak & D. S. Ciccone (Eds.), *Psychological vulnerability to chronic pain* (pp. 137–152). New York: Springer.

Anderson, K. O., Dowds, B. N., Pelletz, R. E., Edwards, W. T., & Peeters-Asdourian, C. (1995). Development and initial validation of a scale to measure self efficacy beliefs in patients with chronic pain. *Pain, 63,* 77–84.

Anderson, L. P., & Rehm, L. P. (1984). The relationship between strategies of coping and perceptions of pain in three chronic pain groups. *Journal of Clinical Psychology, 40,* 1170–1177.

Anderson, R. B., & Taylor, J. F. (1995). *Chronic pain: Taking command of our healing: An approach to the emotional trauma underlying chronic pain.* Minneapolis, MN: New Energy Press.

Anderson, R. M. (1994). *Practitioner's guide to clinical neuropsychology.* New York: Plenum Press.

Andersson, G. B. J., Pope, M. H., Frymoyer, J. W., & Snook, S. (1991). Epidemiology and cost. In M. H. Pope, G. B. J. Andersson, J. W. Frymoyer, & D. B. Chaffin (Eds.), *Occupational low back pain: Assessment, treatment and prevention* (pp. 95–113). St. Louis, MO: Mosby-Year Book.

Arena, J. G., & Blanchard, E. B. (1996). Biofeedback and relaxation therapy for chronic pain disorders. In R. J. Gatchel & D. C. Turk (Eds.), *Psychological approaches to pain management* (pp. 179–230). New York: Guilford Press.

Averill, P. M., Novy, D. M., Nelson, D. V., & Berry, L. A. (1996). Correlates of depression in chronic pain patients: A comprehensive examination. *Pain, 65,* 93–100.

Bandura, A. (1986). *Social foundations of thought in action: A social cognitive theory.* Englewood Cliffs, NJ: Prentice-Hall.

Bandura, A., O'Leary, A., Taylor, C. B., Gauthier, J., & Gossard, D. (1987). Perceived self-efficacy and pain control: Opioid and nonopioid mechanisms. *Journal of Personality and Social Psychology, 53,* 563–571.

Barber, J. (1996). *Hypnosis and suggestion in the treatment of pain.* New York: Norton.

Barnes, D., Gatchel, R. J., Mayer, T. G., & Barnett, J. (1990). Changes in MMPI profiles of chronic low back pain patients following successful treatment. *Journal of Spinal Disorders, 3,* 353–355.

Barnes, D., Smith, D., Gatchel, R. J., & Mayer, T. G. (1989). Psychosocioeconomic predictors of treatment success/failure in chronic low-back pain patients. *Spine, 14,* 427–430.

Basmajian, J. V. (Ed.). (1989). *Biofeedback: Principles and practice for clinicians* (3rd ed.). Baltimore: Williams & Wilkins.

Bates, B. L. (1993). Individual differences in response to hypnosis. In J. W. Rhue, S. J. Lynn, & I. Kirsch (Eds.), *Handbook of clinical hypnosis* (pp. 23–54). Washington, DC: American Psychological Association.

Beals, R. K. (1984). Compensation and recovery from injury. *Western Journal of Medicine, 40,* 276–283.

Beck, A. T. (1967). *Depression: Causes and treatment.* Philadelphia: University of Pennsylvania Press.

Beck, A. T. (1976). *Cognitive therapy and the emotional disorders.* New York: International Universities Press.

Beck, A. T. (1987, 1993). *The Beck Depression Inventory.* San Antonio, TX: The Psychological Corporation/Harcourt Brace.

Beck, A. T. (1990, 1993). *Beck Anxiety Inventory.* San Antonio, TX: The Psychological Corporation/Harcourt Brace.

Beck, A. T., Emery, G., & Greenberg, R. L. (1985). *Anxiety disorders and phobias: A cognitive perspective.* New York: Basic Books.

Beck, A. T., Freeman, A., & Associates. (1990). *Cognitive therapy of personality disorders.* New York: Guilford Press.

Beck, A. T., Kovacs, M., & Weissman, A. (1979). Assessment of suicidal intention: The scale for suicidal ideation. *Journal of Consulting and Clinical Psychology, 47,* 343–352.

Beck, A. T., Rush, A. J., Shaw, B. F., & Emery, G. (1979). *Cognitive therapy of depression.* New York: Guilford Press.

Beck, A. T., Ward, C. H., Mendelson, M., Mock, J., & Erlbaugh, J. (1961). An inventory for measuring depression. *Archives of General Psychiatry, 56*, 53–63.

Beck, A. T., Wright, F. D., Newman, C. F., & Liese, B. S. (1993). *Cognitive therapy of substance abuse.* New York: Guilford Press.

Beck, J. S. (1995). *Cognitive therapy: Basics and beyond.* New York: Guilford Press.

Beckham, J. C., Keefe, F. J., Caldwell, D. S., & Roedman, A. A. (1991). Pain coping strategies in rheumatoid arthritis: Relationship to pain, disability, depression, and daily hassles. *Behavior Therapy, 22*, 113–124.

Beecher, H. K. (1946). Pain in men wounded in battle. *Annals of Surgery, 123*, 96–105.

Bellissimo, A., & Tunks, E. (1984). *Chronic pain: The psychotherapeutic spectrum.* New York: Praeger.

Benedikt, R. A., & Kolb, L. C. (1986). Preliminary findings on chronic pain and posttraumatic stress disorder. *American Journal of Psychiatry, 43*, 908–910.

Benson, H. (1975). *The relaxation response.* New York: Morrow.

Bergner, M., Bobbitt, R. A., Carter, W. B., & Gilson, B. S. (1981). The Sickness Impact Profile: Development and final revision of a health status measure. *Medical Care, 19*, 787–805.

Beutler, L. E., & Clarkin, J. F. (1990). *Systematic treatment selection: Toward targeted therapeutic interventions.* New York: Brunner/Mazel.

Beutler, L. E., Engle, D., Oro-Beutler, M. E., Daldrup, R., & Meredith, K. A. (1986). Inability to express intense affect: A common link between depression and pain. *Journal of Consulting and Clinical Psychology, 54*, 752–759.

Bigos, S. J., Battie, M. C., Spengler, D. M., Fisher, L. D., Fordyce, W. E., Hansson, T. H., Nachemson, A. L., & Wortley, M. D. (1991). A prospective study of work perceptions and psychosocial factors affecting the report of back injury. *Spine, 16*, 1–6.

Blanchard, E. B., & Andrasik, F. (1985). *Management of chronic headaches: A psychological approach.* New York: Pergamon Press.

Blanchard, E. B., & Hickling, E. J. (1997). *After the crash: Assessment and treatment of motor vehicle accident survivors.* Washington, DC: American Psychological Association.

Blanchard, E. B., Kim, M., Hermann, C., & Steffek, B. D. (1993). Preliminary results of the effects on headache relief of perception of success among tension headache patients receiving relaxation. *Headache Quarterly, 4*, 249–253.

Blumer, D., & Heilbronn, M. (1989). Dysthymic pain disorder: The treatment of chronic pain as a variant of depression. In C. D. Tollison (Ed.), *Handbook of chronic pain management* (pp. 197–209). Baltimore: Williams & Wilkins.

Bonica, J. J. (1987). Importance of the problem. In S. Andersson, M. Bond, M. Mehta, & M. Swerdlow (Eds.), *Chronic non-cancer pain* (p. 13). Lancaster, United Kingdom: MTP Press.

Bonica, J. J. (1990). Definitions and taxonomy of pain. In J. J. Bonica (Ed.), *The management of pain* (pp. 18–27). Philadelphia: Lea & Febiger.

Boudewyns, P. A., Stwertka, S. A., Hyer, L. A., Albrecht, J. W., & Sperr, E. V. (1993). EMDR: A pilot study. *Behavior Therapy, 16*, 30–33.

Bower, S. A., & Bower, G. H. (1991). *Asserting yourself.* Reading, MA: Addison-Wesley.

Bradley, L. A. (1995). Biopsychosocial model and the Minnesota Multiphasic Personality Inventory: Even psychologists make cognitive errors. *Pain Forum,* 4(2), 97–100.

Bradley, L. A. (1996). Cognitive-behavioral therapy for chronic pain. In R. J. Gatchel & D. C. Turk (Eds.), *Psychological approaches to pain management* (pp. 131–147). New York: Guilford Press.

Bradley, L. A., Haile, J. M., & Jaworski, T. M. (1992). Assessment of psychological status using interviews and self-report instruments. In D. C. Turk & R. Melzack (Eds.), *Handbook of pain assessment* (pp. 193–213). New York: Guilford Press.

Bromm, B., & Desmedt, J. E. (Eds.). (1995). *Pain and the brain. From nociception to cognition: Advances in pain research and therapy* (Vol. 22). New York: Raven Press.

Brown, D. P., & Fromm, E. (1987). *Hypnosis and behavioral medicine.* Hillsdale, NJ: Erlbaum.

Brown, G. K. (1990). A causal analysis of chronic pain and depression. *Journal of Abnormal Psychology, 99,* 127–137.

Brown, G. K., & Nicassio, P. M. (1987). The development of a questionnaire for the assessment of active and passive coping strategies in chronic pain patients. *Pain, 31,* 53–62.

Brown, G. K., Nicassio, P. M., & Wallston, K. A. (1989). Pain coping strategies and depression in rheumatoid arthritis. *Journal of Consulting and Clinical Psychology, 57,* 652–657.

Bruce, B. K., Rome, J. D., Malec, J. F., Hodgson, J. E., Suda, K. S., Payne, J. E., & Maruta, T. (1992). *Cognitive impairment: A primary reason for the exclusion of the elderly from chronic pain rehabilitation programs?* Paper presented at the meeting of the American Pain Society, San Diego, CA.

Bruera, E., Macmillan, K., Hanson, J., & MacDonald, R. N. (1989). The cognitive effects of the administration of narcotic analgesics in patients with cancer pain. *Pain, 39,* 13–16.

Brussell, E. E. (Ed.). (1988). *Webster's new world dictionary of quotable definitions.* Englewood Cliffs, NJ: Prentice Hall.

Burns, D. D. (1980). *Feeling good: The new mood therapy.* New York: Morrow.

Burns, J. W., Johnson, B. J., Mahoney, N., Devine, J., & Pawl, R. (1996). Anger management style, hostility and spouse responses: Gender differences in predictors of adjustment among chronic pain patien... *Pain, 64,* 445–453.

Butler, R., Damarin, F., Beaulieu, C., Schwebel, A., & Thorn, B. E. (1989). Assessing cognitive coping strategies for acute postsurgical pain. *Psychological Assessment: A Journal of Consulting and Clinical Psychology, 1,* 41–45.

Cairns, D., Mooney, V., & Crane, P. (1984). Spinal pain rehabilitation: Inpatient and outpatient treatment results and development of predictors for outcome. *Spine, 9,* 91–95.

Casten, R. J., Parmelee, P. A., Kleban, M. H., Lawton, M. P., & Katz, I. R. (1995). The relationships among anxiety, depression, and pain in a geriatric institutionalized sample. *Pain, 61*(2), 271–276.

Catalano, E. M., & Hardin, K. N. (1996). *The chronic pain control workbook: A step-by-step guide for coping with and overcoming your pain.* Oakland, CA: New Harbinger.

Caudill, M. A. (1995). *Managing pain before it manages you.* New York: Guilford Press.

Cautela, J. R., & Kearney, A. J. (1986). *The covert conditioning handbook.* New York: Springer Publishing Company.

Cheek, D. B. (1965). Emotional factors in persistent pain states. *American Journal of Clinical Hypnosis, 3*(2).

Cheek, D. B. (1994). *Hypnosis: The application of ideomotor procedures.* Boston: Allyn & Bacon.

Cheek, D. B., & LeCron, L. M. (1968). *Clinical hypnotherapy.* New York: Grune & Stratton.

Chibnall, J. T., & Duckro, P. N. (1994). Post-traumatic stress disorder in chronic post-traumatic headache patients. *Headache, 34,* 357–361.

Childre, D. L. (1994). *Freeze-frame: Fast action stress relief.* Boulder Creek, CA: Planetary Publications.

Childre, D. L. (1996). *Cut-thru: Achieve total security and maximum energy. A scientifically proven insight on how to* care *without becoming a victim.* Boulder Creek, CA: Planetary Publications.

Ciccone, D. S., & Lenzi, V. (1994). Psychosocial vulnerability to chronic dysfunctional pain: A critical review. In R. C. Grzesiak & D. S. Ciccone (Eds.), *Psychological vulnerability to chronic pain* (pp. 153–178). New York: Springer Publishing Company.

Coe, W. C. (1993). Expectations and hypnotherapy. In J. W. Rhue, S. J. Lynn, & I. Kirsch (Eds.), *Handbook of clinical hypnosis* (pp. 73–94). Washington, DC: American Psychological Association.

Coolidge, F. L. (1993). *The Coolidge Axis II Inventory Manual.* Clarmont, FL: Synergistic Office Solutions.

Coolidge, F. L., & Merwin, M. M. (1992). Reliability and validity of the Coolidge Axis II Inventory: A new inventory for the assessment of personality disorders. *Journal of Personality Assessment, 59,* 223–238.

Corey, D., & Solomon, S. (1989). *Pain: Free yourself for life.* New York: Penguin Books.

Cram, J. R. (1986). *Clinical EMG: Muscle scanning and diagnostic manual for surface recordings.* Seattle, WA: Clinical Resources.

Cram, J. R., & Associates. (1990). *Clinical EMG for surface recordings* (Vol. 2). Nevada City, CA: Clinical Resources.

DeBell, C., & Jones, R. D. (1997). As good as it seems? A review of EMDR experimental research. *Professional Psychology: Research and Practice, 28*(2), 153–163.

DeGood, D. E. (1983). Reducing medical patients' reluctance to participate in psychological therapies: The initial session. *Professional Psychology, 14,* 570–579.

DeGood, D. E., & Dane, J. R. (1996). The psychologist as a pain consultant in outpatient, inpatient, and workplace settings. In R. J. Gatchel & D. C. Turk (Eds.), *Psychological approaches to pain management* (pp. 403–437). New York: Guilford Press.

DeGood, D. E., & Kiernan, B. (1996). Perception of fault in patients with chronic pain. *Pain, 64,* 153–159.

DeGood, D. E., & Shutty, M. S. (1992). Assessment of pain beliefs, coping, and self-efficacy. In D. C. Turk & R. Melzack (Eds.), *Handbook of pain assessment* (pp. 214–234). New York: Guilford Press.

Delis, D. C., Kramer, J. H., Kaplan, E., & Ober, B. A. (1987). *California Verbal Learning Test: Adult version.* San Antonio, TX: The Psychological Corporation/Harcourt Brace.

Derogatis, L. R. (1983). *SCL-90-R administration, scoring and procedure manual*. Baltimore: Clinical Psychometric Research.

Deyo, R. A. (1986). Comparative validity of the Sickness Impact Profile and shorter scales for the functional assessment of low-back pain. *Spine, 11*, 951–954.

Dozois, D. J. A., Dobson, K. S., Wong, M., Hughes, D., & Long, A. (1996). Predictive utility of the CSQ in low back pain: Individual vs. composite measures. *Pain, 66*, 171–180.

Dryden, W., & DiGiuseppe, R. (1990). *A primer on RET*. Champaign, IL: Research Press.

Dubuisson, D., & Melzack, R. (1976). Classification of clinical pain descriptions by multiple group discriminant analysis. *Experimental Neurology. 51*, 480–487.

Dworkin, R. H. (1991). What do we really know about the psychological origins of chronic pain? *American Pain Society Bulletin, 1*(5), 7–11.

Dworkin, R. H., & Gitlin, M. J. (1991). Clinical aspects of depression in chronic pain patients. *Clinical Journal of Pain, 7*, 79–94.

Dworkin, R. H., Handlin, D. S., Richlin, D. M., Brand L., & Vannucci, C. (1985). Unraveling the effects of compensation, litigation, and employment on treatment response to pain. *Pain, 23*, 49–59.

Edmonston, W. E. (1986). *The induction of hypnosis*. New York: John Wiley & Sons, Inc.

Eimer, B. N. (1988). The chronic pain patient: Multimodal assessment and psychotherapy. *International Journal of Medical Psychotherapy, 1*, 23–40.

Eimer, B. N. (1989). Psychotherapy for chronic pain: A cognitive approach. In A. Freeman, K. M. Simon, H. Arkowitz, & L. Beutler (Eds.), *Comprehensive handbook of cognitive therapy*. New York: Plenum Press.

Eimer, B. N. (1992). The treatment of chronic pain. In A. Freeman & F. Dattilio (Eds.), *Comprehensive casebook of cognitive therapy*. New York: Plenum Press.

Eimer, B. N. (1993a). Desensitization and reprocessing of chronic pain with EMDR. *EMDR Network Newsletter, 3*(1).

Eimer, B. N. (1993b). EMDR for treating chronic pain. *EMDR Network Newsletter, 3*(3).

Eimer, B. N., & Allen, L. (1995). *Psychological assessment and treatment of chronic pain and related disability. User's guide to the Pain Assessment Battery* (Research ed.). Durham, NC: CogniSyst, Inc.

Eimer, B. N., & Allen, L. (1996). *The Philadelphia Pain Questionnaire User's Manual*. Durham, NC: CogniSyst, Inc.

Eimer, B. N., & Oster, M. I. (1996). *Manual for the Hypnotic Ability and Response Profile (HARP)*. Unpublished manuscript.

Elliot, M. L. (1996). Chronic pelvic pain: What are the psychological considerations? *American Pain Society Bulletin, 6*(1), 1–4.

Ellis, A. (1993). Rational-emotive therapy and hypnosis. In J. W. Rhue, S. J. Lynn, & I. Kirsch (Eds.), *Handbook of clinical hypnosis* (pp. 173–186). Washington, DC: American Psychological Association.

Ellis, A. (1996). *Better, deeper, and more enduring brief therapy: The rational emotive behavior therapy approach*. New York: Brunner/Mazel.

Ellis, A., & Dryden, W. (1987). *The practice of RET*. New York: Springer Publishing Company.

Ellis, A., McInerney, J. F., DiGiuseppe, R., & Yeager, R. J. (1988). *Rational-emotive therapy with alcoholics and substance abusers.* Elmsford, NY: Pergamon Press.

Engel, G. (1959). Psychogenic pain and the pain-prone patient. *American Journal of Medicine. 26,* 899–918.

Erickson, M. (1952). Deep hypnosis and its induction. In L. M. LeCron (Ed.), *Experimental hypnosis* (pp. 70–114). New York: Macmillan.

Erickson, M. (1980). Explorations in hypnosis research. In E. L. Rossi (Ed.), *Hypnotic alteration of sensory, perceptual, and psychophysiological processes: The collected papers of Milton H. Erickson on hypnosis* (Vol. 2, pp. 313–337). New York: Irvington.

Erickson, M. (1986). Symptom-based approaches in mind-body problems. In E. L. Rossi & M. O. Ryan (Eds.), *Mind-body communication in hypnosis* (Vol. 3, pp. 67–202). New York: Irvington.

Ewin, D. M. (1978). Relieving suffering and pain with hypnosis. *Geriatrics, 33*(6), 87–89.

Ewin, D. M. (1986). Hypnosis and pain management. In B. Zilbergeld, M. G. Edelstien, & D. L. Araoz (Eds.), *Hypnosis: Questions and answers* (pp. 282–288). New York: W. W. Norton.

Ewin, D. M. (1992). Constant pain syndrome: Its psychological meaning and cure using hypnoanalysis. *Hypnos, 19*(1), 57–62.

Fairbank, J. C. T., Couper, J., Davies, J. B., & O'Brien, J. P. (1980). The Oswestry Low Back Pain Disability Questionnaire. *Physiotherapy, 66,* 271–273.

Fawzy, F. L., Fawzy, N. W., Arndt, L. A., & Pasnau, R. O. (1995). Critical review of psychosocial interventions in cancer care. *Archives of General Psychiatry, 52,* 100–113.

Fernandez, E., & Towery, S. (1996). A parsimonious set of verbal descriptors of pain sensation derived from the McGill Pain Questionnaire. *Pain, 66,* 31–37.

Fernandez, E., & Turk, D. C. (1989). The utility of cognitive coping strategies for altering pain perception: A meta-analysis. *Pain, 38,* 123–135.

Fernandez, E., & Turk, D. C. (1992). Sensory and affective components of pain: Separation and synthesis. *Psychological Bulletin, 112,* 205–217.

Fernandez, E., & Turk, D. C. (1995). The scope and significance of anger in the experience of chronic pain. *Pain, 61*(2), 165–175.

Festinger, L. (1957). *A theory of cognitive dissonance.* Stanford, CA: Stanford University Press.

Feuerstein, M., & Thebarge, R. W. (1991). Perceptions of disability and occupational stress as discriminators of work disability in patients with chronic pain. *Journal of Occupational Rehabilitation, 1,* 185–195.

Feuerstein, M., & Zastowny, T. R. (1996). Occupational rehabilitation: Multidisciplinary management of work-related musculoskeletal pain and disability. In R. J. Gatchel & D. C. Turk (Eds.), *Psychological approaches to pain management* (pp. 458–485). New York: Guilford Press.

Field, P. B. (1965). An inventory scale of hypnotic depth. *International Journal of Clinical and Experimental Hypnosis, 13,* 238–249.

Figley, C. R., & Carbonell, J. L. (1995, May). *Memory based treatments of traumatic stress: A systematic clinical demonstration program of research.* Paper presented at the fourth European Conference on Traumatic Stress, Paris, France.

Fishbain, D. A. (1996). Some difficulties with the predictive validity of the Minnesota Multiphasic Personality Inventory. *Pain Forum, 5*(1), 81–82.

Fitzhenry, R. I. (1993). *The Harper book of quotations* (3rd ed., p. 283). New York: HarperCollins.

Flor, H., Fydrich, T., & Turk, D. C. (1992). Efficacy of multidisciplinary pain treatment centers: A meta-analytic view. *Pain, 49,* 221–230.

Flor, H., & Turk, D. C. (1988). Chronic back pain and rheumatoid arthritis: Predicting pain and disability from cognitive variables. *Journal of Behavioural Medicine, 11,* 251–265.

Follick, M. J., Smith, T. W., & Ahern, D. K. (1985). The Sickness Impact Profile: A global measure of disability in chronic low back pain. *Pain, 21,* 67–76.

Folstein, M. F., Folstein, S. E., & McHugh, P. R. (1975). "Mini-mental state": A practical method for grading cognitive states of patients for the clinician. *Journal of Psychiatric Research, 12,* 189–198.

Fordyce, W. E. (1976). *Behavioral methods for chronic pain and illness.* St. Louis: Mosby.

Fordyce, W. E. (1988). Pain and suffering: A reappraisal. *American Psychologist, 43,* 276–283.

Fordyce, W. E. (1995). *Back pain in the workplace: Management of disability in nonspecific conditions. Task Force on Pain in the Workplace.* Seattle, WA: IASP Press.

Fordyce, W. E., Bigos, S. J., Battie, M. C., & Fischer, L. D. (1992). MMPI Scale 3 as a predictor of back injury report: What does it tell us? *Clinical Journal of Pain, 8,* 222–226.

Fordyce, W. E., Roberts, A. H., & Sternbach, R. A. (1985). The behavioral management of chronic pain: Response to critics. *Pain, 22,* 113–125.

Fordyce, W. E., Shelton, J. L., & Dunmore, D. E. (1982). The modification of avoidance learning pain behaviors. *Journal of Behavioral Medicine, 5,* 405–414.

Fox, R. M. (1985). Nicotine fading. In A. S. Bellack & M. Hersen (Eds.), *Dictionary of behavior therapy techniques* (p. 156). Elmsford, NY: Pergamon Press.

Frederickson, B. E., Trief, P. M., VanBeveren, P., Yuan, H. A., & Baum, G. (1988). Rehabilitation of the patient with chronic back pain: A search for outcome predictors. *Spine, 13,* 351–353.

Freeman, A., Pretzer, J., Fleming, B., & Simon, K. M. (1990). *Clinical applications of cognitive therapy.* New York: Plenum Press.

Freeman, A., & Reinecke, M. (1993). *Cognitive therapy of suicidal behavior.* New York: Springer Publishing Company.

Freeman, A., & Reinecke, M. (1995). Cognitive therapy. In A. S. Gurman & S. B. Messer (Eds.), *Essential psychotherapies: Theory and practice* (pp. 182–225). New York: Guilford Press.

Fritz, G., & Fehmi, L. (1982). *The open focus handbook. The self-regulation of attention in biofeedback training and everyday activities.* Princeton, NJ: Biofeedback Computers.

Gallagher, R. M., Rauh, V., Haugh, L. D., Milhous, R., Callas, P. W., Langelier, R., McClallen, J. M., & Frymoyer, J. (1989). Determinants of return-to-work among low back pain patients. *Pain, 39,* 55–67.

Gallagher, R. M., Williams, R. A., Skelly, J., Haugh, L. D., Rauh, V., Milhous, R., & Frymoyer, J. (1995). Workers' Compensation and return-to-work in low back pain. *Pain, 61*(2), 299–307.

Gamsa, A. (1990). Is emotional disturbance a precipitator or a consequence of chronic pain? *Pain, 42,* 183–195.

Gamsa, A. (1994). The role of psychological factors in chronic pain: A half century of study. *Pain, 57,* 5–15.

Gamsa, A., & Vikis-Freibergs, V. (1991). Psychological events are both risk factors in, and consequences of chronic pain. *Pain, 44,* 271–277.

Gatchel, R. J. (1994). Occupational low back pain disability: Why function needs to "drive" the rehabilitation process. *American Pain Society Journal, 3,* 107–110.

Gatchel, R. J. (1996). Psychological disorders and chronic pain: Cause-and-effect relationships. In R. J. Gatchel & D. C. Turk (Eds.), *Psychological approaches to pain management: A practitioner's handbook* (pp. 33–54). New York: Guilford Press.

Gatchel, R. J., & Blanchard, E. B. (Eds.). (1993). *Psychophysiological disorders: Research and clinical applications.* Washington, DC: American Psychological Association.

Gatchel, R. J., Polatin, P. B., & Kinney, R. K. (1995). Predicting outcome of chronic back pain using clinical predictors of psychopathology: A prospective analysis. *Health Psychology, 14,* 415–420.

Gatchel, R. J., Polatin, P. B., & Mayer, T. G. (1996). The dominant role of psychosocial risk factors in the development of chronic low back pain disability. *Spine.*

Gatchel, R. J., & Turk, D. C. (Eds.). (1996). *Psychological approaches to pain management: A practitioner's handbook.* New York: Guilford Press.

Geisser, M. E., Robinson, M. E., Keefe, F. J., & Weiner, M. L. (1994). Catastrophizing, depression and the sensory, affective and evaluative aspects of chronic pain. *Pain, 59,* 79–83.

Geisser, M. E., Roth, R. S., Bachman, J. E., & Eckert, T. A. (1996). The relationship between symptoms of post-traumatic stress disorder and pain, affective disturbance and disability among patients with accident and non-accident related pain. *Pain, 66,* 207–214.

Gil, K. M., Williams, D. A., Keefe, F. J., & Beckham, J. C. (1990). The relationship of negative thoughts to pain and psychological distress. *Behavior Therapy, 21,* 349–352.

Goldstein, A., & Feske, U. (1994). Eye movement desensitization and reprocessing for panic disorder: A case series. *Journal of Anxiety Disorders, 8,* 351–362.

Grant, I., & Adams, K. M. (Eds.). (1996). *Neuropsychological assessment of neuropsychiatric disorders* (2nd ed.). New York: Oxford University Press.

Green, W. P., Allen, L. M., & Astner, K. (1996). *The Word Memory Test User's Guide* (U.S. Version 1.1). Durham, NC: CogniSyst, Inc.

Greenberg, M. A., & Stone, A. A. (1992). Emotional disclosure about traumas and its relation to health: Effects of previous disclosure and trauma severity. *Journal of Personality and Social Psychology, 63,* 75–84.

Greene, R. L. (1991). *The MMPI-2/MMPI: An interpretive Manual.* Boston: Allyn & Bacon.

Grzesiak, R. C., Ury, G. M., & Dworkin, R. H. (1996). Psychodynamic psychotherapy with chronic pain patients. In R. J. Gatchel & D. C. Turk (Eds.),

Psychological approaches to pain management (pp. 148–178). New York: Guilford Press.

Guck, T. P., Meilman, P. W., Skultety, M., & Poloni, L. D. (1988). Pain-patient Minnesota Multiphasic Inventory (MMPI) subgroups: Evaluation of long-term treatment outcome. *Journal of Behavioral Medicine, 11,* 159–169.

Haber, J. D., & Roos, C. (1985). Effects of spouse abuse and/or sexual abuse in the development and maintenance of chronic pain in women. In H. L. Fields, R. Dubner, & F. Cervero (Eds.), *Advances in pain research and therapy; Vol. 9, Proceedings of the Fourth World Congress on Pain* (pp. 889–895). New York: Raven Press.

Hagglund, K. J., Haley, W. E., Reveille, J. D., & Alarcon, G. S. (1989). Predicting individual impairment among patients with rheumatoid arthritis. *Arthritis and Rheumatism, 32,* 851–858.

Hall, H. V., & Pritchard, D. A. (1996). *Detecting malingering and deception: Forensic Distortion Analysis (FDA).* Delray Beach, FL: St. Lucie Press.

Hammond, D. C. (Ed.). (1988). *Hypnotic induction and suggestion: An introductory manual.* Des Plaines, IL: The American Society of Clinical Hypnosis.

Hand, D. J., & Reading, A. E. (1986). Discriminant function analysis of the McGill Pain Questionnaire. *Psychological Reports, 59,* 762–770.

Hanson, R. W., & Gerber, K. E. (1990). *Coping with chronic pain: A guide to patient self-management.* New York: Guilford Press.

Harkins, S. W., & Price, D. D. (1992). Assessment of pain in the elderly. In D. C. Turk & R. Melzack (Eds.), *Handbook of pain assessment* (pp. 315–331). New York: Guilford Press.

Harness, D. M., & Donlon, W. C. (1988). Cryptotrauma: The hidden wound. *Clinical Journal of Pain, 4,* 257–260.

Hase, H. D. (1992). McGill Pain Questionnaire: Revised format. In L. Vandecreek, S. Knapp, & T. L. Jackson (Eds.), *Innovations in clinical practice: A source book* (Vol. 11, pp. 285–292). Sarasota, FL: Professional Resource Press.

Haythornthwaite, J. A., Hegel, M. T., & Kerns, R. D. (1991). Development of a sleep diary for chronic pain patients. *Journal of Pain and Symptom Management, 6,* 65–72.

Haythornthwaite, J. A., Seiber, W. J., & Kerns, R. D. (1988). Depression and the chronic pain experience. *Pain, 46,* 177–184.

Hazard, R. G., Haugh, L., Green, P., & Jones, P. (1994). Chronic low back pain: The relationship between patient satisfaction and pain, impairment and disability outcomes. *Spine, 19,* 881–887.

Hekmat, H., Groth, S., & Rogers, D. (1994). Pain ameliorating effects of eye movement desensitization. *Journal of Behavior Therapy and Experimental Psychiatry, 25*(2), 121–129.

Heller, R. F. (1996). Assessment of client beliefs and expectations of hypnosis and treatment. *Psychological Hypnosis, 5*(1), 8–12.

Helmes, E. (1994). What type of useful information do the MMPI and MMPI-2 provide on patients with chronic pain? *American Pain Society Bulletin, 4,* 1–5.

Hendler, N. H. (1981). *Diagnosis and nonsurgical management of chronic pain.* New York: Raven Press.

Hendler, N. H. (1984). Depression caused by chronic pain. *Journal of Clinical Psychiatry, 45,* 30–36.

Hendler, N. H., & Kozikowski, J. G. (1993). Overlooked psychiatric diagnoses in chronic pain patients involved in litigation. *Psychosomatics, 20*(6), 494–501.

Henricks, T. F. (1987). MMPI profiles of chronic pain patients: Some methodological considerations that concern clusters and descriptors. *Journal of Clinical Psychology, 43,* 650–660.

Herbert, J. D., & Mueser, K. T. (1992). Eye movement desensitization: A critique of the evidence. *Journal of Behavior Therapy and Experimental Psychiatry, 23,* 169–172.

Hickling, E. J., Blanchard, E. B., Silverman, D. J., & Schwartz, S. P. (1992). Motor vehicle accidents, headaches, and post-traumatic stress disorder: Assessment findings in a consecutive series. *Headache, 32,* 147–151.

Hilgard, E. R., & Bower, G. H. (1966). *Theories of learning* (3rd ed.). New York: Meredith.

Hilgard, E. R., & Hilgard, J. R. (1994). *Hypnosis in the relief of pain* (Rev. ed.). New York: Brunner/Mazel.

Hill, A., Niven, C. A., & Knussen, C. (1995). The role of coping in adjustment to phantom limb pain. *Pain, 62,* 79–86.

Hill, S. C. (1987). Painful prescriptions. *Journal of the American Medical Association, 257,* 2081.

Holmes, J. A., & Stevenson, C. A. Z. (1990). Differential effects of avoidant and attentional coping strategies on adaptation to chronic and recent-onset pain. *Health Psychology, 9,* 577–584.

Holroyd, K. A., Penzien, D. B., Hursey, K. G., Tobin, D. L., Rogers, L., & Holm, J. E. (1984). Change mechanisms in EMG biofeedback training: Cognitive changes underlying improvement in tension headache. *Journal of Consulting and Clinical Psychology, 52,* 1039–1053.

Horevitz, R. (1993). Hypnosis in the treatment of Multiple Personality Disorder. In J. W. Rhue, S. J. Lynn, & I. Kirsch (Eds.), *Handbook of clinical hypnosis* (pp. 395–424). Washington, DC: American Psychological Association.

Irving, G. A., & Wallace, M. S. (1997). *Pain management for the practicing physician.* New York: Churchill Livingstone.

Jamison, R. N. (1996). *Mastering chronic pain: A professional's guide to behavioral treatment.* Sarasota, FL: Professional Resource Press.

Jamison, R. N., Rock, D. L., & Parris, W. C. V. (1988). Empirically derived Symptom Checklist 90 subgroups of chronic pain patients: A cluster analysis. *Journal of Behavioral Medicine, 11,* 147–158.

Jensen, J. A. (1994). An investigation of eye movement desensitization and reprocessing as a treatment for PTSD symptoms of Vietnam combat veterans. *Behavior Therapy, 25,* 311–326.

Jensen, M. P. (1996). Enhancing motivation to change in pain treatment. In R. J. Gatchel & D. C. Turk (Eds.), *Psychological approaches to pain management* (pp. 78–111). New York: Guilford Press.

Jensen, M. P., & Karoly, P. (1991). Control beliefs, coping efforts and adjustment to chronic pain. *Journal of Consulting and Clinical Psychology, 59,* 431–438.

Jensen, M. P., & Karoly, P. (1992). Self-report scales and procedures for assessing pain in adults. In D. C. Turk & R. Melzack (Eds.), *Handbook of pain assessment* (pp. 135–151). New York: Guilford Press.

Jensen, M. P., Turner, J. A., & Romano, J. M. (1991). Self-efficacy and outcome expectancies: Relationship to chronic pain coping strategies and adjustment. *Pain, 44,* 263–269.

Jensen, M. P., Turner, J. A., & Romano, J. M. (1994). Correlates of improvement in multidisciplinary treatment of chronic pain. *Journal of Consulting and Clinical Psychology, 62,* 172–179.

Jensen, M. P., Turner, J. A., Romano, J. M., & Karoly, P. (1991). Coping with chronic pain: A critical review of the literature. *Pain, 47,* 249–283.

Jensen, M. P., Turner, J. A., Romano, J. M., & Lawler, B. K. (1994). Relationship of pain-specific beliefs to chronic pain adjustment. *Pain, 57,* 301–309.

Jensen, M. P., Turner, J. A., Romano, J. M., & Strom, S. E. (1995). The Chronic Pain Coping Inventory: Development and preliminary validation. *Pain, 60*(2), 203–216.

Karoly, P., & Jensen, M. P. (1987). *Multimethod assessment of chronic pain.* New York: Pergamon Press.

Kee, W. G., Middaugh, S. J., & Pawlick, K. L. (1996). Persistent pain in the older patient: Evaluation and treatment. In R. J. Gatchel & D. C. Turk (Eds.), *Psychological approaches to pain management* (pp. 371–402). New York: Guilford Press.

Keefe, F. J. (1994). Behavior therapy. In P. D. Wall & R. Melzack (Eds.), *Textbook of pain* (pp. 392–406). New York: Churchill Livingstone.

Keefe, F. J., Brown, G. K., Wallston, K. A.,& Caldwell, D. S. (1989). Coping with rheumatoid arthritis pain: Catastrophizing as a maladaptive strategy. *Pain, 37,* 51–56.

Keefe, F. J., Caldwell, D. S., Queen, K. T., Gil, K. M., Martinez, S., Crisson, J. E., Ogden, W., & Nunley, J. (1987). Pain coping strategies in osteoarthritis patients. *Journal of Consulting and Clinical Psychology, 55,* 208–212.

Keefe, F. J., Caldwell, D. S., Williams, D. A., Gil, K. M., Mitchell, D., Robertson, C., Martinez, S., Nunley, J., Beckham, J. C., Crisson, J. E., & Helms, M. (1990). Pain coping skills training in the management of osteoarthritis knee pain: A comparative study. *Behavior Therapy, 21,* 49–62.

Keefe, F. J., Crisson, J. E., Urban, B. J., & Williams, D. A. (1990). Analyzing chronic low back pain: The relative contribution of pain coping strategies. *Pain, 40,* 293–301.

Keefe, F. J., & Dunsmore, J. (1992). Pain behavior: Concepts and controversies. *American Pain Society Journal, 1,* 92–100.

Keefe, F. J., Dunsmore, J., & Burnett, R. (1992). Behavioral and cognitive-behavioral approaches to chronic pain: Recent advances and future directions. *Journal of Consulting and Clinical Psychology, 60,* 528–536.

Keefe, F. J., Lefebvre, J. C., & Beaupre, P. M. (1995). The Minnesota Multiphasic Personality Inventory in chronic pain: Security blanket or sound investment? *Pain Forum, 4*(2), 101–103.

Keefe, F. J., & Van Horn, Y. (1993). Cognitive-behavioral treatment of rheumatoid arthritis pain: Maintaining treatment gains. *Arthritis Care and Research, 6,* 213–222.

Keefe, F. J., & Williams, D. A. (1992). Assessment of pain behaviors. In D. C. Turk & R. Melzack (Eds.), *Handbook of pain assessment* (pp. 275–294). New York: Guilford Press.

Keller, L. S., & Butcher, J. N. (1991). *Assessment of chronic pain patients with the MMPI-2* (MMPI-2 Monographs, Vol. 2). Minneapolis, MN: University of Minneapolis.

Kelly, G. A. (1955). *The psychology of personal constructs* (Vols. 1 and 2). New York: Norton.

Kelly, J. E., Lumley, M. A., & Leisen, J. C. C. (1997). Health effects of emotional disclosure in rheumatoid arthritis patients. *Health Psychology, 16*(4), 331–340.

Kerns, R. D., & Haythornthwaite, J. (1988). Depression among chronic pain patients: Cognitive-behavioral analysis and rehabilitation outcome. *Journal of Consulting and Clinical Psychology, 56,* 870–876.

Kerns, R. D., & Jacob, M. C. (1992). Assessment of the psychosocial context in the experience of pain. In D. C. Turk & R. Melzack (Eds.), *Handbook of pain assessment* (pp. 235–256). New York: Guilford Press.

Kerns, R. D., & Payne, A. (1996). Treating families of chronic pain patients. In R. J. Gatchel & D. C. Turk (Eds.), *Psychological approaches to pain management* (pp. 283–304). New York: Guilford Press.

Kerns, R. D., Rosenberg, R., & Jacob, M. C. (1994). Anger expression and chronic pain. *Journal of Behavioral Medicine, 17,* 57–68.

Kerns, R. D., Turk, D. C., & Rudy, T. E. (1985). The West Haven-Yale Multidimensional Pain Inventory (WHYMPI). *Pain, 23,* 345–356.

Kerr, P. (1993, February 22). The high cost of job injury claims. *New York Times,* C-1.

Kiecolt-Glaser, J., & Williams, D. A. (1987). Self-blame, compliance and distress among burn patients. *Journal of Personality and Social Psychology, 53,* 187–193.

Kiernan, R. J., Mueller, J., Langston, J. W., & VanDyke, C. (1987). The Neurobehavioral Cognitive Status Examination. *Annals of Internal Medicine, 107,* 481–485.

Kinder, B. N., & Curtiss, C. (1988). Assessment of anxiety, depression, and anger in chronic pain patients: Conceptual and methodological issues. In C. D. Spielberger & J. N. Butcher (Eds.), *Advances in personality assessment* (pp. 651–661). Hillsdale, NJ: Erlbaum.

Kleinke, C. L. (1994). MMPI scales as predictors of pain-coping strategies preferred by patients with chronic pain. *Rehabilitation Psychology, 39,* 123–128.

Kleinknecht, R. A. (1992). Treatment of PTSD with EMDR. *Journal of Behavior Therapy and Experimental Psychiatry, 23,* 43–50.

Kleinknecht, R. A. (1993). Rapid treatment of blood and injection phobias with eye movement desensitization. *Journal of Behavior Therapy and Experimental Psychiatry, 24,* 211–217.

Kluft, R. P. (1982). Varieties of hypnotic interventions in the treatment of multiple personality. *American Journal of Clinical Hypnosis, 24,* 230–240.

Koss, M. P., Butcher, J. N., & Hoffmann, N. G. (1976). The MMPI critical items: How well do they work? *Journal of Consulting and Clinical Psychology, 44,* 921–928.

Krishnan, K. R. R., France, R. D., & Davidson, J. (1988). Depression as a psychopathological disorder in chronic pain. In R. D. France & K. R. R. Krishnan

(Eds.), *Chronic pain* (pp. 195–218). Washington, DC: American Psychiatric Press.

Lancourt, J., & Kettelhut, M. (1992). Predicting return to work for lower back pain patients receiving worker's compensation. *Spine, 17*(6), 629–640.

Layden, M. A., Newman, C. F., Freeman, A., & Byers-Morse, S. (1993). *Cognitive therapy of borderline personality disorder.* Boston: Allyn & Bacon.

Lazarus, A. A. (1989). *The practice of multimodal therapy: Systematic, comprehensive and effective psychotherapy.* New York: McGraw-Hill.

Lazarus, R. S., & Folkman, S. (1984). *Stress appraisal and coping.* New York: Springer-Verlag.

Lebovits, A. H., Yarmush, J., & Lefkowitz, M. (1990). Reflex sympathetic dystrophy and posttraumatic stress disorder. *Clinical Journal of Pain, 6,* 153–157.

LeCron, L. M. (1964). *Self-hypnotism: The technique and its use in daily living.* New York: New American Library.

Lefebvre, M. F. (1981). Cognitive distortion and cognitive errors in depressed psychiatric and low back pain patients. *Journal of Consulting and Clinical Psychology, 49,* 517–525.

Lehrer, P. M., & Woolfolk, R. L. (1982). Self-report assessment of anxiety: Somatic, cognitive, and behavioral modalities. *Behavioral Assessment, 4,* 167–177.

Lehrer, P. M., & Woolfolk, R. L. (1993). Research on clinical issues in stress management. In. P. M. Lehrer & R. L. Woolfolk (Eds.), *Principles and practice of stress management* (2nd ed., pp. 521–539). New York: Guilford Press.

Levin, C., Grainger, R. K., Allen-Byrd, L., & Fulcher, G. (1994). *Efficacy of eye movement desensitization and reprocessing (EMDR) for survivors of Hurricane Andrew: A comparative study.* Paper presented at the American Psychological Association annual convention, Los Angeles.

Lezak, M. D. (1995). *Neuropsychological assessment* (3rd ed.). New York: Oxford University Press.

Linton, S. J., & Bradley, L. A. (1996). Strategies for the prevention of chronic pain. In R. J. Gatchel & D. C. Turk (Eds.), *Psychological approaches to pain management* (pp. 438–457). New York: Guilford Press.

Lipke, H., & Botkin, A. (1992). Brief case studies of eye movement desensitization and reprocessing with chronic post-traumatic stress disorder. *Psychotherapy, 29,* 591–595.

Loftus, E. (1993). The reality of repressed memories. *American Psychologist, 48*(5), 518–537.

Lohr, J. M., Kleinknecht, R. A., Conley, A. T., Cerro, S. D., Schmidt, J., & Sonntag, M. E. (1992). A methodological critique of the current status of eye movement desensitization (EMD). *Journal of Behavior Therapy and Experimental Psychiatry, 23,* 159–167.

Long, C. J. (1981). The relationship between surgical outcome and MMPI profiles in chronic pain patients. *Journal of Clinical Psychology, 37,* 744–749.

Love, A. W., & Peck, C. L. (1987). The MMPI and psychological factors in chronic low back pain: A review. *Pain, 28,* 1–12.

Main, C. J. (1983). The Modified Somatic Perception Questionnaire. *Journal of Psychosomatic Research, 27,* 503–514.

Main, C. J., & Spanswick, C. C. (1995). Personality assessment and the Minnesota Multiphasic Personality Inventory: 50 years on: Do we still need our security blanket? *Pain Forum, 4*(2), 90–96.

Main, C. J., & Waddell, G. (1982). Chronic pain, distress and illness behavior. In C. J. Main (Ed.), *Clinical psychology and medicine* (pp. 1–52). New York: Plenum Press.

Malouff, J. M., & Schutte, N. S. (1986). Development and validation of a measure of irrational beliefs. *Journal of Consulting and Clinical Psychology, 54*, 860–862.

Marcus, N. J., & Arbeiter, J. S. (1994). *Freedom from chronic pain.* New York: Simon & Schuster.

Marlatt, G. A., & Gordon, J. R. (1985). *Relapse prevention: Maintenance strategies in the treatment of addictive behaviors.* New York: Guilford Press.

Marquis, J. (1991). A report on seventy-eight cases treated by eye movement desensitization. *Journal of Behavior Therapy and Experimental Psychiatry, 22*, 186–192.

Maruta, T., Swanson, D. W., & Swenson, W. M. (1979). Chronic pain: Which patients may a pain management program help. *Pain, 7*, 321–329.

Maslow, A. H. (1967). A theory of metamotivation: The biological rooting of the value life. *Journal of Humanistic Psychology, 7*, 93–127.

Masson, E. A., Hunt, L., Gem, J. M., & Boulton, A. J. M. (1989). A novel approach to the diagnosis and assessment of symptomatic diabetic neuropathy. *Pain, 38*, 25–28.

Matson, J. (1985). Modeling. In A. S. Bellack & M. Hersen (Eds.), *Dictionary of behavior therapy techniques* (pp. 150–151). Elmsford, NY: Pergamon Press.

Mattis, S. (1976). Mental status examination for organic mental syndrome in the elderly patient. In I. Bellak & T. B. Karasu (Eds.), *Geriatric psychiatry.* New York: Grune and Stratton.

Mattis, S. (1988). *Dementia Rating Scale (DRS).* Odessa, FL: Psychological Assessment Resources.

Maxmen, J. S., & Ward, N. G. (1995). *Essential psychopathology and its treatment* (2nd ed. revised for DSM-IV). New York: W. W. Norton.

McCain, G. A. (1995). Fibromyalgia and myofascial pain syndromes. In P. D. Wall & R. Melzack (Eds.), *Textbook of pain* (pp. 475–493). New York: Churchill Livingstone.

McCann, D. L. (1992). Post-traumatic stress disorder due to devastating burns overcome by a single session of eye movement desensitization. *Journal of Behavior Therapy and Experimental Psychiatry, 23*, 319–323.

McCracken, L. M. (1997). "Attention" to pain in persons with chronic pain: A behavioral approach. *Behavior Therapy, 28*, 271–284.

McCracken, L. M., & Gross, R. T. (1995). The Pain Anxiety Symptoms Scale (PASS) and the assessment of emotional responses to pain. In L. Vandecreek, S. Knapp, & T. L. Jackson (Eds.), *Innovations in clinical practice* (Vol. 14). Sarasota, FL: Professional Resource Press.

McCraty, R., Atkinson, M., Tiller, W. A., Rein, G., & Watkins, A. (1995). The effects of emotions on short-term heart rate variability using power spectrum analysis. *American Journal of Cardiology, 76*(14), 1089–1093.

McCreary, C. P. (1993). Psychological evaluation of chronic pain with the MMPI. *Pain Digest, 3,* 246–251.

McGlynn, F. D. (1985a). Cue-controlled relaxation. In A. S. Bellack & M. Hersen (Eds.), *Dictionary of behavior therapy techniques* (pp. 100–101). Elmsford, NY: Pergamon Press.

McGlynn, F. D. (1985b). Premack principle. In A. S. Bellack & M. Hersen (Eds.), *Dictionary of behavior therapy techniques* (p. 166). Elmsford, NY: Pergamon Press.

McMullin, R. R. (1986). *Handbook of cognitive therapy techniques.* New York: W. W. Norton.

Meichenbaum, D. (1977). *Cognitive-behavior modification: An integrative approach.* New York: Plenum Press.

Meichenbaum, D. (1985). *Stress inoculation training.* New York: Pergamon Press.

Meichenbaum, D. (1994). *A clinical handbook/practical therapist manual for assessing and treating adults with post-traumatic stress disorder (PTSD).* Waterloo, Ontario, Canada: Institute Press.

Meichenbaum, D., & Turk, D. C. (1987). *Facilitating treatment adherence: A practitioner's guidebook.* New York: Plenum Press.

Melding, P. (1991). Is there such a thing as geriatric pain? *Pain, 46,* 119–121.

Melzack, R. (1975). The McGill Pain Questionnaire: Major properties and scoring methods. *Pain, 1,* 277–299.

Melzack, R. (1987). The short-form McGill Pain Questionnaire. *Pain, 30,* 191–197.

Melzack, R. (1996). Gate control theory: On the evolution of pain concepts. *Pain Forum, 5*(2), 128–138.

Melzack, R., & Katz, J. (1992). The McGill Pain Questionnaire: Appraisal and current status. In D. C. Turk & R. Melzack (Eds.), *Handbook of pain assessment.* New York: Guilford Press.

Melzack, R., Terrence, C., Fromm, G., & Amsel, R. (1986). Trigeminal neuralgia and atypical facial pain: Use of the McGill Pain Questionnaire for discrimination and diagnosis. *Pain, 27,* 297–302.

Melzack, R., & Torgerson, W. S. (1971). On the language of pain. *Anesthesiology, 34,* 50–59.

Melzack, R., & Wall, P. (1965). Pain mechanisms: A new theory. *Science, 50,* 971–979.

Melzack, R., & Wall, P. (1982). *The challenge of pain.* New York: Basic Books.

Merskey, H. (1992). The manufacture of personalities: The production of Multiple Personality Disorder. *British Journal of Psychiatry, 160,* 327–340.

Merskey, H., & Bogduk, N. (Eds.). (1994). *Classification of chronic pain: Descriptions of chronic pain syndromes and definitions of pain terms* (2nd ed., p. 210). Seattle, WA: IASP Press.

Millon, T. (1983). *Millon Clinical Multiaxial Inventory manual* (3rd ed.). Minneapolis, MN: NCS Assessments.

Millon, T. (1995). *Disorders of personality: DSM-IV and beyond.* New York: John Wiley & Sons, Inc.

Millon, T., Green, C. J., & Meagher, R. B. (1983). *Millon Behavioral Health Inventory manual* (3rd ed.). Minneapolis, MN: National Computer Systems.

Morey, L. C. (1991). *The Personality Assessment Inventory manual.* Odessa, FL: Psychological Assessment Resources, Inc.

Morey, L. C., Waugh, M. H., & Blashfield, R. K. (1985). MMPI scales for DSM-III personality disorders: Their derivation and correlates. *Journal of Personality Assessment, 49,* 245–251.

Muse, M. (1986). Stress-related, posttraumatic chronic pain syndrome: Behavioral treatment approach. *Pain, 25,* 389–394.

Naliboff, B. D., McCreary, C. P., McArthur, D. L., Cohen, M. J., & Gottlieb, H. J. (1988). MMPI changes following behavioral treatment of chronic low back pain. *Pain, 35,* 271–277.

Nielson, W., Walker, C., & McCain, G. A. (1992). Cognitive behavioral treatment of fibromyalgia syndrome: Preliminary findings. *Journal of Rheumatology, 19,* 98–103.

Norris, P. A., & Fahrion, S. L. (1993). Autogenic biofeedback in psychophysiologic therapy and stress management. In P. M. Lehrer & R. L. Woolfolk (Eds.), *Principles and practice of stress management* (2nd ed., pp. 231–262). New York: Guilford Press.

Novy, D. M., Nelson, D. V., Berry, L. A., & Averill, P. M. (1995). What does the Beck Depression Inventory measure in chronic pain?: A reappraisal. *Pain, 61*(2), 261–270.

O'Donohue, W. O., & Krasner, L. (1995). *Theories of behavior therapy: Exploring behavior change.* Washington, DC: American Psychological Association.

Ofshe, R., & Watters, E. (1994). *Making monsters: False memory, psychotherapy, and sexual hysteria.* New York: Charles Scribner & Sons.

Osterweis, M., Kleinman, A., & Mechanic, D. (Eds.). (1987). *Pain and disability: Clinical behavioral and public policy perspectives* (Report of the Institute of Medicine Committee on Pain, Disability and Chronic Illness Behavior). Washington, DC: National Academy Press.

Parker, J. C., Smarr, K. L., Buescher, K. L., Phillips, L. R., Frank, R. G., Beck, N. C., Anderson, S. K., & Walker, S. E. (1989). Pain control and rational thinking. *Arthritis and Rheumatism, 32,* 984–990.

Parmelee, P. A., Katz, I. R., & Lawton, M. P. (1991). The relation of pain to depression among institutionalized aged. *Journal of Gerontology, 46,* 15–21.

Pennebaker, J. W. (1989). Confession, inhibition, and disease. *Advances in Experimental Social Psychology, 22,* 211–244.

Pennebaker, J. W. (1993). Putting stress into words: Health, linguistic, and therapeutic implications. *Behavior Research and Therapy, 31,* 539–548.

Pennebaker, J. W. (1997). *Opening up: The healing power of expressing emotions.* New York: Guilford Press.

Persons, J. B. (1989). *Cognitive therapy in practice: A case formulation approach.* New York: W. W. Norton.

Philips, H. C., & Rachman, S. (1996). *The psychological management of chronic pain: A treatment manual.* New York: Springer Publishing Company.

Pilowsky, I. (1985). Cryptotrauma and 'accident neurosis.' *British Journal of Psychiatry, 147,* 310–311.

Pilowsky, I. (1994). Pain and illness behavior: Assessment and management. In P. D. Wall & R. Melzack (Eds.), *Textbook of pain* (pp. 1309–1320). New York: Churchill Livingstone.

Pilowsky, I., Chapman, C. R., & Bonica, J. J. (1977). Pain, depression and illness behavior in a pain clinic population. *Pain, 4,* 183–192.

Pilowsky, I., Spence, N., Cobb, J., & Katsikitis, M. (1984). The Illness Behavior Questionnaire as an aid to clinical assessment. *General Hospital Psychiatry, 6,* 123–130.

Pilowsky, I., Spence, N., Rounsefell, B., Forsten, C., & Soda, J. (1995). Out-patient cognitive-behavioral therapy with amitriptyline for chronic non-malignant pain. A comparative study with 6-month follow-up. *Pain, 60,* 19–51.

Pope, K. S., & Brown, L. S. (1996). *Recovered memories of abuse: Assessment, therapy, forensics.* Washington, DC: American Psychological Association.

Portenoy, R. K. (1996a). Basic mechanisms. In R. K. Portenoy & R. M. Kanner (Eds.), *Pain management: Theory and practice* (pp. 19–39). Philadelphia: F. A. Davis.

Portenoy, R. K. (1996b). Opioid analgesics. In R. K. Portenoy & R. M. Kanner (Eds.), *Pain management: Theory and practice* (pp. 248–276). Philadelphia: F. A. Davis.

Portenoy, R. K., & Foley, K. M. (1986). Chronic use of opioid analgesics in non-malignant pain: Report of 38 cases. *Pain, 25,* 171–186.

Portenoy, R. K., & Kanner, R. M. (1996a). Definition and assessment of pain. In R. K. Portenoy & R. M. Kanner (Eds.), *Pain management: Theory and practice* (pp. 3–18). Philadelphia: F. A. Davis.

Portenoy, R. K., & Kanner, R. M. (1996b). Nonopioid and adjuvant analgesics. In R. K. Portenoy & R. M. Kanner (Eds.), *Pain management: Theory and practice* (pp. 219–247). Philadelphia: F. A. Davis.

Portenoy, R. K., & Payne, R. (1992). Acute and chronic pain. In J. H. Lowinson, P. Ruiz, R. B. Millman, & R. G. Langrod (Eds.), *Substance abuse: A comprehensive textbook* (pp. 691–721). Baltimore: Williams & Wilkins.

Porter, J., & Jick, J. (1980). Addiction rare in patients treated with narcotics. *New England Journal of Medicine, 302,* 123.

Poulain, P., Langlade, A., & Goldberg, J. (1997). Cancer pain management in the home. *Pain Clinical Updates, 5*(1), 1–4.

Premack, D. (1959). Toward empirical behavior laws: I. Positive reinforcement. *Psychological Review, 66,* 219–233.

Prochaska, J. O., DiClemente, C. C., & Norcross, J. C. (1992). In search of how people change: Applications to addictive behaviors. *American Psychologist, 47,* 1102–1114.

Ransford, A. O., Cairns, D., & Mooney, V. (1976). The pain drawing as an aid to the psychological evaluation of patients with low back pain. *Spine, 1,* 127–134.

Reading, A. E., Hand, D. J., & Sledmere, C. M. (1983). A comparison of response profiles obtained on the McGill Pain Questionnaire and an adjective checklist. *Pain, 16,* 375–383.

Ready, L. B., & Edwards, W. T. (Eds.). (1992). *Management of acute pain: A practical guide.* Seattle: International Association for the Study of Pain.

Rein, G., McCraty, R., & Atkinson, M. (1995). The physiological and psychological effects of compassion and anger. *Journal of Advancement in Medicine, 8*(2), 87–105.

Renfrey, G., & Spates, C. R. (1994). Eye movement desensitization and reprocessing: A partial dismantling procedure. *Journal of Behavior Therapy and Experimental Psychiatry, 25,* 231–239.

Research overview: Exploring the role of the heart in human performance. (1997). Boulder Creek, CA: Heartmath Research Center.

Revenson, T. A., & Felton, B. J. (1989). Disability and coping as predictors of psychological adjustment to rheumatoid arthritis. *Journal of Consulting and Clinical Psychology, 57,* 344–348.

Rhue, J. W., Lynn, S. J., & Kirsch, I. (Eds.). (1993). *Handbook of clinical hypnosis.* Washington, DC: American Psychological Association.

Richter, J. E., Obrecht, W. F., Bradley, L. A., Young, L. D., Anderson, K. O., & Castell, D. O. (1986). Psychological profiles of patients with the nutcracker esophagus. *Digestive Disorders and Sciences, 31,* 131–138.

Riley, J. F., Ahern, D. K., & Follick, M. J., (1988). Chronic pain and functional impairment: Assessing beliefs about their relationship. *Archives of Physical Medicine and Rehabilitation, 69,* 579–582.

Roberts, A. H. (1986). The operant approach to the management of pain and excess disability. In A. D. Holzman & D. C. Turk (Eds.), *Pain management: A handbook of psychological treatment approaches* (pp. 10–30). New York: Pergamon Press.

Roland, M., & Morris, R. (1983). A study of the natural history of back pain. Part I: Development of a reliable and sensitive measure of disability in low back pain. *Spine, 8,* 141–144.

Romano, J. M., Turner, J. A., Jensen, M. P., Friedman, L. S., Bulcroft, R. A., Hyman, H., & Wright, S. F. (1995). Chronic pain patient-spouse behavioral interactions predict patient disability. *Pain, 63,* 353–360.

Rosenstiel, A. K., & Keefe, F. J. (1983). The use of coping strategies in low-back patients: Relationship to patient characteristics and current adjustment. *Pain, 17,* 33–40.

Rossi, E. L. (1993). *The psychobiology of mind-body healing: New concepts of therapeutic hypnosis.* New York: W. W. Norton.

Rossi, E. L., & Cheek, D. B. (1988). *Mind-body therapy: Methods of ideodynamic healing in hypnosis.* New York: W. W. Norton.

Roth-Roemer, S., Abrams, J. R., & Syrjala, K. L. (1996). Nonpharmacologic approaches to adult cancer pain management. *American Pain Society Bulletin, 6*(5), 1–4.

Rozman, D., Whitaker, R., Beckman, T., & Jones, D. (1995). Initial use of a new intervention program for significantly reducing psychological symptomatology in HIV-seropositive individuals. *Psychosomatics, 36*(2), 207.

Rudy, T. E. (1989). *Multiaxial assessment of pain: Multidimensional Pain Inventory* [Computer program users' manual, Version 2.1]. Pittsburgh: Pain Evaluation and Treatment Institute.

Rudy, T. E., Kerns, R. J., & Turk, D. C. (1988). Chronic pain and depression: Toward a cognitive-behavioral mediation model. *Pain, 35,* 179–183.

Rudy, T. E., Turk, D. C., Kubinski, J. A., & Zaki, H. S. (1995). Differential treatment responses of TMJ patients as a function of psychological characteristics. *Pain, 61*(1), 103–112.

Sanders, S. H. (1995a). Minnesota Multiphasic Personality Inventory and clinical pain: The baby or the bathwater? *Pain Forum, 4*(2), 108–109.

Sanders, S. H. (1995b). Risk factors for the occurrence of low back pain and chronic disability. *American Pain Society Bulletin, 5*(1), 1–5.

Sanders, S. H. (1996). Operant conditioning with chronic pain: Back to basics. In R. J. Gatchel & D. C. Turk (Eds.), *Psychological approaches to pain management* (pp. 112–130). New York: Guilford Press.

Sanderson, A., & Carpenter, R. (1992). Eye movement desensitization versus image confrontation: A single-session crossover study of 58 phobic subjects. *Journal of Behavior Therapy and Experimental Psychiatry, 23,* 269–275.

Scarinci, I. C., Haile, J. M., Bradley, L. A., & Richter, J. E. (1994). Altered pain perception and psychosocial features among women with gastrointestinal disorders and a history of abuse: A preliminary model. *American Journal of Medicine, 97,* 107–118.

Schacter, D. L. (1996). *Searching for memory: The brain, the mind, and the past.* New York: HarperCollins.

Schafer, D. W. (1996). *Relieving pain: A basic hypnotherapeutic approach.* Northvale, NJ: Jason Aronson.

Scheflin, A. W., & Shapiro, J. L. (1989). *Trance on trial.* New York: Guilford Press.

Schiafino, K. M., Revenson, T. A., & Gibofsky, A. (1991). Assessing the impact of self-efficacy beliefs on adaptation to rheumatoid arthritis. *Arthritis Care and Research, 4,* 150–157.

Schinka, J. A. (1986). *Mental Status Checklist for Adults.* Odessa, FL: Psychological Assessment Resources.

Schoenen, J., & de Noordhout, A. M. (1994). Headache. In P. D. Wall & R. Melzack (Eds.), *Textbook of pain* (pp. 495–521). New York: Churchill Livingstone.

Schreiber, S., & Galai-Gat, T. (1993). Uncontrolled pain following physical injury as the core trauma in post-traumatic stress disorder. *Pain, 54,* 107–110.

Schwartz, D. P., & DeGood, D. E. (1983). An approach to the psychosocial assessment of the chronic pain patient. *Current Concepts in Pain, 1,* 3–11.

Schwartz, L., Slater, M. A., & Birchler, G. R. (1990). The role of pain behaviors in the modulation of marital conflict in chronic pain couples. *Pain, 65,* 227–233.

Schwartz, M. S. (1995). Breathing therapies. In M. S. Schwartz & Associates (Eds.), *Biofeedback: A practitioner's guide* (2nd ed., pp. 248–287). New York: Guilford Press.

Schwartz, M. S., & Associates (Eds.). (1995). *Biofeedback: A practitioner's guide* (2nd ed.). New York: Guilford Press.

Seligman, M. E. P. (1975). *Helplessness: On depression, development, and death.* San Francisco: Freeman.

Shapiro, F. (1989a). Eye movement desensitization: A new treatment for post-traumatic stress disorder. *Journal of Behavior Therapy and Experimental Psychiatry, 20,* 2111–2117.

Shapiro, F. (1989b). Efficacy of eye movement desensitization procedure in the treatment of traumatic memories. *Journal of Traumatic Stress, 2,* 199–223.

Shapiro, F. (1995). *Eye movement desensitization and reprocessing: Basic principles, protocols, and procedures.* New York: Guilford Press.

Shealy, C. N. (1976). *The pain game.* Berkeley, CA: Celestial Arts Press.

Shutty, M. S., DeGood, D. E., & Schwartz, D. P. (1986). Psychological dimensions of distress in chronic pain patients: A factor analytic study of Symptom Checklist-90 responses. *Journal of Consulting and Clinical Psychology, 54*, 836–842.

Shutty, M. S., DeGood, D. E., & Tuttle, D. H. (1990). Chronic pain patients' beliefs about their pain and treatment outcomes. *Archives of Physical Medicine and Rehabilitation, 71*, 128–132.

Sifneos, P. (1973). The prevalence of "alexithymic" characteristics in psychosomatic patients. *Psychotherapy and Psychosomatics, 22*, 255–262.

Skevington, S. M. (1990). A standardised scale to measure beliefs about controlling pain (BPCQ): A preliminary study. *Psychology and Health, 4*, 221–232.

Skevington, S. M. (1996). *Psychology of pain.* Chichester, England: John Wiley & Sons Ltd.

Snow-Turek, A. L., Norris, M. P., & Tan, G. (1996). Active and passive coping strategies in chronic pain patients. *Pain, 64*, 455–462.

Social Security Administration. (1987). *Report of the Commission on the Evaluation of Pain.* Washington, DC: U.S. Department of Health and Human Services.

Speculand, B., Goss, A. N., Spence, N. D., & Pilowsky, I. (1981). Intractable facial pain and illness behavior. *Pain, 11*, 213–219.

Spence, D. P. (1982). *Narrative truth and historical truth: Meaning and interpretation in psychoanalysis.* New York: W. W. Norton.

Spiegel, H., & Spiegel, D. (1987). *Trance and treatment: Clinical uses of hypnosis.* Washington, DC: American Psychiatric Press. (Original work published 1978)

Spiegler, M. D. (1983). *Contemporary behavioral therapy.* Palo Alto, CA: Mayfield.

Spinhoven, P., & Linssen, A. C. G. (1991). Behavioral treatment of chronic low back pain: Relation of coping strategy use to outcome. *Pain, 45*, 29–34.

Spreen, O., & Strauss, E. (Eds.). (1991). *A compendium of neuropsychological tests: Administration, norms and commentary.* New York: Oxford University Press.

Sriwatanakul, K., Kelvie, W., Lasagna, L., Calimlin, J. F., Weis, O. F., & Mehta, G. (1983). Studies with different types of visual analog scales for measurement of pain. *Clinical Pharmacology and Therapeutics, 34*, 234–239.

Sternbach, R. A. (1974). *Pain patients: Traits and treatment.* New York: Academic Press.

Strack, S. (1991). *Manual for the Personality Adjective Checklist (PACL).* Pasadena, CA: 21st Century Assessment.

Strub, R. L., & Black, F. W. (1985/1993). *Mental status examination in neurology* (3rd ed.). Philadelphia: F. A. Davis.

Sullivan, M. J., & D'Eon, J. L. (1990). Relation between catastrophizing and depression in chronic pain patients. *Journal of Abnormal Psychology, 99*, 260–263.

Sweet, J. J., Brewer, S. R., Hazlewood, L. A., Toye, R., & Paul, R. P. (1985). The Millon Behavioral Health Inventory: Concurrent and predictive validity in a pain treatment center. *Journal of Behavioral Medicine, 8*, 215–226.

Syrjala, K. L., & Abrams, J. R. (1996). Hypnosis and imagery in the treatment of pain. In R. J. Gatchel & D. C. Turk (Eds.), *Psychological approaches to pain management* (pp. 231–258). New York: Guilford Press.

Tellegen, A., & Atkinson, G. (1974). Openness to absorbing and self-altering experiences ("absorption"), a trait related to hypnotic susceptibility. *Journal of Abnormal Psychology, 83,* 268–277.

The compact edition of the Oxford English dictionary. (1971). Oxford, England: Oxford University Press.

Thorn, B. E., & Williams, D. A. (1993). Cognitive-behavioral management of chronic pain. In L. Vandecreek, S. Knapp, & T. L. Jackson (Eds.), *Innovations in clinical practice* (Vol. 12). Sarasota, FL: Professional Resource Press.

Tollison, C. D., & Langley, J. C. (1995). *P-3 manual.* Minneapolis, MN: National Computer Systems.

Toomey, T. C., Gover, V. F., & Jones, B. N. (1983). Spatial distribution of pain: A descriptive characteristic of chronic pain. *Pain, 17,* 289–300.

Toomey, T. C., Seville, J. L., Abashian, S. W., Finkel, A. G., & Mann, J. D. (1994). Circumstances of chronic pain onset: Relationship to pain description, coping, and psychological distress. *American Pain Society Abstracts,* A-76.

Tunks, E. R., & Merskey, H. (1990). Psychotherapy in the management of chronic pain. In J. J. Bonica (Ed.), *The management of pain* (2nd ed., pp. 1751–1756). Philadelphia: Lea & Febiger.

Turk, D. C. (1996). Biopsychosocial perspective on chronic pain. In R. J. Gatchel & D. C. Turk (Eds.), *Psychological approaches to pain management* (pp. 3–32). New York: Guilford Press.

Turk, D. C., & Fernandez, E. (1995). Personality assessment and the Minnesota Multiphasic Personality Inventory in chronic pain: Underdeveloped and overexposed. *Pain Forum, 4*(2), 104–107.

Turk, D. C., & Matyas, T. A. (1992). Pain related behaviors: Communication of pain. *American Pain Society Journal, 1,* 109–111.

Turk, D. C., Meichenbaum, D., & Genest, M. (1983). *Pain and behavioral medicine: A cognitive-behavioral perspective.* New York: Guilford Press.

Turk, D. C., & Melzack, R. (1992). The measurement of pain and the assessment of people experiencing pain. In D. C. Turk & R. Melzack (Eds.), *Handbook of pain assessment* (pp. 3–14). New York: Guilford Press.

Turk, D. C., Okifuji, A., & Scharff, L. (1995). Chronic pain and depression: Role of perceived impact and perceived control in different age cohorts. *Pain, 61*(1), 92–102.

Turk, D. C., & Rudy, T. E. (1985). *Pain experience: Assessing the cognitive component.* Abstract from the Fifth Annual Meeting of the American Pain Society, Dallas, TX.

Turk, D. C., & Rudy, T. E. (1992). Classification logic and strategies in chronic pain. In D. C. Turk & R. Melzack (Eds.), *Handbook of pain assessment* (pp. 409–428). New York: Guilford Press.

Turk, D. C., & Salovey, P. (1984). "Chronic pain as a variant of depressive disease": A critical reappraisal. *Journal of Nervous and Mental Disease, 172,* 398–404.

Turkat, I. D., & Pettegrew, L. S. (1983). Development and validation of the Illness Behavior Inventory. *Journal of Behavioral Assessment, 5,* 35–47.

Turner, J. A., & Clancy, S. (1986). Strategies for coping with chronic low back pain: Relationship to pain and disability. *Pain, 24,* 355–364.

Turner, J. A., & Romano, J. M. (1984). Self-reported screening measures for depression in chronic pain patients. *Journal of Clinical Psychology, 40,* 909–913.

Turner, J. A., & Romano, J. M. (1990). Cognitive-behavioral therapy. In J. J. Bonica (Ed.), *The management of pain* (2nd ed., pp. 1711–1721). Philadelphia: Lea & Febiger.

Twycross, R. G. (1994). Opioids. In P. D. Wall & R. Melzack (Eds.), *Textbook of pain* (pp. 943–962). New York: Churchill Livingstone.

van der Kolk, B. A., McFarlane, A. C., & Weisaeth, L. (Eds.). (1996). *Traumatic stress: The effects of overwhelming experience on mind, body, and society.* New York: Guilford Press.

Vasudevan, S. V. (1992). Impairment, disability, and functional capacity assessment. In D. C. Turk & R. Melzack (Eds.), *Handbook of pain assessment* (pp. 100–110). New York: Guilford Press.

Vaughan, K., Armstrong, M. F., Gold, R., O'Conner, N., Jenneke, W., & Tarrier, N. (1995). A trial of eye movement desensitization compared to image habituation training and applied muscle relaxation in PTSD. *Journal of Behavior Therapy and Experimental Psychiatry, 25,* 283–291.

Vlaeyen, J. W. S., Kole-Snijders, A. M. J., Boeren, R. G. B., & Van Eek, H. (1995). Fear of movement/reinjury in chronic low back pain and its relation to behavioral performance. *Pain, 62*(3), 363–372.

Waddell, G., Newton, M., Henderson, I., Somerville, D., & Main, G. (1993). A Fear-Avoidance Beliefs Questionnaire and the role of fear-avoidance beliefs in chronic low back pain and disability. *Pain, 52,* 157–168.

Waddell, G., & Turk, D. C. (1992). Clinical assessment of low back pain. In D. C. Turk & R. Melzack (Eds.), *Handbook of pain assessment* (pp. 15–36). New York: Guilford Press.

Walker, E. A., Katon, W., Harrop-Griffiths, J., Holm, L., Russo, J., & Hickok, L. R. (1988). Relationship of chronic pelvic pain to psychiatric diagnoses and childhood sexual abuse. *American Journal of Psychiatry, 145,* 75–80.

Wall, P. D. (1994). Introduction to the edition after this one. In P. D. Wall & R. Melzack (Eds.), *Textbook of pain* (pp. 1–7). New York: Churchill Livingstone.

Wall, P. D., & Melzack, R. (Eds.). (1994). *Textbook of pain.* New York: Churchill Livingstone.

Watkins, J. G. (1992). *Hypnoanalytic techniques: The practice of clinical hypnosis* (Vol. 2). New York: Irvington.

Watkins, R. G., O'Brien, J. P., Draugelis, R., & Jones, D. (1986). Comparisons of preoperative and postoperative MMPI data in chronic back patients. *Spine, 11,* 385–390.

Wechsler, D. (1981). *WAIS-R Manual.* San Antonio, TX: The Psychological Corporation.

Wechsler, D. (1987). *Wechsler Memory Scale–Revised manual.* San Antonio, TX: The Psychological Corporation.

Weissman, A. (1980). *Assessing depressogenic attitudes: A validation study.* Paper presented at the 51st annual meeting of the Eastern Psychological Association, Hartford, CT.

Weitzenhoffer, A. M. (1989a). *The practice of hypnotism: Vol. 1. Traditional and semi-traditional techniques and phenomenology.* New York: John Wiley & Sons, Inc.

Weitzenhoffer, A. M. (1989b). *The practice of hypnotism: Vol. 2. Applications of traditional and semi-traditional hypnotism. Non-traditional hypnotism.* New York: John Wiley & Sons, Inc.

Weitzenhoffer, A. M., & Hilgard, E. R. (1959). *Stanford Hypnotic Susceptibility Scale, Forms A and B.* Palo Alto, CA: Consulting Psychologists Press.

Wickramasekera, I. E. (1988). *Clinical behavioral medicine. Some concepts and proce dures.* New York: Plenum Press.

Williams, D. A. (1996a). Acute pain management. In R. J. Gatchel & D. C. Turk (Eds.), *Psychological approaches to pain management* (pp. 55–77). New York: Guilford Press.

Williams, D. A. (1996b). Psychological screening and treatment for implantables. *Pain Forum, 5*(2), 115–117.

Williams, D. A., & Keefe, F. J. (1991). Pain beliefs and the use of cognitive-behavioral coping strategies. *Pain, 46,* 185–190.

Williams, D. A., Robinson, M. E., & Geisser, M. E. (1994). Pain beliefs: Assessment and utility. *Pain, 59,* 71–78.

Williams, D. A., & Thorn, B. (1989). An empirical assessment of pain beliefs. *Pain, 36,* 351–358.

Williamson, G. M., & Schulz, R. (1992). Pain, activity restriction, and symptoms of depression among community-residing elderly adults. *Journal of Gerontology, 47,* 367–372.

Wilson, S. A., Tinker, R. H., & Becker, L. A. (1994, August). *Eye movement desensitization and reprocessing (EDMR) method in treatment of traumatic memories.* Paper presented at the annual conference of the American Psychological Association (Division 12), Los Angeles.

Wolpe, J. (1990). *The practice of behavior therapy.* Elmsford, NY: Pergamon Press.

Wolpe, J., & Abrams, J. (1991). Post-traumatic stress disorder overcome by eye movement desensitization: A case report. *Journal of Behavior Therapy and Experimental Psychiatry, 22,* 39–43.

Yelin, E. (1986). The myth of malingering: Why individuals withdraw from work in the presence of an illness. *Milbank Quarterly, 64*(4), 622–648.

Young, J. E. (1990/1994). *Cognitive therapy for personality disorders: A schema-focused approach.* Sarasota, Florida: Professional Resource Press.

Zimmerman, M. (1994). *Interview guide for evaluating DSM-IV psychiatric disorders and the mental status exam.* Philadelphia: Psych Products Press.

Zonderman, A. B., Heft, M. W., & Costa, P. T. (1985). Does the Illness Behavior Questionnaire measure abnormal illness behavior? *Health Psychology, 4,* 425–436.

Author Index

Subject Index